Praise for **Blood Brotherhoods**

'[BLOOD BROTHERHOODS] is no dry, scholarly work. Dickie writes with the same distinctive flair that made his book DELIZIA!, on the history of Italian cuisine, so readable.'
—*Daily Telegraph*

'It is almost certainly the most ambitious true-crime assignment ever: to lift the veil of myth, mystery and silence—omertà—shrouding Italy's notorious criminal organisations. The result is a stunning success; a sprawling, powerful historical narrative that is the definitive story of Sicily's Mafia, the Camorra of Naples and Calabria's 'Ndrangheta.'
—*Adelaide Advertiser*

'Both fine social history and hair-raising true crime, this account of the Italian underworld clans tells a grimly fascinating tale.'
—*Independent*

'Exciting and well written, it plays out like a 19th-century Sopranos.'
—*Shortlist*

'Magisterial . . . absorbing . . .'
—*Scotsman*

'[E]nthralling . . . chillingly charts the birth and rise of all three of Italy's mafias.'
—*Dr John Guy*

BLOOD
BROTHERHOODS

Also by John Dickie

Cosa Nostra
Delizia!
Mafia Republic

BLOOD BROTHERHOODS

A History of Italy's Three Mafias

JOHN DICKIE

PUBLICAFFAIRS
New York

Copyright © John Dickie, 2011, 2013, 2014

First half published as *Blood Brotherhoods* in Great Britain in 2011 by Sceptre, an imprint of Hodder & Stoughton, an Hachette UK Company; then published as *Mafia Brotherhoods* in paperback in 2012; and second half first published as *Mafia Republic* in 2013

Published in 2014 in the United States by PublicAffairs™, a Member of the Perseus Books Group
All rights reserved.
Printed in the United States of America.

No part of this book may be reproduced in any manner whatsoever without written permission except in the case of brief quotations embodied in critical articles and reviews. For information, address PublicAffairs, 250 West 57th Street, 15th Floor, New York, NY 10107.

PublicAffairs books are available at special discounts for bulk purchases in the U.S. by corporations, institutions, and other organizations. For more information, please contact the Special Markets Department at the Perseus Books Group, 2300 Chestnut Street, Suite 200, Philadelphia, PA 19103, call (800) 810-4145, ext. 5000, or e-mail special.markets@perseusbooks.com.

Maps by Neil Gower and Clifford Webb
Book Design by Linda Mark

Library of Congress Cataloging-in-Publication Data

Dickie, John, 1963–
    Blood brotherhoods : A History of Italy's three mafias / John Dickie.
     pages cm
    Includes bibliographical references and index.
    ISBN 978-1-61039-427-7 (hardback)—ISBN 978-1-61039-428-4 (e-book)
1. Mafia—Italy—Sicily—History. 2. 'Ndrangheta—History.
3. Camorra—History. 4. Organized crime—Italy—History. I. Title.
    HV6453.I83M326933 2014
    364.1060945'8--dc23
                                                                    2014001947

First Edition

10 9 8 7 6 5 4 3 2 1

Dedicated to the memory of Gilbert Dickie (1922-2011)

The blackest despair that can take hold of any society is the fear that living honestly is futile.

CORRADO ALVARO

CONTENTS

PART IV: THE 'NDRANGHETA EMERGES

PART V: MEDIA DONS

PART VI: MUSSOLINI'S SCALPEL

MAP SECTION APPEARS BETWEEN PAGES 284 AND 285

PART VII: FUGGEDABOUTIT

PART VIII: 1955

PART IX: THE MAFIAS' ECONOMIC MIRACLE

PART X: THE SLAUGHTER

PART XI: MARTYRS AND PENITENTS

SOUTHERN
ITALY

MONDRAGONE
Mazzoni
SANTA MARIA
CAPUA VETERE
AVERSA
○ CASERTA
NAPLES
○ NOLA
Mt.Vesuvius
• SARNO
Procida
○ SALERNO
TORRE DEL GRECO
Capri
CASTELLAMMARE
CAMPANIA

PUGLIA

○ LECCE

T Y R R H E N I A N   S E A

COSENZA
CALABRIA
CATANZARO

Ustica
Aeolian Islands

Favignana
PALERMO
MESSINA
MILAZZO
○ REGGIO CALABRIA
TRAPANI
Straits of
Messina
MARSALA
S I C I L Y
BURGIO
Mt. Etna
○ CALTANISSETTA
SICULIANA
• CANICATTÌ
I O N I A N
• FAVARA
AGRIGENTO
○ SIRACUSA
S E A

0   Miles   100

0   Kilometres   160

Lampedusa

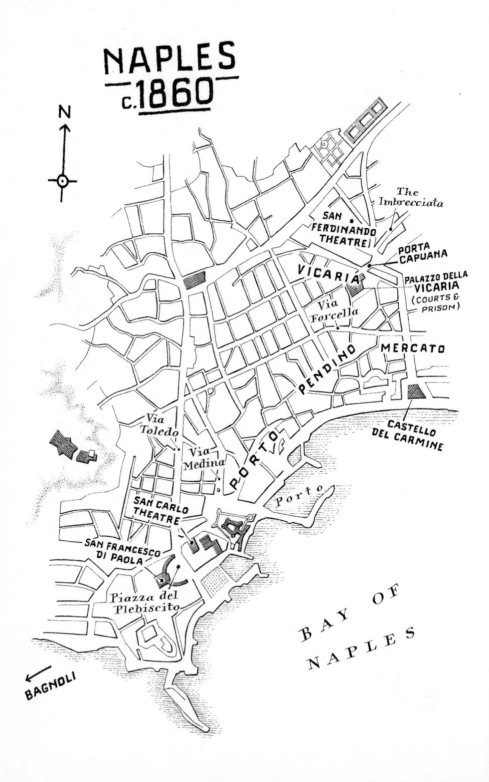

NAPLES
c.1860

N

The Imbrecciata

SAN FERDINANDO THEATRE

PORTA CAPUANA

VICARIA

PALAZZO DELLA VICARIA
(COURTS & PRISON)

Via Forcella

MERCATO

PENDINO

Via Toledo

PORTO

CASTELLO DEL CARMINE

Via Medina

Porto

SAN CARLO THEATRE

Porto

SAN FRANCESCO DI PAOLA

Piazza del Plebiscito

BAY OF

NAPLES

BAGNOLI

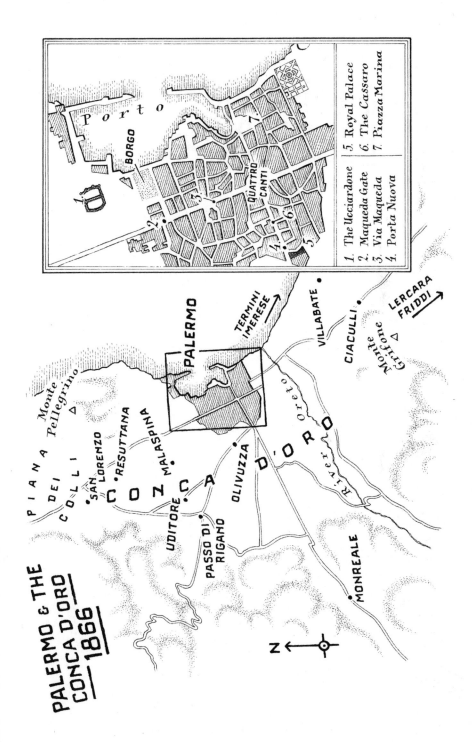

PALERMO & THE
CONCA D'ORO
1866

1. The Ucciardone
2. Maqueda Gate
3. Via Maqueda
4. Porta Nuova
5. Royal Palace
6. The Cassaro
7. Piazza Marina

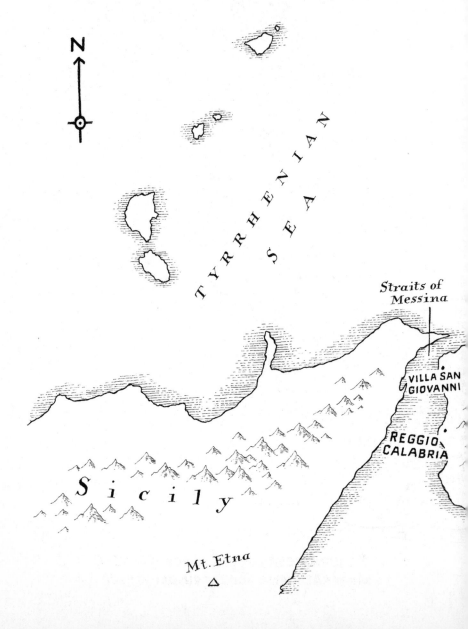

THE 'NDRANGHETA HEARTLANDS

N

TYRRHENIAN SEA

Straits of Messina

VILLA SAN GIOVANNI

REGGIO CALABRIA

Sicily

Mt. Etna

NICASTRO

0 Miles 15

0 Kilometres 25

VIBO VALENTIA

Calabria

NICOTERA

ROSARNO

GIOIA TAURO

POLISTENA

TAURIANOVA ✳

CITTANOVA

GROTTERIA

ALMI

ANTONIMINA

GERACE

SIDERNO

CIRELLA

LOCRI

PLATÌ

PORTGLIOLA

NTO
FANO

omonte

ARDORE

+
Sanctuary
of the Madonna
of Polsi

SAN
LUCA

BOVALINO

AFRICO

CAFORTE
L
RECO

ROGHUDI

BOVA

STAITI

IONIAN

SEA

✳TAURIANOVA CAME INTO BEING IN 1928
WHEN RADICENA AND IATRINOLI MERGED

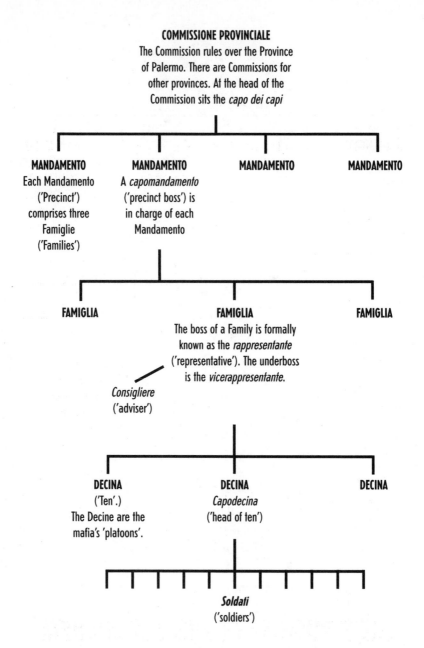

COMMISSIONE PROVINCIALE
The Commission rules over the Province of Palermo. There are Commissions for other provinces. At the head of the Commission sits the *capo dei capi*

MANDAMENTO
Each Mandamento ('Precinct') comprises three Famiglie ('Families')

MANDAMENTO
A *capomandamento* ('precinct boss') is in charge of each Mandamento

MANDAMENTO

MANDAMENTO

FAMIGLIA

FAMIGLIA
The boss of a Family is formally known as the *rappresentante* ('representative'). The underboss is the *vicerappresentante*.

FAMIGLIA

Consigliere
('adviser')

DECINA
('Ten'.)
The Decine are the mafia's 'platoons'.

DECINA
Capodecina
('head of ten')

DECINA

Soldati
('soldiers')

THE STRUCTURE OF COSA NOSTRA
As first described by Tommaso Buscetta in 1984

LA PROVINCIA / IL CRIMINE
The Province (aka Crime or Great Crime) is a
supervisory body headed by the *capocrimine*
(boss of the crime)

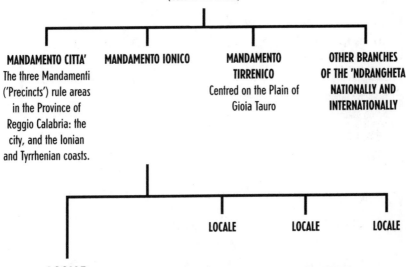

MANDAMENTO CITTA'
The three Mandamenti
('Precincts') rule areas
in the Province of
Reggio Calabria: the
city, and the Ionian
and Tyrrhenian coasts.

MANDAMENTO IONICO

MANDAMENTO TIRRENICO
Centred on the Plain of
Gioia Tauro

OTHER BRANCHES OF THE 'NDRANGHETA NATIONALLY AND INTERNATIONALLY

LOCALE   LOCALE   LOCALE

LOCALE
The 'Locals' into which each
Mandamento is divided govern
territory. For reasons of
secrecy, each Locale is sub-
divided into two compartments:

SOCIETA' MAGGIORE
The 'Major Society' is run by
officers such as:
Capolocale (boss of the local)
Contabile (bookkeeper)
Capocrimine (head of crime)

SOCIETA' MINORE
The 'Minor Society', the
more junior compartment
of the Locale, also has
its officers.

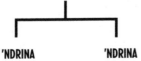

'NDRINA

'NDRINA
The 'ndrine are the cells of
the 'ndrangheta organization.

THE STRUCTURE OF THE 'NDRANGHETA
(Source: 'Operazione Crimine', summer 2010.)

DOTI The 'gifts' (i.e., ranks) that mark the status of an *'ndranghetista*. Being promoted in rank is known as being given a FIORE ('flower').	*Padrino* ('godfather')	Members of the 'ndrangheta have to attain these 'flowers' to be eligible for the most senior positions.
	Quartino	
	Trequartino	
	Vangelista ('gospelist')	*'Ndranghetisti* have to reach these doti to become officials in the Major Society
	Santista ('saintist')	
	Camorrista di sgarro ('*camorrista* who is up for a fight', a.k.a. *sgarrista*)	*'Ndranghetisti* with these ranks belong to the Minor Society
	Camorrista	
	Picciotto ('lad')	
	Giovane d'onore ('honoured youth')	*Giovani d'onore* are being prepared to enter the organisation.

RANKS IN THE 'NDRANGHETA

PREFACE TO THE US EDITION

Once upon a time, three Spanish knights landed on the island of Favignana, just off the westernmost tip of Sicily. They were called Osso, Mastrosso and Carcagnosso and they were fugitives. One of their sisters had been raped by an arrogant nobleman, and the three knights had fled Spain after washing the crime in blood.

Somewhere among Favignana's many caves and grottoes, Osso, Mastrosso and Carcagnosso found sanctuary. But they also found a place where they could channel their sense of injustice into creating a new code of conduct, a new form of brotherhood. Over the next twenty-nine years, they dreamed up and refined the rules of the Honoured Society. Then, at last, they took their mission out into the world.

Osso dedicated himself to Saint George, and crossed into nearby Sicily where he founded the branch of the Honoured Society that would become known as the mafia.

Mastrosso chose the Madonna as his sponsor, and sailed to Naples where he founded another branch: the camorra.

Carcagnosso became a devotee of the Archangel Michael, and crossed the straits between Sicily and the Italian mainland to reach Calabria. There, he founded the 'ndrangheta.

BLOOD BROTHERHOODS IS A HISTORY OF ITALY'S THREE MOST FEARED CRIMINAL organisations, or mafias, from their origins to the present day. But no historian can claim to be the first person drawn towards the mystery of how the Sicilian mafia, the Neapolitan camorra and the Calabrian 'ndrangheta began. *Mafiosi* got there first. Each of Italy's major underworld fraternities has its own foundation myth. For example, the story of Osso, Mastrosso and Carcagnosso (names that mean something like 'Bone', 'Masterbone', and 'Heelbone') is the 'ndrangheta's official account of its own birth: it is a tale told to Calabrian recruits when they prepare to join the local clan and embark on a life of murder, extortion and trafficking.

As history, the three Spanish knights have about as much substance as the three bears. Their story is hooey. But it is serious, sacramental hooey all the same. The study of nationalism has given us fair warning: any number of savage iniquities can be committed in the name of fables about the past. Moreover, in the course of the last 150 years, Italy's criminal brotherhoods have frequently occluded the truth by imposing their own narrative on events: all too often the official version of history turns out to derive from the mafias' myths, which are a great deal more insidious than the hokum about Osso, Mastrosso and Carcagnosso might initially suggest. No ordinary gang, however powerful, has lasted as long as the mafias, nor has it had the same drive to control how its own past is narrated. The very fact that the mafias value history so highly betrays the outrageous scale of their ambition.

Mafia history is filled with many outrages much worse than this. Acts of appalling ferocity are the most obvious. The mafias' cruelty is essential to what they are and what they do; there is no such thing as a mafia without murder, nor has there ever been. Yet violence is only the beginning. Through violence, and through the many tactics that it makes possible, the mafias have corrupted Italy's institutions, drastically curtailed the life-chances of its citizens, evaded justice, and set up their own self-interested meddling as an alternative to the courts. So the real outrage of Italy's mafias is not the countless lives that have been cruelly curtailed—including, very frequently, the lives of the *mafiosi* themselves. Nor is it even the livelihoods stunted, the resources wasted, the priceless landscapes defiled. The real outrage is that these murderers constitute a parallel ruling class in southern Italy. They infiltrate the police, the judiciary, local councils, national ministries, and the economy. They also command a measure of public support. And they have done all this pretty much since the Italian state was founded in 1861. As Italy grew, so too did the mafias. Despite what Fascist propaganda has led many people to believe, the criminal fraternities survived under Mussolini's regime and even infiltrated it. They prospered as never before with the peace and democracy that have characterised the period since 1946. Indeed, when Italy transformed itself into one of the world's wealthiest capitalist economies in the 1960s, the criminal organisations became stronger, more affluent and more violent than ever. They also multiplied and spread, spawning new mafias and new infestations in parts of the national territory that had hitherto seemed immune. Italy is a young country, a modern creation, and the mafias are one of the symptoms of modernity, Italian style.

Today, in the areas of Italy where criminal power is strongest, it constitutes nothing short of a criminal regime. In a secret dispatch from 2008 that found its way onto the Wikileaks site, the United States Consul General in Naples reported on Calabria. One might quibble with one or two of his statistics, but the core of the diagnosis is as true as it is dispiriting:

> The 'ndrangheta organized crime syndicate controls vast portions of [Calabria's] territory and economy, and accounts for at least three percent of Italy's GDP (probably much more) through drug trafficking, extortion and usury . . . Much of the region's industry collapsed over a decade ago, leaving environmental and economic ruin. The region comes in last place in nearly every category of national economic assessments. Most of the politicians we met on a recent visit were fatalistic, of the opinion that there was little that could be done to stop the region's downward economic spiral or the stranglehold of the 'ndrangheta. A few others disingenuously suggested that organized crime is no longer a problem . . . No one believes the central government has much, if any, control of Calabria, and local politicians are uniformly seen as ineffective and/or corrupt. If Calabria were not part of Italy, it would be a failed state.

Italy is and has always been a deeply troubled society. But it is not a banana republic in South America, or an impoverished warlord demesne in Asia, or some remnant of a shattered empire in Eastern Europe. Unless our maps are all calamitously wrong, the famous boot-shaped peninsula is not located in a region of the world where one might expect to find the state's authority undermined by a violent and rapacious alternative power. Italy is a full member of the family of Western European nations. Alone among those nations, it has the mafias. Herein lie both the urgency and the fascination of mafia history.

Yet writing mafia history is a young field of scholarship: it is predominantly a child of the unprecedented mafia savagery of the 1980s and early 1990s, when Italian researchers began to channel their sense of outrage into patient and rigorous study. Overwhelmingly, those historians, whose numbers have grown steadily, hail from the same regions of southern Italy that are worst afflicted by Italy's permanent crime emergency—regions where mafia history is still being made. Some researchers are lucky enough to hold university positions like I do. Others are prosecutors and officers of the law. Some are just ordinary citizens. But all of them are bent on pitting hard evidence and open debate against the lies spread by the mafias and their allies. There can be few other areas where the discipline of understanding the past can make such a direct contribution to building a better future. To defeat the mafias, one has to know what they are; and they are what their history shows us, no more and no less. Thanks to the labours of a number of historians, we can now shine lights into the obscurity of Italian organised crime's development, revealing a narrative that is both disturbing and disturbingly relevant to the present.

Blood Brotherhoods springs from my belief that the findings of this growing body of research are too important to be kept among specialists. It draws together the known documentation and the best research to create a 'choral' work, as the Italians might say: a book in which many voices tell a single tale. My own voice is one of those in the chorus, in that *Blood Brotherhoods* also incorporates substantial new findings that complement and correct the story that has emerged from the exciting work being done in Italy.

This book is also distinctive in another important respect: it seeks to tell the story of *all* the mafias of Italy. Historians have only very rarely done sustained comparative research like this. (For sociologists and criminologists, by contrast, comparison is a stock-in-trade.) Perhaps it is understandable that historians have fallen behind—and not just because writing a unified history of organised crime in Italy is a dauntingly huge job. The criminal fraternities of Sicily, Campania and Calabria each evolved to fit the characteristic features of the territory it fed off. So at various points in their history, they have differed more than the catchall tag 'mafia' might lead us to assume.

Yet the mafias have never existed in isolation. What they share is just as important as the many things that distinguish them. Throughout their history, all three have communicated and learned from one another. So for all their individual peculiarities, studying Italy's underworld organisations in isolation is a bit like trying to figure out the dynamics of natural selection just by staring at beetles impaled on pins in a dusty display case. A broader, comparative context shows us that Italy does not have solitary, static criminal organisms; rather, it has a rich underworld ecosystem that continues to generate new life-forms to this day.

The traces of the mafias' common history are visible in a shared language. *Omertà* is one example—or *umiltà* (humility) to give its original form. Across southern Italy and Sicily, *omertà-umiltà* has denoted a code of silence and submission to criminal authority. 'Honour' is another instance:

all three organisations invoked a code of honour and have at one time or another called themselves the Honoured Society.

The links among the mafias go far beyond words and are one of the reasons for their success and longevity. So the virtues of comparison, and of reading the histories of the mafia, the camorra and the 'ndrangheta in parallel, are perhaps the only lessons in historical method that the fable of Osso, Mastrosso and Carcagnosso has to teach us.

In 2004 I published *Cosa Nostra: A History of the Sicilian Mafia*, in which I brought together the best Italian research on the most notorious of Italy's criminal fraternities. *Blood Brotherhoods* is not a sequel to *Cosa Nostra*: it will stand or fall on its own terms. But readers of *Cosa Nostra* may recognise my retelling of a few episodes from that earlier book, so they deserve to know before starting why the Sicilian mafia is integral to my concerns here. There are two reasons: first, because even in the last ten years or so, new discoveries have radically changed our view of key moments in the history of organised crime in Sicily; second, because there is also a great deal to learn about the Sicilian mafia by comparing it with the camorra and the 'ndrangheta. One thing that the comparison teaches us is that the sinister fame enjoyed by Sicilian *mafiosi* is amply deserved.

Sicily gave the world the term 'mafia', and the fact that that term has entered daily use not just in Italy but across the world is itself a symptom of Sicilian organised crime's pervasive influence. In the dialect of Palermo, the island's capital, 'mafia' denoted beauty and self-confidence: 'cool' comes about as close as English can to its original meaning. In the 1860s, just after the troubled island of Sicily became part of the newly united state of Italy, 'mafia' began to serve as a label for an organisation whose shape briefly became visible through a fog of violence and corruption. The mafia (which would soon disappear into the fog once more) had existed for some time by then, and it had already reached a level of power and wealth that delinquents on the mainland could only aspire to. That power and wealth explains why the Sicilian word 'mafia' became an umbrella term for all of Italy's underworld brotherhoods, including the camorra and 'ndrangheta. Across more than a century and a half—the arc of time covered in these pages—we can chart the fortunes of the peninsula's other two mafias against the heights that the Sicilians reached from the outset.

These days the Sicilian mafia is usually known as Cosa Nostra ('our thing'), a moniker that *mafiosi* in both the United States and Sicily adopted in the 1960s. (The public and the authorities in Italy did not find out about this new name until 1984.) The name 'ndrangheta stuck to the Calabrian mafia in the mid-1950s. (It means 'manliness' or 'courage'.) In both cases, the new names coalesced because post-war public opinion and law enforcement became more searching, and gradually brought into focus a picture that had been blurred by a century of muddle, negligence and downright collusion.

So the first half of *Blood Brotherhoods*, which concludes with the fall of Fascism and the Allied Liberation of Italy, tells a story of underworld regimes that were as yet, if not nameless, then certainly ignored or mysterious, surrounded either by silence (in the case of the 'ndrangheta) or by endless, inconclusive dispute (in the case of the Sicilian mafia).

The camorra had a different relationship to its name. While structured criminal power has waxed and waned through Neapolitan history, the camorra has almost always been called the camorra. The original Honoured Society of Naples was, like the mafias of Sicily and Calabria, a sworn, occult sect of gangsters. Yet it had strangely few secrets. Everyone in Naples knew all about it. Which is one reason why its history has a dramatically different trajectory to the Honoured Societies of Sicily and Calabria.

By taking a comparative approach, *Blood Brotherhoods* will offer answers to some insistent questions. The first and most obvious of those questions is, How did Italy's mafias begin? The worst answers recycle baseless legends that blame Arab invaders in Sicily and Spanish rulers in Naples. Such stories are close to the yarns spun by the Honoured Societies themselves—suspiciously close. Scarcely any better are the answers that evoke abstractions like 'the culture', 'the mentality', or 'the southern Italian family'.

There are explanations, for both the origins and the persistence of mafia crime, that sound rather more sophisticated. University textbooks tend to talk about the fragile legitimacy of the state, the citizens' lack of trust in the government institutions, the prevalence of patronage and clientelism in politics and administration, and so on. As a professor of Italian history, I myself have recited phrases like this in the past. So I know only too well that they rarely leave anyone much wiser. Nonetheless there is one crucial nugget of truth underneath all this jargon: the history of organised crime in Italy is as much about Italy's weakness as it is about the mafias' strength. *Omertà* leads us to the heart of the issue: it is often portrayed as being an iron code of silence, a stark choice between collusion and death. In some cases, it certainly is just as harsh a law as its reputation suggests. Yet the historical sources also show that, under the right kind of pressure, *omertà* has broken again and again. Far from respecting an ancient silence, *mafiosi* have been talking to the police since they first went into business. That persistent weakness is one reason why so many of the underworld's darkest secrets are still there in the archives for us to unearth. And one reason why mafia history is often more about misinformation and intrigue than it is about violence and death.

The best way to divulge those secrets and reconstruct those intrigues is to begin by simply telling stories—documented stories that feature real crimes, real men and women, real choices made in specific times and places. The best historians of organised crime in Italy reconstruct those stories from fragmentary archival sources and from the accounts of people (notably criminals) who often have very good reasons to distort what they say. It is not banal to compare this kind of historical research to detective work. Detectives labour to create a coherent prosecution case by matching the material evidence to what witnesses and suspects tell them. In both tasks—the historian's and the detective's—the truth emerges as much from the gaps and inconsistencies in the available testimonies as it does from the facts those testimonies contain.

But the question that drives research into Italy's long and fraught relationship to these sinister fraternities is not just who committed which crimes. The question is also who knew what. Over the last century and a half, police, magistrates, politicians, opinion formers and even the general public have had access to a surprising amount of information about the mafia problem, thanks in part to the fragility of *omertà*. Italians have also, repeatedly, been shocked and angered by mafia violence and by the way some of its police, judiciary and politicians have colluded with crime bosses. As a result, the mafia drama has frequently been played out very visibly: as high-profile political confrontation, as media event. Yet Italy has also proved positively ingenious in finding reasons to look the other way. So the story of Italy's mafias is not just a *whodunit?* It is also a *whoknewit?* and, most importantly, a *whyonearthdidn'ttheydosomethingaboutit?*

INTRODUCTION: Blood brothers

IN THE EARLY HOURS OF 15 AUGUST 2007, IN THE GERMAN STEEL TOWN OF DUISBURG, six young men of Italian origin climbed into a car and a van, a few yards away from the Da Bruno restaurant where they had been celebrating a birthday. One of them was just eighteen (it was his party), and another was only sixteen. Like the rest of the group, these two boys died very quickly, where they sat. Two killers fired fifty-four shots, even taking the time to reload their 9mm pistols and administer a *coup de grâce* to each of the six in turn.

This was the worst ever mafia bloodbath outside Italy and the United States—northern Europe's equivalent to the St Valentine's Day massacre in Chicago in 1929. As the background to the murders emerged—a long-running blood feud in a little-known region of southern Italy—journalists across the globe began struggling with what the *New York Times* called an 'unpronounceable name': 'ndrangheta.

For the record, the name is pronounced as follows: an-*drang*-get-ah. The 'ndrangheta hails from Calabria (the 'toe' of the Italian boot), and it is oldest and strongest in the province of Reggio Calabria where the peninsula almost touches Sicily. Calabria is Italy's poorest region, but its mafia has now become the country's richest and most powerful. In the 1990s, *'ndranghetisti* (as Calabrian Men of Honour are called) earned themselves a leading position within the European cocaine market by dealing directly with South American producer cartels. The Calabrians have the strongest regime of *omertà*—of silence and secrecy. Few informants abandon the organisation's ranks and give evidence to the state. The Calabrian mafia has also been the most successful of the three major criminal organisations at establishing cells outside of its home territory. It has branches in the centre and north of Italy and also abroad: the existence of 'ndrangheta colonies has been confirmed in six

The Duisburg massacre. Europe finally takes notice of the 'ndrangheta, Italy's richest and most powerful mafia, on 15 August 2007. One of the six victims, Tommaso Venturi, had just celebrated both his eighteenth birthday and his admission into the Honoured Society of Calabria. The partially burned image of the Archangel Michael (inset top), used during the 'ndrangheta initiation ritual, was found in his pocket.

different German cities, as well as in Switzerland, Canada and Australia. According to a recent report from Italy's Parliamentary Commission of Inquiry into mafia crime, the 'ndrangheta also has a presence in Belgium, Holland, Great Britain, Portugal, Spain, Argentina, Brazil, Chile, Colombia, Morocco, Turkey, Venezuela and the USA. Of all southern Italy's mafias, the 'ndrangheta is the youngest and has come the furthest to find its recent success and notoriety; over the course of time, it has learned more than any other Italian criminal group. My research suggests that it absorbed its most important lessons long before the world was even aware that it existed.

The Duisburg massacre demonstrated with appalling clarity that Italy, and the many parts of the world where there are mafia colonies, still lives with the consequences of the story to be told here. So before delving into the past it is essential to introduce its protagonists in the present, to sketch three profiles that show succinctly what mafia history is a history of. Because, even after Duisburg, the world is still getting used to the idea that Italy has more than one mafia. There is only a hazy public understanding of how the camorra and the 'ndrangheta, in particular, are organised.

Blood seeps through the pages of mafia history. In all its many meanings, blood can also serve to introduce the obscure world of Italian organised crime today. Blood is perhaps humanity's oldest and most elemental symbol, and *mafiosi* still exploit its every facet. Blood as violence. Blood as both birth and death. Blood as a sign of manhood and courage. Blood as kinship and family. Each of the three mafias belongs to its own category—its own blood group, as it were—that is distinct but related to the other two in both its organisation and its rituals.

Rituals first: by taking blood oaths, becoming blood brothers, Italian gangsters establish a bond among them, a bond forged in and for violence that is loosened only when life ends. That bond is almost always exclusively between men. Yet the act of marriage—symbolised by the shedding of virginal blood—is also a key ritual in mafia life. For that reason, one of the many recurring themes in this book will be women and how *mafiosi* have learned to manage them.

The magic of ritual is one thing that the 'ndrangheta in particular has understood from the beginning of its history. And ritual often comes into play at the beginning of an 'ndranghetista's life, as we know from one of the very few autobiographies written by a member of the Calabria mafia (a multiple murderer) who has turned state's evidence (after developing a phobia about blood so acute that he could not even face a rare steak).

Antonio Zagari's career in organised crime started two minutes into January 1, 1954. It began, that is, the very moment he issued from his mother's womb. He was a firstborn son, so his arrival was greeted with particular joy: his father, Giacomo, grabbed a wartime heavy machine gun and pumped a stream of bullets towards the stars over the gulf of Gioia Tauro. The barrage just gave the midwife time to dab the blood from the baby's tiny body before he was taken by his father and presented to the members of the clan who were assembled in the house. The baby was gently laid down before them, and a knife and a large key were set near his feebly flailing arms. His destiny would be decided by which he touched first. If it were the key, symbol of confinement, he would become a *sbirro*—a cop, a slave of the law. But if it were the knife, he would live and die by the code of honour.

It was the knife, much to everyone's approval. (Although, truth be told, a helpful adult finger had nudged the blade under the tiny hand.)

Delighted by his son's bold career choice, Giacomo Zagari hoisted the baby in the air, parted his tiny buttocks, and spat noisily on his arsehole for luck. He would be christened Antonio. The name came from his grandfather, a brutal criminal who looked approvingly on at the scene from above a walrus moustache turned a graveolent yellow by the cigar that jutted permanently from between his teeth. Baby Antonio was now 'half in and half out', as the men of the Honoured Society termed it. He was not yet a full member—he would have to be trained, tested and observed before that happened. But his path towards a more than usually gruesome life of crime had been marked out.

The 'social rules'. One of many pages of instructions for 'ndrangheta initiation rituals that were found in June 1987 in the hideout of Giuseppe Chilà. Osso, Mastrosso and Carcagnosso, the three Spanish knights who (according to criminal legend) were the founders of the mafia, camorra and 'ndrangheta, are mentioned.

Zagari grew up not in Calabria, but near Varese by Italy's border with Switzerland, where his father led the local 'ndrangheta cell. As a youth, during his father's occasional jail stints, Antonio was sent back south to work with his uncles who were citrus fruit dealers in the rich agricultural plain of Gioia Tauro on Calabria's Tyrrhenian Sea coast. He came to admire his father's relatives and friends for the respect they commanded locally, and even for the delicacy of their speech. Before uttering a vaguely vulgar word like 'feet', 'toilet', or 'underpants', they would crave forgiveness: 'Speaking with all due respect . . . ' 'Excuse the phrase . . . ' And when they had no alternative but to utter genuine profanities such as 'police officer', 'magistrate', or 'courtroom', their sentences would topple over themselves with pre-emptive apologies.

I have to say that—for the sake of preserving all those present, and the fine and honoured faces of all our good friends, speaking with all due respect, and excusing the phrase—when the *Carabinieri* [military police] . . .

As the son of a boss, Antonio Zagari's criminal apprenticeship was a short one. He took a few secret messages into prison, hid a few weapons, and soon, at age seventeen, he was ready to make the passage into full membership.

One day his 'friends', as he termed them, copied out a few pages of the Rules and Social Prescriptions he was required to learn by heart before being inducted. It was all, he later recalled, like the catechism children have to memorise before Confirmation and First Communion.

The 'catechism' also included lessons in 'ndrangheta history. And having committed the deeds of Osso, Mastrosso and Carcagnosso to memory, Zagari was deemed ready to undergo the most elaborate initiation rite used by any mafia. He was shown into an isolated, darkened room and introduced to the senior members present, who were all arrayed in a circle. For the time being, he had to remain silent, excluded from the group.

'Are you comfortable my dear comrades?', the boss began.
'*Very comfortable. On what?*'
'On the social rules.'
'*Very comfortable.*'
'Then, in the name of the organised and faithful society, I baptise this place as our ancestors Osso, Mastrosso and Carcagnosso baptised it, who baptised it with iron and chains.'

The boss then passed round the room, relieving each '*ndranghetista* of the tools of his trade, and pronouncing the same formula at each stop.

> In the name of our most severe Saint Michael the Archangel, who carried a set of scales in one hand and a sword in the other, I confiscate your weaponry.

The scene was now set, and the Chief Cudgel could intone his preamble to the ceremony proper.

> The society is a ball that goes wandering around the world, as cold as ice, as hot as fire, and as fine as silk. Let us swear, handsome comrades, that anyone who betrays the society will pay with five or six dagger thrusts to the chest, as the social rules prescribe. Silver chalice, consecrated host, with words of humility I form the society.

Another 'thank you' was sounded, as the *'ndranghetisti* moved closer together and linked arms.

Three times the boss then asked his comrades whether Zagari was ready for acceptance into the Honoured Society. When he had received the same affirmative reply three times, the circle opened, and a space was made for the newcomer immediately to the boss's right. The boss then took a knife and cut a cross into the initiate's left thumb so that blood from the wound could drip onto a playing card sized picture of the Archangel Michael. The boss then ripped off the Archangel's head and burned the rest in a candle flame, symbolising the utter annihilation of all traitors.

Only then could Zagari open his mouth to take the 'ndrangheta oath.

> I swear before the organised and faithful society, represented by our honoured and wise boss and by all the members, to carry out all the duties for which I am responsible and all those that are imposed on me—if necessary even with my blood.

The boss then kissed the new member on both cheeks and set out for him the rules of honour. There followed another surreal incantation to wind the ceremony up.

> Oh, beautiful humility! You who have covered me in roses and flowers and carried me to the island of Favignana, there to teach me the first steps. Italy, Germany and Sicily once waged a great war. Much blood was shed for the honour of the society. And this blood, gathered in a ball, goes wandering round the world, as cold as ice, as hot as fire, and as fine as silk.

The 'ndranghetisti could at last take up arms again—in the name of Osso, Mastrosso, Carcagnosso and the Archangel Michael—and resume their day-to-day criminal activity.

These solemn ravings make the 'ndrangheta seem like a version of the Scouts invented by the boys from *The Lord of the Flies* based on a passing encounter with *Monty Python and the Holy Grail*. It would all verge on the comic if the result were not so much death and misery. Yet there is no incompatibility between the creepy fantasy world of 'ndrangheta ritual and the brutal reality of killings and cocaine deals.

Initiation rituals are even more important to the 'ndrangheta than the story of Osso, Mastrosso and Carcagnosso that helps give it an ancient and noble aura. At whatever stage in life they are performed, mafia rites of affiliation are a baptism, to use Antonio Zagari's word. Like a baptism, such ceremonies dramatise a change in identity; they draw a line in blood between one state of being and another. No wonder, then, that because of the rituals they undergo, 'ndranghetisti consider themselves a breed apart. A Calabrian *mafioso*'s initiation is a special day indeed.

15 August 2007, in Duisburg, was one such special day. The morning after the massacre, German police searched the victims' mutilated corpses for clues. They found a partly burned image of the Archangel Michael in the pocket of the eighteen-year-old boy who had just been celebrating his birthday.

The mafia of Sicily, now known as Cosa Nostra, also has its myths and ceremonies. For example, many *mafiosi* hold (or at least held until recently) the deluded belief that their organisation began as a medieval brotherhood of caped avengers called the Beati Paoli. The Sicilian mafia uses an initiation ritual that deploys the symbolism of blood in a similar but simpler fashion to the 'ndrangheta. The same darkened room. The same assembly of members, who typically sit round a table with a gun and a knife at its centre. The aspirant's 'godfather' explains the rules to him and then pricks his trigger finger and sheds a little of his blood on a holy image—usually the Madonna of the Annunciation. The image is burned in the neophyte's hands as the oath is taken: 'If I betray Cosa Nostra, may my flesh burn like this holy woman.' Blood once shed can never be restored. Matter once burned can never be repaired. When one enters the Sicilian mafia, one enters for life.

As well as being a vital part of the internal life of the Calabrian and Sicilian mafias, initiation rites are very important historical evidence. The earliest references to the 'ndrangheta ritual date from the late nineteenth century. The Sicilian mafia's version is older: the first documentary evidence emerged in 1876. The rituals surface from the documentation again and again thereafter, leaving bloody fingerprints through history, exposing Italian organised crime's DNA. They also tell us very clearly what happened to that evidence once it came into the hands of the Italian authorities: it was repeatedly ignored, undervalued and suppressed.

Rituals are evidence of historical change, too. The oldest admission ceremony of all belonged to the Neapolitan camorra. Once upon a time, the camorra also signalled a young member's new status with the shedding of blood. In the 1850s, a recruit usually took an oath over crossed knives and then had to have a dagger fight, either with a *camorrista* or with another aspiring member. Often the blade would be wrapped tightly in rags or string, leaving only the point exposed: too much blood and the duel might stop being a symbolic exercise in male bonding and start being a battle. When the first hit was registered, the fight was declared over, and the new affiliate received both the embraces of the other *camorristi* and the most junior rank in the Honoured Society's organisational hierarchy.

Today's camorra bosses tend not to put their recruits through formal initiation ceremonies or oaths. The traditions have disappeared. The Neapolitan camorra is no longer a sworn sect, an Honoured Society. In fact, as we shall see later, the Honoured Society of Naples died out in 1912 in bizarre and utterly Neapolitan circumstances.

Each of the mafias has evolved its own organisation. The primary aim of these structures is to impose discipline, which can be a huge competitive advantage in the violent turmoil of the underworld. But organisation also serves other purposes, notably that of utilising the loyalties within blood families. Mafias are not kin groups: they are systems for exploiting kin groups for criminal purposes.

Naples and its region of Campania have seen the most dramatic organisational changes of any of the Italian mafias. The camorra that has emerged since the destruction of the Honoured Society of Naples before the First World War is not a single association. Instead it is a vast pullulating world of gangs. They form, split, descend into vicious feuds, and re-emerge in new alliances only to then be annihilated in some new internecine war or police roundup. The Neapolitan underworld is frighteningly unstable. Whereas a Sicilian *capo* has a decent chance of seeing his grandchildren set out on their criminal careers, a senior *camorrista* is lucky if he lives to forty.

Camorra clans lack the formalised job titles, ranks and rituals that can be found in the 'ndrangheta and Cosa Nostra. But that has not stopped *camorristi* from controlling vast swathes of Campanian territory, from turning entire city blocks into fortified no-go zones and drug hypermarkets, from making millions from the trade in bootleg DVDs and designer handbags. It has not stopped them devastating the landscape of Campania with their lucrative trade in illegally dumped waste. Or from infiltrating the national construction industry and dealing internationally in narcotics and weapons.

Camorra clans are organised nonetheless: together they form 'the System', as some on the inside call it. At the centre of the System in each area of the city and its hinterland is a charismatic boss: protector and punisher. Below him there are ranks and specialised roles—like zone chiefs, assassins, drug wholesalers—who are all chosen and nominated by the boss and who will almost invariably live and die with him. Like the other mafias, the camorra clans redistribute some of the profits of their crimes, often pay wages to their troops and set aside funds for those in prison.

Blood, in the sense of kinship, is now the glue that holds the most fearsome camorra clans together. But the individual clans tend not to be led by a Grand Old Man. The core of any camorra group is usually a cluster of relatives—brothers, cousins, in-laws—all roughly the same age. Around them there are friends, neighbours and more relatives.

So, Neapolitan organised crime has seen a great deal of change since the days when the camorra was an Honoured Society. Yet the veins of tradition have never been entirely severed. For one thing, *camorristi* have an enduring weakness for gangster bling. Gold accessories and expensive shirts have been in evidence since the nineteenth century. Now there are also showy cars and motorcycles. The Neapolitan boss's bike of choice was until recently the Honda Dominator. The point of all this conspicuous consumption, then and now, is to advertise power: to proclaim territorial dominion and to be a walking symbol of success to hangers-on.

Cosa Nostra's bosses are generally dowdy compared to the camorra chiefs of Naples, and they spend much more of their time on the kind of organisational formalities that can have a lethal significance in their world.

Each boss (or, strictly speaking, 'representative') of the Sicilian mafia presides over a cell known as a Family. But by no means everyone in a Family is related. Indeed, Cosa Nostra often invokes a rule designed to prevent clusters of relatives from becoming too influential within a Family: no more than two brothers may become members at any one time, so that the boss can't pack the clan with his own kin.

The structure of each Family is simple. (See page xxii.) The representative is flanked by an underboss and a *consigliere* or adviser. The ordinary members, known as soldiers, are organised into groups of ten. Each of these groups reports to a *capodecina*—a 'boss of ten'—who in turn reports to the boss. So the term Family, as Cosa Nostra uses it, is a metaphor for the basic unit in its structure.

Above its base in the Families, Cosa Nostra is shaped like a pyramid. Three mafia Families in adjoining territories form another tier of the organisation's structure, the *mandamento* (precinct), presided over by a *capomandamento* (precinct boss). This precinct boss has a seat on the Commission, which combines the functions of a parliament, a high court, and a chamber of commerce for Cosa Nostra in each of Sicily's four most mafia-infested provinces. Presiding over them all, at the very apex of the mafia pyramid, there is a *capo di tutti i capi*—the 'boss of all bosses'. The *capo di tutti i capi* is invariably from the province of Palermo, the island's capital, because about half of Cosa Nostra's manpower, and about half of its Families, are based in the Palermo area.

So much for the diagram. But in the underworld, more even than in the upper world inhabited by law-abiding citizens, power is invested in people, and not in the nameplates on office doors. Comparisons between a mafia boss and the managing director of a capitalist enterprise are not only trite; they completely fail to capture the acutely cagey and political world in which *mafiosi* operate.

Cosa Nostra has gone through phases of greater and lesser coordination; different bosses have had different styles of leadership and have had all manner of external limits placed on their power. Confusion, double-dealing, mutual suspicion, and civil war have been constants in the mafia from the get-go. The cast of character-types is vast. There are certainly party leaders, policy-makers, reformers and legislative tinkerers. But also a good many rebels, grey eminences, impatient tycoons, Young Turks, and isolationists. And of course everyone in the mafia is also both a conspirator and a near-paranoid conspiracy theorist. All of these characters may choose to twist the mafia's precedents, traditions and rules; they may even trample and deride them. But no boss, however powerful, can do so without calculating the political price.

One of the big issues in the history of the Sicilian mafia is just how old the organisation's pyramidal structure is. Some of the most disquieting recent research has shown that it is a lot older than we thought until only a couple of years ago. The mafia would not be the mafia without its inborn drive to formalise and coordinate its activities. As I write, to the best of our knowledge, the Palermo Commission of Cosa Nostra has not met since 1993, a fact that is symptomatic of the worst crisis in the organisation's century and a half of history. Quite whether today's crisis turns into a terminal decline depends, in part, on how well Italy absorbs the lessons of the mafia's history, lessons that spell out the Sicilian mafia's astonishing power to regenerate itself.

In Calabria, just as in Sicily, there is a fraught relationship between the gangland rulebook and the expediency determined by the sheer chaos of criminal life. When I began writing this book, there was a consensus in both the law courts and the criminology textbooks that the 'ndrangheta's structure was very different to Cosa Nostra's. The 'ndrangheta is a federal organisation, it was said, a loose fellowship of local gangs.

Then in July 2010 the police and *Carabinieri* arrested more than three hundred men, including the eighty-year-old Domenico Oppedisano, who, investigators claim, was elected to the 'ndrangheta's highest office in August 2009. Since their arrest, Oppedisano and most of his fellows have availed themselves of the right to remain silent. So we cannot know what defence they will mount against the charges. Nor can we know whether the courts will decide that those charges have substance. Operation Crime, as the investigation is called, is in its early stages. Yet whatever its final result, it constitutes a lesson in humility for anyone trying to write about the secret world of Italian gangsterism. At any moment, historical certainties can be overturned by new policework or by discoveries in the many unexplored archives.

The magistrates directing Operation Crime allege that Oppedisano's official title is *capocrimine*, or 'chief of the crime'. The 'Crime', which *'ndranghetisti* also refer to as the 'Province', is thought to be the 'ndrangheta's supreme coordinating body. It is subdivided into three *mandamenti*, or precincts, covering the three zones of the province of Reggio Calabria.

Many newspapers in Italy and abroad that covered Operation Crime portrayed the Crime as the 'ndrangheta version of the Sicilian mafia Commission, and Domenico Oppedisano as a Calabrian *capo di tutti i capi*: the peak of the 'ndrangheta pyramid, as it were. But that image does not correspond to what the magistrates are claiming. Instead, they paint a picture of Oppedisano as a master of ceremonies, the speaker of an assembly, a wise old judge whose job is to interpret the rules. The head of crime's responsibilities relate to procedure and politics, not to business.

But then procedure and politics can easily have fatal consequences in Italian gangland. The Crime has real power: it may be based in the province of Reggio Calabria, but *'ndranghetisti* across the world are answerable to it, according to the investigating magistrates. In the spring of 2008, the boss, or 'general master', of the 'ndrangheta's colonies in the Lombardy region (the northern heart of the Italian economy) decided to declare independence from the Crime. In July of that year, the police bugged a conversation in which one senior boss reported to his men that the Crime had decided to 'sack' the insubordinate general master. A few days later the sacking took effect, when two men in motorcycle jackets shot the Lombardy boss four times just as he was getting up from his usual table at a bar in a small town near Milan. Shortly afterwards, the *Carabinieri* secretly filmed a meeting at which the Lombardy chiefs raised their hands in unanimous approval of their new general master; needless to say, he was the Crime's nominee.

It seems that the textbooks on the 'ndrangheta may have to be rewritten. And historians will have to take up a new prompt for research. My own findings suggest that the links—procedural, political and business links—between the 'ndrangheta's local cells have been there right from the beginning and that the Crime—or something like it—may be as old as the 'ndrangheta itself.

Despite all the new information about the Crime, much of what we knew about the lower reaches of the 'ndrangheta's structure remains valid. (For the organisational structure and ranks of 'ndrangheta, see pages xxiii–xxiv.) The 'ndrangheta of today is closely entwined with family, in that each unit, or 'ndrina, forms the backbone of a broader clan. (The term 'ndrina may well originate from the word malandrina, which used to refer to the special cell in prison reserved for gangsters.) The boss of an 'ndrina, often called a capobastone ('chief cudgel'), is typically a father with a good number of male children. Unlike his peers in Cosa Nostra, the chief cudgel can bring as many boys into the 'ndrangheta as he is able to sire. Clustered around the core members in the 'ndrina are the boss's kin and other families, often bound in by blood, marriage or both. Accordingly, 'ndrangheta clans take their names from the surname(s) of its leading dynasty or dynasties, such as the Pelle-Vottari and the Strangio-Nirta—respectively the victims and per-petrators of the massacre in Duisburg.

A number of 'ndrine report up to a locale or 'Local', whose boss is known as the capolocale and who is assisted by other senior officers. For exam-ple, the contabile ('bookkeeper') handles the gang's common fund, or what 'ndranghetisti rather quaintly call the valigetta ('valise'). The capocrimine ('head of crime') is in charge of surveillance and day-to-day criminal activ-ity. When the time comes, the head of crime also acts as the clan's Minister of War. For extra security the Local is divided into two compartments, insu-lated from one another: the lower ranking 'ndranghetisti are grouped in the Minor Society, and the higher ones in the Major Society.

So far, so (relatively) straightforward. But at this point the 'ndrangheta's peculiar fondness for arcane rules and procedures takes over again. In Cosa Nostra, holding office is the only official measure of a Man of Honour's status. In the 'ndrangheta, if a member is to hold one of the official posi-tions of power in a Local, a Precinct, or in the Crime, then he has to have reached a certain degree of seniority. Seniority is measured in doti, meaning 'qualities' or 'gifts', which are the ranks in the organisation's membership hierarchy. Sometimes, more poetically, rising a rank in the 'ndrangheta is referred to as receiving a fiore—a flower. The offices in the Local are tem-porary appointments, whereas the flowers are permanent marks of status.

As he steals, extorts and kills, an *'ndranghetista* wins new flowers. Every new flower means yet another protracted induction ceremony and after it a greater share of power and secrets. The young initiate starts at the bottom as a *picciotto d'onore* ('honoured youth') and ascends through a series of other ranks like *camorrista* and *camorrista di sgarro* (which means something like 'camorrist who is up for a fight') and then on to the more senior ranks, such as *santista, vangelista* and *padrino* (or saintist, gospelist and godfather).

As if this were not complicated enough, *'ndranghetisti* disagree about how many ranks there are and what rights and responsibilities they bring with them. There has also been floral inflation in recent years: inventing new badges of status is a cheap way to resolve disputes. For instance, *gospelist* (so called because the initiation ritual for this flower involves swearing on a bible) seems to have been created recently.

None of this is harmless etiquette. The rituals and organisational structures are a liturgical apparatus that is intended to turn young men into professional delinquents and transform a mere life of crime into a calling in savagery. A calling that, despite the antique origins its members boast, is only a century and a half old. Only as old, that is, as Italy itself.

PART I

VIVA LA PATRIA!

1

HOW TO EXTRACT GOLD FROM FLEAS

SIGISMONDO CASTROMEDIANO, DUKE OF MORCIANO, MARQUIS OF CABALLINO, LORD OF seven baronies, sat on the ground with his right calf resting on an anvil. Rangy and blue-eyed, he seemed like an entirely distinct order of being from the Neapolitan jailers who stood before him under a lean-to roof, toying with their ironmongery. Next to the Duke, his fellow patriot Nicola Schiavoni sat in the same undignified position, with the same look of dread on his face.

One of the jailers grabbed the Duke's foot and slipped a stirrup-shaped metal shackle over it. He then enclosed the ankle entirely by pushing a rivet through the small holes at each end of the shackle; sandwiched between them was the last link of a heavy chain. Laughing and singing, the jailer smashed the rivet flat with blows that could have splintered bones.

The Duke flinched repeatedly, and was assailed by the jailers' mocking cheers: 'Give 'em some more! They're enemies of the king. They wanted to get their hands on our women and our property.'

Ordered to stand, Castromediano and Schiavoni lifted their fetters for the first time: some twenty pounds of chain in twelve feet of oblong links. For both of them, this moment marked the beginning of a prison sentence of thirty years in irons for conspiring against the government of the Kingdom of Naples, one of the many states into which the Italian peninsula was divided. The two prisoners embraced before mustering a show of their undaunted belief in the sacred cause of Italy: 'we kissed those chains tenderly', the Duke wrote, 'as if they were our brides'.

The guards were briefly taken aback. But they soon got on with the rituals that marked admission to the Castello del Carmine, one of the worst prisons in the Kingdom of Naples. Civilian clothes were replaced by uniforms comprising brown breeches and a red tunic, both in the same rough wool. Heads were scraped bald and bloody with a sickle-shaped razor. Into each pair of hands were thrust a rag-stuffed mattress, a donkey-hair blanket, and a bowl.

It was sunset by the time the Duke and his companion were led across the prison yard and shoved through the door of the dungeon.

What they saw inside, Castromediano recalled, was a sight fit to 'annihilate the most generous soul, the most steadfast heart'. It could have been a sewer: a long room with a low ceiling, its floor set with sharp stones, its tiny windows high and heavily barred, its air sick and clammy. A stench like rotting meat emanated from the filth smeared everywhere, and from the figures of misery skulking in the half-light.

As the new arrivals were nervously looking for a place to lay their mattresses, another shackled pair approached from among the crowd. One was tall and handsome, with a swagger in his walk. He was dressed in black plush trousers, with polished buttons at the haunches, and a brightly coloured belt; his matching waistcoat displayed a watch and chain. With elaborate civility, he addressed the two patriots.

> Well, well, gentlemen! Fortune has smiled on you. All of us here have been waiting to honour you. Long live Italy! Long live Liberty! We *camorristi*, who share your sad and honourable fate, hereby exempt you from any camorra obligation . . . Gentlemen, take heart! I swear by God that no one in this place will touch a hair on your head. I am the boss of the camorra here, and so I'm the only one in charge. Absolutely everyone is at my beck and call, including the commander and his jailers.

Within an hour the new prisoners learned two stark lessons: that the camorra boss had made no hollow boasts about his power; and that his promise to exempt them from any 'camorra obligation' was utterly worthless. The *camorrista* did get them back their purses, which had been confiscated on arrival at the prison. But that courtesy was a self-interested one: it meant that he could cajole the bewildered Duke into paying an exorbitant sum for revolting food.

That first exaction was crushing. Castromediano visualised his future as an endless ordeal by protection racket, and found himself contemplating suicide.

The Duke of Castromediano was clapped in irons on 4 June 1851. The scene is true but also irresistibly metaphorical for it was in prison, in the mid-1800s, that Italy was first chained to the hoodlums that have hampered its every step, ever since.

The camorra was born in prison. By the time the Duke of Castromediano entered the Castello del Carmine, gang rule behind bars had been a fact of life in southern Italy for centuries. Under the *ancien régime* it was easier and cheaper to devolve day-to-day control of the prisons to the toughest inmates. Then in the 1800s the prison extortionists turned themselves into a sworn secret society and gained a foothold in the world beyond the dungeons. The story of how that happened is thick with intrigue, but in essence it involves picking out every nuance and irony in the opening encounter between Duke Castromediano and the *camorrista*. For now, that story can be summarised in one word: Italy.

In 1851, what we now call Italy was still only a 'geographical expression' rather than a state; it was divided between one foreign power (Austria), two Dukedoms, a Grand Dukedom, two Kingdoms, and one Papal State. The biggest of those territories was also the southernmost: the Kingdom of Naples, or the Kingdom of the Two Sicilies, to use its official name.

From the Kingdom's capital, Naples, a King born of the Bourbon dynasty reigned over the southern Italian mainland and the island of Sicily. Like most princes in Italy, the Bourbons of Naples were haunted by the memory of what had happened to them in the years following the French Revolution of 1789. In 1805 Napoleon deposed the Bourbons and put his own nominees on the throne. French rule brought a whole series of innovations in the way the Kingdom was run. Out went feudalism, and in came private property. Out went a messy assemblage of local customs, baronial and church jurisdictions, and public ordinances: in came a new code of civil law and the beginnings of a police force. The southern part of the Italian peninsula began to resemble a modern, centralised state.

In 1815 Napoleon was finally vanquished. When the Bourbons returned to power, they caught on to the big advantages that the French-style reforms could have for securing their own authority. But the theory and the practice of modern administration were hard to reconcile. The throne of the Kingdom of the Two Sicilies was still shaky. There was widespread opposition to the new, more centralised system. Moreover, the French Revolution had not only introduced continental Europe to new ways of administering a state, it had also spread volatile ideas about constitutional government, the nation, and even democracy.

Duke Castromediano was one of a generation of young men who dedicated themselves to building an Italian *Patria*, a Fatherland that would embody the values of constitutional government, liberty, and the rule of law. After trying and failing to turn those values into a political reality during the revolts of 1848–49, many patriots like Castromediano paid for their beliefs by being hurled into the dungeon realm of the *camorristi*.

Such treatment of political prisoners, of *gentlemen* prisoners, soon became a scandal. In 1850 a highly strung Member of the British Parliament, William Ewart Gladstone—the future Grand Old Man—began a long sojourn in Naples for the sake of his daughter's health. Gladstone was drawn into local issues by the plight of men like Castromediano. Early in 1851 the authorities in Naples unwisely allowed Gladstone to visit some of the city's jails. He was horrified by the 'beastly filth' he witnessed. Here political detainees and common criminals of the worst kind mingled indiscriminately, and without any kind of supervision. The prisoners ran the place themselves.

> They are a self-governed community, the main authority being that of the *gamorristi*, the men of most celebrity among them for audacious crime.

Gladstone's unfamiliar spelling did not change the truth of what he wrote. Or indeed the polemical force of his argument: no sooner had he emerged from the Neapolitan prisons than he unleashed two open letters condemning the rule of the Bourbon King as 'the negation of God, erected into a system of Government'. *Camorristi* were now a diplomatic stick with which to beat the Bourbons. Any government that farmed out the management of its prisons to violent thugs surely did not deserve to stand. Courtesy of Gladstone, Italy's organised criminal gangs became what they have never ceased to be since: a detonator of political controversy.

The international sympathy aroused by the jailed patriot martyrs came to play an important role in the almost miraculous sequence of events that finally turned Italy into a *Patria*, or something like it. In 1858 the Prime Minister of the northern Italian Kingdom of Piedmont-Sardinia struck a secret deal with France to drive Austria out of northern Italy by force. The following year, after appalling bloodshed at the battles of Magenta and Solferino, Piedmont-Sardinia absorbed the former Austrian domain of Lombardy. Piedmont's military success triggered uprisings further south, in the various central Dukedoms, as well as in part of the Pope's territory. Much of the north of the peninsula had now become Italy. Europe held its breath and awaited the next move.

Then in May 1860 Giuseppe Garibaldi launched one of idealism's greatest ever feats when he landed at Marsala, at Sicily's furthest western shore, with just over 1,000 red-shirted patriotic volunteers. After his first touch-and-go victories, the momentum of revolution began to build behind Garibaldi's expedition. He soon conquered the Sicilian capital Palermo, and then turned his growing army eastwards to invade the Italian mainland. In early September, he entered Naples. Italy would henceforth, for the first time in history, be one country.

With Italy unified, the patriotic prisoners of the Kingdom of the Two Sicilies could now convert their long sufferings into political credibility. They travelled north, to the Piedmontese capital of Turin at the foot of the Alps, and joined the new country's first national elite.

The tale of the *Risorgimento*, of how Italy was unified, has been told countless times. Much less well-known is its sinister subplot: the emergence of the camorra. Most of the multiple threads of that subplot were set in motion in the dungeons where the patriots met the *camorristi*. So the patriotic prisoners are our most important witnesses to the camorra's early history. Not only that: some of them stepped bodily into the historical fray, as both heroes and villains.

A united Italy was still a formless dream when Duke Sigismondo Castromediano was clapped in irons in 1851. But as his traumatic first hours in prison turned into days, months, and years, he found sources of resilience to add to his political dreams: the companionship of his fellows in degradation; but also a determination to understand his enemy. For the Duke of Castromediano, making sense of the camorra was a matter of life and death.

His discoveries should be ours, since they still hold good today. In prison, Castromediano was able to observe the early camorra in laboratory conditions as it perfected a criminal methodology destined to infiltrate and subvert the very nation that Duke Castromediano suffered so much to create.

Castromediano began his study of the camorra in the most down-to-earth way: he followed the money. And the thing that most struck him about what he called the camorra's 'taxes' was that they were levied on absolutely every aspect of a prisoner's life, down to the last crust of bread and the most miserable shred of clothing.

At one end of most dungeons in the Kingdom was a tiny altar to the Madonna. The first tax extracted from a newly arrived prisoner was often claimed as a payment for 'oil for the Madonna's lamp'—a lamp that rarely, if ever, burned. Prisoners even had to rent the patch of ground where they slept. In prison slang, this sleeping place was called a *pizzo*. Perhaps not coincidentally, the same word today means a bribe or a protection payment. Anyone reluctant to pay the *pizzo* was treated to punishments that ranged from insults, through beatings and razor slashes, to murder.

Duke Sigismondo Castromediano, who analysed the camorra's methods while in prison in the 1850s. He called it 'one of the most immoral and disastrous sects that human infamy has ever invented'.

Duke Castromediano witnessed one episode that illustrates how the camorra's prison funding system involved something far more profound than brute robbery—and something much more sinister than taxation. On one occasion a *camorrista*, who had just eaten 'a succulent soup and a nice hunk of roast', threw a turnip into the face of a man whose meagre ration of bread and broth he had confiscated in lieu of a bribe. Insults were hurled along with the vegetable.

> Here you go, a turnip! That should be enough to keep you alive—at least for today. Tomorrow the Devil will take care of you.

The camorra turned the needs and rights of their fellow prisoners (like their bread or their *pizzo*) into favours. Favours that had to be paid for, one way or another. The camorra system was based on the power to grant those favours and to take them away. Or even to throw them in people's faces. The real cruelty of the turnip-throwing episode is that the *camorrista* was bestowing a favour that he could just as easily have withheld.

Duke Castromediano had an acute eye for episodes that dramatised the underlying structures of camorra power in the prisons. He once overheard two prisoners arguing about a debt. There were only a few pennies at stake. But before long, a *camorrista* intervened. 'What right have you got to have an argument, unless the camorra has given you permission?' With that, he seized the disputed coins.

Any prisoner who asserted a basic right—like having an argument or breathing air—was insulting the camorra's authority. And any prisoner who

Camorra code book. Reportedly confiscated from a prison *camorrista* who kept it secreted in his anus, this secret table explains the symbols *camorristi* used in messages they smuggled in and out of prison. From a nineteenth-century study of the Honoured Society of Naples.

tried to appeal for justice to an authority beyond the prison was committing treason. The Duke met one man who had had his hands plunged into boiling water for daring to write to the government about prison conditions.

Much of what Castromediano learned about the camorra came from his time in a prison on Procida, one of the islands that, like its beautiful sisters Capri and Ischia, is posted at the mouth of the Bay of Naples. When he later looked back at his time on Procida, the Duke unleashed an undigested anger.

The biggest jail in the southern provinces. The queen of jails, the camorra's honey pot, and the fattest feeding trough for the guard commanders and anyone else who has a hand in supporting the camorra; the great latrine where, by force of nature, society's most abominable scum percolates.

It was in Procida prison's own latrine, which fed straight into the sea, that the Duke came across another crucial facet of the camorra system. One day he noticed two human figures sketched in coal on the wall. The first had wide, goggling eyes and a silent howl of rage issuing from his twisted mouth. With his right hand he was thrusting a dagger into the belly of the second, who was writhing in excruciating pain as he keeled over. Each figure had his initials on the wall above his head. Below the scene was written, 'Judged by the Society', followed by the very date on which the Duke had come across it.

Castromediano already knew that the Society or Honoured Society was the name that the camorra gave itself. But the doodle on the wall was obscure. 'What does that mean?' he asked, with his usual candour, of the first person he came across.

> It means that today is a day of justice against a traitor. Either the victim drawn there is already in the chapel, breathing his last. Or within a few hours the penal colony on Procida will have one less inmate, and hell will have one more.

The prisoner explained how the Society had reached a decision, how its bosses had made a ruling, and how all members except for the victim had been informed of what was about to happen. No one, of course, had divulged this open secret.

Then, just as he was warning the Duke to keep quiet, from the next corridor there came a loud curse, followed by a long and anguished cry that was gradually smothered, followed in turn by a clinking of chains and the sound of hurried footsteps.

'The murder has happened,' was all that the other prisoner said.

In a panic, the Duke bolted for his own cell. But he had hardly turned the first corner when he stumbled upon the victim, three stab wounds to his heart. The only other person there was the man the victim was chained to. The man's attitude would remain seared into Castromediano's memory. Perhaps he was the killer. At the very least he was an eyewitness. Yet he gazed down at the corpse with 'an indescribable combination of stupidity and ferocity' as he waited calmly for the guards to bring the hammer and anvil they needed to separate him from his dead companion.

Castromediano called what he had witnessed a 'simulacrum' of justice; this was murder in the borrowed clothes of capital punishment. The camorra not only killed the traitor. More importantly, it sought to make that killing legitimate, 'legal'. There was a trial with a judge, witnesses, and advocates for the prosecution and the defence. The verdict and sentence that issued from the trial were made public—albeit on the walls of a latrine rather than in a court proclamation. The camorra also sought a twisted form of democratic approval for its judicial decisions, by making sure that everyone bar the victim knew what was about to take place.

The camorra courts did not reach their decisions in the name of justice. Rather, their lodestar value was *honour*. Honour, in the sense that the Society understood it (a sense that Castromediano called an 'aberration of the human mind'), meant that an affiliate had to protect his fellows at all costs, and share his fortunes with them. Disputes had to be resolved in the approved fashion, usually by a dagger duel; oaths and pacts had to be respected, orders obeyed, and punishment accepted when it was due.

Despite all the talk of honour, the reality of camorra life was far from harmonious, as Castromediano recalled.

Relations between those accursed men seethed with arguments, hatred, and envy. Sudden murders and horrible acts of vengeance were perpetrated every day.

A murder committed as a vendetta was a murder to defend one's personal honour, and as such it could easily be sanctioned by the camorra's shadow judicial system. Quite whether a vendetta was legitimate or not depended partly on the Society's rules and legal precedents, which were transmitted orally from one generation of criminals to the next. More importantly, it depended on whether the vendetta was committed by a *camorrista* fearsome enough to impose his will. In the prison camorra, even more than anywhere else, the rules were the tool of the rich and powerful. Honour was law for those who placed themselves above the law.

Camorra 'taxation'. Camorra 'justice'. Castromediano also talks of the camorra's 'jurisdiction', its 'badges of office', and its 'administration'. His terminology is striking, consistent and apt: it is the vocabulary of state power. What he is describing is a system of criminal authority that apes the workings of a modern state—even within a dungeon's sepulchral gloom.

If the camorra of the prisons was a kind of shadow state, it had a very interventionist idea of how the state should behave. Duke Castromediano saw that *camorristi* fostered gambling and drinking in the full knowledge that these activities could be taxed. (Indeed the practice of taking bribes from gamers was so closely associated with gangsters that it generated a popular theory about how the camorra got its name. *Morra* was a game, and the *capo della morra* was the man who watched over the players. It was said that this title was shortened at some stage to *ca-morra*. The theory is probably apocryphal: in Naples, *camorra* meant 'bribe' or 'extortion' long before anyone thought of applying the term to a secret society.)

Card games and bottles of wine generated other moneymaking opportunities: the camorra provided the only source of credit for unlucky gamblers, and it controlled the prison's own stinking, rat-infested tavern. Moreover, every object that the camorra confiscated from a prisoner unable to afford his interest payments, his bottle, or his bribe, could be sold on at an eye-watering markup. The dungeons echoed to the cries of pedlars selling greasy rags and bits of stale bread. A whole squalid economy sprouted from exploiting the prisoners at every turn. As an old saying within the camorra would have it, '*Facimmo caccia' l'oro de' piducchie*': 'We extract gold from fleas.'

The camorra system also reached up into the prisons' supposed command. Naturally, many guards were on the payroll. This corruption not only gave the camorra the freedom it needed to operate, it also put even more favours into circulation. For a price, prisoners could wear their own clothes, sleep in separate cells, eat better food, and have access to medicine, letters, books and candles. By managing the traffic in goods that came in and out of prison, the camorra both invented and monopolised a whole market in contraband items.

So the prison camorra had a dual business model designed to extract gold from fleas: extortion 'taxes' on the one hand and contraband commerce on the other. The camorra of today works on exactly the same principles. All that has changed is that the 'fleas' have become bigger. Bribes once taken on a place to lay a mattress are now cuts taken on huge public works contracts. Candles and food smuggled into prison are now consignments of narcotics smuggled into the country.

Duke Castromediano's years as a political prisoner were spent in several jails but everywhere he went he found the camorra in charge. So his story is not just about the origins of what today is called the *Neapolitan* camorra. Prisoners from different regions mingled in jails across the southern part of the Italian peninsula, on Sicily, and on many small islands. They all referred to themselves as *camorristi*.

The Duke did however notice distinctions in the dress code adopted by *camorristi* from different regions. Sicilians tended to opt for the black plush look. (The *camorrista* who introduced himself to the Duke on his first day in the Castello del Carmine was Sicilian.) Not long before, Neapolitans had dressed in the same way. But for some time now they had preferred to signal their status with clothes that could come in any colour, as long as it was of good quality and accessorised in gold: gold watch and chain; gold earrings; chunky gold finger rings; all topped off with a fez decorated with lots of braid, embroidery and a golden tassel.

There were strong loyalties and rivalries between *camorristi* from different regions. In Duke Castromediano's experience, the Neapolitans nurtured an 'inveterate antipathy' towards the Calabrians. When this antipathy exploded into open hostilities, *camorristi* from elsewhere tended to take sides in a familiar formation: with the Neapolitans would stand the men from the countryside near Naples and from Puglia; everyone else would side with the Calabrians. The Sicilians 'loved to keep themselves to themselves', said Castromediano. 'But if they came down in favour of one side or the other, oh! the savage vendettas!' In the worst cases, 'tens of dead bodies took their places in the prison cemetery'.

For all their vicious rivalries and their many distinctive qualities, Sicilian *mafiosi*, like Neapolitan *camorristi* and Calabrian *'ndranghetisti*, have all referred to themselves as members of the 'Honoured Society'. Their shared vocabulary is a sign of shared origins in the prison system of the Kingdom of the Two Sicilies. In fact, everything Castromediano discovered in prison about the camorra not only still holds good—it still holds good for the Sicilian mafia and the Calabrian 'ndrangheta too. Italy's criminal organisations both engage in illegal commerce and act as a shadow state that combines extortion 'taxes' and alternative judicial and political systems. If they had their way, Italy's Honoured Societies would turn the whole world into a giant prison, run by their simple but brutally effective rules.

Seven and a half years after Sigismondo Castromediano was admitted to the Castello del Carmine, the diplomatic pressure on the Bourbon government finally paid off for the patriotic prisoners; like others, the Duke had his sentence commuted to permanent exile. By then his hair had turned completely white. One of the last things he did before being freed was to bribe a jailor to let him keep two mournful souvenirs: his shackles and his red tunic. The humiliations of his prison years would remain with him for the rest of his life.

The Duke spent just over a year in exile. Then came Garibaldi: the Bourbon state collapsed and its territory became part of Italy. In Turin, on 17 March 1861, Castromediano was in parliament to see Victor Emmanuel, the King of Piedmont-Sardinia, pronounced hereditary monarch of the new Kingdom. The ideal for which he had suffered so long was now an official reality.

But Castromediano soon lost the parliamentary position his prison martyrdom had earned. He returned to his ancestral seat in Puglia, the region that forms the heel of the Italian boot. While he was in jail his castle near the city of Lecce had fallen into serious disrepair. But he had been leeched to near penury by the camorra and would never have the money to renovate. The Duke's occasional visitors over the years found the castle a fitting setting for a man who had endured so much in the national cause: it became a semi-ruin like those in the romantic novels that had so fired the Duke's patriotism when he was young. In one corner of the castle chapel, on permanent display, were what he called his 'decorations': the prison chain and tunic. The camorra had seeped into the Duke's soul, infecting him with a recurring melancholy: 'the spawn of hell', he called it. 'One of the most immoral and disastrous sects that human infamy has ever invented.'

The Duke began writing a memoir of his captivity only days after he was released; yet it remained unfinished when he died in his castle thirty-six years later. Castromediano's *Political Prisons and Jails* reads like the work of a man still struggling to come to terms with his past. The Duke's narrative is occasionally jumbled and repetitive but at its best, it is a vivid firsthand account of where Italy's mafias began.

What Castromediano could not appreciate while in jail was that the camorra had already made its first steps out from the dungeon and into the streets.

2

Co-managing crime

Naples teemed. There were just under half a million inhabitants in the 1850s, making the capital of the Kingdom of the Two Sicilies the biggest city in Italy. With the highest population density in Europe, it packed more misery into each square metre than any other town on the continent. Every grotto and cellar, every nook and doorway had its ragged and emaciated inhabitants.

The quarters of Porto, Pendino, Mercato and Vicaria held the most notorious concentrations of indigence; they made up the so-called 'low city'. Some of the alleyways were so narrow it was impossible to open an umbrella. Many of the low city's poorest lived in tenements known as *fondaci* ('depositories') where whole families and their animals were crammed into single, windowless rooms. Vermin were rife and the stench unholy: sewage overflowed the ancient cesspits and ran through the alleys. In the 1840s close to 30 per cent of infants in the low city died before their first birthday. None of these four quarters had a life expectancy above twenty-five years.

But unlike London, Naples did not hide its poor away. Under the southern sun, in every street and piazza, tradesmen and pedlars of all conceivable varieties put on daily performances. Slum-dwellers scraped their living picking rags, weaving straw or singing stories; they hawked snails and pizza slices, collected cigar butts, or portered the occasional box.

Nowhere was the variety of this starveling economy more apparent than in the via Toledo, the city's main thoroughfare and 'the noisiest street in Europe'. Here, each morning, the city's life would seep from the hovels and palazzi, spill through the side streets and converge to form a roiling flood of people. Poor and wealthy, the scuttling urchin and the promenading bourgeois, all dodged the carriages on via Toledo. The din of haggling was immense. And to add to it, everyone from the sausage vendors with their braziers to the sellers of ice water in their grandly decorated pagodas, had a distinctive, sonorous cry.

There was also a less picturesque side to the industry of the Neapolitan poor. Tourists were most vexed by the crowds of beggars who thrust their maimed limbs at anyone likely to surrender a coin. Veteran travellers considered that the child pickpockets of Naples set an international standard for dexterity. Theft, swindling and prostitution were crucial survival strategies for many of the poor. The low city, in particular, lived almost entirely outside the law.

Not even the world's most zealous and honest constabulary could have imposed order on this swarm. So in Naples, the nineteenth century's proud new science of policing quickly became a modest routine of minimising the nuisance caused by the plebs. Because Naples was so vast and so poor, the police learned that the best way to contain that nuisance was to collaborate with the hardest plebeian thugs.

In 1857 Antonio Scialoja wrote a pamphlet on policing that continued the patriotic propaganda offensive against the Kingdom of the Two Sicilies. Scialoja was a brilliant Neapolitan economist living in political exile in Turin. Because he was himself a veteran of the Bourbon jails, the prison camorra was a centrepiece of his polemic. He claimed that 'the Society of *camorristi*' was so powerful that it could carry out death sentences in any prison in the Kingdom. The Society made other prisoners pay for everything, Scialoja reported, even for escaping what he delicately referred to as the 'turpitudes' of their fellow detainees: he meant rape.

But Scialoja's diagnosis of the malaise in Naples went far beyond the prison walls. Using his accounting skills, he identified a slush fund that did not appear in the official police budget. He then showed how some of this cash was spent hiring ruffians and spies. Nor did the corruption stop there. For decades the Bourbons had recruited their police from among the city's most feared criminals. The ordinary people of Naples referred to them as the *feroci*, the 'ferocious ones'. There were 181 *feroci* at the time Scialoja was writing. Although they were paid their meagre wages out of the official police budget, they nonetheless habitually supplemented their income with bribes.

Italian has a useful piece of jargon to describe this kind of arrangement: it is called 'co-managing' crime. And if the *feroci* who co-managed crime with the police are beginning to look rather like the *camorristi* who co-managed the prison system with the warders, that is because they were sometimes

The flashy dress and strutting posture of a *guappo*, or street-corner boss. By the 1850s, when these illustrations were published, the camorra was already a highly visible presence on the streets of Naples.

one and the same thing. But policing the streets with the cooperation of the toughest delinquents was always a messy affair. Some *camorristi* proved to be more loyal to their criminal comrades than they were to their police paymasters, while others provoked intense suspicion and hatred in the underworld. Nevertheless, thanks to co-management, the bosses who had been left in charge of the dungeons for centuries now held a government licence to be a power on the streets. By the early 1850s, *camorristi* decked out in the latest gangster uniform of slicked hair, velvet jacket and flared trousers were as conspicuous a part of the life of Naples as pizza-pedlars and strolling players.

Once the camorra of the prisons had been given its foothold in the outside world, it began doing what it was best at: extracting gold from fleas. Just as in prison, extortion was the basis of the camorra's power. Illegal or semi-illegal activities were particularly vulnerable. *Camorristi* would demand a cut of any thief's takings and they came to occupy a dominant position in prostitution. Gambling was another lucrative racket.

Large sections of the *lawful* economy also came to be subject to extortion rackets. Outsiders would often encounter *camorristi* in action without really understanding what they were seeing. As the visitor stepped from a hired boat, his oarsman would be approached by a gaudily dressed man, often wearing lots of jewellery, who would silently expect and receive an offering. As the visitor arrived at his hotel, his porter would discreetly slip a coin into the hand of a stocky stranger. And as the visitor stepped into a hackney carriage, the driver would pay up to yet another waiting heavy.

Camorristi demanded their taxes at the pressure points of the urban economy: at the quays where cargo, fish, and passengers were landed; at the city gates where produce arrived from the countryside; at the markets where it was distributed. Boatmen and stevedores, customs officers and cart-drivers, wholesalers and hawkers: all were forced to pay in the same way that had long been familiar for prison inmates.

The heart of the camorra's Naples became the Vicaria quarter, located at what was then the city's eastern boundary. The slums of the Vicaria were where every criminal sphere of influence overlapped, as if at the intersection of a Venn diagram. The quarter took its name from the Palazzo della Vicaria, a medieval block that housed the courtrooms and, in its basement, a notorious dungeon. The walls of the Vicaria prison looked solid enough but in reality they were a membrane through which messages, food and weapons constantly slipped into and out of the surrounding slums.

Near the prison was the Porta Capuana, a stone archway adorned with friezes and frescos through which much of the produce from the hinterland arrived ready to be 'taxed'. But the criminal epicentre of the Vicaria was what is now a stretch of via Martiri d'Otranto that, with the alleys running

Camorristi settle their differences over a card game; gambling was one of the Honoured Society's primary rackets.

off it, was known as the Imbrecciata. The Imbrecciata was a kasbah of cheap carnal pleasures; its inhabitants were almost all involved in prostitution and live sex shows. The area was so notorious that the authorities tried several times to cordon it off by building walls at its exits.

With all these opportunities for illegal income close to hand in the Vicaria, it is not surprising that the first supreme bosses of the Honoured Society in the outside world came from here.

The 'co-management' of crime in Naples was indeed scandalous. But the exiled economist Antonio Scialoja was particularly angered by the way the Bourbon authorities gave their spies, *feroci* and *camorristi* a free rein to harass and blackmail liberal patriots. In fact these rough and ready cops were no respecters of political affiliation: even Bourbon royalists had to cough up to avoid what the *feroci* smilingly called 'judicial complications'. In this way, amid the uncertainties of the 1850s, with the Bourbon monarchy vulnerable and wary, the camorra was given the chance to meddle in politics.

Scialoja concluded his pamphlet with an exemplary tale drawn from his own memories of life as a political prisoner in the early 1850s. He recalled that the common criminals in jail referred to the captive patriots simply as 'the gentlemen', because their leaders were educated men of property like him. But by no means everyone who got mixed up in liberal politics was a gentleman. Some were tough artisans. A case in point was one Giuseppe D'Alessandro, known as *Peppe l'aversano*—'Aversa Joe' (Aversa being an agricultural settlement not far north of Naples). Aversa Joe was sent to jail for his part in the revolutionary events of 1848. When he encountered the camorra, he quickly decided that joining the ranks of the extortionists was preferable to suffering alongside the gentlemen martyrs. He was initiated into the Honoured Society and was soon swaggering along the corridors in his flares.

In the spring of 1851, at about the time when Gladstone was thundering about the *gamorristi* to his British readers, one particularly zealous branch of the Neapolitan police conceived a plan to kill off some of the incarcerated patriots. But not even the police could carry out such a scheme without help from the prison management—the camorra. In Aversa Joe they found the perfect man for the job; in fact they didn't even have to pay him since he was still under sentence of death for treason and was glad simply to be spared his date with the executioner.

Aversa Joe twice attempted to carry out his mission, with a posse of *camorristi* ready to answer his call to attack. But both times the gentlemen managed to stick together and face down their would-be killers.

The political prisoners then wrote to the police authorities to remind them of the diplomatic scandal that would ensue if they were torn to pieces by a mob. The reminder worked. Aversa Joe was transferred elsewhere, then released, and finally given the chance to swap his velvet jacket for a police uniform: he had completed the transformation from treasonable patriot, to *camorrista*, to policeman in the space of a couple of years.

For Scialoja, the Aversa Joe story typified everything that was bad about Bourbon rule, with its habit of co-managing crime with mobsters. The Italian *Patria* would stand in shining contrast to such sleaze. The new nation of Italy, whenever it came, would finally bring good government to the benighted metropolis in the shadow of Mount Vesuvius.

But Naples being Naples, forming the *Patria* turned out to be a much stranger and murkier business than anyone could have expected.

3

THE REDEMPTION OF THE CAMORRA

THE SUMMER OF 1860 WAS THE SUMMER OF GARIBALDI'S EXPEDITION, WHEN MARVELS of patriotic heroism finally turned the Kingdom of the Two Sicilies into part of the Kingdom of Italy. In Naples, history was being made at such a gallop that journalists scarcely had time to dwell on what they saw and heard. This was a moment when the incredible seemed possible, and thus a time for narrative. Explanation would have to wait.

There was consternation in Naples when news broke that Garibaldi and his Thousand redshirted Italian patriots had invaded Sicily. On 11 May 1860 the official newspaper announced that what it called Garibaldi's 'freebooters' had landed in Marsala. By the end of the month it was confirmed that the insurgent forces had gained control of the Sicilian capital, Palermo.

The ineffectual young king, Francesco II, was scarcely a year into his reign. As the *garibaldini* consolidated their grip on Sicily and prepared to invade the Italian mainland and march north, Francesco dithered in Naples and his ministers argued and schemed.

Only on 26 June did Neapolitans find out how the Bourbon monarchy planned to respond to the crisis. Early that morning, posters were plastered along the major streets proclaiming a 'Sovereign Act'. King Francesco decreed that the Kingdom of the Two Sicilies was to cease being an absolute monarchy and embrace constitutional politics. A government comprising liberal patriots had already been formed. There would also be an amnesty for all political prisoners. And the flag would henceforth comprise the Italian tricolour of red, white and green, surmounted by the Bourbon dynasty's coat of arms.

The early risers who came across the Sovereign Act on the morning of 26 June were afraid to be seen reading it: there was always the chance that it was a provocation intended to force liberals out into the open, and make them easy targets for the *feroci*. But within hours Neapolitans had absorbed what the posters really meant: the Sovereign Act was a feeble and desperate attempt to cling onto power. The gathering momentum of Garibaldi's expedition had put Francesco in a hopeless position, and the Bourbon state was tottering.

The day the Sovereign Act was published was a bad day to be a policeman in Naples. For years the police had been feared and despised as corrupt instruments of repression. Now they were left politically exposed when there was almost certain to be a battle for control of the streets.

The evening of the day that the Sovereign Act posters appeared, clusters of people from the poorest alleyways came down onto via Toledo to jeer and whistle at the police. Shopkeepers pulled down their shutters and expected the worst. They had good reason to be afraid. Mass disorder visited Naples with what seemed like seasonal regularity, and pillaging inevitably accompanied it.

Serious trouble began the following afternoon. Two rival proletarian crowds were looking for a confrontation: the royalists yelling 'long live the King', and the patriots marching to the call of 'viva Garibaldi'. One colourful character, difficult to miss in the mêlée, was Marianna De Crescenzo, who went by the nickname of *la Sangiovannara*. One report described her as being 'decked out like a brigand', festooned in ribbons and flags. Responding to her yelled commands was a gang of similarly attired women brandishing

The pivotal figure in the murky Neapolitan intrigues of 1860. At age 30, Marianna De Crescenzo, a.k.a. *la Sangiovannara*, was a prosperous tavern owner who became famous for her charismatic leadership of the patriotic mob.

knives and pistols. Loyalists to the Bourbon cause suspected that *la Sangiovannara* had stoked up the trouble by handing out cheap booze from her tavern, as well as large measures of subversive Italian propaganda.

On via Toledo, two police patrols found themselves caught between the factions. When an inspector gave the unenforceable order to disarm the crowd, fighting broke out. Some onlookers heard shots. After a running battle, the police were forced to withdraw. Only the arrival of a cavalry unit prevented the situation degenerating even further.

There were two notable casualties of the clash. The first was the French ambassador, who was passing along via Toledo in his carriage when he was accosted and cudgelled. Although he survived, no one ever discovered who was responsible for the attack.

The second victim was Aversa Joe, the patriot, turned prison *camorrista*, turned Bourbon assassin, turned policeman. He was stabbed at the demonstration and then hacked to death while he was being carried to hospital on a stretcher. The murder was clearly planned in advance, although again the culprits remained unknown.

Everyone thought that this was only the overture to the coming terror. Fearing the worst, many policemen ran for their lives. There was no one left to resist the mob. Organised gangs armed with muskets, sword-sticks, daggers and pistols visited each of the city's twelve police stations in turn; they broke down the doors, tossed files and furniture out of the windows, and lit great bonfires in the street.

The Neapolitan police force had ceased to exist.

But by the afternoon, a peculiar calm had descended. The London *Times* correspondent felt safe enough to go and see the ruined police station in the Montecalvario quarter and found the words 'DEATH TO THE COPS!' and 'CLOSED DUE TO DEATH!' scrawled on either side of the entrance. These bloodcurdling slogans did not match what had actually happened, though. Witness after witness related how unexpectedly peaceful, ordered and even playful the scenes of destruction were. The mob did rough up the few cops they caught. But instead of lynching their uniformed captives, they handed them over to the army. The *London Daily News*'s man at the scene wrote that, although rumours suggested that many policemen had been murdered, he had been unable to verify a single fatality. Around the bonfires of police paraphernalia there was cheering, laughing and dancing; street urchins cut up police uniforms and handed the pieces out as souvenirs. This was less a riot than a piece of street theatre.

The most unexpected part of it all was that there was no stealing. On every previous occasion when political upheaval had come to Naples, a predatory mob had risen from the low city. Yet this time, outlandishly, rioters

The Neapolitan camorra's cue to take to the streets. In desperation, on 25 June 1860, Francesco II of the Kingdom of the Two Sicilies issued the *Atto Sovrano* (Sovereign Act).

from the same slums even handed over any cash and valuables they found to army officers or parish priests. Moving through the streets from one target to the next, they shouted reassurance to the traders cowering behind their shutters. 'Why close up your shops? We aren't going to rob you. We only wanted to drive off the cops.' According to the *Times* correspondent, one man took several watches from the wreckage of a police station. But instead of pocketing them, he threw them on the bonfire burning outside. 'No one shall say that I stole them', he proclaimed.

These were strange days, and they were about to get even stranger. The evening before the police stations were attacked in such carnivalesque style, King Francesco II appointed a new Prefect of Police, a lawyer by the name of Liborio Romano.

Miracle worker, Liborio Romano, who kept order in Naples after June 1860 by recruiting the camorra to replace the police.

Like Duke Sigismondo Castromediano and economist Antonio Scialoja, Liborio Romano was sent to jail in the early 1850s for his liberal, patriotic beliefs. But he was already nearing sixty and suffered from excruciating gout so he was released early in 1852; and in 1854 he was allowed to return to Naples after signing an oath of loyalty to the throne. Romano thus owed the Bourbon monarchy a debt of honour. In June 1860 when King Francesco was looking for tame patriots to take up positions in the liberal cabinet announced by the Sovereign Act, Romano's obligation seemed to make him the perfect candidate. So he was put in charge of the police—the toughest job of them all.

Within hours of taking office Romano launched one of the boldest initiatives in the history of policing: he offered the camorra the chance to 'rehabilitate itself' (his words) by replacing the police. The Honoured Society's bosses accepted the offer with alacrity, and soon *camorristi* sporting cockades in the red, white and green of the Italian flag were on patrol. Naples remained calm as a result, and Liborio Romano became a hero. The Piedmontese ambassador gushed that he 'is deeply loved by the public and has very Italian feelings'. *The Times* called Romano a statesman 'who has gained the confidence of all by his ability and firmness', and said that, but for him, the city would be in chaos. On 23 July his saint's day was marked with public illuminations and a lantern-lit parade. Indeed, so successful was Romano's policy that many *camorristi* were subsequently recruited into the new National Guard. The risky summer between a crumbling Bourbon regime and the arrival of Garibaldi passed more peacefully than anyone could ever have hoped.

The camorra's extraordinary role in the Naples drama made news in Turin, the new Italy's capital city. One magazine even marked the occasion by

The redemption of the camorra. Crime bosses become patriotic heroes and have flattering portraits printed in the press. Among them is Salvatore de Crescenzo, the most notorious *camorrista* of the era.

publishing flattering pictures of three leading camorra bosses. One of them, Salvatore De Crescenzo, is worth looking at closely.

In the 1860 engraving, De Crescenzo is shown sporting a tricolour rosette, his right hand resting Napoleonically inside his waistcoat, his hair parted neatly and his earnest expression framed by a fuzzy, chin-strap beard. De Crescenzo's police files allow us to add some facts to these impressions. They tell us that he was a shoemaker by trade, probably born in 1822. He was manifestly a violent man, first jailed in 1849 for seriously wounding a sailor, and strongly suspected of killing a fellow inmate later the same year. He spent the 1850s in and out of prison, and the last arrest before his picture appeared in the press was in November 1859. Despite this frightening CV, the Turin magazine declared that De Crescenzo and the other *camorristi* were now 'honest men who were held in high regard by both the national party and the people'.

In the south, Garibaldi was performing miracles, conquering a whole Kingdom with a handful of volunteers. In Naples, it seemed to some observers, there was a miracle before Garibaldi even arrived. The camorra had been redeemed, converted in the sacred name of the *Patria*.

But in the shadows where politics, mob violence and organised crime overlap, there had been no miracle, and no redemption of the camorra. The truth—or at least fragments of it—would only emerge later. Many of those fragments were in the possession of one of the more sympathetic characters in the history of Italian organised crime, a myopic, bearded Swiss hotelier called Marc Monnier.

Monnier never spent time in jail, and never held political office. Yet he knew the camorra as well as anyone in Naples thanks to his job: he ran the Hôtel de Genève, which stood amid the hubbub of via Medina. The hotel catered mainly for commercial travellers; Herman Melville, author of *Moby Dick*, was one of its few notable guests. The family business put Monnier in daily contact with the camorra's territorial control: with the porters, carriage drivers, greengrocers and butchers who paid kickbacks to the mob. From the very windows of the Hôtel de Genève, Monnier could watch hoodlums taking their 10 per cent cut on street card games.

The hotel business gave Marc Monnier a priceless knowledge of how the city worked, as well as a reliable source of income. Reliable, but dreary. Monnier's real passion was writing, particularly drama. In the mid-1850s he was converted to the patriotic cause and thereby acquired a journalistic mission: to explain Italy to the rest of the world. The unfolding story of Italy's unification was by turns inspiring and confusing to foreign onlookers—not to mention to Italians themselves. Being both an insider and an outsider, Monnier had a perspective that Italians and foreigners alike could trust.

Monnier's *The Camorra* was published in 1862. As a guide to the Neapolitan Honoured Society of the nineteenth century, it has never been surpassed. One of the key testimonies in *The Camorra* is from a patriot, one of a number who had returned to Naples to conspire in secret for the overthrow of the Bourbon monarchy. Many of these conspirators joined an underground group called the 'Committee of Order' (a name chosen so as to disguise the revolutionaries' real intentions). Monnier knew the conspirators well because the Committee of Order used to hold some of its meetings in the Hôtel de Genève. And what Monnier learned from his contacts in the Committee of Order was that there was a secret pact between the movement for Italian unification and the camorra that dated back to the mid-1850s.

Here, then, is our first lesson in Neapolitan politics: while some patriots were being persecuted by the camorra in jail and others were decrying it from exile as the worst product of the Bourbons' sordid despotism, back in Naples still others were trying to strike a deal with the gangland leaders.

But why on earth would the Committee of Order want to befriend the gangsters of the camorra? Because they knew the lessons of Neapolitan history. Time and time again the Bourbon monarchy had enlisted the urban poor to defend itself from change: rabble-rousers were plied with cash and told to direct the mob at political enemies. Any political revolution would fail if it could not control the streets. The camorra was organised, violent and rooted in the very alleyways that generated the notorious mobs. With the camorra on its side—or at least a substantial faction within the camorra—Italy could win

Naples and thus the whole of the south. The Committee of Order was set to compete with the Bourbon police for the camorra's friendship.

Not all of the patriotic leaders agreed with this Machiavellian tactic. And by no means all *camorristi* went along with it. But the prospect of a deal between patriots and hoodlums raised genuine fears for the Bourbon authorities. In October 1853 the police (themselves of course riddled with *camorristi*) reported that 'the liberals are trying to recruit from among a pernicious class of individuals from the plebs, who go by the name of *camorristi*.' Among the list of politically suspect *camorristi* was Salvatore De Crescenzo: the boss whose 'redemption' would make headlines seven years later.

Marc Monnier learned about the pact between the Committee of Order and the Honoured Society from a source he referred to only as the 'Neapolitan gentleman'. The Neapolitan gentleman told Monnier that at some time in the mid-1850s, he himself had arranged to meet leading *camorristi* on the northern outskirts of the city. He watched them arrive, one by one, each with a hat pulled down low, each announcing himself with the same signal: a noise made with the lips that sounded like a kiss.

The Neapolitan gentleman reported that his first meeting with the leaders of the Honoured Society started badly and very quickly got much worse. The *camorristi* began by berating him: he and his well-dressed and well-educated friends had ignored the needs of the poor. The 'holy rabble', they said, had no intention of letting people like him, who were already rich, glean all the fruits of revolution. After this opening verbal assault, the *camorristi* got down to business. It would take money to provoke a patriotic revolt against the Bourbon monarchy. A lot of money. To start with, they demanded a bounty of 10,000 ducats each. In 2010 values, by a very rough calculation, the bosses were demanding $170,000 per head to help bring down the Bourbon state.

The Neapolitan gentleman splutteringly pleaded with the *camorristi* to take a less materialistic view of things, but his protest was in vain. The patriots agreed to pay the camorra. Thereafter, each underworld chief received regular sums according to the number of men he commanded.

As it turned out, the camorra's preparations for the coming revolution were less than wholehearted. They gave their followers ranks, as if they were in an army, and emblazoned large parchment signs with the patriots' watchword: ORDER. Yet somehow they never quite made the leap from preparing for a revolt to actually starting one. In fact, they were more interested in blackmailing the patriotic conspirators by threatening to tell the Bourbon police everything unless they were given more money.

Things were looking very bleak for the patriots of Naples, when suddenly in 1859 the situation changed, with the completion of the first stage of Italian

Anarchy in Naples? A mob orchestrated by the camorra ransacks the city's police stations in June 1860.

unification in the north. In the south, the Kingdom of the Two Sicilies suddenly looked very vulnerable. The relationship between the Bourbon police and street thugs broke down in the new climate of fear. In November 1859, the government ordered a big roundup of *camorristi*, and many of them, including Salvatore De Crescenzo, were transported to prison islands off the Italian coast.

The camorra bosses—some of them at least—realised that an alliance with the Committee of Order might actually prove useful, rather than merely lucrative.

Garibaldi's invasion of Sicily in May of the following year, and the Bourbon government's desperate lurch towards constitutional politics, brought the situation to a climax. The police chief who had masterminded the November roundup of gangsters was sacked. Political prisoners were released, as were many *camorristi*—all of them spitting bile about the Bourbon police. Then the government issued the Sovereign Act, and the street theatre began.

The reason why the armed crowd that attacked the police stations showed such remarkable self-discipline was that many of them were *camorristi* allied with the patriots, who wanted to take the Bourbon police out of the game, but did not want the city to descend into anarchy. *La Sangiovannara* was a key figure here. She was rumoured to have helped patriotic prisoners smuggle messages out of Bourbon jails. More importantly, she was camorra boss Salvatore De Crescenzo's cousin. As our Swiss hotelier Marc Monnier said of her

Without being affiliated to the Society, she knew all of its members and brought them together at her house for highly risky secret parleys.

The parleys between the patriots and the camorra entered a new phase once the Neapolitan police force melted away, and Liborio Romano took control of enforcing order in the city. Why did Romano ask the camorra to police Naples? Several different theories circulated in the aftermath. Marc Monnier, generous soul that he was, gave a very charitable explanation. Romano, like his father before him, was a Freemason, as were some other patriotic leaders, as indeed was Garibaldi himself. The typical Masonic cocktail of fellowship, high ideals and ritualistic mumbo-jumbo fitted very well with the seemingly far-fetched project of creating a common *Patria* out of Italy's disjointed parts. Garibaldi's conquest of the Kingdom of the Two Sicilies seemed to be turning those ideals into a reality. Perhaps, argued Monnier, Liborio Romano saw the Honoured Society as a primitive version of his own sect, and hoped it could be turned to the same humanitarian ends. Perhaps.

Less generous and much more realistic commentators said simply that the camorra threatened Romano that they would unleash anarchy on the streets unless they were recruited into the police. It was also claimed that the camorra threatened to kill Romano himself. Other voices—bitter Bourbon supporters it must be said—claimed that Romano was not threatened at all, and that he and some other patriots were the camorra's willing partners all along.

For several years Romano squirmed silently as others tried to make sense of what he had done. Over time, his public image as the saviour of Naples was upended. Most opinion-formers came to regard him as cynical, corrupt and vain; the consensus was that Romano had colluded with the camorra all along. Finally, several years later, Romano made his bid to tell his side of the story and to magnify his history-making role in the turbulent summer of 1860. But his memoir, with its mixture of self-dramatisation and evasive bluster, only served to fuel the worst suspicions, showing that at the very least he was a man with a great deal to hide.

Romano's explanation of how he persuaded the camorra to replace the Bourbon police is so wooden and devious as to be almost comic. He could have reasoned that Naples was an unruly city, and that to keep the peace after the fall of the Bourbons he had had to resort to any means necessary— including recruiting criminals into the police. Few would have criticised him if he had opted for that line of argument. But instead, Romano set out a curious story. He tells us that he asked the most famous *capo* of the Honoured Society to meet him in his office at the Prefecture. Face-to-face with the notorious crook, Romano began with a stirring speech. He explained that the previous government had denied all routes to self-improvement for

Two more redeemed *camorristi*:
Michele 'the Town Crier' (left)
and 'Master Thirteen' (right).

hardworking people with no property. (The *camorrista* could be forgiven a blush of recognition as it sank in that this meant him.) Romano pressed on: the men of the Honoured Society should be given a chance to draw a veil over their shady past and 'rehabilitate themselves'. The best of them were to be recruited into a refounded police force that would no longer be manned by 'nasty thugs and vile stoolpigeons, but by honest people'.

Romano tells us that the mob boss was moved to tears by this vision of a new dawn. Camorra legend has it that he was none other than Salvatore De Crescenzo.

The tale is far-fetched enough to be a scene from an opera. Indeed the whole memoir is best read in precisely that way: as an adaptation, written to impose a unity of time, place and action—not to mention a sentimental gloss—on the more sinister reality of the role that both Liborio Romano and the camorra played in the birth of a united Italian nation. The likelihood is that Romano and the Honoured Society were hand in glove from the outset. The likelihood is, in other words, that Romano and the camorra together planned the destruction of the Neapolitan police force and its replacement by *camorristi*.

Ultimately the precise details of the accord that was undoubtedly struck between gangsters and patriots do not matter. As events in Naples would soon prove, a pact with the devil is a pact with the devil, whatever the small print says.

4

UNCLE PEPPE'S STUFF: The camorra cashes in

THE LAST BOURBON KING OF NAPLES ABANDONED HIS CAPITAL ON 6 SEPTEMBER 1860. The following morning, the city's population poured into the streets and converged on the station to hail the arrival of Giuseppe Garibaldi. Bands played, banners fluttered. Ladies of the highest rank mixed with the rankest plebs, and everyone shouted 'viva Garibaldi!' until they could do little more than croak. Marc Monnier left his hotel early to join the throng. 'I didn't believe that national enthusiasm could ever make so much noise', he recorded. Through a gap in the rejoicing multitude he glimpsed Garibaldi from close enough to make out the smile of tired happiness on his face. He did not have to peer to see *la Sangiovannara*, with her large following of armed women. Or indeed the *camorristi* who stood above the crowd in their carriages, waving weapons in the air.

Liborio Romano shared Garibaldi's glory. The camorra's great friend had been the first to shake Garibaldi's hand on the platform at Naples station; the two of them later climbed into the same carriage and rode together through the rejoicing crowds.

Garibaldi's Neapolitan triumph was also the cue for 'redeemed' camorra bosses like Salvatore De Crescenzo to cash in on the power they had won, and to turn their tricolour cockades into a licence to extort. After Garibaldi arrived in Naples a temporary authority was set up to rule in his name while the south's incorporation into the Kingdom of Italy was arranged.

A French journalist found *la Sangiovannara* (with flag) hard to pin down: 'a young woman's innocent smile alternates on her face with a wolfish cackle'. He described her tavern, adorned with patriotic flags and religious icons, as a hang-out for thugs. He did not know that she was a powerful figure in the Neapolitan underworld.

The short period of Garibaldian rule saw the camorra reveal its true, unredeemed self. As Marc Monnier wryly noted

> When they were made into policemen they stopped being *camorristi* for a while. Now they went back to being *camorristi* but did not stop being policemen.

The *camorristi* now found extortion and smuggling easier and more profitable than ever. Maritime contraband was a particular speciality of Salvatore De Crescenzo's—he was the 'the sailors' *generalissimo*', according to Monnier. While his armed gangs intimidated customs officials, he is said to have imported enough duty-free clothes to dress the whole city. A less well-known but no less powerful *camorrista*, Pasquale Merolle, came to dominate illegal commerce from the city's agricultural hinterland. As any cartload of wine, meat or milk approached the customs office, Merolle's men would form a scrum around it, shouting '*È roba d' o si Peppe*'. 'This is Uncle Peppe's stuff. Let it through'. Uncle Peppe being Giuseppe Garibaldi. The camorra established a grip on commercial traffic with frightening rapidity; the government's customs revenue crashed. On one day only 25 *soldi* were collected: enough to buy a few pizzas.

The camorra also found entirely new places to exert its influence. Hard on the public celebrations for Garibaldi's arrival there followed widespread feelings of insecurity. Naples was not just a metropolis of plebeian squalor. It was also a city of place-seekers and hangers-on, of underemployed lawyers and of pencil-pushers who owed their jobs to favours dished out by the powerful. Much of Naples's precarious livelihood depended heavily on the Bourbon court and the government. If Naples lost its status as a capital it would also forfeit much of its economic *raison d'être*. People soon began wondering whether their jobs would be safe. A purge, or just a wave of carpet-baggers eager to give jobs to their friends could bring unemployment for thousands. But if no job seemed safe, then no job seemed beyond reach either. The sensible thing to do was to make as much fuss as possible and to constantly harass anyone in authority. That way you were less likely to be forgotten and shunted aside when it came to allocating jobs, contracts and pensions.

In the weeks following Garibaldi's triumphant entry the ministers and administrators trying to run the city on his behalf had to fight their way through crowds of supplicants to get into their offices. *Camorristi* were often waiting at the head of the queue. Antonio Scialoja, the economist who had written such an incisive analysis of the camorra back in 1857, returned to Naples in 1860 and witnessed the mess created under Garibaldi's brief rule.

> The current government has descended into the mire, and is now smeared with it. All the ministers have dished out jobs hand over fist to anyone who pleads loudly enough. Some ministers have reduced themselves to holding court surrounded by those scoundrel chieftains of the people that are referred to here as *camorristi*.

'Some ministers' undoubtedly included Liborio Romano. Not even under the discredited Bourbons had *camorristi* had such opportunities to turn the screws of influence and profit.

5

SPANISHRY: The first battle against the camorra

ON 21 OCTOBER 1860, AN AUTUMN SUNDAY BLESSED WITH JOYOUS SUNSHINE AND A clear blue sky, almost every man in Naples voted to enter the Kingdom of Italy. The scenes in the city's biggest piazza—later to be re-baptised Piazza del Plebiscito (Plebiscite Square) in memory of that day—were unforgettable. The basilica of San Francesco di Paola seemed to stretch its vast semi-circular colonnade out to embrace the crowds. Under the portico, a banner reading 'People's assemblies' was stretched between the columns. Beneath there were two huge baskets labelled 'Yes' and 'No'.

In incalculable numbers, yet with patience and good humour, the poorest Neapolitans waited their turn to climb the marble steps and vote. Ragged old men too infirm to walk were carried, weeping with joy, to deposit their ballot in the 'Yes' basket. The tavern-owner, patriotic enforcer and camorra agent known as *la Sangiovannara* was again much in evidence. She was even allowed to vote—the only woman given such an honour—because of her services to the national cause. Etchings of her strong features were published in the press: she was 'the model of Greco-Neapolitan beauty' according to one observer.

Shortly after, the plebiscite Garibaldi relinquished his temporary dictatorship and handed over the appalling mess that Liborio Romano had created to the interim authority managing the integration of Naples into the Kingdom of Italy. Over the coming months the camorra would face the first determined drive to break its stranglehold. Naples was set for a struggle to decide who really controlled the streets.

The man given the job of tackling the policing crisis in Naples was another southern Italian patriot, another veteran of the Bourbon jails: Silvio Spaventa. But Spaventa was a very different politician to his predecessor Liborio Romano. A squat man with a black beard suspended below his flabby cheeks, Spaventa applied moral standards as rigidly to his own behaviour as he did to other people's. Where Romano pandered to the crowd, Spaventa was a model of self-containment with an acute aversion to self-display. On one oc-

Silvio Spaventa, who led the first crackdown on the Honoured Society and the first investigations into its mysterious origins.

casion back in 1848 he had attended a political banquet held in a theatre. The climax of the evening came when he was supposed to parade across the stage. Annoyed and flustered, he failed to notice the prompter's box and fell straight into it.

Spaventa responded to the hardships of prison by forcing himself to pore over the philosophies of Hegel and Spinoza. Like the Duke of Castromediano, he was only freed in 1859. When the King of Naples issued the Sovereign Act he returned to Naples to work with the underground Committee of Order. But the incorruptible Spaventa would have nothing to do with any deal with *camorristi*. To avoid the Bourbon police he slept in a different bed every night; the Hôtel de Genève, owned by his friend Marc Monnier, was one of his refuges. Then the fall of the Kingdom of the Two Sicilies gave him the long-awaited chance to implement the lofty conception of the state's ethical role that he had learned from his prison studies. Spaventa was not just a formidable intellect, he was also an adept networker who knew how much personal loyalty could count in building a power base. But Spaventa's character, his principles and his networking skills would all be tested to breaking point when he became the first Italian politician to face down the camorra. Where Liborio Romano had made himself the most loved politician in Naples by cosying up to organised crime, Silvio Spaventa's crackdown earned him nothing but revulsion.

It did not take Spaventa long to realise how hard his task was going to be. On 28 October 1860 he wrote to his brother.

The stench and the rotting mess here are polluting my senses. You just can't imagine what is happening, what they are up to. Everywhere you turn there are people begging and grasping for as much as they can. Everywhere there is wheeler-dealing, intrigue and theft. I see no earthly way this country can return to some reasonable state of affairs. It seems like the moral order has been torn off its hinges . . . The Kingdom is full of murders, robberies and all kinds of disorder.

Southern Italy was sliding towards anarchy. Prices began to rise steeply as new free-market policies were implemented. The economic downturn sharpened latent conflicts between peasants and landowners. The remains of two armies—Garibaldi's and King Francesco II's—were roaming the countryside. Many *garibaldini* gravitated towards Naples, creating another source of trouble. The bulk of Garibaldi's army resented the fact that they had conquered southern Italy only to lose it to sly political manoeuvres directed by a conservative government in far-off Turin. Mingling with them were hangers-on who hoped that putting on a red shirt might help them get a job or just beg a few coins. The new Italian government tried to create jobs in public works to soak up some of the pool of hungry labour. But as the value of government bonds fell, it proved impossible to raise the funds needed.

Given this daunting disarray, Silvio Spaventa deserves great credit for fighting the camorra with such brio. The first mass arrests came on 16 November 1860. Large quantities of arms and police uniforms were recovered. Salvatore De Crescenzo, the 'redeemed' camorra chieftain and *generalissimo* of maritime contraband, was returned to jail. There he would continue his rise to the top. Nearly two years later, on the morning of 3 October 1862 at the very threshold of the Vicaria jail, De Crescenzo would have his main rival in the Honoured Society stabbed to death. In so doing, he became the first supreme *capo* of the Society who did not come from the Vicaria quarter.

But even with De Crescenzo in prison the camorra was not about to buckle under Spaventa's assault. On the night of 21 November 1860 *camorristi* attacked the Prefecture in the hope of liberating their bosses from the cells.

Spaventa pressed on into the New Year, purging the police and sacking many of the corrupt old turnkeys in the prisons. His rigour rapidly made him the focus for Neapolitans' frustration. Although he was a southerner, he seemed like just the kind of haughty northern politician they had feared would be imposed on them from Turin. *The Times* (London) reported that he was widely regarded as 'obnoxious'. In January 1861 there was a street demonstration against him. Many of those shouting 'Down with Spaventa!' were *camorristi* in National Guard uniforms. There followed a petition with several thousand signatures calling for him to be sacked. Oblivious to his own unpopularity, Spaventa responded with more arrests.

In April 1861, in the heat of the battle between the new Italian state and the Neapolitan camorra, Silvio Spaventa received the order from Turin to conduct an investigation into how the camorra operated. Everyone knew it had begun in the prisons but there were still many questions. How did it come to be a secret society, a sect? When was it founded? In search of answers, Spaventa's civil servants began to rummage in the Neapolitan archives and speak to a number of confidential sources.

All of this research produced two outstanding short reports: the Italian government's first ever dossier on the camorra. Keen to generate publicity for his battle, Spaventa later passed on many of the documents he gathered to Marc Monnier. Monnier added his own material by interviewing everyone he could, including Liborio Romano and several *camorristi*.

Spaventa discovered that the camorra in Naples had different chapters, one for each of the city's twelve quarters. Its power, nevertheless, was heavily concentrated in the four quarters of the low city. The *capo camorrista* of each chapter was elected by his peers. Holding office at the *capo*'s side was a *contarulo* or bookkeeper, who was charged with the highly sensitive task of gathering and redistributing the Society's money.

Anyone who aspired to become a member of the camorra had to show that he met the Society's criteria: there was a ban on passive homosexuals, for example, and on any man whose wife or sister was a prostitute. (Although this, more even than other clauses in the underworld's rulebook, was honoured almost entirely in the breaking.) Candidates for membership also had to be put to the test and observed by their superiors in the Society. They might be required to commit a murder or administer a disfiguring razor slash to the face of one of the Society's enemies. These razor slashes were used as a form of punishment both for outsiders and members who had broken the rules. They became a horribly visible trademark of the camorra's power in the slums of Naples.

Once a new affiliate was deemed ready, he had to swear an oath over crossed knives and fight a duel by dagger against a *camorrista* who was chosen by lot. If the new recruit proved his courage he became a *picciotto di sgarro* (meaning either 'lad who is up for a fight' or 'lad who rubs you up the wrong way').

Knife fights were so important to the Society that its members spent a great deal of time practising their skills; some *camorristi* even became specialised teachers of the art. Duelling to the death was relatively rare. More often the fight had a ceremonial function, so the participants would be told to aim only for the arms. A dagger fencing contest also marked each criminal's elevation to the Society's more senior rank: *camorrista* proper. Becoming a *camorrista* meant gaining access to decision-making power within the Society, and to a greater share of the profits of crime.

Marc Monnier added some very important riders to this organisational sketch. He explained that the various ranks were inherently flexible.

> The members of the sect do not know how to read, and therefore do not have written laws. They hand down their customs and regulations orally, modifying them according to the time and place, and according to the bosses' will and the decisions taken by their meetings.

Underlying the hierarchies within the camorra there was nevertheless a single principle: exploitation. The *camorristi* pitilessly exploited their juniors, the *picciotti di sgarro*. Monnier describes the life of a 'lad who is up for a fight' as a blend of 'toil, humiliation and danger', all endured in the hope of being promoted to *camorrista* at some point. One common test of a *picciotto di sgarro*'s mettle was to take the blame for a felony committed by a senior member of the Society. Ten years of prison was a price worth paying for the chance to become a *camorrista* in your own right.

What about the sect's origins? The civil servants burrowed further into the archives, but found nothing. Spaventa was puzzled.

> Neapolitan police took action against *camorristi* on many occasions. Yet it is strange but true that they did not leave a single important document that might be useful in deducing the origins of this social plague.

Spaventa did not know that in 1857, for unknown reasons, the Bourbon authorities had burned the police archives that would have told him, and us, a great deal more about how the 'social plague' came into being. The holes in the historical record left space only for suspicion. And suspicion, for Spaventa and his civil servants, centred on Spain.

Monnier and Spaventa together propounded a theory that the camorra arrived in Naples at some point during the sixteenth or seventeenth centuries when the Kingdom of Naples, including Sicily, was part of the Spanish empire, ruled by Viceroys appointed in Madrid. The same theory has been in circulation ever since. The evidence Monnier and Spaventa found to support it is very thin, and comes down to four points that scarcely withstand scrutiny.

First, that *camorra* is a Spanish word, meaning 'quarrel' or 'fight'—which it certainly is, and certainly does. But the origins of the Spanish word are Italian anyway, putting us back where we started: in Naples.

Second, that Miguel de Cervantes, the author of *Don Quixote*, published a short story entitled 'Rinconete and Cortadillo' in 1613 that is set in Seville and concerns a criminal confraternity that looks very like the camorra. The obvious problem here is that Cervantes's story is a fiction, and even if it were based on reality, that hardly constitutes proof of any relationship with the camorra two centuries later.

Third, that there was a secret criminal society in Spain called the *Garduña*, which emerged in the early 1400s. But recent research has shown that the *Garduña* was a fiction too, an intellectual con trick. There is no reference to the supposedly medieval sect before 1845, when it appears from nowhere in a very successful French pulp novel about the terrors of the Spanish Inquisition. The novel was translated into Italian in 1847. Its author seems to have got the idea from Cervantes's 'Rinconete and Cortadillo'.

And last, that Spanish rule was proverbially corrupt, which is the weakest point of all. For our tastes, Spanish rule in Italy may well have been arrogant, ostentatious and devious. In fact, Spain became a byword for a government that showed a haughty contempt for the people it ruled. *Spagnolismo* ('Spanishry') was an Italian political insult that evoked lavish displays of power coupled with deadly manoeuvres behind the scenes. But Spain surrendered control of Naples in 1707. There is absolutely no trace of the camorra before the nineteenth century—well over a hundred years later. Spanish influence would have to be very, very devious indeed to have generated the camorra.

The story of the camorra's Spanish origins is nonsense. Indeed in all probability it is nonsense from the jailbird school of history, a story first put about by the *camorristi* themselves. Rather like the tale of the Spanish knights Osso, Mastrosso and Carcagnosso that we have already encountered in the 'ndrangheta's official account of its own roots, the tale of the *Garduña* and all that is a criminal foundation myth that was likely cobbled together in the mid-nineteenth century at precisely the time that the camorra was asserting itself outside the prison system.

If the story of the camorra's Spanish origins is indeed a foundation myth, how come intelligent people like Silvio Spaventa, Marc Monnier and many others after them were fooled by it? It may be that Spaventa simply lowered his formidable intellectual guard, and this piece of hooey sneaked through unanalysed. But there is an alternative theory: all the talk of Spain was a convenient cover story, and the real origins of the camorra were a little too close for comfort for Italian patriots.

As a historical witness, the Swiss hotelier Marc Monnier had the advantage of his outsider's capacity to be amazed by what he saw, while still being able to get close to many of the leading players. Nevertheless, there are moments when he gets too close to be entirely dispassionate. Monnier was Spaventa's mouthpiece, and as such he dutifully repeated and elaborated what he had learned from the official reports about the camorra's Spanish beginnings. To his credit he also hints at a much more convincing and rather more disturbing theory. As if he knows the truth unconsciously, but cannot quite allow himself to utter it, Monnier compares some camorra rituals to a 'pseudo Masonic fantasmagoria' without elaborating on his point. This is more than an idle comparison: the rules and rituals of the Honoured Society were almost certainly derived not from the mythical *Garduña* but from Freemasonry and other Masonic-style sects.

Masonic organisations were integral to the way politics was done in the early nineteenth century. When the French were in charge in Naples they tried to recruit their elite administrators into the Freemasons as a way of flattering and controlling them. But Masonic groups subsequently became a centre of resistance to French rule and were banned in 1813. The Bourbons were highly suspicious of the secret societies when they were restored to the throne—and with good reason. A Masonic sect of patriots called the *Carbonari* ('Charcoal Burners') infiltrated the army and instigated an unsuccessful revolution in Naples in 1820. When the revolution collapsed, many Charcoal Burners ended up in jail where they came into contact with *camorristi*. Interestingly, Liborio Romano was once a Charcoal Burner.

So, while we will never know *exactly* when and how the camorra of the prison system came to ape the patriotic secret sects of the *Risorgimento*, it seems certain that they did. In short Italy, and Italy's chronic problem with organised crime, were profoundly intertwined from the nation's birth. In 1860 the precise moment when the camorra adopted Masonic-style rituals was still recent enough for the truth to bleed through the words still used by *camorristi*. The camorra's local chapters were sometimes called 'lodges', for example, and *camorristi* referred to the members of their Society as the *Patria*: in other words, the camorra saw itself as a 'nation' of elite criminals.

Even by the 1850s, this criminal *Patria* had its own national anthem, a song summarising the spirit in which the Society viewed the whole business of Italian Unification. It goes something like this:

> The Charcoal Burners are a travesty;
> The Bourbon party's a farce.
> We are the *camorristi!*
> And we take them both up the arse.

Camorristi connived with the Bourbons against the patriots, and then with the patriots against the Bourbons. In doing so, they played a key role in making Naples into part of the new Italy. But through all those murky dealings, *camorristi* held true to the methods that Duke Sigismondo Castromediano had observed in jail. Their aim was to extort and smuggle, to 'extract gold from fleas'. Politics—even the inspiring politics of the *Risorgimento* and Garibaldi's heroism—were only a means to that sordid end.

While his civil servants were researching the secrets of the camorra's past, the incorruptible Silvio Spaventa continued his efforts to curtail its present power. One measure he adopted annoyed *camorristi* more than anything else: he stopped National Guardsmen wearing their uniforms when they were not on duty. For the hoodlums who had infiltrated the National Guard, this ban meant that they could not use the uniform as a cover for extortion operations.

Revenge followed swiftly. On 26 April 1861 an angry mob comprising many *camorristi* invaded the ministry building. This time, the cry was not 'Down with Spaventa!' but 'Death to Spaventa!' They forced their way past the guards and into his office but his loyal secretaries managed to buy time while he escaped down a secret staircase. The mob then followed him to his house and smashed its way in. Spectators in the street looked up to see a man appear on the balcony; he waved a long knife and cried, 'Here's the blade I killed him with, and here is his blood!'

In reality, Spaventa had escaped once more. But the attack was so shocking as to make him overcome his deep-seated abhorrence of public attention. The following day he put on a show of courage by going to lunch at the Caffè d'Europa. That evening he sat in a second tier box on the first night of a new production of Bellini's *Norma* at the Teatro San Carlo—the theatre where the rulers of Naples had traditionally made themselves visible to the public that counted. Spaventa even left by the main staircase, under the eyes of a stupefied crowd. He had learned the hard way that Naples could not be governed without a little Spanishry, a little ostentation.

Three months later it became clear that he had learned some other lessons too. In July 1861, in a busy street a short walk from Spaventa's house, a senior police officer called Ferdinando Mele was stabbed behind the ear in broad daylight; he was dead within hours. Mele embodied all the contradictions of the time and place: a *camorrista* who had allied himself with the patriots, he was one of the chief suspects in the murder of Aversa Joe; he was then recruited into the police by Liborio Romano in June 1860 and put in charge of law and order in a whole city quarter.

Mele's killer was soon caught and dragged through the streets into custody. His name was De Mata; he had killed Mele out of revenge because Mele had arrested his equally thuggish brother. De Mata also embodied some very strange contradictions. Although he was not a member of the Honoured Society, he was still an extortionist who had escaped from prison. Yet somehow, thanks to a powerful friend, this dangerous man had found a no-show job at the Post Office.

That powerful friend, it turned out, was Silvio Spaventa. Both De Mata brothers were members of Spaventa's personal bodyguard. There were rumours that Spaventa used the De Matas and their gang to close down politically dangerous newspapers and beat up uncooperative journalists. So it seems that even the incorruptible Spaventa had ended up 'co-managing' Naples with criminals.

Spaventa resigned in the wake of the scandal—although the government spun out a cover story to conceal the real reason why he had stepped down. *The Times* commented glumly on the whole affair for its perplexed readers back in London.

> Nothing will bear examination in Naples. Under the fairest aspects you will find nothing but rottenness; and any man who expects order and tranquillity in this province during the next generation must be very slightly acquainted with the country and the people.

Spaventa's story did indeed foreshadow a sombre future for law and order in Naples. Although the authorities would never again ask the camorra to keep order as Liborio Romano had done, there would be the same dreary swings of the policing pendulum for years to come: first towards repression, with mass arrests accompanied by loud anti-camorra rhetoric; then back towards 'co-management', as the bosses reasserted their hold over the low city. Italian unification in Naples had been a chaotic and unpredictable affair, but it had nonetheless set a simple and lasting pattern for the future history of the camorra.

The events of 1860–61 also heralded the future in ways that were still more worrying. Marc Monnier, our Swiss hotelier, saw the evidence with his own eyes during Spaventa's crackdown.

> I can tell all: every *camorrista* that was arrested could call on influential protectors who issued certificates of good conduct for him. The moment a member of the sect was led to the Vicaria prison, the Chief of Police

was sure to receive twenty letters defending the 'poor man'; the letters were all signed by respectable people!

Politicians were prominent among these 'respectable people' who had befriended the camorra.

> During elections the *camorristi* stopped some candidates from standing; and if any voter objected to this on grounds of conscience or religion, they would appease him with their cudgels. What is more, the *camorristi* were not content to send a deputy to Parliament, and then just watch over his behaviour from a distance. They kept a beady eye on what he did, and had his speeches read aloud to them—since they could not read themselves. If they were not happy with what they heard, they would greet their Member of Parliament on his return from Turin with a bestial chorus of whistling and shouting that would burst out suddenly under the windows of his house.

Clearly the Honoured Society had learned an important lesson from everything that had happened during the crisis of the Bourbon regime and the foundation of a united Italy: a lesson in wedding its own opportunism to the opportunism of the more unscrupulous politicians.

Where once the camorra had lurked, cockroach-like, in the seamiest corners of the Kingdom of the Two Sicilies, now it had begun to climb up through the cracks in the social structure and infest the representative institutions of the Kingdom of Italy. At the end of all the intrigues of Italian Unification, the camorra was no longer just a problem that lay where the state could not reach: it was a problem within the state itself.

In 1864, Marc Monnier, who had done so much to explain the camorra to readers across Italy, was awarded honorary citizenship following a recommendation by a friend and patriotic hero, Gennaro Sambiase Sanseverino, Duke of San Donato. San Donato had known prison and exile during the 1850s. He became a colonel in the National Guard under Liborio Romano in 1860. After the plebiscite, during Silvio Spaventa's campaign against the camorra, San Donato was given charge of the city's theatres; in the course of his duties, a *camorrista* stabbed him in the back outside the Teatro San Carlo. We do not know why the camorra tried to kill San Donato, but we can guess, because we have met the Duke already: he was the 'Neapolitan gentleman' and patriotic conspirator who told Monnier about his secret meeting with the camorra bosses in the 1850s. He was one of the minds behind the patriots' deal with the Honoured Society. San Donato would go on to be mayor of Naples from 1876 to 1878, and was a key figure in the city's sleazy machine politics until the end of the century. The camorra was part of his patronage network. San Donato became what the camorra's redeemer, Liborio Romano, might have become had he not died in 1867.

Marc Monnier had passed through the intrigues of the 1850s and early 1860s with the serenity of an inert particle in a raging chemical reaction. After receiving his honorary citizenship there was little left for him to write about in Italy, so he sold the Hôtel de Genève and moved his young family to Switzerland. He could now finally realise his ambition to be a Genevan author rather than a Neapolitan hotelier. He went on to write a great deal more journalism (for money) and tens of plays (for literary immortality). None of his works has enjoyed anything like the lasting success of his book on the camorra.

Italy was governed between 1860 and 1876 by a loose coalition known as the Right. The Right's leaders were typically landowning, conservative free-marketeers; they favoured rigour in finance and in the application of the law; they admired Britain and believed that the vote was not a right for all but a responsibility that came in a package with property ownership. (Accordingly, until 1882, only around 2 per cent of the Italian population was entitled to vote.)

The men of the Right were also predominantly from the north. The problem they faced in the south throughout their time in power was that there were all too few southerners like Silvio Spaventa. Too few men, in other words, who shared the Right's underlying values.

The Right's fight against the Neapolitan camorra did not end with Spaventa's undignified exit from the city in the summer of 1861. There were more big roundups of *camorristi* in 1862. Late in the same year Spaventa himself became deputy to the Interior Minister in Turin, and began once more to gather information on the Honoured Society. While the publication of Marc Monnier's *The Camorra* kept the issue in the public mind, Spaventa made sure that the camorra was included within the terms of reference of a new Parliamentary Commission of Inquiry into the so-called 'Great Brigandage', a wave of peasant unrest and banditry that had engulfed much of the southern Italian countryside. The outcome of the Commission's work was a notoriously draconian law passed in August 1863—a law that heralds the most enduring historical irony of Silvio Spaventa's personal crusade against organised crime, and of the Right's time in power. The name for that irony is 'enforced residence'.

The new law of August 1863 gave small panels of government functionaries and magistrates the power to punish certain categories of suspects without a trial. The punishment they could hand down was enforced residence—meaning internal exile to a penal colony on some rocky island off the Italian coast. Thanks to Spaventa, *camorristi* were included in the list of people who could be arbitrarily deprived of their liberty in this way.

Enforced residence was designed to deal with *camorristi* because they were difficult to prosecute by normal means, not least because they were so good at intimidating witnesses and could call on protectors among the elite of Neapolitan society. But once on their penal islands, *camorristi* had every opportunity to go about their usual business and also to turn younger inmates into hardened delinquents. In 1876 an army doctor spent three months working in a typical penal colony in the Adriatic Sea.

> Among the enforced residents there are men who demand respect and unlimited veneration from the rest. Every day they buy, sell and meddle without provoking hatred or rivalry. Their word is usually law, and their every gesture a command. They are called *camorristi*. They have their statutes, their rites, their bosses. They win promotion according to the wickedness of their deeds. Each of them has a primary duty to keep silent about any crime, and to respond to orders from above with blind obedience.

Enforced residence became the police's main weapon against suspected gangsters. But far from being a solution to Italy's organised crime emergency as Silvio Spaventa hoped, it would turn out to be a way of perpetuating it.

In 1865, before these ironies had time to unfold, rumours of another criminal sect began to reach the Right's administrators—'the so-called Maffia' of Sicily. The mafia would soon penetrate Italy's new governing institutions far more thoroughly than did the camorra in Naples. So thoroughly as to make it impossible to tell where the sect ended and the state began.

PART II

GETTING TO KNOW THE MAFIA

6

Rebels in Corduroy

Like the camorra, the Sicilian mafia precipitated out from the dirty politics of Italian unification.

Before Garibaldi conquered Sicily in 1860 and handed it over to the new Kingdom of Italy, the island was ruled from Naples as part of the Kingdom of the Two Sicilies. In Sicily, as in Naples, the prisons of the early nineteenth century were filthy, overcrowded, badly managed, and run from within by *camorristi*. Educated revolutionaries joined secret Masonic sects like the Charcoal Burners. When the sect members were jailed they built relationships with the prison gangsters and recruited them as insurrectionary muscle. Soon those gangsters learned the benefits of organising along Masonic lines and, sure enough, the Bourbon authorities found it hard to govern without coming to terms with the thugs. In Sicily, just as in Naples, Italian patriots would overthrow the old regime only to find themselves repeating some of its nefarious dealings with organised crime.

But the Sicilian mafia was, from the outset, far more powerful than the Neapolitan camorra, far more profoundly enmeshed with political power, far more ferocious in its grip on the economy. Why? The short answer is that the mafia developed on an island that was not just lawless: it was a giant research institute for perfecting criminal business models.

The problems began before Italian unification, when Sicily belonged to the Kingdom of the Two Sicilies. The authority of the Bourbon state was more fragile in Sicily than anywhere else. The island had an entirely justified reputation as a crucible of revolution. In addition to half a dozen minor revolts there were major insurrections in 1820, 1848, and of course in May 1860, when Giuseppe Garibaldi's redshirted invasion triggered the overthrow of Bourbon rule on the island. Sicily lurched between revolution and the restoration of order.

Under the Bourbons, Naples completely failed to impose order on the Sicilians, and the Sicilians proved too politically divided to impose order on themselves. Once upon a time, before the invention of policing, private militias beholden to great landowners kept the peace on much of the island. In the early nineteenth century, despite the attempt to introduce a centralised, modern police force, the situation began to degenerate. All too often, rather than being impartial enforcers of the law, the new policemen were merely one more competing source of power among many—racketeers in uniform. Alongside the cops were private armies, groups of bandits, armed bands of fathers and sons, local political factions, cattle rustlers: all of them murdered, stole, extorted and twisted the law in their own interests.

To make matters worse, Sicily was also going through the turmoil brought about by the transition from a feudal to a capitalist system of land ownership. No longer would property only be handed down from noble father to noble firstborn son. It could now be bought and sold on the open market. Wealth was becoming more mobile than it had ever been. In the west of Sicily there were fewer great landowners than in the east and the market for buying land, and particularly for renting and managing it, was more fluid. Here becoming a man of means was easier—as long as you were good with a gun and could buy good friends in the law and politics.

By the 1830s there were already signs of which criminal business model would eventually emerge victorious. In Naples the members of patriotic sects made a covenant with the street toughs of the camorra. But in lawless Sicily, scattered documentary records tell us that the revolutionary sects themselves sometimes turned to crime. One official report from 1830 tells of a Charcoal Burner sect that was muscling its way into local government contracts. In 1838 a Bourbon investigating magistrate sent a report from Trapani with news of what he called 'Unions or brotherhoods, sects of a kind': these Unions formed 'little governments within the government'; they were an ongoing conspiracy against the efficient administration of state business. Were these Unions the mafia, or at least forerunners of the mafia? They may have been. But the documentary record is just too fragmentary and biased for us to be sure.

The condition of Sicily only seemed to worsen after it became part of Italy in 1860. The Right governments faced even graver problems imposing order here than they did in the rest of the south. A good proportion of Sicily's political class favoured autonomy within the Kingdom of Italy. But the Right was highly reluctant to grant that autonomy. How could Sicily govern

Palermo, 1860: freed prisoners parade their warder through the streets before shooting him. The Sicilian mafia was incubated in the political violence of the early to mid-1800s.

its own affairs, the Right reasoned, when the political landscape was filled with a parade of folk demons? A reactionary clergy who were nostalgic for the Bourbon kings; revolutionaries who wanted a republic and were prepared to ally themselves with outlaws in order to achieve it; local political cliques who stole, murdered and kidnapped their way to power. However, the Right's only alternative to autonomy was military law. The Right ruled Sicily with both an iron fist and a wagging finger. In doing so, it made itself hated.

In 1865 came the first news of 'the so-called Maffia or criminal association'. The Maffia was powerful, and powerfully enmeshed in Sicilian politics, or so one government envoy reported. Whatever this new word 'Maffia' or 'mafia' meant (and the uncertainty in the spelling was symptomatic of all manner of deeper mysteries), it provided a very good excuse for yet another crackdown: mass roundups of deserters, draft dodgers and suspected *maffiosi* duly followed.

Then, on Sunday 16 September 1866, the Right paid the price for the hatred it inspired in Sicily. On that morning, Italy—and history—got its first clear look at what is now the world's most notorious criminal band.

Palermo in 1866. Almost the entire city was sliced into four quarters by two rectilinear streets, each lined with grimy-grand palaces and churches, each perhaps fifteen minutes' walk from one gated end to the other. At the city's centre, the meeting point of its two axes, was the piazza known as the Quattro Canti. The via Maqueda pointed north-west from here, aiming towards the only gap in the surrounding ring of mountains. Palermo's one true suburb, the Borgo, ran along the north shore from near the Maqueda gate. The Borgo connected the city to its port and to the looming, bastioned walls of the Ucciardone—the great prison.

Palermo's other principal thoroughfare, the Cassaro, ran directly inland from near the bay, across the Quattro Canti, and left the city at its south-western entrance adjacent to the massive bulk of the Royal Palace. In the middle distance it climbed the flank of Monte Caputo to Monreale, a city famed for its cathedral's golden, mosaic-encrusted vault, which is dominated by the figure of Christ 'Pantocrator'—the ruler of the universe, in all his kindly omnipotence.

The magnificent view inside Monreale Cathedral was matched by the one outside: from this height the eye scanned the expanse of countryside that separated Palermo from the mountains. Framed by the blue of the bay, the glossy green of orange groves was dappled with the grey of the olives; one-storey cottages threw out their white angles among the foliage, and water towers pointed at the sky. This was the Conca d'Oro ('golden hollow' or 'golden shell').

More than any other aspect of Palermo's beautiful setting, it was the Conca d'Oro that earned the city the nickname *la felice*—'the happy', or 'the lucky'. Yet any outsider unwise enough to wander along the lanes of the Conca d'Oro would have soon detected that there was something seriously wrong behind the Edenic façade. At many points along the walls surrounding the orange groves a sculpted crucifix accompanied by a crude inscription proclaimed the point where someone had been murdered for reporting a crime to the authorities. The Conca d'Oro was the most lawless place in the lawless island of Sicily; it was the birthplace of the Sicilian mafia.

So no one was surprised that when trouble entered Palermo on the morning of 16 September 1866, it came from the Conca d'Oro. Specifically, it came down the long, straight, dusty road from Monreale, through the citrus gardens, and past the Royal Palace. The vanguard of the revolt was a squad from Monreale itself; it comprised some 300 men, most of them armed with hunting guns and wearing the corduroy and fustian that were habitual for farmers and agricultural labourers. Similar squads marched on Palermo from the satellite villages of the Conca d'Oro and from the small towns in the mountains behind. Some sported caps, scarves and flags in republican red, or carried banners with the image of the city's patron, Saint Rosalia.

By seven o'clock even the heaviest sleepers in the farthest corners of Palermo had been woken by the sound of musketry and shouting. There was confusion. But the urban masses quickly grabbed the chance to vent their frustrations.

Seven and a half days passed before troops restored order. Seven and a half days when barricades went up in the streets, when arms depots and official buildings were ransacked, when police stations and law courts were raided and criminal records burned, when respectable citizens were robbed at gunpoint in their homes, or forced to make contributions to support the insurrection.

The revolt of September 1866 came at a terrible time for Italian national morale. One of the reasons for the rebels' initial success was that Palermo was lightly garrisoned. All available military forces had been sent to the north-eastern frontier where the Austrians inflicted humiliation by both land and sea at the battles of Custoza and Lissa. The anarchy down in western Sicily was a stab in the back.

Things could easily have been much worse. One of the revolt's primary targets was the Ucciardone, housing two and a half thousand prisoners; many of them would have swollen the ranks of the squads. The rebels surrounded the jail and tried to blow a breach in the walls. But just in time, on the morning of 18 September, the steam corvette *Tancredi* arrived to shower the besiegers with grapeshot and grenades. One of the first men to be hit in this bombardment, his legs grotesquely mangled by shrapnel, was Turi Miceli, the fifty-three-year-old leader of the Monreale crew that had spearheaded the rebellion; he took hours to die of his injuries, and did so without uttering the slightest murmur of complaint.

Turi Miceli was a *mafioso*. He was a tall, imposing figure with a distinctive large scar on his face. Violence was his livelihood. The very sight of him, with his arquebus over his shoulder, had struck terror into the countryside around Palermo. Yet by the time Miceli died he was also a man of money and property, one of the wealthiest people in Monreale.

The camorra was, in its origins, a proletarian criminal association, incubated among the scum of the Neapolitan jails and slums. *Mafiosi* like Turi Miceli were, by contrast, 'middle-class villains'—as one early mafia expert would term them. In much of the rest of western Europe this would have sounded like a contradiction in terms: 'it seemed to subvert every single principle of political economy and social science', as one bewildered observer noted. Men of property had a stake in maintaining the law—that much was surely a self-evident truth. Yet in Palermo's environs, landowners had become criminals and accomplices. In western Sicily, violence was a profession for the upwardly mobile.

So before we retrace the path of *mafioso* Turi Miceli's rise up the social ranks, it is worth highlighting the other striking contrasts between him and someone like Salvatore De Crescenzo, the 'redeemed' camorra boss. Early *camorristi* like De Crescenzo almost invariably had a long stretch inside on their underworld *curriculum vitae*. Yet prison does not appear in the documentary records that Turi Miceli left in his wake. As far as we know, Miceli did not spend a single day in jail, and the same can be said of many of the other bosses we will meet. Sicily certainly had its prison *camorristi*, and the mafia's leaders willingly recruited such men. But some of the most important bosses perfected their skills elsewhere.

The first secret of Turi Miceli's upward mobility lay in the business he was involved in. The land around Miceli's hometown of Monreale was typical of the Conca d'Oro. It was divided up into smallholdings and the dominant crops were olives, vines and particularly oranges and lemons. Citrus fruit trees certainly appealed to the aesthetic senses of visitors, but they also furnished Sicily's most important export business. From Palermo the lemons were mainly shipped across the Atlantic to the burgeoning market of the United States. There was serious money in citrus fruit: in 1860 it was calculated that Palermo's lemon plantations were the most profitable agricultural land in Europe.

The big profits attracted big investment. To create an orange or lemon garden from nothing involved far more than just sticking a few trees in the ground; it was an expensive, long-term project. High walls had to be built to protect the plants from cold. There were roads to lay, storage facilities to construct and irrigation channels to dig. In fact, sophisticated irrigation was vital because if they were watered correctly, citrus fruit trees could crop twice a year instead of once. Yet after all this groundwork was done, it still took around eight years for the trees to start to produce fruit, and several more before the investment turned a profit.

In the Conca d'Oro, as everywhere else in the world, investment and profit came with a third indispensible ingredient of capitalism: risk. But in the Conca d'Oro, risk came dressed in corduroy.

The *mafiosi* of the Palermo hinterland learned the art of the protection racket by vandalising fruit groves, or threatening to vandalise them. Rather than extracting gold from fleas, they squeezed it from lemons. The options were many and varied: they could cut down trees, intimidate farmhands, starve irrigation channels of water at crucial moments of the season, kidnap landowners and their families, threaten wholesalers and cart drivers, and so on. So *mafiosi* wore many hats: they were the men who controlled the sluices of the precious irrigation channels; the guards who protected the groves at night; they were the brokers who took the lemons to market; the contractors who managed the groves on behalf of landowners; and they were also the bandits who kidnapped farmers and stole their highly valuable crops. By creating risk with one hand, and proffering protection with the other, *mafiosi* could infiltrate and manipulate the citrus fruit business in myriad ways. Some of them, like Turi Miceli, could even vandalise and murder their way to ownership of a lemon grove.

Turi Miceli the *mafioso* was both a criminal and a market gardener. But, as the events of September 1866 showed, he was a revolutionary too—as were the other early mafia bosses. Sicily's revolutions provided the other crucial propellant for the mafia's ascent.

For when revolution came along, as it regularly did, it proved good for criminal business. The typical *mafioso* understood that fact better even than the typical *camorrista*. The inevitable confusion of revolution offered men like Turi Miceli the chance to open prisons, burn police records, kill off cops and informers and rob and blackmail wealthy people associated with the fallen regime. Then, once the bloodletting had passed, new revolutionary governments whose leaders needed enforcers would grant amnesties to powerful men 'persecuted' under the old order. In Sicily, much more than in Naples, revolution was the test bed of organised crime, and the launch pad for many a mobster's rise up the social scale.

Turi Miceli's rebel opportunism during the *Risorgimento* was breathtaking. When revolution against the Bourbons broke out in January 1848, Miceli was a known bandit—meaning that he indulged in cattle rustling and armed robbery. But he grasped the chance offered by the revolt with impressive daring: his squad, mostly comprising market gardeners, captured the Bourbon garrison in Monreale before trooping down the hill to Palermo. There, Miceli was celebrated by local poets and lauded in official dispatches for defeating a Bourbon cavalry unit near the Royal Palace. Despite disturbing reports of crimes committed by his men, Miceli was awarded the rank of colonel by the new revolutionary government, partly because his goons packed the meeting at which the officers were elected. The Monreale bandit had 'remade his virginity', as the Sicilian saying goes.

The following year, when the revolution began to fall apart and Bourbon troops were advancing on Palermo, Miceli promptly swapped sides: he toured the main streets and defensive entrenchments persuading the populace not to offer any resistance. His reward from the restored Bourbon authorities was yet another virginity: he was amnestied and given the chance to stuff his pockets. First he was made customs officer, paid 30 ducats a month to pick his own band of men and patrol a long stretch of coastline in eastern Sicily, presumably confiscating contraband and taking hefty bribes at the same time. Not long after that he won the tax-collecting franchise in Lercara Friddi, a sulphur-mining town not too far from Palermo. A senior government official gave him a job reference that said—in blatant contradiction of the facts—that Miceli played no part whatsoever in the 1848 revolution.

In 1860 Miceli nonchalantly changed sides once more and supported Garibaldi's fight against the Bourbons. Naturally, he was then recruited into the National Guard. Under Miceli's control, the National Guard in Monreale was described in an official report of July 1862 as being made up of 'robbers, *cammoristi* [*sic*], Bourbon royalists and corrupt men'.

Miceli did not have the same success in building his career under the Italian government as he had done under the Bourbons. And like everyone else, he could see how detested Italian government authority in Sicily was. So in September 1866, Miceli staked his fortunes on revolution for what turned out to be the last time. The revolt's aims were confused: Bourbon restoration, or a republic—no one was very sure. That did not matter to Turi Miceli. Politics, of whatever stripe, was just a way to convert ferocity into influence, position and money.

In September 1866, for the first and last time, Turi Miceli backed the wrong side and found an agonising death. The revolt was crushed. There were to be no more revolutions in Sicily. For good or ill, Italy was in the island to stay. Other mafia bosses understood that better than Miceli. Instead of forming squads and leading the revolt, they formed what were called 'countersquads' and defended the Italian status quo. Their strategy echoed the moves made by 'redeemed' camorra boss of Naples, Salvatore De Crescenzo: like De Crescenzo, most top *mafiosi* calculated that supporting the cause of Italy was now the surest way to guarantee their criminal fortunes. September 1866 was to be a crucial transitional moment in the history of the mafia.

7

THE BENIGN MAFIA

IN NINETEENTH-CENTURY NAPLES, NOBODY EVER QUESTIONED WHETHER THE CAMORRA existed. Of course there was occasional reticence about the contacts between the early camorra and the Masonic societies of the *Risorgimento*. But nobody ever tried to pretend that 'camorra' meant anything other than what it really was: a secret criminal sect.

Yet for most of the Sicilian mafia's history, most people did not believe it was a sworn criminal fraternity, a Freemasonry of delinquents. 'Mafia', or better, 'mafiosity'—it was said—was a characteristic Sicilian mentality, an island syndrome. If you were *mafioso* you suffered from a swelling of the ego that made you reluctant to settle your disputes through official channels. The symptoms of this strange malady were probably inherited from Sicily's ninth-century Arab invaders.

Late-twentieth-century sociologists had their own versions of the same spurious theory. *Mafiosi* were affiliates of self-help groups in poor, isolated villages—who just happened to kill people occasionally. Or they were local problem solvers and mediators, judges whose courtroom was the piazza and whose law book was an ancient, unwritten code of honour. Meadow Soprano, daughter of TV mafia boss Tony, summed up the theory nicely when she said that the mafia was 'an informal method of conflict resolution in Mediterranean societies'.

As we shall see, this tangle of mystifications was deliberately spun by the mafia and its allies in the Sicilian ruling class. One of the main reasons why the Sicilian mafia was for so long Italy's most powerful criminal organisation was because of its ability to perpetuate the illusion that it did not even exist. The illusion was first created in the years following the Palermo revolt of 1866.

From the Right government's point of view, the miserable story of the 1866 revolt did at least have a hero in Antonio Starabba, Marquis of Rudinì, and Mayor of Palermo. Like all mayors at this time, he was appointed directly by the king rather than being elected by the local people. Rudinì got the Palermo job because despite being a Sicilian, indeed one of the island's biggest landowners, he was a man of the Right. His rectitude and courage amid the mayhem did honour to the Italian flag, and drew the admiration of the European press.

When the squads descended on the city Rudinì mustered the members of his administration to defend the town hall from the rebels. His house at the Quattro Canti was ransacked; his father died from shock as a result; and his wife only just escaped by clambering through a window with their baby in her arms. When the town hall became indefensible, Rudinì led its occupants to the safer surroundings of the Royal Palace. There, with other beleaguered government loyalists, he survived for the rest of the week on horse meat, and shot back at the insurgents with musket balls made from melted down gas pipes. Tall, blonde and handsome, with an easy authority to his manner, Rudinì was not yet thirty years old but his political career was set on a steep, upward trajectory. He was now a poster boy for the Right's project to civilise Sicily. Soon after the revolt he was promoted from Mayor to Prefect. In other words, he was the eyes and ears of central government in the provinces, an official with access to high-level police intelligence. When it came to the problems of Sicily, nobody could command the attention of central government more than him.

Marquis Rudinì was given a platform for his opinions eight months after the Palermo revolt of September 1866, when a parliamentary commission of inquiry came to Sicily to learn the lessons. The commissioners assembled in the comfort of the Hotel Trinacria set back from the marina, its doors protected by a picket of troops. They heard Rudinì give a testimony that addressed the mafia issue with shocking clarity.

> The Mafia is powerful—perhaps even more powerful than people believe. Uncovering it and punishing it is very often impossible, because there is no proof, either of the crimes, or of who is to blame . . . We've never been able to pull together enough evidence to prepare a trial and bring it to a successful conclusion.
>
> Only people who have the Mafia's protection can move around freely in the countryside . . . The lack of security has brought about the following situation: anyone who wants to go into the countryside and live

there has to become a brigand. There is no alternative. To defend your-self and your property, you have to obtain protection from the criminals, and tie yourself to them in some way.

The Ucciardone—the Palermo prison—is a kind of government. That's where rules, orders, etc. are issued. In the Ucciardone they know everything. So that might lead us to believe that the Mafia has formally recognised bosses.

In the countryside around Palermo criminal gangs are very wide-spread, and there are many different bosses. But they often act in agree-ment with one another and look to the Ucciardone for leadership.

Their aim is to get rich in the disorder and bump off their enemies. Robbery and vendetta, in short.

Rudinì was right. Or at least he was as right as he could feasibly be at this early stage in the mafia's history. Granted, talking about the mafia was polit-ically convenient for the young Marquis. For one thing, it saved his having to address his own share of the blame for the revolt. His high-handed pol-icies as mayor had made him as loathed in Palermo as Silvio Spaventa was in Naples.

Nevertheless, we can now appreciate just how far towards a full under-standing of the mafia Rudinì had advanced. He was particularly astute in identifying how the property owners of the area had to 'tie themselves' to the mafia. The threats and promises that won the mafia such a big slice of the citrus fruit business also won them freedom from the law and friends in high places. Here lay the genuine shock effect of Rudinì's words: the land-owners who had become 'brigands' were also the ruling class of the province of Palermo, its political leadership.

The self-assured young Marquis Rudinì did not have all the answers, of course. He was sensible enough to acknowledge as much: he confessed that he could not tell how many bosses and affiliates the mafia had, for instance. 'To really appreciate the Mafia's power and influence, we would need to get to know this mysterious organisation better.'

A decade later, another parliamentary inquiry squinted into the murk of Sicilian affairs. In March 1876, this time in Rome (which had become the capital city in 1870), Marquis Rudinì was called to demonstrate whether he had indeed managed to get to know the mysterious mafia organisation any better.

Rudinì's political career had made further progress in the meantime: he became Minister of the Interior for a while in 1869. Yet the years seemed to have eroded his confidence. His views on the mafia were now hesitant, slippery, and confusing.

He began by saying that, in Sicily, public opinion had been 'led astray' in such a way that criminals had become 'likeable' to the local population. Perhaps sensing that these words might not play well in Sicily, he tried to claim that the same thing 'happens in every country in the world'. Ignoring the puzzled frowns of the commission members sitting before him, he blundered on.

> Now when public opinion and indeed the very moral sense of any population is led astray in the way I have described, the result is the maffia. The famous maffia! But what is this maffia? Let me say first of all that there is a benign maffia. The benign maffia is a sort of bravado. It is a strange inclination not to allow yourself to be bullied; instead, you bully others. It's about striking an attitude—the attitude of the *farceur*, or practical joker, as the French would say. Thus I myself could be a benign *maffioso*. Not that I am one. But, in a nutshell, anyone who respects himself, who has a dash of exaggerated haughtiness, could be one.

Rudinì's waffling testimony then moved on to what he called the 'malign maffia', which was, he asserted, the unfortunate result of the 'atmosphere' created by the benign maffia. As if he had not already done enough to baffle his listeners, he further divided the malign mafia into two distinct and apparently unconnected types. First there was the prison mafia—but that had all but disappeared anyway; then there was what he called a 'high mafia'. Unlike the prison mafia, the high mafia was not a genuine criminal association. Instead, it was what he termed a 'solidarity in crime'.

It was all about as clear as a glass of black Sicilian wine. No mention of an organisation. No mention of bosses or links between the prisons and criminals on the outside. No reference to landowners who become 'brigands' or to protection rackets. No mention of lemon groves, witnesses being intimidated, or robbery and vendetta. Not even a suggestion that there might be more to learn.

Between 1867 and 1876, Marquis Rudinì's views on the mafia had retreated from clarity into muddle, from forthright condemnation into woolly apologia.

Rudinì was not the only witness to spin out such verbiage in 1876. Some flatly denied that the mafia even existed. Many others talked about a 'good mafia' and a 'bad mafia', about the islanders' proud way of taking the law into their own hands, and so on. If the mafia did exist, it was something shapeless and hard to explain to an outsider, something that Sicilians felt in their bones. Nobody could ever hope to get to know the mafia better.

Rudinì had very good reasons for being flustered when he came before the 1876 commission of inquiry. The commission itself had been instituted in the aftermath of a scandal involving the chief of police of Palermo, a man called Giuseppe Albanese. In 1871 Albanese went on the run to avoid being arrested for arranging several murders in concert with the mafia chief of Monreale, who was presumably Turi Miceli's successor as boss of the town. While in hiding, Police Chief Albanese was received in Rome by no less than the Prime Minister, who promised him the government's protection. Not surprisingly there was an outcry in Sicily when Albanese was acquitted for lack of evidence some months later. Then in June 1875 further scandalous details about the police chief emerged. His favourite underworld informer led a gang of criminals who had perpetrated a series of burglaries from aristocratic palaces, from the offices of the Court of Appeal, from a pawnbroker's, and even from the city museum. The loot was recovered in the house of a policeman who worked in Albanese's office.

Rudinì was profoundly implicated in the scandal since he had appointed Albanese in the first place. Rudinì had also been Interior Minister, with direct responsibility for law and order policy, when Albanese was employing the mafia to murder people in Monreale. (Albanese's aim, once more, was to co-manage crime with the underworld elite.)

Rudinì also had political reasons for unlearning what he knew about the mafia. As Member of Parliament for a Sicilian constituency, he was one of only a small handful of Right MPs that the island had sent to Rome in the last general election. The Right had bludgeoned Sicily to get rid of the mafia, but then hired the mafia to help in its repressive work. Now it was paying the political price for its hypocrisy and double-dealing. Rudinì was trying desperately to fit in with the new mood, but his efforts proved futile. Eight days after Rudinì's testimony, on 18 March 1876, the Right coalition government split over the issue of railway nationalisation and the Left entered government for the first time. Rudinì was destined for a long spell in the political wilderness.

Like the Right, the Left was a very loose coalition: its unifying themes were the desire to extend democracy and to invest more money in the country's backward infrastructure. The Left was also more southern than the Right, and in particular more Sicilian. With the advent of the Left, Sicilian politicians gained access to power, and the Italian state finally won consent for its authority on the island. Yet among the politicians who now represented Sicily in a Left-dominated chamber were the 'brigands' that Rudinì had spoken of in 1867—landowners who, willingly or not, had struck a deal with the *mafiosi* to protect and manage their land. The mafia was now able to offer other services to its patrons: election management, for one. Once the Left was in power, the mafia's political sponsors enjoyed purchase with central government.

After the Bourbons, the Right. After the Right, the Left. Whether in times of revolution or in times of peace, no government could control Sicily without going through *mafiosi*.

8

A SECT WITH A LIFE OF ITS OWN:
The mafia's rituals discovered

ON 29 FEBRUARY 1876, ELEVEN DAYS BEFORE MARQUIS RUDINÌ PUT FORWARD HIS abstruse theories about the 'benign mafia', the Italian government discovered the most important piece of evidence in the entire history of Sicilian organised crime. The Palermo police chief wrote to the Minister of the Interior to describe, for the first time, the initiation ritual used by *mafiosi* in a settlement in the Conca d'Oro called Uditore.

Uditore was a suburban village, a *borgata*, of only 700–800 souls, but there had been no less than thirty-four murders there in 1874, as rival mafia factions fought for a monopoly over the lucrative business of 'protecting' the market gardens. The local boss was don Antonino Giammona, described by the chief of police as 'almost completely lacking in education, but with a natural intelligence'. Another witness described him as 'taciturn, puffed up, and wary'. Giammona even fancied himself as something of a poet and wrote verse in Sicilian dialect.

He also made each of his gang's members-to-be undergo a kind of baptism into a new, more exalted life of crime, the chief of police explained. The aspiring *mafioso* was taken to a secluded spot and shown into the company of Giammona and his underbosses. The recruit offered his finger or arm to be punctured with a dagger, and then dripped blood onto a small picture of a saint. The picture was then burned and its ashes scattered to signify the total obliteration of traitors, while the recruit swore eternal loyalty to the sect.

The Police Chief of Palermo was in no doubt about how significant this find was: it utterly discredited all the waffle about the 'benign mafia', the mafia as an inborn Sicilian egotism.

It shows that the maffia is not only an individual manifestation of an instinctive tendency to bully people, but is instead a sect with a life of its own, which operates in the shadows.

The same ritual recurs throughout the history of the mafia in Sicily and North America. But the rules by which individual mafia gangs or *cosche* (pronounced *kos-keh*) live are very rarely written down. So, because they are transmitted by word of mouth, they are susceptible to minor local variations: in the wording of the oath taken by the initiate, for example. Sometimes the bottom lip was pierced, more often the trigger finger. Most *cosche* use a pin to draw blood, some use the thorn from a Seville orange-tree. Different figures appeared on the sacred image that was consumed by the flames, although the Madonna of the Annunciation is by far the most frequent. There is nevertheless a strong family resemblance between all the variants. That family resemblance is the clearest possible demonstration that the mafia is not just a haughty attitude or some vague 'solidarity in crime', as Marquis Rudinì would try to claim. It is an organisation. And that organisation has a history—a single line of continuity that runs from the lemon groves of the Palermo hinterland to the streets of New York and beyond.

In the months following the first unearthing of the initiation rite, news of very similar oaths arrived from elsewhere in the province of Palermo and even across the island in the province of Agrigento. Curiously, one of the *cosche* using these rites was discovered in the town of Canicattì, where Marquis Rudinì had his constituency.

The resemblances between the different mafia gangs were striking. Like the Giammona crew in Uditore, the other *cosche* also used a coded dialogue so that *mafiosi* who did not know one another personally could recognise one another as brothers in crime. The dialogue began when one *mafioso* complained about a toothache and pointed to one of the canines in his upper jaw. The second *mafioso* would reply that he too had a toothache. The two would proceed to tell one another where they were when the tooth began to hurt, who was present, and so on. The 'toothache' signified membership of the mafia; and the references to the time and place the toothache began recalled the moment when the *mafioso* was initiated.

All of this evidence arrived at a politically sensitive time. The Left was consolidating itself in power and discovering that the mafia was something rather more menacing than a peculiar Sicilian form of bravado. Then in November 1876 the state of law and order in Sicily became an international embarrassment when the English manager of a sulphur company was kidnapped in the province of Palermo; there were strong suspicions of mafia involvement.

The Left's new Prefect of Palermo, Antonio Malusardi, became convinced that there was a link, or as he termed it, 'a real correspondence' between the various mafia cells. On 30 January 1877 the Prefect wrote to the Chief Prosecutor, the man in charge of the whole judicial system in Palermo, and urged him to unify the different mafia investigations so that the connections between the different *cosche* could be explored. In short, the Prefect of Palermo was asking the Chief Prosecutor to answer a simple but crucial question. Were there many criminal sects in Sicily, or was there just one single Freemasonry of delinquency? One Sicilian mafia, or many?

No Sicilian old enough to remember the 1980s can read Prefect Malusardi's words without a shiver of recognition. For only in 1983, amid a terrifying upsurge in mafia violence, did Palermo investigators finally begin to base their strategy on the 'real correspondences' between the mafia gangs across western Sicily. To trace and document those correspondences, they formed an anti-mafia 'pool' of four specialised prosecutors.

In the summer of the following year, a leading Man of Honour called Tommaso Buscetta, who had lost many of his relatives in the ongoing slaughter, turned state's witness. Buscetta, who was known as the 'boss of the two worlds' because of his transatlantic influence, gave the pool of investigators a deeper insight into the mafia than they had ever had. Among the many vital revelations provided by Buscetta was the initiation ritual that he, like every other Man of Honour, had undergone. In 1992, a verdict from the Court of Cassation, Italy's Supreme Court, finally accepted the boss of two worlds' testimony; it confirmed for *the first time in history* that the mafia was not a loose ensemble of local gangs but a single organisation, bound by an oath of loyalty until death. There was only one Sicilian mafia.

Two of Italy's most courageous and able men would soon pay for this truth with their lives. Within weeks of the Supreme Court's ruling, the leading members of the anti-mafia pool, Giovanni Falcone and Paolo Borsellino, were both blown up. Tragically, Prefect Malusardi's hunch had finally been proven incontrovertibly—more than a century of bloodshed later. New research tells us that Italy could and should have answered Malusardi's question shortly after he asked it.

The Chief Prosecutor's reply to Prefect Malusardi's letter about the mafia's rituals took more than a month to arrive—a strange delay given the importance of the matter. Its conclusions were absolutely categorical.

Doubtless there are groups or associations of criminals of various sizes here and there in Sicily. But they are *not* confederated or bound to one another by links of mutual complicity.

The Chief Prosecutor was very hostile to the suggestion that there should be large-scale mafia prosecutions—Italians today call them 'maxi-trials'. Such trials would trample on the autonomy of the magistracy, he protested, and open the way for politically motivated abuses of the law by the government. This argument won the day. In courts across Sicily over the following six years, a few *mafiosi* were put on trial, many of them for the first time. But they were tried as members of separate, locally based criminal organisations.

The Chief Prosecutor's letter has often been cited by historians sceptical about the existence of a unified criminal network called 'the mafia'. Falcone and Borsellino may have demonstrated beyond doubt the existence of the organisation known as Cosa Nostra, they argue, but it is naïve to project that finding back into the past. In 1877 the far-fetched theory that there was only one mafia suited the government's purposes all too well, it has been claimed. There are few better pretexts for an authoritarian crackdown than the fantasy of a mysterious clandestine sect of murderers with links right across western Sicily. The Chief Prosecutor had access to all the available police evidence on the early mafia, much of which has since been lost. So if someone as knowledgeable as him thought that the different gangs were not 'confederated', who are we, at more than a century's distance, to cast doubt on his conclusions?

Yet on closer inspection, the Chief Prosecutor's letter is hardly a shining example of forensic logic. The different associations could not be linked, he argued, because fighting often broke out between them. The toothache dialogue was not a recent discovery, he added: tough guys across the island had been using the same formulaic exchange for a while to check whether the people they met shared a similar mindset; they had started doing it in the prison in Milazzo, and had probably copied the idea from a story about a noble bandit written by Alexandre Dumas, author of *The Three Musketeers*. The Chief Prosecutor concluded by conceding that on one occasion, and one only, the different gangs had indeed shown a sense of shared purpose: in the revolt of September 1866, when they united in the cause of overthrowing what they called the 'despicable government'.

Quite why these points make for a decisive rebuttal of the theory that there was a single, unified mafia network is not entirely clear.

Mafiosi killed one another before 1877, and they have done so ever since. But that does not stop them being members of the same brotherhood.

The fact that the toothache routine may have been invented in prison does nothing to diminish the suspicions that surround it—quite the contrary. Nor indeed does the fact that it may have been copied from a novel, an opera, or whatever. As we know from the fable of the camorra's Spanish origins, Italian criminal organisations like to create a rich mythology for themselves; we can hardly be surprised if they are unscrupulous enough to do it by plagiarising bits and pieces from the culture around them.

Last but not least, if many of the gangs were able to coordinate sufficiently well to rise up in simultaneous revolt in September 1866, did that not provide deeply worrying evidence of the links between them?

It is time we met the Chief Prosecutor who put his name to these shaky arguments. He was Carlo Morena, a highly respected magistrate who had been given many decorations during his distinguished career. He came from a place immune to Sicily's 'exaggerated haughtiness', its proudly truculent attitude to official legality: he was born in 1821 in a village in the north, not far from the Ligurian coastal town of Savona.

In March 1876, just after being appointed to the most senior judicial position in Sicily, Morena was interviewed by a parliamentary inquiry about the state of justice in the Palermo area. His replies were frank—as befitted a magistrate who clearly believed in upholding the rule of law. Sicilian magistrates were weak or corrupt, Morena said; there was a wall of *omertà* among witnesses and even victims; and the courts handed out feeble punishments for violent crimes that undermined the authority of the state.

But by the time he came to reply to Prefect Malusardi ten months later, Carlo Morena was a *mafioso*. He did not have a 'toothache', and was not part of the sworn criminal fraternity. Nor was he necessarily even a willing aide to the gangsters. But he was nonetheless a 'friend of the friends', as the Sicilian expression has it.

Quite what the mafia did to win Morena over in 1876 is not known. He may have been subjected to any mixture of threats, bribery, blackmail and political pressure. As with the landowners that Marquis Rudinì labelled 'brigands', or indeed with Rudinì himself, many different scenarios are possible. But we can at least be sure that Chief Prosecutor Morena was working for the Honoured Society of Sicily. To find out why, we need to move much, much deeper into the world of the mafia—deeper than was ever possible before the discovery in 2009 of a quite exceptionally revealing document. That document is in the neat handwriting of the first genuine hero in the history of Italian organised crime, a man whose long and eventful career we will follow from now on.

If there is one thing that the mafia fears, it is good police. Despite all the co-management of crime in Naples and Palermo, nineteenth-century Italy did produce some very good police. Among the best of them was a blonde, square-jawed officer called Ermanno Sangiorgi. Sangiorgi's bulky personal file is kept among the endless Ministry of the Interior papers in Rome's Central State Archive. It covers a career that lasted nearly five decades. Sangiorgi retired in 1907, by which time he was the country's most experienced and decorated mafia-fighter. Sangiorgi embodies all the tribulations of the fight against the mafia after Italian unification.

For very good personal and professional reasons, Sangiorgi had no doubts about what the mafia was: a clandestine sect of murderers with links right across western Sicily. For one thing, it was Sangiorgi who led the inquiry into the Uditore mafia whose boss was the dialect poet, don Antonino Giammona, and Sangiorgi who first discovered the initiation ritual and the 'toothache' dialogue.

What follows in the next chapter is the story of a previously unknown investigation that ran in parallel to the case of the Uditore mob. The mafia did not lightly forgive Ermanno Sangiorgi for exposing its initiation ritual. As the mafia's vengeance played itself out, Sangiorgi was to discover just how subtle and ramified was its authority, and just how wrong Carlo Morena was to deny the existence of a unified criminal brotherhood in western Sicily.

Sangiorgi's investigation also reveals the sinister manoeuvrings during the early years of the Left, which saw the mafia put on trial for the first time, but which also saw Sicilian politicians, among them the mafia's friends, step onto the national political stage.

There is one background political issue that is worth keeping in mind from the outset of this story: discontinuity. The problem has bedevilled Italy's response to organised crime for much of the last century and a half. After 1860, whether under the Right or the Left, the Italian system generated one fragile coalition government after another, and therefore a dizzying turnover of officials and policies.

Policing policy is a prime example. The short chain of command that concerns us here descends as follows: from the Prime Minister and then the Interior Minister in Rome, down to the Prefect of Palermo and then through the city's chief of police to his officers on the ground. The following story is set over three and a half years, from November 1874 to June 1878. It was a bad period for policy discontinuity, but not unrepresentative: there were three Prime Ministers, four Interior Ministers, six Prefects of Palermo and three chiefs of police. Some of them barely had time to hang their jackets up before they were transferred. All the time, at every level, policy swung unpredictably between repressing the mafia and cultivating it. For frontline policemen like Ermanno Sangiorgi, these rapid changes in the political weather could have terrifying consequences.

9

DOUBLE VENDETTA

Like most Italian policemen, Ermanno Sangiorgi badly wanted to win the favour of the civil servants who controlled his destiny and monitored every detail of his private life. Pay was poor. Conditions were tough. The Public Security Service had a national career structure and a habit of moving its officers rapidly between postings, so that even the rank and file could spend their entire careers in wandering exile among alien communities where the locals spoke incomprehensible dialects and regarded the cops with contempt.

Sangiorgi was from the centre-north of the country; he was born in 1840 in the Romagnol spa town of Riolo. He knew only too well how a police career could play havoc with family life. His first wife died, probably in childbirth, leaving him with a son, Achille, to care for on his own when he was not yet out of his teens. He got married for a second time in 1861, to Enrica Ricci, a girl from a respectable lower-middle-class Faenza family, and the couple gave their children the patriotic names of Italo and Italia. After 1863, much of Sangiorgi's service was spent fighting brigand bands in the south. Posted to primitive mountain communities, he and his wife could not keep Achille with them much of the time. Promotion was the only path to a less arduous life, yet every step up the career ladder had to be twisted from the grasp of politicians and bureaucrats by means of strenuous hard work, string pulling, and sob stories. Sangiorgi had a high sense of his own worth and was dogged in the pursuit of his ambition. As a Prefect would later write of him, 'he seeks out every possible means of getting himself noticed'.

In December 1874 Sangiorgi tried to get himself noticed by the Minister of the Interior, no less. For nine months he had been acting inspector in Trapani, on the westernmost tip of Sicily, he wrote. The permanent promotion to inspector that he had been promised had not yet materialised. Of course he had absolute confidence that this promise would be kept—so much so that he had not hesitated to dip into his own pocket to supplement his police pay. After all, he had a wife and three children to support. But his 'intense desire' was to show his gratitude to the minister with further services, and 'to make himself ever more worthy of the Royal Government's consideration'. Would it be possible, therefore, for him to be transferred 'to a place where the conditions of law and order leave more to be desired'?

Sangiorgi was looking for action, and he got all the action he could ever have hoped for. In March 1875 he took charge of the biggest, most heavily populated, and most mafia-infested police district in Sicily: Castel Molo, covering the northern part of the Conca d'Oro. Within its administrative boundaries lay the Piana dei Colli—a fertile plain bounded on one side by the small mountains to Palermo's north-west, and on the other by Monte Pellegrino, an isolated mass of rock that surges from the shore just to the city's north. The Piana dei Colli was dotted with the villas and gardens of the wealthy. Yet, like the rest of the Conca d'Oro, its settlements had a fearsome reputation for lawlessness. A little further to the west, Castel Molo cops also policed the lemon groves of Passo di Rigano and Uditore. These satellite villages were, in Sangiorgi's words, 'sadly renowned for criminal associations and bloody crimes'. Sangiorgi diagnosed the cause of the bloodshed in Castel Molo with incisive calm.

> The mafia dominated the situation, and it had even managed to infect the police station. In fact the main mafia bosses had all been granted gun licences. When murders and other serious crimes happened in the Castel Molo district, as they did frequently, the police chose its informers from among these men . . . They turned to the most notorious *mafiosi* for confidential information on who was guilty, with the frequent result that poor, honest families were sacrificed, criminals went unpunished, and the general public was disheartened and distrustful.

Clearly the policy of co-managing crime with the mafia was still fully operative. One of the most egregious cases of this policy concerned Sangiorgi's immediate predecessor in charge of the Castel Molo police station, Inspector Matteo Ferro. Ferro had a close friendship with the *mafioso* who was to occupy a central role in Sangiorgi's story: Giovanni Cusimano, known as *il nero* ('Darky') because of his complexion.

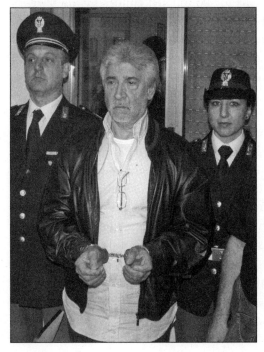

Salvatore Lo Piccolo, arrested in November 2007, in possession of a mafia rulebook (see p. 80). Lo Piccolo's territory included the Piana dei Colli, where many of the earliest dramas of the Sicilian mafia's history took place.

Inspector Ferro had already done a great deal to obstruct investigations into the Uditore mafia before Sangiorgi arrived; he had also gone on record to defend Darky, denying that he was a *capomafia*, calling him instead 'an upright man, an individual who is completely devoted to law and order'. This despite the fact that Darky, among his many other crimes, had recently terrorised one landowner into granting him a lease on a villa worth 200,000 lire for the derisory annual fee of one hundred litres of olive oil. (A rent which, needless to say, Darky did not even deign to pay.) Once installed in the villa, Darky regularly received visits not only from the friendly local police inspector, Matteo Ferro, but also from a sergeant in the *Carabinieri*, and the editor of the local newspaper, *L'Amico del Popolo* (*The People's Friend*). Everyone with any influence in the Piana dei Colli was a friend of Darky's.

Soon after establishing himself in Castel Molo police station, Sangiorgi acted.

I quickly grasped that I needed to adopt a method diametrically opposed to the one that the police had used thus far. So at once I started openly fighting the mafia.

An open fight against the mafia. The simplicity of these words should not mislead as to just how difficult the task really was. When Sangiorgi revoked the mafia bosses' gun licences and handed out police cautions to them all, he had to overcome opposition on a scale that the police fighting the camorra in Naples had never encountered: Sangiorgi referred to 'the intervention of Senators, MPs, senior magistrates and other notables' in defence of the crime bosses. In other words, the mafia was already part of a network that reached up towards the higher echelons of Italy's governing institutions. Sangiorgi's story is a parable of just how difficult an open fight against that network can be.

At first, Sangiorgi achieved excellent results. 'The mafia went into its shell', he later recalled, 'there was a positive reawakening of public morale, and a marked reduction in the number of crimes.'

Then in November 1875, eight months after Sangiorgi arrived in Palermo, a crippled old man, leaning heavily on a lawyer's arm, was shown into his office. His name was Calogero Gambino, and he was the owner of a lemon grove in the Piana dei Colli, near the *borgata* of San Lorenzo. He began by saying that he had heard of Sangiorgi's reputation as an honest and energetic cop, and so was now turning to him to obtain justice against the mafia.

Gambino had two sons, Antonino and Salvatore. Some eighteen months earlier, on 18 June 1874, Antonino had been ambushed and killed—shot in the back from behind the wall of a lemon grove as he was on his way to spray the family's vines with sulphur. Gambino's other son Salvatore was about to stand trial for his brother's murder. But this 'fratricide' was nothing of the sort, old man Gambino explained. The mafia, in the shape of Darky Cusimano, had killed one son and framed the other: this was its last, cunning act of vengeance against his family.

Without needing to be told, Sangiorgi understood why Gambino had come to see him now: Giovanni 'Darky' Cusimano was dead, a recent victim of the semi-permanent mafia war to control the lemon groves. The bloody end to Cusimano's reign in the Piana dei Colli left Calogero Gambino free to tell his extraordinary story.

A story that was a stick of political dynamite with a fizzing fuse. For old man Gambino also claimed that the police had helped the mafia arrange the fake fratricide. The national scandal surrounding former Chief of Police Albanese had reached its peak only a few months earlier. If what Gambino said was true, it would prove that the corruption had not ended with Albanese; it would prove that the mafia's infiltration of the police in Palermo was still well-nigh systematic.

The 'fratricide' plot against Gambino's surviving son was only the climactic moment of a campaign of vengeance that stretched back over fourteen years, to the time when Garibaldi's expedition to Sicily made the island part of a unified Italian kingdom. The old man said that the mafia had originally targeted him because he was a well-to-do outsider who was not born in San Lorenzo. His son-in-law, Giuseppe Biundi, was the original source of his troubles; Biundi was the nephew of Darky's underboss. In 1860 Biundi kidnapped and raped Gambino's daughter to force a marriage. A few months after the wedding, Gambino's new son-in-law stole several thousand lire from his house. The young man's family connections made old man Gambino too afraid to report the burglary to the authorities, he said.

Then, in 1863, Giuseppe Biundi kidnapped and murdered Gambino's own brother. The old man could no longer keep quiet: following his tip-off to the police, Biundi and his accomplice were caught and sentenced to fifteen years' hard labour.

Sitting in Sangiorgi's office eleven years later, Gambino explained the dread consequences of his actions.

First the mafia persecuted me for vile reasons of economic speculation. But after what I revealed to the police, there came another, much more serious reason for turning the screw on me: personal vendetta.

But vendetta did not arrive immediately: Giovanni 'Darky' Cusimano had to wait three years, until the revolt of September 1866.

At the outbreak of the revolt, Gambino was confidentially warned that he was in grave danger, and had to leave San Lorenzo immediately. His sons threw the family's cash, clothes, linen, cooking implements and chickens onto a mule cart, and set off to take refuge at another farm managed by a friend of theirs. On the way, they were attacked by a party of seventeen *mafiosi*. A fierce gun battle followed; Salvatore Gambino was wounded in the left thigh. But both brothers knew the area well, and managed to escape over the wall of a nearby estate, abandoning the family's possessions to be ransacked by their tormentors.

The Palermo countryside was by then almost completely in the hands of the rebellious squads. Fearing that their chosen place of safety no longer offered sufficient protection, the Gambino family went to Resuttana, the village next to San Lorenzo in the Piana dei Colli. There they were taken in by one Salvatore Licata. It was in Salvatore Licata's house, the following day, that the Gambinos took delivery of a package from Giovanni 'Darky' Cusimano: it contained a hunk of meat from their own mare. As a mafia message, the horse flesh may not have had the cinematic flair of the decapitated stallion deployed in *The Godfather*, but its meaning was very similar all the same: Darky had not yet concluded his business with the Gambino family.

Inspector Sangiorgi does not tell us what his thoughts were as he listened to old man Gambino—he was far too savvy a policeman to write those thoughts down. Yet to appreciate the full drama of what Sangiorgi was hearing, and the intrigue that he was being drawn into, we have no choice but to figure out how his mind began to work when he learned who had offered sanctuary to the beleaguered Gambinos in Resuttana in September 1866. Sangiorgi was an outsider to Sicily, a northerner. But he had been in Palermo long enough to know the baleful power of the Licatas. The very mention of the Licata name told him, more clearly than any other detail, that Gambino was hiding a crucial part of the truth.

Salvatore Licata, aged sixty-one at the time he took in the Gambinos, was one of the most venerable and best-connected *mafiosi* in the Conca d'Oro.

Like many important mafia bosses, including Turi Miceli from Monreale, Darky Cusimano from San Lorenzo, and don Antonino Giammona from Uditore, Licata had led a revolutionary squad into Palermo in 1848 and 1860. But during the 1866 revolt Licata mobilised his heavies to oppose the insurgents. They formed a countersquad. Licata, in other words, was one of the smart *mafiosi* who realised that he had more to lose than to gain by rebelling.

His son Andrea was an officer in the Horse Militia, a notoriously corrupt mounted police force. His three other sons were armed robbers and extortionists who were guaranteed impunity by the family's connections.

Like the Licatas, and like don Antonino Giammona who was a pillar of the National Guard, many Palermo bosses broke their remaining links with revolutionary politics during the revolt of 1866.

Old man Gambino's friendship with the fearsome Licata clan raises the very strong suspicion that Gambino and his sons were also *mafiosi*. Several aspects of his story stretched credulity too far. He was asking Inspector Sangiorgi to believe that he was entirely an innocent victim. Fear alone, according to Gambino, had kept him from going to the law when persecuted by Darky, even though that persecution had been going on for nearly a decade and a half. The way he described his murdered son Antonino was also suspicious.

My son Antonino was a young man who was full of courage. He had too much respect for himself to lose his composure and allow his enemies, and his family's enemies, to assume too much familiarity with him. That is why Darky and his allies were constantly worried, afraid that my son had in mind to take out his revenge against them.

A man of bravado and self-respect who would not stand for being bullied. A 'benign maffioso', to use Marquis Rudinì's term. This is how the mafia likes to represent itself to the outside world.

The conclusion forming in Sangiorgi's mind was inexorable: old man Gambino and his two sons were not being persecuted *by* the mafia, they were participants in a struggle for power *within* the mafia. It was only when they faced final defeat in that struggle that old man Gambino got his lawyer to take him to the police. Sangiorgi was to be his instrument of revenge against his former comrades; turning to the state was a vendetta of last resort.

Fear must have honed Sangiorgi's concentration as he listened to the rest of the story.

Once again, after sending the hunk of horseflesh to old man Gambino, Darky Cusimano was forced to postpone his campaign against the Gambino family. When the revolt of September 1866 was subdued there was a brutal crackdown by the authorities. Fearing that they had exposed themselves with their open assault on the Gambinos, Cusimano's people made peace overtures. Emissaries approached Gambino, who was still living with countersquad leader Salvatore Licata, to propose what Darky termed a 'spiritual kinship': two of his lieutenants were to become godfathers to Gambino's grandchildren.

Reluctantly—according to his own very selective narrative of events— old man Gambino agreed to the proposal, and decided not to report the attack he had suffered to the authorities. Much more likely, the 'spiritual kinship' was in reality an alliance between mafia bloodlines.

In Sicily, and in much of the southern Italian mainland, a godfather is called a *compare*, literally a 'co-father'. *Comparatico* ('co-fatherhood') was a way of cementing a family's important friendships, of extending the blood bond further out into society. Often a poor peasant would ask a wealthy and powerful man to become 'co-father' to his child as a sign of deference and loyalty. But ever since the days of old man Gambino and 'Darky' Cusimano, *mafiosi* too have taken advantage of *comparatico*: senior bosses establish 'spiritual kinships' as a way of building their following within the sect.

The Gambino family's enforced stay with Salvatore Licata during the 1866 revolt produced another intriguing development: old man Gambino's son Salvatore married one of Licata's daughters.

Naturally Gambino did not say as much to Sangiorgi, but this marriage was in all probability as political as the 'spiritual kinship' with Darky Cusimano: it bound the Gambinos firmly into the Licata clan. Mafia bosses in more recent and better-documented times have used marriages in exactly the same way that the crowned heads of Europe did for centuries: to end or prevent wars, to forge military alliances, to earn money and prestige, and to secure their power and wealth down the generations.

Sangiorgi was learning that, through 'co-fatherhood' and marriage, the bosses of the Conca d'Oro were developing a *dynastic* strategy. Although they were profoundly immersed in short-term mafia politics, in the blood-letting and alliance building that are a constant in the mafia's world, they were also thinking for the long term, trying to project their power into the future. Mafia patriarchs shaped their families to meet the peculiar needs of their business in a way that made their behaviour very distinct from other Sicilians. (Contrary to a widespread stereotype, in Sicily at this time the nuclear family was dominant, rather than the extended family.)

Calogero Gambino's story tells us that, where women and marriage were concerned, the difference between early *camorristi* and early *mafiosi* was striking and very important. *Mafiosi* used their wives and daughters as political pawns and by doing so built their illicit gains into patrimonies. *Camorristi*, by contrast, consorted with prostitutes and spent money as soon as they had stolen it.

Marc Monnier (as always the Swiss hotelier is one of the most insightful sources on the Honoured Society of Naples) tells us that the average *camorrista*'s wife was 'a power in her own right' who had the authority to collect protection racket payments.

> Even the toughest among the common people would tremble before the petticoats of these female hoods. Everyone knew that one day their husbands would leave prison and, cudgel in hand, visit reluctant payers to demand an explanation for the outstanding debts.

Such *camorriste* also ensured that their children 'made themselves respected right from the cradle'. So the camorra was trying to use its women and to think to the future too. But they were not as strategic, either in their use of marriage as a dynasty-building tool, or in their preservation of family life from the potentially destabilising effects of contact with prostitution.

The early crime bosses of Naples almost invariably had pimping on their criminal records, whereas profiting from the sex trade was notably *absent* from the biographies of the Sicilian mafia's first bosses. Palermo certainly had its pimps, known by the revolting nickname of *ricottari*—literally 'ricotta cheese makers'. But Turi Miceli, don Antonino Giammona and the other mafia chieftains of the 1860s and 1870s never had anything to do with the *ricottari*. In the city of Palermo, just as in Naples, many prostitutes and their pimps could be seen wearing the serpentine facial scars that were the sex trade's ugly signature. But just outside Palermo, among the lemon groves where the mafia dominated, the *sfregio*, or disfiguring razor slash, was all but unknown.

Cosa Nostra today forbids its members to profit from prostitution because, as murdered anti-mafia magistrate Giovanni Falcone explained, they have to ensure that their womenfolk 'are not humiliated in their own social environment'. A disaffected woman, as the bearer of gruesome family secrets, is a great danger to the organisation.

It seems that it was always thus: the Sicilian mafia of the 1860s may have brutalised and used women domestically but it did not humiliate them publicly—as any involvement with prostitution would have done—because it needed them; it needed them to keep quiet, breed sons and educate those sons in the ways of honour.

It is noticeable that no female personality in Sicily earned the upper world fame or underworld status that surrounded some of the women in the early camorra's orbit: like *la Sangiovannara* and her armed female band, or the brothel keepers who won the title of *matrona annurrata*—'honoured madam'. It seems that the mafia's women wielded less overt power because, in their domestic role, they were *more* important to the organisation. The mafia's iron strategic control over women is a vital secret of its extraordinary resilience over time. A resilience that the Honoured Society of Naples, with its persistent weakness for the short-term profits of pimping, would ultimately prove unable to match.

Old man Gambino's tale was moving towards its conclusion. The 'spiritual kinship' between the Gambinos and Darky Cusimano held for six years. Then, on 17 December 1872, the Gambino brothers were once more ambushed in the Piana dei Colli. Following an initial volley of shots, they fought the six assailants hand-to-hand. Again the brothers escaped through the lemon groves. Despite receiving a head wound, Antonino Gambino managed to wrestle a rifle away from one of the attackers.

The Gambinos knew who had waylaid them: they recognised all six attackers. Predictably, five of them were Darky's men. Less predictably, and much more worryingly, a *mafioso* called Giuseppe 'Thanks be to God' Riccobono was also part of the firing party. Riccobono was son-in-law to Antonino Giammona, the poet-*capo* of Uditore. What this meant to old man Gambino was that his family now faced the combined wrath of *two* mafia factions based in different *borgate*: their old enemies the Cusimano group from San

Lorenzo; but now also the Giammona group from Uditore. Gambino referred to these factions as 'parties' or 'associations'. Today we would refer to them as mafia Families.

Yet at the same time that the attack revealed a worrying new alliance ranged against the Gambinos, it also offered them a potentially devastating weapon against their enemies: the rifle that Antonino Gambino had captured. Here was concrete proof of the attackers' identity—as long as the Gambinos could find the right person in law enforcement to offer that proof to.

Still pretending to Sangiorgi that he was an innocent victim of mafia persecution, old man Gambino explained that he turned to the Licatas, his dynastic allies, to make the best use of the rifle captured from Darky Cusimano's men.

But what seemed like a smart move only exposed the Gambinos' isolation even more cruelly. The senior police connected to the Licatas ignored the rifle. Much worse than that, they made moves that suggested to old man Gambino that they were going to try and frame him for stealing it.

The Gambinos were now being targeted by the three most powerful mafia *cosche* in the Piana dei Colli. Their protection, the web of 'spiritual kinships' and marriage pacts, had been torn apart, isolating the family completely. Eighteen months later, at dawn on 18 June 1874, the lethal consequences of that isolation hit home, when Antonino Gambino was shot dead.

As Sangiorgi listened, the old man described his response to his son's death in tones that were both genuinely moving and creepily manipulative. When news of the murder reached him, grimly certain that Giovanni 'Darky' Cusimano had accomplished his vendetta, Gambino hobbled as fast as he could to embrace the bleeding corpse. He then sat holding his son for hours.

After a while, Darky himself appeared. Leaning over the corpse, he roughly pushed back an eyelid, turned to the distraught father and told him that there was nothing more to be done.

Some time later the police arrived in the person of Inspector Matteo Ferro, Sangiorgi's predecessor as inspector in the Castel Molo district, and the very man who had defined Darky as 'an individual completely devoted to law and order'.

By this time, Gambino was 'crying out as if he was obsessed'. He heard Inspector Ferro tell him to pull himself together, and felt Darky's hands try to tug him to his feet. Gambino scrambled away from them, yelling 'Get back! Don't touch me!' He then listened, in rage and despair, as Inspector Ferro asked him if he could 'shed any light' on the murder. Of course, with the *mafioso* who ordered the killing looking on, he could say nothing in reply.

Inspector Ferro left old man Gambino to his grief and went to the nearby villa that was 'rented' by Giovanni 'Darky' Cusimano. He was joined by the sergeant of the local *Carabinieri* who, as we know, was also a regular guest of Darky's.

At that point, Calogero Gambino's other son Salvatore also came to weep for the murdered Antonino. Word of Salvatore's arrival quickly reached the *mafiosi* and police in Darky's villa. At which point, the *Carabiniere* sergeant came out and promptly arrested Salvatore for killing his own brother. The mafia's fratricide plot had been set in motion—a 'double vendetta', the old man called it.

Many times, through forty-eight years of service to the cause of law and order, Sangiorgi would make pleas for promotion. Many times, his superiors would give him glowing references: brave, able and tactful, they called him. These were precisely the attributes that he had to call on during his first months as a mafia-fighter when Calogero Gambino hobbled into his office on his lawyer's arm.

Brave. Sangiorgi knew that, even though Giovanni 'Darky' Cusimano was now dead, the investigation implicated many other violent and well-connected *mafiosi*.

Able. Sangiorgi needed all his investigative skills to verify what old man Gambino had told him. He quickly ascertained that the old man's story tallied perfectly with the facts.

And, most of all, tactful. The case took Sangiorgi deeper and deeper into the sinister nexus between the state and the criminal sect that had brought death to the lemon groves of the Conca d'Oro.

Sangiorgi found damning evidence about the *Carabiniere* sergeant who emerged directly from Darky's villa to arrest Salvatore Gambino. His source within the *Carabinieri* explained how the mafia had entrapped the sergeant by using a two-pronged strategy it deployed frequently against law enforcement. Cusimano and other mafia bosses first buttered the sergeant up: they took him out into the countryside on what Sangiorgi referred to as 'frequent *tavulidde*'. The inspector had evidently picked up some Sicilian dialect during his time on the island. A *tavulidda* was (and is) a languorous al fresco lunch at which men bond over roast goat, artichokes, *macco* (broad bean purée), and wine as dark as treacle. The mafia was introducing the sergeant to a bit of local culture.

The second prong involved the mafia's womenfolk, who sidled up to the sergeant's wife and told her

```
GIURO DI ESSERE FEDELE "A COSA NOSTRA" SE DOVESSI TRADIRE LE MIE
CARNI DEVONO BRUCIARE - COME BRUCIA QUESTA IMMAGINE.

          DIVIETI E DOVERI.

NON CI SI PUO' PRESENTARE DA SOLI AD UN'ALTRO AMICO NOSTRO - SE NON
E' UN TERZO A FARLO.

NON SI GUARDANO MOGLI DI AMICI NOSTRI.

NON SI FANNO COMPARATI CON GLI SBIRRI.

NON SI FREQUENTANO NE'TAVERNE E NE'CIRCOLI.

SI E' IL DOVERE IN QUALSIASI MOMENTO DI ESSERE DISPONIBILE A COSA
NOSTRA.ANCHE SE CE LA MOGLIE CHE STA PER PARTORIRE.

SI RISPETTANO IN MANIERA CATEGORICA GLI APPUNTAMENTI.

SI CI DEVE PORTARE RISPETTO ALLA MOGLIE.

QUANDO SI E' CHIAMATI A SAPERE QUALCOSA SI DOVRA' DIRE LA VERITA'.

NON CI SI PUO' APPROPRIARE DI SOLDI CHE SONO DI ALTRI E DI ALTRE
FAMIGLIE.

CHI NON PUO' ENTRARE A FAR PARTE DI COSA NOSTRA.
```

```
·HA UN PARENTE STRETTO NELLE VARIE FORZE DELL'ORDINE.
·HA TRADIMENTI SENTIMENTALI IN FAMIGLIA.
·HA UN COMPORTAMENTO PESSIMO - E CHE NON TENE AI VALORI MORALI.
```

```
SAN MAURO CASTELVERDE.
TRABIA. I PAESI DI APPARTENENZA:CACCAMO,VICARI,ROCCA PALUMBA E ALTRI
BAGHERIA. " "  " VILLABATE,CASTELDACCIA,MILICIA,
BELMONTE MEZZAGNO. " " " MISILMERI,
BRANCACCIO. " " " CORSO DEI MILLE,ROCCELLA,CIACULLI.
SANTA MARIA DI GESU'. " " " VILLA GRAZIA DI PALERMO.
PALERMO CENTRO. " " " PORTA NUOVA,BORGO VECCHIO:
RESUTTANA " " " ACQUASANTA,ARENELLA.
VILLAGRAZIA " " " MOLARA,CORSO CALATAFIMI,
PARTANNA " " "
ARENELLA DI FALCO." " " UDITORE,TORRETTA.
CRUILLAS. " " " NOCE,ALTARELLO.
TOMMASO NATALE." " " SAN LOR.PARTANN,CAPACI,CARINI,CINISI,TERRASINI.
PARTINICO. " " " BORGETTO,BALESTRATE,MONTELEPRE?
SAN GIUSEPPE JATO." " " MORREALE,ALTOFONTE,SAN CIPIRELLO
CORLEONE. " " " PRIZZI,FICUZZA,
```

Mafia morality. A very rare Cosa Nostra rulebook from 2007. Among the regulations crammed onto a single, badly typed page are: 'Respect your wife' and 'The following people cannot become part of Cosa Nostra: Anyone who has a close relative in the police. Anyone who has emotional infidelities in their family. Anyone who behaves very badly or does not keep to moral values.'

In the Piana dei Colli, any woman who likes to keep out of all sorts of bother needs to stay close to her husband.

An oblique threat, but a blood-freezingly clear one all the same. Over a century and a half this form of wheedling intimidation has done more to protect the mafia than any other form of corruption in its wide repertoire. There is no better way to incapacitate the state than to nullify the effectiveness of its operatives on the ground.

Sangiorgi's investigations then concentrated on the key prosecution witness in the fratricide case. Standing guard not far from the point where Antonino Gambino was murdered was a soldier who heard the shots and ran to the scene. When he arrived, he saw two men standing over the victim, who was still emitting his dying groans. The two men took to their heels. But the soldier got a good view of one of them, who was wearing a straw hat with a black ribbon round it. Later he picked Salvatore Gambino out of an identity parade and said that he was the man in the straw hat.

Old man Gambino told Sangiorgi that the witness was lying, and that the identity parade was fixed. Sangiorgi soon found evidence to back up the old man's accusations. He discovered that, when Darky Cusimano was shot dead, a receipt for a 200 lire loan was found on his body. The beneficiary of the loan was the commander of an army platoon stationed in San Lorenzo—the same platoon that the key witness came from. The loan made the framing of Salvatore Gambino look very much like one token in a murky exchange of favours between the mafia boss and the platoon commander. Sangiorgi could add the army to the long list of organisations that had been infiltrated by the mafia of the Conca d'Oro.

Tact, indeed.

Inspector Sangiorgi now faced the delicate task of telling the magistrates what he knew. If he exposed the Gambino case as a mafia plot, he risked trampling on some very important toes inside the Palace of Justice, because the 'fratricide' prosecution was already scheduled to come before the Court of Assizes.

When Sangiorgi approached the magistrates he received a reassuring response: they told him he was right to let them know, and asked him to submit a full report. In the meantime, the fratricide case kept being adjourned because the soldier who was supposed to have recognised Salvatore Gambino in the straw hat twice failed to appear as a witness.

During this delay, there was a change in the political weather.

In March 1876 the Right fell from government, and the first Left administration, including Sicilian politicians, took office in Rome. A new Prefect was sent to Palermo, and the Right's senior personnel were rapidly purged, irrespective of their competence and honesty. The chief of police under whom Sangiorgi had worked was sent to Tuscany.

Sangiorgi was now exposed: he, more than any officer in Sicily, had been in the front line of the struggle against the mafia; he had even discovered the mafia's secret initiation ritual. Without the backing of his superiors, his career, and possibly his life, were in danger. The corrupt elements within the Palermo police were already lobbying against him, pouring poison in the new Prefect's ear. In July 1876 the Prefect sent an urgent telegram to the Minister of the Interior.

> Above all, I beg you, get rid of young Sangiorgi for me. He is able, but a schemer and gossiper who boasts that he has protectors in the Ministry and in Parliament. I prefer timewasters to cops like him.

Sangiorgi put in a transfer request that was quickly granted: in August 1876 he took up a posting in Syracuse, the least crime-ridden province of Sicily, in the opposite corner of the island to Palermo. The mafia was both very well informed of this development and delighted by it: even before confirmation of the transfer came through, the news was trumpeted to the Piana dei Colli by *L'Amico del Popolo*, whose editor had been spotted consorting with Darky in his 'rented' villa. The mafia's rumour mill spread the falsehood that Sangiorgi had been moved for disciplinary reasons.

While Sangiorgi was in Syracuse the Gambino case dragged on in perfunctory hearings, through 1876 and into 1877. Old man Gambino got the chance to tell his story directly to the magistrates. But the new atmosphere in Palermo began to turn the case against Sangiorgi. Some of the witnesses he had interviewed lost confidence and changed their stories. Nothing was done to verify whether the soldier had really seen Salvatore Gambino in a straw hat at the murder scene. Corrupt cops, whom Sangiorgi had removed for incompetence or collusion with the mafia, seemed to get their fingers into the case again. As Sangiorgi noted wistfully

> If I were fatalistic, I would regrettably have to admit that an evil spirit, an arcane and pernicious influence overcame all the procedures I went through to investigate the deductions I had based on old man Gambino's evidence.

Inspector Sangiorgi had yet to experience just how pernicious that 'evil spirit' could be.

A few more months passed and once again the political weather around Sangiorgi changed. The Left found that it was not as easy to enforce the law in Sicily as it had been led to believe during fifteen years of noisy Sicilian protests against the hated Right's repressive measures. The kidnap of the English sulphur-mining company manager in November 1876 meant that something had to be done. So early in 1877 the Left reversed its policy and sent yet another new Prefect to Palermo to crack the whip. Across Sicily, a vast new anti-mafia campaign—as big as anything under the Right—was set in motion.

Given this transformation in the Left's official attitude to organised crime in Sicily, Inspector Sangiorgi was too valuable an asset to be parked in peaceful Syracuse. Early in 1877 he was reassigned to the province of Agrigento, home turf of yet another recently discovered mafia sect. He was given a pay raise and recommended for a decoration. Sangiorgi was back in the front line, and soon renewed his 'open fight against the mafia'—and against one *mafioso* in particular: Pietro De Michele, the boss of the town of Burgio, near Agrigento, where Sangiorgi was now stationed. De Michele insisted on being called 'Baron', although he seems to have had no real claim on the title. His CV displayed the *mafioso's* typical combination of crime and opportunistic political thuggery. More than that, it showed that the province of Palermo was not the only place where Men of Honour had used sexual violence as a shortcut to wealth and position, and indeed that there were close business links between *mafiosi* from different provinces.

In 1847 De Michele kidnapped and raped the daughter of a rich landowner who had refused his advances. But the rape backfired. De Michele's reputation was so bad that the girl's family refused to repair the damage to her honour by conceding a wedding: family disgrace was far better than a marriage to a known hood. But De Michele would not accept defeat. In 1848, he allied himself to the revolution of that year, and took advantage of it to take back the girl, forcibly marry her and rob her family of a large dowry. He served a short time in jail after the authority of the Bourbon state was restored; and he was suspected of many murders after being released.

The 'Baron' joined the revolution again in 1860 when Garibaldi invaded. At some point during the upheaval, all the town's police and judicial documents were burned.

When Sicily became part of Italy, De Michele went on to manage the cattle rustlers and bandits who operated between the provinces of Palermo, Agrigento and Trapani in the 1860s and 1870s. He armed them, fed them and hid them from the authorities. Most importantly, he used his mafia connections to sell their stolen cattle in far distant cities: animals robbed near Palermo would end up butchered in Trapani, where they could never be traced.

This was an exceptionally lucrative traffic. By the time Sangiorgi caught up with De Michele, he was the richest landowner in town and completely

controlled the local council. The fearless inspector showed no deference
to De Michele. Sangiorgi took away his firearms licence, placed him under
police surveillance, and ordered his arrest when he went on the run. Baron
or not, the boss of Burgio was to be subject to the law like everyone else.

The bad news about the Gambino fratricide case arrived soon after 28
August 1877. In Agrigento, Inspector Sangiorgi read the report on the
long-delayed trial in the *Gazzetta di Palermo*. It is not hard to imagine his
emotions as he did so. Disappointment first: the court had not believed old
man Gambino's story; Salvatore Gambino was found guilty of murdering
his brother and sentenced to hard labour for life. Then resignation: the outcome was not a surprise.

Sangiorgi's eyes then moved down the page to read the *Gazzetta di Palermo*'s admiring paraphrase of the prosecution's summing up. As they did, his
heart began to thump with shock.

> The honourable magistrate then had extremely grave things to say about
> the behaviour of a Police Inspector, a certain Ermanno Sangiorgi. Be-
> cause he wanted to take advantage of the position that he still undeserv-
> edly holds, Sangiorgi tried to throw justice off its course by denying that
> Salvatore Gambino had committed the crime, and claiming instead that
> the culprit was someone or other called Darky Cusimano.
>
> This is not the first case that shows us that there are police officers
> who have become the maffia's protectors. They make a big show of want-
> ing to strike at some other, hypothetical maffia; and to do so they con-
> trive investigations that have no basis in fact.
>
> Then the prosecuting magistrate said that Sangiorgi had deceived,
> mystified and duped justice by trying to find a way to give someone else
> the blame. On the eve of the first hearings Sangiorgi haughtily sent a
> report to the Chief Prosecutor's Office that made out that Gambino was
> not guilty of his brother's murder.
>
> Sangiorgi's dishonest conduct (the word is the prosecutor's) was mo-
> tivated by his desire to pay back the dirty services that Calogero Gam-
> bino had provided to the police.
>
> Thus, in effect, the prosecuting magistrate's eloquent speech to the
> court was making two separate accusations: the first against Salvatore
> Gambino, and the second against Ermanno Sangiorgi who has made
> himself into the maffia's protector. He signs off gun licences for people

who have police cautions hanging over them and he releases dangerous criminals from police surveillance.

Any policing system that is represented by men like Sangiorgi is absolutely pitiful. This is government banditry—no more and no less. It is the police maffia that has imposed itself on the law.

The presiding judge used the prosecutor's own solemn words to bring his highly fluent précis of the case to a conclusion: 'If the jury award the accused a verdict of not guilty, it will amount to a crown of plaudits awarded to this corrupt police officer for the dirty services performed by Calogero Gambino.'

Dishonest. Corrupt. Deceiver of justice. Broker of dirty services. Protector of the maffia. There was an unnervingly symmetrical irony to the charges against Sangiorgi, as if the judicial system and the *Gazzetta di Palermo* were mocking his 'open fight' against the mafia. It was alleged that he had indulged in precisely the kind of shady policing that he had overturned when he first came to the Castel Molo district. That he was precisely the kind of double-dealing cop that he had expelled from among his subordinates.

Police like Albanese and Ferro had used *mafiosi* by siding with the winners in the underworld's internal power struggles; they had co-managed crime with the victorious mafia bosses. What Sangiorgi had done with old man Gambino was very different: he had sought to adopt the mafia's losers so as to attack the very basis of the sect's authority. The difference between these two approaches was as clear as the difference between wrong and right.

Yet together, the judiciary and the *Gazzetta di Palermo* had obliterated any distinction. The new villain of the story, Inspector Sangiorgi, came out as just another scheming northern cop. Meanwhile, the real mafia, the mafia of Darky Cusimano, of the poet-boss Giammona, of Salvatore Licata and his sons, the mafia whose blood-spattered victims Sangiorgi had seen lying among the lemon trees, was dismissed as a 'hypothetical maffia', a mere pretext, a fiction dreamed up by a policeman in the cynical pursuit of power and influence.

Inspector Ermanno Sangiorgi was in very serious trouble.

The mortifying allegations made against Inspector Sangiorgi in the Palermo Court of Assizes were bound to reach the ears of his superiors. Dispatches were duly sent, reports were requested and collated: the Gambino case became the Sangiorgi case. The Minister of the Interior asked the Minister of Justice to make inquiries. On 12 October 1877 the Minister of Justice gave his verdict: 'the accusations against Inspector Sangiorgi are, alas, true'. Sangiorgi now faced disgrace, dismissal and possibly jail.

The principal witness against him, the man who investigated the case on behalf of the Minister of Justice, was also the magistrate to whom Sangiorgi had turned when Calogero Gambino's testimony first raised such grave doubts about the 'fratricide': Chief Prosecutor Carlo Morena—the same Carlo Morena who just a few months earlier had dismissed the theory that there could be any kind of 'confederation' between the different mafia cells across Sicily. Carlo Morena, a man with responsibility for supervising the justice system across the whole of Sicily, was exacting a vendetta on behalf of the mafia against Ermanno Sangiorgi.

On behalf of one *mafioso* in particular: 'Baron' Pietro De Michele, the Burgio boss. Chief Prosecutor Morena knew all about the Baron's past, but spent his credibility in spadefuls to defend him from Sangiorgi. De Michele had made a few mistakes in the past, Morena reported. But now he was a friend of the law and the government, who had become a victim of political persecution. To accuse the Baron of raping his future wife back in 1847 was unfair: the families had made peace afterwards. So the accusation of rape was based on an ignorance of Sicilian customs, Morena argued.

> Kidnap and rape of this kind constitute a primitive phenomenon that occasionally crops up even in the most civilised societies. Sometimes there are no bad consequences arising from it. Indeed sometimes the very family who were supposedly harmed by the rape actually approve of it by agreeing to a subsequent marriage. Society readily approves of such arrangements. When that happens, the state should forget about the whole affair.

Morena went on to explain that the mafia was a local tradition of the same kind as kidnapping and raping young girls, albeit a much vaguer one.

> The word mafia is such an ill-defined concept, which is spoken much more often than its meaning is understood.

Thanks to Chief Prosecutor Morena, the order to arrest *capomafia* 'Baron' De Michele was rescinded.

Of course Morena knew perfectly well that the mafia was no 'ill-defined concept'. It was a secret criminal organisation whose influence stretched right across western Sicily. At the lowest level, the network linking the local mafia gangs was held together by the long-distance business of banditry and cattle rustling. Sangiorgi discovered that the same cattle rustlers who were sheltered by De Michele were also friends with Palermo *mafiosi* like don Antonino Giammona, the Licatas, and Darky Cusimano. At an intermediate level, the mafia sought to control the market for buying and renting land, which had its hub in Palermo. At the highest level, the mafia network's strength came from the favours it could call in from 'friends of the friends' in politics and the legal system. Favours like persecuting policemen who had the temerity to mount an open fight against organised crime and the foolish courage to discover the Honoured Society's secret initiation ceremony.

There was only one Sicilian mafia.

On 18 October 1877, the Minister of the Interior wrote to Sangiorgi's boss, the Prefect of Agrigento, relaying the details of the case exactly as it had been set out in the *Gazzetta di Palermo*. Sangiorgi could and perhaps should have been prosecuted, the Minister explained. But he was still an important witness in some outstanding cases. Did the Prefect consider that a severe reprimand was sufficient punishment for his behaviour?

Only then did Sangiorgi's luck change. The Prefect of Agrigento urged the Minister to hear the other side of the story. Sangiorgi rapidly put together a long and precise account of the 'fratricide' affair. This is the documentation I have drawn on to tell his story here.

The Prefect backed up Sangiorgi's report by telling the Minister that Sangiorgi was one of his most intelligent and energetic officers, one who had gone beyond the call of duty to fight organised crime and to bring order to the province of Agrigento. He even recommended the supposed 'protector of the mafia' for a promotion.

Meanwhile the Minister of the Interior also received alarming reports on Chief Prosecutor Carlo Morena. In addition to defending the mafia boss De Michele, Morena had been sending urgent memos to magistrates around western Sicily, digging up every technicality possible to secure the release of *mafiosi* subject to police surveillance and 'enforced residence'. The Minister pronounced himself 'profoundly shocked' by Morena's behaviour.

The Interior Ministry now held a compelling body of evidence. The saga of Sangiorgi's dealings with old man Gambino exposed gangland infiltration not only of the police, but also of the magistrature; it provided new evidence that the different *cosche* that used the same rituals were actually part of *one* criminal brotherhood; it made for the most vivid picture of the mafia yet assembled by any police investigation. For a moment, it seemed that someone in power in Rome was going to take notice.

But nothing happened. The Minister of the Interior who was 'profoundly shocked' by Morena was soon toppled, and his successor had other priorities.

There was no inquiry into the systematic mafia infiltration of the police and magistrature that Sangiorgi had uncovered. No one took the time to make the connection between the whole 'fratricide' affair and the crucial role that Chief Prosecutor Carlo Morena had played in blocking any attempt to treat the mafia as a single criminal brotherhood. Morena kept his job, but for unknown reasons he volunteered for early retirement in 1879, at age fifty-eight. He was granted all the honours his prestigious legal career had earned.

Old man Gambino was left to the tender mercies of the Piana dei Colli mafia; it is not known what happened to him. His son Salvatore, aged thirty-four when he was wrongly convicted of murdering his own brother, broke rocks for the rest of his life.

The two *mafiosi* that Sangiorgi believed were the real culprits in the Antonino Gambino murder were not investigated; neither were the people responsible for framing his brother, Salvatore.

'Baron' De Michele became mayor of Burgio in 1878; his son would become a Member of Parliament.

Then there were the unspoken victims of the tragedy. Victims on whom not even Sangiorgi wastes enough ink for the historian to be able to cite their names: the women. We have no resource but the imagination to reconstruct their hellish fate. First, in Palermo, there was the Gambino daughter forced to marry the *mafioso* who raped her—a *mafioso* who was part of the same Cusimano clan that would end up murdering both her uncle and her brother. Then there was the Licata girl given in expedient marriage to a Gambino son who was destined to be framed for fratricide. Finally, in Burgio, there was the wife of 'Baron' De Michele: kidnapped, disgraced, kidnapped again, and forcibly married to the man who robbed her family. We can only presume that all of these women spent the rest of their lives performing their marital duties—duties which, as Sangiorgi had learned, included issuing smiling threats to the wives of policemen.

It is a sad truth that Inspector Sangiorgi himself bears some of the responsibility for the fact that the 'fratricide' affair went nowhere but the archives. Responsibility, but not blame. It was a question of tact. It seems certain that Sangiorgi believed that the Gambinos were *mafiosi*. But he was hardly stupid enough to say so in his report to the Minister of the Interior, when his career was on the line. For that would have given ammunition to those who accused him of being a protector of the mafia. He pitched his report with the utmost care, making it clear that he knew that the Gambinos were no angels, or no 'saint's shin-bones', as the Italian phrase has it. But he had to stop short of drawing the obvious conclusion that they were deeply immersed in the mafia world.

Inspector Sangiorgi's tact helped preserve his career. It may, just may, have helped preserve his life too. An obvious question that arises from the 'fratricide' affair is why the mafia did not just kill Sangiorgi. The answer is probably a cost-benefit calculation: killing a prominent cop would probably have brought more trouble than rewards for the Honoured Society. Far better to just discredit him. But then, for the mafia, discrediting someone is often only a prelude to killing them. Shamed murder victims are not mourned and not remembered.

As it was, the police authorities gave Sangiorgi the very mildest of warnings about his future conduct but turned him down for a promotion on the grounds that he was not old enough. In 1878, he had to defend himself again when the same accusations of colluding with the mafia appeared once more in the press. It turned out that 'Baron' De Michele was the author of the defamatory pieces. But Sangiorgi had much graver worries at this point: his life was thrown into turmoil when his wife died; he was a single parent once more. But he did not stop fighting the mafia. In 1883 he dismantled a *cosca* known as the Brotherhood of Favara, which controlled the infernal sulphur mines of the Agrigento area by using the same tactics the *mafiosi* of the Conca d'Oro used in the lemon groves. Hereafter, Sangiorgi's unfolding career will lead us through another twenty-five years of mafia history.

The Left's 1877 crackdown did not destroy the mafia, far from it. Granted, most of the bandits who roamed the Sicilian countryside were shot down or betrayed to the authorities. But the *mafiosi* who protected them—men like 'Baron' De Michele—were left unmolested. With a relative calm now restored in Sicily, the political agenda could move on. The Left's great law and order campaign was to be the last for two decades. As in the low city of Naples, in Sicily it proved easier to govern with organised crime than against it. *Mafiosi* learned to keep their violence within levels that were suited to the new political environment. With the Left in power, Sicilian politicians could exercise their elbows in jostling for a share of the funds now being spent on roads, railways, sewers, and the like. With the help of their friends in the mafia, they could convert those funds from lire into the south's real currency: the Favour.

Meanwhile the trials that had been triggered by Sangiorgi's discovery of the mafia initiation ritual went ahead, with very mixed results. Many juries were profoundly and understandably suspicious of the police and were reluctant to issue guilty verdicts. As a rule, only the losers in mafia wars were successfully prosecuted. Losers like the Gambinos: *mafiosi* who had spent all their favours, who had lost their 'friends of friends', whose 'spiritual kinships' and marriage alliances had broken down, and whose enemies within the mafia proved shrewder, more violent and better connected than them. And above all, thanks to Chief Prosecutor Carlo Morena, the trials treated the mafia as an unconnected and temporary ensemble of local gangs.

The country had been on a long journey between the Palermo revolt of 1866 and the anti-mafia campaign of 1877. Two parliamentary commissions of inquiry and countless police and judicial investigations had tried to define the mafia. But despite all the compelling evidence that had surfaced, the mafia was destined to remain what Carlo Morena had called it: 'an ill-defined concept'. Within a few years, the Honoured Society's initiation ritual would slip from Italy's institutional memory. *Il tempo è galantuomo*, as they say in Italy: 'Time heals all wounds' or, more literally, 'Time is a gentleman'. Perhaps it would be better to say that, in Sicily, time is a Man of Honour.

PART III

THE NEW CRIMINAL NORMALITY

BORN DELINQUENTS: Science and the mob

IN BOTH NAPLES AND PALERMO, THE LATE 1870S INAUGURATED A QUIET PERIOD IN THE history of organised crime. Successive Left governments seemed to find an accommodation with the camorra and mafia. The underlying problems that had made the new state such a welcoming host to the underworld sects became endemic: political instability and malpractice; police co-management of delinquency with gangsters; criminal rule within the prison system. But the issue of underworld sects did not disappear from public debate. Indeed *mafiosi* and *camorristi* loomed large in Italian culture during the 1880s and 1890s. Their deeds, their habits, and above all their faces were displayed for all to see—whether on the page or on stage. Italians were often fascinated and horrified by what they saw. But they deluded themselves that the spectacle was merely a primitive hangover, a monument to old evils that was about to crumble into the dust of history. Thus, while Italy could not eradicate the gangs, it could at least change the way it thought about them: the organised crime issue became a matter of perceptions. Unfortunately, illegal Italy showed itself to be even more adept at perception management than legal Italy. This was the new criminal normality. A normality that, with all its ironies, was set to welcome a third criminal brotherhood into its midst.

The Right had viewed criminal organisations, understandably enough, as something much more threatening than mere crime. The camorra and the mafia (at least to those prepared to accept that the mafia was something more than an 'ill-defined concept') constituted a challenge to the state's very right to rule its own territory; they were a kind of state within the state that no modern society could tolerate.

This view had always faced opposition, not least from lawyers who thought that the fight against the 'anti-state' did not give the government the right to trample over individual rights. One piece of legislation, passed in 1861, made lawyers particularly nervous: it targeted 'associations of wrongdoers'. This was the law used in the anti-mafia trials of the late 1870s and early 1880s. It stipulated that any group of five or more people who came together to break the law were now deemed to be committing an extra crime—that of forming an 'association of wrongdoers'. The government's tendency to use this law as a catchall for clamping down on groups of polit- ical dissidents helped increase the lawyers' anxiety.

The law was revised in 1889, and rephrased as a measure against 'asso- ciating for delinquency'. But some fundamental legal dilemmas survived the rewrite. What exactly was an 'association for delinquency'? How could it be proved, beyond reasonable doubt, that one existed? Rivers of legal ink were spilt in the search for a solution. The crime of 'associating for delinquency' only attracted quite minor penalties in any case—a couple of extra years in prison. So it was much easier to forget the elaborate busi- ness of dragging the mafia and camorra before a judge. Better to fall back on 'enforced residence', and send any conspicuous offenders off to a penal colony without a trial. Put another way, organised crime was to be pruned, and not uprooted.

The nitpicking legalistic approach to the mafia and camorra was a dead end. From the late 1870s until the end of the century, sociology seemed to have far greater purchase on the problem. And at that time, sociology largely meant *positivist* sociology—positivism being a school of thought that dreamed of applying science to society. From a properly scientific perspec- tive, the positivists reasoned, lawbreakers were creatures of flesh and blood; they were human animals to be observed, prodded, weighed, measured, pho- tographed, and catalogued. If only science could identify these 'born delin- quents' *physically*, then it could defend society against them—irrespective of what the legal quibblers said.

The most optimistic, and most notorious, attempt to identify a 'delinquent man' and a 'delinquent woman' by their physical appearance was articulated by the Turinese doctor Cesare Lombroso. He claimed to have identified cer- tain anomalies in criminal bodies, like sticky-out ears or a bulky jaw. These 'stigmata', as he termed them, revealed that criminals actually belonged to an earlier era of human development, somewhere between apes and Negroes on the evolutionary ladder. Lombroso made a great career out of his theory and defended it doggedly, even when some other sociologists demonstrated what claptrap it was.

Lombroso was not the only academic who thought science could unlock the crime issue. Others sought the key in factors like diet, overcrowding, the weather, and of course race. Southern Italians and Sicilians seemed to be made of different stuff from other Europeans, if not physically, then at least psychologically. In 1898 one celebrated young sociologist, Alfredo Niceforo, gave a derogatory twist to the mafia's own propaganda when he argued that the Sicilian psyche and the mafia were one and the same thing.

> In many respects the Sicilian is a true Arab: proud, often cruel, vigorous, inflexible. Hence the fact that the individual Sicilian does not allow others to give him orders. Hence also the fact that Saracen pride, conjoined with the feudal hankering after power, turned the Sicilian into a man who always has rebellion and the unbounded passion of his own ego in his bloodstream. The *mafioso* in a nutshell.

Neapolitans emerged in just as unflattering a light from Niceforo's research: they were 'frivolous, fickle and restless'—just like women, in fact. But the camorra was distinct from the Neapolitan 'woman-people' among whom it lived. After all, there was wide agreement that the camorra, unlike the mafia, was a secret society. The camorra's weird rituals, its duels and the elaborate symbolic language with which *picciotti* addressed their *capo-camorrista* showed that the camorra was nothing less than a savage clan, identical to the tribes of central Africa as described by Livingstone or Stanley.

Camorra tattoos particularly fascinated 'scientists' like Lombroso and Niceforo. As far as anyone knew, *camorristi* had always adorned their skin with the names of the prostitutes they protected, the vendettas they had sworn to perform and the badges of their criminal rank. Tattoos served a double purpose: they were a sign of loyalty to the Honoured Society that also helped intimidate its victims. Like the flashy clothes early *camorristi* wore, tattoos tell us a great deal about the nature and limits of camorra power. At a time when the Society was rooted in places where the state scarcely bothered to extend its reach—in prison, or among the plebeian labyrinth of central Naples—it mattered little that these bodily pictographs could also be deciphered by the prison authorities and the police. However,

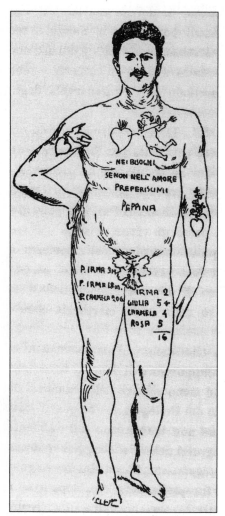

'Camorra pimp', with signature body adornments. Taken from one of many prurient studies of gangland tattooing published in the late nineteenth century.

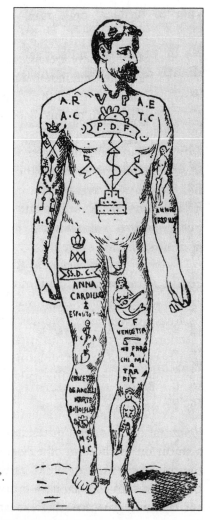

'Bloodthirsty camorrista'.

needless to say, these subtleties escaped the criminologists, who just took tattoos to be one more bodily symptom of degeneracy.

Positivist criminology became a fashion; in the name of scientific inquiry it pandered to the public's fascination for secret societies and gruesome misdemeanours. A hungry readership was fed with titles like: *The Maffia in its Factors and Manifestations: A Study of Sicily's Dangerous Classes* (1886); *The Camorra Duel* (1893); *Habits and Customs of Camorristi* (1897); and *Hereditary and Psychical Tattoos in Neapolitan Camorristi* (1898). Naples had a particularly avid market for guides to the structure and special vocabulary of the camorra. It was as if these were textbooks, part of an informal curriculum on the Honoured Society that the locals had to digest before they could lay claim to knowing Naples, to being truly Neapolitan.

Some of the authors of these guides were police officers and lawyers who brought a great deal of hard evidence to the debate about organised crime. For instance, it was shown that for reasons of secrecy, affiliates of the Honoured Society were actually grouped into two separate compartments: the junior *picciotti* belonged to the 'Minor Society' and the more senior *camorristi* formed the 'Major Society'. Yet the same authors who relayed insights such as this also blithely threw in recycled folklore (about the camorra's Spanish origins, for example), pseudo-scientific speculation, and plain old titillation. Many of the books carried garish illustrations of delinquent ears, prostitutes disfigured by horrendous scars, or torsos tattooed with arcane gang motifs. Underlying it all was the simplistic but seductive belief that seeing and knowing are the same thing. As one police officer-cum-sociologist wrote

> The majority of *camorristi* have a dark complexion with pale tones, and abundant frizzy hair. Most have dark, sparkling, darting eyes, although a few have clear, frosty eyes. Their facial hair is sparse. Apart from a few harmonious physiognomies (which are in any case often spoiled by long scars), one can observe many noses that are misshapen, large or snubbed. There are also many low or bulbous foreheads, large cheekbones and jaws, ears that are either enormous or tiny, and finally rotten or crooked teeth.

Positivist criminology treated crime as if it were no more complicated than a smear on the bottom of a Petri dish. Yet *mafiosi* and *camorristi*, just like the rest of us, are capable of rational, strategic planning. And, more even than the rest of us, they have every reason to be fascinated by tales of secret societies and gruesome misdemeanours . . .

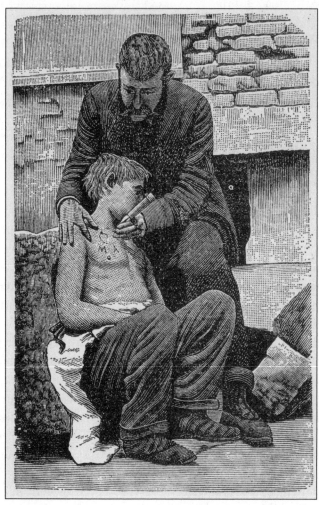

A youngster gets his first criminal insignia. A street tattooist at work in Naples.

11

An Audience of Hoods

Among the more intriguing items held in the National Library in Naples is a photograph, no less, of the moment when the camorra was founded. Or at least, that is what it appears to be. With remarkable clarity it shows the camorra's founding members—all nine of them—arranged in a semi-circle in a large prison cell. They are evidently taking an oath by swearing on the sacred objects that lie on the floor before them: a crucifix with crossed daggers arranged at its foot. The new members have their gaze fixed on the man who seems to be leading the ceremony. He is a confident figure with a brimmed hat pushed to the back of his head, who is shown pointing at the dagger and crucifix and placing a reassuring hand on the shoulder of one nervous-looking novice.

The photograph was taken during rehearsals for *The Foundation of the Camorra*, a play first performed on the evening of 18 October 1899. It may well have been a publicity shot. If so, it certainly did the trick. Interest in the play was such that tickets for the second night sold out by midday and the *Carabinieri* had to be called in to calm the scrum of frustrated theatregoers.

The script for *The Foundation of the Camorra* is lost, alas. But the reviews give us some idea of why it generated such excitement.

The audience was intensely interested in the episodes that led to the establishment among us of the evil sect. Returned travellers came here to transplant it from Spain, and chose the Vicaria prison as the place to

The Honoured Society conducts its first ever initiation ritual. A scene from Edoardo
Minichini's highly successful play, *The Foundation of the Camorra*, from 1899.

found what someone, perhaps ironically, once called the 'Dishonoured
Society'. In any case, the Vicaria was for some time after that the seat of
its supreme command and its tribunal.

The drama reproduces the affiliates' first feats, their first oaths, their
first acts of extortion, their first ritualised knife fights, and their fierce
early struggle to establish themselves and spread their rule. Their brand
of criminality disguised as heroism was designed to unnerve and frighten
the weak. The second performance is tonight.

The Foundation of the Camorra could have been scripted from one of the
criminological guidebooks to the Honoured Society.

The audience captivated by this spectacle was peculiarly knowledgeable. For *The Foundation of the Camorra* was staged at the San Ferdinando
theatre, which stood just a few metres from the infamous Vicaria prison
where the play was set. During any given performance the spectacle in the
auditorium was as colourful as whatever happened on stage. And as noisy:
the din of chatter, catcalls and fragments of song was incessant. In the
stalls, under a constant rain of orange peel and seed husks from above, ink-

stained printers argued with smoke-blackened railwaymen, and breastfeeding mothers gossiped with fat prostitutes. Surveying it all from the rickety boxes just above was what passed for a middle class in the Vicaria quarter: shabby-smart teachers, or pawnbrokers with their wives and kids decked out lavishly in unreclaimed loan collateral. Here in the San Ferdinando was a hyper-condensation of the already impossibly cramped life of the Vicaria quarter. So it is hardly surprising that when *The Foundation of the Camorra* was on, *camorristi* came to see it too.

So many *camorristi* came, in fact, that the play drew the attention of law enforcement. On 4 November the local inspector wrote to the chief of police to express his concerns.

> Given that the aforementioned theatre is frequented by an audience entirely made up of members of the underworld and men with prison records, the action being performed there is one big lesson at the school of crime.

What worried him was the play's dangerously ambiguous message. Of course it had a happy and morally instructive ending, as did everything else staged at the San Ferdinando. But the audience seemed far more excited by what came before: displays of delinquent bravado that mirrored their own twisted values. Worse still, certain passages in the play were little more than propaganda for the Honoured Society. The police inspector's letter quotes from one offending speech by the stage *capo*.

> Our rulers act like *camorristi* on a big scale. So there's nothing wrong if the people do it on a small scale.

Nonsense, of course; but alluring nonsense all the same.

Popular melodramas were churned out at staggering speed for the unruly punters at the San Ferdinando. Edoardo Minichini, the author of *The Foundation of the Camorra*, is thought to have written around 400 plays; he died in poverty, leaving his wife and ten children to fend for themselves. (The fact that the camorra notoriously took protection payments from theatres probably helps explain his economic difficulties.) Many of Minichini's plays featured *camorristi*. In fact there was a fashion for such dramas in 1890s Naples. Titles like *The Boss of the Camorra* (1893) and *Blood of a Camorrista* (1894) sucked in large and enthusiastic audiences from the tenements. In fact these plays were only the latest manifestations of Honoured Society folklore. Ever since the 1860s, singers, storytellers and puppet shows had been thrilling plebeian audiences with phoney tales of camorra honour and derring-do.

The star of the San Ferdinando stage, an actor appropriately named Federigo Stella, always played the good guy, and always played him in the same histrionic, declamatory style. One of Stella's stock characters became what one contemporary man of the theatre called the 'old-school, valorous *camorrista* who dishes out good deeds, clubbings and oratory with the same spirit of fair play'. It mattered little to Stella's audience that there was no such thing as the noble *camorrista*, nor had there ever been.

Mafiosi and *camorristi* have always had a narcissistic fascination with their own image as reflected on stage, in verse and in fiction. There is nothing at all new about the feedback loop that links gangster art and gangster life. The Hollywood filmmakers who are fascinated by the mob, and the mobsters who make their villas look like the house in the climactic scene of *Scarface* (I know of three cases in Italy), are both heirs to a tradition as old as organised crime itself. As we have already seen, the camorra assembled a myth of its own Spanish origins from whatever cultural flotsam and jetsam it could find. The mafia was scarcely less stage-struck. The very name 'mafia' almost certainly entered common use in Palermo because of an enormously successful play in Sicilian dialect first performed in 1863, *I mafiusi di la Vicaria* ('The mafiosi of Vicaria prison'—the Vicaria being, as well as the notorious Naples prison, the other name for Palermo's Ucciardone jail). *I mafiusi* is the sentimental tale of an encounter between prison *camorristi* and a patriotic conspirator in the years before Italian unification. In other words, the play that gave the mafia its name has eerie echoes of the real meetings between patriots and prisoners that played such a crucial role in the history of Italian gangland. It is said that a Man of Honour was consulted on the script.

Mafiosi also loved adventure stories. Their favourite author was not Alexandre Dumas, as Chief Prosecutor Morena claimed, but the Sicilian, Vincenzo Linares, famous for his fictional tale of *The Beati Paoli,* which was first published in 1836.

The Beati Paoli of Linares's imagination was a mysterious brotherhood in the Palermo of the 1600s. They would meet before a statue of the goddess Justice in a grotto full of weaponry under a church in piazza San Cosimo; here they would pass solemn and lethal judgement on anyone who abused the weak and innocent.

The fable proved so popular in Palermo that in 1873 piazza San Cosimo was renamed piazza Beati Paoli. Then in April 1909 the police discovered that *mafiosi* were holding their own tribunals in a cellar just off

Francesco Schiavone, arrested in 1998, was boss of the camorra's *casalesi* clan. He was known as 'Sandokan', because he looked like a heroic pirate from a 1970s TV series.

Schiavone's brother Walter modelled his villa (left, below) on the house from the final scene of *Scarface*. But in Italy, the interplay between gangster fiction and gangster reality is nothing new.

piazza Beati Paoli—the very cellar that popular legend identified with the HQ of the secret society in Linares's story. Later still, in the 1980s, many Sicilian Men of Honour who turned state's evidence would tell the authorities, with not a hint of irony, that the mafia and the Beati Paoli were the same thing. Clearly, *mafiosi* had long since begun to believe their own propaganda.

The play that gave the Sicilian mafia its name. A poster advertising *The Mafiosi of Vicaria Prison* (1863). Set in the 1850s, it tells the story of an honourable sect of prison extortionists who are recruited to the cause of a unified Italy.

12

THE SLACK SOCIETY

PSEUDO-SCIENTIFIC CRIMINOLOGISTS AND OPPORTUNISTIC MEN OF THE THEATRE DID not have a monopoly on public discussion of the mob in the new criminal normality of the 1880s and 1890s. A pioneer of serious-minded analysis of the issue was Pasquale Villari, a Neapolitan historian who held a university chair in Florence.

Villari was a lifelong campaigner for good government and social progress in the south. The squalor of the low city and the camorra that grew out of it was his consistent concern. In 1875 he created a furore by writing an open letter in which he claimed that the state of Naples was so desperate that the camorra was 'the only normal and possible state of things, the natural form that the city takes'. One of the most revealing passages in the letter was an interview with a former deputy mayor who told him that most public works contracts were impossible to implement without the approval of the camorra.

Villari's call to moralise Naples from top to bottom gained new resonance when the Left assumed power, with a brand of pork-barrel politics that gave *camorristi* even greater access to public spending. Villari inspired a generation of radical conservative campaigners to raise what became known as the 'Southern Question'. One of those to follow Villari's call was Pasquale Turiello, who in 1882 diagnosed what he termed the individualism, indiscipline and 'slackness' in Neapolitan society. Turiello argued that the Left's shambolic sleaze both reflected and cultivated Neapolitan 'slackness'. The city was being divided up between bourgeois political clienteles from above and proletarian camorra gangs from below.

The events of the 1880s and 1890s would confirm Turiello's grim diagnosis and demonstrate his belief that it applied across much of southern Italy and Sicily, and even to the national political institutions. In 1882, the right to vote in general elections was finally extended to include about 7 per cent of the population. Any male who paid some tax or had a couple of years of primary school education could now go to the polls. Another reform followed in 1888: the electorate for town and provincial councils was broadened; and the mayors of larger towns were now to be elected. The spread of democracy swelled the market in political favours. *Mafiosi* and *camorristi*—either directly, or through their friends in national and local government—gained the power to share out such appetising perks as exemptions from military service, reduced local authority tax assessments, and town hall jobs. Other quasi-public bodies, like charities, banks and hospitals, helped grease the wheels of patronage.

Meanwhile, in Naples, the paradigm of the slack society, an appalling cholera epidemic struck in 1884. The entire bourgeoisie and aristocracy fled in panic. Some 7,000 people died, most of them from the alleys and tenements of the low city, which one contemporary said were like 'bowels brimming with ordure'. In the epidemic's aftermath the call went up to 'disembowel' the city. Tax incentives and public money were quickly allocated to support ambitious plans for slum clearance and sewer construction. For the next twenty-five years, the modernisation of Naples proceeded with agonising slowness and inefficiency. All the while, the city's political cliques squabbled over the trough.

At every level of government, the slack society had enormous trouble creating and enforcing good reforms that benefitted everyone. Instead, it produced endless political fudges that fed temporary alliances of greedy politicians and their hangers-on. Indeed, when it came to dealing with the mafia and the camorra, the most important reforms were often the least likely to be implemented: policing is a prime example. On this point, as on others, there is no clearer way to illustrate the weaknesses of the slack society than through the life of an individual policeman.

In 1888 Ermanno Sangiorgi, the policeman who had first discovered the Sicilian mafia's initiation ritual, was working in Rome as a special inspector at the Ministry of the Interior. By that time he had found happiness in his personal life, although that happiness once more brought down trouble from above. While he was still in Sicily, six years after his wife's death, he began an affair with a colleague's wife. He was punished for what a senior civil servant called his 'scandalous conduct' by being transferred immediately, in December 1884. (The Ministry evidently regarded sexual morality as a more serious matter than consorting with gangsters.) Sangiorgi's new love, a Neapolitan called Maria Vozza, twenty years his junior, followed him. She had to live in separate accommodation to avoid damaging his career any further. The two would remain together for the rest of his life.

In September 1888 Sangiorgi was sent back to Sicily on a secret mission to inspect the island's unique mounted police corps, in preparation for a root and branch reform. He found that Palermo police headquarters was 'in a complete state of confusion and disorder'; Trapani was worse. The mounted police corps did not even keep proper records of what crimes had been committed. Two of its most senior officers in Palermo had 'intimate relationships with people from the mafia'. The result was not a surprise. As Sangiorgi wrote, 'It would be dangerous to be deceived: the mafia and banditry have incontrovertibly raised their heads.'

No action was taken. Not for the last time, Sangiorgi's hard work failed to produce any political effects.

The results for Sangiorgi's career were positive, however. In 1888 he was picked to manage security when the King visited the turbulent region of Romagna. He did the job so well that in 1889, in Milan, he became Italy's youngest chief of police. His rapid progress earned him the rare accolade of a newspaper profile.

> Sangiorgi is only forty-eight. He is reddish-blonde, likeable, and knows how to conceal the cunning required by his job beneath a layer of affable bourgeois calm. He is as alert as a squirrel, an investigator endowed with a steady perspicacity.

The year after this profile was published he was transferred to Naples, a city where the police still enjoyed one of the worst reputations of any force in Italy, a city in ferment in the aftermath of the cholera epidemic of 1884 and the 'disembowelling' that followed it. As he had done in Sicily, Sangiorgi immediately set about breaking up the traditionally cosy relationship between the police and organised crime. On 21 February 1891, one of Sangiorgi's officers, Saverio Russo by name, paid the ultimate price for this 'open fight' against the camorra when he was murdered by a *camorrista* he was trying to arrest. One well-informed newspaper commentator warned his readers against taking this shocking incident as an indication that gangsterism was out of control. Indeed, crime had decreased considerably in recent months:

Without any doubt a great deal of the credit for this must be given to the new Police Chief Sangiorgi. Of course it is no easy matter purifying the environment inside Police Headquarters and the local stations. Nor is it an easy job to shake up officers who are not always diligent and who previously went as far as to protect gangland. But the good results that Police Chief Sangiorgi has obtained so far, his sharp sagacity and great experience, constitute a guarantee for the government and citizenry alike.

Trouble cropped up in Sangiorgi's personal life while he was in Naples. In February 1893 he was mortified to learn that his son from his first marriage, Achille, by now a coal merchant in Venice, had been arrested for cheque fraud; to Sangiorgi's great shame, the story was reported in the press. The Ministry of the Interior looked into the case, but could only express sympathy for a hard-pressed father's lot.

The supreme boss of the Honoured Society when Sangiorgi arrived in Naples was Ciccio Cappuccio, known as 'Little Lord Frankie'. His specialism was a traditional area of camorra dominance: the market in horses, particularly the army surplus nags that were occasionally auctioned off to the general public. Rigging auctions was easy: the *camorristi* only had to bully other bidders. But the camorra's control over the horse trade was also more insidious.

Marc Monnier's father had been a keen equestrian and occasional horse dealer back in the 1840s and 1850s, so the Swiss hotelier had witnessed firsthand how *camorristi* used the uncertainties of the business to wheedle themselves into every possible economic transaction. Buying a horse from a stranger in Naples was always risky. No one could guarantee that, once the money had been handed over, the animal would not turn out to be frightened of the city's clamour or too weak to cope with its hills. No one, that is, except a *camorrista*. For a share of the price, *camorristi* promised to make business deals run smoothly—on pain of a beating, or worse. The camorra also controlled the supply of horse fodder: many bosses, including Little Lord Frankie, doubled as dealers in bran and carobs. From this base they could exercise total control over the city's ragged army of hackney-carriage drivers.

Little Lord Frankie passed away, of natural causes, in early December 1892. His death became the occasion for a disturbing display of just how deeply dyed by illegality was the slack fabric of Neapolitan society. From Police Headquarters, Sangiorgi could do little more than watch.

Little Lord Frankie's obituary in an important new Neapolitan daily, *Il Mattino*, was lavish in its praise. Here was a righter of wrongs, a proletarian

Day-to-day criminal business in Naples: a *camorrista*, in typical flared trousers, takes protection money from a cab driver (1880s).

justice of the peace. With a flush of pride, *Il Mattino* recalled the time when he had single-handedly downed twelve Calabrian *camorristi* in a knife fight in prison. But it was wrong to call him a 'bloodthirsty, born delinquent'.

> He was exceptionally nice: a model of decorum, respectful and deferential. He had a grim look in his grey eyes. But he strove constantly to moderate it by applying the sweetness and docility of a man who knows his own strength—a man who is absolutely sure that nothing in the world can resist his will.

Evidently it was not only the *lumpenproletariat* of the Vicaria quarter who embraced the myth of the noble, old-style *camorrista*. *Il Mattino*, like its notorious editor Edoardo Scarfoglio, was hysterically right wing and utterly corrupt—the mouthpiece of the worst elements in the Neapolitan political class. But what is both shocking and revealing about its coverage of Little Lord Frankie's death is the way it tolerates, and even celebrates, the private statelets that camorra bosses were able to carve out in large areas of the city.

Little Lord Frankie's last journey was a statelet funeral. Six horses drew an elaborate hearse, covered in wreaths, on a tour of half the city. The mourners were led by every cab driver in Naples, and a procession of sixty hackney carriages. Then came a huge crowd of awestruck followers, all telling tales of the dead man's 'heroic and chivalrous deeds', according to *Il Mattino*. The paper even published a poetic lament for Little Lord Frankie.

> *Who will defend us now?*
> *Without him, what will we do?*
> *Whoever can you run to*
> *If a wrong is done to you?*

Naples was still a city where the rule of law and honesty in public affairs seemed alien concepts.

A few months after Little Lord Frankie's posthumous show of force, Sangiorgi found himself at the centre of a riot that, for one brief moment, laid bare the contorted entrails of the slack society. And despite his 'steady perspicacity', and 'sharp sagacity', the notorious hackney-cab-drivers' strike of August 1893 would prove too tough an assignment for the determined Police Chief. For the first time in decades, the camorra took to the streets in force.

The events of the strike itself can be quickly related. The cab drivers' anger was triggered by a proposal to extend the city's tram system. So on 22 August three thousand cabbies launched a violent street protest to coincide with patriotic demonstrations against the murder of some Italian workmen in southern France. Socialists, anarchists and a hungry mob from the low city soon joined in. Sangiorgi was in bed with a severe fever when the disorder broke out. While he was away from work, a scrum of his officers on the hunt for rioters assaulted customers in the Gambrinus, the most prestigious café in the city. Sangiorgi crawled back to his desk the following morning to find that the police had become the targets of mass fury: there were pitched battles in the alleys between rioters and the forces of order. A boy of eight, Nunzio Dematteis, was shot in the forehead by a *Carabiniere* defending a tram from the mob. News quickly spread that the police were to blame for the boy's death. The crowd carried his bleeding body aloft and marched on the Prefecture. Sangiorgi's officers blocked their path and a grotesque tug of war over the corpse ensued. Some local parliamentarians demanded that the police withdraw their 'provocative' presence from the streets. The army was called in to restore calm.

Thus far, with the possible exception of the botched police operation, there is little that is particularly Neapolitan about the events of August 1893. Trams represented an obvious threat to the hackney-carriage business. A violent industrial dispute like this could have happened in any big city in

The camorra takes to the streets again. A mob battles with police during the hackney-cab-drivers' strike of August 1893.

Europe, where police aggression would have been the likely response. But in Naples there were of course many *camorristi* among the cab drivers. After all, these were the same men who had filed along behind Little Lord Frankie's coffin just a few months earlier. Sangiorgi's police learned that the riot of August 1893 had been planned the night before, at a meeting between *camorristi* and anarchists. The chief of police compiled a list of several hundred cabbies involved in the disturbances, marking out many of them as *camorristi* and men with criminal records.

And where the camorra had interests, so too did its eminent friends. Street gangsters may have performed the strike but it was orchestrated by city politicians. Those politicians had two notable beefs against the central government in Rome: first, the proposal to award the contract for extending the tram network to a company from Belgium, of all places; and second, the threat to take away control over the reconstruction programme set in motion after the cholera epidemic of 1884. One of Sangiorgi's officers later reported that the origins of the riot lay in 'the great shifting of interest groups caused by the disembowelling work'. By engineering anarchy in the streets of Naples, the interest groups clustered around city hall and the building industry hoped to win concessions from Rome.

Over subsequent days the strike was quelled by a mixture of negotiation and deceit. First the negotiations: the cab drivers were invited to talks with the town council. Then, presumably on the orders of the Interior Ministry, and 'in order to favour the resolution of the dispute', as Sangiorgi put it, he released the cabbies who had been arrested—*excluding* the ones with criminal records. A camorra-backed politician called Alberto Casale then acted as intermediary during the talks; in all likelihood, Casale was one of the politicians who had helped orchestrate the strike in the first place. Concessions were duly made: the tram timetable would be curtailed, and the tram network would not be extended.

Then came the deceit: a few weeks later this agreement was torn up and the original plans for the tram network were reinstated. It would later emerge that Alberto Casale had accepted a sturdy backhander from the Belgian tram company. His favourite *camorristi* received their share of the cash too—or at least we can surmise as much because the town council's flagrant bad faith during the negotiations did not reignite the cab drivers' protest. More importantly, the city council retained its control over a large chunk of the reconstruction funds. The manoeuvrings behind the scenes of the hackney-cab strike showed, as Turiello had argued, that the camorra and the political clienteles were operating at different ends of the same market for favours. The slack society was also the sly society.

By the time the dispute was resolved, Sangiorgi had left Naples. The disastrous way the cab drivers' protest had been tackled led to a purge in Police Headquarters. Sangiorgi was transferred to Venice only two weeks after the end of the strike. The rioting of August 1893 was one of the worst moments of his career, but he took much more than his fair share of the blame for the chaos.

Meanwhile, among the many jails, penitentiaries and penal colonies of the peninsula, mob rule persisted unchecked throughout the last quarter of the nineteenth century. Overhauling the prisons would have been an incisive reform directed against organised crime, drying up its traditional sump of strength. Yet the forces of law rarely concerned themselves with the mafia and camorra's prison activities. One exception was a case in the late 1870s: following the murder of a police informer in Naples that had been ordered from behind bars, fifty-three prison *camorristi* were successfully convicted, a rare investment of precious institutional resources in trying to tackle this chronic problem.

Evidently the prisons still hosted a dense gangster network. In 1893 a positivist criminologist published *The Story of a Born Delinquent*, an autobiography—no less—by a senior prison *camorrista* known only as Antonino M. Antonino M recounted taking part in several vicious battles in prison, including one that saw Neapolitans and Sicilians line up against Calabrians and Abruzzesi: many were killed and a warden was left holding his intestines in his hands.

But it is the unity of the prison confraternity, rather than its divisions, that emerges most clearly from Antonino M's account. He related that every time he was transferred from one jail to another (usually for violent conduct), he used code words to prove his camorra credentials. His status was duly recognised wherever he went: in jails in Puglia and the Marche, as in the Castello del Carmine in Naples (the very jail where Duke Castromediano had been clapped in irons in 1851). Nor was this the only way that *camorristi* in different regions were connected: punishments decreed in a prison in Cosenza, northern Calabria, could be carried out in the penal colony on Favignana, an island off the western coast of Sicily.

There was plenty more evidence where Antonino M's story came from. Undeniably, all the things that Duke Castromediano had observed back in the 1850s were still going on in Italy's prisons: organised violence and vendettas; corruption, extortion, smuggling and the trade in favours; ritual initiations and knife fights; and training in the skills and protocols of the sect. But instead of reform, such information only triggered a depressingly repetitive pattern of political failure. Now and again a particularly savage prison riot or an unusually alarming government report would generate fervent calls for change. Just as predictably, those calls would echo pointlessly into silence: lack of funds and the sheer political irrelevance of the prisons issue meant that Italy's slack society could not muster the will to tackle the problem.

Soon Italy would pay a very heavy price for failing to reform the prisons.

The criminologist who published Antonino M's autobiography also subjected him to a close physical examination. Not surprisingly, the tests came up positive: Antonino M was a born delinquent, a mixture of 'the savage, the epileptic and the moral lunatic'. He had a series of tell-tale bodily deformities, such as jug-handle ears, large testicles and slow reflexes in his pupils. He also had tattoos, including the slogan 'DOWN WITH DISHONOURED SCUM' across his chest. But the giveaway was the specimen's broad, flat skull—his brachycephaly, to use the scientific term. Antonino M was Calabrian, the criminologist explained; and typical Calabrians were dolichocephalic, meaning that they had long, thin heads. Manifestly, Antonino M was a degenerate member of the Calabrian race.

Many Italians would probably have believed the criminologist if he had said that Calabrians had four arms and a single eye in the middle of their brow. Calabria was Italy's poorest region, its most politically marginal. But by the time Antonino M came to have the criminological callipers applied to his cranium, born Calabrian delinquents like him had already surfaced from the prison system to form a new criminal fraternity.

PART IV

THE 'NDRANGHETA EMERGES

13

Harsh Mountain

A SINGLE GEOGRAPHICAL FACT DEFINES THE LANDSCAPE AT THE SOUTHERNMOST TIP OF Calabria: Aspromonte. The 'Harsh Mountain' is a place of bitter beauty. To the south, where Aspromonte looks down past Mount Etna and out towards North Africa, its flanks are toasted by the sun. Here valleys gouge their descent, spilling cement-grey grit towards the turquoise expanse of the Ionian Sea. In spring, the more sheltered hollows host embattled blooms of pink oleander and yellow broom. Aspromonte's higher reaches, by contrast, are dark with pine and slender beech. Among the trees, tortuous paths seek out the peaks and exquisite high meadows before skirting down into sudden gorges that springtime fills with the smell of oregano. The woodland canopy extends down the lush western and northern slopes where the panoramas are even more captivating: the Straits of Messina separating Calabria from Sicily, the smoky Aeolian Islands, and the Tyrrhenian Sea.

Nothing in this landscape is permanent. Human inhabitants cling to the coastal strips or create improbable, eagle's nest villages above the gorges. Every winter torrents tear rocks from the fragile valley sides and landslips rake brutal shortcuts down through the roads' painstaking meanders. Whole villages, like Roghudi and Amendolea, have been abandoned from one day to the next, their inhabitants pushed down from the mountain to the coast.

Massive earthquakes give history a deadly, arrhythmic beat in southern Calabria. In 1783 as many as 50,000 people died, and there was a sequence of lethal quakes in 1894, 1905, 1907 . . .

Even to the north-east of Aspromonte the mountains hog most of the terrain in Calabria, leaving precious little space for the coastal plains, and posing a formidable obstacle for travellers. As a result, most nineteenth-century tourist guides covered the region with little more than a cursory reference to its rugged scenery and stubborn inhabitants. Baedeker, the obligatory companion volume for the well-to-do northern European traveller, all but told its readers not to bother going to Calabria in 1869.

> The length of the journey, the indifference of the inns and the insecurity of the roads, which has of late increased, at present deter all but the most enterprising.

Such words of warning were not misplaced. At that time the railway stopped at Eboli. But Eboli was still a long way above Calabria's northern border, and 327 miles from Reggio Calabria, the small city at the tip of Italy's toe where Aspromonte overlooks the Straits of Messina. At Eboli, if the visitor were lucky enough to grab one of the three places available in the coach and then lucky with the roads, the weather and the outlaws, he could make the journey to Reggio in three and a half days. Along the route, he would stare nervously out at the forests and crags, recalling recent tales of bandit atrocities.

In 1871 the government census recorded that 87 per cent of Calabrians could not read or write. Across much of the region, callous landowners imperiously exploited vast swarms of peasants. Leopoldo Franchetti, a Tuscan Jewish intellectual who was one of the few men intrepid enough to investigate Calabrian society, wrote in 1874 that

> Among the oppressed there is no middle stage between two extreme states of being: on the one hand, fear, obedience and the most abject docility; and, on the other, the most brutal and ferocious rebellion.

Franchetti tells us that local government was a grubby and violent business in Calabria. There were many places where the mayor and his relatives cornered common land for themselves, or lived off the trade in timber stolen from common woodland. Any forest wardens who tried to impose the law, 'ran a serious risk of getting a bullet'. The 'grain banks' created to lend seed corn and money to the poor at planting time often served only as a source of easy credit for the rich. As elsewhere in the south and Sicily, the government in Rome tolerated such abuses because Calabria's corrupt mayors mustered votes for the ruling national factions. Calabria was one of the slackest parts of the slack society.

Yet one thing that Franchetti was not particularly worried about was organised crime. In the 1860s and 1870s, at a time when copious evidence attests to the shocking extent of mafia and camorra power, there are only a few intermittent reports of gangsterism in Calabria. Together, those reports do nothing to suggest that southern Calabria would become a hoodlum fief on a par with Sicily and Campania. There is no government document from the 1860s or 1870s, no traveller's tale, no faded local memoir that speaks of a strong and insistent mafia presence here. The region had many serious problems but delinquent fraternities were not among them.

By the mid-1880s, there were some signs of improvement in Calabria's fortunes. Trains now crawled to Reggio along a single-track railway that clung to the Ionian coast; and the line along the Tyrrhenian coast was under construction. Yet it was precisely at this historical moment that the first official reports tell us that 'a nucleus of *mafiosi* and *camorristi*' was in operation in Reggio Calabria and 'the ranks of the maffia's criminal associations' were growing elsewhere in Aspromonte's shadow. As if from nowhere, a new criminal sect was being born. By the end of the 1880s the province of Reggio Calabria and some adjoining parts of the province of Catanzaro were enduring an explosion in gang crime from which they have never recovered.

Mafiosi and *camorristi*: the earliest labels were borrowed from Sicily and Naples. Other names would soon be used: Calabrian mafia, Honoured Society, Society of *Camorristi*, and so on. But as police and magistrates became more knowledgeable about this new threat to public order in southern Calabria, they most often referred to it as the picciotteria. The word is pronounced roughly 'peach-otter-ear', and there is no mystery to its derivation. *Picciotto* ('peach-otto') was a southern Italian or Sicilian dialect word for 'lad'. *Picciotti* were also the lower ranking members of the Neapolitan camorra. Picciotteria sometimes means a young man's air of arrogant self-confidence. So 'Lads with Attitude' is a handy translation of the new association's informal title.

The Lads with Attitude were a lowly bunch: herdsmen and farmhands, by and large, men whose grandest ambition was a flask of wine and a piece of goat meat. At the time when the picciotteria first appeared, the great Sicilian novelist Giovanni Verga was evoking the lives of poor people like them in some of the greatest fiction in the Italian language. Verga knew that he faced a hard task convincing his bourgeois readership to dare an imaginative leap into the mental universe of the peasantry. 'We need to make ourselves tiny like them', Verga pleaded. 'We need to enclose the whole horizon between two clods of earth, and look through the microscope at the little causes that make little hearts beat.'

From today's perspective, we need to make a similar imaginative leap. But we have no need to be patronising towards the 'little hearts' of the farm hands and woodcutters who became members of the picciotteria. For these humble folk were the direct ancestors of a fearsome Calabrian criminal brotherhood whose definitive name would only become commonly used in the 1950s: the 'ndrangheta, Italy's third mafia, and now its richest, its most secretive and the most successful at spreading vile metastases around the globe.

Soon after it was born, the picciotteria was subjected to a judicial offensive that was sporadic but nonetheless more effective than any faced so far by organised crime in either Naples or Sicily. In the years following the first signs of alarm, around Aspromonte and on either side of the first stretch of the Apennines, hundreds of Calabrian *picciotti*—precisely 1,854 of them between 1885 and 1902 according to one local prosecutor—were tried, convicted and put behind bars. This fact alone tells us something significant: Calabria's gangsters did not yet enjoy the same degree of VIP protection enjoyed by the Neapolitan camorra, let alone the Sicilian mafia.

Yet the picciotteria remained almost entirely unknown in the rest of Italy. Unlike the mafia and camorra, it provoked no parliamentary inquiries or debates, no bouts of national newspaper outrage, no investigations by sociologists, no poems or plays. Nobody cared: this was Calabria, after all.

The lack of interest in the picciotteria together with Calabria's history of maladministration and natural disaster often leaves historians with a shortage of evidence. The city of Reggio Calabria was undoubtedly where the picciotteria was first spotted in the early 1880s, but there is not enough surviving documentation to explain how and why. Yet elsewhere the early trials did deposit a thin but precious seam of paper that can now be mined for clues about how organised crime in Calabria began. And as it turns out, the 'ndrangheta's beginnings were much more straightforward than the camorra's or mafia's. There are two places in particular where enough nineteenth-century policework survives to give us a clear picture of those beginnings. A later chapter deals with the most notorious of those places: the village of Africo, sited 700 metres above the Ionian coast. Until it was finally abandoned in 1953 as a result of devastating floods, Africo was a byword for the isolation and poverty of Calabria's highland communities— and a byword for organised crime.

But before going to Africo, the story of the 'ndrangheta's origins takes us to the opposite flank of Aspromonte, and to a place of relative wealth and power. One of the secrets of the 'ndrangheta's survival and success over the years has been its ability to straddle the distance between prosperity and hardship, as between the contrasting faces of the Harsh Mountain.

14

THE TREE OF KNOWLEDGE

PALMI SITS ON A SHELF WHERE ASPROMONTE MEETS THE TYRRHENIAN SEA. GAZING to the north-east, it affords a seductive panorama over the Plain of Gioia Tauro, a fertile amphitheatre of land descending gently from the mountains. The Plain was Calabria's answer to the 'Golden Shell' around Palermo in the late nineteenth century. Land was owned in smaller farms rather than great estates, partly because a great deal of Church property was confiscated and privatised after Italian unification. There were many citrus fruit groves in the Plain too, although the irrigation was not as sophisticated as it was in Sicily. More important to the economy of towns like Palmi were the famous olive trees, as tall and venerable as oaks. Recently the wine industry had come to the fore, after French vineyards were devastated by phylloxera, an aphid-like insect that feasted on the roots and leaves of vines. Italian producers moved to fill the gap in supply, and in the plain of Gioia Tauro they even cut down olive trees to make room for the grape.

In the 1880s Palmi was a town of some eleven or twelve thousand inhabitants, which was not small by the standards of the region. Southern Calabria is a place where the population is spread out in little centres, and in the 1880s few of them housed more than five thousand people. Even the provincial capital, Reggio Calabria, could only muster its 40,000 population by including the villages that surrounded it. Palmi was the administrative capital for the whole of the Plain of Gioia Tauro, an area encompassing 130,000 souls. And as the administrative capital it had an outpost of the Prefecture, a police station, a courtroom, and a prison. Men from that prison

Christ and the thieves overlook an 'ndrangheta heartland. Palmi, one of the centres from
which the 'ndrangheta first emerged in the 1880s, can be seen in the middle distance. Beyond
and below it lies the notorious plain of Gioia Tauro.

would turn Palmi into Calabria's most notorious mafia stronghold in the
1880s and 1890s.

It all began in the spring of 1888. The local newssheet started to report
razor slashings and ritual knife duels. In Palmi's taverns and brothels, gang
members battled it out with clubs and blades. In classic mafia and camorra
fashion, the bleeding losers refused point blank to name the men who had
wounded them.

Within weeks of these first reports, Palmi's hoodlum problem was out
of control. Ordinary citizens were afraid to leave their homes. Anyone who
stood up to the thugs received the razor treatment. The *picciotti* settled their
bloody accounts in the centre of town, on corso Garibaldi and in piazza
Vittorio Emanuele. They had begun by extorting money from gamblers and
prostitutes. Now they also fleeced landowners who were afraid to report
thefts and vandalism for fear of worse: the Lads with Attitude were setting
up protection rackets, the very foundation of any mafia's territorial authority. The gang threatened a local *Carabiniere*, and pelted him with stones;
they even silenced the local newspaper, whose editor received a threatening
letter telling him not to 'persecute the lads'. From Palmi the sect spread to

the smaller towns and villages right across the Plain of Gioia Tauro, and up onto the surrounding mountain slopes.

Only in June 1888, when a clerk at the local branch of the Prefecture was slashed across the face as he came out of the theatre, did the police round up the first large batch of suspects. The twenty-four men arraigned early in 1889 give us our first glimpse of the *kind* of person who became a Lad with Attitude. Many of them were young—late teens or early twenties—and all of them were labourers or artisans: the legal documents list job titles such as peasant, wagon driver, waiter, tailor, mule driver, shepherd. There were also one or two men who farmed their own plot. The boss, one Francesco Lisciotto, was a cobbler; at sixty, he was comfortably the oldest man in the gang. More importantly, like all but three of the Palmi *picciotti*, he had already spent time behind bars.

The police and magistrature continued their fight. In June 1890 one trial targeted a picciotteria network based in Iatrìnoli and Radicena, two towns that sat one just above the other about fifteen kilometres from the coast at Gioia Tauro. Many of the ninety-six defendants were workers and craftsmen like their fellow *picciotti* in Palmi. The judges in the case explained that the sect began in 1887; they had no doubts about where it came from.

> The association originated in the district prisons [in Palmi], under the name of 'Sect of *camorristi*'. From there, as and when its bosses and promoters were released, it spread to other towns and villages where it found fertile soil among the callow youth, old jailbirds, and especially goatherds. The Society, with the protection it afforded to its comrades, offered this last group a way to pasture their animals illegally on other people's land, and to impose themselves on landlords.

Men like the Palmi *capo* Francesco Lisciotto came out of jail with their status in the Society already well established. The 'ndrangheta was not founded, in other words; it *emerged* almost fully formed from inside the prison system.

More arrests and further trials followed over the coming years. Early in 1892 the court in Palmi tried some 150 men from right across the Plain of Gioia Tauro. The *picciotti* did their best to evade justice by killing one witness and threatening many others into silence. But the evidence against them proved overwhelming. The new boss of Palmi, Antonio Giannino, aged only 20, was his gang's knife-fencing instructor. Indeed he was so proud of his skills that he had himself photographed in fighting pose. The image helped convict him.

The 1892 trial added more detail to what the police knew about the picciotteria: the characteristic appearance of its affiliates, for example. The *picciotti* had tattooed hieroglyphs that signalled their rank. They also wore tight trousers that flared over their shoes, tied their silk scarves in a special way to leave the ends fluttering as they swaggered, and combed their hair into a distinctive butterfly-shaped pompadour.

If peace returned to Palmi following the huge and successful prosecution of 1892, it certainly did not return for long. In 1894 the town was reduced to rubble by an earthquake. By the following year the picciotteria was active again, robbing and extorting among the temporary shacks in which much of the population still lived. Yet the police seemed inert. Commentators in the press muttered that the police in Palmi had 'evening conversations' in the very wine cellars where the hoods hung out, and that the forces of law and order were less interested in tackling organised crime than they were in arresting opposition voters during elections. In Calabria's bigger towns, just as in Naples and Sicily, the police soon learned to co-manage crime with gangsters.

Eventually, in September 1896, another wave of arrests elicited more confessions. Early in 1897 the resulting trial provided full details of the Calabrian mafia's ranks and rituals for the first time. The picciotteria formed itself into locally based cells or 'sections'. Each cell was subdivided between a Minor Society and a Major Society. The Minor Society contained men bearing the lower rank of *picciotto*. The Major Society contained the more senior criminals, known as *camorristi*. Both the Major and the Minor had their own boss and a *contaiuolo*, or bookkeeper, who gathered and redistributed the gang's income from crime. Each new member had to undergo an initiation ritual to join the Society before he was awarded the lowest rank of all, that of 'Honoured Youth'. The boss of the Major Society would call his men into a darkened room, form them into a circle and begin the long ceremony with the words, 'Are you comfortable?' to which the assembled gangsters would reply, 'Very comfortable!'

On 24 February 1897 a crucial witness in the resulting trial, a man by the name of Pasquale Trimboli, took the stand in Palmi's courthouse. The defendants in their cage, and the public squeezed into the tiny gallery, all craned to hear what he had to say. Trimboli had been a member of the picciotteria, and therefore knew everything about the sect—including the terrible secret of its origins. Mention of the mysterious genesis of the picciotteria transfixed the court. But the mood of intense concentration soon gave way to puzzled laughter as he told his childish tale of how the Calabrian mafia was born.

The society was born from three knights, one from Spain, one from Palermo, and one from Naples. All three of them were *camorristi*. The Spanish knight took a camorra, a bribe, on every hand of cards the other two played. With time, he gathered in all their money and the others could not play anymore. So he gave 10 lire back to each one, and told them, 'Here are 10 lire for you, and I've got all the rest in my hand, so that means that I'm the strongest.'

Metaphorically speaking, these three *camorristi* were a *tree*. The boss, the Spanish knight, was the *trunk* of the tree. The Palermo knight, who was the oldest, was the masterbone, *Mastrosso*. And the third knight, the one from Naples, was the bone, *Osso*. The other members were the *branches* and the *leaves*. The 'honoured youths', who aspired to become *picciotti*, were the *flowers*.

To my knowledge, this is the first recorded (and garbled) version of the 'ndrangheta's founding myth. What it suggests is that Calabrian gangsters were seeking out fables to build their *esprit de corps*, to endow their newly surfaced fraternity with the same aura as their brethren in Campania and Sicily.

The success of the judicial assault on the picciotteria can be judged from the testimony of a priest who was called to give evidence in yet another trial just three years later. He said that in Palmi,

the criminals' audacity makes walking through the streets extremely dangerous, even before the Angelus [i.e., sunset]. Honest people are now in the habit of going home as soon as they can, because at any time in the busiest parts of town you can hear the wails of the wounded and dying.

But if the trials in Palmi failed to shake the grip of the picciotteria in the Plain of Gioia Tauro, they did at least provide historical documentation that has a familiar ring. Doubly familiar, in fact. On the one hand there is a great deal about the picciotteria that resembles the Honoured Society of Naples. (One early picciotteria trial in 1884 even found that the criminal boss of the small town of Nicastro 'had relations with the famous Neapolitan *camorrista* Ciccillo ["Little Lord Frankie"] Cappuccio'.) Like their Neapolitan cousins, the Calabrians duelled with knives, and slashed their victims' faces with razors. Both sects exploited prostitution and gambling; both blew their illicit earnings on feasting and getting drunk; both had a similar dress code (flared trousers and all that); and both divided their gangs between a Minor Society and a Major Society, between aspiring 'Honoured Youths', junior *picciotti*, and senior *camorristi*. Like the Neapolitans, the Calabrians punished their members' transgressions with a distinctively disgusting punishment they called *tartaro* ('Tartarus' or 'Hell'): it involved daubing the culprit with urine and faeces. There are many, many other similarities that it would be tiresome to list here: in the coded jargon they spoke to try and conceal what they were talking about, for example. What these likenesses confirm is that both the Neapolitan camorra and the Calabrian mafia share the same genealogy. Both were born from the *same* prison camorra.

On the other hand the picciotteria is also familiar in that it closely resembles the 'ndrangheta of today, with its Minor Society and its Major Society, its foundation myth of the three Spanish knights, and so on. In fact even the most confused bits of Pasquale Trimboli's testimony chime strongly with what we know about the 'ndrangheta's contemporary practices. *'ndranghetisti* habitually refer to their organisation metaphorically, as what they call a 'Tree of Knowledge': the trunk being the boss, the branches the officers, and so on.

The 'ndrangheta of today, with its unique admission rituals for every rank in the organisation, is more obsessed with ceremony than any other Italian mafia. The archival papers tell us that the Calabrian mafia of the late 1800s was developing the same obsession. Today's 'ndrangheta also has a great variety of specialised job titles within each local gang—far more than either the Sicilian mafia or the Neapolitan camorra. Echoes of that level of specialisation reach us from the nineteenth century too. Both the Minor Society and the Major Society of the Palmi section of the picciotteria had other posts in addition to the boss and the bookkeeper: such as the '*Camorrista* of the Day', whose duty was to inform the boss of local goings on; and the '*Picciotto* of Correspondence,' who handled communications between members in prison and members at large. In short, there can be no doubt that the Lads with Attitude were the 'ndrangheta by an earlier name.

A long and gruesome history had begun.

15

DARKEST AFRICO

THE ZAMPOGNA, OR SOUTHERN ITALIAN BAGPIPE, IS AN ANCIENT AND UNLOVELY instrument. It is made from a whole goat- or sheepskin that has been cured, turned wool side in, and sealed. A cluster of wooden pipes lolls where the sheep's head was once attached and a mouthpiece protrudes from the stump of a front leg. When the zampogna is pressed under the player's arm, nasal melodies are emitted over a hypnotic wheeze that sounds like the infinite bleat of the departed animal's soul.

In the hilltop towns of nineteenth-century Calabria, dancing to the *zampogna* was one of the few things that passed for entertainment. So any student of Calabrian folklore who had ventured into the streets of Africo on the mild evening of All Saints, 1 November 1894, would not have been surprised to see a circle of men taking turns to perform a skipping dance around the local *zampogna*-player. But as the *zampognaro* himself—his name was Giuseppe Sagoleo—would later tell an investigating magistrate, there was nothing folkloristic about his performance that evening. This bagpipe party was a carefully choreographed prelude to a murder that would precipitate one of the biggest early picciotteria trials. By luck, the complete papers from that trial have survived the upheavals of Calabrian geology and history to give us a priceless insight into this newly emerged criminal organisation in one of its heartlands.

But to make sense of the bagpipe party of All Saints, we need to take a few steps further back in time. For the brutal execution carried out that evening was the culmination of a campaign by the recently established Africo section of the picciotteria to take control of the town for the first time. The *zampogna* had a central role in that campaign. Combined with the testimonies of witnesses, Giuseppe Sagoleo's story takes us deep into the world of the 'ndrangheta in its primitive form.

The *zampognaro*'s woes began, he testified, early the same year when Domenico Callea, age thirty-four, returned to his home town after serving ten years in prison for the kidnap and violent rape of a woman. Once his hair grew back from his prison crew cut, Callea cultivated a butterfly-shaped pompadour. He made the transition from prison *camorrista* to senior Lad with Attitude smoothly: he immediately became both the bookkeeper for the Africo section, and also its duelling instructor.

Domenico Callea approached the *zampognaro*, offering to propose him for membership of a 'society' that existed in Africo. Because Callea was one of the society's leaders, he said, he could even offer to waive the 7½ lire enrolment fee. But Sagoleo was smart enough to make inquiries about the society before accepting Callea's invitation. When he was told that the members were obliged to follow the bosses' orders, even if that meant committing robbery or murder, he refused to join.

Across southern Calabria, Lads like Callea were making similar offers. They nearly always charged a membership fee of 7½ lire—about three quarters of the value of a goat, or about 8 per cent of the price of a pig. They usually claimed that the society just existed to drink wine and have a good time. And very frequently they beat people up or flicked them with a razor if they refused to pay. Sagoleo the *zampognaro* was lucky.

This simple method of squeezing money from new recruits was a classic prison camorra technique. The picciotteria would use it for years to come. So the early 'ndrangheta was based partly on a kind of pyramid selling scam that benefitted only the bosses at the top. As the case of the bagpipe player of Africo also illustrated, this method had an inbuilt weakness in that it created a great many new members who had little genuine loyalty to the picciotteria. One of the reasons we can know so much about the early 'ndrangheta is that so many of these new recruits would confess everything to the police. The 'ndrangheta came into the world with a birth defect that would take decades to shed.

Although the *zampognaro* refused Domenico Callea's offer, he did not save himself from the attentions of Callea's friends. As he explained to the investigating magistrate

> The association's members were always coming to me and asking me to play. There were times when they told me I had to do it whether I wanted to or not because they were in charge. Sometimes they paid me, and

sometimes they didn't. And I couldn't complain because they threatened to break my bagpipes.

Domenico Callea's *picciotti* were subjecting the bagpipe player to what the police called a *prepotenza*, an act of petty bullying—like refusing to pay in a shop or pestering another man's wife. But this *prepotenza* had a clear strategic purpose. The picciotteria may have been a secret sect, but its secrecy, like that of other Italian criminal fraternities, was of a paradoxical kind: the Lads were, after all, not yet so guarded that they could resist sporting distinctive haircuts and trousers. This is because their power depended on their ability to make their presence felt in the most public of ways. Indeed by strong-arming the poor *zampognaro* into playing at their parties, the Lads were imposing themselves on one of the few expressions of a collective social life in Africo. This was a flagrant *prepotenza* committed against the whole community. More than that, it was a deliberate attempt to undermine any sense of community, and replace it with fear.

On 12 May 1894, the day devoted to Africo's patron, Saint Leo, Domenico Callea called upon the bagpiper to welcome a very important guest: Filippo Velonà, a 38-year-old cobbler from the nearby village of Staiti. The official files on Velonà give us a clear but hardly very expressive description: he was 5'7" tall with brown hair and eyes, a 'regular' forehead, a 'natural' complexion, a 'robust' physique and no distinguishing marks. In short, Velonà could have been any one of the countless artisans who eked out a life by servicing the poor mountain communities of Calabria. The only clue to his real identity is in the local mayor's description of his conduct as *cattivissima*—'exceptionally bad'. This after all, was a man who had two convictions for wounding and who had served seven years in jail for dishing out a beating from which the victim subsequently died. When he was released in 1892 he led the emergence of the picciotteria in the district of Bova, which lay either side of the rugged valley blasted out by the Amendolea torrent.

The villages of the Bova district, including Africo, were a cultural island even on Aspromonte: their inhabitants spoke not Calabrian dialect, but Greek—or at least Grecanico, an archaic dialect of Greek that survives from the early Middle Ages when Calabria was part of the Byzantine Empire. One sign of how important this cultural island is to the Calabrian mafia today is the fact that the word 'ndrangheta derives from the word for 'manliness' or 'heroism' in Grecanico.

But boss Velonà's prestige extended beyond the Grecanico-speaking area: further round the coast to the north-east, he was acknowledged in Bovalino,

San Luca and even as far as Portigliola and Gerace. This was a huge stretch of the Calabrian coast—as big as the Plain of Gioia Tauro just over the mountains; it corresponds more or less to the *Mandamento ionico*, or 'Ionian Precinct', which is one of the three areas into which the 'ndrangheta's jurisdiction is divided today. No wonder the rank and file called Velonà 'President'.

Velonà came to Africo on 12 May to initiate a new Lad with Attitude. The formalities were completed indoors. The young man ritually submitted himself to the boss's authority by kneeling before him, kissing his hand, and uttering the following words: 'Father forgive me if I have strayed in the past, and I promise not to stray in the future.'

The initiation, as always, was celebrated with a banquet attended by members from across the area. They drank a great deal of wine and ate a goat purloined from the man who had been forced to put Velonà up during his stay. Everyone laughed when one *picciotto* loudly asked the wife of the very man from whom the animal had been stolen for some salt to preserve a piece of it. The lads clearly appreciated such a creatively framed *prepotenza*. Then, after eating copiously, the bosses settled down to play cards while the younger affiliates danced to the sound of the bagpipes. 'All of this happened publicly, in front of everyone', as one witness explained.

By stealing animals, and eating stolen meat in such demonstrative assertions of their *esprit de corps*, the *picciotti* were proclaiming themselves to be at the top of the food chain; for this was a part of the world where the peasant diet was mostly vegetarian. Elsewhere, the picciotteria went to even greater lengths to show that its members were in the protein elite. In Bova, the town's mayor would indignantly testify, one local mobster (a cobbler like his boss) once treated his brethren from other towns to a fish banquet. Now, Bova is only about nine kilometres from the sea, as the crow flies. But those 9 kilometres may as well have been 900: nothing perishable could be relied upon to survive the arduous trip on a mule's back up into the mountains from the coast. As the mayor explained, fish 'arrives only very rarely in our town, and people from a humble background are not accustomed to eating it'. For a cobbler to serve fish to his guests was the dietary equivalent of gangster bling.

On Aspromonte, there were many who were impressed by these rudimentary advertisements for power. While the boss Velonà was in Africo he was approached by a woman who presented him with a sheep and begged him 'to do her the honour of admitting her son to the association'.

Callea's crew were doing more to earn such admiration than bullying the bagpiper and pinching the odd goat for their team-building banquets. According to the mayor of Africo, seventy pigs had been stolen in 1893 alone. Many other beasts went missing too. The victims—men like the schoolteacher, the archpriest, and the mayor himself—were too afraid even to report their losses to the authorities. Rumours said that the animals were sold cheaply to butchers who were also in the association; goats had been found with their ears—and therefore their owners' marks—cut off. Butchers in Bova later reported that the legal livestock trade had virtually collapsed because people were just too afraid to go around buying and selling animals.

The accumulating evidence from Africo points inexorably to an important conclusion: even in the most isolated mountain villages of Grecanico-speaking Aspromonte, the Lads with Attitude were part of an organisation that was much bigger, and more coordinated, than some loose constellation of local gangs. Not only did they have common rituals and structures and a shared past behind bars, in Filippo Velonà they also had a charismatic boss whose prestige traversed a wide territory. They even placed themselves under the jurisdiction of a single judge: his name was Andrea Angelone.

Angelone was an old prison *camorrista*, fifty-nine years old to be precise. He was released from jail for the last time following a twelve-year stretch in 1887 and immediately set up a branch of the picciotteria in his home village of Roccaforte del Greco, in the Grecanico-speaking district. Although he did not take an active role in the sect's day-to-day criminal activity thereafter, he still received his regular cut of the takings in return for dispensing his wisdom at tribunals. The Grecanico-speaking Lads also had contacts in Reggio Calabria and in the district of Palmi.

The authorities in Palmi reported similar long-range connections. The various sections of the organisation on the Plain of Gioia Tauro had 'emissaries so they could correspond with one another'. And while the local branches each had their own boss and underboss, clusters of them operated under the authority of one gang.

As in Sicily, cattle rustling was almost certainly one of the main reasons for these links. Many of the Calabrian *mafiosi* were woodcutters and herdsmen who thought nothing of spending days on end in the mountains, and who were born with a map of Aspromonte's numberless pathways imprinted on their minds. The rustling technique was simple and virtually foolproof: steal animals in one place, and then avoid detection by sending them off through the mountains to trusted brethren in other towns who could put them on the market. The *picciotti* also moved around the area to exact an extortion tribute on the regular fairs that were still an important part of the Calabrian mountain economy.

What were the authorities doing in the late 1880s and early 1890s, while the picciotteria was building its numbers and thickening its networks? The answer is, very little. Africo, Roccaforte, Bova and the other centres of gang activity were still among the many places in the peninsula where 'Italy' did not mean very much beyond taxes, military service and the occasional visit from *Carabinieri* on patrol. In April 1893, two forest guards (auxiliary policemen) sent a letter to the local magistrate denouncing the existence of 'a terrible sect of so-called maffiosi' in Africo and the surrounding area. Their warning was ignored and buried in a pile of paperwork.

Which is where, more than a year later, it was found by a dynamic new representative of the Italian state's feeble authority in Calabria: Sergeant Angelo Labella, commander of the Bova station of the *Carabinieri*. On 21 June 1894, Labella wrote his first report on the criminal association he had unearthed: he named fifty members, including Domenico Callea and Filippo Velonà. Over the coming weeks Labella added to his roll call of suspects, and laid the groundwork for a huge prosecution by detailing witnesses who could provide evidence against the gang. At last, it seemed, the Italian state was set to challenge the picciotteria regime in this forgotten place.

In September 1894 investigating magistrates came to the district capital of Bova and began summoning the witnesses Labella had cited. The Lads quickly mobilised in response to this challenge to their authority. They verbally threatened anyone prepared to give evidence against them, including the wealthier citizens of Africo. They slaughtered animals and left them in the fields for the owners to find; they vandalised vines. In late October they cut down twelve fruit trees belonging to one landowner and carved funeral crosses into the stumps, just in case the message in the damage was not clear.

The *picciotti* also enlisted the bagpiper to their campaign of intimidation. He was forced to play while they went through the streets improvising menacing songs about their enemies, including literate folk like town councillors, the archpriest, the tax collector, and Sergeant Angelo Labella. They were heard bellowing the following clumsy ditty outside one landowner's balcony.

> Now take up your pen and inkpot to do a new trial. But if we win our freedom, we'll take vengeance with our own hands.

While their Lads were intoning their threats, Domenico Callea and the other bosses had already decided on the fate of the most dangerous of the witnesses named in Sergeant Labella's first report: a fifty-year-old swineherd named Pietro Maviglia.

Maviglia did not cut a very impressive figure. His crippled leg meant that he walked with the aid of a stick and he could not hobble very far without gasping for breath. (The post-mortem would identify the signs of pleurisy in his wounded lungs.) But Maviglia's importance lay in the fact that he was a member of the gang—one of the earliest members, in fact.

Back in 1892 Maviglia had become involved in a dispute with Domenico Callea's equally nasty younger brother Bruno, who had beaten him up as a result. To take revenge, Maviglia leaked news of a burglary that Bruno Callea had committed. As a result of Maviglia's testimony, Callea was sentenced to two years for the burglary, and another fourteen months for beating the crippled old swineherd up a second time.

Maviglia was expelled from the picciotteria. From that point on, he lived his life under the threat of death. With Sergeant Labella's detective work continuing, and prosecuting magistrates conducting their first interrogations in the case, silencing Maviglia now became an urgent priority for the bosses.

In a place like Africo, rumours took the place of newspapers, especially when it came to informing the citizenry about the internal affairs of the criminal fraternity. In October 1894 whispering voices began to relate the surprising news that the Calleas had settled their quarrel with Pietro Maviglia. In the face of the ongoing judicial investigation, harmony had returned to the brotherhood, it was said. Maviglia himself was unsure of how to respond to the peaceful proposals directed at him; he asked his brother for advice, confiding that the *picciotti* wanted to readmit him into what he referred to as 'the sect'.

The *picciotti* held the bagpipe party on the evening of All Saints for two reasons. First, to reassure Maviglia that the offer to readmit him to their fraternity was genuine. Second, to provide cover for his killers. While the members of the gang danced and drank and sang in the streets that evening, one *picciotto* approached Maviglia and explained to him that the Lads had stolen a goat and would eat it together in a shack out in the countryside to celebrate the swineherd's return to the brotherhood. Pulling his fist from his pocket, he showed its contents: 'I've even got some salt', he smiled.

About an hour after dark that night, Pietro Maviglia was seen for the last time by anyone but his assassins. Leaning on his walking stick, with his jacket slung over his shoulder, he set off along the via Anzaro that led towards the cemetery.

Shortly afterwards, one of the Lads told the bagpiper to bring the dancing to an end and then followed the direction that his intended victim had taken.

Late on the morning of 4 November 1894 the local deputy magistrate and doctor arrived in Africo to perform a grisly duty. They were 'local' in the sense that they had only had to trudge for four hours to reach Africo from the district capital of Bova, along mountain tracks that horses refused to tackle. They found Pietro Maviglia lying where he had been found the previous evening: face down on top of his walking stick, in a field about fifteen minutes from where he had last been seen among the *picciotti* dancing to the bagpipes.

The doctor worked quickly once the body had been moved to the cemetery and formal identification had taken place. Five lesions spoke the likely narrative of Maviglia's last minutes. The old man was stabbed in the small of his back first. Perhaps the head injury came next: a hatchet blow had notched the back of his skull. Maviglia was then stuck twice with a dagger, both blows entering the chest cavity just to the left of the breastbone. The heart was pierced through both ventricles. Either of these injuries would have been fatal, but the killers—at least three of them—were remorseless, inflicting the fifth and final wound when their victim was already prostrate. It seemed a reasonable deduction that, as Maviglia's head was heaved backwards by the hair, his throat was cut by a very sharp blade: a clean-edged, ten-centimetre gash bisected his right jugular vein, his voice box and his oesophagus. 'Undigested food is coming out', the doctor jotted dispassionately.

> I must also point out that there was coarse cooking salt on the throat wound. The authors of the murder sprinkled it there, perhaps in order to achieve greater satisfaction for their feelings of vendetta.

Pietro Maviglia was butchered like a goat. In the days following his death, the people of Africo said that his butterfly pompadour had been sliced off too, 'so as to demonstrate that he was not fit to belong to the association'. The doctor neither confirmed nor denied the rumour.

The revolting details of Pietro Maviglia's murder give the lie to the first of many historical misconceptions about the picciotteria. The early Calabrian mafia, it is still sometimes said, had a social function. In a desperately deprived and backward part of the country, *mafiosi* got together to create a source of authority and a system of mutual assistance. Or so the argument goes.

It may be true that, on the slopes of Aspromonte, the early 'ndrangheta moved into a vacuum where the state should have been. But they ruled by fear—that much is evident from one statement after another that the magistrates collected in the aftermath of Maviglia's death. That fact is not changed if, in the absence of state authority, some people—including landowners—

made the best of their situation, and allied themselves with bullies they could not fight. Pietro Maviglia's murderers, it is worth remembering, made no attempt to hide his corpse: those horrific injuries and even the fistful of salt thrown on his slit gullet, were meant as a warning to others—a public, poetic 'justice'.

After the post-mortem, investigations into the picciotteria in Africo finally began to make real progress. More *Carabinieri* arrived in the village, and were billeted in a house right next door to Domenico Callea's. The picciotteria's bookkeeper and fencing instructor had gone on the run after ordering Pietro Maviglia killed. His new wife was left alone in the house. She kept the *Carabinieri* awake all night with the sound of her sobbing.

The strong military presence in Africo encouraged more witnesses to come forward. With Sergeant Labella's energetic help the magistrates preparing the prosecution case were able to tease out more and more evidence. Maviglia's murderers were arrested. Under interrogation, they broke: blaming one another at first, and then finally confessing. In the Grecanico-speaking communities, the wall of *omertà* around the picciotteria collapsed.

Perhaps the most historically significant truth to surface after Maviglia's brutal demise was that the criminal network that the Lads with Attitude rapidly created in the 1880s and 1890s had an enthralling religious symbol at its centre.

The Sanctuary of the Madonna of Polsi lies hidden in a valley in Aspromonte's upper reaches. Legend has it that in 1144 a shepherd came to this secluded spot looking for a lost bullock. He was greeted by a miraculous vision of the Blessed Virgin. 'I want a church erected', she declared, 'to spread my graces among the devout who will come here to visit me'. For centuries, in early September, poor pilgrims have made their way up the twisting mountain roads to Polsi in joyous conformity with the Virgin's wishes.

Calabria's greatest writer, Corrado Alvaro, described Polsi as it would have been in the late nineteenth century, when twenty thousand men and women flooded the churchyard and the woods round about in preparation for the Festival. Some had walked barefoot all the way; others came wearing crowns of thorns. The men drank heavily and fired their guns in the air. Everyone feasted on roast goat, bellowed ancient hymns, and danced all night to the music of the bagpipe and the tambourine.

On the day of the Festival itself, the tiny church was filled with the imploring wails of the faithful, and with the bleating and mooing of the animals brought as votive offerings. Hysterical women shrieked vows as they elbowed their way through the crowd to place eerie *ex-votos* at the Madonna's feet: brass jewellery, clothes, or babies' body parts modelled from wax. When evening came and the Madonna was paraded around the

The Sanctuary of the Madonna of Polsi, on Aspromonte. Since at least 1894, the 'ndrangheta's annual gathering has coincided with the Festival of the Madonna of the Mountain held here.

sanctuary on a bier, the pilgrims prayed, wept, beat their chests, and cried out 'viva Maria!'

The Festival of the Madonna of Polsi has a special symbolic significance for the 'ndrangheta. To this day the Chief Cudgels from across the province of Reggio Calabria use the Festival as cover for an annual meeting. In September 2009, prosecutors maintain, the newly elected 'Chief of the Crime', Domenico Oppedisano, came to have his appointment ratified at Polsi. Senior positions in the 'ndrangheta's coordinating body, the Crime, come into force at midnight on the day of the Festival.

The nearest town to the Sanctuary at Polsi is San Luca, where the writer Corrado Alvaro grew up, and where the 'ndrine (local mafia cells) involved in the Duisburg massacre of 2007 originated. 'Ndranghetisti refer to San Luca as their Mamma; the 'ndrangheta there is traditionally the guardian of the whole association's rules, and the arbiter in disputes. San Luca has been called the 'Bethlehem' of Calabrian organised crime.

We can now be sure that the Polsi crime summit is a tradition as old as the 'ndrangheta itself. For in June 1895 a shopkeeper from Roccaforte del Greco told the magistrates investigating Pietro Maviglia's murder what he had seen in Polsi.

On 3 September 1894 I went to the Festival of the Madonna of the Mountain. There I saw several members of the criminal association from Roccaforte in the company of about sixty people from various villages who were all sitting in a circle eating and drinking. When I asked who paid for all that food and wine at the Festival, I was told that they paid for it with the camorra they collected.

Evidently the pilgrimage to the Sanctuary at Polsi was, from the outset, a chance for the Lads to make a profit and talk shop rather than to worship.

Sergeant Labella's investigations also threw up more scattered evidence about how the picciotteria began. Although he could not be precise about the year of its emergence, he thought that it was no later than 1887, the year that the sect's 'judge', Andrea Angelone, was released from prison. Other witnesses pushed the starting date back further. One resident of the same village said he thought Angelone had been a member of a criminal association 'sixteen or seventeen years back' (i.e., in about 1879).

The elementary-schoolteacher in Africo proved to be a particularly insightful witness. He had first taken up his post in the mid-1880s and had immediately heard talk of a criminal sect in town. But 'this association, it was said at the time, comprised three or four people'. Its numbers increased rapidly over the coming years, particularly during Domenico Callea's recruitment drive in 1893–94.

The story that these fragments of evidence tell—a story that was being repeated in Palmi, and indeed all around Aspromonte—goes something like this. Until the mid-1880s, a few Calabrian ex-cons, the senior *camorristi* from within the prison system, would keep in touch when they returned home from jail. They might offer one another help and even get together for the odd criminal venture: the trial records and other sources tell us of occasional outbreaks of gang activity in various parts of the province of Reggio Calabria in the 1870s and even before. But the *picciotti* as yet lacked the numbers and the strength to impose themselves on other felons in the outside world in the way that they had done in the confined environment of prison. Needless to say, they also lacked the power to browbeat whole towns. Then in the 1880s there were changes that gave Calabria's prison camorra the chance to project itself into the outside world. The question, of course, is what exactly those changes were.

It is telling that no representative of the state seemed at all curious to answer that question. In 1891, Palmi's Chief Prosecutor wrote his annual report on the work of the court during the previous year. The picciotteria did not even merit a mention: it was only a superficial symptom of Calabria's chronic backwardness, after all. The reason for the high rate of violence in the Palmi district was not organised crime, he wrote, but the 'ardent and lively nature of this population, their touchiness, the stubborn way they stick to their plans, the unwavering tenacity of their feelings of hatred— which very often drive them to vendetta'.

If a Sicilian Chief Prosecutor had written such claptrap we would have very good reason to be suspicious of his motives. But in Calabria, such suspicions are probably not merited. (Not yet, at any rate.) After all, the Palmi court had just sent dozens of *picciotti* back to jail. But the Chief Prosecutor's stereotypical views of the Calabrian psyche are significant all the same. Railway or no railway, Calabria was still seen as a semi-barbaric, faraway land about which Italy knew very little and cared even less. Despite its ties to the international market for olive oil, wine and lemons, Palmi was simply not important enough to draw much government curiosity down on the picciotteria, which means that historians have to work harder to solve some outstanding mysteries about its emergence.

Sworn sects have dominated prisons in many different times and places. The long-established South African number gangs, the 26s, the 27s, and the 28s, for example, who take their mythology from the story of a Zulu chief. Or the vast network of *vory-v-zakone* ('thieves with a code of honour') who infested the Soviet Gulag system from the 1920s. The *vory* had a 'crowning' ritual for new members, sported tattoos, and had a distinctive look comprising an aluminium cross round the neck and several waistcoats.

But by no means do all of these gangs manage to establish their authority in the world outside the prison gates. The 26s, the 27s, and the 28s only did it in the 1990s, when Apartheid fell and the country was opened to narcotics traffickers who needed local manpower and a local criminal 'brand'. When the Soviet Union collapsed the *vory-v-zakone* did not simply step out of the Gulag to assume leadership of the crime bonanza that ensued. Rather they had their traditions hijacked by a new breed of gangster bosses who wanted to add an air of antiquity to their territorially based bands: the result was the Russian mafia. Examples like these show just what an achievement it was for Calabria's prison *camorristi* to carve up territory in the outside world between themselves.

The economy is surely a big part of the reason why they pulled it off. An economic crisis hit Calabrian agriculture with increasing force in the 1880s. Phylloxera reached Italy and the wine boom went sour. Then a trade war with France threw agricultural exports into crisis. Some smallholders, like those in the Plain of Gioia Tauro, had run up debts to buy a plot of former Church land and plant it with vines: they now faced penury. Others had bullied or bribed their way to ownership, and now faced the wrath of their factional enemies. Meanwhile, the poorest labourers, like those in Africo, struggled even harder to feed themselves. There were plenty of recruits for the picciotteria, and plenty of landowners and peasants vulnerable or un-scrupulous enough to consider striking a deal with the men of violence.

The arrival of the steam train was also partly to blame, in Palmi at least. Contemporaries noted that the initial upsurge of razor attacks and knife fights coincided with the presence of navvies working on the Tyrrhenian branch of the railway in the spring of 1888. A dozen years later, in around 1900, some observers began to claim that the Lads with Attitude had been *imported* into the Plain of Gioia Tauro by Sicilian *mafiosi* among the navvies. But since none of the men convicted in Palmi's court house were Sicilians, this theory is almost certainly wrong. A more likely scenario is that there were ex-con *camorristi* among the railway workers. The fighting in Palmi could have been the result of competition for jobs with local *picciotti*.

Either way, the role that the railways played in the emergence of the Ca-labrian mafia makes for a bitter historical irony. As one magistrate opined at the time

> Whether the railway brought more evil than advantage is unclear. It is painful to ascertain that such a powerful influence for civilisation and progress served to trigger the cause of so much social ignominy.

The 'ndrangheta began just when Calabria's isolation ended.

There is a third likely reason why the picciotteria appeared when they did. In my view, it is the most important. In 1882 and 1888 two impor-tant electoral reforms inaugurated the era of mass politics in Italy. The number of people entitled to vote increased. Local government obtained both more freedom from central control, more responsibilities for things like schooling and supervising charities, and with them, more resources to plunder. With around one quarter of adult males now entitled to have a say in who governed them, politics became a more expensive and more lucrative business.

More violent too. Shootings, stabbings and beatings had always been part of the language of Italian politics, particularly in the south. Much of the vio-lence was administered from Rome. On orders from the local Prefect, the po-lice would rough up opposition supporters, arrest them or simply take away their gun licences, leaving them vulnerable to attack by goons who worked for the candidate the government wanted to win. The reforms of the 1880s greatly increased the demand for violence at election times and encouraged more aspiring power brokers to enlist support from organised enforcers.

Strong-arm politics was not something that the police were particularly keen to investigate, understandably enough. But there are nonetheless clear signs from deep within the dusty folders of trial papers that even in Africo the picciotteria had friends among the elite. The press remarked that the men who sliced up the crippled old swineherd Maviglia were defended by the best lawyers in Reggio Calabria. And among the *picciotti* in the case were 'people who, because of their prosperous financial state, can only have been driven to crime because they are innately wicked'.

The 'innately wicked' inhabitants of Africo included the former mayor, Giuseppe Callea, whose sons were prominent *picciotti*: Domenico, the sect's bookkeeper and fencing instructor who tried to recruit the bagpiper into the gang; and his brother Bruno, the *picciotto* who was sent to prison for robbery on the evidence provided by the crippled swineherd Pietro Maviglia. Former mayor Callea clearly endorsed his sons' criminal career path: he himself physically threatened Maviglia.

The rise of the picciotteria brutally exposed the fragmentation of Calabria's ruling class. At war with one another over local politics and land, the Calabrian social elite proved utterly incapable of treating the newly assertive criminal brotherhood as a common enemy. In Africo, some men of education and property testified against the *picciotti*, and were duly threatened to the music of the *zampogna*. Others, like Giuseppe Callea, were more than happy to ally themselves with the gang. But it would be naïve of us to think that such cases saw good citizens pitted against shady protectors of gangsters. Legality and crime were not what divided Calabrians; ideology of one colour or another was not what brought them together. On Aspromonte, family, friends and favours were the only cause of conflict, and the only social glue. The law, such as it was, was just one more weapon in the struggle. The few sociologists who took an interest in Calabria after Italian unification noted that the propertied class 'lacked a sense of legality', and even 'lacked moral sense'. Whatever terms one used to describe it, the rise of the picciotteria showed that the lack was now infecting the other social classes.

Despite this proliferation of organised criminal activity, the prosecution of the early 'ndrangheta in Africo was a success, in the very short term. The butchers of Maviglia were convicted, as were dozens and dozens of the *picciotti*. Across southern Calabria the police and *Carabinieri* registered similar results, and would continue to do so for years to come. But the struggle to assert the state's right to rule was close to futile from the start. The Lads convicted of 'associating for delinquency' served their risibly short sentences in the very same jails where they had learned their Attitude in the first place.

And there was no sign of an end to the fundamental weaknesses in Calabrian society that gave them their foothold outside the prisons.

The criminal emergency in Calabria utterly failed to capture the attention of national public opinion. All too few Italians were prepared to 'look through the microscope at the little causes that make little hearts beat'. In the long term, Italy would pay the price for this collective failure of the imagination. Nothing that happened to Calabrian shepherds and peasants could ever be news. Nothing that is, until the exploits of a woodsman called Giuseppe Musolino turned him into the Brigand Musolino, the 'King of Aspromonte', and perhaps the greatest criminal legend in Italian history.

16

THE KING OF ASPROMONTE

THE FACTS OF GIUSEPPE MUSOLINO'S LIFE WOULD COUNT FOR LITTLE, IN THE END. BUT the facts are nonetheless where we must begin.

Musolino was born on 24 September 1876 at Santo Stefano in Aspromonte, a village of some 2,500 inhabitants situated 700 metres up into forests overlooking the Straits of Messina. His father was a woodsman and a small-time timber dealer just successful enough to set himself up as the owner of a tavern. Musolino grew into a woodsman too. But it was the violent tendencies of his youth that would most attract the attention of later biographers: before his twentieth birthday he got into trouble several times for weapons offences and for threatening and wounding women.

The Musolino saga really began on 27 October 1897, in his father's tavern, when he became involved in an argument with another young man by the name of Vincenzo Zoccali. The two arranged to have a fight and Musolino suffered a badly cut right hand. Musolino's cousin then fired two shots at Zoccali, but missed.

Two days later, before dawn, Zoccali was harnessing his mule when someone shot at him from behind a wall. Again the bullets failed to find their target. Musolino, whose rifle and beret were found at the scene, went on the run in the wilds of Aspromonte. He was recaptured just over five months later, and in September 1898 he was given a harsh twenty-one-year sentence for attempted murder. Enraged at the verdict and proclaiming himself the innocent victim of a plot, Musolino swore vendetta. He would eat Zoccali's liver, he cried out from the dock.

Giuseppe Musolino,
the 'King of Aspromonte'.

On the night of 9 January 1899 Musolino and three other inmates, including his cousin, escaped from prison in Gerace by hacking a hole in the wall with an iron bar and lowering themselves to the ground with a rope made from knotted bedsheets. The promised vendetta began on the night of 28 January, when Musolino gunned down Francesca Sidari, the wife of one of the witnesses against him. He apparently mistook her for his real target as she stooped over a charcoal mound. When the gunshots and screaming attracted the attention of her husband and another man, Musolino shot them too. He left them for dead, and fled once more into the mountains.

The Brigand Musolino (as he soon became known) now entered a twin spiral of vengeance: his targets were both the witnesses against him in the Zoccali case and the informers recruited by the police in their efforts to catch him.

A month after his first murder, Musolino killed again, stabbing a shepherd whom he suspected of being a police spy. In mid-May the bandit returned to Santo Stefano and caught up with Vincenzo Zoccali—the man whose liver he had vowed to eat. He planted dynamite in the walls of the house where Zoccali was sleeping with his brother and parents; but the charge failed to detonate. (The family subsequently fled to the province of Catanzaro.) Musolino badly wounded another enemy a few days later.

The sequence of attacks continued through the summer of 1899. In July he killed one suspected informer with a single shotgun blast to the head. A week later he shot another in the buttocks.

In August the brigand went all the way to the province of Catanzaro in pursuit of Vincenzo Zoccali and his family and succeeded in killing Zoccali's brother. He then returned quickly to a village just below Santo Stefano where he murdered another man he may have suspected of being an informer.

Musolino then vanished for six months.

The next the world heard of Musolino was in February 1900 when he reappeared on Aspromonte with two young accomplices; he shot and wounded his own cousin by mistake. The brigand apparently kneeled before his bleeding cousin, offered him his rifle, and begged him to take vengeance for the error there and then. The request was declined and the brigand continued with his attacks.

Musolino found his next prey in the Grecanico-speaking village of Roccaforte, blasting him in the legs with a shotgun. The prostrate victim then managed to convince the bandit that he was not, as suspected, a police spy. Musolino tended the man's wounds for half an hour and then sent a passing shepherd to fetch help.

On 9 March 1900 one of Musolino's accomplices, a man from Africo called Antonio Princi, betrayed him to the police. As part of the plan to capture Musolino, Princi left some *maccheroni* laced with opium in the bandit's hideout, which at the time was in a cave near Africo cemetery. Princi then went to get the police. Five policemen and two *Carabinieri* followed him back to the hideout. But the opium had been sitting on the shelf of a local pharmacy for so long that it had lost much of its narcotic power. Even after eating the *maccheroni*, Musolino still had sufficient command of his faculties to fire at his would-be captors and then escape across the mountain, with the police and *Carabinieri* in pursuit.

In the early hours of the following morning Musolino was surprised while urinating by Pietro Ritrovato, one of the two *Carabinieri*; the brigand fired first from close range. The young *Carabiniere* suffered a gaping wound in his groin, and died in torment several hours later.

After another six months of silence Musolino and another two accomplices killed again on 27 August 1900. They chased their victim, Francesco Marte, onto the threshing floor of his own house, where he stopped, turned and begged them to be allowed the time to make his peace with God before dying. They allowed him to kneel down, and then shot him repeatedly in front of his mother, continuing to fire even when he was already dead. Musolino would claim that Marte was a traitor who was involved in the *maccheroni* plot against him.

Subsequently the same two accomplices, perhaps acting on his behalf, also tried and failed to kill the former mayor of Santo Stefano who had testified when Musolino went on trial for attempted murder.

The brigand's last violent attack came on 22 September 1900, when he wounded yet another alleged informer in Santo Stefano.

Musolino's bloody rampage and the continuing failure to arrest him had long since become a political scandal. The Aspromonte woodsman was discussed in parliament. The government's credibility was at stake. Hundreds of uniformed men were sent to southern Calabria to join the hunt. Yet still, for another year and more, Musolino would manage to evade them all . . .

There is one more important fact about Musolino: he was a Lad with Attitude.

At the height of the political furore over the brigand, Italy's most valiant journalist, Adolfo Rossi, took the very rare step of actually going down to Calabria to find out what was going on. From police and magistrates he learned all there was to know about the new mafia.

Rossi toured the prisons and saw the *picciotti* in their grey- and tobacco-striped prison uniforms. He went to Palmi, which he learned was 'the Calabrian district where the picciotteria was strongest'. Palmi's Deputy Prefect glumly explained that, 'one trial for "associating for delinquency" has not even finished by the time we have to start preparing the next one'.

Rossi visited Santo Stefano, Musolino's home village, and even climbed all the way up to Africo. He was shocked by the squalor he found there, writing that 'the cabins are not houses being used as pig sties, but pig sties used as houses for humans'. The *Carabinieri* told him how, a few years earlier, members of the sect had 'cut a man to pieces, and then put salt on him like you do with pork'.

Adolfo Rossi's long series of reports from Calabria is still the best thing ever written about the early 'ndrangheta; it deserved to be read far more widely than in the local Venetian newspaper in which it appeared. And everyone Rossi interviewed agreed that Musolino was an oathed member of the picciotteria—albeit that opinions varied on when exactly Musolino was oathed, and what rank he held. Rossi saw reports that showed how the *Carabinieri* in Santo Stefano had Musolino down for a gangster from the beginning. On the day after Musolino's first knife fight with Vincenzo Zoccali, they wrote that he belonged to the 'so-called maffia'.

While Musolino was in custody awaiting trial for attempted murder, the jailers observed him behaving like a *camorrista*. One guard stated to Rossi that

Musolino entered this prison on 8 April 1898. Later some of his cellmates informed me that in June of the same year he was elected a *camorrista* [i.e., a senior member of the Society].

In Africo Rossi spoke to a police commander who explained that Musolino had avoided capture for so long because he had the support of the picciotteria network across Aspromonte and beyond. One man who confessed to Rossi that he had sheltered Musolino was the mayor of Africo, a shady figure who testified *against* the picciotteria back in 1894. In Santo Stefano, Rossi learned that some of the brigand's accomplices were Lads, and that some of his escapades, including his original spat with Vincenzo Zoccali, had more to do with the internal politics of the mob than with his personal programme of vengeance.

Despite these facts Musolino became a hero: a wronged avenger, a solitary knight of the forest, a Robin Hood, the 'King of Aspromonte'.

His fame began to grow rapidly after his prison breakout in 1899. It was a local phenomenon at first. Most people on Aspromonte firmly believed that Musolino was innocent of the charge for which he was originally imprisoned—that of attempting to murder Vincenzo Zoccali. And, in truth, there are one or two residual doubts about how sound the conviction was. Musolino's 'innocence', genuine or not, proved to be the seed of his fame. The peasants of Aspromonte, ignorant and pitiably poor, regarded the state with inborn suspicion. For such people, in such circumstances, a renegade hero who only killed false witnesses was all too captivating a delusion.

Musolino found food and shelter everywhere he went on Aspromonte. For his sake, women kept lanterns lit for the Madonna of Polsi and for Saint Joseph (San Giuseppe, the patron saint of woodworkers, from whom Musolino took his Christian name). Much of this support was managed by the picciotteria. Much of it can be explained by perfectly understandable fear. Some of it—and it is impossible to tell just how much—was down to the brigand's burgeoning popular aura.

Stories soon spread that aura further afield. Stories about how, while Musolino was in prison, Saint Joseph came to him in a miraculous vision and revealed the weak points in his cell wall. Stories about how he never stole from anyone, always paid for what he ate, never abused women, and always outwitted the clodhopping *Carabinieri*.

From Aspromonte, the Musolino legend was broadcast by the oral folklore of the entire south. He became a star of the puppet theatre. Children played at being Musolino in the street. Wandering players dressed up as brigands to sing of his adventures or had their poems in praise of him printed on grubby sheets of paper to be sold for coppers. The authorities arrested some of these minstrels, but the cult was now unstoppable. The 'King of Aspromonte' himself capitalised on it. Musolino sent a letter to a national newspaper in which he impudently put himself on the side of the ordinary people against authority.

I am a worker, and the son of a worker. I love people who have to sweat in the fields from morning until night so as to produce society's riches. In fact I envy them, because my misfortune means I cannot make a contribution with my own hands.

The Italian state now found itself losing a propaganda war against the delinquent artisans and peasants of Aspromonte. The whole Musolino affair was turning into what today we would call a PR disaster for the rule of law. Perhaps its most worrying dimension was that the illiterate were not the only people seduced by the myth. Although right-thinking opinion-formers of all political persuasions condemned the popular cult of Musolino as a sign of Italy's backwardness, books and pamphlets about him still sold in their thousands. In Calabria, only one newspaper dared to suggest that the King of Aspromonte might actually have been guilty of attempting to murder Vincenzo Zoccali. In Naples, where the myth of the noble *camorrista* had such currency, the *Corriere di Napoli* reported fables about the brigand's supposed acts of generosity without critical comment and came very close to justifying his campaign of retribution.

Musolino only harms his enemies, because he thinks he has a mission and wants to carry it through to the end.

Between the brigand and the law, there was right and wrong on both sides—so went the argument. Accordingly, some press commentators entertained the idea that a fair solution would be to offer Musolino safe passage to the United States.

Eventually the authorities acted on the intelligence that told them Musolino was no lone wolf. Early in 1901, a zealous young police officer, Vincenzo Mangione, was sent to Santo Stefano to implement a more radical strategy than blindly chasing the bandit around the mountain and trying to bribe informants (especially *picciotti*) to betray him.

Mangione compiled a series of highly revealing reports on the picciotteria in Musolino's home village. Drawing on sources who were mostly disaffected *picciotti*, he describes a 'genuine criminal institution', with its own social fund, tribunal, and so on. There were 166 affiliates of the mafia in Santo Stefano. It was founded in the early 1890s by Musolino's father and uncle, who both now sat on the organisation's 'supreme council'. In other words, the evidence collected by Mangione, together with the fact that Musolino was able to rely on a region-wide support network, strongly indicate that the 'ndrangheta has always been a single organisation, and not a rag-bag ensemble of village gangs.

Musolino's possible motives emerged with a new clarity from Mangione's research. The bandit was of course an affiliate like his father. Nothing he had done could be separated from his role inside the criminal brotherhood. For example, the attempt on Zoccali's life that began the Musolino saga was ordered by the picciotteria as punishment because Zoccali had tried to duck out of his duties as a *picciotto*. Musolino was now a roving contract killer for the whole sect.

Most revealingly of all, Mangione learned how the Lads earned favours from 'respectable people . . . political personalities, lawyers, doctors, and landowners'. The most important of those favours were character references and false witness statements. A more tangible example of the favours that the picciotteria could command stood, ruined and smoke-blackened, at the very entrance of the village. It was the Zoccali family's house. When Musolino failed to dynamite it, the *picciotti* simply burned it to the ground and then persuaded the town council to deny the Zoccali family a grant to rebuild.

The notables of Santo Stefano were not remotely concerned to keep their friendship with the picciotteria secret. When the King of Aspromonte's sister Anna got married, the new mayor and his officers, the town councillors, the general practitioners, teachers, municipal guards, and the town band all came to the wedding reception. The mayor chose the occasion to circulate a petition asking the Queen to grant Musolino a pardon.

The outcome of Mangione's intelligence was a two-pronged strategy to capture Musolino: first, his support network would be attacked; second, the whole picciotteria in Santo Stefano would be prosecuted. Accordingly, there was a series of mass arrests in the spring and summer of 1901. With many of his supporters in custody, Musolino struggled to find a place to hide on his home territory.

On the afternoon of 9 October 1901, in the countryside near Urbino—more than 900 kilometres from Santo Stefano—a young man in a hunting jacket and cyclist's cap was spotted acting suspiciously by two *Carabinieri*. He fled across a vineyard when they hailed him and then tripped over some wire. He pulled out a revolver but was smothered before he could pull the trigger. 'Kill me', he said as the handcuffs went on. He then tried bribery, unsuccessfully. When searched he was found to be carrying a knife, ammunition and a large number of amulets, including a body pouch full of incense, a crucifix, a medallion showing the Sacred Heart, a picture of Saint Joseph, and an image of the Madonna of Polsi. Five days later he was identified as the brigand Giuseppe Musolino.

Musolino was sent for trial in the pretty Tuscan city of Lucca for fear that a Calabrian jury might be too swayed by the myth surrounding him.

His long-delayed encounter with justice was set to be one of the most sensational trials of the age.

But before it could begin, the second arm of the government's strategy failed. The witnesses Mangione had relied upon to gather evidence about the picciotteria in Santo Stefano were intimidated into retracting their statements. The case never even reached court.

So when national and international correspondents gathered in Lucca to report on the eagerly awaited Musolino trial in the spring of 1902, what they witnessed turned out to be a prolonged exercise in self-harm for the law's reputation in Italy. The problem was that Musolino's lawyers objected vociferously every time the prosecution tried to demonstrate that he was a sworn member of a criminal sect. After all, had not the case against this supposed sect in Santo Stefano been thrown out before it reached court? Where was the evidence? In this way, the real context of the Musolino saga was obscured. So a multiple murderer was largely left free to pose as the heroic outlaw that the marionette theatres of southern Italy had made him out to be.

Musolino had spent the time since his capture the previous October writing a verse narrative of his adventures and having his body meticulously measured by positivist criminologists. Over the same period he received countless admiring letters and postcards, particularly from women. They pledged their love, sent him religious tokens and sweets, promised to pray for him and begged for locks of his hair. The judge in Lucca was so concerned about Musolino's effect on the morals of the town's womenfolk that he stipulated that only men would be allowed into the hearing. But the stream of fan mail only increased once the trial started. Mysteriously, signed postcard portraits of the King of Aspromonte went on sale near the courtroom. Interviewed by journalists in his cell, Musolino would relish recounting his erotic adventures while he was on the run.

From the outset, Musolino's lawyers did not contest the fact that he had committed a long trail of murders and attempted murders after escaping from prison. Their defence rested instead on the claim that he was innocent of the crime for which he had been imprisoned in the first place: the attempted murder of Vincenzo Zoccali. The lawyers reasoned that his bloody deeds could be explained, and perhaps even justified, by the conspiracy against him in the Zoccali case.

A visiting French judge was understandably astonished that this argument could even be considered a defence at all; it seemed like evidence of Italy's 'moral backwardness' to him. Musolino did not share the same doubts. When he was called to the dock he told the court that he had concluded his

IL PREFETTO
DELLA PROVINCIA DI REGGIO CAL.

RENDE NOTO

Che per disposizione del Ministro dell'Interno furono versate alla Banca d'Italia, sede di Reggio, le **LIRE 20,000** come premio promesso dal Governo per la cattura di

GIUSEPPE MUSOLINO.

I Sindaci della Provincia daranno la massima pubblicità al presente manifesto valendosi anche dei pubblici banditori.

Reggio Cal. 12 aprile 1901.

il Prefetto
LA MOLA

Wanted poster for Giuseppe Musolino, the 'King of Aspromonte'.

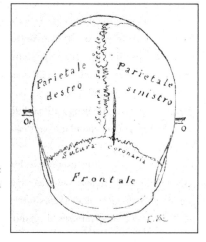

At right, a diagram showing the damage inflicted on Musolino's skull in infancy by a falling flowerpot.

Below: Sketches of Musolino made in court.

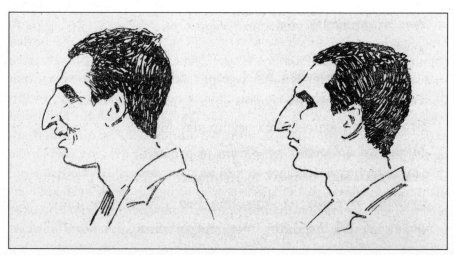

A scene from the Musolino trial in Lucca, 1902. Despite his ferocious deeds, he aroused much public sympathy. 'Poor Musolino!' wrote one leading man of letters. 'I'd like to write a poem that shows how every one of us has a Musolino inside.'

campaign of righteous retaliation now, and would never break the law again if he were allowed to go free. He claimed to be the descendant of a French prince and compared his plight to that of Jesus Christ.

Now and again Musolino did blot the script that portrayed him as a noble desperado: such as when he repeatedly screamed 'slut!' at Vincenzo Zoccali's mother as she came to the witness stand. But that did not prevent many onlookers from sympathising with him. One of Italy's greatest poets, a sentimental socialist called Giovanni Pascoli, lived in the countryside not far from Lucca and observed the trial with his habitual compassion. 'Poor Musolino!' he wrote to a friend. 'You know, I'd like to write a poem that shows how every one of us has a Musolino inside.'

Many commentators on the trial argued that the underlying problem in the Musolino case was not one lone brigand but the isolation of Calabrian society as a whole. Modern means of communication like the railway would surely bring the light of civilisation to the primitive obscurity of Aspromonte. The sun-weathered peasant witnesses who came up to Lucca for the case made for a spectacle that seemed only to confirm this view. Most of them were Calabrian dialect speakers who had to testify through an interpreter. There was loud laughter on one occasion when, as a witness started to talk, the interpreter turned to the judge and admitted that even he could

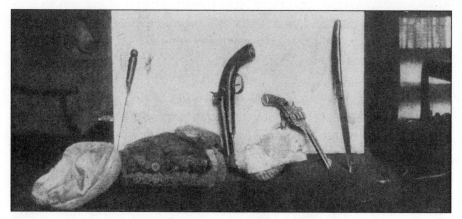

Musolino's weapons displayed for an avid press.

not understand a word of what was being said. There was probably not a single Grecanico-Italian interpreter available in the whole of Italy.

Positivist criminologists were called on to explain the results of their painstaking physical and psychological examination of Musolino. He had a contradictory mix of symptoms, they explained. There seemed to be no clear aetiology for his criminaloid tendencies. Musolino had suffered a head injury at age six when a flowerpot fell on his head. The accident caused a dent in his skull, and may have given him epilepsy—an obvious delinquent trait. But then again he did not masturbate at all frequently and was very intelligent. Racially speaking, they concluded lamely, he was an exaggeration of the 'average Calabrian type'.

The most moving speech of the trial came from the lawyer representing the parents of Pietro Ritrovato, the young *Carabiniere* who had died of the horrible injuries inflicted on him by Musolino the morning after the drugged *maccheroni* episode. The old Ritrovato couple had filed a civil suit against the 'King of Aspromonte'. But they sobbed so much in court that they often had to withdraw. Their lawyer explained that his aim was not to ask for money, but to 'bring a flower to the memory of a victim who fell in the line of duty'. To that end, he wanted to destroy what he called 'the legend of Musolino' by insisting on the one crucial thing that the trial had neglected: Musolino was a member of a criminal association called the picciotteria.

The most squalid testimony came from the mayor of Santo Stefano—the one who had attended Musolino's sister's wedding and circulated a petition for a royal pardon. Aurelio Romeo was a chubby man with a sleek black beard who was a major player in one of the two dominant political factions in Reggio Calabria. In court he affected a flaming moral outrage about how the people of Santo Stefano had been mistreated by brutal and incompetent police. 'The picciotteria is an invention, an excuse for the police's weakness,' he said. Asked about the character of Musolino's two accomplices who were accused of trying to kill his predecessor as mayor, he said they were just honest, hard-working men.

The trial's outcome was inevitable: Musolino was found guilty and sentenced to life imprisonment. But equally inevitably Italy had lost a priceless opportunity to draw public attention to the acute criminal emergency in southern Calabria. The early 'ndrangheta would remain shrouded in obscurity and confusion, a little-known curiosity of a little-known region.

Musolino, by contrast, was destined for enduring fame, even as he languished in confinement. Just before the First World War, the English writer Norman Douglas went walking on Aspromonte and heard tale after tale about the brigand's adventures from his peasant guides.

God alone can tell how many poor people he helped in their distress. And if he met a young girl in the mountains, he would help with her load, and escort her home, right into her father's house. Ah, if you could have seen him, sir! He was young, with curly blonde hair, and a face like a rose.

Musolino's hair was actually black. That, at least, the criminologists at the trial had demonstrated beyond doubt.

PART V

MEDIA DONS

17

BANKERS AND MEN OF HONOUR

ONE REASON WHY ITALY BARELY NOTICED THE RISE OF THE PICCIOTTERIA WAS THAT THE country had much graver worries. In the late 1880s a building bubble burst, leaving lending institutions with huge liabilities. In 1890 the economy went into recession, piling further pressure on the financial system. Several banks subsequently failed, including two of Italy's biggest. Another, the Banca Romana, tried to stave off implosion by effectively forging its own money and then using the phoney cash to buy off dozens of politicians. 'Loans' from the Banca Romana also helped the King maintain his lavish lifestyle. The Prime Minister was forced to resign in November 1893 when his involvement in the scandal was exposed in parliament.

To many, it seemed as if it was not just the Italian banking system that was about to collapse, but the monarchy and even the state itself. The politician called upon to save the nation was Francesco Crispi, an old warhorse of the Left, a Sicilian who had been one of the heroes of Garibaldi's expedition back in 1860. Crispi also faced an unprecedented political challenge in the form of the trades unions, the Socialist Party and other organisations recruiting among the peasants and labourers. Crispi responded with repression, proclaiming martial law in some areas of the country and banning the Socialist Party in 1894. Desperate for military glory to reinforce the feeble credibility of the state, Crispi launched a reckless colonial adventure in East Africa. In March 1896, at the battle of Adowa, the Italian army that Crispi had spurred into action was destroyed by a vastly superior Ethiopian force. Crispi resigned soon after the news from Adowa reached Rome.

After Crispi the clampdown on the labour movement was relaxed, but politics continued on its reactionary course. For the next few years conservative politicians would talk openly of putting Italy's slow and hesitant advance towards democracy into a brusque reverse. In the spring of 1898 a hike in food prices caused rioting. Cannon fire resounded in the streets of Milan as troops mowed down demonstrators. Another new Prime Minister then embarked on a long parliamentary battle to pass legislation restricting press and political freedoms.

In the summer of 1900 a Tuscan anarchist called Gaetano Bresci returned to Italy from his home in Patterson, New Jersey; he was bent on revenge for the cannonades of 1898. On 20 July he set a suitably violent seal on the most turbulent decade in Italy's short history when he went to Monza and assassinated the King.

By that time, though, Italy was already striding into a very different age. An overhauled banking system, including the newly established Bank of Italy, helped the economy revive. The north-west was industrialising rapidly: in Turin, FIAT started making cars in 1899; in Milan, Pirelli started making car tyres in 1901. Over the next few years Italian cities would fill with noise and light: automobiles, electric trams, department stores, bars, cinemas, and soccer stadia. In politics, reform was the order of the day. More people became literate and thereby earned the right to vote. The Socialist Party, though still small, was strong enough to bargain for concessions in parliament. In 1913, Italy would hold its first general election in which, by law, all adult men were entitled to vote.

A surge in newspaper readerships was another symptom of the new vitality. In 1900, the year that Bresci shot the King, the *Corriere della Sera* had a print run of 75,000 copies. By 1913, it was up to 350,000. So the Italy that followed the King of Aspromonte's trial in 1902 was a country undergoing a media revolution. Indeed all three of Italy's Honoured Societies now had to test their aptitude for brutality, networking and misinformation in a much more democratic society—one where public opinion shaped the political decisions that in turn shaped criminal destinies.

The Neapolitan camorra would not survive the challenge.

But in the case of the Sicilian mafia, the new media era made no more impact than the puff of a photographer's flash powder: it illuminated a crepuscular landscape of corruption and violence for an instant, and then plunged it back into a darkness deeper than before.

The Sicilian mafia dramas of the early twentieth century all arose from the single most sinister moment of the banking crisis of the early 1890s, a murder that would remain the most notorious of mafia crimes for the best part of the next century. Notorious partly because the victim was one of

Sicily's outstanding citizens, and partly because the killers got away with it, but mostly because the resultant scandal, known as the Notarbartolo affair, briefly exposed the mafia's influence in the highest reaches of Sicilian society.

Marquis Emanuele Notarbartolo di San Giovanni fought with Garibaldi in 1860 but he was constitutionally averse to violence. In an age when questions of honour were often settled with swords at sunrise, Notarbartolo was only ever drawn into one duel: it lasted three hours because he only fought defensively. He was a devoted family man who wrote his wife short, tender notes every day of their life together. Notarbartolo was also a public servant of rare dedication. As Mayor of Palermo between 1873 and 1876, he tackled corruption. In 1876 he began a long stint as Director General of the Bank of Sicily, where he made himself unpopular with a policy of tight credit. The reputation for rigour that Notarbartolo earned at the Bank of Sicily would lead directly to his atrocious murder.

Notarbartolo's fine record found its malevolent shadow in the career of don Raffaele Palizzolo, whom the police would define as 'the mafia's patron in the Palermo countryside, especially to the south and east of the city'. Palizzolo's fiefdom centred on the notorious *borgate* of Villabate and Ciaculli, where he owned and leased land, and where his friends exerted their characteristic control over the citrus fruit groves and coordinated the activities of bandits and cattle rustlers.

In the 1870s don Raffaele began amassing a fortune by installing himself in town and provincial councils and on the boards of countless charities and quangos (quasi-autonomous non-governmental organisations). When Notarbartolo was mayor of Palermo, he caught Palizzolo palming money from a fund that stockpiled flour for the poor.

Palizzolo was a master of what Italians now call *sottogoverno*—literally 'under government'—meaning the bartering of shady favours for political influence. Come election time he would tour the area on horseback, flanked by the mafia bosses and their heavies. Indeed the Villabate mafia would often disguise their sect summit

Emanuele Notarbartolo, the honest Sicilian banker stabbed to death by the mafia in 1893.

as political meetings in support of their patron. In 1882 Palizzolo was elected to parliament.

At the Bank of Sicily, Emanuele Notarbartolo also found Palizzolo in his path. As Director General, Notarbartolo was supposed to be supervised in his work by a General Council of forty-eight dignitaries from local government, chambers of commerce and the like. Palizzolo was one of them, as were other notorious shysters linked to organised crime, and a number of businessmen with a manifest conflict of interests: they were among the people that owed money to the bank. No wonder Notarbartolo's policy of tight credit was unpopular.

In 1882 Notarbartolo was kidnapped by four men dressed as soldiers, and only released on payment of a ransom. Acting on a tip-off, the police found the kidnappers hiding out in any empty house. The ransom was never recovered, although we can make a good guess at who took a hefty share of it: both the site of the kidnapping and the kidnappers' hideout lay on territory controlled by the same Villabate *mafiosi* who made Palizzolo the guest of honour at their banquets.

In 1888 Notarbartolo found himself working alongside his great enemy day-to-day when Palizzolo was voted onto the Bank of Sicily's board. The smouldering confrontation between the Director General and the General Council exploded when Italy's building boom collapsed. Notarbartolo tried to persuade ministers to have the Bank of Sicily's constitution amended so as to lessen the power of the General Council and give the Director General the power to respond to the credit crisis. But he was out-lobbied by Palizzolo *et al*, and lost his job in February 1890. His victorious enemies then tried to withhold his pension.

With Emanuele Notarbartolo out of the way, the bank's money was used illegally to inflate the share price of Italy's biggest shipping company, *Navigazione Generale Italiana*, or NGI. NGI's major shareholder happened to be the wealthiest man in Sicily. Who happened to be a great supporter of the dominant politician of the moment, the Sicilian Prime Minister Francesco Crispi. Who happened to have a close ally in the Bank of Sicily's new Director General. Who happened to have a pot of NGI shares of his own.

Palizzolo greased the cogs of this mechanism. As a Member of Parliament, don Raffaele lobbied hard, as he had always done, for NGI's cause. As a member of the Bank of Sicily's board, he approved the NGI share operation. As a member of the mafia, he took some of the bank's cash to buy more of those artificially boosted NGI shares, and made generous loans to friends of his who exported lemons and oranges for a living.

Then, late in 1892, the sleaze at the Banca Romana (the bank that was forging its own money) was exposed in parliament. Credit institutions across the country were wobbling. The calls for a clean-up in the banking system were now too loud to ignore. Emanuele Notarbartolo was strongly rumoured to be about to return to the Bank of Sicily with a mandate to crack down on corruption once more. And if Notarbartolo regained his job as Director General of the Bank of Sicily, he would surely expose a fraud that implicated the most powerful economic and political interest group on the island—and linked them squarely with Raffaele Palizzolo and the mafia.

At dusk on 1 February 1893 Emanuele Notarbartolo was stabbed twenty-seven times on a train heading for Palermo; his body was thrown out onto the track.

Months later, Notarbartolo's wife was seen, still in tears, as she burned the hundreds of notes he had sent her. While she wept, and Italy descended into a financial, social and political crisis that threatened to bring the young country to its knees, the mafia and its accomplices quietly covered the murderers' tracks, burying the story in artful layers of deceit and obfuscation.

The reason we know all about the shenanigans at the Bank of Sicily, indeed the reason why Emanuele Notarbartolo's murder ever came to court at all, was because of the grief-stricken determination of his son Leopoldo, a young naval officer who was a man in his father's mould.

Right from the outset, no one seriously doubted that Emanuele Notarbartolo was a victim of the mafia, although the mafia had never killed anyone of such status before. (Nor would it do so again until the 1970s.) Right from the outset, the authorities heard the strong rumours that the Honourable don Raffaele Palizzolo had orchestrated the murder. Leopoldo Notarbartolo, well aware of Palizzolo's long history of run-ins with his father, had more reasons than anyone to suspect the notorious MP of being involved. Yet nothing was done. In 1894, just over a year after Notarbartolo was found lying on the trackside, a senior magistrate wrote to the Minister of Justice to explain the reasons why no one had yet been charged.

> This failure can be attributed to the following two causes: first, the high mafia planned the murder long in advance, and carried it out with the greatest of care; second, the authorities receive no help from society, because all the witnesses are either reticent or afraid.

Knowing what we know about the mafia's history so far, we can also add a third cause that the magistrate neglected to mention: the police and judiciary in Palermo were profoundly infiltrated.

Leopoldo Notarbartolo witnessed the scandalously lax handling of the investigation and began to make inquiries of his own. He was one of many Italians whose quest for truth and justice was a long and solitary one: it took over a decade out of his life. Like most such quests, Notarbartolo's was a tale of meticulous endeavour: sifting through his father's papers, interviewing reluctant witnesses, travelling far and wide to check dubious alibis. And like most such quests, it was also a search for political help.

Leopoldo Notarbartolo knew that his only chance of exposing the high-level intrigues that had led to his father's death, and protected the murderers from the law, would come if he exploited high-level contacts of his own. Sometimes, in Italy, the forces for good have to operate through the same personal channels as the forces for evil.

When Francesco Crispi—the Prime Minister close to the NGI shipping lobby—fell from power following Italy's humiliating defeat at the battle of Adowa in March 1896, his successor as Prime Minister was another Sicilian: someone that Leopoldo thought he might just be able to talk to; someone who has already had a part to play in the history of the mafia.

Antonio Starabba, Marquis of Rudinì, was the mayor of Palermo who made his name by defending the Royal Palace during the Palermo revolt of September 1866. Standing side-by-side with Rudinì during the siege was Emanuele Notarbartolo—indeed Notarbartolo had carved the mould from which the Royal Palace's defenders made musket balls out of lead piping. We last saw Rudinì as he stood on the edge of the political wilderness, desperately expounding his baffling theory about the 'benign maffia' to the parliamentary inquiry of 1876. By the 1890s Rudinì's trim blonde beard had become broad, grizzled and forked. The financial and political crises of the day had pushed Italy rightwards, and in doing so had revived the Marquis's fortunes.

Leopoldo Notarbartolo had few illusions about Rudinì: 'slimy' was the adjective he used to describe him. In truth Rudinì was now so powerful he could rely on someone else to wade through the slime on his behalf. His constituency campaign manager at the time was one Leonardo Avellone, a local mayor. In 1892 a Sicilian newspaper gave an unforgettable portrait of Avellone.

Commendatore Avellone is a well-to-do man who is nearing sixty. He is chubby, friendly, with the cunning of a peasant and the polite, helpful nature of a Jesuit priest. But he is also vengeful and treacherous with everyone, especially his friends. He is ignorant, but quick-witted and equally adept in doing good as in doing harm. He makes friends with the virtuous and the wicked alike, without the slightest distinction. He is a father figure not just to his numerous children, but also to his relatives and hangers-on who, in his shadow, exercise an absolute tyrannical do-minion in the Termini area. He always strikes the pose of a man of order who is extremely conservative, a classic figure of the Right. On occasion, he has given the police some excellent assistance. But then at other times he has had no scruples about helping or setting free criminals of all kinds who are either employed by him or have placed themselves under his protection.

Avellone, in short, was the very archetype of a mafia boss; he was happy to take care of local business—both legal and criminal—while his sponsor Rudinì dealt with grand affairs of state in Rome. Avellone did very well out of Rudinì's return to the forefront of Italian politics. He acquired a decisive influence over everything that moved in his little realm: from giving out licences to sell lottery tickets and tobacco to awarding government positions and public sector jobs; he was even said to control policing policy. This then, was what Rudinì had meant by a 'benign *maffioso*' back in 1876. There were many such benign *maffiosi* in western Sicily—don Raffaele Palizzolo being the most influential of them all.

The one thing that persuaded Leopoldo Notarbartolo that it was worth talking to Rudinì was that the new Prime Minister was a sworn political enemy of the previous premier, Francesco Crispi. So Notarbartolo used his family name to get access to Rudinì's study and then set out the gist of his case against Raffaele Palizzolo. Could Rudinì do anything to bring justice?

Rudinì's reply was brief, jocular and chilling: Notarbartolo should find 'a good *mafioso*', pay him well, and let him take care of Palizzolo.

The Prime Minister subsequently called on don Raffaele's services in Palermo when it came to ousting Crispi's supporters from their positions in the city.

Only in 1898, more than five years after his father's death, did Leopoldo finally find the political help he needed. Rudinì fell from power soon after the events of May of that year, when troops fired cannons into the crowds in Milan. His successor was a military man, General Luigi Pelloux. Pelloux had no political interests in Sicily and he was also a friend of the Notarbartolos. Through General Pelloux, Leopoldo Notarbartolo got access to the documentation he needed: from inside the Bank of Sicily, from Palermo police headquarters, and even the Interior Ministry. Finally, the murdered banker's son could look forward to his day in court.

Within weeks of taking office, General Pelloux also opened another front against the mafia. He recruited the country's foremost mafia-fighter to lead the most serious assault on organised crime's territorial dominance in Sicily since the 1870s.

18

FLORIOPOLIS

ON 4 AUGUST 1898 THE NEW PRIME MINISTER TELEGRAPHED A PEREMPTORY ORDER TO the Prefect of Genoa: 'Chief Police Ermanno Sangiorgi transferred Palermo. He must go as soon as. With expenses.'

Ermanno Sangiorgi was now fifty-eight years old and Italy's most experienced senior police officer. Since leaving Naples following the cab drivers' strike in 1893 he had been posted to Venice, Bologna, Livorno and Genoa. While his career resumed its upward course, he found moments of great happiness in his personal life. He had another daughter, Maria Luigia, in 1890. In 1895 he married her mother, Maria Vozza, in a civil ceremony: the two could finally live together without causing a scandal. But Sangiorgi's older children were still a source of anguish. His daughter Italia was often unwell. His son Italo had turned out to be a ne'er-do-well: abandoning one steady job after another, roaming the Orient in search of something to do, constantly begging his father for cash to save him from what he called his 'squalid poverty'.

Sangiorgi's transfer to Palermo was to be his last posting, the culmination of nigh on four decades of service to the cause of law and order. A month after he arrived back in Sicily, a new Prefect was installed too. The Prefect announced the radical new policy that he and Sangiorgi would be implementing: an attack on the protection rackets that were the very base of mafia power.

> The crime of extorting money with menaces is the most terrible curse
> pervading the rural territory of the province of Palermo. The mafia has

found a way to live an easy life by shaking down landowners; it has organised what amounts to nothing less than a tax system in its own favour.

Suddenly, in the middle of Italy's darkest political crisis, Sangiorgi had
the political backing to carry through the 'open fight against the mafia'
he had first embarked on all those years ago. His efforts would be concentrated in the Piana dei Colli, to the north-west of Palermo—the same
beautiful and dangerous landscape that was the theatre of Giovanni
'Darky' Cusimano's persecution of old man Gambino and his sons in the
1860s and 1870s.

Sangiorgi arrived in Palermo in the middle of a mafia civil war. At stake,
as always, was territory in the rich citrus fruit groves of the Conca d'Oro.
The trail of death and bereavement was not particularly long by the mafia's
standards: five *mafiosi* shot dead, another driven to suicide and a seventh
poisoned when he escaped to New Orleans. There were also two innocent
victims: an eighteen-year-old shop girl and a seventeen-year-old cowherd
who were both murdered in case they talked. But what was historically unprecedented about the mafia war of the late 1890s was that Sangiorgi skilfully used it to recruit witnesses, among both the *mafiosi* and their innocent
casualties. He then used their evidence to put together the most detailed
and convincing description of the criminal sect's structure that had ever
been compiled. Sangiorgi set out that description in a report he sent back to
Rome in instalments between November 1898 and January 1900.

The first striking thing about Sangiorgi's report is that it started from
scratch. He had to assume that his readers (notably senior magistrates and
the Prime Minister) knew nothing about the mafia because nothing had yet
been proved. Accordingly he began with the basics.

> The association's aim is to bully landowners, and thereby to force them to
> hire stewards, guards, and labourers, to impose contractor-managers on
> them, and to determine the price paid for citrus fruit and other produce.

From these simple first steps, Sangiorgi advanced a long way. He got the
chance to confirm what he knew about the mafia's initiation ritual. And he
ended by listing the bosses, underbosses and over two hundred soldiers in
eight separate mafia cells. He exposed their links beyond Palermo—even as
far as Tunisia, an outpost of the citrus fruit business. He explained how they
came together for meetings and trials, and how they performed collective
executions of any members deemed to have broken the rules—especially
the rule that stipulated blind obedience to the bosses' wishes. Sangiorgi

even named the mafia's 'regional or supreme boss', the fifty-year-old citrus fruit dealer and *capo* of the Malaspina *cosca*, Francesco Siino.

The Siino name echoed in Sangiorgi's memory. Francesco's older brother Alfonso, now in charge of the Uditore branch of the sect, was one of the two hit men who shot dead old man Gambino's son in 1874, and then went unpunished thanks to the 'fratricide' plot. Many other names in Sangiorgi's report rang a malevolent bell: names like Cusimano, and above all Giammona. Antonino Giammona was the poetry-writing boss whose gang's initiation ritual Sangiorgi had exposed in 1876. The old mobster was now close to eighty, but he still carried huge authority.

> He gives direction through advice based on his vast experience and his long criminal record. He offers instructions on the way to carry out crimes and construct a defence, especially alibis.

Linking these surnames there was now much more than a shared history of murder and extortion. While Ermanno Sangiorgi, beset by the stresses of his police career, was struggling to hold his own small family together, the hoodlum clans of the Palermo hinterland had intermarried, and many had passed on their wealth and authority to their offspring: Antonino Giammona's son Giuseppe was *capo* in Passo di Rigano; Alfonso Siino's boy Filippo was underboss in Uditore. A generation on from his last encounter with the Palermo mob, Sangiorgi could see that the mafia's marriage strategising had founded criminal dynasties. If the structure of bosses, underbosses and *cosche* gave the mafia its skeleton, then these kinship ties were its bloodstream.

Sangiorgi also identified intimate ground-level contacts between this new criminal nobility and some of Palermo's longer established dynasties, among them the richest family in Sicily, the Florios. The head of the house of Florio, Ignazio, was a fourth generation entrepreneur whose father had married into some of the bluest blood in Sicily. The fortune that Ignazio inherited included the principal stake in NGI, the shipping company whose share price was covertly pumped up with Bank of Sicily money. A man of dash and style who was not yet out of his twenties when Sangiorgi became chief of police, Ignazio set the decadent tone in the Sicilian *monde*. Florio turned Palermo—or Floriopolis, as it became known—into a prime destination for the European yacht set. His sumptuous villa, located in its own parkland amid the fragrant hues of the Conca d'Oro, was the epicentre of polite society. But as Sangiorgi discovered, the Florio villa was also an important place for the Sicilian Honoured Society.

The men responsible for security at the Florio villa were the 'gardener', Francesco Noto and his younger brother Pietro—respectively the boss and underboss of the mafia's Olivuzza *cosca*. Sangiorgi did not discover just what were the terms of the deal between the Noto brothers and Ignazio Florio. But protection was almost always how *mafiosi* got their foot in the garden gate. Kidnapping was a serious risk, the Notos would have explained to Ignazio Florio, deferentially. But we can make sure of your safety. And once the Florios' safety was in the hands of the mafia, there was no limit to the turns the relationship might take—many of them mutually beneficial. Having murderers to call on can be a very tempting resource.

One morning in 1897 Ignazio Florio woke to learn that his safety had been scandalously compromised: the villa had been broken into, and a large number of *objets d'art* were missing. He summoned the Noto brothers and delivered a humiliating tirade. A few days later, Florio woke up again and found that the stolen valuables had reappeared during the night—in exactly their original positions. This was a criminal gesture of astonishing finesse: both an apology, and a serene reminder of just how deeply the mafia had penetrated the Florio family's domestic intimacies.

Sangiorgi learned that the culprits in the Florio burglary were two of the Notos' own soldiers, who were unhappy because they felt they had not received a fair share of some loot from a kidnapping. The Notos strung the burglars along, promising more money on condition that the Florios' property was put back—which it duly was. Then they reported the episode to a sitting of the mafia tribunal, which ruled that it was an outrageous act of insubordination. Several months later, in October 1897, an execution squad comprising representatives from each of the eight mafia *cosche* lured the burglars into a trap, shot them dead, and heaved their bodies into a deep grotto on a lemon grove.

What shocked even Sangiorgi about the whole story was that the Noto brothers had told the Florios just what they had done to the burglars. In November 1897, soon after the police had found the bodies in the grotto, but before anyone outside the mafia had the slightest idea how and why they had ended up there, Ignazio Florio's mother was heard explaining that the dead men had been punished for the break-in earlier in the year. Justice had been done—discreetly and with due force—to the satisfaction of both the Florios and the hoodlums they sponsored. A kind of justice that could never have anything to do with the police.

The Florios inhabited a world of garden parties and gala balls, of royal receptions and open-top carriage rides, of whist soirées and opera premieres. An inconceivable distance separated their milieu from the rat-run tenements where the Neapolitan camorra was incubated, or from the dung-strewn hovels of Africo's *picciotti*. Yet between the Florios and the Sicilian mafia there was almost no distance at all. If it came to an 'open fight' between the state and the mafia, there was little doubt about which side the House of Florio would take.

On the night of 27 April 1900 Sangiorgi ordered the arrest *en masse* of the Men of Honour named in his reports. He hand-picked his officers, trusting his judgement of their honesty and courage. Even so, Sangiorgi had to keep the operation a secret until the last minute to avoid leaks: the mafia's spies were everywhere. By October the Prefect of Palermo reported that Sangiorgi had reduced the mafia to 'silence and inactivity'. That silence was the reward for months of brilliant policework. But it was also the mafia's response to what had now happened to its favourite Member of Parliament, don Raffaele Palizzolo.

FOUR TRIALS AND A FUNERAL

BETWEEN NOVEMBER 1899 AND JULY 1904 THE MAFIA ISSUE WENT ON A NATIONAL tour. Prime Minister General Luigi Pelloux had to put direct pressure on the Palermo prosecutors' office to make sure the Notarbartolo murder finally came to court. The case was transferred away from Palermo lest the peculiar local atmosphere influence the outcome. There would, in the end, be three Notarbartolo murder trials, each in a different Italian city, each covered in depth by the country's growing press corps. For the first time, Sicily's shadiest machinations became a scandal across the whole country.

The first trial took place in the north, in foggy Milan, which was still a political tinderbox following the army massacre of the previous year. Here the ground itself seemed to throb with industry: hydroelectric power, Italy's 'white coal', was cabled in from the Alps; smoke stacks were reaching skywards in the periphery; and a grand stock exchange building was taking shape in the city's core. Milan was Italy's shop window to the world. With its strong radical traditions, home of the Socialist Party and its mordant newspaper *Avanti!*, Milan would also turn into the perfect resonance chamber for the Notarbartolo scandal.

Yet when the trial finally opened, only two people were in the dock: the brakeman and the ticket collector on the train where Notarbartolo had been stabbed to death more than six and a half years earlier. General Pelloux would only apply so much leverage on the Palermo judiciary. For the prosecution, the two railwaymen were accomplices to the mafia's assassins. For the defence, they were, at worst, merely terrified witnesses. For Leopoldo

Poor Sicilians summoned to chilly Milan to give evidence in the first Notarbartolo murder trial. Fourteen of them were hospitalized with bronchitis, and one died. A local newspaper took pity on them and arranged a collection.

Notarbartolo, they were a chance to spark a publicity firestorm that would finally drive don Raffaele Palizzolo into the open.

On 16 November 1899, from the witness stand in Milan, Leopoldo Notarbartolo gave an assured testimony of which his father would have been proud. Speaking briskly in his deep voice, Leopoldo explicitly accused Palizzolo of ordering his father's murder and then went on to set out everything he had learned about the mafia and the Bank of Sicily. He also cast grave suspicions over the police and magistrates who had never even interviewed Palizzolo about the case.

Calls for Palizzolo to resign began immediately. The political pressure on him intensified day-by-day, until Parliament voted in a special session to remove his immunity from prosecution. The very same evening, Chief of Police Ermanno Sangiorgi enacted the order to arrest him.

Leopoldo Notarbartolo got the publicity firestorm he wanted. The newspapers at home and abroad carried lurid stories about Palizzolo, real or imagined. He seemed like a satirical grotesque come to life. One American resident in Italy, who understandably chose to remain anonymous, claimed to have gained access to one of the open receptions that Palizzolo held every morning at his sumptuous house on Palermo's main thoroughfare.

Raffaele Palizzolo, the mafia politician strongly suspected of ordering the Notarbartolo murder. He was photographed only reluctantly, complaining, 'We have become the object of public curiosity'.

The American visitor explained that Palizzolo's bed was his throne: its heavy mahogany frame was inlaid with mother of pearl and surmounted by a baldachin; it stood, surrounded by numerous gaudily ornamented spittoons and shaving mirrors on stands, at the centre of a hall hung with pink silks. A crowd of petitioners gathered round about: council commissioners in search of seats on committees, policemen who wanted to win a promotion, and former convicts still sporting their penitentiary crew cuts. One by one, Palizzolo's major-domo would pick out the supplicants and guide them to a perch on one of the great bed's broad, upholstered flanks. Palizzolo greeted them all effusively, sitting up in his nightgown, holding a cup of chocolate with one hand and making extravagant gestures with the other.

Palizzolo is a small man with the short, thick neck of a bull and black, shining hair, parted in the middle. Except for his bushy eyebrows, he has few masculine features. His chin is weak and his forehead denotes cunning rather than breadth of thought and strength of character.

The fingers of both his fat, stubby hands were covered with rings— rings of all sorts, marquis, snake and signet rings, set with diamonds, rubies and opals, a whole jeweller's tray full. Yet under this rather vulgar display, under this half-womanish, half-foppish mask, lies hidden a

Giuseppe Fontana, citrus fruit entrepreneur, *mafioso* and alleged assassin of Emanuele Notarbartolo.

shrewd personality and a calculating mind of no mean order.

As the trial in Milan progressed, there were more and more sensational revelations. A stationmaster turned out to have recognised one of the killers in an identity parade, but his testimony was ignored until he was frightened into retracting it. A police inspector close to Palizzolo was arrested in the witness stand for concealing evidence; some twenty other witnesses faced charges of perjury. The Minister of War was forced to resign when a Republican paper exposed that he had lobbied to have an influential *mafioso* released from jail in time for the elections. The court learned that former Prime Minister Rudinì had bestowed an official decoration on Palizzolo in 1897.

One of the men suspected of actually stabbing Emanuele Notarbartolo to death was named in the Milan courtroom too: Giuseppe Fontana was a lemon trader and a member of Palizzolo's favourite Villabate *cosca* of the mafia. He also turned out to be the manager on an estate owned by an aristocrat and Member of Parliament.

When the order went out to arrest Fontana, his aristocratic sponsor had to have his arm twisted by Chief of Police Sangiorgi before he would agree to talk to Fontana about surrendering. In the end, the *mafioso* Fontana did give himself up to Sangiorgi; but only on his own terms, and only in a style that confirmed the wildest journalistic guesswork about the mafia's influence in high places. Fontana came to town in a coach bearing his protector's family crest, in the company of his protector's lawyers. He then refused to enter Police Headquarters, insisting instead that Sangiorgi receive him in his own home. On hearing how Fontana dictated the terms of his own surrender, Leopoldo Notarbartolo acidly quipped that the *mafioso* had forgotten to demand that the guard at Sangiorgi's gate present arms as he passed.

The whole country was shocked by what was emerging in Milan. Even Prime Minister Pelloux began to worry about how far the scandal might reach, and thought it might be necessary to call a general election early. The Notarbartolo case reeked of a cover-up, and that reek increased public revulsion at the political system: while politicians were ordering troops to shoot at starving demonstrators and trying to quash press freedom, they were also pocketing illegal loans from banks and consorting with *mafiosi*.

Palizzolo had become a political leper. On 15 December 1899 an estimated 30,000 people filed through the streets of Palermo to show their support for the Notarbartolo cause. A hastily sculpted bust of the murdered banker was born aloft at the head of the procession and then set in a little temple opposite the Politeama theatre in the city centre; soon afterwards it was moved to the atrium of the Bank of Sicily's headquarters. As well as the Socialists and representatives from Palermo schools and clubs, the city's political class were out in force—even many whose conduct was called into question in the Milan hearings. Clearly there had been some shamelessly swift conversions to the cause of law and order in recent weeks. London's *Morning Post* pinpointed the hypocrisy.

> If any one of the numerous politicians who now compete in doing honour to Signor Notarbartolo's memory had energetically set about forcing the Government to punish his murderers, justice would have been done long since.

In January 1900, two months after the Milan trial began, proceedings were halted to allow a much more far-reaching case to be prepared. Here was a significant victory for the Notarbartolo cause, and for the struggle against Sicilian organised crime. Leopoldo Notarbartolo later recalled these moments as 'the culmination of the short-lived tide in our favour'.

In the summer of 1900 Prime Minister General Pelloux resigned. Leopoldo Notarbartolo had lost his key supporter in the Roman palaces of power. But the public indignation at the Notarbartolo cover-up was still strong. The destiny of the whole case hung in the balance.

The second important mafia trial of the day began back in Palermo in the spring of 1901. It did not arise directly from the Notarbartolo-Palizzolo affair, but from the determined policework of Chief of Police Sangiorgi: the *mafiosi* named in his reports stood accused of forming a criminal association.

Because Sangiorgi's investigations had no direct bearing on the banking scandal he did not benefit from the public fury that still resonated from Milan. There were no foreign correspondents in Palermo when the trial began, and proceedings barely rated a mention in the mainland press. Yet in many ways the Sangiorgi trial was just as historically important as the

The great enemy of the early Sicilian mafia: Ermanno Sangiorgi. A newspaper described this career cop as being 'as alert as a squirrel, an investigator endowed with a steady perspicacity'.

Men of Honour briefly caught in Chief of Police Sangiorgi's net in 1900.

Giuseppe Giammona, boss of Passo di Rigano, and son of the venerable *capo* Antonino Giammona.

Francesco Siino, the recently deposed 'regional or supreme boss'.

Brothers Francesco and Pietro Noto, respectively boss and underboss in Olivuzza, and responsible for 'security' at the home of Sicily's wealthiest family, the Florios.

Courtroom sketches from newspapers of the day.

Notarbartolo affair: this was a case that could have proved once and for all that the mafia existed.

Sangiorgi, veteran of Sicilian affairs that he was, must have had a weary sense of inevitability about the outcome of the trial he had spent the best part of three years preparing. With General Pelloux gone Sangiorgi was once more vulnerable to the system of friendships that the mafia had created to protect itself in its capital. Most of the *mafiosi*, including the venerable *capo* Antonino Giammona, were acquitted before the case even reached court. The likely explanation for these acquittals was that, just as during the 'fratricide' affair in 1876–77, Sangiorgi faced insidious opposition from Sicily's most senior magistrate. Days before proceedings began, the Chief Prosecutor of Palermo, one Vincenzo Cosenza, wrote to the Minister of Justice to explain that 'in the course of exercising my duties I have never noticed the mafia, because the mafia has no desire to ensnare the priests of Themis'. (He meant magistrates, because Themis was the ancient Greek personification of order and justice.) Any Palermo judge who was incapable of imagining why the mafia might want to corrupt the legal system was, at best, culpably naïve. But Vincenzo Cosenza was not naïve: he was identified by Leopoldo Notarbartolo as a protector of Palizzolo's, the main obstacle in the way of bringing don Raffaele and his hit men to justice.

The trial itself went as badly as Sangiorgi feared. One after another, most of his key witnesses retracted their statements. The mafia's protectors among the elite took the stand to give immaculate character references for their friends in the criminal sect: 'the Giammonas are highly esteemed in the area', one local politician explained. Another man of property was effusive.

> The Giammonas have been very generous to anyone who has a business relationship with them, and no one has a bad word to say about them.

An utterly implausible statement, of course, but understandable given that this particular witness owned land next to both Francesco Siino and the Giammona clan.

The House of Florio was simply too powerful to get mixed up in the case: no one from the shipping baron's family was called to court to explain what *exactly* the Florios' relationship was with the Olivuzza mafia. Ignazio Florio limited himself to a written statement, denying everything.

Defence lawyers portrayed the mafia war as a feud between unconnected families. One after another, they ridiculed Sangiorgi's theory that men who had been at one another's throats could secretly be members of the same sect. *Omertà*, they said, was not part of the rulebook of an organisation. As anthropologists had ascertained, it was a typically Sicilian 'hypertrophy of individualism—something that undoubtedly has its positive side'. Mafia was a kind of *cavalleria rusticana*, of 'rustic chivalry', and as such it was merely the degenerate form sometimes taken by the most noble features of the Sicilian character; getting rid of it—if that were even possible—would mean changing Sicily entirely.

Most of the *mafiosi* were acquitted, and the rest received the usual short prison terms that went with the crime of 'associating for delinquency'. Sangiorgi had been beaten again.

In September 1901 the second Notarbartolo murder trial opened. The city chosen to host the eagerly awaited proceedings was Bologna. With its arcades and ancient university, Bologna was one of the best-administered towns in Italy. Like Milan, it was still safely distant from the judicial snake pit in Palermo. But unlike Milan, it was conservative: a Bolognese jury was unlikely to be swayed by subversive propaganda.

Perhaps it was an optical illusion generated by the publicity. Or perhaps it was the toll taken by months of confinement before the trial. But when don Raffaele Palizzolo stood up to give evidence just a few days into proceedings, he seemed to have shrunk. There were no rings on his fingers and for a prop he only had the back of a chair rather than his mahogany bed. Whether he was pleading with the jury, shouting to the gallery or rambling to himself, Palizzolo seemed incapable of striking the right tone. It was as if he were so habituated to the body language of pork-barrelling—the gladhands and corridor mutters—that he could find no pose to strike for open, public discourse.

> I was the only Member of Parliament who was accessible to the voters . . . I went down and lived among the people, trying to be their adviser and friend. And the people felt grateful.

In London, *The Times* commented on his uneasy performance with typical understatement, saying that Palizzolo's testimony lacked the 'element of simple straightforwardness which carries conviction'. Leopoldo Notarbartolo, still dressed in his navy uniform, was the same assured witness in Bologna that he had been in Milan. *The Times* again:

> The statement of Lieutenant Notarbartolo, with its sobriety, scrupulous attention to fact and careful separation of deduction from premise, held the Court spellbound.

Chief of Police Sangiorgi was also called to the witness stand, although to my knowledge his testimony did not rate a single mention in any foreign newspaper. At least he was well known in Bologna, where he had served as chief of police in the mid-1890s. The local press commented that he had changed little: only a few more grey hairs in the blonde of his beard and receding hair. He was forthright in his account of the mafia's power.

> The mafia is powerful and it has relations across five Sicilian provinces and also abroad, where there are colonies of Sicilians.

Lawyers for the defence swept his testimony aside: the recent trial in Palermo hardly backed up this highly improbable assertion.

Sicily's wealthiest man, Ignazio Florio, may not have appeared in court in Palermo, but he could not avoid giving evidence in Bologna. He said that the mafia was 'an invention created to calumny Sicily'. An 'invention', of course, that was protecting his luxurious villa and helping him boost the share price of his shipping line, NGI. Florio was a figure at the very heart of the prosecution case. The NGI stocks scam involving the Bank of Sicily's money was thought to be the whole reason why Palizzolo ordered Emanuele Notarbartolo murdered. Yet Florio somehow avoided being interrogated on the whole subject. One historian has wryly called his easy ride 'miraculous'.

The verdict, which finally arrived after nearly eleven months of hearings, came as a surprise to most. Palizzolo folded his arms and laughed convulsively when he heard that he, like the alleged assassin Giuseppe Fontana, had been sentenced to thirty years in jail. By a majority, the jury had evidently deduced that Palizzolo's guilt was the only possible explanation for the whole cover-up, despite the lack of positive proof against him.

Palizzolo's conviction marked the climax of a countrywide debate about the mafia that had been set in motion two and a half years earlier in Milan. There was a minor publishing boom, and a major outbreak of muddle. Most commentators agreed that the mafia could not possibly be a single criminal fraternity. That was surely preposterous. But if there was broad agreement about what the mafia was not, then only riddles lay in store for any Italian reader curious to know what the mafia actually was.

The very worst book on the subject was one of the most prominent. Its author was Napoleone Colajanni, a firebrand Republican MP from central Sicily who had been the first to lift the lid on the scandal at the Banca Romana back in 1892. Colajanni explained that the mafia was a 'particular moral criterion' left over from feudal times, an underlying feature of the Sicilian character. The isolated gangs that cropped up in Sicilian villages from time to time were merely surface manifestations of this archaic mentality. The Arab invasions of the early Middle Ages were a factor here, probably. Poverty and illiteracy were obviously to blame, mostly. Although there were sometimes rich and well-educated *mafiosi*. And politicians. And aristocrats. But in any case, Colajanni mused

> The *mafia* does not always have evil as its aim; on occasion, indeed not infrequently, it works towards what is good and just. But the methods it uses are immoral and criminal—especially when its actions include violent crime. It would also be false to say that all *mafiosi* are shirkers who live an easy life based on violence, deceit and intimidation. In fact often a *mafioso*, in order to keep his standing as a *mafioso* and show it off, will deliberately stop being wealthy and embrace poverty.

The hopelessly misinformed public debate over the Notarbartolo affair raises one of the most vexing puzzles about the mafia—one that would become more vexing over the decades as Italy's other criminal fraternities acquired power to rival the Sicilian mafia's. The Notarbartolo trial triggered the first organised crime scandal to take place in the era of modern media and mass politics. The vast majority of Italians did not take kindly to the murder and corruption that the word 'mafia' conjured up—whatever that word really meant. So why did the mafia not shrivel, like a vampire, when it was trapped by the rays of the media dawn?

The befuddlement created by books like Colajanni's counted for a great deal. And although Colajanni was not one of them, the mafia also had its own ideologists—lawyers and hired pens keen to spread fallacies about 'mafiosity' and the Sicilian mentality. Their views were eagerly amplified by one of Sicily's most important newspapers, *L'Ora*, which was founded, owned and controlled by none other than Ignazio Florio.

The mafia's influence on the fourth estate could also be brutally direct. On the day after the Milan trial was suspended, the head of the Sicilian press association wrote to Prime Minister General Pelloux to explain that he had twice been threatened, and challenged to a duel, by Palizzolo supporters. 'Timid journalists are keeping quiet, and honest ones are afraid', he warned.

But it is the political backstory to the Notarbartolo affair that really explains why media attention does not hurt the mafia nearly as much as one might expect. The new press of the early 1900s in Italy was ideologically riven, and its divisions reflected a divided nation.

The Notarbartolo cause had the Socialists among its most vocal supporters. Most grassroots Sicilian Socialists were inveterate enemies of *mafiosi*. In the 1890s the mafia had used all of its tricks—corruption, infiltration and violence—to undermine new labour organisations that recruited among the peasantry. So we should not be surprised that Leopoldo Notarbartolo, despite being a man of the Right like his father, employed a highly able Socialist lawyer.

But other conservatives, who lacked Leopoldo's intimate yearning for justice, were loath to reach out across the political gulf. The barricades of 1898 may have come down, but early twentieth-century Italy remained a country permanently at risk of internal conflict. For men of both Right and extreme Left, the Italian state was a ramshackle edifice that could only be salvaged by being rebuilt. Both sides thought it was naïve to invest much hope in such a state when it came to enforcing real justice. As a result, when mafia issues were at stake in the game of political power, ideology trumped the rule of law.

And Italy's notorious regional divisions often trumped them both. Even the bestselling newspapers, like Milan's *Corriere della Sera*, spoke overwhelmingly to a local readership. There was no such thing as a 'national' public opinion. Prejudices were rife. In Milan, even some of the Socialist Party's leaders viewed the whole south with open disgust, as a land peopled by aristocratic reactionaries, parliamentary pettifoggers, and racially degenerate peasant morons. All the inscrutable talk about how 'mafiosity' was part of Sicilians' make-up only served to harden the stereotypes.

Even the most open-minded Italians from the north and centre did not feel that the mafia, however dastardly it might be, had much bearing on their lives. Sure, they were indignant when they read how Sicilian politicians got into bed with toughs and crooks. But it was hard to sustain that indignation when the people they themselves voted for then got into bed with suspect Sicilian MPs. For most Italians outside the south and Sicily, the mafia lay at two removes.

Regionalism worked in both directions. The Florio family organ, *L'Ora*, stuck to a consistent line throughout the Notarbartolo affair: the mafia was a fiction, a pretext for northerners to get one over on Sicily. Partly because of *L'Ora*'s influence, when Raffaele Palizzolo was found guilty in Bologna in the summer of 1902, a broad section of opinion in Sicily greeted the news with a show of hurt regional pride. The Notarbartolo murder verdict, they lamented, was only the latest haughty swipe that the north had taken at the island. A *Pro Sicilia* Committee was set up, recruiting quickly from the constituency created by Florio wealth and mafia traction, but also drawing in support from many conservatives. The Palizzolo cause became the latest excuse to crank up Sicilian indignation, and thereby lever more money and favours out of the government in Rome. As a side effect of the *Pro Sicilia* turn in the island's politics, Palizzolo was cured of his leprosy and converted into a martyr to northern prejudices.

The old regionalist ploy worked. Someone in Rome almost certainly had a quiet word with the senior judiciary, and within six months Italy's Supreme Court quashed the whole Bologna trial on a tiny and highly questionable technicality.

Palizzolo and the mafia cut-throat Giuseppe Fontana faced a third jury, amid the Renaissance glories of Florence this time. But by now public opinion was exhausted. Not even the death of a crucial new witness, who was found hanging from the stairs of his Florence hotel, raised many eyebrows.

Ermanno Sangiorgi, still chief of police in Palermo, testified once more in Florence, despite the recent death of his beloved daughter Italia following a long illness. For his pains, Sangiorgi immediately became the target of a mafia smear campaign. The allegations—a convoluted yarn about bad debts, bully-boy policing, and favours to *mafiosi*—appeared first in a long letter published in the Florios' newspaper *L'Ora*. The story was soon picked up in Naples where the *Tribuna Giudiziaria*, a local rag specialising in courtroom dramas, told its readers that the episode shed a disturbing light on Sangiorgi, who had attracted such attention to himself by delivering 'a testimony against the defendants in Florence that was as fierce as it was slanderous'.

> Our conclusion? In Palermo, you won't find the real mafia among the People, but among the police. Just like in Florence, where the real *camorristi* are standing outside the dock, not inside it.

The original slurs were made by an ex-con in the orbit of organised crime. The brains behind him belonged to Palizzolo's lawyer, and possibly also to Vincenzo Cosenza, the Chief Prosecutor of Palermo who claimed never to have noticed the mafia during his career as a 'priest of Themis'—Cosenza was known to be close to the *Tribuna Giudiziaria's* editors.

The Florentine jury acquitted Palizzolo and Fontana in July 1904. In London, the *Daily Express* gave the news in a few weary lines, under the title 'Victory for the mafia'. In Palermo, that victory was celebrated by a procession with flags and music: men wore Palizzolo's picture on their lapels, women waved handkerchiefs from the balconies. The mafia-backed *Pro Sicilia* Committee hailed the verdict as a great confirmation of patriotic harmony, and sent the mayor of Florence a telegram of thanks.

A most solemn and imposing meeting of this Committee acclaims the city of Florence, which, by giving heart to Sicily's juridical conscience, has reunited the Italian People in the ideal of justice.

Leopoldo Notarbartolo was almost destroyed psychologically by the outcome of his eleven-year struggle. In 1900, after the Milan trial, when Palizzolo was first arrested and Chief of Police Sangiorgi rounded up the *mafiosi* of the Conca d'Oro, the murdered banker's son had been lured into believing that the mafia could be defeated in one swift strike, like a monster run through by a knight's lance. The second and third trials ground those illusions into a bitter dust.

What is the result of my efforts? Palizzolo free and serene. As for the mafia and its methods: the *Pro Sicilia* Committee proclaims and glorifies them; the government bows down to them and sustains them; and the wretched island of Sicily reinforces them ever more . . . Do I live on an earth that is watched over by God the Father, or amid a chaos of brutal forces unleashed by loathsome, wicked gnomes like the ones in Scandinavian legends?

Leopoldo continued his naval career but spent a further seven years reflecting on his experience, and then another five pouring his anguish into a meticulous and moving account of his father's story, and his own. He found little consolation other than in contemplating sea life, which offered him a less heroic metaphor of how the forces of good might one day defeat the mafia. He observed how, over generations and generations, tiny undersea creatures live and die, all the while creating their miniature dwellings from limestone deposits, piling them higher and higher until, following some minor seismic shift, an entirely new island appears above the waves.

The people working humbly in the cause of good are like those ocean creatures. One day, the marvellous little island will emerge! God has written his promise in the holy book of nature.

Back on the 'wretched island' of Sicily, Ermanno Sangiorgi, one of the people working in the cause of good, took until the summer of 1905, a year after the conclusion of the Notarbartolo affair, to win a libel suit against his accuser.

Italy reserves a peculiar cruelty to those that love it the most. Soon afterwards Sangiorgi's son-in-law, who worked in Pisa as an administrator for the royal family, the House of Savoy, committed suicide after being caught with his hand in the till. Sangiorgi was entirely blameless in the disgrace of his daughter's widower. But the Royal Household held him liable for some of the losses, which cost him more than a month's salary.

In March 1907, Sangiorgi formally requested permission to retire from his position as chief of police of Palermo; he was showing signs of ill health, in the form of a creeping paralysis. His life in law enforcement—forty-eight years of service, eighteen of them as chief of police—had begun even before Italian unification. But passing time had not made him any coyer: he bluntly asked for a special pension and the honorary title of Prefect. He concluded the letter in a typically patriotic fashion.

> I began my career during the war of Italian Independence when Northern Italy was echoing to the cry of 'Long live King Victor Emmanuel II!' I now end it with another cry on my lips and in my heart, 'Long live Victor Emmanuel III! Long live the House of Savoy!'

Sangiorgi retired in May 1907, with his honorary title but without his special pension. The creeping paralysis that had hastened his retirement also hastened him to his death, in November 1908. The press in Naples and Palermo recalled him to readers as the police chief whose botched handling of the cab drivers' strike in 1893 had brought anarchy to the streets.

Sangiorgi's passing marked the loss of a unique store of expertise on the mafia's early years: the hugely important report on the mafia that he had written for Prime Minister Pelloux would remain hidden in the archives until the 1980s. Fundamentally, the knowledge he had worked so hard to accumulate would remain valid long after his death: as times changed, the Sicilian mafia changed remarkably little. Nevertheless, the ingenuity and ferocity with which the mafia adapted to the changing times to come would have astonished even Sangiorgi.

Sangiorgi had played by the rules in Palermo; he had fought a clean, 'open fight' against the mafia, and it had ended in defeat. He died in his wife's city, in Naples, where the *Carabinieri* had already begun a campaign against the camorra that was both devious and very dirty—a campaign that would end in victory.

20

THE 'HIGH' CAMORRA

IN NAPLES, JUST AS IN PALERMO, CORRUPTION AND ORGANISED CRIME REACHED THE top of the news agenda as the economic and political crises of the 1890s petered out. In 1899 a new Socialist newspaper, *La Propaganda*, began a campaign against sleaze and gangsterism. Certain high-minded politicians joined in from the Right. The campaign was such a success that a Socialist MP was elected in Vicaria—the most densely populated constituency in Naples and, of course, the very cradle of the camorra.

The main target of *La Propaganda*'s vitriol was Alberto Casale, a Member of Parliament and influential local government power broker who had extensive contacts with the Neapolitan underworld. We have already had a passing encounter with Casale: back in 1893, he used his purchase with the Honoured Society to bring an end to the camorra-backed cab drivers' strike. Casale responded to *La Propaganda*'s attacks by reporting the newspaper to the authorities for slandering him, and a criminal trial ensued.

The outcome of the Casale case was a disaster for a whole crooked system that linked the city's politicians, bureaucrats, businessmen and journalists. *La Propaganda* successfully defended itself against the slander charge by proving that Casale, among many other corrupt deals, had banked a kickback from a Belgian tram company for his role in the cab drivers' strike.

The shock waves from Casale's judicial humiliation sped to Rome. Casale resigned, the Naples city council was dissolved, and an official investigation into corruption in city government was launched under the leadership of an owlish old law professor from Liguria, Senator Giuseppe Saredo. The Saredo inquiry would once more lay bare the 'slack society'; indeed it would prove to be one of the starkest portraits of political and bureaucratic malpractice in Italian history.

Shining a light into the tenebrous passages of Naples city hall was no easy task. Senator Saredo and his team needed to study the paperwork to discover why the system was so corrupt and inefficient. But the paperwork was in chaos because of all the corruption and inefficiency. Bagfuls of official files had been smuggled away by bureaucrats keen to cover their tracks. The commissioners received a sullen or angry response from many of the key people it interviewed.

Despite all the obstacles, after ten months of wading through a slobland of documents and testimonies, Senator Saredo and his team dredged up hard evidence aplenty. Appointments to public service were supposed to be made on an impartial, competitive basis. In Naples the regulations had been systematically evaded. Half of all local government employees had no educational qualifications whatsoever. Staggeringly, even the chief accountant whose job it was to draw up the council's budget had no qualifications. Some local government employees drew two or even three separate salaries. Several well-known journalists had no-show jobs with the council.

The reason why government posts in Naples existed was *not* so that services could be carried out for the citizenry. Services like fighting fires, teaching children, caring for the parks, collecting taxes and rubbish, building sewers: these were secondary concerns, at best. For that reason, they were left to the minority of idiots who actually felt bound to do an honest day's work. No, the real reason a job existed in Naples was so it could be handed out to people who had the right friends or relatives. A post with the council was a favour bestowed in return for other favours. In a package with these posts came the power to give and withhold yet more favours: to move an application for a trading licence to the top of the in-tray, or to consign it in perpetuity to the bottom; to give a contract to one tram company rather than to another. Because most local government bureaucrats were not particularly interested in doing anything for anyone they did not know, a whole parasitical swarm of intermediaries grew up: the *faccendieri*, they were called. (They still are.) The term means 'hustlers', 'wheeler-dealers'. The only expertise these *faccendieri* had was knowing which ear to whisper in. In return for a small consideration, they would arrange for someone they knew to get you what you wanted—as a *favour*.

A system of political patronage made this foul mess possible. Politicians stood at the business end of the chains of favours that snaked through the corridors of the Naples municipality. Explosively, the Saredo report referred to the men who operated this patronage system as 'the high camorra'.

The original *low camorra* held sway over the poor plebs in an age of abjection and servitude. Then there arose a *high camorra* comprising the most cunning and audacious members of the middle class. They fed off trade and public works contracts, political meetings and government bureaucracy. This high camorra strikes deals and does business with the low camorra, swapping promises for favours and favours for promises. The high camorra thinks of the state bureaucracy as being like a field it has to harvest and exploit. Its tools are cunning, nerve and violence. Its strength comes from the streets. And it is rightly considered to be more dangerous, because it has re-established the worst form of despotism by founding a regime based on bullying. The high camorra has replaced free will with impositions; it has nullified individuality and liberty; and it has defrauded the law and public trust.

As a direct result of the inquiry's findings a corruption trial was launched and twelve people, including Alberto Casale and the former Mayor of Naples, were convicted.

Low camorra / high camorra. No encapsulation of the Neapolitan malaise could have been better calculated to make headlines. Whereas 'mafia' was still a vague notion, one enmeshed in woolly fibs about Sicilian culture, the term 'camorra' carried the distinctive reek of the dungeon, the tavern, and the brothel; it spoke clearly of primitive rituals and knife fights; it conjured up stark pictures of violent men with crude tattoos on their torsos and arabesques of scar tissue on their faces.

At the very same time, during the Notarbartolo affair, the press were referring constantly to a 'high mafia'. Raffaele Palizzolo was without doubt a *mafioso*, who profited from cattle rustling and kidnapping; and he was also, without doubt, at home in the 'high' world of banking and politics. So the label 'high *mafioso*' fitted him as snugly as did his expensively tailored frock coat.

But was 'high camorra' really an accurate description of the systematic malfeasance the Saredo inquiry had unearthed in Naples? The politician at the centre of the whole scandal, Alberto Casale, was a proven crook and a master of undergovernment like Palizzolo. But it was not strictly true to call him a *camorrista*. While Casale was certainly a politician who was shameless about doing business with the camorra, he was not an integral part of the camorra in the same way that don Raffaele was an integral part of the mafia.

What this amounts to saying is that the camorra was not as powerful as the mafia. The camorra certainly had a steady partnership with pieces of the state. But it had not *become* the state in the way that the mafia had done in Sicily.

Senator Saredo did not give any evidence to back up his use of the phrase 'high camorra'. His inquiry found no trail of blood or money leading from the upper world of politics down into the underworld where the camorra, in the strict sense, operated. In fact the low camorra remained a mere peripheral blur in Saredo's field of vision.

Saredo's provocative language was therefore misleading, but understandable. Ever since Italy had found out about the criminal sect called the camorra, it had also used 'camorra' in a much vaguer way, as an insult. The c-word was a label for any shady clique or faction—for *other people's* cliques or factions. As the nineteenth century drew to a close, this term of abuse was steeped in new bile. Italians were growing bitterly frustrated with the way their politics worked. The mysterious deal brokering, the jobbery, the strong-arm tactics: 'camorra', it sometimes seemed, was everywhere in the country's institutional life. A hostility towards politics—*antipolitica* as it is sometimes called—has been a constant feature of Italian society ever since. With his talk of a 'high camorra', the old law professor showed that he had a mischievous streak: he was knowingly appealing to what was by now a conditioned reflex in public opinion.

As soon as it became clear that the Saredo inquiry was doing its job seriously, some leading politicians began briefing against it: what Saredo had termed the 'high camorra' was mobilising to defend itself. Tame journalists heaped abuse on Senator Saredo. Knowing the threat posed by a wave of 'antipolitics', they appealed to another conditioned reflex of Italian collective life: a suspicious, defensive local pride. So the northerner Saredo had besmirched the image of Naples, the editorials wailed. There may have been a few cases of corruption. But that was because Naples was poor and backward. What the city needed was not haughty lectures, but more money from government. Lots more.

In Italy, public indignation has a short half-life. When it fails to catalyse change, it steadily decays into less volatile states of mind: fatigue, forgetting, and sullen indifference. By 1904 the indignation about political corruption and organised crime that marked the turn of the century had all but totally degenerated. Raffaele Palizzolo was finally acquitted of ordering the murder of banker Emanuele Notarbartolo in July of that year. In Naples too, the Casale trial and the Saredo inquiry no longer provoked the same anger. The Socialist Party, having tried to ride the scandals, was now divided and discredited by a failed general strike. The chiefs of the 'high camorra' could now go on the offensive.

The Prime Minister of the day was Giovanni Giolitti—*the* dominant figure in Italian politics between the turn of the century and the First World

War. Giolitti was a master of parliamentary tactics, better than anyone else at the devious game of coaxing factions into coalitions.

In the early 1900s Giolitti presided over an unprecedented period of economic growth and introduced some very welcome social reforms. But his cynicism made him as loathed as he was indispensable. 'For your enemies, you apply the law. For your friends, you interpret it', Giolitti once said: a manifesto for undermining public trust in the institutions, and all too accurate an encapsulation of the pervading values within the Italian state. He also compared governing Italy to the job of making a suit of clothes for a hunchback. It was pointless for a tailor to try and correct the hunchback's bodily deformities, he explained. Better just to make a deformed suit. Italy's biggest deformity was of course organised crime, and Giolitti showed himself to be as expedient as any previous statesman in tailoring his policies around it. One later critic, incensed at the way the Prefects used thugs to influence elections in the south, called Giolitti 'the Minister of the Underworld'.

In the general election of November 1904, Giolitti (whose lieutenants in Naples had orchestrated the drive to undermine the Saredo inquiry's authority) deployed all the dark arts of the Interior Ministry to turn the vote. In Vicaria, the constituency in Naples that had elected a Socialist MP in 1900, *camorristi*—real *low camorristi*—were enlisted to bully Socialist supporters. On polling day, alongside the police, gangsters stood guard outside the places where votes were changing hands for government cash.

Someone deep within police headquarters that day was endowed with a cynical historical wit. For *camorristi* who enjoyed official approval were given tricolour cockades to wear in their hats. So, just as they had done in the days before Garibaldi's Neapolitan triumph in 1860, *camorristi* in patriotic red, white and green favours formed a flagrant alliance with the police. The traditional trade in promises and favours between the 'low camorra' and the 'high camorra' had resumed. Nothing, it seemed, had changed.

Barely eighteen months later, things changed more dramatically than they had done at any point in the camorra's history.

Among the *camorristi* in tricolour cockades on election day in 1904 was the boss of the Vicaria chapter of the Honoured Society, Enrico Alfano, known as Erricone—'Big 'Enry'. In the summer of 1906, Big 'Enry became caught up in what the *New York Times* would call 'the greatest criminal trial of the age'.

The Cuocolo trial, as it was known, was the stuff of a newspaperman's dreams. Tales of a secret sect risen from the brothels and taverns of the slums to infiltrate the salons and clubs of the elite. Police corruption and political malpractice. A cast of heroic *Carabinieri*, villainous gangsters, histriònic lawyers and even a camorra priest. The drama that unfolded in Viterbo seemed to have been fashioned expressly for the new media age. Foreign correspondents, news agencies, and the fibrillating images of Pathé's *Gazette* could now relay the excitement to every corner of the globe. Nor was the Cuocolo trial just a media event: unlike the Notarbartolo affair, it was a turning point in the history of organised crime. Not only did it reignite the political controversy and emotion that the Saredo inquiry had generated. Not only did it threaten, once more, to expose the sordid deals between *camorristi* and politicians. It actually killed off the camorra. With the Cuocolo case, the secret sect known as the camorra ceased to exist. Big 'Enry was to be the last supreme boss of the Honoured Society in Naples. And it all began with the discovery of two bodies.

21

THE CAMORRA IN STRAW-YELLOW GLOVES

JUST BEFORE 9 A.M. ON 6 JUNE 1906 POLICE ENTERED AN APARTMENT IN VIA Nardones, central Naples. They found the occupant, a former prostitute called Maria Cutinelli, on a bed soaked in blood; she was in her nightshirt and had died of multiple stab wounds—thirteen in total—to her chest, stomach, thighs and genitals. The police suspected a crime of passion and immediately began looking for the victim's husband, Gennaro Cuocolo. (Like most Italian women then as now, Maria Cutinelli had kept her maiden name.)

The hunt was over before it began. News soon arrived from Torre del Greco, a settlement squeezed between Mount Vesuvius and the sea some fifteen kilometres from the city: Gennaro Cuocolo had been found dead at dawn. His body lay in a lane that ran along the coast behind the slaughterhouse. He had been stabbed forty-seven times and his skull had been smashed with a club. Much of Torre del Greco was still smothered in ash from a recent volcanic eruption. Traces of a struggle in the black-grey carpet allowed Cuocolo's last seconds to be outlined: there were several attackers; after killing their victim, they lugged the body onto a low wall overlooking the sea—as if to put it on display. Cuocolo's blood mingled with the gore seeping through a gutter that ran from the slaughterhouse onto the crags.

There were good grounds for guessing the real motive for the murders. Cuocolo made his living commissioning burglaries and fencing the resulting booty. He was notoriously enmeshed with organised crime—a former member of the Honoured Society in the Stella quarter, in fact. The conclusion was surely plain: the camorra killed the Cuocolo couple.

The chief suspects were soon identified. At the same time that Gennaro Cuocolo was being stabbed and bludgeoned to death, five men were eating a leisurely dinner of roasted eel at Mimì a Mare, a picturesque trattoria only a couple of hundred metres from the murder scene. The five were arrested: at least three of them were known gangsters, including Big 'Enry who, as the police were well aware, was the effective supreme boss of the Honoured Society.

Yet initial investigations failed to unearth anything concrete to connect the diners at Mimì a Mare with the carnage behind the slaughterhouse. None of the five had left the dinner table long enough to kill Cuocolo. Big 'Enry and his friends walked free, much to the outrage of the Neapolitan public.

The decisive breakthrough came only at the beginning of the following year, as a result of the longstanding rivalry between the two branches of Italian policing. The *Pubblica Sicurezza*, or ordinary police force, was run from the Ministry of the Interior. The *Carabinieri*, or military police, operated under the Ministry of War. In theory the two forces patrolled different areas: the police were based in the towns and cities and the *Carabinieri* in the countryside. In practice, their duties often overlapped. The Cuocolo investigation was to be a classic case of the tensions and turf wars that often resulted.

In 1907, the *Carabinieri* wrested control of the Cuocolo murder probe from the police, and soon submitted a startling testimony by an informer: he was a young horse trader, groom, habitual thief, and *camorrista* called Gennaro Abbatemaggio.

Gennaro Abbatemaggio made history when he broke the code of *omertà*. He recounted every detail of the Cuocolo murders: motive, plan and execution. But his evidence was far more important than that. There had never been a witness like him. Of course plenty of gangsters had spoken to the authorities before, and plenty of trials had drawn on evidence from deep within the Sicilian mafia, the Neapolitan camorra, and the Calabrian picciotteria. But no one before Gennaro Abbatemaggio had stood up in court to denounce a whole sect. Before him, no self-confessed mobster had made his own life and psychology into an object of public fascination and forensic scrutiny. Gennaro Abbatemaggio would become the biggest of the many celebrities created by the Cuocolo affair.

Abbatemaggio explained to the *Carabinieri* that the murder victim, Gennaro Cuocolo, first became the target of the camorra's anger because he broke its most sacred rule by talking to the authorities. Cuocolo's breach of *omertà* came after he commissioned a burglary by one Luigi Arena. In order to keep all the loot, Cuocolo betrayed his partner in crime to the police.

The hapless thief Arena was sent to a penal colony on the island of Lampedusa, situated between Sicily and the North African coast. From there, smarting
with understandable rage, he wrote two letters
to a senior *camorrista* to demand justice.

The thief's plea for vendetta was debated
at a camorra tribunal, a meeting of the entire
leadership of the Honoured Society, which
took place in a trattoria in Bagnoli in late May
1906. The tribunal sentenced Cuocolo to
death and ruled that his wife, who knew many
of his secrets, should die too. Big 'Enry, boss
of the Vicaria quarter and the most authoritative *camorrista* in the city, took on the job of
organising the executions. He nominated six
killers, in two teams, to do away with Cuocolo and his wife. Big 'Enry also set up the
eel dinner in Torre del Greco so that he could
keep an eye on the gruesome proceedings.

So Abbatemaggio asserted. He also said
he knew all of this because he had served as
a messenger to Big 'Enry in the build-up to
the Cuocolo slayings. He also claimed to have
been present, both when the death squads
were debriefed by their boss, and when the   Enrico Alfano, or 'Erricone' (Big
camorristi shared out the jewellery stolen from   'Enry), the camorra's dominant boss.
Maria Cutinelli's blood-spattered bedroom.

There was a subplot to Abbatemaggio's narrative, a subplot that would
become the most loudly disputed of his many claims. He said that Gennaro
Cuocolo always wore a pinkie ring engraved with his initials. Cuocolo's
killers were supposed to have pulled the ring from his dead hand and sent
it to the penal colony of Lampedusa as proof that camorra justice had been
done. However, said Abbatemaggio, one of the killers disobeyed orders and
kept the trinket for himself. Many months later, when *Carabinieri* following
Abbatemaggio's tip-off raided the house where the killer lived, they slit open
his mattress and out fell a small ring bearing the initials G.C. Here was crucial material corroboration of the stool pigeon's testimony.

With Abbatemaggio on their side, the *Carabinieri* could turn a simple murder investigation into a frontal assault on the whole Honoured Society. A huge
roundup of *camorristi* followed. The people of Naples cheered from the side-lines.

Yet doubts about the evidence against Big 'Enry and his cohorts surfaced quickly after the *Carabinieri* handed over Abbatemaggio's testimony

to the magistrates who would have the job of preparing and evaluating the prosecution before the case could come to court. The *Carabinieri* had very obviously trampled over the procedural rule book. The search that had led to the discovery of Cuocolo's pinkie ring looked particularly irregular. And the main motive for the murders, in Abbatemaggio's tale, was questioned when it became clear that Gennaro Cuocolo had played no part whatsoever in getting the thief Luigi Arena sent to the penal colony of Lampedusa. Why would Arena write to the camorra asking for vengeance against Cuocolo, when Cuocolo had done nothing wrong?

For the *Carabinieri* who were driving the prosecution, trouble also came from within their own ranks. One officer got wind of the real story of Cuocolo's pinkie ring. As it turned out, Abbatemaggio the stoolpigeon had bought the ring himself and arranged for it to be engraved with G.C. The *Carabinieri* had then planted it where their pet *camorrista* said it would be. This was the 'Ring Trick', as sympathisers with the defendants would come to call it.

The *Carabiniere* who discovered the Ring Trick threatened to expose it to the press. He was immediately straitjacketed and deposited in a lunatic asylum on the orders of his commanding officer. The poor man eventually proved his sanity and a sympathetic magistrate arranged for him to be released. But he decided not to tell what he knew about the Ring Trick after some comfy wadding was added to his pension package. Retirement on the grounds of ill health, went the official version.

The Naples police, fuming at having been elbowed out of the case by the *Carabinieri*, relaunched their investigations following a completely different line of inquiry: they believed that the Cuocolos were killed by two thieves whom Gennaro Cuocolo had cheated of some government bonds stolen in an earlier robbery.

But there was a big problem with the police's 'government bonds' theory too: it was based largely on evidence from a certain don Ciro Vittozzi, an obese priest who was godfather to one of Big 'Enry's children; don Ciro also had a record of helping *camorristi* evade justice. So the *Carabinieri* accused the police of believing a fib that the camorra had fed them. The government bonds story, they said, was fabricated by the camorra to protect the real culprits. The *Carabinieri* even prosecuted two police officers for falsifying evidence. They upped the stakes further still by bullying the robbers accused by the police into suing their accusers. New tangles were thus added to a case already matted with legal complexities.

Despite the best efforts of Abbatemaggio's handlers, his story was clearly a rickety construction. So he changed it. A year after his initial testimony, he issued a new improved version. The pivotal figure in Abbatemaggio's new narrative was now one Giovanni Rapi, known in camorra circles as 'Johnny the Teacher' because, when young, he had worked in local schools. He had also been a champagne dealer in France. Now in his fifties, Johnny the Teacher had risen to become Big 'Enry's *contaiuolo*—bookkeeper; he also ran a prestigious social club and gambling den. According to Abbatemaggio, Johnny the Teacher side-lined in fencing stolen goods. In other words, he was a rival in the same trade as the murder victim Gennaro Cuocolo. Because of this rivalry, and because Cuocolo was blackmailing him, Johnny the Teacher had asked Big 'Enry to do away with Cuocolo and his wife.

The obvious question raised by this new story was why Abbatemaggio had not accused Johnny the Teacher before, even though he had been one of the five men known to have dined on eel at Mimì a Mare on the night of the murders. Abbatemaggio replied that he had originally been afraid of two things: that no one would believe that an apparently respectable figure like Johnny the Teacher could be capable of such a horrific deed; and that he could not point the finger at the Teacher without implicating himself in some robberies he had carried out at the Teacher's behest. Abbatemaggio duly confessed to the robberies in question, and was arrested.

The stakes in the Cuocolo murder inquiry were rising inexorably.

Much of the prosecution evidence for the Cuocolo trial was made public while the case was still going through its drawn-out preparatory phases. (This is still the norm in Italy.) So the public followed the developing story closely, and newspapers quickly divided into opposing camps. Were Big 'Enry and his friends guilty or innocent? Who was right, the police or the *Carabinieri*? Some sensed a miscarriage of justice and mounted their own parallel investigations into both the crime and how the *Carabinieri* had obtained Abbatemaggio's confession. Others supported a clampdown on gangsters, regardless of the legal etiquette.

Much of the Socialist press joined the hue and cry, as was predictable given the success of the campaign that had led to the Casale trial and the blows struck against the 'high camorra' a few years earlier. But the Socialists now found they had a very unexpected ally in the right-wing daily, *Il Mattino*—the biggest-selling newspaper in Naples.

As we have already seen, *Il Mattino* liked to give flattering coverage to the Honoured Society's funerals; as the mouthpiece of the 'high camorra', it had also been among the most vocal in blasting the Saredo inquiry for throwing muck at Naples. *Il Mattino*'s venal but brilliant editor Edoardo Scarfoglio had close friends among the 'high camorra' politicians—men who helped him pay for his beloved yacht: with its permanent crew of eleven, it cost more than a Prefect's annual salary to run. Yet just a few years later, here was

Scarfoglio's paper cheering the *Carabinieri* on as they launched a new drive to cleanse the city. The turnaround in the newspaper's line was something of a mystery.

One part of the solution to that mystery is that the alliance between 'high' and 'low' camorras was inherently weak and messy. Those 'high camorra' politicians were quite prepared to make use of the 'low camorra' at election time, and to trade squalid favours and promises with them whatever the season. But they had no second thoughts about turning on their gangland auxiliaries when there was a public outcry demanding a few felons' heads on posts. (In Sicily, where the mafia was so intimately tied to the ruling class, such betrayals were much less likely.)

Sales are another reason for *Il Mattino*'s switch to an anti-camorra line. The grisly Cuocolo murders made the city flinch with fear, and turned organised crime into a red meat issue for a canny editor like Scarfoglio. Unnervingly for many Neapolitans, even the 'low camorra' now seemed to operate behind a façade of respectability. Gone were the bell-bottom trousers, garish waistcoats and pompadours that had marked the early *camorristi* out among the urban unwashed. Gangsters now blended in with the bourgeoisie and even the upper echelons. The expression 'camorra in straw-yellow gloves' (*in guanti gialli*, or *in guanti paglini*) was often used at the time and still provides a useful tag for the new breed of gentleman mobster. Gloves in a delicate, light-coloured suede were an accoutrement of wealth. So 'to wear straw-yellow gloves' meant to put on a false appearance of refinement, to disguise yourself among your social betters. If the 'high camorra'—one lodged within the government institutions like the mafia—did not really exist, the camorra in straw-yellow gloves certainly did. By the early twentieth century, *camorristi* were covering their tattoos in respectable garb and turning up uninvited among the well-to-do.

Johnny the Teacher, with his high-society gambling den, was an obvious example. As were the dead couple: Gennaro Cuocolo was a gangland fence, and his wife, Maria Cutinelli, was a former dockers' tart. Yet they lived in a well-furnished apartment across the road from the local police station. Cuocolo's *modus operandi* was to win the trust of well-off families so that he could enter their homes and find out what was worth stealing. He then gave precise instructions to his team of housebreakers on how to get in and what to take: tailored burglary.

But the most alarming embodiment of the *camorrista* in straw-yellow gloves to be revealed by the Cuocolo investigation was Gennaro De Marinis, known in criminal circles as '*o Mandriere* ('the Cowherd'), because he once worked in an abattoir. According to Abbatemaggio, the Cowherd had been the recipient of the letters from Lampedusa. The Cowherd certainly had an interesting underworld CV: he was now a jeweller, fence, loan shark and pimp so successful that he lived in a big house with servants.

The Cowherd was portrayed in the press as a new 'ultra-modern' type of *camorrista*. Sophisticated crooks like him infiltrated the cafés and clubs frequented by wealthy and dissolute young men. By offering introductions to attractive 'actresses', invitations to exclusive gambling dens, and cash loans 'between friends', they laid out a cushioned velvet path to blackmail and financial ruin for their victims.

There were also strong rumours in Naples that the Cowherd had inadvertently incurred the anger of royalty, and in doing so brought the wrath of the *Carabinieri* down upon the Honoured Society. The dashing Duke of Aosta, who was one of the most head-turning presences on the Neapolitan ball circuit, was shocked to find himself mixing with *camorristi* at sporting galas; and he was incandescent to hear that the Cowherd had even been bed-hopping among the ladies of the blue-blood set. So the Duke complained to his cousin the King, who had the police surrender control of the Cuocolo investigation to the *Carabinieri*. Faced with the camorra in straw-yellow gloves, the King told the *Carabinieri* to take the gloves off.

Like so much about the Cuocolo trial, these rumours are destined to remain unverified. Be that as it may, the Honoured Society had long since ceased to be confined to the slum quarters. The drama of the Cuocolo murders unfolded amid the scenery of bourgeois city life. Under the pergola of Mimì a Mare in Torre del Greco, where Big 'Enry and his men ate eel, and where the legendary tenor Caruso once lauded the *maccheroni alle vongole*. Or beneath the marble columns and ornamental lamps of the Galleria Umberto I, a prestigious new arcade built as part of the massive reconstruction programme following the cholera epidemic of 1884. Abbatemaggio explained that Big 'Enry and his cohorts had planned the Cuocolo murders here in the Galleria, in full view of the public, at the tables of the elegant Caffè Fortunio. The police confirmed that the Galleria was a regular camorra hang-out. Troublingly, the biggest rats from the alleyways now had the run of the city's swankier milieus too.

These were only the most visible symptoms of the sickness. Naples may not yet have produced a 'high camorra' to match the 'high mafia' of Palermo, but the *camorristi* still lurked in the city's every recess. Money lending was the key. Debt was a way of life in a city with little productive economic activity. The poor lived on the edge of destitution, addicted to the regular buzz of an illegal lottery ticket. The middle classes teetered just above the humiliations of poverty, addicted to the little luxuries that proclaimed their status to the ragged folk who lived on the lower floors. Upper-class betting addicts borrowed to keep betting. The whole town was in hock. As one local journalist commented, usury was to the Neapolitans what absinthe was to the French. The Honoured Society specialised in feeding that addiction.

As the Cuocolo investigation ground along, amid exposés and controversies, the publicity that figures like the Cowherd generated was only magnified by the squalid way the evidence was being gathered. The *camorristi* listed among the accused tried to buy their way out of jail—as was only to be expected. But newspapers, especially *Il Mattino*, were also happy to pay for a scoop, however much truth or falsity it contained. The *Carabinieri* seemed to be involved too. Crooks from across Naples gravitated towards the *Carabinieri* barracks where the investigation was based, hoping to sell a specially crafted witness statement. The shrewdest witnesses touted their story to all three sides, it was said.

The *Carabinieri* converted the strong rumours of a bidding war for testimonies into political leverage. In December 1910, in a secret report sent to their high command in Rome, they complained that the camorra was using every trick it knew to thwart their investigations. Even some newspapers had become hang-outs for crooks. Who could tell how high the camorra's influence now reached? Defeat in the Cuocolo case would do 'irreparable damage' to the Corps, and to the future of public order in Naples. The report cashed out in a revealing plea for 'moral and material support'.

> We regard it as necessary, for now, that funds in the region of 20,000 lire be made available. We need to subsidise able, well-paid and trustworthy informants so that they do not just sell themselves to the highest bidder. Otherwise they could provide false information that could give rise to serious incidents during the trial.

Or, put bluntly: 'Can we have more cash to pay our witnesses please?'

It is scarcely a surprise that, in the end, four years and nine months of investigation and legal preparation would be required to prosecute the camorra for the murders of Gennaro Cuocolo and Maria Cutinelli.

22

THE CRIMINAL ATLANTIC

THOSE YEARS OF INVESTIGATION WERE PACKED WITH INCIDENT. WHEN GENNARO Abbatemaggio gave his original statement to the police early in 1907, Big 'Enry fled to New York disguised as a stoker on a steamer.

By that time, Italian organised crime had long since entered a transoceanic age. The first mafia murder on American soil—the first we know about, at any rate—took place on Sunday 14 October 1888: the victim, a Palermitan by the name of Antonio Flaccomio, had just had a drink in a Sicilian restaurant when he was stabbed to death right in front of Manhattan's celebrated Cooper Union building. But the history of the mafia in America was under way well before that date. Sicilian fugitives from justice had been hiding out in the United States since before Italy was unified; New York and New Orleans were major outlets for Sicily's lemons, and therefore became the mafia's first bases in the USA.

At the turn of the twentieth century the tens of thousands who crossed the Atlantic every year became hundreds of thousands: an awe-inspiring 870,000 at the peak of the exodus in 1913. Emigration transformed the economy of the rural south: migrants sent money home and their absence drove up the wages of those who stayed behind.

Among the new tide of migrants there were also members of all three of Italy's major criminal associations. From being a local nuisance in New Orleans or Mulberry Bend, Italian organised crime quickly grew into a national problem for the United States.

The two shores of the criminal Atlantic were bound together by uncountable cunning threads. Just by tugging at one of those threads—Big 'Enry's dash to New York—we can glimpse just how vast and densely woven the history of Italo-American gangsterism really is. (Too vast to be told in these pages.)

Big 'Enry's bid for freedom did not last long: he was soon tracked down and sent back to Naples by Lieutenant Giuseppe 'Joe' Petrosino, a Salerno-born policeman who had risen through the ranks of the New York police by fighting Italian organised crime. We can think of Petrosino as a potential heir to the mantle just relinquished by Ermanno Sangiorgi: Petrosino was a suitably transatlantic cop for the new transatlantic crime.

In 1909, while the Cuocolo investigation was still progressing, Petrosino paid a brief visit to Italy in order to set up an independent information network on Italian-born gangsters. On 12 March 1909 he was standing under the Garibaldi statue in Palermo's piazza Marina when two men shot him dead. He left a widow, Adelina, and a daughter of the same name who was only four months old.

No one would ever be convicted of Petrosino's assassination. There were many lines of inquiry. The first, and most plausible, related to a gang of Sicilians whose counterfeiting operation Petrosino had disrupted in 1903 following the notorious 'body in the barrel' mystery—the body in question being one of the *mafiosi*'s victims. In 1905 the gang thought to be responsible for the 'body in the barrel' were joined by a *mafioso* and lemon dealer called Giuseppe Fontana—the same Giuseppe Fontana outrageously acquitted of killing banker Emanuele Notarbartolo the previous year. (In 1913, Fontana was shot dead in East Harlem.)

The chief suspect for the murder of Lieutenant Petrosino was, and still is, don Vito Cascio-Ferro, a Man of Honour who shuttled back and forth across the Atlantic in the early 1900s. Cascio-Ferro never stood trial because he had a seemingly impregnable alibi provided for him by a Sicilian MP who said that Cascio-Ferro was at his house when Petrosino died. The MP in question was called Domenico De Michele; as chance would have it, he was the son of 'Baron' Pietro De Michele, the Burgio rapist and *capomafia* involved in the 'fratricide' plot against Ermanno Sangiorgi in 1877.

In the course of their protracted investigations into the Petrosino murder, Italian police also questioned a Calabrian gangster: Antonio Musolino, the younger brother of the King of Aspromonte, whose cousin was suspected of having taken the contract to kill Lieutenant Petrosino. With surprising candour Antonio Musolino said he fled Santo Stefano in 1906 because he was afraid that his family's many enemies were trying to kill him. In Brooklyn, he joined up with some of his brother's former support team, among them the cousin suspected of the Petrosino murder. In a basement room in Elizabeth Street, the heart of Manhattan's Italian community, Musolino was initiated into a mafia gang that included both Calabrians and Sicilians. His name for the gang was the Black Hand—a catchall label for Italian gangsterism in America that derived from the menacing symbols (bloody daggers, black hands, and the like) that *mafiosi* sometimes drew on their extortion letters.

Musolino's brief story is typical of the way that the *picciotti* who travelled from Aspromonte to New York were absorbed into a much more powerful and well-established Sicilian organisation: the poor Lads with Attitude came under the influence of the 'middle-class criminals'. Where the Sicilian presence was not so strong, such as amid the lunar landscape of the mining districts of Pennsylvania and Ohio, the Calabrians brought across the Atlantic to cut coal were able to organise among themselves, and directly apply the methods and traditions they had learned at home.

Big 'Enry's brief trip to New York set in motion a third theory about the murder of Lieutenant Joe Petrosino, one implicating the camorra: Big 'Enry himself was the suspect. Interest in the Cuocolo case in the United States became intense after the Petrosino murder. The huge investigation in Naples seemed to have exposed something much more powerful than even the most disquieting speculation about the Black Hand in the United States. In the *New York Times*, journalist Walter Littlefield boldly asserted that Big 'Enry had issued the order to kill Petrosino, and that the Honoured Society he ruled was the umbrella organisation for all Italian-American criminals on both sides of the Atlantic.

> It is the fond hope of modern, civilised Italy that the trial will stamp out forever the largest and most perfectly organised society of criminals on earth, with its profitable ramifications in America and its willing slaves in Sicily. If this object shall be attained, it will be like severing the head from the body. It will mean the dissolution of the brains of the Black Hand in America and the Mafia in Sicily.

Around the world, the expectations surrounding the Cuocolo affair were becoming as acute as they were unrealistic.

The latest historical research reaches less panic-striken conclusions than Walter Littlefield. *Camorristi* from Naples and its surrounds were certainly operative in the United States at the time of Big 'Enry's visit, and some of them even created autonomous territorial pockets in Brooklyn, next door to the dominant Sicilian gangs. Johnny the Teacher, Big 'Enry's bookkeeper, seemingly had links with a savings institute in New York that gathered immigrants' money and sent it back home. Once Big 'Enry had been extradited, New York *camorristi* toured Italian-owned restaurants to pay for his lawyers.

Meanwhile the man at the centre of the approaching Cuocolo trial, the stoolpigeon Gennaro Abbatemaggio, spent his time in custody reading a serialised life of Joe Petrosino.

As the preparations for the Cuocolo trial ground on, the most newsworthy event of Italy's new media era occurred shortly after 5.20 a.m. on 28 December 1908 when a massive earthquake, with its epicentre in the narrow Straits separating Sicily and Calabria, devastated Messina, Reggio Calabria, and many of the towns and villages of Aspromonte. It is estimated that some 80,000 people died; many of the traumatised survivors emigrated to the New World. This cataclysm, the most lethal seismic event in the history of the west, aroused the whole world's sympathy for weeks.

Once the media agenda had moved on, the drab and sorry story of the reconstruction began. The stricken zones of Calabria had been a slack society before the disaster, they became slacker still in its aftermath. In Reggio Calabria, it took eleven years to rebuild the Prefecture, and six more to finish the Palace of Justice where the criminal courts were housed. The protracted struggle over reconstruction funding from the state became the new centre of gravity of political and economic life in much of the disaster area. The picciotteria wanted a share of the spoils. In Reggio Calabria, mobsters were spotted in the shebeens where the builders drank: such a large workforce offered plentiful opportunities to profit from gambling, extortion, robbery and gangmastering. In 1913 the police would go on to successfully prosecute eighty-three members of a mafia group operating across the city. They had a hierarchy of ranks, like *picciotto, camorrista*, bookkeeper and *fiorillo*—little flower. But of course this was a matter of interest only for the local press, as were other trials of the early twentieth century that showed that the picciotteria was spreading north into the other provinces of Calabria.

Of the people who saw the way the picciotteria was quietly entrenching itself in Calabrian society in the years before the First World War, precious few have left us any kind of testimony. One of them is the San Luca–born writer Corrado Alvaro. In 1955 he retrieved a vivid memory from his adolescence that encapsulated how the picciotteria had become what he called an 'aspect of the ruling class', a normal and broadly accepted part of community life—scarcely a generation after it emerged. On one occasion Alvaro returned home to San Luca, which had avoided the worst of the 1908 earthquake, from a term spent at his distant grammar school. His mother casually told him that his father was busy in the upstairs room with 'men from the association'. Alvaro, full of his textbook notions of public-spiritedness, assumed she meant a group promoting some kind of local interest. 'So there is an association in our village at long last?' His mother gave a flat reply: 'It's the association for delinquency'.

23

GENNARO ABBATEMAGGIO: Genialoid

AT LAST, IN MARCH 1911, THE CUOCOLO TRIAL OPENED IN THE CAVERNOUS BAROQUE church that served as the Court of Assizes in Viterbo, a small city between Rome and Florence that had been chosen to host the whole show for fear that a Naples jury might be swayed either by camorra threats, or by the camorra fever the case was generating.

Newspaper readers and newsreel viewers around the world could finally see the eloquent pictures of the defendants crammed into a large cage in the court, and put faces to the quirky nicknames in the Cuocolo story.

For his own protection, Gennaro Abbatemaggio was confined to a smaller cage by himself. Now twenty-eight years old, small and well-dressed, he had a long razor-slash scar running down his cheek to the point of his chin. He wore a short, pomaded moustache that turned perkily upwards at its points to form inverted commas around his mouth.

'The camorra is a career', he began in an attractive baritone, 'which goes from the rank of *picciotto* to that of *camorrista*, passing through intermediate ranks.' He joined the camorra in 1899, at age sixteen, as a *picciotto*. In 1903 he was promoted to the rank of *camorrista* in the Stella section of the Honoured Society.

> *Camorristi* in Naples exploit prostitution greedily . . . They demand a *camorra* [a bribe] on everything, and especially on all the shady activities that, precisely because they are illegal, have to pay the camorra's tax. They extort the *camorra* on illegal betting, on the gambling dens that cover Naples like a rash. They extort the *camorra* on sales at public

The stool pigeon who destroyed the camorra: a dapper Gennaro
Abbatemaggio gives evidence from the cage built to protect him
from his former comrades, 1911.

auctions, and even show their arrogance during national and local elections . . . The camorra is so base that it takes money, sometimes even
really tiny payments, to massacre or disfigure people. The camorra is involved in loan sharking. In fact its biggest influence is on loan sharking.

Abbatemaggio went on to describe the camorra as 'a kind of low-grade
Freemasonry'. His description of the camorra's rules, structure and methods
confirmed the criminological 'textbooks' that had been so popular in Naples
for years. He ended with a passionate plea.

My assertions are the absolute truth. I want to carry my head high, and
look anyone who might dare to doubt them straight in the face.

Abbatemaggio then began to reel off his account of how the Cuocolos
came to be so brutally slain on that June night nearly five years previously.

The letters from the Lampedusa penal colony. The lobbying by Johnny the Teacher and the Cowherd to have Gennaro Cuocolo punished. How the plenary meeting of the camorra's top brass at the Bagnoli trattoria approved the decision. How Big 'Enry organised the executions in a series of meetings in the Galleria. The savage actions of the two teams of killers. The dinner at Mimì a Mare. The story of Cuocolo's G.C. pinkie ring.

Abbatemaggio stood and spoke for so long that he had to cut a hole in his shoe to relieve the pressure on a severe blister. During breaks he passed his fan mail on to friendly hacks and explained that, if he had ever had the chance to study, he too would have become a journalist.

Il Mattino's correspondent had no doubts about Abbatemaggio's sincerity. Here was 'a man endowed with marvellous physical and mental solidity, and with balanced and robust willpower' the Neapolitan daily opined. It was inconceivable that he could have dreamed everything up as the defence claimed.

> Even the most audacious imagination would not have been able to create all the interconnecting lines of this judicial drama. Every detail he gives is a page taken directly from life—albeit from a life of crime: it is intense, keen, overwhelming.

The defence also thought that Abbatemaggio's testimony was dramatic, although in a very different sense. In cross-examination, one lawyer announced that he would prove that this supposed inside witness had gleaned all he knew about the Honoured Society from downmarket plays. 'Has Abbatemaggio ever been to the San Ferdinando Theatre to see a performance of *The Foundation of the Camorra*?' Abbatemaggio replied calmly that he only liked comic opera—*The Merry Widow* and the like. 'Besides, why would I need to watch the camorra performed in the theatre, when I was part of it?'

The quip was greeted with approving laughs from the public gallery.

The defence also tried to discredit Abbatemaggio by questioning his sanity: he was a 'hysterical epileptic', they claimed, in the dubious psychological jargon of the day. One expert who closely examined him disagreed, but said nonetheless that he was a particularly fascinating case. Again and again Abbatemaggio responded to those who doubted his evidence with names, dates, and a torrent of other particulars. Perhaps he could be classified as a 'genialoid', a rare blend of the genius and the lunatic; his 'mnemonic and intuitive capacities are indeed phenomenal'.

Abbatemaggio's credibility as a witness also depended on his ability to tell a story about himself, a story of redemption. He claimed to have found personal moral renewal by exposing the camorra's secrets to the law. He had been saved, he said, by his love for the young girl he had recently married. 'Camorrist told all to win his bride', was the *New York Times* headline.

Meanwhile, in the defendants' cage, camorra boss Big 'Enry scowled and scoffed. Wiry, sunken eyed and heavy jawed, he had a disconcerting horizontal scar that ran from the corner of his mouth out towards his right ear. He wore mourning black because his younger brother Ciro, one of the five men who ate at Mimì a Mare on the night of the murders, had died of a heart attack in custody. During Abbatemaggio's testimony Big 'Enry was heard to mutter the occasional comment. 'This louse is like a gramophone, and if you turn his handle he goes on and on.' The label stuck: for the rest of the trial, the defendants would refer to Abbatemaggio as 'the gramophone'.

When Big 'Enry's own turn to give evidence came he made an impression that initially surprised many by how eloquent and convincing it was. He explained that he ran a shop in piazza San Ferdinando selling horse fodder—bran and carobs. He was also a horse dealer who traded with military supply bases in Naples and surrounding towns; he had made a lot of money exporting mules to the British army in the Transvaal during the Boer war. He denied being a *camorrista* but admitted that he was rather hot-headed and did sometimes lend money at very high interest rates. It was all a question of character.

Gentlemen of the jury, you need to bear in mind that we are Neapolitans. We are sons of Vesuvius. There is a strange violent tendency in our blood that comes from the climate.

The *Carabinieri*, Big 'Enry concluded, were victimising him and had bribed witnesses. He had suffered so much in prison that he was losing his hair.

Several policemen of various ranks were subsequently called to testify, and reeled off Big 'Enry's catalogue of convictions. He had begun his career as a small-time pimp. Like many other *camorristi*, Big 'Enry dealt in horse fodder because it provided a good front for extorting money from hackney carriage drivers and rigging the market in horses and mules. They explained that he provided the protection for the high society gambling den run by Johnny the Teacher, and confirmed that he was the effective boss of the camorra. They noted that the nominal boss was one Luigi Fucci, known as *'o gassusaro*—'the fizzy drink man'—for the prosaic reason that he ran a stall selling fizzy drinks. Big 'Enry used him as a patsy, while keeping the real power in his own hands.

Big 'Enry began to look like what he really was: a villain barely concealed behind a gentlemanly façade. Not many of the other defendants came across

The accused arrive in Viterbo for the most sensational camorra trial in history, 1911. Following the brutal slaying of a former *camorrista* and his wife, the Cuocolo case generated worldwide interest. The man in the bowler hat is Luigi Fucci, 'the fizzy drink man', and nominally the supreme boss of the Honoured Society.

much better. Arthur Train, a former assistant District Attorney in New York, was one of many American observers at the trial. He noted that

> the Camorrists are much the best dressed persons in the court room. Closer scrutiny reveals the merciless lines in most of the faces, and the catlike shiftiness of the eyes. One fixed impression remains—that of the aplomb, intelligence, and cleverness of these men, and the danger to a society in which they and their associates follow crime as a profession.

The Cowherd, the 'ultra-modern *camorrista*' whose sexual conquests among the ladies of the aristocracy had reputedly so enraged the Duke of Aosta, was a particularly elegant figure. He too tried to present himself as an honest businessman who had begun by selling bran and carobs and had risen to become a successful jeweller. Only a freakish chain of bad luck had led him to spend several short spells in jail for extortion, theft and taking part in a gunfight, he said. The Cowherd's refined appearance was compromised by the two long scars on his cheek. 'Fencing wounds', he protested. He did at least make a telling point about the notorious ring engraved with Gennaro Cuocolo's initials: he demonstrated that it was not big enough to fit on his own little finger—and he was a much smaller man than Cuocolo.

Individui della mala vita sfregiati
(*Riproduzione dal vero mercè il metodo foto-xilografico*)

The *sfregio*, or disfiguring scar, was one of many visible signs of camorra power in Naples. *Camorristi* handed out *sfregi* as punishments both to one another and to the prostitutes they pimped. Sicilian *mafiosi*, by contrast, refrained from both pimping and the *sfregio*.

Few of the accused had plausible alibis. Some denied knowing Abbatemaggio, only to be flatly contradicted by other credible witnesses. One *camorrista* thought it was a good idea to have his defence printed in pamphlet form. In it he admitted that the camorra existed but claimed that it was a brotherhood of well-meaning individuals who liked to defend the weak against bullies. This brotherhood's ruling ethos was what he termed *cavalleria rusticana*—'rustic chivalry'. Evidently this particular defendant was trying to apply the lessons from the Sicilian mafia's successful ploy in earlier trials. He cited camorra history too, concluding his pamphlet on a patriotic note by recalling how, half a

A CONTRAST TO THE DECORUM OF A BRITISH CRIMINAL TRIAL: TURBULENCE IN THE CAMORRA CASE.

Disorder in court. The chaotic scenes at the Cuocolo trial baffle and repulse observers across the world. From the *Illustrated London News*.

century ago, when Italy was unified, *camorristi* had fought Bourbon tyranny and contributed to 'the political redemption of Southern Italy'.

The judge in Viterbo attracted much criticism for allowing the defendants themselves to cross-examine witnesses. These exchanges prolonged proceedings enormously, and sometimes descended into verbal brawls. One *camorrista*, a fearsome one-eyed brute who stood accused of smashing Gennaro Cuocolo's skull with a club, shrieked colourful insults across the court at Abbatemaggio.

You're a piece of treachery! And you've sold yourself just so you can eat good *maccheroni* in prison. But you'll choke on those nice tasty bits of mozzarella. You'll see, you lying hoaxer!

Shut up you louse! Shut up you pederast! I'd spit in your face if I wasn't afraid of dirtying my spit.

Abbatemaggio had no such worry, and spat back across the court into the defendants' cage.

Weeks and weeks of witness statements, angry cross-examinations, and scuffles went by. Public interest slowly flagged as spring turned to summer. But it revived in July and August 1911 when the two great heroes of the Cuocolo spectacular were called to give their statements. In the words of the *New York Times*, these were the *Carabinieri* who 'finally succeeded in penetrating the black vitals of the criminal hydra and are now ready to exhibit the foul, noxious mass at the Viterbo Assizes'. They were Sergeant Erminio Capezzuti and Captain Carlo Fabroni.

Sergeant Capezzuti was Abbatemaggio's handler: he had persuaded the informant to break the code of *omertà* and protected him afterwards; he had also led the search team that claimed to have found the G.C. pinkie ring.

Ludicrously overblown tales of Capezzuti's heroism had circled the globe between the murders and the trial. It was said that he had disguised himself as a *camorrista* and even undergone a ritual knife fight and been oathed into membership of the Honoured Society. The *New York Times* claimed he had pulled off 'one of the most remarkable feats of detection ever accomplished'. The *Washington Times* reported that Capezzuti was set to become a monk after the trial because this was the only way he could protect himself from the camorra's revenge. Every newspaper in the world seemed to compare Capezzuti to Sherlock Holmes.

It is not clear quite where some of these fables about the 'Sherlock Holmes' of Naples began. Certainly little to justify them surfaced when Capezzuti came to Viterbo. The Sergeant stuck calmly to every detail of the prosecution case, including the G.C. ring story. His evidence was measured and, for those expecting Sherlock Holmes, rather dull.

Captain Carlo Fabroni's time on his feet was anything but dull. The *Carabiniere* officer who was in charge of the whole Cuocolo investigation hailed from the Marche region, and had arrived in Naples only shortly after the Cuocolo murders. One of the first things he did, he explained, was to read up on all the criminology published about the camorra. What he had learned during the course of his investigations precisely corresponded with what he had read.

As Captain Fabroni's testimony continued, his self-confidence tumesced into arrogance. He brushed aside any suspicions that Abbatemaggio might not be telling the whole truth.

With my extremely honourable past in the military I would blush at the very thought of inducing a man to commit an act of nameless infamy by inventing an accusation.

Captain Carlo Fabroni, who turned the
Cuocolo murder case into an assault on
the whole Honoured Society.

Under cross-examination, Fabroni provoked the defence at every opportunity, and scattered accusations that the police, politicians and even the judiciary were in cahoots with the camorra. On one occasion, he claimed that
Big 'Enry had only been acquitted on an earlier extortion charge because his
defence lawyer was the judge's brother; the lawyers all took off their robes
and walked out in protest at this collective insult to their profession.

But Captain Fabroni's most startling move was to drop a hand grenade
in the lap of his key witness. Since the first hearings, there had been much
comment on the sheer vividness of Abbatemaggio's narrative. The 'gramophone' told the court the order in which the *camorristi* stabbed each of the
victims, and even the abuse they had shouted while they were doing it. Was
it really plausible that the killers would tell Abbatemaggio about their own
bloody actions in such detail?

Captain Fabroni's counter to this question was a highly risky move to
undercut the stoolpigeon's character, but keep the testimony intact. Abbatemaggio had not broken the code of *omertà* because he wanted a cleaner life
with his new wife, Fabroni explained: that was just a cover story. Fear was
Abbatemaggio's real motive—fear that the camorra would kill him as it had
done the Cuocolos. The reason for this fear was that he had tried to blackmail
his fellow criminals. And the reason he knew enough to blackmail them was
because, in all probability, he had been present at one or both of the murder
scenes. Perhaps Abbatemaggio was himself one of the killers. As Captain Fabroni concluded, 'It's just not possible to reconstruct such an appalling tragedy in every particular unless you have taken part in it in some way.'

Having taken in Captain Fabroni's words, the world's press immediately upended their sentimental opinions of the 'gramophone'. One Australian newspaper called the informer 'a rascal of almost inconceivably deep dye'. Nor was Captain Fabroni the only man in Viterbo to point the finger at Abbatemaggio: the Cowherd also accused him of the murders, and referred to him constantly as 'the assassin'. Thus both prosecution and defence seem to have believed that Abbatemaggio was one of the Cuocolo hit men. Quite what proportions of truth and cynical tactics were in these allegations may never be known. What is certain is that Abbatemaggio was never formally indicted with the murders.

The Viterbo trial still had a year to run when Captain Fabroni finished giving evidence. Through the months that followed, each of the defendants and many of the witnesses were called back time and again to answer further questions. But a decisive shift in the burden of proof had already taken place. For all its unfathomable obscurities, the Cuocolo case was now a simple credibility contest: either the accused were guilty, or the *Carabinieri* were slanderers. On one side was a cage full of crooked figures with scarred faces who gave mutually contradictory statements. On the other side were Captain Fabroni and Sergeant Capezzuti. Granted, these two *Carabinieri* had failed to live up to their 'Sherlock Holmes' billing. But it was hard to believe that they could be so devious as to fabricate the whole prosecution case.

24

The Strange Death of
The Honoured Society

At just after five thirty in the afternoon of 8 July 1912, the forty-one accused were summoned back into the packed Viterbo courtroom to hear their fate. Almost all of them failed to move, immobilised by dread. Their nerves were understandable given the scale of the proceedings that were about to reach a climax: 779 witnesses had been heard in the course of sixteen exhausting months of hearings.

Finally, the familiar gaunt figure of Big 'Enry appeared, alone, in the defendants' cage. He looked around him. The lugubrious tension was broken only by the staccato sobs emitted by one of the defence lawyers. Big 'Enry saw, heard and understood which way the verdict had gone. He then destroyed the silence by aiming a shrill cackle across at the elevated box where the jury sat.

You've found us guilty. So we are murderers? But why, if you are our judges, have you got your heads bowed? Why won't you look me in the face? *We* are the ones who have been murdered! *You* are the murderers!

More of the accused filed into the cage and began bawling, pleading with the jury and the public, screaming at Abbatemaggio. Suddenly a long jet of blood spurted out onto the marble floor. The Cowherd had used a piece of glass to cut his own throat. Doctors rushed to save him and the guards carried him away to recover.

One by one the defendants gave up their protests and flopped down onto their benches to weep. The loudest and angriest of them, Johnny the Teacher, also took the longest to exhaust himself. He alone was still raving when the Clerk of the Court could finally make himself audible and read out the guilty verdicts. The judge handed down more than four centuries of prison to those found guilty of murder and membership of a criminal association, among other crimes.

A crusade for justice, with no prisoners taken? Or a gross abuse of the state's power? In the aftermath of the Cuocolo trial, public opinion remained divided as to what this courtroom spectacular actually meant. The Cuocolo trial certainly achieved the highly desirable aim of striking at the camorra. Yet everyone in Italy could see that it had achieved that aim by lengthy, shambolic and perhaps even dubious means. The Cuocolo murders presented the Italian state with a unique opportunity to show off its fight against organised crime to a vast new audience at home and abroad. The result was confusion at home and national embarrassment abroad. Newspaper leader writers all over the globe lamented the state of Italian justice. The press in the United States was scornful: the trial had been a 'bear garden', a 'circus', a 'cage of monkeys'. Even an observer more sympathetic to Italy, like Arthur Train, could only plead with his readers to understand how difficult it was to administer justice when 'every person participating in or connected with the affair is an Italian, sharing in the excitability and emotional temperament of his fellows'. Still more sober, and no less damning, was the appraisal of the *Bulawayo Chronicle* in what is now Zimbabwe, where cinemagoers had seen newsreels from Viterbo.

> The Camorra trial stands as monumental evidence to the incapacity and inadequacy of the present system of criminal procedure in Italy.

Had more than a tiny minority of magistrates and lawyers been ready to heed them, there were plenty of legal lessons about the fight against camorra-type crime to be learned from the Cuocolo trial: about Italy's hazy laws against criminal associations; about the ungainly, agonisingly slow, and peculiarly Italian marriage of investigative justice with an adversarial system.

The most important lessons came from the story of Gennaro Abbatemaggio. Even on the *Carabinieri's* account, his treatment was a legal outrage: for example, after first talking to the *Carabinieri*, he spent many months hiding out in a remote part of Campania in what happened to be Sergeant 'Sherlock Holmes' Capezzuti's home village. As Ermanno Sangiorgi found out as long ago as the 'fratricide' case of the 1870s, the authorities had absolutely no guidelines on how to handle defectors from the ranks of the criminal brotherhoods. What kind of deal should the law strike with them in return for what they knew? How could there be any certainty that what they said was true? Italian legislation offered no answers to these questions, and no way of distinguishing good police intelligence gathering from co-managing crime. Because the lessons of the Cuocolo trial were never learned, those questions would continue to vex, and continue to undermine the struggle against organised crime in southern Italy.

And yet remarkably, after the trial in Viterbo, there were to be no more reports of criminal activity by the sect that had plagued Naples since before Italy was unified. Somehow Gennaro Abbatemaggio, and the judicial monster he helped create, ended the history of the Honoured Society.

The trial in Viterbo left a legacy of puzzles. The hardest of them all is why, when so many earlier camorra prosecutions had merely pruned the branches of the Honoured Society, the Cuocolo case actually struck at its root.

One possible answer lies in the evidence given by the Neapolitan police, who had not enjoyed a good press in the build up to the Viterbo trial. Not only had they been overshadowed by the *Carabinieri*, in the persons of Sergeant Capezzuti and Captain Fabroni; but they had been discredited by the insinuation that some of them were hand in glove with *camorristi*. Italians were quite ready to believe that this charge had purchase. Everyone knew that the police used the camorra to lend a hand at election time on behalf of the Interior Ministry. In Naples, as in Palermo, the police and gangsters co-managed crime. For all these reasons, evidence from policemen received only desultory media coverage.

Yet for the same reasons, the police understood better than anyone else how the Honoured Society worked. Just as importantly, because of their acrimonious rivalry with the *Carabinieri*, the police who gave evidence in the Cuocolo trial had no corporate interest in backing up either the *Carabinieri's* textbook account of the camorra, or Abbatemaggio's story. So, in retrospect, the picture of the camorra the police gave the Viterbo jury becomes all the more credible—a picture of a criminal organisation that was already in serious decline before Gennaro Cuocolo and his wife were knifed to death.

Take agent Ludovico Simonetti, who spent four years as a street cop in Big 'Enry's own quarter of the city. Simonetti had no problem admitting to the judge in Lucca that the police regularly used camorra informers, and he was happy to confirm Big 'Enry's leading rank inside the criminal organisation. But Simonetti's evidence was most interesting where it diverged from the prosecution's line; it displays none of the frozen, 'idiot's guide' quality of what Captain Fabroni and the 'gramophone' testified.

Agent Simonetti explained that the Honoured Society was founded on two principles: dividing the profits of crime out among the members; and blind obedience or *omertà*. 'The camorra was so powerful that it could be called a state within a state.' *Was* so powerful: the camorra's supremacy was emphatically a thing of the past. Simonetti went on to say that the principles upon which the criminal sect had been founded were crumbling.

> Now the booty goes to whoever did the job, not to the collectivity. Except on the odd occasion when some more energetic boss manages to extract a bribe. The underworld doesn't have the blind obedience it once did: there are no longer any punishments.

Agent Simonetti pinpoints a crucial new weakness here. The Honoured Society had lost its ability systematically to 'tax' criminals—to extract bribes from them, in other words. Once, by means of this kind of extortion, *camorristi* had presided over petty criminals in the same way that a state presides over its subjects. Now that the power to tax crime had faded, the camorra was beginning to look like just one gang among many. For that reason, it had become more vulnerable to the kind of humdrum underworld rivalries that regularly tore other gangs apart. Blind obedience had gone.

Simonetti made it clear that clusters of *camorristi* still did all the things they had done for decades: robbing, pimping, loan sharking, rigging auctions, bullying voters, extorting money from traders, running the numbers racket. Almost all the most important fences in the city were still members of the Honoured Society. *Camorristi* still respected one another. The individual camorra cells in each quarter of the city still existed. But these days their power came simply from the ferocity and charisma of the individual criminals. In Simonetti's words, the camorra as an 'organised collectivity' did not exist anymore.

The old sacraments were losing their magic. In the past, for a criminal to be elevated to membership of the Honoured Society was a life-changing rite of passage. Now existing members used the initiation ritual as a way of flattering other hoods and wheedling cash out of them. As agent Simonetti put it, 'Once it was a serious business that required a blood baptism. Now it's just a baptism in wine.'

Other grassroots police officers enriched Simonetti's account. One of them, Giovanni Catalano, had often seen Abbatemaggio eating pizza with Big 'Enry, Johnny the Teacher and other top *camorristi* in the old days. The camorra certainly still existed, Catalano went on to stress: in virtually every convicted felon's police file there was a telegram from a prison governor wanting to know if the crook in question was a member of the Honoured Society so he could be put in the segregated wing reserved for *camorristi*. But, Catalano went on, the potboilers on the camorra that filled the shelves of Neapolitan bookshops were based on out of date sources, and designed only to satisfy 'readers' morbid curiosity'. The chiefs of the Honoured Society were simply not capable of imposing total obedience now. Camorra tribunals had gone for good. The very fact that a *camorrista* like Gennaro Abbatemaggio could go over to the law was itself a sign of how much things had changed.

The most vivid police testimony of all was the last. A third officer, Felice Ametta, began by joking that he had started his career at the same time as many of the men in the cage had started theirs. He reeled off a list of the Honoured Society's top bosses since he had first arrived in Naples in 1893; he knew them all. But this was a time of crisis for the organisation, a time of infighting. Ametta then recalled the bizarre and revealing incident that led directly to the rise of the new supreme boss, Big 'Enry—an incident that beautifully encapsulates the divided state of the camorra in the early years of the twentieth century.

Needless to say, Big 'Enry was listening intently as Ametta began to tell his tale to the court.

The story revolved around a thief who wanted to be admitted to the Honoured Society. What made his case unusual and controversial was that many *camorristi* suspected the thief of being a pederast. In the old days there would have been no debate: cuckolded husbands, thieves and pederasts were all banned. Accordingly, the then *contaiuolo* (bookkeeper) of the Honoured Society invoked the old rules and obstinately refused to make him a member. But opinion within the camorra was split; the 'pederast' was lobbying hard among his *camorrista* friends. The dispute rumbled on until one evening, in a tavern in the Forcella quarter, the 'pederast' provoked a fight in which the *contaiuolo* suffered serious head injuries. The Honoured Society was suddenly on the brink of a civil war.

Felice Ametta heard news of this potentially explosive rift soon after the fight. Hard-nosed cop that he was, and very used to the business of using the camorra to manage crime, he called Big 'Enry in for a meeting in a coffee bar in via Tribunali.

Hardly had these words sounded across the Lucca courtroom, than the jury swivelled in their seats at the sound of Big 'Enry detonating with rage.

Called *me* in for a meeting? I'm no stoolie! Never! I'd go to jail a thousand times before I stained myself by arranging a meeting with a policeman!

From a man who denied even being a *camorrista*, this was a highly revealing outburst.

When calm was restored, Ametta went on to explain that Big 'Enry took control of the Honoured Society at precisely this delicate moment, presenting himself as the man who could bring about peace. His leadership platform involved turning the clock back. In Ametta's words

> Big 'Enry wanted to found a kind of old-style camorra, with rigid regulations and statutes, with a tribunal including two advocates for first trials, four advocates for appeal hearings and a general secretary.

There were guffaws when the court heard this elevated legal vocabulary being applied to the sordid affairs of hoodlums. But Ametta's point was a serious and extremely insightful one. What he was implying was that the textbook camorra as Captain Fabroni and Gennaro Abbatemaggio had portrayed it in Viterbo was no longer a reality on the streets of Naples. Instead it existed only as a political project put forward by a new leader desperate—for his own selfish reasons, no doubt—to hold the Honoured Society's rapidly fragmenting structure together.

Thus when Big 'Enry was arrested, the last paladin of the old order was brought down and the Honoured Society was allowed to fall into ruin. The Cuocolo trial did not exactly destroy the camorra, it destroyed the only man who still believed in the camorra, who still wanted to take the criminological textbooks on the Honoured Society and make reality fit them once more.

The street cops who gave evidence at the Cuocolo trial give us a close-up description of the Honoured Society's decline. But being street cops, they did not have to try and *explain* that decline. So their vivid evidence begs a bit of educated guesswork from the historian.

In essence, it seems, the old Honoured Society could not cope with the way Naples was modernising. With Italy becoming more democratic, politicians were gaining access to greater sources of patronage of jobs, housing, and other favours. As a result, undergovernment could reach further down into the low city, competing with the camorra to win clienteles among the poor. The camorra's bosses were unable to respond by mutating into a 'high camorra', by producing their *own* politicians, by *becoming* the state rather than just performing services for *pieces* of the state. The Honoured Society remained at heart what it had always been: a criminal elite among the ragged poor. The leap from the tenements to the salons was just too great. And in the new, more-democratic age, when Neapolitan political life became as visible as it was volatile, the camorra had no political mask, leaving it too conspicuous and isolated to survive a serious onslaught by the forces of order. In short: the top *camorristi* might put on their straw-yellow gloves, but they could not cover the scars on their faces.

Here a comparison with the Honoured Societies of Calabria and Sicily is instructive. The picciotteria shared the camorra's lowly origins. But they did rapidly merge with local politics and—just as importantly—Calabria was all but invisible to public opinion in the rest of the country. The Sicilian mafia orbited around a city that rivalled Naples for its importance to national political life: Italy could not be governed if Palermo and Naples were not governed. Yet unlike the camorra, the mafia had its own politicians, its Raffaele Palizzolos and Leonardo Avellones, to say nothing of the Prime Ministers and shipping magnates who were its friends. Even the mafia's killers could rely on being shrouded by the elite if they fell afoul of the law. Big 'Enry and the other *camorristi* were left naked by comparison.

Camorra legend has it that not long after the Cuocolo verdict, on the evening of 25 May 1915, the few remaining *camorristi* met in a cellar bar in the Sanità area of the city and dissolved the Honoured Society forever.

What of Gennaro Abbatemaggio? Once the newsreel cameras had ceased to whirr, the man who had snuffed out the Honoured Society followed an eccentric and even self-destructive path through life. The redemption parable that he tried to sell to the Viterbo jury would return to mock him.

Abbatemaggio was caught defrauding two members of the Cuocolo trial jury in a strange deal to buy some cheese, and spent time in jail as a result. Subsequently, during the Great War, he won a sergeant's stripes with the *arditi* ('the audacious'), a volunteer corps of shock troops who raided trenches with grenade and dagger. In 1919 he returned victorious from the front into the arms of the wife who had reputedly saved him from a life of crime—only to discover that she had been having an affair with one of the *Carabinieri* ordered to protect him from the camorra's vengeance. His marriage fell apart, and he attempted suicide in January 1920.

Then came Fascism. Abbatemaggio embraced the Fascist revolution in Florence, murdering and plundering with one of Mussolini's most militant and corrupt squads.

Perhaps, through all these vicissitudes, Gennaro Abbatemaggio was trying to make a fresh start, to fashion a new self. If so, his efforts failed. Something was gnawing away inside his mind. On 9 May 1927, he finally found release from the inner torment when he deposited a statement with a lawyer in Rome. The statement began as follows.

I feel it is my duty, dictated by my conscience, to make the following declaration. I do so belatedly, but still in time to bring an end to the worst miscarriage of justice in the legal annals of the world.

I proclaim that the defendants found guilty in the Cuocolo trial are innocent.

The man Big 'Enry had called 'the gramophone' went on to explain that he had played a pre-recorded lie of fabulous complexity and detail in Viterbo. The reason he had made up all that evidence was that the *Carabinieri* had threatened to charge him with the Cuocolo murders unless he helped them. They had arranged his release from prison and given him money and wedding presents. They had bribed key defence witnesses and leading journalists, spending a grand total of 300,000 lire on sweeteners during the case. In particular, they had spent 40,000 lire on a bribe for *Il Mattino* editor Edoardo Scarfoglio who, in return for this hearty contribution towards the cost of running his yacht, became the prosecution's cheerleader through the whole affair.

The trial that destroyed the Honoured Society of Naples was a giant bluff. An early release was rapidly granted to the *camorristi* convicted a decade and a half earlier—or at least to those who had not died or gone insane in the interim.

The uncertainties about the Cuocolo case remain legion to this day. Ultimately, there is no way to tell whether even Gennaro Abbatemaggio's 1927 confession exposed the full facts. He was an unreliable witness in Viterbo, and is doomed to remain one. We still cannot know for certain whether Big 'Enry and his crew murdered the Cuocolo couple. We still cannot explain the sheer ferocity with which the Cuocolos were slain that June night in 1906. Why stab Gennaro Cuocolo so many times? Why move his body and put it on display? Why mutilate his wife's genitals? Why risk the public outcry and political pressure that would inevitably follow such unprecedented acts of butchery?

My own view, for what it is worth, is that Big 'Enry was indeed guilty: the *Carabinieri* got the right man, but fabricated the evidence they needed to convict him. Even the street cops who testified in Lucca thought that the Cuocolo murders were a camorra vendetta.

The Cuocolo murders might make sense as part of Big 'Enry's political project, his plan to inject new vigour into the Honoured Society's wilting traditions. Big 'Enry's reasoning in the run-up to the murders ran along the following lines. Gennaro Cuocolo used to be a big player in the Honoured Society, an impresario of highly lucrative burglaries. But he had left the camorra and gone his own way; he now belonged to a bigger, less rule-bound criminal world. His wife could now be a partner rather than a streetwalker to be exploited and expended as camorra traditions demanded. Gennaro Cuocolo therefore represented a double threat: he was both a rival in the struggle to control the strategic market in stolen goods; and he was a living demonstration that the Honoured Society was falling apart. So camorra justice had to be done as it was in the old days. More flagrantly than the old days. More savagely than the old days. In a last, hopeless attempt to bring back the old days.

Whoever really murdered the Cuocolos, the whole affair became an awkward and contested memory for Naples. Abbatemaggio's final confession certainly reversed the verdicts, but in doing so it only compounded the debacle. Thus, even in Italy's epoch-making moment of victory over the Neapolitan Honoured Society, truth and the law had been disgraced. For that reason, among many others, the camorra was destined to enjoy a long and bloody afterlife.

Between the crises of the 1890s and the First World War, Italy had lurched towards democracy and an open arena for public debate in the press. At the same time it had tried to fight organised crime. The results, in both cases, were distinctly mixed.

Italy entered the Great War as a deeply divided country. It emerged from it victorious, but on the brink of falling apart: its fragile democracy soon collapsed under the political strains that were the war's immediate legacy. Fascism took power. And where democracy failed in the battle with organised crime, Fascist dictatorship would trumpet success.

Two weeks after Gennaro Abbatemaggio's final confession, on 26 May 1927, Benito Mussolini delivered one of the most important speeches of his life—the Ascension Day speech, as it was known. In it he welded his political credibility to the war against gangsters with more conviction than any of his liberal predecessors. Not only that, he proclaimed that the end of mob rule on Italian territory was imminent.

PART VI

MUSSOLINI'S SCALPEL

25

SICILY: The last struggle with the mafia

FASCISM WAS FOUNDED IN MARCH 1919 BY A HANDFUL OF AGGRESSIVELY NATIONALISTIC war veterans in Milan. The first stage of the movement's rise was the most overtly violent: Fascist squads broke strikes, ransacked trades union offices, killed and crippled selected leftists, and generally posed as defenders of the *Patria* against the red menace. The typical *squadrista* dressed in a black shirt and fez and his signature weapons were the cudgel and the can of castor-oil, an industrial lubricant that was force-fed to victims, bringing on violent stomach cramps and diarrhoea.

Many industrialists and landowners were delighted at this ruthless purge of the Left. Prefects and senior police officers often stood by and did nothing. The old schemers in parliament were confident that they could domesticate the black-shirted bully-boys once the left-wing subversives had been humbled.

Mussolini soon showed that this confidence was badly misplaced. In October 1922, the Duce staged the 'March on Rome', daring a vacillating government to hand over power to him, or face a black-shirted invasion of the capital and the risk of civil war. Mussolini did not blink, and was duly installed as Prime Minister.

Before the March on Rome, the Blackshirt movement was overwhelmingly concentrated in the north and centre of Italy. However, when Fascism took power, it suddenly found that it had won lots of new southern supporters. With their traditional shamelessness, the old political grandees of southern

223

Calabria and western Sicily, along with their mafia campaign-managers and tawdry clienteles, rushed to cosy up to Fascism now that it promised access to the Roman patronage trough. In the south, the *Partito Nazionale Fascista* risked being hollowed out into an alibi for the same old politics of faction and favour that so suited the gangsters. The few original Fascists were dismayed. Just a few weeks after the March on Rome, the Fascist groups in Reggio Calabria and Palmi were found to be suffering from 'acute factionitis'. In Sicily, early uptake Blackshirts decried the 'Fascistised mafias' that now took control of some town councils.

Fascism welcomed fair-weather supporters like these in the early days. But Mussolini had bigger ambitions. In 1924 he changed electoral law to guarantee the *Partito Nazionale Fascista* an outright parliamentary majority. Just a few weeks after the subsequent election victory, Fascist agents kidnapped and murdered the Socialist Party leader Giacomo Matteotti. Outrage spread across the country. But once again the King and leading liberal politicians vacillated at the prospect of throwing the Duce out. Democracy's last chance had gone. On 3 January 1925 Mussolini declared himself dictator. Now he looked south to find an exemplary enemy for his new regime: the mafia. The fight against criminal associations was to be a vital front in the Duce's belligerent nation-building project.

As so often, the tempo of criminal history was set in Sicily: in October 1925 Mussolini bestowed full powers to attack the mafia across the whole island on an ambitious northern policeman called Cesare Mori. Mori had dragged himself up the career ladder from nowhere, or rather from the orphanage in Pavia, near Milan, where he had been brought up. The Sicilian mission was his chance to make history; history has come to know him as the 'Iron Prefect' and his anti-mafia campaign as the Mori Operation.

The Iron Prefect began with a highly publicised assault on the hilltop town of Gangi, at the very eastern edge of the province of Palermo. All access to Gangi was denied, all communications cut. Criminals were flushed out of their hiding places with flagrant ruthlessness: their women and children were taken hostage, their goods sold off for pennies, their cattle butchered in the town square. There were as many as 450 arrests.

The Mori Operation involved deploying the same methods among the lemon groves of the Conca d'Oro, and among the many mafia-infested satellite towns of Palermo like Bagheria, Monreale, Corleone and Partinico. The roundups continued into the provinces of Agrigento, Caltanissetta and Enna.

The Mori Operation was still in full swing when the Duce decided it was time to tell the world about what he had achieved.

On 26 May 1927—for Catholics, the anniversary of Jesus's ascent into heaven—Italy witnessed a little apotheosis of its own.

With his barrel chest and bull neck crammed into a frock coat and wing collar, Mussolini entered the Chamber of Deputies to be greeted with volleys of cheering and applause. The effusive reception was to be expected: this was now the Duce's fifth year in power, and Italy's parliament had been entirely tamed. All the same, this was not a routine institutional event. The speech Mussolini was about to give was heralded as the most important he had ever delivered: a progress bulletin on the building of the world's first Fascist dictatorship. To mark the occasion, the ushers set a huge bouquet of roses before Mussolini's chair. And to mark the occasion, the dictator modulated his usual pout and strut. Toying almost meditatively with one of the roses, he addressed the chamber in a low, even voice.

Mussolini's Ascension Day speech betrayed what the *New York Times* diagnosed as 'signs of increasing megalomania'. But the speech was also undeniably seductive to many Italian ears. In 1922, Mussolini asserted, the Fascists had inherited a democratic governing apparatus that was shambolic, weak and seedy; it was merely 'a badly organised system of Prefects' offices in which each Prefect's only worry was how to hustle votes effectively'. In five short years, Mussolini claimed, his regime had done 'something enormous, epoch-making, and monumental': for the first time since the fall of the Roman Empire, it had established genuine government authority over the Italian people. The Fascist regime had finally imposed order and discipline on an Italy debilitated for so long by politicking and corruption. The country now marched as one to the thumping beat of a totalitarian ideology: 'Everything within the state. Nothing against the state. Nothing outside the state.'

The supreme authority of the state was Fascism's blazon motif. The Sicilian mafia constituted a state within a state. Therefore Fascism and the mafia were on a collision course.

A centrepiece of the Ascension Day speech was Mussolini's proud bulletin on the Mori Operation. Sicily, he told parliament, was lying on the operating table, its torso sliced open by the Duce's 'scalpel' so that the cancer of delinquency was exposed. Thousands of suspected *mafiosi* had been captured in tens of Sicilian towns and villages. The result was a dramatic fall-off in crime. Murders had come down from 675 in 1923 to 299 in 1926, and episodes of cattle rustling from 696 to 126 over the same

period. The Duce fired off more statistics before concluding with an ora-
torical flourish.

> Someone is bound to ask me, 'When will the struggle against the mafia
> come to an end?'
>   It will come to an end *not just* when there are no longer any *mafiosi*,
> but when Sicilians can no longer even *remember* the mafia.

Here was a long-awaited show of political willpower: there was to be 'no
holding back' against the mafia that was 'dishonouring Sicily', in Mussolini's
words. After six decades of collusion and connivance, Italy seemed finally
to have a leader who made it priority business to destroy the country's most
notorious criminal organisation.

Mussolini's scalpel continued to slice into the island's flesh for another
two years after the Ascension Day speech: by 1928, according to some
calculations, there had been 11,000 arrests. Then in June 1929, the Iron
Prefect was recalled to Rome. His part of the job of eradicating the mafia,
Mussolini declared, had been completed; it was up to the judiciary to finish
off the task. A long cycle of major mafia trials, the biggest of them with 450
defendants, began in 1927 and would not come to an end until 1932. By
that time many people felt able to talk about the Sicilian mafia in the past
tense. Among them was the Iron Prefect himself.

Cesare Mori published a memoir in 1932 and it was rapidly translated
into English with the title *The Last Struggle with the Mafia*. Having bran-
dished the scalpel against organised crime in Sicily, Mori now took up the
chisel, with the intention of carving his own narrative of the mafia's demise
into the marble of history.

The Iron Prefect told his readers that Sicilian psychology, which he called
'childlike', was at the root of the mafia problem. Sicilians, Mori believed,
were easily impressed by haughty figures like *mafiosi*. So to win the Sicilians
over, the Fascist state had awed them; it out-mafiaed the mafia; it had given
itself a physical presence, and become embodied in men tougher and more
charismatic than the *mafiosi* themselves—men like Cesare Mori.

The Iron Prefect was sceptical about the theory that the mafia was a sworn
criminal association, an Honoured Society.

> The Mafia, as I am describing it, is a peculiar way of looking at things
> and of acting which, through mental and spiritual affinities, brings to-
> gether in definite unhealthy attitudes men of a particular temperament,
> isolating them from their surroundings into a kind of caste . . . There are

no marks of recognition; they are unnecessary. The *mafiosi* know one another partly by their jargon, but mostly by instinct. There are no statutes. The law of *omertà* and tradition are enough. There is no election of chiefs, for the chiefs arise of their own accord and impose themselves. There are no rules of admission.

In order to repress this 'peculiar way of looking at things', a certain amount of brutality was necessary, if regrettable. With their awe-inspiring toughness, Mori wrote, the great roundups of 1926 and 1927 caused the felons' morale to crumple.

> Dismayed and panic-stricken, they fell like flies, with no other gesture of resistance but a feeble attempt at flight to well-concealed hiding places. They were all struck down.

If Mori had bothered to follow the trials that had just concluded in Palermo, he would have found reams of evidence that the mafia was indeed more than a 'mental and spiritual affinity' between men with an 'unhealthy attitude'. But that did not matter much now. In his book's closing lines, Mori declared that Sicily, having won its last struggle with organised crime, had now begun an 'irresistible march towards her victorious destiny'.

The Iron Prefect was showily magnanimous to those he had vanquished and imprisoned, expressing the hope that *mafiosi* would 'come back to the bosom of their families better and wiser men, and then spend their life in honest toil until the mantle of forgiveness and oblivion is thrown over the past'. If the island had not yet had the mafia erased from its memory, as Mussolini promised, then that day could at least be envisaged with confidence. Fascism had beaten the mafia. Whatever the mafia was.

So confident was the regime of its success that, in the autumn of 1932, in celebration of the tenth anniversary of the Fascist March on Rome, hundreds of *mafiosi* convicted during the Mori Operation were released in an amnesty. The Sicilian mafia's history was not quite over yet.

26

CAMPANIA: Buffalo soldiers

WHAT REMAINED OF THE CAMORRA AFTER IT WAS DISMANTLED BY THE CUOCOLO TRIAL? Although the trial marked the end of the Honoured Society, it did not eliminate gang crime in some of the city's nerve centres, such as the wholesale markets or the docks at Bagnoli, where extortion and smuggling were endemic.

Another thing that survived was the myth of the good *camorrista*. Risen from among the poor, the good *camorrista* enforced a rough and ready justice in the alleyways, or so it was believed. Above everything else, such 'men of respect' protected the honour of women. One tale became an archetype in popular memory: the *camorrista* who, seeing a local girl seduced and abandoned, collars her rogue *innamorato* and forces him to do the decent thing. With telling and retelling, such stories hardened into a tableau utterly removed from reality and impervious to contrary evidence. What camorra honour had really meant for women was pimping, beatings, and disfigurement.

When the *camorristi* of the Honoured Society had gone, *guappi* were invested with the aura of 'men of respect'. A *guappo* was a street-corner boss. He may have lacked the formal investiture of Honoured Society membership; he may have lacked contacts with a brotherhood far beyond the alleys of his tiny fief. But the typical *guappo* certainly carried on in much the same way as the typical *camorrista* had done: contraband, usury, pimping, receiving stolen goods and of course farming his turf for votes. Many *guappi* were former *camorristi*, or the sons of *camorristi*.

228

But to discover the real forebears of the cocaine barons, building industry gangsters and political fixers who make up the camorra today, we need to return for a moment to the days of the Cuocolo trial; more importantly, we need to leave Naples and explore a very different criminal landscape.

On 4 August 1911, two jewellers, father and son, were waylaid by armed robbers on the fruit-tree lined road leading out of Nola, a town perhaps 30 kilometres north-east of Naples. There was a struggle when the father refused to give up the jewellery he was carrying. The attackers responded by shooting his son several times in the face, causing the old man to faint with shock. It was the kind of crime that would not normally have generated a great deal of interest in Naples. But with the Cuocolo trial priming the public's taste for camorra stories, journalists were drawn out into the countryside to cover the story. Nola, after all, hosted the livestock market where Big 'Enry sourced the mules he once sold to the British army fighting the Boers.

Even *Il Mattino*'s wonder-worn hacks were taken aback by what they found when they got there: 'a reign of terror, a kind of martial law'. The territory around Nola displayed all the tell-tale symptoms of a well-rooted criminal organisation: large numbers of crimes unsolved and unreported (meaning that witnesses and victims were being intimidated); vines and fruit trees cut down (meaning that extortion demands had been made). Mayors who tried to do something about the growing power of the bosses had been beaten up. An uncooperative priest had had his arms broken. Any man who protested to the authorities was liable to have his wife or daughter kidnapped, or his house or business dynamited. Bandits openly patrolled the roads, their rifles slung over their shoulders. And according to the police there was an organisation of only 100–150 men behind it all; they formed a federation of gangs, and divided the booty from their crimes equally.

For all these terrifying details, *Il Mattino*'s exposé barely skimmed the surface. Mobsters infiltrated the fields, market towns and supply routes that enveloped and nourished Naples. *Camorristi* were active down the coast in Castellammare and Salerno and in Nocera, Sarno and Palma Campania just beyond Mount Vesuvius. But the problem was at its worst to the city's north, in a vast expanse of hyper-productive land that catered for virtually every item on the Neapolitan menu. From the livestock centre of Nola in the east; to Acerra, which was particularly known for its cannellini beans and for the eel that flourished in its water courses; to the peach orchards around Giugliano; on to Marano, with its peas; and then up the coast to Mondragone, which was known for its onions, endive and chicory. All around Naples a population of farmers, guards, butchers, cart-drivers, brokers and speculators doubled as extortionists, vandals, fraudsters, smugglers, armed robbers and murderers. Out here, the line between legitimate and illegitimate business scarcely had a meaning: theft and racketeering were as valid a source of income as squeezing a profit from the peasantry.

But of all the agricultural bounty that issued from the Neapolitan hinterland, one product was more tightly controlled by hoods than any other.

South of the Garigliano river, north-west of Naples, there lay a malaria-cursed wilderness called the Mazzoni. Lush, flat, interminable and oppressively quiet, the Mazzoni were pocked by quagmires. The land's other features were few and strange. An isolated water channel threaded through lines of poplar trees; or a dust road, white as a scar, tracing a bullet-straight path to the horizon. Solitary herders were the only travellers: they galloped with their bellies flat to their ponies' bare backs, as if they had fled a stable fire and forgotten to stop. Once in a while the dust they kicked up would settle upon a bridge over a reed-choked ditch, with a gate propped between two posts. These marked the entrance to a *difesa*, in the local parlance—literally a 'defence'—which was a kind of boggy farm. Inside, beyond holm oak and cane thicket, were the buffalo: black, short-haired and massive, they stood in filthy water and glowered at nothing through the shimmering air. At the centre of each compound there was a thatched, whitewashed single-storey shed. Inside, where the air was gamey with the reek of buffalo milk, the herders thumbed mozzarella cheese into balls and dropped them into brine tuns ready for the journey to market in Santa Maria Capua Vetere.

Sallow and sullen with fever, the herdsmen worked the *difese* in teams, living little better than their animals, not seeing their womenfolk for weeks or months on end. Their boss, known as a *minorente*, was a rough and ready entrepreneur. Naples and Caserta paid good money for the creamily fragrant cheeses that miraculously issued from the muck and stench of the Mazzoni. The boss rented his *difesa* from a landowner who was probably too scared to go anywhere near his property. For the Mazzoni were among the most lawless areas in the whole of Italy, and the herdsmen who made the mozzarella also made much of the trouble. In 1909, a government inquiry into agriculture evoked the teams of buffalo herdsmen in the Mazzoni in the language of folk terror. 'For centuries these local tribes have hated one another and fought one another like prehistoric peoples.'

Yet as so often in Italy, lazy talk of 'primitives' served only to mask a far-from-primitive criminal logic. Violence was integral to the buffalo dairy economy. Bosses intimidated their competitors so they could negotiate a lower rent with the landowner. The herders set up protection rackets: if their threatening letters were not understood, they slaughtered buffalo, cut down trees, and burned buildings until they had made their position clear. Highway robbery was a constant risk for the men taking the cheese to market, and bringing the money back. In other words, mozzarella was for the Mazzoni what lemons were for Palermo's Conca d'Oro.

During the Cuocolo trial, *Il Mattino* reporters visited the Mazzoni to be cursorily horrified by the 'crass ignorance' and 'bloodthirsty instincts' of the buffalo herdsmen. What they failed to mention was that the camorra in the Mazzoni, and in the Aversa area between the Mazzoni and Naples, was integral to a political and business machine whose handles were cranked by the local Member of Parliament, Giuseppe Romano, known as Peppuccio ('Little Joey'). It just so happened that Little Joey was a friend of *Il Mattino* editor, Edoardo Scarfoglio.

Despite the obliging reserve of Scarfoglio's journalists, Little Joey's career was doomed. Partly as a result of the fuss around the Cuocolo trial, he became too notorious to be tolerated even by Prime Minister Giovanni Giolitti (the 'Minister of the Underworld') who had been happy to accept his support in the past. During the 1913 national elections, there was an anti-camorra campaign in Little Joey's constituency (the cavalry were sent into the Mazzoni), and he was unseated. But with Little Joey out of the way, gangster life in the Neapolitan hinterland returned to normal.

From the Mazzoni to Nola, and down beyond Mount Vesuvius, *camorristi* were as at home in the towns and villages around Naples as they were in the prisons and alleys of the city itself. Indeed, there were close ties between the rural and urban organisations. The tomatoes, lettuces, salami and mozzarella that *camorristi* cornered in the countryside went first to the criminal cartels who controlled little portions of the city's wholesale distribution. It was all staggeringly inefficient, a system designed only to fatten the cut taken by middlemen. Poor Naples paid cruelly high food prices as a result. But official Italy hardly took any notice.

Until Fascism, that is.

During his Ascension Day speech in 1927, Mussolini introduced parliament to the Mazzoni. He assumed, naturally enough, that his audience would not have heard of them before: who in his right mind would bother leaving the city to find out where the delicious mozzarella actually came from?

The Mazzoni are a land that lies between the provinces of Rome and Naples: they are a marshy terrain, a malarial steppe.

The inhabitants, the Duce continued, had a terrible reputation even in ancient times: *latrones*, they were called in Latin— 'highwaymen' or 'brigands'. As was his wont, Mussolini then hurled statistics: between 1922 and 1926, the Mazzoni had seen 169 murders and 404 instances of extortion-related vandalism. But the Fascist scalpel was already cutting away at this millennial legacy of lawlessness. The Duce's orders had been abrupt: 'Free me from this delinquency with iron and fire!' Now, with yet another salvo of statistics, the Duce could announce the triumph of state authority: 1,699 underworld figures had been arrested in the Mazzoni; just to the south, among the vines and fruit trees of Aversa, another 1,278 had been brought to book. In rural Campania, just as in Sicily, Fascism was on the verge of victory.

The press called it Fascism's campaign of 'moral drainage' in the bogs of the Mazzoni. The man charged with conducting the campaign was Major Vincenzo Anceschi, a fifty-year-old *Carabiniere*. Anceschi was the son of a *Carabiniere*, and his own son would become one too: a lineage that testifies to the devotion that the *Arma*, as Italians call this military police force, can inspire in its members. Anceschi's anti-camorra operation was huge, entirely comparable to what Mori was doing in Sicily: between December 1926 and May 1928, 9,143 people were arrested and two suspects died in gunfights with the *Carabinieri*.

Anceschi's men patrolled the countryside in mounted squads, disarming notoriously dangerous families, arresting renegades and breaking up corrupt factions in local government. Although the toughest assignments were in the Mazzoni, their roundups also included the countryside as far east as Nola.

Anceschi could hardly have known this territory better: he was born in Giugliano, right on the edge of the Mazzoni. And on New Year's Eve 1926 he deployed that local knowledge in his most spectacular strike, at a gangland funeral that was intended to be a show of force, just like the Honoured Society funerals of the 1890s in Naples.

Vincenzo Serra was the most notorious *camorrista* in the Aversa countryside. An elegant figure with a lordly bearing, he had spent thirty-six of his seventy years in prison, and was particularly well known for shooting two *Carabinieri* in a tea house. Serra died in Aversa hospital following a mysterious accident. His open coffin was set up in a ground-floor mortuary, surrounded by black drapes, exotic plants and fat candles. Hoods from all around came to pay their respects. They then assembled in the hospital atrium, where (according to the press) the acting boss decided their positions according to rank: first the older *camorristi*; then the *picciotti*; and finally the 'honoured youths' lugging large wreaths. Vincenzo Serra's funeral procession was to be a solemn collective tableau of a structured criminal organisation.

But it never even began. The *Carabinieri* simply bolted the door of the hospital, locking the mobsters in the atrium until they could be herded onto a truck and taken to prison.

Major Anceschi made something of a speciality of raiding camorra funerals. This was a dangerous tactic: officers received frequent death threats.

Carabinieri dressed in mufti would mingle with the crowds, while Anceschi supervised operations from an unmarked car parked nearby. He had the car wired so that anyone who tried to get in uninvited would receive an electric shock. But the rewards made the risks of this kind of operation worthwhile. The arrests were important, of course. Perhaps more important still was the chance to transform a show of force for the camorra into a show of force for the law.

What these reports suggest is that, even after the Honoured Society died out in the city of Naples as a result of the Cuocolo trial, its structures and traditions lived on in the countryside fifteen years later. Anceschi reported to Mussolini that, in the Mazzoni, the camorra had 'a rigid system based on hierarchy and *omertà*'. 'The country around Aversa and Nola', he went on, 'very close to Naples, was a daily destination for the members of the city's underworld, which was intimately linked to the rural criminals'. The countryside had become a kind of life-support system for urban organised crime.

Anceschi and his men discovered no less than twenty criminal associations and sent 494 men for judgement in eighteen separate trials, but historians have so far managed to locate only a few pages of the resulting documentation. Until more research is done and the archives surrender more of their secrets, we cannot know exactly what kind of criminal organisations dominated the Mazzoni, or indeed the successes and failures of Fascism's 'moral drainage'. What seems certain is that there were no further traces of an Honoured Society in the Neapolitan countryside after the 1920s.

To his credit, Major Anceschi gave a proud but sober assessment of his own work in a report to *Carabinieri* High Command in May 1928. The roads were now safe, the fields were once again filled with peasants, and the barrels of mozzarella cheese could make their way to market without being stolen or 'taxed' by the camorra. Public order was normal, all the way from Mondragone to Nola—for now. But Anceschi detailed a number of things that would need to happen before peace could settle definitively over this troubled territory. Extraordinary policing would need to continue. In the 'malign and fearful moorland' of the Mazzoni, there would have to be education, land reclamation, and road building. Above all—and here lay the most uncomfortable message for the Fascist state—there would have to be much more careful supervision of the personnel within both the government bureaucracy and the Fascist Party. Anceschi's operation had courageously exposed a number of corrupt functionaries who tried to influence the magistrature on behalf of *camorristi*, and who were involved in obscure dealings with the Freemasonry. The report ended with a brusque imperative: 'Prevent political infiltration in favour of organised crime.'

Despite Major Anceschi's caution, Mussolini decided by the late 1920s that the camorra, like the mafia, had been beaten. He also decided that he had solved the whole Southern Question—the persistent scandal of the backwardness, poverty and corruption of Italy's south. Further public discussion of these issues was therefore pointless. So pointless that it was banned. Between 1931 and 1933, the head of the Duce's press corps wrote frequently to newspaper editors exhorting them not to print the words 'southern Italy' and '*Mezzogiorno*' (another term for the south). From now on, Fascism would have other concerns: building a cult of the Duce, for example, and militarising the Italian people in preparation for imperial war. From this point on, whatever surprises mafia history might have in store were to be stifled by a subservient media.

CALABRIA: The flying boss of Antonimina

DOMENICO NOTO HAD A LOVELY TIME IN THE GREAT WAR. NOT FOR HIM THE LICE and shrapnel that millions of his fellow soldiers endured in the trenches scoured into the Alpine foothills between 1915 and 1918. Most of the Italians recruited to fight Austria were country folk, barely literate, whose mental horizon simply could not encompass the reasons for this mechanised slaughter. Noto had a loftier perspective. He had a good secondary school education, and used it to become a non-commissioned aviator. His duty was to patrol the breathtaking skies between Calabria and Sicily on the lookout for Austrian mines in the Straits below. On one occasion he even overflew his home village of Antonimina, which clings to an Aspromonte outcrop above Calabria's Ionian coast. Noto's gesture won him the lasting reverence of the herdsmen who had shaded their eyes to see the local prodigy soar by. Aviators were the very epitome of a dashing, virile modernity. Domenico Noto seemed like the harbinger of a heroic Italian future. And he even had a good disciplinary record during the war.

Which is why it is striking that, on 19 December 1922 (that is, just after Mussolini became Prime Minister) Noto was convicted of being the boss of the local mafia. If the judges in the case are to be believed, Noto drew on his prestige as a wartime flyer to assume leadership of Antonimina's underworld.

Noto's gang had methods, rituals and a structure that were identical to those of the picciotteria discovered three decades or so earlier around

Aspromonte. Thus, despite everything that had happened since then—a communications and transport revolution, mass emigration, the destruction of the Honoured Society in Naples, and the titanic military slogging match with Austria—the 'ndrangheta's forefathers remained obstinately themselves.

Like their predecessors of the 1880s and 1890s, Noto's men took a blood oath and were ranked into two sub-groups: the *picciotti* and the *camorristi*. They had specific job titles, like the boss and the *contaiuolo*. They stole a great many farm animals: some of which they sent to connected livestock traders and butchers in distant towns; some they roasted and ate in banquets designed to nourish the gang's *esprit de corps*; some they miraculously 'found' and returned to the rightful owners—in return for cash and a solemn promise to say nothing to the *Carabinieri*.

Whole passages of the judges' ruling against Noto's *'ndrina* could have been copied from documents dating from thirty years before. The gang contained a few quite wealthy members, and some who had relatives in local government: a former mayor, called Monteleone, counted at least two nephews among the affiliates. The sect had strict rules: wrongdoers were punished with fines, acts of vandalism, or a deft flick of the blade.

Noto's men were also part of a great network of Calabrian mafia gangs. That much was clear from the occasion when he heard from his friends in Palmi, on Calabria's other coast, that one of their brethren had been imprisoned for attempting to murder a *Carabiniere*. Noto ordered his men to make a welfare contribution, and one member who refused was heavily fined. Boasting far-lying contacts like these, the Antonimina mob could demand, and get, 'resignation and respect', from the people at home, as the judge put it. Thefts and beatings were not reported to the police.

So the flying *capo* of Antonimina was a throwback, not a harbinger. Or rather, the future his example heralded was a depressingly familiar one: it was a future in which even educated young men from the mafia heartlands of Calabria, those who had seen the world and taken the chances offered by the national institutions that were supposed to turn them into good Italians, would prefer the career routes afforded by mafia violence.

Domenico Noto's group also betrayed many of the same weaknesses as the Lads with Attitude of the late nineteenth century. There was an admission fee for new members (which had now gone up to 25 or 50 lire). Like the first *picciotti*, Noto and his men browbeat the vulnerable into paying the fee. One victim of this kind of extortion was a sixteen-year-old chicken thief. If the traditional rules of the Honoured Society had been respected, this boy would never have been allowed to join at all because both his sisters were prostitutes. But he was initiated, and exploited, all the same. Aggrieved by the treatment he received, he subsequently gave a vital testimony to the authorities. Nobody in the police and judicial system was remotely surprised by this kind of egregious breach in the code of silence. As a judge in another trial wearily opined, 'as judicial psychology teaches us, members of criminal associations always betray one another, and the solidarity between them is only superficial'. Clearly the Calabrian mafia was still a long way from becoming the byword for *omertà* that it is today.

Across the picciotteria's home territory the courts were encountering similar cases, similar gangs that mixed former soldiers with veteran mobsters, similar infractions of the law of silence. In Rosarno, on the plain of Gioia Tauro, 'the population was terrorised': in broad daylight there were knife fights, acts of sabotage, robberies, attacks on the *Carabinieri*. The picture was very similar in and around Africo, where a judge noted that there was 'a very marked and sudden resurgence in crimes against property' when the troops came home. In the mayhem of demobilisation and the accompanying economic crisis, the *picciotti* were resurgent.

After 1925, just as it did in Sicily and Campania, Fascism mounted an anti-mafia drive in Calabria. Once again, there were hundreds and hundreds of arrests, and some very big trials, especially in the years from 1928 to 1930. But compared to the Mori Operation in Sicily and to Major Anceschi's roundups in the Mazzoni, Fascism's crackdown in Calabria barely rated more than a few lines in the local press, let alone nationally—and that even before the media blackout on the 'Southern Question' from the early 1930s. Fighting organised crime in Italy's most neglected region provided no more political kudos under Fascism than it had done before.

In his 1927 Ascension Day speech, Benito Mussolini gave Italy a monumentally simple picture of his anti-mafia campaign: Fascism set against organised crime—two great blocks facing one another in mutual antagonism. Yet he did not mention the picciotteria at all. The silence is telling, not least because in Calabria the reality on the ground shattered Mussolini's marmoreal rhetoric into fragments. In some times and places, the state manifested its power in brave policework and shrewd investigation. But in others, it showed its weakness through gross naivety, cowardly brutality, idiotic posturing, and lazy collusion.

The archives from the Fascist era allow historians to identify a pattern in the fragments of Fascist anti-mafia policy. Continuity is undoubtedly part of that pattern: in some areas of southern Calabria the *picciotti* were still behaving like the flying boss of Antonimina and his men did after the First World War, and they would continue to do so after Fascism fell. But elsewhere the picciotteria was growing, transforming itself into something altogether more formidable than the sect of ex-cons and tavern rats of the 1880s and 1890s.

Calabrian hoodlums were not new to the mass arrests and major trials that came with Fascism. Comparatively unprotected from the state's wrath, they had always been vulnerable to the kind of repression that the Sicilian mafia eluded as a matter of course. Italy cut them back, but never managed to eliminate them. Under Fascism, the *picciotti* began to show that they were learning from this long and harsh experience. Wherever they could avoid the capricious swing of the Fascist axe, they infiltrated the institutions and bent justice to their own ends. If they had first emerged as a provincial version of the prison camorra of Naples, by the end of Fascism the most powerful Calabrian gangsters looked rather more like Sicilian *mafiosi*.

Looking back at the Lads with Attitude during the Fascist era is like watching ants. With an energy that at first seems utterly myopic, each indistinguishable insect scuttles, explores, fights and dies. Yet somehow, from their multiplied frenzy, the colony as a whole grows stronger and more numerous. Somewhere in the DNA of all Italy's mafias is the ability to think strategically and not just tactically, to evolve over time. A form of natural selection—namely the constant and ferocious competition for predominance within the ranks of each criminal organisation—partly explains this ability. But collective adversity can play a part too: it seems to me that the 'ndrangheta's long-term success was in good part the result of what it endured early in its history at the hands of the state. If 'ndranghetisti had a motto, it would be one drawn from the philosophy of Friedrich Nietzsche. Ironically, it was a maxim of which the Duce himself approved: *what does not destroy me makes me stronger.*

CALABRIA: What does not kill me makes me stronger

FASCIST REPRESSION HIT HOME ACROSS THE VARIOUS MOB NURSERIES OF CALABRIA. For example, in 1931 the chief of police of Catanzaro felt able to report that the mafia had 'almost been crushed' in his area, although he did add that the 'impetuous and primitive character' of the locals meant that there was still a very high level of bloodshed. Another notable success came in 1932 when the police in Reggio Calabria dismantled a whole criminal system: the bosses of five 'ndrine were convicted.

But Fascism's early operations against the picciotteria were temporary successes at best. In fact in some places, ironically, they merely created a power vacuum in which other criminals could wreak havoc. Take the particularly nasty gang who ran riot on the plain of Gioia Tauro in the mid-1930s. As well as committing many robberies and acts of violence, their boss, a certain Michele Barone, was also convicted of smothering an old lady in her bed and throwing a prostitute off a bridge for giving him syphilis. Nasty this crew may have been, but it was *not* a cell of the picciotteria.

Michele Barone was a former member of the tax and customs branch of the police—a CV that would automatically have debarred him from membership of the picciotteria. Yet Barone and his friends operated unmolested for three years in the traditional mafia towns of Polistena and Taurianova. In other words, for a while, in this highly significant corner of Calabria, Fascist repression took away the mafia's monopoly of thuggery.

The picciotteria would not accept defeat. The crackdown had to continue throughout the Fascist era: there was another peak in the number of trials in 1937 and 1938. During the mid and late 1930s, the police and *Carabinieri* were sending suspects into internal exile in greater numbers than almost anywhere else in Italy.

Fascism's drive against the Calabrian mob all too often lost its momentum where it really counted: in court. Already in 1923, one judge remarked that the *picciotti* relied on the 'acquiescence of the wealthiest classes who often use the criminals to further their own goals of personal supremacy and to guard their estates'. Just as in Sicily, the Lads with Attitude had used the subtle art of the protection racket to win friends among the upper echelons—friends who, as witnesses, could swing trials in the gangsters' favour. But as time went on, an increasing number of strange rulings were handed down by judges themselves, suggesting strongly that the picciotteria was beginning to subvert the workings of justice from the inside. One example comes from Villa San Giovanni, a port township that lies just north of Reggio Calabria. In 1927 a group of local *mafiosi* were acquitted of forming a criminal association, despite the fact that some of the mobsters had had themselves photographed, pistols pointed and palms raised, as they took an oath.

Among the big gangster trials of 1928 was the prosecution of fifty-two men from Africo. Some of them were almost certainly the sons and nephews of the *picciotti* whose killing crew took a razor to Pietro Maviglia's oesophagus in 1894. Africo was still, as one Fascist official admitted, 'real barbarian country, isolated from the world'; there were few places in Calabria with such a notorious history of mafia activity. Yet the judge's ruling in the 1928 case shows absolutely no memory of the criminal association's deep roots in the town. He even handed out reduced sentences on the grounds that

> The criminal association was partly the result of social causes such as the poverty of the Great War's aftermath and the moral upheaval that resulted from the war itself.

Obligingly, the judge went on to declare that the defendants were now 'changed men, morally and socially'. No Fascist iron and fire in Africo then, because society was to blame.

Two cases from the notorious Locri area on the Ionian coast also betray a suspicious degree of judicial leniency. In 1928 copious testimony from an insider who had gone through the picciotteria initiation ritual was not enough to convince the judge that a mafia gang was actually a criminal organisation. Yes, they were an association, the judge conceded. But they could have just got together, as they claimed, 'to defend one another from other people's violent attacks'. Acquittal on the grounds of insufficient evidence was the decision.

In 1929 two prosperous citizens were among forty-eight suspected *mafiosi* charged with 'associating for delinquency' and extortion in Ardore: one was an entrepreneur, the other a former cobbler who had become politically powerful. Both were freed on no more solid grounds than that 'it was implausible that they would have shady dealings with what was essentially a bunch of beggars'. The chief 'beggar', as it happens, was caught with a mafia rule book in his house.

Some of these rulings may be down to ignorant judges, or to displays of class prejudice. More likely, they are the end product of the Calabrian mafia's increasing power to infiltrate the judicial system through the state administration. For since Fascism's earliest months in power, when Blackshirts in the region had gone down with 'acute factionitis', the *Partito Nazionale Fascista* in Calabria had proved exasperatingly prone to the local vices of corruption, cronyism, and in-fighting. In Calabria, Fascism not only struggled to govern society, it struggled to govern its own ranks.

Predictably, the malaise was worst around Aspromonte, where cliques still squabbled over the funds allocated to repair the damage caused by the catastrophic 1908 earthquake a *generation* earlier. Mussolini dispatched a rapid succession of special commissioners from Rome to put an end to jobbery and mud-slinging. But what passed for 'Fascism' in the toe of the peninsula remained obstinately unruly throughout the twenty-year regime.

So the single most important weakness in Fascism's campaign against the Calabrian mafia was that it could not cut the tendrils that organised crime had wound around the hollow branches of the state. As early as 1933 the national Fascist Party Secretary in Rome was told that the local Party Secretary in Reggio was 'notoriously affiliated to the organised crime that still infects the province'; the man in question had a strong influence within the Prefect's office and police headquarters. In 1940 a special commissioner reported that a 'high number' of citizens were members of criminal associations, or had relatives who were members. Even his predecessor as special commissioner had several men in his circle who were suspected of involvement in organised crime.

The *picciotti* were growing stronger by sucking energy from the Fascist state. But their increasing vigour also came from within, from bonds that made the *'ndrine* even tougher to prise from the mountain crags and coastal plains where they had first marked out their territory. The Lads with Attitude were learning how to make crime a family business.

CALABRIA: A clever, forceful and wary woman

ITALY'S UNDERWORLD NETWORKS HAVE ALWAYS BEEN WOVEN FROM MANY DIFFERENT strands, all of them stolen from other parts of the social fabric: Masonic rituals, male bonding, patronage, godparenthood, the language and rituals of a religion hollowed of any spiritual meaning, feasting, the glamour reflected back from literature . . . Anything will do, as long as it knits the organisation together. But the strongest criminal ties of all have been those braided from the purloined threads of kinship. Families lend gangs the kind of loyalty that more impersonal forms of organisation can rarely match. It is one thing to betray a comrade to the police: it is quite another when that comrade is also your cousin, your uncle, or your father-in-law.

Among Sicilian *mafiosi*, births, marriages and baptisms have never been *private*; that is, they are not purely domestic affairs that a gangland leader only turns his mind to once the day's extorting and smuggling are done. Rather, family is at the heart of quotidian underworld scheming: a wedding can seal a pact ready for war or end a season of bloodshed and signal the birth of a new alliance. Dynastic politics have always been integral to what the mafia is about. The *mafiosi* that Inspector Sangiorgi encountered during the 'fratricide' affair already cultivated the arts required to sire their own criminal bloodlines, to make their surnames echo fear down through the generations. Sangiorgi also discovered the first known occasion on which a Man of Honour was offered the distinctively Sicilian choice between murdering a relative and being killed himself: it was in 1883, when an uncle was made to take part in the murder of his own nephew, who was also a *mafioso*. In the Brotherhood of Favara, the mafia of the sulphur mines, those were the rules.

In Calabria, back in the 1880s and 1890s, family matters were handled very differently. The 'ndrangheta was originally a sect in which prisoner enlisted prisoner, rather than father enlisting son. Once they emerged from jail, *picciotti* did begin to spread along the pathways of kinship. The earliest picciotteria trial papers list brothers, cousins and other relatives among the members—it could hardly be otherwise given the tangle of intermarriage in some of the isolated Calabrian communities. Before long, a first generation of sons were joining their fathers in the criminal ranks. For example, if the police were right about the King of Aspromonte, Giuseppe Musolino, then his father founded the picciotteria in Santo Stefano. So family and gang crime were interlaced very quickly. But in the early days there seems to have been little strategic and legislative thought behind that interlacing: the *picciotti* did not call meetings about family matters; they did not make rules about who could marry whom; they did not cut faces for breaches of dynastic etiquette.

Today the 'ndrangheta is more resistant to repression than the Sicilian mafia or the Neapolitan camorra; its secrets are more closely guarded, because fewer of its members turn state's evidence. Ask any magistrate or policeman in Calabria why that should be, and they will reply with one word: family. These days, the 'ndrangheta is even more family-oriented than the Sicilian mafia: each *'ndrina* is deliberately *built* from one clan, often a single boss and his male offspring. In bugged conversations from 2010, *'ndranghetisti* can be heard discussing what they call the principle of 'the line', meaning the hereditary principle, when it comes to deciding who will become the boss (of Roghudi, in this case). The rule that a son should inherit from his father is not inviolable but it is a rule all the same. No such statute exists in the Sicilian mafia, although the sons of bosses often follow their fathers into leadership positions.

So although the Lads with Attitude had very similar rituals and a similar structure to the 'ndrangheta as it is known and feared today, they lacked the strong basis in kinship for which the 'ndrangheta is most renowned. In fact the picciotteria was slow to take on board the full criminal potential of blood relationships. From the beginning, deaths were part of the Calabrian mafia's collective business; but it was only during the two decades of Fascism that births and marriages really entered the ledger too. The transformation was slow and patchy, but absolutely fundamental to the growing strength of the picciotteria.

By the time the Fascist dictatorship had asserted itself in Rome, judges were beginning to hear new kinds of family stories among the hoodlums of Calabria. In Vibo Valentia, to the north of the Plain of Gioia Tauro, a *Carabiniere* was murdered in 1927 for trying to stop a marriage alliance between two criminal kinship groups, one of which had colonised the local Fascist state.

Three years later, in Nicotera just to the south, one boy was initiated into the Honoured Society at only eleven years old.

Across the mountains to the south-east, in Grotteria in 1933, the local boss heard rumours that his fiancée was pregnant by another *picciotto*. So the gang met to discuss this smear on their *capo's* honour, and decided to put a contract out. Contrary to what one might expect, the target was not the woman's alleged lover, but the man thought to be spreading the rumours. Hearsay, after all, has always been the most dangerous of weapons in dynastic struggle. The chosen killer, a sixteen-year-old boy, took six goes before he managed to cut his victim's throat properly.

Such stories are undoubtedly significant. Yet an even clearer way to trace the evolution of the early 'ndrangheta's sexual politics is by following the changing role of women. Italy's criminal organisations were from their inception overwhelmingly masculine and inherently sexist. Mafia honour has always been a men-only quality. Nevertheless, as we have already seen, women had important uses to *mafiosi* and *camorristi*, and there was significant variety in the ways they were used.

Whores were the women most frequently found in the company of the early 'ndranghetisti. Whereas Sicilian *mafiosi* have never had anything to do with prostitution, the first Calabrian *picciotti* tended to be ponces. As ponces do, they partied with the girls whose earnings they creamed off. (They raped and sometimes even married them too—because the business relationship between a pimp and his girls is also, very often, an intimate one.) So unlike their contemporaries in the Sicilian mafia, and unlike 'ndranghetisti of today, the Calabrian gangsters of the late 1800s and early 1900s did not view profiting from sex as dishonourable.

In this respect, the picciotteria was exactly like the Honoured Society of Naples had been in the nineteenth century. Neapolitan camorra slang bristled with derogatory synonyms for 'prostitute': *bagascia, bambuglia, bardascia, drusiana, risgraziata, schiavuttella* ('little slave'), *vaiassa* and *zoccola* ('sewer rat'). There was also a whole nomenclature for different kinds of streetwalkers. A new girl was a *colomba* ('dove'); one from the provinces was a *cafona* ('yokel'). A *gallinella* ('young hen') was a woman with kids; whereas a *pollanca* ('young turkey') was the term for a virgin set to be put on the market. In addition, there were several names for an old woman, like *carcassa* ('carcass') and *calascione* ('a battered old mandolin'). This was the jargon of an exploitative industry central to the camorra economy. We know little about the family lives of Neapolitan *camorristi* in the 1800s. But it seems unlikely that men so profoundly embroiled in the flesh trade could sire dynasties to compare with those of the Sicilian dons.

Like their Neapolitan peers, who had accorded *la Sangiovannara* exceptional honour in recognition of her vital role in the events of Italian unification, the *picciotti* of Calabria also sometimes hung around with strong women. A few women involved with the picciotteria in its early days directly participated in criminal actions. Female names leap out now and again from among the defendants listed in the trial documents. There were two 'Lasses with Attitude' found guilty in Palmi in 1892, for example: Concetta Muzzopapa, age 40, and Rosaria Testa, age 26. Both were from Rosarno, at the opposite end of the Plain of Gioia Tauro from Palmi. Both had taken the oath to become members of the Calabrian mafia 'by making blood come out of the little finger of their right hand as they promised to maintain secrecy', the judges explained. Both also dressed up in men's clothing to take part in robberies and violent attacks. Rosaria Testa confessed her part in the organisation, and told prosecutors many of its secrets before she retracted after being threatened by the male members of the gang.

There were other oathed women too, such as in the King of Aspromonte's home town of Santo Stefano: investigations into the picciotteria during the brigand Musolino's rampage found that 12 of the 166 initiated members were women; they included Musolino's lover, Angela Surace, and his three sisters, Ippolita, Vincenza and Anna (who, it is worth recalling, were also the boss's daughters). 'Safe in the criminal association's moral and material support', the police wrote, 'women from the members' families are also able to issue threats and impose their will'. The oldest of the Musolino sisters, Ippolita, was particularly feared and it seems that she even advised her brother on who his targets should be. These are all fascinating cases, and we would know a lot more about the early 'ndrangheta if we had more documents on which to base a study of them. There is nothing quite like these Calabrian *mafiose* in the history of the other criminal organisations.

Some of the Calabrian hoodlums that came to trial in the 1920s and 1930s still displayed the same taste in women as the *picciotti* of the 1880s and 1890s. Like Domenico Noto, the flying boss of Antonimina: his gang pimped, forced whores to take part in robberies and regularly held meetings and parties in a hooker's house. But Noto was not content with 'wandering Venuses' (in the judge's delicate phrase). He arm-twisted his way into other beds, including those of an emigrant's wife, her fourteen-year-old daughter, and a vulnerable deaf-mute girl. But it was hard to keep the criminal brotherhood's secrets when you carried on like this. In court, the emigrant's wife gave crucial evidence against Domenico Noto and more than forty of

Musolino's sister Ippolita. According to the police, she had also been oathed into the Calabrian mafia.

his comrades. Other Calabrian mafia cells were undone on the say-so of streetwalkers. For Calabrian judges showed no reluctance to believe evidence given by sex workers against the men who extorted money from them. As early as 1890, a judge in Reggio Calabria handed down severe sentences to a group of *picciotti*, and his ruling waved aside the defence's attempts to discredit the testimonies of four prostitutes: 'It is no use attacking what those unfortunate women have declared—for the reason that their repugnant trade cannot destroy their personality, which is the very substance of truth.' The habit of making money from prostitution, like the technique of browbeating young boys into being initiated, was a structural weakness in the picciotteria: both were bound to generate witnesses for the prosecution.

But elsewhere during the Fascist era there are clear signs of change in women's role. There are fewer prostitutes, and the gun-toting girl gangsters disappear. Instead, a cannier brand of gender politics begins to emerge. And with it, a new type of Calabrian mafia woman. Not a harlot. Or a cross-dressing brigandess. Instead a mother and wife whose nurturing energies are single-mindedly bent to building the honour of her menfolk, young and old.

It is often assumed that the 'ndrangheta's heavy reliance on family bonds grows from the culture of 'familism' in Calabrian society. The available evidence suggests this is wrong. The 'ndrangheta had to *learn* to base itself on kinship ties. The apparently traditional function of 'ndrangheta women—as the cult of honour's domestic priestesses—is actually a modern invention.

But even when this new model *mafiosa* first appears in the trial records during Fascism, she could wield real power and influence behind the scenes of picciotteria life. Maria Marvelli was one such woman. She was, to use a judge's words once again, a 'clever, forceful and wary woman', one well used to the ways of the Honoured Society. Not even these qualities stopped her husband meeting his gory end. But they did allow her to have her revenge. The following story comes from beneath Fascism's media blackout, and it draws heavily on Maria Marvelli's own evidence to dramatise the role women were playing in the evolution of the picciotteria.

As it happens, Maria Marvelli's story also exposes the most savage face of Fascism's countermeasures.

Just south west of Antonimina, home of the flying boss, lies Cirella, yet another tiny settlement clinging to the flanks of Aspromonte. Cirella was isolated in an inhospitable terrain; without roads fit for wheels, it was a village prey to the forces of nature and all but ignored by the forces of order.

The men of Cirella's Honoured Society did all of the things that might be expected of them: they robbed, vandalised, raped, mutilated and murdered. But they were also developing softer forms of power. Remarkably, they had elbowed the local priest aside: crooks, and not the cleric, ran Cirella's religious festivals. Anyone who wanted to do business with the local *picciotti* or marry one of their womenfolk had to join their ranks as a precondition.

Paolo Agostino was among the most influential men in Cirella's Honoured Society. Even among their number his ferocity stood out, as a judge would later note:

> He was one of those men who combines a robust and vigorous body with an audacious mind, a rare propensity for bullying, a strong tendency to commit all kinds of abuses, and the courage needed to make all these qualities count.

Paolo Agostino also had another quality that the judge did not identify, a quality that was becoming increasingly important for successful Calabrian bosses: he had a sharp eye for a smart woman. Those who went through the mafia initiation ritual in Cirella, as elsewhere in Calabria, had to swear to 'renounce family affections, putting the interests of the Society before their parents, siblings and children'. But Calabrian gangsters were also beginning to learn that families have advantages. Paolo Agostino made a particularly good choice of wife: the 'clever, forceful and wary' Maria Marvelli.

La Marvelli had been married before; she was a widow. Her son from her first marriage, Francesco Polito, joined her as part of the new family she made with the 'robust and vigorous' Paolo Agostino. If the judge is to be believed, the marriage was not an equal one, at least within the walls of the Agostino home. Maria apparently 'exercised a commanding authority over her husband and son. And she was obeyed without debate.' Paolo Agostino's return on the union was a new heir, and a wealthy one too: Maria's son, Francesco Polito, had already inherited property worth one hundred thousand lire from his late father.

The marriage seems to have been happy, and Maria had more children. Moreover her older boy, Francesco Polito, was initiated into the Honoured Society when he came of age, as befitted the stepson of a senior gangster.

However his mother, smart and suspicious woman that she was, would not allow him to handle any money. So he had to steal twenty-four bottles of olive oil from his grandfather by way of a membership fee.

Francesco Polito, with his money and his powerful stepfather, was clearly a catch in the mafia marriage market. Before long, no less a felon than the boss of the Honoured Society in Cirella offered young Francesco his daughter's hand, along with a promotion from *picciotto* to *camorrista*. A marriage to the *capo*'s daughter and a promotion seemed like a very respectable offer. But young Francesco's stepfather, Paolo Agostino, put a stop to the alliance. It is not clear why, or whether Maria Marvelli had anything to do with the decision. The best guess is that he preferred to bind himself to another criminal lineage. But refusing such an offer would inevitably seem like a snub. If there were no divisions within the ranks of the Cirella Honoured Society before, they certainly appeared now.

At this point in the story, Mussolini intervened. The dire state of public order in Cirella came to the attention of the authorities in 1933. The local boss—and everyone knew he was the boss, for what need would he have had to be coy about his power?—was sent to enforced residence. His destination was the tiny island penal colony of Ustica, which lies some 80 kilometres north of Palermo. But as so often, this measure proved inadequate to stem the tide of violence. So the following year Paolo Agostino was also sent to Ustica to join his *capo*—the very man whose generous offer of a marriage alliance he had spurned. Rumours filtered back to Cirella that when the two had met, Paolo Agostino had smashed a bottle over the boss's head. Although the rumours were probably false, they were also a very real symptom of a potentially explosive power struggle: the issue of who Maria Marvelli's son was going to marry was an open sore in Cirella.

Soon other rumours began to fly in the opposite direction, from Cirella to the penal colony on Ustica, and this time sex was what generated the gossip. Before departing for Ustica, 'robust and vigorous' Paolo Agostino left his affairs in the hands of a trusted deputy, Nicola Pollifroni. Pollifroni very soon became very close to Agostino's wife, Maria Marvelli—close enough to set off some wry smiles: they were seen riding the same horse and he was seen sitting on her lap. The judge, rather primly, would later say that the gossip was 'not without plausibility'. When these reports reached Paolo Agostino on Ustica, he made his own inquiries as to how plausible they really were. Strangely, he was told by two separate witnesses, including his own brother, that nothing was wrong. Even more strangely, he believed them.

Paolo Agostino's relaxed attitude to his wife's infidelity contradicts all the stereotypes about the southern Italian male's violent possessiveness. It also transgresses the behavioural norms among gangsters. The picciotteria had already shown that mere rumours about marital infidelity could easily send a *mafioso* to a gruesome death. Yet in this case, Paolo Agostino was prepared to discount the rumours even when everyone else saw they were at the very least 'plausible'. One explanation of this failure to defend his own reputation is that Agostino realised that, as both a husband and a criminal, Maria Marvelli was just too valuable to him. With the tensions building within the *clan*, he needed to keep his family compact, and had no choice but to overlook the affair. Mafia rules of honour, as always, were elastic.

While Paolo Agostino and his boss were in the penal colony on Ustica—the one pondering the subject of his wife's fidelity, and the other dwelling on how the offer of his daughter's hand had been rejected—back in Cirella the political terrain within the Honoured Society shifted. Three brothers, Bruno, Rocco and Francescantonio Romeo emerged as the new centre of power. The Romeo brothers decided they needed to hide their newly acquired authority behind a figurehead leader. So they began the search for a new boss, a dummy don who would not attract attention to himself, who would not be very *visible*, as the Romeo brothers stipulated.

Now, *visibility* is one of the great themes in the history of Italian organised crime. Absolute invisibility, absolute anonymity, is not an option for *mafiosi*, whose aim is to control their territory. However they do it, they have to let the local people know that it is *they* who must be feared, *they* who must be paid. But there are a thousand ways to carve out a profile, to cultivate respect. A gangster, like some colourful territorial animal, can save a lot of energy by being easy to identify: potential rivals quickly learn to spot the danger signs, and learn that flight rather than fight is the wisest reaction. So early *camorristi* advertised their power with pompadours, bell-bottom trousers, and tattoos. As did their cousins in the Calabrian picciotteria. But of course visibility brings risks—especially when the police are in the mood to repress the mafia rather than cohabit with it. It is one thing to flash your criminal rank and battle honours in a dungeon, where everyone is a felon, or in the police no-go areas of Naples's low city, or in some godforsaken Calabrian hill village. It is quite another to do so when the eyes of the *Carabinieri* are upon you, or when you want to pass through Ellis Island, or when your dealings with politicians and entrepreneurs demand a less showy façade. The 'middle-class villains' of Sicily have always tended to dress inconspicuously and to intimate their authority with little more than a stare, a stance or a stony silence. The other criminal associations, whose origins were humbler, took a while to master the visibility game's subtler stratagems. The learning process was already well under way by the dawn of the Fascist era. In Naples, the silly clothes and butterfly pompadours were gone by the time of the Cuocolo trial. The Calabrian mafia abandoned them not long afterwards: there is little sign of them in the Fascist era.

Faced with more unwelcome police attention than they had ever known, the Romeo brothers looked for a new and less visible patsy, one without a criminal record whose wealth put him beyond suspicion. Their chosen candidate, a young man called Francesco Macrì, accepted without hesitation, despite not having even been a member of the gang before, and despite being rich enough to provide lawyers for his new co-conspirators. The judge later said that Macrì regarded being nominated boss as a 'special honour'. It is a telling testament to the prestige that this criminal association had now acquired that Macrì took on the job of *capo* so readily. As the judge explained, 'entry into the association was an essential condition if you wanted to win public esteem'. The picciotteria, less visible than it once had been, but more poisonous, was seeping further still into the bloodstream of Calabrian life. The Romeo brothers formed a committee to 'advise' the enthusiastic but inexperienced appointee, while retaining the real power for themselves. And with that arrangement, the politics of organised crime in Cirella reached a new equilibrium.

Meanwhile, criminal business carried on as usual. And as usual, even the simplest criminal business could have lethal consequences. The local doctor had had a valuable yearling bull stolen a while earlier and he was still making strenuous and unsuccessful efforts to find out who had taken it. Eventually he approached Maria Marvelli, asking her to ask her exiled husband Paolo Agostino (a relative of the doctor's) to make inquiries among the inmates on Ustica. Prison, as ever, was the great junction box of mafia communications.

A letter soon came back from the prison island: Paolo Agostino wrote that the thieves were Bruno, Rocco, and Francescantonio Romeo—the men behind the 'invisible boss' who were now the most influential *picciotti* in Cirella.

Naively, the doctor passed Paolo Agostino's letter on to the *Carabinieri*. Someone from inside the *Carabinieri*—whether a spy or an agent provocateur—told the three Romeo brothers that Paolo Agostino had tried to get them into trouble. Even before this tip-off arrived, the Romeos knew that Agostino would pose a threat to them once he was released from Ustica. So they swiftly issued a warning by burning down Maria Marvelli's house and stealing thirty of her goats.

As Agostino's return from Ustica neared, the Romeo brothers began to plan for more drastic action to defend their position. They introduced a motion with the Honoured Society to kill Maria Marvelli's husband; in support of it, they cited the impeccable legal logic that he had broken the code of *omertà* by telling the doctor who had stolen the yearling bull.

After two years away, Paolo Agostino finally arrived home on 2 March 1936. He was immediately summoned to a meeting of the Honoured Society: how could he justify his breach of the rules? His self-defence was a desperate show of chutzpah. He said that he no longer feared anyone in Cirella, because on Ustica he had found 'new and more powerful friendships by joining a mighty association that was represented there'.

What was this 'mighty association' on Ustica? A bluff? Or was Paolo Agostino hinting that he had become a member of the Sicilian mafia since last he saw Aspromonte? Ustica was more than usually full of Sicilian *mafiosi* at the time. Whether Agostino was bluffing or not, the Romeo brothers became even more determined to eliminate him. When Paolo Agostino flagrantly insulted the Honoured Society's protocols by failing to turn up for a second hearing into his case, the Romeos got their motion through, and a death sentence against Agostino was passed. The problem now for the Romeo brothers became a practical rather than a political one: how to carry out the hit—a task that would require both a carefully prepared trap and a narrative to bait it.

While waiting for their opportunity, the Romeo brothers had to content themselves with insults. They broke Paolo Agostino's gramophone at a gangland celebration to mark the engagement of his stepson, Francesco Polito. (After turning down the boss's daughter, Maria Marvelli's boy had finally found a suitable girl from a suitably delinquent family.) Only the presence of so many witnesses stopped the gramophone incident degenerating into a bloodbath.

If Paolo Agostino did not realise before that his time was running out, he certainly realised now. He became gloomy. Among friends he referred to himself wistfully as 'a bird just passing through life'. He refused to spank his children, saying that he did not want to leave them with bad memories of him. His despondency was apparent to Maria Marvelli, who took charge of security at home, forcing her husband to sleep elsewhere when danger threatened.

The first attempt on Agostino's life involved the staged theft of his ox. The Romeo brothers sent men to steal the animal, making plenty of noise as they did, in the hope that Agostino would rush out of his house. If all went well, he could then be shot down, as if by anonymous robbers. But in the event it was the redoubtable Maria Marvelli who came out of the house, gun in hand, and chased off the would-be assassins.

A far more rigorously conceived plot would be needed to do away with Paolo Agostino. The Romeo brothers called a meeting of senior *mafiosi* in an abandoned shack on 30 April 1936. After much discussion their plan was agreed and a ten-man firing party picked to execute it. The dummy don, Francesco Macrì, volunteered to stand shoulder-to-shoulder with the Romeo brothers in the upcoming action; evidently he wanted to earn the lofty rank that he had so recently been given. But the crucial figure in the scheme, the man set up to betray Paolo Agostino to his enemies, was to be Nicola Pollifroni—the man who had a 'plausible' affair with Maria Marvelli. Pollifroni was made to kneel before his brethren, with his arms crossed flat on his chest, and swear to help kill his friend.

On 2 May Pollifroni invited Paolo Agostino along on an expedition to raid some beehives, thereby insulting their owner with whom Pollifroni had an old beef. No member of the Honoured Society could refuse such an invitation. The raid was a success, and Pollifroni and Agostino returned along an isolated path, carrying pots of fragrant honey. The route took them through a narrow pass between two giant boulders covered in gorse. The judge would subsequently explain that the path reminded him of the ever-narrowing gulleys in an abattoir floor that isolate a single pig, forcing it to walk between two walls until it can no longer turn round or go back. By the time the butcher's knife comes into view, there is no longer any escape. The pass had a name locally: Agonia ('Agony').

Just as the two honey thieves were entering the pass, Pollifroni stopped. He had to take a pee. Agostino should walk on ahead, into the narrow walls of the pass.

The last thing Agostino ever heard came from somewhere on the boulder above him: a strangled cry of warning, both sudden and familiar. Agostino's stepson Francesco Polito was being forced to watch the murder, a dagger pressed to his throat. He had the courage and desperation to cry out a warning before a large hand was clamped over his mouth, and a shotgun chorus drowned out all other sound.

What gives an undeniably Fascist flavour to the story of the Cirella mafia was what happened to the Romeo brothers, the dummy don Francesco Macrì, and the others once they were arrested. Under interrogation, as their blood oaths dictated, they denied any knowledge of the criminal association they belonged to. So they were punched and whipped and beaten with anything that came to hand, like a heavy ruler and a blotter. They were forced to drink a clay pot full of piss. To muffle their screams, their own socks were stuffed in their mouths and secured with their own belts. Then they were pushed to the floor, and their legs chained up on chairs so that the soles of their feet could be beaten and their toenails pulled out. (Later, some would have amputations as a result.) Their wounds were doused in salt and vinegar. The most uncooperative among them were electrocuted: wires attached to a car battery were applied to their inner thighs, leaving them barely conscious. They were then hurled into damp, filthy cells in Locri jail with no food or water. All requests for medical visits were denied.

One by one, they confessed. Every time they were called on to confirm their confessions, the beatings began again. The men of Cirella's Honoured Society had found their own place called Agony.

Only in court could the allegation of police violence finally emerge. When the judge heard of the horrors he treated them as just that: mere allegation. Somehow, he deemed it no job of his to weigh up whether what the defendants alleged was true. Not even, it seems, by checking on their amputated toes. But the sheer detail of the judge's description, and the squirming of his logic, tell us he knew what had really happened: the accused before him had been brutally tortured by the *Carabinieri*.

Of course the judge had plenty of other evidence to draw on: the testimonies of Maria Marvelli and her son Francesco Polito; the suspects' utterly unconvincing alibis; and the jumble of patently false testimonies, mostly from their womenfolk, that the *mafiosi* had marshalled in their defence. The prosecution could also point out that the dummy don Francesco Macrì kept a list of the Honoured Society's members in a suitcase, and wrote down the names of the ten men chosen to kill Paolo Agostino.

The judge concluded that all of the evidence confirmed the confessions, 'without any regard to the way in which the suspects' initial statements were gathered'. So he felt able to 'put his conscience to rest', and take no further action about a blindingly clear case of police brutality. Torture or no torture, the verdict against the Lads with Attitude in Cirella was guilty.

Everything within the state. Nothing against the state. Nothing outside the state. Fascism's totalitarian ideology clearly gave the cops a licence to go far beyond any acceptable means of interrogation. No doubt the torture used here was also deployed elsewhere against *mafiosi* and *camorristi*. But it is rare to find such graphic and unambiguous evidence of it as there is in the trial papers from Cirella. More often, false claims about police brutality were made by mobsters. Fascism's battle with organised crime could be a very dirty fight indeed, but quite how frequently the authorities really abused their power is anyone's guess.

Maria Marvelli's story is but an isolated tableau of the piecemeal changes happening in Calabrian organised crime: the marriage politics that the *picciotti* were learning, and the new power behind the scenes that some women gained as a result. Marvelli was, without doubt, a loser: her house had been torched; her husband murdered. She lost her son too: despite his confession, the boy who had once been the most eligible criminal batchelor in Cirella was sentenced to six years and eight months under new, tougher Fascist laws against criminal associations. It is not known whether he was among the men who had their toenails extracted by the *Carabinieri*; it is not known what happened to him in prison.

But Maria Marvelli did at least have something to put in the scales to counterbalance her losses. The satisfaction of vendetta, for one thing. And even some money: she sued the defendants on her children's behalf, and won 26,000 lire—roughly equal to the value of her house.

We do not know what happened to Maria Marvelli later. She is like thousands of other faceless mafia women in history, in that we can only wonder what became of her after the court records fall silent. If she did go back to Cirella, she would certainly have found a village still in the grip of the picciotteria. The same judge who was too timid to confront the *Carabinieri* about their repeated assaults on the prisoners was also too timid to pass a harsh verdict on the mafia: he acquitted 104 of the *picciotti* whose names appeared on the dummy don's list, on the less than convincing grounds that 'public rumour' was the only evidence against them. What this amounted to saying was that everyone in Cirella had seen these men strutting around the square; everyone knew at the very least that they were in cahoots and up to no good. They were visible, in other words. But even under Fascism, visibility alone was not enough to convict.

CAMPANIA: The Fascist Vito Genovese

ON 8 JULY 1938 THE NEAPOLITAN DAILY *IL MATTINO* PUBLISHED THE FOLLOWING short notice.

FASCIST NEWSBOARD

The Fascist Vito Genovese, enlisted in the New York branch of the Fascist Party and currently resident in Naples, has donated 10,000 lire. The Roccarainola branch received 5,000 lire as a contribution to the cost of the land required to build the local party headquarters. The other 5,000 lire is for building Nola's Heliotherapy Centre.

Vito Genovese would later reportedly subsidise the building of Nola's Fascist party HQ to the tune of $25,000 (in 1930s values). Visitors to Nola—and there are not many—can still see the building in piazza Giordano Bruno: a white block, long since stripped of its Mussolinian badges, it houses a local branch of the University of Naples, the Faculty of Law in fact.

Genovese was born in Risigliano, near Nola, on 21 November 1897. We do not know whether his family had any connections with the Campanian underworld before they emigrated to the United States in 1912. Nonetheless, New York offered bounteous opportunities for violent young immigrants. Vito rose rapidly through the ranks of gangland, alongside his friend, the Sicilian-born Charles 'Lucky' Luciano. A now famous mug shot of Genovese from this period shows a bug-eyed enforcer with a skewed crest of black hair.

In 1936, Lucky Luciano received a thirty-to-fifty-year sentence on compulsory prostitution charges. (Which of course he would have avoided had he followed the conventions in force in the mafia's homeland.) Vito Genovese was scheduled to take over from Luciano at the apex of the New York mafia, an organisation still dominated by Sicilians. But he was also due to face a murder charge, and was afraid that it might result in comparably harsh treatment. So in 1937 he fled to a gilded exile in the land of his birth.

In Italy, Vito Genovese's generosity, like his Fascism, were self-interested. Strong rumours suggest that he was busy shipping narcotics back to the United States. With the profits, Genovese made his contribution to the Fascist architectural legacy in Campania and lavishly entertained both Mussolini and Count Galeazzo Ciano, the Duce's son-in-law and Foreign Minister. It is only logical to assume that Genovese had excellent top-level contacts in Nola too.

Evidently, in Campania Fascism lacked the integrity and the attention span needed to follow up on Major Anceschi's recommendations following his operations in the Mazzoni in 1926–28. One way or another, in Campania Fascism lapsed from the crusading zeal of the Ascension Day speech into a quiet political accommodation with gangsters. As later events would prove, Vito Genovese was now part of a flourishing criminal landscape.

'The Fascist Vito Genovese', the New York boss who enjoyed a profitable homecoming in Campania in the 1930s and 1940s.

31

SICILY: The slimy octopus

WE HAVE KNOWN FOR A LONG TIME THAT CESARE MORI'S BOAST THAT HE HAD BEATEN the mafia would turn out hollow, and that the Mori Operation was a failure in the long-term. After all, once Fascism fell and democracy was restored, Sicily's notorious criminal fraternity began a new phase of its history that would prove more arrogant and bloodthirsty than any yet seen. A great deal of energy has been devoted to dishing out responsibility for the mafia's revival after the Second World War. Conspiracy theorists said it was all the Americans' fault: the mafia returned with the Allied invasion in 1943. Pessimists put the blame on Italian democracy: without a dictator in charge, the country was just not capable of staging a thoroughgoing repression of organised crime.

Whoever was to blame for the subsequent revival in the mafia's fortunes, most memories of the campaign to eradicate it were more or less in tune with Fascism's own trumpet calls. Even some *mafiosi* recalled the alarums of the late 1920s with a shudder. One Man of Honour, despite being too young to remember the Mori Operation, said in 1986 that

> The music changed [under Fascism]. Mafiosi had a hard life . . . After the war the mafia hardly existed anymore. The Sicilian Families had all been broken up. The mafia was like a plant they don't grow anymore.

So, until recently, the historical memory of the Iron Prefect's titanic campaign of repression in Sicily was fundamentally united: even if the mafia had not been destroyed, it had at least bowed its head before the thudding might of the Fascist state.

Until recently. Until 2007, that is, when Italy's leading historian of the mafia unearthed a startling report that had lain forgotten in the Palermo State Archive. Because of that report—many hundreds of pages long if one includes its 228 appendices—the story of Fascism's 'last struggle' with the mafia must now be completely rewritten. Some of the best young historians in Sicily are busy rewriting it. The Mori Operation, it turns out, involved the most elaborate lie in the history of organised crime.

The report dates from July 1938, and it addresses the state of law and order in Sicily since the last big mafia trial concluded late in 1932. It had no less than forty-eight authors, all of them members of a special combined force of *Carabinieri* and policemen known by the unwieldy title of the Royal General Inspectorate for Public Security for Sicily—the Inspectorate, for short. And the majority of its members were Sicilians, to judge by their surnames.

The report begins as follows.

> Despite repeated waves of vigorous measures taken by the police and judiciary [during the Mori Operation], the criminal organisation known in Sicily and elsewhere by the vague name of 'mafia' has endured; it has never really ceased to exist. All that happened is that there were a few pauses, creating the impression that everything was calm . . . It was believed—and people who were in bad faith endeavoured to make everyone believe—that the mafia had been totally eradicated. But all of that was nothing more than a cunning and sophisticated manoeuvre designed by the mafia's many managers—the ones who had succeeded in escaping or remaining above suspicion during the repression. Their main aim was to deceive the authorities and soften up so-called public opinion so that they could operate with ever greater freedom and perversity.

The mafia had sold Fascism an extravagant dummy, the Inspectorate claimed. Some bosses had used the very force and propagandistic éclat of the Mori Operation to make believe that they had gone away. The mafia had its own propaganda agenda—to appear beaten—and its message was broadcast by the Fascist regime's obliging megaphones. The Palermo *capi* may just as well have ghostwritten Cesare Mori's *The Last Struggle with the Mafia*.

The story of the 1938 report dates back to 1933, well within a year of the last Mori trial, when there was a crime wave so overwhelming as to make it obvious that the police structures put in place by the Iron Prefect were no longer fit for purpose. The police and *Carabinieri* were reorganised into an elite force to combat it: the Royal General Inspectorate for Public Security for Sicily. Thus the Fascist state started the struggle with the mafia all over again. Only this time the national and international public that had lapped up reports of the Iron Prefect's heroics were not allowed to know anything about what was going on.

The men of the Inspectorate picked up again where Mori's police had left off in 1929. As they did, they slowly assembled proof that the mafia across western Sicily was more organised than anyone except perhaps Chief of Police Ermanno Sangiorgi would ever have dared imagine: the 'slimy octopus', they called it.

The chosen starting point was the province of Trapani, at the island's western tip, where the Mori Operation had made least impact and where criminal disorder was now at its worst: here the mafia 'reigned with all of its members in place', the Inspectorate found. When they arrested large numbers of Trapani *mafiosi*, the bosses still at liberty held a provincial meeting to decide on their tactical response. A letter was sent urging everyone in the organisation to keep violence to a minimum until this new wave of repression had crested and broken.

The Inspectorate's next round of investigations discovered a mafia livestock-smuggling network, 300 strong, that extended across the whole of the west of the island; *mafiosi* referred to it as the *Abigeataria*—something like 'The Cattle-Rustling Department'. As they always had done, Sicilian *mafiosi* worked together to steal animals in one place and move them to market far away.

Then came the southern province of Agrigento. The Inspectorate's investigations into an armed attack on a motor coach gradually revealed that the mafia had a formal structure here too. *Mafiosi* interrogated by the Inspectorate used the term 'Families' for the structure's local cells. The Families often coordinated their activities. For example, the men who attacked the motor coach came from three different Families; they had never met one another before their bosses ordered them to participate in the raid, but they nonetheless carried it out in harmony. Even more alarmingly, the Inspectorate discovered that, just as the Mori Operation trials were coming to their conclusion in 1932, bosses in Agrigento received a circular letter from Palermo telling them 'to close ranks, and get ready for the resumption of large-scale crimes'.

Among the most revealing testimonies gathered by the Inspectorate was that of Dr Melchiorre Allegra, a family doctor, radiographer and lung specialist who ran a clinic in Castelvetrano, in the province of Trapani. Allegra was arrested in the summer of 1937, and dictated a dense twenty-six-page confession that shone the light of the Inspectorate's policework back into the past. Allegra was initiated in Palermo in 1916 so he could provide phoney medical certificates for Men of Honour who wanted to avoid serving in the First World War. The *mafiosi* who were formally presented to Dr Allegra as 'brothers' included men of all stations, from coach drivers, butchers and fishmongers, right up to Members of Parliament and landed aristocrats. After the Great War, the provincial and Family bosses would often come from across Sicily to meet in the Birreria Italia, a polished café, pastry shop and bar situated at the junction of via Cavour and via Maqueda, in the very centre of Palermo. For a few years, until the Fascist police became suspicious, the Birreria Italia was the centre of the mafia world, a social club for the island's gangster elite.

The Inspectorate were well aware that the men Dr Allegra called brothers were in a permanent state of war among themselves, whether open or declared. The mafia was prone to 'internecine struggles deriving from grudges which, whether they were recent and remote, nearly always revolved around who was to gain supremacy when it came to distributing the various positions within the organisation'. An 'internecine struggle' of just this kind would give the Inspectorate its route into the mafia's very nucleus, the lemon groves of the Conca d'Oro around Palermo.

When the Iron Prefect first came to Palermo in October 1925, his attention was immediately drawn to the Piana dei Colli, the northern part of the Conca d'Oro where Inspector Ermanno Sangiorgi first tussled with the mafia in the 1870s. Half a century later, the Piana dei Colli was the site of a particularly ferocious battle between two mafia factions. The conflict left bodies in the streets of central Palermo, many of them belonging to senior bosses. Some of the mafia dynasties that had ruled the area since the 1860s did not survive the carnage. Those that did, and who didn't manage to escape to America, Tunisia or London, were rounded up by the Iron Prefect's cops. Then Mori left, and calm returned.

The Inspectorate discovered that the *mafiosi* from the Piana dei Colli who had been released, or returned from exile after the Mori Operation ended, could not reorganise their Families because of the residual tensions between them. The tit-for-tat killings resumed. In 1934, a boss named Rosario Napoli was slain; the culprits tried to frame Napoli's own nephew for the murder. This nephew was the first Palermitan *mafioso* to give information to the Inspectorate. His testimony slowly tipped into a cascade of confessions from other mobsters, some of whom described the initiation ritual they had undergone when they were first admitted. As so often, *omertà* had cracked. By bringing together these confessions, and patiently corroborating them, the Inspectorate then assembled a narrative of the war in the Conca d'Oro that shed an even more withering light on Mussolini's portentous Ascension Day claims.

The protagonists of this new narrative were the Marasà brothers, Francesco, Antonino, and above all Ernesto—the *generalissimo*, as the Inspectorate dubbed him. The Marasà brothers had their power base in the western section of the Conca d'Oro, between Monreale and Porta Nuova. That is, along the road travelled by Turi Miceli and his mafia squad when they launched the Palermo revolt back in September 1866. Like Turi Miceli, the Marasà brothers had money. In fact the Inspectorate estimated that they owned property, livestock and other assets worth 'quite a few million lire'. One million lire was worth some $52,000 at the time, and that amount in 1938 had the purchasing power of some $1.7 million today.

What the men of the Inspectorate found most disturbing about the Marasà brothers was their ability to collect friendships among the island's ruling class, to place themselves above suspicion, to cloak the power they had won through violence, and to cover the bloody tracks that traced their ascent.

By poisoning the political system under the pre-Fascist governments, they carried out their shady criminal business on the agricultural estates, in

After the mafia's defeat, 1937: Mussolini makes a triumphal visit to Sicily to open a new aqueduct. By this time the island's criminal Families had returned to full operation under the leadership of Ernesto 'the *generalissimo*' Marasà.

the lemon groves, in the city, in the suburban townships, in the villages. They always managed to stay hidden in the shadows cast by baronial and princely coats of arms, by medals and titles. Thanks to the shameful complaisance shown by men who are supposed to be responsible for the fair and efficient administration of the law, they always slipped away from punishment. But behind the politician's mask, behind the honorific title, behind the all-pervasive hypocrisy and the imposing wealth, there lurked the coarsest kind of criminal, with evil, grasping instincts, whose warlike early years in the ranks of the underworld have left an indelible mark of infamy.

It is a testament to the Marasà brothers' success in shrouding their 'indelible mark of infamy' that, until the discovery of the Inspectorate's report in 2007, their names had hardly been mentioned in the chronicles of mafia history. No photographs, no police descriptions, hardly even any rumours: a criminal power all the more pervasive for being unseen and unnamed.

In the late 1920s, while the bosses of the Piana dei Colli were busy ambushing one another, and then falling victim to the Mori Operation, Ernesto Marasà and his brothers remained entirely untouched. Indeed, *generalissimo* Ernesto showed a breathtaking Machiavellian composure in the face of the Fascist onslaught: he actually fed incriminating information about his mafia rivals to the Iron Prefect's investigators. Mussolini's Fascist scalpel had been partially guided by a *mafioso's* hand.

Ernesto Marasà's rise to power continued after the Mori Operation ended. While his enemies were held in jail, seething about being betrayed, Marasà constructed an alliance of supporters across the mafia Families of Palermo's entire hinterland, including the Piana dei Colli where he continued to undermine his enemies by passing information to the police. His plan was, quite simply, to become the mafia's boss of all bosses. The Inspectorate spied on the *generalissimo* as he ran his campaign from room 2 of the Hotel Vittoria just off via Maqueda, Palermo's main artery. Now and again, he and two or three of his heavies would clamber aboard a little red FIAT *Balilla* and set off to meet friends and arrange hits in one of Palermo's many mafia-dominated *borgate*.

After five years of work, the Inspectorate could conclude its 1938 report with a chillingly clear description of the mafia's structure that reads like a line-by-line demolition of the Iron Prefect's own views.

The mafia is not just a state of mind or a mental habit. It actually spreads this state of mind, this mental habit, from within what is a genuine organisation. It is divided into so-called 'Families', which are sub-divided into

'Tens', and it has 'bosses' or 'representatives' who are formally elected. The members, or 'brothers', have to go through an oath to prove their unquestioning fidelity and secretiveness.

The oath, no one will be surprised to learn, involved pricking the finger with a pin, dripping blood on a sacred image, and then burning the image in the hands while swearing loyalty until death.

The mafia was organised 'in the form of a sect, along the lines of the Freemasons'. Its Families in each province had an overall 'representative' whose responsibilities included contacts with the organisation's branches abroad, in the United States, France and Tunisia. The Families in the provinces of Trapani, Agrigento and Caltanissetta looked to Palermo for leadership at crucial times. The mafia, declared the Inspectorate, 'had an organic and harmonious structure, regulated by clearly defined norms, and managed by people who were utterly beyond suspicion'. At the centre of the mafia web, there was a 'boss of all bosses' or 'general president': *generalissimo* Ernesto Marasà.

The Inspectorate's 1938 report was sent in multiple copies to senior figures in the judiciary and law enforcement. The forty-eight brave men who put their names to the document were desperate for their sleuthing to make a real difference in Sicily. Their desperation was evident in an indignant, impassioned turn of phrase: in the lurid talk of a 'slimy octopus' (as if a beast as sophisticated as the mafia could ever have just one head); and also in the conclusion, which deliberately parroted the catchphrases of Mussolini's Ascension Day speech. Somewhere, they hoped, their plea would meet the eyes of someone determined to make Fascism's results match up to its battle cries: there must be 'no holding back' against an evil that was 'dishonouring Sicily'; the state must once again wield the 'scalpel' against the mafia.

The passion and insight that went into the Inspectorate's 1938 report makes its every word chilling, for two reasons. First, because it provides the earliest absolutely indisputable evidence that the Sicilian mafia was a single highly structured organisation that extended right across western Sicily. Terms like 'Family', 'representative', and 'boss of all bosses' had never appeared before in the historical record. Second, because many years would pass, and the lives of many brave police, *Carabinieri* and magistrates would be sacrificed, before the moment in 1992 when a diagram of the Sicilian mafia that was *identical* to the one assembled by the Inspectorate would finally be accepted as the truth within the Italian legal system.

But in 1938 there was not the slightest hope that the Fascist state would return to a war footing against organised crime. In fact the signs that Fascism would fail to beat the mafia were there to be seen all along. In the Iron Prefect's refusal to believe that his enemy was an Honoured Society, for example.

The many faces of 'Iron Prefect' Cesare Mori, who spearheaded
Mussolini's attack on the Sicilian mafia in the 1920s.

Man of action, and scourge of the
mafia.

Fascist role model.

Wannabe socialite . . .

. . . and friend to the Sicilian
aristocracy.

Or in his crass view of Sicilian psychology. Or in Fascism's preference for bundling suspects off into enforced residence on penal colonies: no noise, and no judicial process. For, as anyone with a historical memory for anti-mafia measures would have known, fighting organised crime in this way was like fighting weeds in your garden by transplanting them into your greenhouse.

The Mori Operation was only ever going to be a short-term measure. The aim was to draw a decisive line between the new regime and the corrupt democratic past; it was to show that Fascism was still vigorous even though the cudgels and the castor oil had been cast to one side. Fascist 'surgery' on Sicily was never intended to prepare the patient for a life of law and order. It was about putting on a propagandistic spectacle; it was about winning for Mussolini the support of the island's landed elite—the very aristocrats whose 'baronial and princely coats of arms' had shielded the Marasà brothers, like so many other *mafiosi* before them.

The Iron Prefect, the orphan boy from Pavia, was besotted with the sumptuous decadence of Palermo's *beau monde*. When Mori socialised in the Sicilian capital, he went out in a luxurious carriage, its lustrous black bodywork bristling with gilt, intaglio, and all manner of baroque ornamentation. He was 'on heat for the nobility'—to use an enemy's crude phrase—as he swished from ball to ball, from salon to salon. The Iron Prefect believed, or chose to believe, that the landowners he played *baccarà* with were exactly what their lawyers had always said they were when, from time to time, their underworld connections were exposed: they were *victims* of the thugs, and not their strategic protectors.

The charges against the 'slimy octopus' that were meticulously assembled in the Inspectorate's 1938 report took until 1942 to come to court. By that time the Men of Honour who had told their secrets to the Inspectorate had retracted their confessions. Before the trial most of the *mafiosi* named in the 1938 report were released for lack of evidence—including the *generalissimo* Ernesto Marasà, with his brothers. And in the trial itself, most of the fifty-three men who were eventually convicted received only short sentences. The case set out in the 1938 report had slowly crumbled until it became a comparatively minor inconvenience for the Sicilian mob. As Ermanno Sangiorgi could have told the men of the Inspectorate, many earlier anti-mafia cases had fallen apart in the same way. What was different in 1942 was that the Fascist regime, which was busy crowing about dazzling feats of bravura by the Italian army in the Second World War, completely suppressed all mention of the Inspectorate's report and the resultant court proceedings. Once again, Italy had proved just how resourceful it could be when it came to denying the truth about the Sicilian mafia.

32

Master Joe dances a *Tarantella*

If there is a servant of the state who encapsulates all the contradictions of Fascism's long fight against the Honoured Society in Calabria, but also elsewhere, then perhaps it is Giuseppe Delfino.

Delfino was a homespun hero of law enforcement. In August 1926, just as Fascism was first cranking up its clampdown, he took command of the *Carabiniere* station in Platì, overlooking the Ionian Coast. This was the territory where Delfino was born and he knew it as well as anyone. Both the picciotteria citadel of San Luca and the Sanctuary of the Madonna of Polsi were on his beat. Cussed and smart, Delfino would disguise himself as a shepherd to patrol the mountain unobserved, or slip into taverns so he could overhear the *picciotti* as they bragged. Among the peasants he earned the respectful nickname *Massaru Peppi* ('Master Joe')—*massaru* being the word for a farm overseer or factor. Master Joe dismantled a cattle-rustling network centred on San Luca in January 1927, and thereby—despite the murder of his key witness—brought seventy-six *mafiosi* to justice. Among them were men called Strangio, Pelle and Nirta: perhaps not coincidentally, families with these surnames would much later be caught up in the blood feud that led to the massacre at Duisberg on 15 August 2007.

The Calabrian press, which was generally sparing in its coverage of the anti-organised crime campaign, said that Delfino had 'brought honour on himself'.

Meanwhile this resourceful station commander has not even allowed himself a day's rest, and is pressing on with his pursuit of the lawbreakers.

Shortly afterwards, once the rustlers he had arrested had their convictions confirmed on appeal, 'Master Joe' Delfino even earned himself a walk-on part in the canon of Italian literature. Corrado Alvaro, the San Luca–born author who was our witness to the pilgrimage to the Sanctuary at Polsi, also wrote a vignette about Master Joe's relentless hunt for a small-time goat thief. Borrowing the peasants' own spare vocabulary, Alvaro evoked the holy terror that Delfino inspired on Aspromonte throughout Fascism's twenty-year rule.

> Delfino was the *Carabiniere* who couldn't hear a robber's name mentioned without setting off in pursuit as if he'd staked money on it . . . With his short cloak, his rifle, and his sparkly eyes, he rummaged everywhere: he knew all the hiding places, he knew every renegade's habits like he knew his own pocket—the hollow trunks, the grottoes that no one apart from the mountain folk could find, the perches high in ancient trees.

As publicity goes, this may not seem much. Indeed, compared to the Iron Prefect, the inveterate blowhard whose battle with the mafia in Sicily received glowing worldwide press, Master Joe's profile was positively meek. But the odd line in local newspapers and the hushed respect of the peasants amounted to about as much fame as anyone could possibly hope to accumulate by serving the law in far-off Calabria, even at the height of Fascism's short-lived enthusiasm for facing down the bosses.

Local legend and family memory are the only source we have to draw on to reconstruct much of Master Joe's long career on Aspromonte. But that memory, however much time may have embroidered it, gives us access to a truth that the newspapers and trial documents disguise. Even Master Joe's son, the current guardian of Delfino lore, portrays him as a man with very violent methods. This was a part of the world where there were two paths in life—'Either you became a *Carabiniere*, or you entered the 'ndrangheta'— and brutality lay along both of them.

The story goes that Master Joe once waited until Christmas for a runaway *picciotto* to return home, and did not swoop until his target had hunkered down over a plate of *maccheroni* with goat meat sauce. Master Joe then stood below the window, disguised as a shepherd, and played a wistful song on the bagpipes. The *picciotto* was so moved that he stopped eating and leaned out of the window to offer the minstrel a drink of wine, only to find a pistol pointed at his face. Recognising Master Joe, he said, 'Let me finish my *maccheroni*, at least'. The reply was blunt. 'That would be pointless, because back at the barracks we'd only make you vomit them all up again anyway'.

Master Joe, it is said, was as good as his word: the thief spent a week on his back being punched and forced to drink salt water. When a doctor was finally allowed in, he saw the man's grotesquely swollen stomach, shook his head, and said, 'You don't need a GP here, you need an obstetrician'.

If this story sounds far-fetched then perhaps we should recall that Cirella, where the members of the picciotteria who killed Maria Marvelli's husband were tortured until they confessed, was also part of Master Joe's beat.

There is one more family memory of Master Joe that shows us another side of his, and Fascism's, battle with the 'ndrangheta.

In the autumn of 1940 station commander 'Master Joe' Delfino was still on duty. With only one officer to help him maintain order during the annual pilgrimage to the Sanctuary of the Madonna of Polsi, it is said that he took a Chief Cudgel aside and made a deal so that there would be no trouble. If there were any murders decreed at Polsi that year, then they were performed at a polite distance in time and space from the Sanctuary. Indeed Delfino's son later recalled that, 'for all the years my father was in charge, nothing happened' at Polsi. The station commander would even join the celebrating crowds during the pilgrimage, taking his turn to dance a *tarantella* with the members of the Honoured Society. The picture Delfino's son paints in our

Don 'Ntoni Macrì, the most powerful of post-war *'ndranghetisti*, and Master Joe's dance partner at Polsi.

'Master Joe' (seated). The *Carabiniere* who fought the Calabrian mafia under Mussolini.

mind's eye is vivid. The sanctuary set amid the chestnut trees. The hectic trilling of a squeeze box. A circle of swarthy grins, some of them traversed by ghastly razor-blade tracery. And there in the middle, the *Carabiniere*, kicking out the bold red stripes on his black uniform trousers.

Se non è vero, è molto ben trovato: if the picture isn't true, it's a very smart invention—one that historians should cherish. What official sources can scarcely ever record is just this kind of informal accord between the authorities and the mob. A cagey mutual respect. An improvised agreement to share power and territory. At Polsi, as in so many other parts of Sicily and southern Italy, after the roundups, and the beatings, and the trials, and the propagandistic speeches had passed, the Fascist state settled back into Italy's traditional dance with organised crime.

33

LIBERATION

THE SECOND WORLD WAR WAS THE GREATEST COLLECTIVE TRAGEDY EVER ENDURED BY the Italian people. Between 1935 and 1942, Italian armies visited death and destruction on Ethiopia, Albania, France, Greece and Russia. In 1943, death and destruction came home to the peninsula with vengeful fury.

Italian territory was invaded for the first time on 10 July when seven Allied divisions launched a seaborne assault on Sicily. Up in Rome, in the early hours of 25 July, a meeting of the Fascist Grand Council voted to bring twenty years of Fascist rule to an end; Benito Mussolini was arrested the following evening. As news spread across the country, Italians tore down Fascist symbols; many people thought the war was over. But the catastrophe had only just begun.

On 17 August the last Axis troops completed their evacuation of Sicily. On 3 September the Allies crossed the Straits of Messina into Calabria, where they met only token resistance. On 8 September the Allied Supreme Commander, General Dwight D. Eisenhower, announced Italy's surrender. The very next day saw the beginning of Operation Avalanche—the landing at Salerno, just south of Naples. The Germans—no longer allies but invaders—rumbled down the peninsula to carry on their war. Italy's king fled. All semblance of his government's civil and military authority dissolved and the Italian people were left to find their own path to survival.

Naples was liberated on 1 October. But the Allied advance ground to a halt soon afterwards. For the next twenty months Italy was a battleground, as the *Reich* and the Allies slogged out a slow and bloody contest. Behind German lines in the north and centre, a civil war pitted recalcitrant Fascists against the Resistance. There were collective reprisals and atrocities, mass deportations of Italian workers and troops, and a campaign of racial extermination directed at Italy's Jews.

The south scarcely fared better under Allied Military Government in the Occupied Territories, known as AMGOT. In preparation for AMGOT, the War Office had drafted *Zone Handbooks* on the society and mores of Sicily, Calabria and Campania. Those *Handbooks* are revealing in two ways. First, they tell us what the world knew about organised crime after a century of history. Second, they allow us to measure how shocked the Allies were by the chaos that followed liberation and the rapid collapse of the Italian state. Score settling, hunger, contagion, corruption, black-marketeering and banditry: these were ideal conditions in which Italy's gangsters could announce to the world that, whatever Mussolini might claim, they still had a role to play on the historical stage.

War Office, London: Directorate of Civil Affairs.

Sicily Zone Handbook.

Secret.

*The information contained herein is believed
to be correct as at May 1st, 1943.*

*The head of the Palermo police has said that if a cross were
to be placed on every spot where a victim lies buried in the plain
of Palermo, the Conca d'Oro would appear as a vast cemetery.*

*Mafia never was a compact criminal association, but a
complex social phenomenon, the consequence of centuries of
misgovernment. The Mafiuso is governed by a sentiment akin to
arrogance, which imposes a special line of conduct upon him. A
Mafiuso is thus not a thief or a rascal in any simple sense. He
desires to be respected, and nearly always he respects others.
Mafia is the consciousness of one's individuality, the exaggerated
conceit of one's strength.*

*All Italian governments have been anxious to suppress this
scourge of Sicilian life. The Fascist regime did its best to destroy
Mafia, and the ruthless efforts of Mori, the Prefect of Palermo,
resulted in many arrests. However, it is difficult to change the
spirit of a people by mere police measures, and the Mafia may
still exist in Sicily.*

Nicola (Nick) Gentile was born in 1885 in Siculiana, in the province of Agrigento, Sicily's notorious sulphur country. In 1906 he was initiated into the Honoured Society in Philadelphia, USA. An extortionist, murderer, bootlegger and drug dealer, he spent the next three decades of his life shuttling to and fro across the Atlantic as the demands of his criminal business, and the need to avoid his enemies in the police and mafia, dictated. Arrested on a narcotics charge in New Orleans in 1937, Gentile jumped bail and fled to Sicily.

Gentile was back in the province of Agrigento in the momentous month of July 1943, in his wife's hometown of Raffadali. When the American troops passed through, he smilingly offered them his services as a translator and guide to their commanding officer. Soon he and the officer had formed what he called 'an administration, a government' across many of the surrounding towns.

Thus began the Allies' crash course in the techniques for infiltrating state authority that the mafia had refined over the previous century. Nick Gentile's story is typical: across western Sicily *mafiosi* made friends with combat troops and then with the utterly bewildered military administrators who followed in behind. Amid an explosion of prison breakouts and armed robbery, AMGOT sought authority figures untainted by Mussolini's regime to help them deal with the anarchy. As 'middle-class villains', Men of Honour are very good at creating the respectable façade that AMGOT was looking for. Nick Gentile could even pose as a victim of Fascist oppression because he had spent a couple of years on remand during the Iron Prefect's anti-mafia drive of the late 1920s. Many of his brethren had similar tales of woe to tell. So when AMGOT looked to replace Blackshirted mayors with more friendly locals, there was often an obvious candidate to hand. As Major General Lord James Rennell Rodd, the British head of AMGOT, later admitted

> With the people clamouring to be rid of a Fascist *Podestà* [mayor], many of my officers fell into the trap of selecting the most forthcoming self-advertiser . . . The choices in more than one instance fell on the local 'Mafia' boss or his shadow, who in one or two cases had graduated in an American gangster environment.

Lord Rennell had a huge amount to cope with, in an uncertain and fast-moving situation. But he was also being parsimonious with the truth. The most insidious overtures to AMGOT were those made by the members of the island's landowning elite. Lord Rennell, the 2nd Baron Rennell, could hardly have been more patrician: a multilingual former diplomat and banker who was educated at Eton and Balliol College Oxford, he was also an enthusiastic member of the Royal Geographical Society who had travelled among the Touareg in the Sahara as a young man, and was a devoted Italophile. To a man of Lord Rennell's breeding it would scarcely have seemed credible that the suave noblemen who invited him to dinner in their grand palazzi in Palermo could have intimate connections with mafia thuggery.

One of those aristocrats was Lucio Tasca Bordonaro, Count of Almerita, who emanated a distinct odour of mafia (as the Italian phrase has it). Back in 1926–27, with the Mori Operation rounding up hoodlums by the hundreds, a mob war was raging in the Conca d'Oro and threatening to bring the Fascist axe crashing down on the very cradle of the Honoured Society. No less than three special commissions of *mafiosi* had come over from the United States, but failed to bring the warring factions together. The Inspectorate discovered that Count Tasca then approached the Iron Prefect on the mafia's behalf. He promised on his honour that the violence would soon end. So what need was there to go to all the trouble of arresting everyone involved?

In the summer of 1943, Lord Rennell, unaware of Count Tasca's record as a mafia mediator, appointed him Mayor of Palermo.

Seeing the mafia's intimacy with the Allies, Sicilians quickly lost faith in AMGOT's ability to impose law and order. And a state that has lost the faith of its citizens is just the kind the mafia likes.

Some American intelligence agents working for the Office of Strategic Services (or OSS, the forerunner of the CIA) came up with what they clearly thought was a smart and highly original scheme to address the crisis. Less than a week after Allied armies occupied the last corner of Sicily, in an enthusiastic bid to win more clout for his young and hitherto unimportant intelligence corps, the OSS's man in Palermo reported as follows.

> Only the Mafia is able to bring about suppression of black market practices and influence the 'contadini' [peasants] who constitute a majority of the population . . . We have had conferences with their [the mafia's] leaders and a bargain has been struck that they will be doing as we direct or suggest. A bargain once made here is not easily broken . . . We lent a sympathetic ear to their troubles and assured them, however feeble our cooperation, that it was theirs for the asking.

In other words, the OSS was suggesting, the Allies should use the mafia to co-manage crime. Throughout the AMGOT period in Sicily, as former agents have since confessed, the OSS continued to lend a 'sympathetic ear' to mafia bosses. The understanding between them, it seems, was based on an exchange of favours: the OSS received information in return for precious little tokens of trust—like tyres, which the *mafiosi* needed for the trucks they deployed in black market operations. In short, with the kind of naivety of which only those most determined to be cunning are capable, the OSS had fallen for the mafia's oldest trick. As had always been the case, robbery and smuggling did not just fill the mafia's coffers; they also had a handy political purpose from the bosses' point of view. A crime wave weakened the state and meant that the state had to seek help in ruling Sicily. Help from the mafia, that is.

Within weeks of the Allied landings in Sicily, much of what little Fascism had achieved against the mafia was obliterated. The AMGOT authorities had little time for the OSS's cynicism. Once Lord Rennell realised the terrifying speed with which the mafia had reasserted its grip, he took what counter-measures he could. But it was already too late. Where a mafia mayor was dismissed, other leading citizens were often afraid to take his place. Sicily's Men of Honour could now plot their course into a post-war world that would bring them greater power and wealth than even they had ever known before.

War Office, London: Directorate of Civil Affairs.

Calabria Zone Handbook.

Secret.

*The information contained herein is believed
to be correct as at May 15th, 1943.*

*Physically, the Calabrian has his own look and build. He is
dark and whiskered, short and wiry; and in Calabria it is the man
who counts. The wife is a beast of burden or a slave, the mother
a nurse . . . Flirting and courting in the English manner are not
understood, and may cost you your life . . . The tough natural
conditions in which a Calabrian lives and works have made
him hard and matter-of-fact . . . The Calabrian is a man of few
words, and those straight to the point. He is scornful of comfort
and luxury, which never enter his own life, and indifferent to pain
and suffering . . . Public justice according to English ideals the
Calabrian does not understand, never having experienced it . . .
Thus no Calabrian, however well born and bred, can be expected
to be on the side of the police as a matter of course.*

*It is natural that in a country where feelings are apt to run
high, crimes committed on a sudden violent impulse are far more
numerous than those arising from cool deliberate malice. Indeed
the latter class of crime is almost unknown in Calabria.*

The fighting between the Allies and the Germans in much of Calabria was
brief. And after the fighting was over, AMGOT kept only a skeleton staff
there. The *Calabria Zone Handbook* made no mention of a mafia in the region. No intelligence reports identified any organised criminal activity in
1943–44. Even Lord Rennell, who toured Calabria in early October 1943,
failed to spot anything seriously amiss. If mayors linked to the picciotteria
were appointed, which seems certain to have been the case, nobody noticed. The Honoured Society of Calabria entered the post-war era stronger
than ever, and—as it had always been—far, far below the radar of public
awareness.

The rise of one Calabrian Chief Cudgel gives us the measure of what
the Allies could not see. Don Antonio ('Ntoni) Macrì was born in 1904 in
Siderno, the economic heart of the notorious Locri region on the Ionian
Coast. His career began in the late 1920s with repeated arrests for assault
and carrying an illegal weapon—the classic profile of the enforcer. In 1933,
with Fascism now claiming victory over the mafias, he was released from
a five-year prison sentence on an amnesty. The obliging governor of his
prison said that he had been 'well behaved and assiduously hard-working',
and therefore deserved to be encouraged further along the path to complete
rehabilitation. There was no rehabilitation: in 1937, he was categorised as a
'habitual delinquent', convicted of being the boss of a criminal association
known by its members as the Honoured Society, and sent to an agricultural
colony for three and a half years.

Once this 'habitual delinquent' was free again, the *Carabinieri* reports
suddenly change their tone dramatically: 'irreproachable and hard-working',
he was called. Don 'Ntoni was the boss that Master Joe danced the *tarantella* with in the last years of Fascism. So now we have an idea what he
received in return for keeping control of his men during the pilgrimage
to Polsi.

In August 1944, with the AMGOT period over and Calabria back under
Italian control, don 'Ntoni was once more identified as the leader of a criminal organisation and recommended for enforced residence. The reports on
him say that he was running protection rackets in the most valuable agricultural land of the Ionian Coast. A judge wrote that he 'dictated the price
of oranges and lemons to suit his own whim and to serve his own interest
as a dealer in the citrus fruit sector'.

Don 'Ntoni 'went on the run', but such was the control he exercised over his territory that he was able to stay exactly where he was. In April 1946 he was finally spotted and arrested in the centre of Locri, near to the Palace of Justice, with a revolver and a dagger in his pockets. In July of the same year magistrates dismissed the case against him because of 'insufficient evidence'. *Insufficient evidence*: since the 1870s, this had been the proud motto beneath many a Sicilian crime dynasty's family crest. Now don 'Ntoni Macrì had acquired the same degree of power and influence. Along with the same self-interested strain of family values. When don 'Ntoni's wife passed away not long after, his men forced large numbers of local people to attend her funeral. In a judge's words, the ceremony became 'the opportunity to stage a public demonstration of the Honoured Society's omnipotence'.

In this corner of Calabria at least, the humble picciotteria, the sect of brawlers, pimps and petty extortionists that had crawled out from the prisons in the 1880s, had completed its ascent.

By the 1960s don 'Ntoni had a criminal record—a shelf-bowing 900 pages long—that read like the bill for the decades since the 1880s in which Calabria's gangster emergency had been ignored. He was murdered in 1975, just after finishing a game of bowls in what was the most significant hit in 'ndrangheta history. For by that time, don 'Ntoni Macrì had become the most notorious *'ndranghetista* of them all—referred to by some Men of Honour as the boss of all bosses, and probably also an initiated member of Sicily's Cosa Nostra. But then that is a story for another era.

War Office, London: Directorate of Civil Affairs.

Campania Zone Handbook.

Secret.

*The information contained herein is believed
to be correct as on July 1st, 1943.*

Chapter VI, 'Folklore and Feasts'

*The real camorra, once a powerful secret society, does in fact
no longer exist, though there is much underground life in Naples.
One must beware of pickpockets; if one is on the lookout for the*

singers one can listen to the songs in the streets, 'o bambeniello
nasciuto' or 'l'amore non è più bagnato', when many people cluster
round, or, if one can stomach it, one can even eat mussels and
snails at a 'bancarella de maruzzaro' or 'purpetielli veraci'.

The war brought horrors of all kinds on Italy, from the most viciously personal (mass rape), to the most terrifyingly impersonal (carpet bombing).
In September 1943 Naples was a hungry city battered by air raids that left
some 200,000 people homeless and destroyed much of the sewage system.
The Germans then began a policy of deportation and summary executions.
The Neapolitans rose in revolt, and freedom was already within their grasp
when they greeted the first Allied tanks on 1 October.

But the traumas of war did not cease with the Wehrmacht's departure.
Naples had always been a shambolic city, one that seemed to teeter on the
edge of breakdown. Under AMGOT, it tipped headlong into squalor and
degradation. To many in Naples at the time it felt as if all standards of human self-respect had been abandoned in the scramble to get a little food
to eat, a little water to drink, and something to wear. The scenes of misery
made a profound impression on the great movie director John Huston, who
was in Naples making army newsreels. He later recalled that

> Naples was like a whore suffering from the beating of a brute—teeth
> knocked out, eyes blackened, nose broken, smelling of filth and vomit.
> There was an absence of soap, and even the bare legs of the girls were dirty.
> Cigarettes were the medium of exchange commonly employed, and any-
> thing could be had for a package. Little boys were offering their sisters and
> mothers for sale. At night, during the blackouts, rats appeared in packs
> outside the buildings and simply stood there, looking at you with red eyes,
> not moving. You walked around them. Fumes came out of the alleyways,
> down which there were establishments featuring 'flesh' acts between ani-
> mals and children. The men and women of Naples were a bereft, starving,
> desperate people who would do absolutely anything to survive. The souls
> of the people had been raped. It was indeed an unholy city.

The facts from the archives back up Huston's memories. Prostitution was
a very common survival tactic. The British Psychological Warfare Branch
(PWB), which had responsibility for keeping tabs on civilian morale, estimated that there were around 40,000 prostitutes in Naples—about 10 per
cent of the city's women. Nor was it just women. In the alleys, pimps were
heard shouting 'Two dollars the boys, three dollars the girls!' to uniformed

men who were openly eyeing and pawing the children lined up before them. Needless to say, venereal disease joined typhus among the scourges assailing liberated Naples.

Kleptomania gripped the city too. Anything of any conceivable value vanished: telegraph wires, manhole covers, railway tracks, even whole trams. It is said that a Papal Legate's car was found to be running on pilfered tyres.

Profiteers controlled much of the food supply from what the PWB called 'the almost miraculously fertile land in the low-lying ground around Naples'. The PWB referred to a 'fantastic gangland situation' between Nola and the coast north of the city. There were armed bands, many of them made up of deserters, but with widespread backing in this 'traditionally violent' area: 'they have the support of a whole organisation which includes prostitutes, receivers, Black Market specialists, etc.'

Among the worst offenders in Naples itself were rich industrialists, especially pasta manufacturers and millers. Spaghetti factories took to producing two varieties of product: a good one for the black market, and one that was 'almost black and of an unpleasant taste' for legal distribution. In March 1944 Antonio and Giuseppe Caputo, the owners of one of the city's biggest flour mills in the industrial quarter of San Giovanni a Teduccio, were sentenced to seven years for black market activities; investigators discovered machine guns and grenades in their house.

Floating comfortably on this tide of illegality, at least for a few months, was the Fascist Vito Genovese. 'Fascist', that is, only until the Allied armies reached Campania, at which point he shed his Mussolinian credentials like a worn-out suit, and stepped into a new disguise as a translator and guide to the US Army.

In May 1944 a sergeant from the US Army's Criminal Investigation Division received a tip-off and began looking hard at Genovese's interests. Before the war, the sergeant in question—Orange C. Dickey—had a job patrolling the leafy campus of Pennsylvania State College. His new assignment took him into the even leafier but rather more dangerous surroundings of Nola.

Sergeant Dickey's first breakthrough came when he found an elephants' graveyard of burned out military trucks in a vineyard outside Nola. He then heard two Canadian soldiers confess that they had delivered the trucks, with their priceless cargo of flour and sugar, with the transparent password 'Genovese sent us'.

By the end of August 1944 Sergeant Dickey had enough evidence to make an arrest: he picked Genovese up just after watching him collect a travel permit from the Mayor of Nola. A search of the gangster's wallet brought to light several enthusiastic letters of reference written by American officials in Nola on Genovese's behalf.

Mr Genovese met me and acted as my interpreter for over a month. He would accept no pay; paid his own expenses; worked day and night and rendered most valuable assistance to the Allied Military Government.

Despite these letters, and a great deal more alarming evidence of Genovese's influence within the US Army, Sergeant Dickey's investigations would prove arduous and ultimately futile. After long months during which nobody seemed to want to take responsibility for the case, Genovese was eventually escorted back to the United States to face the murder charge that had originally provoked his flight to Italy. But one poisoned witness later, he was freed to resume his stellar career in American gangsterdom.

The intriguing thing about the Genovese story, from the Italian point of view, is the glimpse it affords of re-emergent criminal organisations in the Neapolitan hinterland. Sergeant Dickey's evidence showed that Genovese's black market network ran in many directions. The branches that most concerned Dickey were in AMGOT, of course. But Genovese also sheltered local thieves and smugglers from prosecution, assiduously cultivated friends in the Neapolitan judiciary, and even found protection from the chief of police of Rome. Sergeant Dickey also believed that Genovese partly controlled the electricity supply in the Nola area, giving him a stranglehold on manufacturing.

But if Genovese had links with existing criminal gangs in Nola, the signs are that things were not always friendly between them. Among the letters of recommendation written by Allied military officials for Genovese was one, dated June 1944, that contained the following curious phrase.

[Vito Genovese] has been invaluable to me—is absolutely honest, and as a matter of fact, exposed several cases of bribery and blackmarket operations among so-called trusted civil personnel.

In traditional mafia fashion, Genovese was using his contacts with the authorities to eliminate his rivals.

Then there also is the mysterious informer whose tip-off first put Sergeant Dickey onto Genovese's black market empire. The man in question is likely to remain anonymous—his name was removed from the documentation for his own protection. Whoever he was, he spun Sergeant Dickey a particularly intriguing story. He said he was 'a former member of the Camorra' who had bought himself out of the organisation after marrying an American girl. The camorra, he went on to explain, was 'the Italian counterpart of the Mafia Sicilian Union of the United States', and Vito Genovese was now its supreme boss.

At least two things about this story are odd. First, in 1944 there was almost certainly no such thing as the camorra, in the traditional sense of an Honoured Society. Second, the camorra—even if it did exist—was nothing like Italy's equivalent of the mafia in the United States. It sounds to me as if the informer cooked his story to suit the tastes of his American interlocutor. If so, we can only guess at his motives. But it would be no surprise if he turned out to be an emissary of one of Genovese's local competitors. Perhaps the valiant Sergeant Dickey was lured into action by hoods from Nola or the Mazzoni who were eager to expel the American cuckoo from their Campanian nest. With the Fascist repression a fading memory, and Vito Genovese out of the way, the gangs of the Neapolitan hinterland could begin their history anew.

Meanwhile, in the hovels of the city centre, a contraband bonanza was changing the urban ground rules. In each tiny quarter, the street-corner boss or *guappo* was at the hub of the black market. Anyone who had under-the-counter goods to sell would turn to the *guappo*, whose assistants would dart out into the alleys to find the right outlet at the right price. The profits to be made were enormous. PWB reported that the illiterate lumpen proletarians of the low city who made it rich in profiteering were too ignorant to count the bags of money they collected, so they weighed them instead. 'I have 3 kilos of thousand lire notes.' On one occasion a passing bank clerk was stopped by an old crone and asked to help her count a great wicker basket of cash; when he had finished, she gave him a tip of 2,000 lire. The story is poignant because it was so typical: bank clerks, factory workers, pensioners and bureaucrats—people on fixed incomes that is—suffered worst in the wild black market inflation of the Liberation period. In Naples, the PWB noted, 'class distinctions are disappearing'. Crime paid.

For much of the war in Italy Naples was the most important port of arrival for the colossal volume of provisions consumed by the advancing Allied armies. That deluge was simultaneously the city's deliverance and its damnation. By April 1944 an astonishing 45 per cent of Allied military cargo was being stolen. Only systemic corruption within Allied Military Government and among the Anglo-American forces can account for the industrial scale of the robbery. In September 1944 the PWB reported that Allied troops were openly ferrying packages of goods to market, and that the Military Police were doing nothing to stop them. The Italian police and *Carabinieri* who served under AMGOT at least had the defence of being as hungry as the rest of the local population. But they were just as likely to be venal as their British and American superiors. In May 1944 the PWB said that policemen were taking a cut of 20–30,000 lire on every lorry load of goods that disappeared from the port. Everyone in Naples acquired a wily expertise on the relative merits of American and Canadian blankets, or British and French army boots. There was such a big racket in penicillin that the soldiers at the front went short.

The most visible retail outlets for stolen Allied goods were in via Forcella, near an American military depot. The street became a multinational, open-air, army surplus bazaar where anything intended for the Allied forces could be bought. And 'anything' included weaponry, it was said, as long as you knew whom to ask.

Via Forcella runs through the cramped heart of the city; it lies only a few metres from the old Palazzo della Vicaria, the former prison and court house where, on 3 October 1862, Salvatore De Crescenzo, the gangland chieftain 'redeemed' at the time of Italian unification, had his rival stabbed to death and became the supreme boss of the Honoured Society of Naples. Eighty-one years later, at the time of AMGOT, the *guappi* in charge of via Forcella were the Giuliano boys, Pio Vittorio, Guglielmo and Salvatore. Today the Giuliano family name means only one thing: camorra.

In the ensuing decades new clans like the Giulianos, drawing on their experiences during the chaos of Liberation, would find different answers to the challenges that had ultimately defeated the old Honoured Society of Salvatore De Crescenzo, of Ciccio 'Little Lord Frankie' Cappuccio, of Enrico 'Big 'Enry' Alfano. How to organise tightly and network widely. How to infiltrate the economy and the political apparatus of the state. How to tame the police and courts. How to control and exploit women, and with them breed sons, and even daughters, able to perpetuate the system's power. How, by all these means, to turn mere delinquency into enduring territorial authority. 1943 was year zero for the rule of law in Naples. The Allied Liberation restarted the clock of camorra history.

Organised crime is Italy's congenital disease. The Honoured Societies of Naples and Sicily were born from the prison system in the middle decades of the nineteenth century. The violence and conspiratorial politics of Italian unification gave the hoodlums their passage out of the dungeons and into history.

The legacy of the *Risorgimento* in parts of the South and Sicily was a sophisticated and powerful model of criminal organisation. The members of these brotherhoods deployed violence for three strategic purposes. First: to control other felons, to farm them for money, information and talent. Second: to leech the legal economy. And third: to create contacts among the upper echelons—the landowners, politicians and magistrates. In the environs of Palermo the mafia, boosted by the island's recent history of revolution, did not just have contacts with the upper class, it formed an integral facet of the upper class.

The new Kingdom of Italy failed to address that legacy. Worse, it lapsed into sharing its sovereignty with the local bosses. Italy allowed a criminal ecosystem to develop. It tried to live out the dream of being a modern state; but it did so with few of the resources that its wealthier neighbours could draw on, and with many more innate disadvantages. The result was political fragmentation and instability: an institutional life driven less by policies designed to address collective problems than by haggling for tactical advantage and short-term favours. This was a political system that frequently gave leverage to the worst pressure groups in the country—the ones sheltering men of violence. At election time the government sometimes used gangsters to make sure the right candidates won. Parliament produced bad legislation, which was then selectively enforced: the practice of dealing with *mafiosi* and *camorristi* by sending them into 'enforced residence' is one prime instance. Urgently needed reforms never materialised: an example being the utter legislative void around the likes of Calogero Gambino (from the 'fratricide' case of the 1870s) and Gennaro Abbatemaggio (from the Cuocolo trial of the early 1900s)—*mafiosi* and *camorristi* who abandoned the ranks of their brotherhoods and sought refuge with the state. Italy also had enough lazy and cynical journalists, wrong-headed intellectuals and morally obtuse writers to mask the real nature of the emergency, give resonance and credibility to the underworld's own twisted ideology, and allow gangsters to gaze at flattering reflections of themselves in print.

The criminal ecosystem spawned a new Honoured Society, the picciotteria, to retrace the evolutionary path of its older cousins: in the 1880s, it quickly progressed from prison to achieve territorial dominance in the outside world.

Yet to say that Italy harboured a criminal ecosystem is not to say that the country was run by gangsters. Italy has never been a failed state, a mafia regime. The reason why the mafias of southern Italy and Sicily have such a long history is *not* because they were and are all-powerful, even in their heartlands. The rule of law was not a dead letter in the peninsula, and Italy *did* fight the mafias. *Omertà* broke frequently. Sometimes the mafias' territorial control broke too, leading to a reawakening in what good police like Ermanno Sangiorgi called the *spirito pubblico*—the 'public spirit': in other words, the belief that people could trust the state to enforce its own rules. Such moments offered a glimpse of an underlying public hunger for legality, and showed what could have been achieved had there been a more consistent anti-mafia effort.

But alas, Italy fought the Honoured Societies only for so long as their overt violence kept them at the top of the political agenda. It fought them only until the mafias' wealthy and powerful protectors could exert an influence. It fought them only enough to sharpen the gangster domain's internal process of natural selection. Over the years, weaker bosses and dysfunctional criminal methodologies were weeded out. Hoodlums were obliged to change and develop. The Sicilian mafia had the least to learn. In Naples, the Honoured Society failed to learn enough. Perhaps against the odds, the Calabrian picciotteria, that working museum of the oldest traditions of the prison camorras, proved itself capable of adapting to survive and grow.

In the underworld competition not just to dominate, but to endure, the mafias found perhaps their most important resource in family. Through their kin, *mafiosi*, *camorristi* and *picciotti* gained their strongest foothold in society, the first vehicle for their pernicious influence. Thus the lethal damage that the mafias caused to so many families—their own and their victims'—is the most poignant measure of the evil they did.

From 1925 Benito Mussolini styled his regime as the antithesis of the squalid politicking of the past, the cure for Italy's weak-willed concessions to the gangs. But Fascism ended up repeating many of the mistakes committed during earlier waves of repression. The same short attention span. The same reliance on 'enforced residence'. The same reluctance to prosecute the mafias' protectors among the elite. The same failure to tackle the endemic mafia presence in the prisons. Political internees in the 1920s and 1930s told *exactly* the same stories of mob influence behind bars as poor Duke Sigismondo Castromediano and the other patriotic prisoners of the *Risorgimento* had done three generations earlier.

The only thing that Mussolini did markedly better than his liberal predecessors was to pump up the publicity and smother the news. With a little help from the Sicilian mafia, he created the lasting illusion that Fascism had, at the very least, suppressed the mob. So when it came to organised crime, Fascism's most harmful legacy was its determination to keep quiet about the problem. The *Zone Handbooks* with which the Allied forces arrived in Sicily, Calabria and Campania accurately reflect the desperately limited state of public knowledge that Fascism bequeathed. (They were based on published Italian sources after all.)

Fascism's legacy was indeed a damaging one. Amid the chaos of war and Liberation, the country was immediately faced with the reality of endemic criminal power that lay behind the dumb bluster of the regime's propaganda.

When the Second World War ended, Italy quickly became a democracy. Not long afterwards, it would develop into a major industrial power. Here was a very different country from the *Italietta*—the 'mini Italy'—that had first confronted the mafias after 1860, or from the deluded, strutting Italy of the Blackshirt decades. The transition of 1943–48 was the most profound in the country's entire history: from war to peace; from dictatorship to freedom. Yet some things about Italy did not change—and the history of organised crime in the post-war period is the most disturbing measure of the continuities. The same political vices that had helped give birth to the mafias would propel them to even greater power and violence during the era of democracy and prosperity. After 1945, just as it had done since 1860, Italy's political class settled into a messy accommodation with the mob.

Fascism can be blamed for many things, but certainly not for that accommodation. The *Zone Handbooks* did not represent the full extent of the knowledge about the mafias that Mussolini's regime bequeathed. The police and magistrates who had spent much of the 1920s and 1930s fighting organised crime knew exactly how dangerous the gangland organisations of Campania, Calabria and Sicily were: theirs was a bank of experience and understanding from which a fledgling post-Fascist Italy had a great deal to learn. Yet almost everything they knew was ignored or repressed. The new Italian state proved itself more reluctant than Fascism to stand up to the mafias, and even keener than Fascism to unlearn the lessons of the past. Once the Second World War was over, mafia history began all over again—with an act of forgetting.

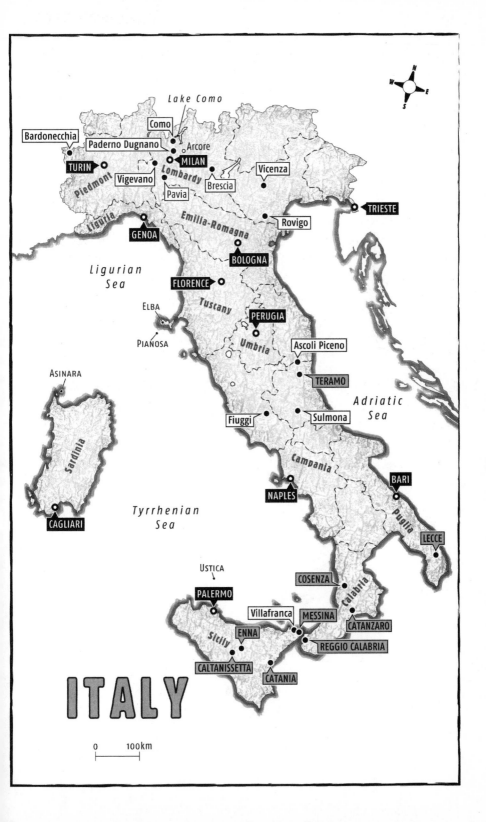

Lake Como

Bardonecchia
Paderno Dugnano
Como
Arcore
TURIN
Piedmont
MILAN
Vicenza
Vigevano
Lombardy
Pavia
Brescia
TRIESTE
Liguria
Emilia-Romagna
Rovigo
GENOA
BOLOGNA
Ligurian
Sea
FLORENCE
Tuscany
ELBA
PERUGIA
PIANOSA
Umbria
Ascoli Piceno
ASINARA
TERAMO
Adriatic
Sea
Fiuggi
Sulmona
Sardinia
Campania
BARI
NAPLES
Tyrrhenian
Sea
Puglia
CAGLIARI
LECCE
USTICA
COSENZA
PALERMO
Calabria
Villafranca
MESSINA
CATANZARO
Sicily
ENNA
REGGIO CALABRIA
CALTANISSETTA
CATANIA

ITALY

0   100km

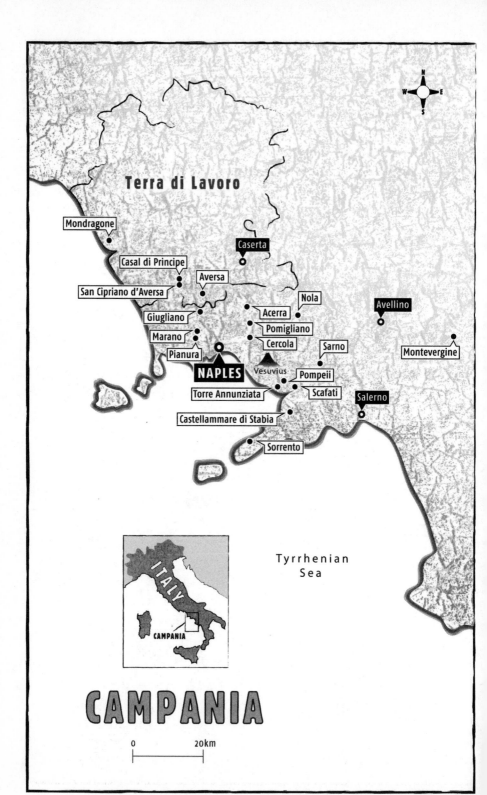

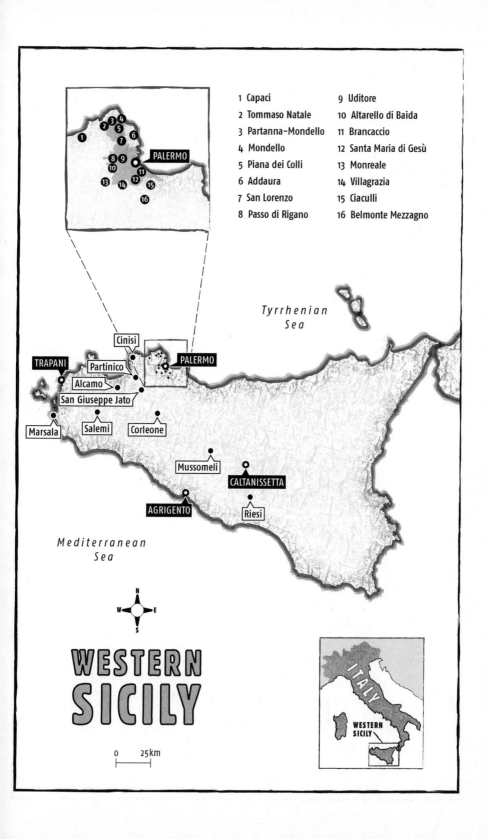

1 Capaci
2 Tommaso Natale
3 Partanna-Mondello
4 Mondello
5 Piana dei Colli
6 Addaura
7 San Lorenzo
8 Passo di Rigano

9 Uditore
10 Altarello di Baida
11 Brancaccio
12 Santa Maria di Gesù
13 Monreale
14 Villagrazia
15 Ciaculli
16 Belmonte Mezzagno

PALERMO

Tyrrhenian Sea

Cinisi
TRAPANI
Partinico
PALERMO
Alcamo
San Giuseppe Jato
Marsala
Salemi
Corleone
Mussomeli
CALTANISSETTA
AGRIGENTO
Riesi

Mediterranean Sea

N
W E
S

WESTERN
SICILY

0   25km

ITALY

WESTERN
SICILY

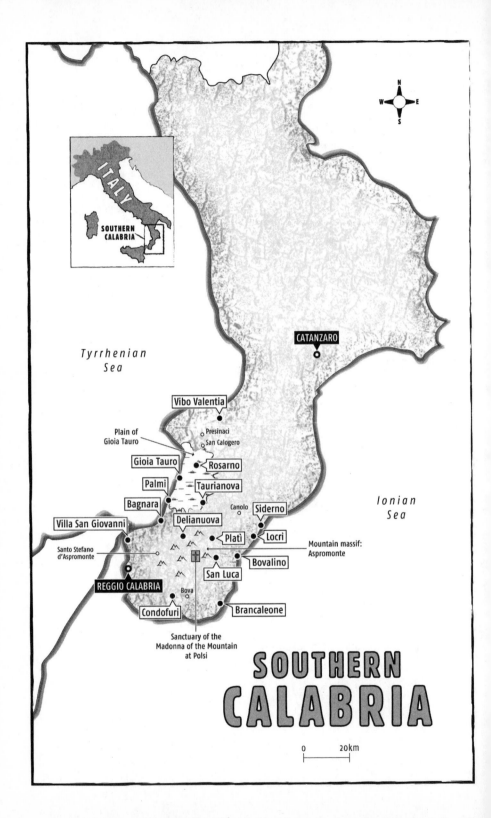

ITALY

SOUTHERN
CALABRIA

*Tyrrhenian
Sea*

CATANZARO

Vibo Valentia

Plain of
Gioia Tauro

Presinaci
San Calogero

Gioia Tauro   Rosarno

Palmi   Taurianova

Bagnara

Canolo   Siderno

*Ionian
Sea*

Villa San Giovanni   Delianuova

Platì   Locri

Santo Stefano
d'Aspromonte

Mountain massif:
Aspromonte

Bovalino

San Luca

REGGIO CALABRIA   Bova

Condofuri   Brancaleone

Sanctuary of the
Madonna of the Mountain
at Polsi

SOUTHERN
CALABRIA

0   20km

PART VII

FUGGEDABOUTIT

34

SICILY: Banditry, land and politics

TODAY'S ITALY CAME INTO BEING ON 2 AND 3 JUNE 1946, WHEN A PEOPLE BATTERED BY war voted in a referendum to abolish a monarchy that had been profoundly discredited by its subservience to Fascist dictatorship. Here was a clean break with the past: Italy would henceforth be a Republic. In the same poll, Italians elected the members of a Constituent Assembly who were charged with drafting a new constitution for the Republic based on democracy, freedom and the rule of law.

The camorra, the 'ndrangheta and Cosa Nostra are a monstrous insult to the Italian Republic's founding values—the same values that underpin Italy's, and Europe's, post-war prosperity. But in Italy, alone among Western European nations, mafia power has been perfectly compatible with the day-to-day reality of freedom, democracy and prosperity. The story of how that happened began as soon as Italy embarked on the difficult transition from war to peace.

AMGOT came to an end in February 1944: Sicily and much of the South came under the authority of the coalition of anti-Fascist forces making up the new civilian government. So it was southerners, people from the traditional heartlands of organised crime, who were the first Italians to reacquire the power to shape the country's future. The path towards that future was marked by four milestones:

> April 1945: the war in Italy came to an end, only a few days before Hitler's suicide.
> June 1946: the monarchy was abolished and the Republic was born.

> March 1947: President Harry S. Truman announced that the United States would intervene to check Soviet expansion across the globe. In Italy, the *Partito Comunista Italiano* had won great prestige from its role in the Resistance, and was promising to create a Communist Party branch for every bell tower. The peninsula found itself right on the front line of the newly declared Cold War.

> April 1948: Italy's first democratic parliamentary election was decisively won by the American-backed *Democrazia Cristiana* (DC—the Christian Democrats) and decisively lost by the Communists.

Nowhere in Italy was the post-war transition more turbulent than in Sicily. Nowhere was organised crime more profoundly involved in the turbulence. In southern Calabria and Campania, as we will see, *'ndranghetisti* and *camorristi* carved out their own niche in the post-war settlement. But in Sicily, the mafia had grander designs. Many Sicilians are inclined to express doubts when the label 'organised crime' is applied to the mafia. *Mafiosi* are all criminals, and they always have been. But ordinary criminals, however organised they may be, do not have remotely the kind of political friendships that senior *mafiosi* have always enjoyed. It would be far, far beyond the mental horizon of any common-or-garden crook to try and shape the institutional destiny of his homeland in the way Sicilian *mafiosi* tried to do.

The most clamorous and bloody crime in which the mafia was involved was banditry. At the peak in 1945, hundreds of bandit bands roamed the Sicilian countryside, many of them well armed enough to best the police and *Carabinieri* in a firefight. Robbery, extortion, kidnapping and the black market gave these outlaws a rich income stream. As was traditional, rather than joining the bandits, *mafiosi* preferred, wherever they could, to 'farm' them through an exchange of favours. For example, the bandits might kick back a percentage of their earnings to the *mafiosi*, who in return offered tips on lucrative kidnapping or robbery targets, advance news on police round-ups, and mediators who could broker ransom payments with the necessary discretion.

Soon after the Allied invasion, *mafiosi* set about re-establishing their time-honoured stranglehold over the 'protection', rental and management of agricultural land in western Sicily. Many of Sicily's biggest landowners lived in decadent splendour in Palermo while leaving the running of their vast farms to brutal mafia middlemen. Hence, after the war, the landowners appointed men who would become some of the most notorious bosses of the 1950s and 1960s as leaseholder-managers of their land: like Giuseppe Genco Russo from Mussomeli, and the twenty-year-old killer Luciano Liggio from the agricultural town of Corleone, in the province of Palermo.

(Liggio already had an arrest warrant out against his name when, after his predecessor's mysterious death, he became manager of the Strasatto estate in 1945.)

The business of land inexorably drew the mafia into politics. At every moment of political upheaval in recent Sicilian history, peasants had made loud claims to fairer contracts or even a share of the estates owned by the Sicilian aristocrats. In the end, mafia shotguns always voiced the definitive response to the peasants' demands.

The land issue was bound to resurface after the war and, when it did, the landowners and *mafiosi* turned terror into a political tool. With the pistol, the machine gun and the hand grenade, *mafiosi* went all out to eliminate peasant militants and intimidate their supporters into passivity. The appalling roll call of murdered trade unionists and left-wing activists began in the summer of 1944 and had not run its course a full decade later. For example, in the autumn of 1946, at Belmonte Mezzagno near Palermo, the peasants formed a cooperative to take over the management of land from a nearby estate. On 2 November, a death squad of thirteen men turned up in a field where many ordinary members of the cooperative were labouring. The brothers Giovanni, Vincenzo and Giuseppe Santangelo were led away to be executed one after another with a single shot to the back of the head.

Both the landowners and the mafia feared that a new, democratic Italian government would be forced to make concessions to the Communists, and therefore to the left-wing peasants in Sicily. Accordingly, from as early as 1943, the landowners and the mafia sponsored a movement to separate the island off from the rest of the peninsula. The road to Sicilian independence was plotted at a series of meetings held over the coming years. Scions of some of the oldest family lineages in Sicily welcomed the island's most senior mobsters to their luxurious country villas. At one of those meetings in September 1945, the bosses negotiated a deal to integrate some bandits into the Separatist movement's army. Salvatore Giuliano, the leader of the most notorious bandit gang of all, was offered a large sum of money, the rank of colonel, and the promise of an amnesty once the flag of a free Sicily was raised. There followed a series of assaults on *Carabinieri* barracks that were intended to prepare the ground for an insurrection.

In the end, there was no Separatist insurrection. The movement's ramshackle military wing was dispersed. More importantly, its political leadership was outmanoeuvred: in May 1946 Sicily was granted autonomy, and its own regional parliament, while remaining *within* Italy. *Mafiosi* who had supported Separatism began the search for new political partners.

If Separatism was in decline in 1946, Sicily's criminal emergency had become more serious than ever. Bandit gangs, often operating under the mafia's wing, were robbing and kidnapping at will. The police and *Carabinieri* in Sicily were sending information aplenty to Rome. Many of them had taken a leading role in Fascism's secret war on the mafia in the 1930s. For that reason they were under no illusions about what the mafia really was, as this report from October 1946 makes clear:

> The mafia is an occult organisation that traverses Sicily's provinces and has secret tentacles that reach into all social classes. Its exclusive objective is getting rich by unlawful means at the expense of honest and vulnerable people. It has now reconstituted its cells or 'Families', as they are referred to here in the jargon, especially in the provinces of Palermo, Trapani, Caltanissetta, Enna and Agrigento.

So these were the violent years that decided Sicily's future. Not coincidentally, these were also the years when Italy's rulers decided to forget everything they knew about Sicily's notorious 'occult organisation'. The most revealing illustration of that process of forgetting is not a mafia massacre or a secret report. To understand how the Sicilian mafia really worked in the late 1940s, to understand its unique ability to vanish into thin air, while at the same time seeping into the state apparatus, we need to watch Italy's first-ever mafia movie.

35

SICILY: *In the Name of the Law*

It is September 1948, but the scorched expanses of the Sicilian interior that stretch out before the camera seem timeless. A young man in a double-breasted jacket, his chiselled face shaded by a fedora, sits erect in the saddle. Suddenly, he swivels to look out across a lunar landscape of dust and rock. He sees eight figures on horseback emerge over a hilltop to stand silhouetted against the sky.

'The mafia.' The young man speaks the dread word aloud to himself, and his jaw sets with determination. His name is Guido Schiavi, and he is a magistrate, a champion of the law. This is the confrontation he has been expecting.

The *mafiosi*, riding beautifully curried thoroughbred mares, come down the hill towards the magistrate at a stately canter. The soundtrack provides an accompaniment of stirring trumpets and driving strings to their cavalcade. As they approach, Schiavi sees that each is dressed in corduroy and fustian; each has a flat cap pulled down over a craggily impassive face; and each has a shotgun slung over his shoulder.

The *mafiosi* come to a halt on a low bridge. Their boss, who goes by the name of Turi Passalacqua, is unmistakeable on his statuesque white mount. He raises his cap courteously to address the magistrate.

> Good day to you, *voscenza*. Welcome to our land. You do us a great honour.

> You are very young, sir. And my friends and I are very happy about that. Because we know that the young are pure of heart. You are intelligent, and I'm sure you have already understood the way of the world here. Things have been like this for more than a hundred years, and everyone is content.

The magistrate Schiavi is not impressed by this homily. He objects that there are plenty of people who are far from 'content' with this 'way of the world': the victims of murder and blackmail and their families, for example; or the brutalised farm labourers and sulphur miners. But his words fail to provoke even a flicker of irritation on the *mafioso*'s serene countenance:

> Every society has its defects. And besides, it's always possible to reach an agreement between men of honour . . . You need only express your desires.

Now it is the magistrate's turn to remain unmoved. In tones of measured defiance he affirms that he has only one desire, only one duty: to apply the law.

Clearly, there can be no compromise. Two opposing value systems have deployed their forces in the field. A great clash between the state and the mafia is inevitable. All that remains is for the *capomafia* Turi Passalacqua to restate his credo:

> You are a brave man, but we make the law here, according to our ancient traditions. This is an island. The government is a long way away. And if we weren't here, with our own kind of severity, then criminals would end up spoiling everything, like rye-grass spoils the wheat. Nobody would be safe in their own home any more. We are not criminals. We are honourable men: as free and independent as the birds in the sky.

And with that, the trumpets and strings swell once more. We watch as the posse of Men of Honour wheels round and gallops off into the distance.

In 1940s Italy, the movies meant much more than just entertainment. The US studios had boycotted the Italian market in protest at Mussolini's attempts to control imports. During the last five years of Fascism, Italians were denied their weekly dose of Californian celluloid. When the theatres were reopened after the Liberation, and the supply from Hollywood resumed, Italians were soon going to the movies in greater numbers than ever—greater than in any other European country. The glamour of Rita Hayworth and Glenn Ford held out the promise of what freedom and democracy might bring to a country racked by war and demoralised by the debacle of Fascism.

Yet no country that had lived through such traumatic changes could ever be entirely satisfied with the products of the US studios. So, in the cinema, the years 1945–50 have come to be defined by the gritty homegrown poetry of Roberto Rossellini's *Rome, Open City* or Vittorio De Sica's *Bicycle Thieves*. Neorealism ('new realism') was the cultural buzzword of the day. Neorealist directors took their cameras out into the bomb-shattered streets; they found moving dramas among the peasants toiling on the terraces or wading through rice paddies. Neorealist cinema seemed so true to life that it was as if the skin of history had peeled off as film (to quote what one critic evocatively wrote at the time). There has never been a moment when the movie screen was more important to how Italy imagined the light and the dark within itself.

Released in Italian cinemas in March 1949, *In nome della legge* (*In the Name of the Law*) was Italy's first mafia film. It is a strange muddle of a movie: it has many of the accoutrements of Neorealist cinema, notably in its use of the sun-blasted Sicilian landscape; but it also straddles the divide between Neorealism and Hollywood. The film's director, Pietro Germi, had never been to Sicily before his film went into production in 1948. Then again, his ignorance mattered little. Because when he got off the ferry and set foot on the island for the first time, he already knew exactly what he was going to find: Arizona. *In the Name of the Law* stages a shotgun marriage between Neorealism and the cowboy movie genre. Germi's Sicily is *Tombstone* with Mediterranean trimmings: a place of lone lawmen, long stares, and ambushes in gulches. Here trains pull into desert stations, gunshots echo across vast skies, and men stride into bars and drink glasses of Sicilian aniseed liqueur as if they were knocking back fingers of hooch whiskey.

Germi's reasoning was that the quasi–Wild West setting would dramatise the head-to-head between the lone lawman and his criminal foe. Muscular heart-throb Massimo Girotti, playing the young magistrate Guido Schiavi, was to be Italy's answer to John Wayne. But Germi's camera is even more obsessed with mafia boss Turi Passalacqua, played by French veteran Charles Vanel: he is always framed from below, cut out against a pale sky—as if he were part craggy rancher, and part Apache sage.

The cowboys-cum-*capos* formula clearly worked. 'Frenetic applause' was reported at the first public screenings. *In the Name of the Law* went on to become the third most popular movie of the 1948–9 season in Italy, taking a bumper 401 million lire (roughly $9.3 million in 2011 values) at the box office, and standing toe-to-commercial-toe with such Hollywood classics as *Fort Apache* and *The Treasure of the Sierra Madre*.

As mob movies go, *In the Name of the Law* may seem quaint at first glance—now that our tastes are attuned to *GoodFellas* and *Gomorrah*. Yet Germi's film is sinister too: it has a back-story full of dark surprises, and a context of unprecedented mafia violence and arrogance. More recent classics of the mafia movie genre, like *The Godfather*, are often criticised for glamourising organised crime. But in this respect Coppola's film has nothing on *In the Name of the Law*. The opening credits display a familiar disclaimer: 'Any reference to events, places and people who really exist is purely coincidental'. But that is some distance from the truth.

In the Name of the Law was based on a novel, and inspired by the example of the novel's author. Written in the early months of 1947, *Piccola Pretura* (*Local Magistrate's Office*) was the work of Giuseppe Guido Lo Schiavo, one of the country's foremost authorities on the Sicilian mafia. Born and brought up in Palermo, Lo Schiavo was a hero of the First World War who, when the war ended, went into the front line of the fight against organised crime on his island home.

Lo Schiavo's life was closely intertwined with the history of the Sicilian mafia under Fascism. In 1926 he was himself a young magistrate, like the hero of his novel. (The similarity between the names of author and protagonist—Giuseppe Guido Lo Schiavo/Guido Schiavi—is no accident.) In that year, Benito Mussolini's dictatorship launched a long overdue attack on the mafia. The 'cancer of delinquency' was to be cut out of Sicily by the Fascist 'scalpel', the Duce boasted. The police and *Carabinieri* led the assault, and prosecuting magistrates like Lo Schiavo had the job of preparing the evidence needed to convert thousands of arrests into convictions.

Lo Schiavo was among the most enthusiastic instruments of the Fascist repression. In 1930, one of the mobsters' defence lawyers, Giuseppe Mario

Puglia, published an essay claiming that the mafia was *not* a secret criminal society. Indeed *mafiosi* were not even criminals. Rather the *mafioso* was an incorrigible individualist, 'a man who instinctively refuses to recognise anyone superior to his own ego'. What is more, the *mafioso* was a typical Sicilian, because this exaggerated pride and self-containment had seeped into the island's psyche as a form of resistance to centuries of foreign invasions. Therefore to repress the mafia was inevitably to repress the Sicilian people. Puglia's essay, in short, reads like the words uttered by countless other mafia apologists since the 1870s, and indeed like the words Lo Schiavo would later put into the mouth of mafia boss Turi Passalacqua in *In the Name of the Law*.

Lo Schiavo refused to let the defence lawyer's claims pass unchallenged, responding to them in a pamphlet that is a little masterpiece of controlled anger. The mafia, Lo Schiavo argued, was 'a criminal system'; it was not just illegal, it was an 'anti-legal organism whose only aim was getting rich by illicit means'.

Lo Schiavo went on to give the mafia lawyer a lesson in mafia history. He explained how the Sicilian mafia first emerged from the political violence of the Risorgimento, when patriotic conspirators found the revolutionary muscle they required among the fearsome wardens, overseers and bravoes of the Sicilian countryside. From those conspirators, the criminals learned to organise themselves like the Freemasons. Lo Schiavo had also delved into the economic history of the mafia. His research showed that it had first grown rich by establishing protection rackets over the valuable lemon and orange groves surrounding Palermo.

Fear of the mafia pervaded society in western Sicily, reaching right up into parliament. Anything unfavourable said about the mafia would inevitably reach hostile ears. And that, argued Lo Schiavo, is why so many Sicilians could be found spouting the same drivel, along the lines that: 'the mafia does not exist; at worst, *mafiosi* are local problem solvers who embody the typically Sicilian pride and truculence towards authority'. Even the landowners who were, in theory, the mafia's most prominent victims, had bought into this fiction and espoused the belief that the mafia was somehow good for social peace, for law and order. On the contrary, Lo Schiavo asserted, the mafia was 'a programme to exploit and persecute honest members of society while hiding behind a reputation for courage and welfare that was only so much lying garbage'.

So, in the early 1930s, the man who would later inspire *In the Name of the Law* was an anti-mafia crusader with the bravery to engage in a public spat with the crime bosses' own defence lawyers. By 1948, Lo Schiavo had become one of the country's most senior magistrates, a prosecutor at the

Supreme Court in Rome. In that year he published his novel, which was immediately adapted into a film.

Both novel and film tell a simple story about a young magistrate, Guido Schiavi, who is posted to a remote town deep in the arid badlands of the Sicilian interior. In this lawless place, the mafia rules unchecked, and runs a protection racket over the estate of the local landowner. When bandits kill one of the landowner's men, *capomafia* Turi Passalacqua hunts them down: the bandits are trussed up and tossed into a dried-up well, or simply shot-gunned in the back in a mountain gully.

The young magistrate investigates this series of slayings, but he is frozen out by the terrified townspeople. When the courageous Schiavi confronts *capomafia* Turi Passalacqua on his white mare, he resists the boss's attempts to win him over to the mafia's way of thinking (the scene with which I began this chapter).

Eventually, Schiavi narrowly survives an assassination attempt. Resigned to defeat, he decides to abandon his post. But just as he is about to board the train to safety, he learns that his only friend in town, an honest seventeen-year-old boy called Paolino, has been murdered by a renegade *mafioso*. Indignant and distraught, Schiavi strides back into town. He rings the church bells to summon the whole population into the piazza for a do-or-die engagement. The state and the mafia are set to have their high noon—in what turns into perhaps the most bizarre climactic scene in the long history of gangster movies.

> The church bell clangs out a continuous, urgent summons across the dust of the piazza, over the sun-weathered rooftops, and out into the surrounding fields. We are shown the unemployed sulphur miners, sitting and dozing in a line at the kerb, who raise their heads to listen. The camera then cuts to the women, young and old, who come out into the street wrapped in their black shawls; and then to the elegant club where the mayor and his cronies forget their game of baccarat and turn towards the source of the alarm.
>
> Without discussion, everyone ups and walks towards the bells. The mule drivers scarcely pause to tether their beasts. Labourers drop their mattocks in the furrows. Soon streams of people are converging on the piazza. Led by Turi Passalacqua on his white mare, even the *mafiosi*–accompanied as always by the rhythmical trumpets of their signature theme–gallop into town to join the crowd gathering before the church steps.

There are loud murmurs of anxious curiosity as the young magistrate Guido Schiavi emerges from the church doors. Silence falls as he begins his address:

> Now that you are all here, I declare that this is a trial.
> Half an hour ago we found Paolino's body, blasted by a double-barrelled shotgun. He was seventeen years old and he had never harmed anyone.

Schiavi scans the crowd as he speaks, seeking to look directly into the eyes of every person there. Then, staring with still greater intensity, the magistrate hails the group of stony-faced men on horseback.

> You there, men of the mafia. And you, Turi Passalacqua. Your bloody and ferocious brand of justice only punishes those who give you offence, and only protects the men who carry out your verdicts.

At these words, one of the *mafiosi* levels his shotgun at the magistrate. But with a firm but gentle hand his boss pushes the barrels downwards again.

Guido Schiavi does not hesitate for an instant:

> And you chose to put your brand of justice before the true law—the only law that allows us to live alongside our neighbours without tearing one another to pieces like wild beasts.
>
> Isn't that true, *massaro* Passalacqua?

Everyone in the piazza cranes to see how the *capomafia* will react to this breathtaking challenge. A subtle change in his expression shows that he is troubled: his habitual composure is gone, replaced by solemnity. Silhouetted once more against the sky, Turi Passalacqua begins to make a speech of history-making gravity:

> Those were tough words, magistrate. Until now, no one had ever spoken such tough words to us.

But I say that your words were also just. My people and I
did not come into town today to listen to your speech . . .
But listening to you made me think of my son, and made
me think that I would be proud to hear him talk in that way.

So I say to my friends that in this town the time has come
to change course and go back within the law. Perhaps
everyone here did kill Paolino. But only one person pulled
the trigger. So I hereby hand him over to you so that he
may be judged according to the state's law.

He turns and, with a mere flick of his head, gives the order to
his crew. Amid clattering hooves, the Men of Honour corner the
murderer before he can run away: it is the renegade *mafioso*,
Francesco Messana.

The magistrate advances, flanked by two Carabinieri:

Francesco Messana, you are under arrest, in the name
of the law.

The murderer is led away. The magistrate then turns, and with a
look of glowing appreciation, gazes up towards the mafia boss to
utter the film's final words:

In the name of the law!

And with that we cut to yet another shot of Turi Passalacqua
silhouetted against the sky. His serenity has returned, and the
suggestion of a smile plays on his lips. The mafia cavalcade music
rises yet again. As the credits begin to roll, the boss turns his white
mare to lead the *mafiosi* in their heroic gallop towards the sunset.

Mafiosi are not criminals, *In the Name of the Law* tells us. Turi Passalacqua is a man devoted to living by a code of honour that, in its own primitive
way, is as admirable a law as the one Magistrate Guido Schiavi is trying to
uphold. If only *mafiosi* like him are addressed in the appropriately firm tone
of voice, they will become bringers of peace and order. The mafia finds its
true calling at the end of the film, the best way to live out its deeply held
values: it becomes an auxiliary police force. If Sicily were really Arizona,

and *In the Name of the Law* were really a cowboy film, then we would not know which of the two men should wear the sheriff's badge.

In the Name of the Law is not *about* the mafia; rather it is mafia propaganda, a cunning and stylish variant of the kind of 'lying garbage' upon which Giuseppe Guido Lo Schiavo had poured vitriol in the 1930s. In the 1940s, each day of chaos in Sicily was adding to a mountain of proof that *mafiosi* were anything but friends to the rule of law. Yet this was precisely the time that Lo Schiavo's views on the mafia underwent an astonishing reversal. Lo Schiavo became a convert to the mafia's lies.

Now, anyone inclined to be generous to Giuseppe Guido Lo Schiavo might suppose that Pietro Germi's movie had twisted the meaning of the magistrate's novel by grafting a happy Hollywood ending onto a grimmer Sicilian tale. And it is certainly true that, in 1948, it would have been tough to create a genuinely realistic portrayal of the mafia. Rumours circulated during production that, when director Pietro Germi first arrived in Sicily, he was approached by several senior *mafiosi* who would not allow him to begin work until they had approved the screenplay. After the movie's release, during a press conference, a young Sicilian man in the audience argued with Germi about how true to life the Men of Honour in the film were: was the director not aware that the real mafia had killed dozens of people? Germi could only give a lame reply, 'So did you expect me to meet the same end?'

But the local difficulties that Germi faced in Sicily actually do nothing to excuse Giuseppe Guido Lo Schiavo. Indeed, his novel is *even more* pro-mafia than *In the Name of the Law*. In Lo Schiavo's tale, mafia boss Turi Passalacqua is 'the very personification of wisdom, prudence and calm . . . pot-bellied, shaven-headed and smiling like a benevolent Buddha'.

The conclusion is unavoidable: a magistrate who was a scourge of the mafia in the early 1930s was, by the mid-1940s, an enthusiastic mouthpiece for mystifications that could easily have been voiced by the mafia's slyest advocates. Once Giuseppe Guido Lo Schiavo had been scornful about the way 'literature and drama glorified the figure of the *mafioso*'. Now he was himself writing fiction that did precisely that.

But why? What caused Lo Schiavo to upend his views so shamelessly?

Lo Schiavo was a conservative whose political sympathies had made him a supporter of Mussolini's regime in the 1920s and 1930s. After the Liberation, his conservatism turned him into a friend of the most murderous criminals on the island. The magistrate-novelist's bizarre rewriting of the mafia records in *Local Prosecutor's Office* testified to an unspoken and profoundly cynical belief: better the mafia than the Communists. This simple axiom was enough to drive Lo Schiavo to forget his own hard-won knowledge about Sicily's 'criminal system', and to relinquish the faith in the rule of law that was the grounding ethos of his calling as a magistrate.

Turi Passalacqua, the heroic bandit chieftain of *In the Name of the Law*, was laughably unrealistic. But, in a peculiarly Sicilian paradox, he was also horribly true to life. *In the Name of the Law* may have been a cinematic fantasy, but it nonetheless glorified a very real deal between the mafia and the state in the founding years of the Italian Republic.

Sicily is a land of strange alliances: between the landed aristocracy and gangland in the Separatist movement, for example. And once Separatism had gone into decline, the political and criminal pressures of 1946–8 created a still stranger convergence of interests: between conservatives, the mafia and the police. It is that alliance that is celebrated by *In the Name of the Law*, through the fictional figure of mafia boss Turi Passalacqua, sermonising from the saddle of his thoroughbred white mare.

In 1946, the police and *Carabinieri* were warning the government in Rome that they would need high-level support to defeat the mafia, because the mafia itself had so many friends among the Sicilian elite—friends it helped at election time by hustling votes. But these warnings were ignored. It may have been that conservative politicians in Rome were daunted by the prospect of taking on the ruling class of an island whose loyalty to Italy was questionable, but whose conservatism was beyond doubt. Or more cynically still, they may have reasoned that the mafia's ground-level terror campaign against the left-wing peasant movement was actually rather useful. So they told the police and *Carabinieri* in Sicily to forget the mafia (to forget the real cause of the crime emergency, in other words) and put the fight against banditry at the top of their agenda.

The police knew that to fight banditry they would need help—help from *mafiosi* prepared to supply inside information on the movement of the bands. For their part, *mafiosi* appreciated that farming bandits was not a long-term business. So when outlaws outlived their usefulness, *mafiosi* would betray them to the law in order to win friends in high places. Thus was the old tradition of co-managing crime revived in the Republican era.

Through numerous occult channels, the help from the mafia that the police needed was soon forthcoming. In the latter months of 1946, the bandits who had made Sicily so lawless since the Allied invasion in 1943 were rapidly eliminated. Until this point, police patrols had ranged across the wilds of western Sicily without ever catching a bandit gang. Now they mysteriously stumbled across their targets and killed or captured them. More frequently outlaw chiefs would be served up already dead. Just like the bandits of *In the Name of the Law*, they would be trussed up and tossed into a dried-up well, or simply shotgunned in the back in a mountain gully.

So at the dawning of Italy's democracy, the mafia was *exactly* what it had always been. It was *exactly* what the anti-mafia magistrate Giuseppe Guido Lo Schiavo and any number of police and *Carabinieri* had described it as: a secret society of murderous criminals bent on getting rich by illegal means, a force for murder, arson, kidnapping and mayhem.

Yet at the same time, give or take a little literary licence, the mafia was also *exactly* what the novelist Giuseppe Guido Lo Schiavo and the film director Pietro Germi portrayed it as: an auxiliary police force, and a preserver of the political status quo on a troubled island. Without ceasing to be the leaders of a 'criminal system', the smartest mafia bosses were dressing up in the costume that conservatives wanted them to wear. Hoisting themselves into the saddles of their imaginary white mares, *mafiosi* were slaughtering bandits who had become politically inconvenient, or cutting down peasant militants who refused to understand the way things worked on Sicily. And of course, most of the mafia's post-war political murders went unsolved—with the aid of the law.

The Cold War's first major electoral battle in Italy was the general election of 18 April 1948. One notorious election poster displayed the faces of Spencer Tracy, Rita Hayworth, Clark Gable, Gary Cooper and Tyrone Power, and proclaimed that 'Hollywood's stars are lining up against Communism'. But it was predominantly the Marshall Plan—America's huge programme of economic aid for Italy—that ensured that the Partito Comunista Italiano and its allies were defeated. The PCI remained in opposition in parliament; it would stay there for another half a century. The election's victors, the Christian Democrats (Democrazia Cristiana, DC), went into government—where they too would stay for the next half a century. Like trenches hacked into tundra, the battle-lines of Cold War Italian politics were now frozen in place.

A few weeks after that epoch-making general election, the most senior law enforcement officer in Sicily reported that, 'The mafia has never been as powerful and organised as it is today.' Nobody took any notice.

The Communist Party and its allies were the only ones not prepared to forget. In Rome, they did their best to denounce the Christian Democrat tolerance for the mafia in Sicily. Left-wing MPs pointed out how DC politicians bestowed favours on mafia bosses, and used them as electoral agents. Such protests would continue for the next forty years. But the PCI never had the support to form a government; it was unelectable, and therefore impotent. In June 1949, just a few weeks after *In the Name of the Law* was released in Italian cinemas, Interior Minister Mario Scelba addressed the Senate. Scelba had access to all that the police knew about the mafia in Sicily. But he scoffed at

Communist concerns about organised crime, and gave a homespun lecture about what mafia really meant to Sicilians like him:

> If a buxom girl walks past, a Sicilian will tell you that she is a *mafiosa* girl. If a boy is advanced for his age, a Sicilian will tell you that he is *mafioso*. People talk about the mafia flavoured with every possible sauce, and it seems to me that they are exaggerating.

What Scelba meant was that the mafia, or better the typically Sicilian quality known as 'mafiosity', was as much a part of the island's life as *cannoli* and *cassata*—and just as harmless. The world should just forget about this mafia thing, whatever it was, and busy itself with more serious problems.

For over forty years after the establishment of the Republic, Scelba's party, the DC, provided the mafias with their most reliable political friends. But the DC was by no means a mere mafia front. In fact it was a huge and hybrid political beast. Its supporters included northerners and southerners, cardinals and capitalists, civil servants and shopkeepers, bankers and peasant families whose entire wealth was a little plot of land. All that this heterogeneous electorate had in common was a fear of Communism.

In Sicily and the South, the DC encountered a class of political leader who had dominated politics since long before Fascism: the grandees. The typical southern grandee was a landowner or lawyer who was often per-

Friends in politics. *Mafioso* Giuseppe Genco Russo stands as a Christian Democrat (DC) candidate (late 1950s).

sonally wealthy, but invariably richer still in contacts with the Church and government. Patronage was the method: converting public resources (salaries, contracts, state credit, licences . . . or just help in cutting through the dense undergrowth of regulations) into private booty to be handed out to a train of family and followers. Through patronage, the grandees digested the anonymous structures of government and spun them out into a web of favours. *Mafiosi* were the grandees' natural allies. The best that can be said of the DC's relationship with the mafias is that the party was too fragmented and faction-ridden to ever confront and isolate the grandees.

Under Fascism, as on many previous occasions, police and magistrates had painstakingly assembled a composite image of the mafia organisation, the 'criminal system'. Now, in the era of the Cold War and the Christian Democrats, that picture was broken up and reassembled to compose the Buddha-like features of Turi Passalacqua. Better the mafia than the Communists. Better the Hollywood cowboy fantasy land of *In the Name of the Law* than a serious attempt to understand and tackle the island's criminal system of which many of the governing party's key supporters were an integral part.

Thanks to the success of *In the Name of the Law*, and to his prestigious career as a magistrate, Giuseppe Guido Lo Schiavo went on to become Italy's leading mafia pundit in the 1950s. He never missed an opportunity to restate the same convenient falsehoods that he had first articulated in his novel. More worryingly still, he became a lecturer in law at the *Carabinieri* training school, the chairman of the national board of film censorship, and a Supreme Court judge.

In 1954 Lo Schiavo even wrote a glowing commemoration of the venerable *capomafia* don Calogero Vizzini, who had just passed away peacefully in his home town of Villalba. Vizzini had been a protagonist in every twist and turn of the mafia's history in the dramatic years following the Liberation. By 1943, when he was proclaimed mayor of Villalba under AMGOT, the then sixty-six-year-old boss had already had a long career as an extortionist, cattle-rustler, black-marketeer and sulphur entrepreneur. In September of the following year, Vizzini's men caused a national sensation by throwing hand grenades at a Communist leader who had come to Villalba to give a speech. Vizzini was a leader of the Separatist movement. But when Separatism's star waned, he joined the Christian Democrats. The old man's grand funeral, in July 1954, was attended by mafia bosses from across the island.

Giuseppe Guido Lo Schiavo took Calogero Vizzini's death as a chance to reiterate his customary flummery about the mafia. But intriguingly, he also revealed that, one Sunday in Rome in 1952, the fat old boss had paid a visit to his house. He vividly recalled opening the door to his guest and being struck by a pair of 'razor-sharp, magnetic' eyes. The magistrate issued a polite but nervy welcome: '*Commendatore* Vizzini, my name is—'

'For you, I am not *commendatore*,' came the reply, as Vizzini waddled into the book-lined study and lowered his meaty frame onto the sofa. 'Call me Uncle Calò.'

Uncle Calò's tone was firm, but his manner open-hearted. He praised Lo Schiavo as a man of the law who had played hard but fair. The two men shook hands as a sign of mutual respect. Lo Schiavo tells us that, as he gazed at Uncle Calò, he was reminded of a picture from the past, from his first years as an anti-mafia magistrate in Sicily, when he first met a corpulent old mafia boss who always rode a white mare. He concluded his memories of Uncle Calò with good wishes for his successor within the mafia: 'May his efforts be directed along the path of respect for the state's laws, and of social improvement for all.'

Lo Schiavo's account of the conversation between himself and don Calogero Vizzini is as heavily embroidered as any of his novels. But the meeting itself really happened. The reason for Uncle Calò's visit was that he was caught up in a series of trials for the hand-grenade attack back in 1944. Only three days earlier, the Supreme Court had issued a guilty verdict against him. But the legal process was due to run on for a long time yet, and Uncle Calò knew that he would almost certainly die before he saw the inside of a jail. The real reason that he called in on Lo Schiavo may simply have been to say thank you. For the celebrated magistrate-novelist was involved in presenting the prosecution evidence at the Supreme Court. The suspicion lingers that, behind the scenes, he gave the mafia boss a helping hand with his case.

In today's Italy, if any magistrate received a social call from a crime boss he would immediately be placed under investigation. But in the conservative world of Christian Democrat Italy, affairs between the Sicilian mafia and magistrates were conducted in a more friendly way. The state and the mafia formed a partnership, in the name of the law.

36

CALABRIA: The last romantic bandit

WHEN IT CAME TO ORGANISED CRIME, POST-WAR ITALY'S AMNESIA WAS AS DEEP AND complex as the country's geology: its layers were the accumulated deposits of incompetence and negligence; the pressures of collusion and political cynicism sculpted its elaborate folds. By the time the Second World War ended, this geology of forgetfulness had created one of its most striking formations in Calabria.

In 1945, Italy's best-loved criminal lunatic returned to the land where he had made his name. Aged seventy, and now deemed harmless, Giuseppe Musolino, the 'King of Aspromonte', was transferred from a penal asylum in the north to a civil psychiatric hospital way down south in Calabria.

Musolino's new home was an infernal place. Although it was a Fascist-era building, it was already crumbling by the time the Fascist dictator's battered corpse was swinging by its heels from the gantry of a Milanese petrol station. Bare, unsanitary and overcrowded, the psychiatric hospital's rooms and corridors echoed with the gibbering and shrieking of afflicted souls. But in the late 1940s and early 1950s, before today's encrustation of motorways and jerry-built apartments had sprouted around the Calabrian coast, the hospital did at least afford a lovely panorama: before it, the view down to the city of Reggio Calabria, across the Straits of Messina, and over towards Sicily; behind it, the wooded shoulders of Aspromonte—the 'harsh mountain' that had once been Musolino's realm.

The new arrival attracted a great deal more attention and sympathy than the other patients. He was, after all, one of the most famous Calabrians alive. 'Don Peppino', the doctors and nurses all called him, combining a

305

respectful title and a fond nickname. Despite his mind's desolation, his frail body did its best to live up to this lingering aura. Musolino was thin, but unbowed by decades of incarceration. His scraggy beard stood out strikingly white against the olive darkness of his skin, making him look part Athenian philosopher and part faun, as one journalist noted. An actress drawn to visit the hospital was struck breathless by his resemblance to Luigi Pirandello, the great Sicilian dramatist, whose tales of masks and madness had earned him a Nobel Prize.

Musolino's own madness bore the blundering labels of mid-twentieth century psychiatry: 'progressive chronic interpretative delirium' and 'pompous paranoia'. He thought he was the Emperor of the Universe. He spent most of his day outside, smoking, reading, and contemplating the shadow of the cypress trees in the nearby cemetery. Yet when he found anyone with the patience to talk, he would grasp the chance to expound the hierarchy over which he presided: from the kings, queens and princes enthroned at his feet, to the cops and stoolies who grovelled far below.

Don Peppino had an obsessive loathing of cops and stoolies. And somehow, when he spoke to visitors, that very loathing often became a pathway to the corners of his mind that were still lucid. 'Bandits have to kill,' he would concede, 'but they must be honourable.' For Musolino, honour meant vendetta: all the crimes that had led to his imprisonment had been carried out to avenge the wrong he had endured at the hands of the police and their informers. Even in his insanity, he prized honesty above all: he would proudly point out that he had never denied any of his murders. After all, the victims were only cops and stoolies.

The newspapermen who made the long journey to the mental hospital in Reggio relished the chance to delve into the past and fill the gaps in don Peppino's fragmented memory for their readers. They told how this woodcutter's son had escaped his wrongful imprisonment in 1899, and spent two and a half years as a renegade up in the Aspromonte massif. They told how he killed seven people and tried to kill six more, all the while proclaiming that he was the victim of an injustice. The longer he evaded capture, the more his reputation grew: he came to be seen as the 'King of Aspromonte', a wronged hero of the oppressed peasantry, a symbol of desperate resistance to a heartless state.

But the heartless state, the journalists explained, had its revenge in the end. During the years of solitary confinement that followed his capture, Musolino lost his mind. His insanity only threw his tragic stature into starker relief.

Then, in 1936, a Calabrian-born emigrant to the United States made a deathbed confession: it was he, and not Musolino, who had shot at Vin-

A noble and tragic desperado? Giuseppe Musolino was known as the 'King of Aspromonte'. His famous story was acted out by major Italian star, Amedeo Nazzari, in the 1950 crime drama, *The Brigand Musolino*.

cenzo Zoccali all those years ago. The King of Aspromonte had stuck heroically to the same story from the start of his murderous rampage, during his trial, and even through his descent into insanity. Now that story had been proved right.

Perhaps it is no wonder that the psychiatrist in Reggio Calabria was so angry on his behalf. 'Was Musolino antisocial?' he asked in one newspaper interview. 'Or was it society that forced him to become what he became?'

Don Peppino received many presents. The most generous—food, clothes and dollars—came from Calabrians who had emigrated to America and made it big. Occasionally, he was even allowed day release—when a sentimental Italian-American businessman in a fedora and pinstriped suit turned up to take the old bandit out on a motor tour of the mountain.

Looking back now, one has to suspect that the Americans who came to pay homage to Giuseppe Musolino may have known the truth. He was no lone bandit hero: he was a member of the Calabrian mafia, an Honoured Society killer. And the whole fable of the 'King of Aspromonte' had served only to keep what was really going on in Calabria hidden from the public eye.

After 1945, with the war over, the transition to democracy under way, and the King of Aspromonte residing in Reggio Calabria mental hospital, the organisation that is today known as the 'ndrangheta operated in very much the same way that it had done when he was in his murderous prime. *Carabinieri* 'co-managed' petty crime with the underworld bosses. Grandees used the mafia to round up electors, and then returned the favour by

Meanwhile, the real Musolino lived
out his last years in a Reggio Calabria
mental hospital.

testifying in court that there was no such organisation. For successive governments, it proved easy to just bank the votes of Calabria's mafia-backed
members of parliament, and ignore the Honoured Society. And while politicians looked the other way, the police and magistracy had time to forget all
they had learned about the Calabrian mafia during the Fascist era from—
among other people—the King of Aspromonte's own brother, Antonio Musolino. In the early 1920s, Antonio engaged in a long battle with his cousin
and *capo* Francesco Filastò (the same cousin suspected of killing Lieutenant
Joe Petrosino in 1909). In the end, defeated, impoverished and paralysed (a
revolver shot cost him the use of his left leg and arm), Antonio Musolino
went over to the state. He told the authorities everything he knew about the
criminal organisation to which he, like his infamous brother, belonged. In
1932, his evidence fed into the trial of ninety men. Prosecutors in the 1932
case believed that the Calabrian mafia had its own governing body, known
as the *Gran Criminale* (the Great Criminal), which intervened to settle disputes within the various *'ndrine* across the province of Reggio Calabria—but
which had failed to settle the dispute between Antonio Musolino and his
cousin. The surviving evidence suggests that the Great Criminal served the
same purposes as what is now called the Crime, which would only finally
be revealed to the world by investigators in 2010. In other words, post-war
amnesia may well have cost Italy eighty wasted years when it came to understanding the unitary structure of Calabria's Honoured Society.

Meanwhile, just as during Giuseppe Musolino's homicidal rampage, lazy
journalists were content to churn out the King of Aspromonte fable, even
now that their primary source was a crazy geriatric killer. Musolino, for
his part, lived as the Emperor of the Universe, commanding interplanetary

ships and deploying devices more destructive than the atomic bomb. In his psychologically damaged state, he became a metaphor for Italy's own cognitive failure. The reasons for that failure were ultimately very simple. In southern Calabria, the conflict between Left and Right had nowhere near the explosiveness that propelled Sicily up the political agenda and created such devilish intrigues between *mafiosi* and men of the law. Calabria remained Italy's poorest and most neglected region. The 'ndrangheta could be forgotten because the region it came from simply did not count.

Cinema proved unable to resist the story of the King of Aspromonte, however. Under Fascism, Benito Mussolini blocked any attempt to make a film of Musolino's life because of the similarity in their surnames. Finally, in 1950, two of Italy's biggest stars, Amedeo Nazzari and Silvana Mangano, were cast in *Il brigante Musolino*. Filmed on location on Aspromonte, the movie told how Musolino was unjustly imprisoned for murder on the basis of false testimonies, and then escaped to become an outlaw hero. The film did well among the Italian community in the United States.

Giuseppe Musolino died in January 1956 aged seventy-nine. Up and down Italy, the newspapers told his story one more time, and called him 'the last romantic bandit'.

The wealthy Italian-American visitors who came to pay him homage may just have known the truth behind the myth: Musolino was an 'ndrangheta killer.

37

NAPLES: Puppets and puppeteers

IN 1930, ITALY'S FIRST GREAT NATIONAL ENCYCLOPEDIA, THE *ENCICLOPEDIA TRECCANI*, included the following entry under *Camorra*:

> The camorra was an association of lower class men, who used extor-
> tion to force the vice-ridden and the cowardly to surrender tribute. Its
> branches spread through the old Kingdom of Naples; it had laws and
> customs, a rigidly organised hierarchy, specific obligations and duties,
> and a jargon and court system of its own . . . Moral education and en-
> vironmental improvements succeeded, in the end, in destroying the
> camorra . . . Only the word remains today, to indicate abuses or acts of
> bullying.

The camorra was dead: for once, this proud claim had a strong basis in
truth rather than in the propaganda needs of the Fascist regime. Whereas
Calabria's gangsters had climbed the social ladder until they merged with
the state, *camorristi* in Naples never quite left the alleys behind. Unable to
call on the kind of political protection that the mafias of Sicily and Calabria
could boast, the camorra was vulnerable. By the time the First World War
broke out, the Honoured Society (in the city, at least) had collapsed.

In Naples in the late 1940s, one of the few places where the word 'camorra'
was regularly used was in a tiny theatre, the San Carlino. Its entrance was
hard to find: a doorway hidden among the bookstalls that crowded about
the Porta San Gennaro. Inside, the auditorium could barely contain seven
dilapidated benches. The stage was only just wider than the upright piano

310

standing before it. This was the last poky outpost of a beleaguered art form for the illiterate: the only remaining puppet playhouse in the city.

Puppet theatre had been popular in Sicily and southern Italy for more than a century. Its stock stories told of chivalry and treachery among Charlemagne's knights as they battled against their Saracen foes. The marionettes, in tin armour and with bright red lips, would speechify endlessly about honour and betrayal, and then launch into a wobbly dance that signified mortal combat.

In Naples, the puppet theatres had another speciality too: tales of chivalry and treachery set in the world of the Honoured Society. Indeed, if the San Carlino was still holding out against the cinemas, it was largely because of the enduring appeal of camorra dramas. Outside, badly printed posters proclaimed the dramatic delights on offer:

TONIGHT

THE DEATH OF PEPPE AVERZANO THE WISE GUY.

WITH REAL BLOOD

Inside, the audience was integral to the spectacle. The loud cries of 'Traitor!' and 'Watch out!' from the stalls could as well have been written into the script. The audience knowledgeably applauded the knife-fighting skills of some *camorristi*, and angrily denounced the cowardly tricks of others: 'You should be ashamed of yourself! Ten against one!' The plots were repetitive: *camorristi* taking blood oaths, or fighting dagger duels, or saving marionette maidens from dishonour. The dramatic pay-off was always the same: good versus evil, the surge of righteous indignation versus the prurient thrill of violence. When the action was particularly moving, the San Carlino rocked and creaked like a railway carriage trundling over points.

Everyone knew the camorra heroes' names: the gentleman gangster, don Teofilo Sperino, and the mighty boss Ciccio Cappuccio ('Little Lord Frankie'); the devious Nicola Jossa, endlessly pitting his wits against the greatest *camorrista* of them all, Salvatore De Crescenzo. All of these puppet heroes and villains had once been real gangsters rather than gaudily painted puppets. Genuine episodes of nineteenth-century camorra history were reimagined on the stage of the San Carlino. The 'real blood' that spurted from the puppet's chest at the dramatic conclusion of the piece was in fact a bladder full of aniline dye. And whereas the good-guy *camorristi* would be given bright red gore, the bad guys bled a much darker shade, almost black.

Outside the San Carlino, in the bomb-ravaged streets of Naples, the real Honoured Society had not been seen for over thirty years. There were still a few old *camorristi* around. The most notorious of them was a familiar and pitiful sight, who recalled both the old camorra and the strange story of its demise: he was Gennaro Abbatemaggio, the controversial 'gramophone' whose testimony during the Cuocolo trial in 1911–12 had inflicted a fatal blow on the Honoured Society.

The years since the Cuocolo trial had not been kind to Abbatemaggio. He had become a tubby little old man, almost bald. At first glance he seemed dapper in a suit and open-necked shirt, or in a dark turtle-neck, sports jacket and sunglasses. But the threadbare tailoring fooled no one who saw him up close. For don Gennaro, as journalists called him with ironic reverence, was all but indigent. He lived hand-to-mouth, on petty theft and scams. No one would have cared about his fortunes—but for the fact that he was a living relic of a once fearsome criminal power.

After the Second World War, Abbatemaggio did everything he could to keep himself in the limelight—at least he did when he was not in prison. In 1949 he staged a suicide attempt, and a conversion to religious faith; he later gave interviews on the steps of the Roman church where he was due to receive his First Holy Communion. When religion failed, he tried show business. But his repeated efforts to get his own story turned into celluloid came to nothing. In 1952 he had to be content with being snapped with the stars at the premiere of *The City Stands Trial*, a 1952 film retelling the story of the 1911 case that had destroyed the Honoured Society.

Shut out of the cinema, Abbatemaggio's last resort was to try and revive his moment of glory. He claimed to have sensational revelations about one of the biggest murder mysteries of 1953: the death of a Roman girl, Wilma Montesi. But it soon emerged that the old stool pigeon was at it again. He was arrested and tried for false testimony. Thereafter, he was seen begging. The press began to ignore him.

So if the word 'camorra' was used in post-war Naples, it was only to evoke its memory with the same mixture of amusement and pity that was conjured up by newspaper stories about the puppet theatre or Gennaro Abbatemaggio.

Today, more than half a century after Abbatemaggio's death, 'camorra' has changed its meaning. In the decades since the end of the Second World War, the camorra has re-emerged and adopted a new identity; it has become stronger and more insidious than ever. It is no longer an Honoured Society—a single sect of criminals with its initiation rituals, its formalised dagger duels, its ranks and rules. Today *camorrista* means an affiliate of one of many structured, but frequently unstable, gangster syndicates. The camorra is not just one secret society like the mafias of Sicily and Calabria, therefore. Rather it is a vast and constantly shifting map of gangs ruling different territories in Naples and the Campania region. Like the Honoured Society of old, these organisations run protection rackets and trafficking operations. But—at least when things are going well for them—they are far more successful than the old Honoured Society ever was at infiltrating the state institutions, politics and the economy.

To the audiences at the San Carlino in the late 1940s, such a future incarnation of the camorra would have seemed a highly unlikely prospect. Hoodlums were certainly active in Naples in the post-war years. But they were much less powerful than they are today—or indeed than they were in Sicily or Calabria at the time. Naples could not manage anything like the great Sicilian ruling-class conspiracy of silence about the mafia. There was no Neapolitan equivalent of a senior magistrate like Giuseppe Guido Lo Schiavo, who was prepared, in the teeth of everything he knew, to deny the mafia's very existence. And the great and troubled city of Naples was far from politically invisible in the way the towns and villages of Calabria were.

However, under closer examination, the hoodlums of post-war Naples do turn out to be the progenitors of today's Kalashnikov-wielding, cocaine-smuggling, suit-wearing *camorristi*. The seeds of the camorra's future revival had already been planted. Indeed, there was already something menacing there in the city's underworld—something that made it abundantly clear that the camorra was not as dead as all the encyclopedias claimed. A careful look at Neapolitan gangland in the 1940s and early 1950s also shows that Italy in general, and Naples in particular, had a guilty conscience when it came to organised crime. This was a city that refused to use the 'c' word (unless it was talking about the past, of course—about the San Carlino theatre or Gennaro Abbatemaggio). In short, Naples had *both* its own distinctive mobsters, *and* its own characteristic style of forgetting that they were there.

Stereotypes were the most powerful way to forget about the camorra. Naples is Italy's hardest city to decipher. Countless visitors have been lured into judging it by appearances, because those appearances are so obvious and so diverting. For hundreds of years, Europe has found the sunlit spectacle of Neapolitan street life irresistible. Here was a place where squalor seemed to come in colour, and sweet music to emerge miraculously from a constant din. The poor of the city had the reputation of using any shabby trick, putting on any demeaning act, in order to fill their bellies and live a life of *dolce far niente* ('sweet idleness'). The reason Gennaro Abbatemaggio appeared in the papers so often in the late 1940s was not just because he had destroyed the Honoured Society; it was also because, with his tragicomic ducking and diving, he seemed like a personification of everybody's archetypal Neapolitan. The San Carlino attracted attention because it too seemed peculiar and typical of the city. The Neapolitan poor were viewed as imps living in paradise: mischievous, sentimental, naïve, and endlessly inventive to the point of being unabashed about playing up to all the stereotypes about them. Before the war, Neapolitan urchins would charge a fee to foreigners who wanted to photograph them eating spaghetti with their hands, as a century and more of stereotypes dictated that they should.

The post-war generation also had its travellers keen to revive these commonplaces. The simple trick was to show a city encapsulated only in what first met the eye in the poor neighbourhoods like Forcella or Pignasecca. A city of beggars and pedlars, where from every windowsill or doorway, from orange boxes or trays, somebody would be trying to sell you something: chestnuts, or fragments of fried fish, or single cigarettes, or prickly pears, or *taralli* (pretzels). Poor Naples was an open-air bazaar where barbers and tailors plied their trade out in the street, and where passers-by could look in at the single-family sweatshops making shoes or gloves.

Foreigners were not the only ones responsible for rehashing the old clichés: there were always professional Neapolitans prepared to chip in too. One such was Giuseppe Marotta. He knew precisely how hard life in Naples could be: he and his two sisters had been brought up by a seamstress in one of the notorious *bassi*—the one-room apartments that opened directly onto the street. In 1926 he went north to become a writer in Italy's industrial and literary capital, Milan. By the late 1940s, after years of hack-work, he had made it: he was a regular newspaper columnist, and the man to whom editors turned when they wanted a colourful piece on some aspect of Neapolitan life.

In the stereotypical Naples that Marotta served up for his readers, lawlessness was not really crime, it was a part of the urban spectacle. Here pickpockets and endlessly inventive rip-off artists expressed a picturesque form of dishonesty—one that grew from hardship and not malice. There was something both creative and endearing about crime here. The poor of Naples could steal your heart as easily as lift your wallet.

In one article from 1953, Marotta marvelled at the agility of the *correntisti*—daring, agile young crooks who would swing themselves up onto the back of a passing lorry so as to offload the contents as it rumbled along. This type of crime was known in the alleys as *la corrente* ('the stream') because of the fluidity of the whole operation. A good *correntista*, Marotta remarked, needed a freakish range of skills:

The legs of a star centre forward, the eye of a sailor, the ear of a redskin, the velvet touch of a bishop, and the iron grip of a weightlifter—as well as hooked feet, rubber ribs, and the balance of a jockey. And to coordinate it all, the brain of the conductor Arturo Toscanini.

Marotta also smirked indulgently at the teetering pyramids of stolen tin cans that were the fruits of the *corrente*.

The truth that Marotta's stereotypes concealed was that criminal power was a threatening presence in Naples. The poor, the very inhabitants of those alleys who so charmed onlookers, were often its first victims, as one revealing episode from the everyday life of Naples allows us to see.

At around 6.30, one hot summer evening in 1952, Antonio Quindici, known as 'O Grifone (the Griffon), decided to buy some mussels. He presented himself at a stall in via Alessandro Poerio, not far from the station, but he found five workers from a nearby building site in front of him. He demanded to be served first, and the mussel-seller meekly obeyed. But the builders, who were from a different part of the city, obviously did not know whom they were dealing with, because they objected loudly. 'O Grifone responded by grabbing the mussel-seller's knife and stabbing the most vocal builder twice in the heart. He then fled. He was chased by the victim's friends, but their pursuit was blocked by a coordinated group of accomplices. 'O Grifone vanished into the side streets. His victim bled to death where he lay, leaving a wife and a baby daughter.

The story of 'O Grifone is interesting for several reasons. First because the murderer was one of the *correntisti* that Giuseppe Marotta so admired. Men like 'O Grifone had learned their skills during the war, when Naples had been the major supply port for the Allied forces in Italy: around half of those supplies found their way off the backs of army lorries and onto the black market. The crowded area around via Forcella, where 'O Grifone came from, was where the wartime trade in stolen military supplies was concentrated: not for nothing did the Forcella area become known as the kasbah of Naples. Significantly, Forcella was once also a stronghold of the Honoured Society: it was home to all the earliest bosses. *Correntisti* like 'O Grifone would become protagonists of the camorra's revival.

When the war ended, everyone confidently expected the *correntisti* to disappear. Yet they were still very much in business in 1952, when one newspaper commented:

The *corrente* is fluid, as everyone knows, and omnipresent, especially in the streets where there is most traffic. Communications between the city and its outskirts are watched over by squads of criminals. Quick,

well-equipped and scornful of danger, these men remove all kinds of
goods from vehicles. It can be said that no road-train, lorry or car es-
capes the clutches of the *correntisti*.

Around each *correntista* there was a whole organisation that included teams
of spies who tracked the path of valuable cargoes, porters who smuggled
the goods away once they were dropped from the lorry, and fences who put
the swag on the market. Long after the great days of military contraband
came to an end, goods stolen by the *corrente* were still openly on sale in via
Forcella.

The *correntisti* were not just agile, but also violent. They were often
armed, for practical reasons: to protect themselves from gun-wielding truck
drivers and rival gangs; and to discourage passers-by from trying to pick
up anything they might have seen falling off the back of a lorry. But they
were also armed because they had to impose themselves on the community
around them, and establish a reputation for toughness. Back in the days
of the Honoured Society, this reputation would have been referred to as
'honour'. It is one of the key ingredients of the mafias' power—of 'territorial
control', as it is termed. 'O Grifone's row at the mussel stall displayed that
'honour' in an individualistic, undisciplined form.

After the stabbing, 'O Grifone spent several days on the run. Eventually
he had a last breakfast in the bar next to the police station and gave himself
up, having first concocted a story about how he had been grievously insulted and provoked by the man he knifed to death. Evidently his support
network could not stand the strain of a high-profile police investigation and
a public outcry. 'O Grifone and his friends still had limits to their territorial
control.

Strikingly, the newspapers in Naples referred to 'O Grifone as a *camorrista*. Or at least they did so initially. This is one of the rare occasions when
the word slipped into print in the late 1940s and early 1950s. Curiously,
as the manhunt for 'O Grifone continued over the following days, the early
references to the camorra disappeared. 'O Grifone started off as a *camorrista*,
and then became a mere criminal.

There was a palpable unease about using the word 'camorra' in Naples
in the years after the war, as there was about admitting just how serious the
city's crime problem was. Naples was a key political battleground, where
the soul of the Italian Right was being fought over by opposing political
machines. On the one hand, there was the creeping power of the Christian
Democrats. On the other, there were the Monarchists, under the war profiteer, shipping magnate and soccer mogul Achille Lauro. (Naples, like many
southern cities, had voted against the Republic in the referendum of 1946.

Thereafter, the monarchy remained a powerful rallying cause for the city's right wing.)

The Naples these two political machines contested was scarred by chronic unemployment and homelessness, poor health and illiteracy. Neapolitan industry and infrastructure had not recovered from the devastations of the war, which were worse here than in any other Italian city. Yet politics found no answers because it was beset with instability and malpractice, mostly rotating around the lucrative construction industry. These were the years of 'maccheroni politics'. At election time, political grandees would order their local agents to set up distribution centres in the kasbahs of the centre. Here, packets of pasta, or cuts of meat, or pieces of salt cod would be wrapped in the vague promise of a job or a pension and handed out in exchange for votes. Achille Lauro's campaign managers came up with the scheme of handing out pairs of shoes to their would-be supporters: the right shoe before the poll, and the left one afterwards, when the vote had been safely recorded.

The poor who sold their support so cheaply seemed almost as resistant to the benefits of education, social improvement and conventional party politics as they had been when Italy was unified in 1860. Their political loyalties were understandably fickle. One of the few ways of trying to win them over, other than maccheroni or shoes, was a tear-jerking local patriotism: the claim that the city's problems were all the fault of northern neglect. Achille Lauro, who also owned the second-biggest newspaper in Naples, Roma, was a master at playing up to the stereotype of Naples as a big-hearted city that history had treated harshly. Any talk of the camorra or organised crime was just old-fashioned northern snobbery.

There was another reason why Neapolitans insisted on confining the word camorra to the past: criminals were part of the ruling political machines. Even the old camorra stool pigeon Gennaro Abbatemaggio was an occasional electoral runner for Achille Lauro. But much more important than these grassroots agents were the so-called guappi. As we have seen, guappi were fences and loan sharks, runners of illegal lotteries: they were the puppeteers of the city's lively criminal scene. But they were not just criminal figures: guappi also pulled political strings, fixing everyday problems by calling in favours from the politicians on whose behalf they raked in votes come election time.

The most famous guappo of them all was Giuseppe Navarra, known as the King of Poggioreale. He was a loyal electoral chief for the Monarchists and Achille Lauro, and collected honorific titles from his political protectors: Commendatore, and Knight of the Great Cross of the Constantinian Order. During the war, he had operated in the black market, making friends with the Allied authorities. He also made a great deal of money in iron and other scrap, which his people took (mostly illegally) from bombed-out buildings.

Navarra lived among the coffin-makers on the main thoroughfare of Poggioreale, the neighbourhood where the cemetery and the prison stand. He held court on wooden chairs on the pavement. It is said that on his saint's day, the tram would stop outside his house so that all the passengers could sample the sweets and liqueurs he offered. Navarra drove a gigantic Lancia Dilambda limousine with running boards down the side, a car of the kind we are used to seeing in American gangster movies of the inter-war years. Navarra bought it at an auction in Rome after the fall of Fascism; it used to belong to the Duce's oldest son, Vittorio Mussolini. In 1947, one northern newspaper gave a tongue-in-cheek portrait of this street-corner monarch:

> He is about fifty, dumpy, with a square face and thick salt-and-pepper hair. One of his eyes is lazy, and his nose starts off from a very wide base on his face, but comes to a rapid end in a sharp point—as if it started off wanting to be a huge Bourbon nose, and then repented along the way.

Navarra owed his fame, and quite a part of his popularity, to an extraordinary episode earlier in 1947, when he rescued the treasure of the city's patron saint, San Gennaro (Saint Januarius). San Gennaro is the martyr whose 'blood' is kept in a glass box in Naples cathedral so that it can miraculously liquefy a couple of times a year. Or not, if the citizens meet with the Almighty's displeasure for whatever reason. The saint's treasure is a collection of gifts from the faithful, which was taken to the Vatican for safe-keeping during the war. Firsthand details of the King of Poggioreale's supposed act of heroism are sketchy because almost all newspapers, rather suspiciously, did not report it until later. But the story told is that, when the mayor asked the chief of police to help bring the treasure home, he was refused: the police could not spare the money or resources to send the armoured car, ten trucks and twenty-man armed escort that it would take to carry the treasure over the dangerous roads between the capital and Naples. At that point, the *guappo* Navarra volunteered his services, and did the job stealthily by car, with an aged Catholic aristocrat on the passenger seat next to him. He reportedly travelled in a FIAT 22, which was less conspicuous than his limo. But quite how he fitted all the treasure in its tiny boot is not entirely clear. Bizarrely, Ernest Borgnine later recreated the escapade when he played the title role in the 1961 movie, *The King of Poggioreale*.

Navarra was a figure enveloped in layers of legend and theatrical self-promotion—yet another picturesque landmark of the Neapolitan streets. Accordingly, the 'professional Neapolitan' journalist Giuseppe Marotta penned a typically indulgent portrait of him in 1947, saying that he was 'a man dedicated to charity work no less than he was to his wife and the Monarchist cause'. But Navarra had very real power, sustained by the threat of violence. Locals later remembered him strutting up and down the street in a fedora and waistcoat, brandishing a pistol.

So Navarra, like other *guappi* in the city, was a bridge between the streets, including the underworld, and the city's palaces of power. One of the things that sets Italy's mafias apart from ordinary criminal gangs is precisely this link with politics. Put the *correntisti* and the *guappi* together in a single system, and you would have every justification in using the 'c' word that the Neapolitan newspapers were determined not to use.

38

GANGSTERISMO

THE MAFIA IN THE UNITED STATES WAS FOUNDED BY SICILIAN EMIGRANTS IN THE LATE nineteenth century. In the big cities, crooks from Calabria and Naples were also recruited into what was soon an Italian-American mob. Ever since that time, Men of Honour have shuttled back and forth across the Atlantic, trafficking, investing and killing—and then running from the law or from their mafia enemies. The story of the mafia in the United States is not one I can hope to tell here. Nevertheless, some aspects of that story have a bearing on events in Italy.

America was a synonym for modernity in the backward Italy of the years that followed the Second World War. According to their political loyalties, Italians were either grudging or wholehearted in their admiration for the United States' awesome warrior might, inconceivable wealth and unreachable movie stars. As one commentator wrote in 1958:

> People all over the world are looking to America, waiting expectantly for everything: for their daily bread or their tin of meat; for machines or raw materials; for military defence, for a cultural watchword, for the political and social system that can resolve the evils of the world. America provides the models for newspapers, scientific manuals, labour-saving devices, fashion, fiction, pop ditties, dance moves and dance tunes, and even poetry . . . Is there one single thing that we don't expect America to provide?

In fact there *was* one thing that Italy as yet refused to accept from across the Atlantic: a lesson in how to fight the mafia. In 1950, just when Italy had managed to forget about its organised crime problem, America started talking about the mafia again. For the first time in a very long time, Italian-American crime became news. But the perverse circumstances of the Cold War conspired to ensure that the noise surrounding the mafia in America only made the silence in Italy even more deafening.

On 6 April 1950, Kansas City gambling baron and local Democratic kingmaker Charles Binaggio, together with his enforcer Charles 'Mad Dog' Gargotta, were shot dead in a Democratic clubhouse. The press printed embarrassing photographs of Binaggio slumped at a desk under a large picture of President Harry S. Truman. On Capitol Hill, the Binaggio episode caused an outcry that removed the last opposition to Bible Belt Senator Estes Kefauver's efforts to set up a Senate Special Committee to Investigate Crime in Interstate Commerce, with the mafia as one of its main targets.

The Kefauver hearings, as they became known, were held in fourteen cities across the States over the following year. But it was the climactic nine days of testimonies in New York, in March 1951, that really propelled the mafia issue into the public domain. Underworld potentates such as Meyer Lansky and Frank Costello, plus a real live gangster's moll, and a host of other shady hangers-on, were hauled before the Senator and his sharp-tongued deputy Charles Tobey. At Kefauver's insistence, their testimonies were televised to a national audience that peaked at seventeen million. Housewives held afternoon 'Kefauver parties', their husbands left bars deserted to catch the evening résumé of the day's scandals, sales of home-popping popcorn more than doubled, and the Brooklyn Red Cross had to install a television set to prevent blood donations drying up.

The testimony of Frank Costello (born Francesco Castiglia in Calabria) made for a particularly captivating spectacle. While he refused to have his face on screen, the camera nonetheless showed lingering close-ups of his hands as they cruelly twisted pieces of paper or fiddled deviously with a pair of spectacles. This 'hand ballet', together with a voice 'like the death rattle of a seagull', made Costello loom far larger in the public imagination than if his rather nondescript features had been visible.

In Italy, the Communist press reported with undisguised glee on the evidence of political collusion with organised crime that was being uncovered by Kefauver. 'The "heroes" of American democracy on parade', ran one sarcastic headline.

Everything is mixed up inextricably: political intrigues and police intrigues. The entire American system of government, both local and central, is prey to the gangs.

Mafia media frenzy. Calabrian-born mobster Frank Costello testifies before the Kefauver Hearings, New York, 1951.

While the Cold War enemy was washing its dirty laundry in public, in Italy there had been no washing at all. The 1943–50 period had seen mafia violence and political collusion with organised crime on a scale greater even than the United States. Yet, in parliament as in the law courts, the Left had failed to take advantage from the mafia issue in their battle with the Christian Democrats. Kefauver, by contrast, exposed the long-standing mafia ties of William O'Dwyer, a former mayor of New York who was currently Ambassador to Mexico, and brought his political career to an end. Frank Costello, who at one time had been the 'respectable' face of the American mafia, its hinge with Democratic machine politics in New York, received a short stretch in prison for contempt of Congress, and his tax affairs attracted the unwelcome attentions of the Internal Revenue Service. Costello's 'hand ballet' also gave him the kind of notoriety that Sicilian *mafiosi* had repeatedly managed to dodge. 'Kefauver is a master of publicity,' *L'Unità* commented. So while the PCI relished what the Kefauver hearings exposed, it also quietly envied their impact.

Many of the underworld figures interviewed by Estes Kefauver refused to incriminate themselves at the hearings—so many that the phrase 'take the Fifth Amendment' entered common parlance. To fill the huge gaps in these firsthand testimonies, the crusading Senator relied on several sources: information from the Federal Bureau of Narcotics, whose ambitious head, Harry J. Anslinger, had been seeking to ramp up the mafia issue for years; the often muddled testimonies of a cluster of mafia informers; and a great deal of supposition. As a result, the profile of the mafia published in Kefauver's findings was alarming:

> Behind the local mobs which make up the national crime syndicate is a shadowy, international criminal organization known as the Mafia, so fantastic that most Americans find it hard to believe it really exists. The Mafia, which has its origins and its headquarters in Sicily, is dominant in numerous fields of illegal activity . . . and it enforces its code with death to those who resist or betray it . . . The Mafia is no fairy tale. It is ominously real, and it has scarred the face of America with almost every conceivable type of criminal violence, including murder, traffic in narcotics, smuggling, extortion, white slavery, kidnapping, and labor racketeering . . . The Mafia today actually is a secret international government-within-a-government. It has an international head in Italy—believed by United States authorities to be Charles (Lucky) Luciano . . . The Mafia also has its Grand Council and its national and district heads in the countries in which it operates, including the United States.

America was living through a period of Cold War paranoia at the time, and there is more than a hint of the Reds-under-the-bed worldview in what Kefauver wrote. The mafia: a sophisticated criminal conspiracy against America; a single, global organisation whose 'Kingpin' or 'Tsar of Vice' was Lucky Luciano.

Lucky Luciano's true story does not really fit Kefauver's image of him. In 1946, he had been released suspiciously early from a long sentence for pimping; he was expelled from the country and set up shop in Naples. There he did a bit of drug dealing with his Sicilian and Neapolitan friends, but he was certainly not the ruler of a criminal conspiracy, a super-boss whose every order was faithfully implemented in every corner of the world.

Many in the United States remained understandably unconvinced by Kefauver's sensationalist account, and some of them refused to believe that the mafia existed at all. Even the man charged with drafting the committee's recommendations called it a 'romantic myth'. The FBI would continue to remain sceptical about the existence of the mafia for several years yet. Kefauver had overplayed his hand.

Giuseppe Prezzolini, a professor at Columbia University, was the Italian press's most prominent American correspondent. His views on organised crime were much more representative of the most widespread attitudes in Italy than were those of the Communists. When he received calls from worried Americans wanting to know if the mafia really existed in Italy, he was moved to write a withering dismissal of Kefauver's 'grotesque legend'. The mafia in Sicily, Prezzolini explained, was not really a criminal organisation, but a product of centuries of bad government; it was 'a state of mind that expressed the resentment of a people that wanted to take justice into its own hands because it believed it had not received justice from its rulers'. Only in the dynamic capitalist environment of the United States could *mafiosi* be considered hoodlums:

> The modern felon in America, even if he bears an Italian name, is no longer an Italian felon. Rather he is a felon brought up in America and schooled in lawbreaking in America; he earned his degree at the American university of crime. America transformed his character.

The notorious Brooklyn waterfront gangster, Albert 'the Mad Hatter' Anastasia was a very good example. The fact that he was born Umberto Anastasio in Calabria in 1902 meant nothing because, 'I have never heard it said that a mafia has taken root in Calabria.'

Early in 1953, Kefauver's findings were translated into Italian as *Il gangsterismo in America*, the first book on the mafia to be published in Italy since the Second World War. Many commentators on all sides of the political spectrum passed over Kefauver's mafia-as-global-conspiracy in embarrassed silence, concentrating instead on what the Senator had to say about the United States. For most Italians, *gangsterismo*, as the ugly linguistic import implied, remained an exclusively American affair.

Something spectacularly newsworthy would be needed to succeed where the Kefauver hearings had failed, and break Italy's silence. Something like a homicidal maniac. Or a gangland beauty queen. Or an alien invasion of Calabria. Suddenly, in 1955, all three of these things arrived, exposing at last just how deep-rooted the new Republic's mafia problem really was.

PART VIII

1955

39

THE MONSTER OF PRESINACI

LATE ON THE MORNING OF 17 APRIL 1955, A PEASANT CALLED SERAFINO CASTAGNA from the Calabrian village of Presinaci ate two fried eggs without even stopping to cut himself a slice of bread. He then kissed the crucifix on the wall before hugging his wife and nine-year-old son. 'The things of this world are no longer for me,' he told them. 'God has given them, and God takes them away.'

Moments later, armed with a Beretta pistol, a service rifle with bayonet fixed, and a haversack of ammunition, he loped out into the Sunday sunshine to find his first victim.

In a hovel just metres away lived Castagna's distant cousin Domenicantonio Castagna. When Serafino got there, he found only Domenicantonio's sixty-year-old mother, so he shot her six times.

He then caught sight of Francesca Badolato, who had once been his brother's fiancée. He fired and missed, and she managed to escape, scooping a baby into her arms as she ran. Castagna was not a quick mover because a congenital disability had made his right leg three centimetres shorter than the left. But he pursued Francesca all the same, and saw her take refuge in the house belonging to an aged barber. Castagna battered at the door and smashed a window while the barber and his wife pleaded with him to spare the girl. Finally, frustrated, he took a step back and shot the couple dead. Their names were Nicola Polito (71) and his wife, Maria (60), and only two weeks earlier they had been reunited following Nicola's three-year stint in Argentina.

Castagna then followed the tinny murmur of a radio to the Communist Party centre. Peering in, he saw no one who had done him any harm and

327

moved on. When he approached the Christian Democrat HQ nearby, they saw his pistol and begged for mercy. 'Don't be afraid,' he told them. 'I'm only looking for some friends of mine to say hello.'

Castagna now headed out of the village, making for the hay-barn where he had hidden more ammunition. When it dawned on him that his route ran past his father's plot, bitter childhood memories began to flash through his mind. His father had abandoned the family for other women, and wasted what little money the Castagnas had. Minutes later, Serafino was staring at his father and uttering a tearful sentence of death: 'Can you see what you've brought me to? You didn't give us a proper upbringing. Look at the abyss I'm in, at thirty-four years old . . . As a father, I adore you. But as a man, you must die.'

A single shot left the old man writhing on the ground. Serafino bayoneted him to end the agony, and then stooped to plant a farewell kiss on his father's hand.

On his way to the next target, he passed an old cowherd who enquired, 'What brings you by these parts, Serafino?' 'I'm hunting two-footed wolves,' came the reply. A short time later, Castagna found Pasquale Petrolo, who was sitting on the threshing floor in front of his farmhouse and chatting happily to his wife. Castagna shot him five times.

Then he went on the run.

Within hours, reporters across Italy were updating their readers on the manhunt. There were roadblocks at every crossroads. Patrols of *Carabinieri* scoured the slopes of Mount Poro, stopping to level burp guns at the goatherds, scrutinising each sun-weathered face to see if it matched the description: 'Medium height, robust physique, blond hair, blue eyes. Affected by heart disease and a duodenal ulcer.' The press called Castagna 'the Monster of Presinaci'.

Castagna's home village was a place of stunted peasants, black pigs and fat flies, a mountain hamlet of scarcely a hundred crude stone houses lost in a neglected corner of Italy's most neglected region. Inasmuch as most Italians knew anything about Calabria, they knew it as a region whose timeless poverty generated periodic explosions of peasant savagery. Serafino Castagna's homicidal rampage bore all the signs of being just another Calabrian tragedy. Indeed local legend even provided a script for the slaughter. 'Castagna has certainly read the story of the brigand Musolino, and would like to imitate his deeds', proclaimed the policeman in charge of the search. The 'Monster of Presinaci' became the 'Second Musolino', a candidate for the succession as King of Aspromonte. (At the time, the original King of Aspromonte was living out the last months of his life in the Reggio Calabria mental hospital.) Castagna even followed Musolino in issuing messages to the authorities. Before setting out on his rampage, he scribbled a list of twenty people he intended to murder, and left it behind for his wife to hand in to the police. He later wrote to the local sergeant of the *Carabinieri* to proclaim his plan of vengeance: 'I'll kill until my last cartridge.'

On the day Castagna's victims were buried, the only people in Presinaci who dared join the funeral procession were *Carabinieri* in their dark parade uniforms. A single child was spotted scuttling out from a doorway to throw a bunch of flowers onto the last coffin of the five. The sound of his mother's imploring wail followed him into the street, and he immediately hurried back indoors.

As the search for the Monster went on, the press began to ask questions. Something about the calm with which he had gone about the slaughter suggested that he was not entirely insane. But what logic could there possibly be to the murder of five seemingly innocent people, two of them women, and all of them old? Who were the 'friends' and 'two-footed wolves' that he said he was looking for? Initial speculation concentrated on Castagna's criminal record: he had served three years in prison for attempting to murder Domenicantonio Castagna, the distant cousin whose mother was the first to fall on that terrible Sunday. Some of the other victims seemed to have a connection with the same case. Was the Monster, like the King of Aspromonte all those years ago, taking vengeance on those who had testified against him? Another theory was that he was restoring his family's slighted honour by killing the woman who had spurned his brother.

The Communist press saw things differently, emphasising the social background to the tragedy. The correspondent for *L'Unità*, the Partito Comunista Italiano's daily, interviewed a comrade from the area who complained that bourgeois journalists from the north were having fun portraying Calabrians as a 'horde of ferocious people'. The real cause of Serafino Castagna's madness was poverty and exploitation. Why couldn't they make the effort to understand that?

Fragments of a more far-fetched explanation for Serafino Castagna's rage also surfaced from the well of village gossip. The first person to speak to journalists was, like Castagna, a farm labourer. Skulking by a wall, and refusing to give his name, he warily muttered something about a secret society in Presinaci. But the press remained sceptical:

> There have been rumours that Serafino Castagna is affiliated to the 'Honoured Society', a kind of Calabrian mafia. But the society's existence is very problematic. Supposedly this 'society' gave Castagna until 20 April to eliminate a man who had come into conflict with it. But it seems that these reports are baseless.

The Monster of Presinaci could not be a member of the Calabrian mafia for the simple reason that there was no such thing. On that count, the most authoritative voices were unanimous.

Then, some three weeks after going on the run, Castagna sent a forty-page memoir to the *Carabinieri* that explained that he was a sworn affiliate of what he called the 'Honoured Society of the Buckle'; he also referred to it as the 'mafia'.

Castagna was finally arrested after sixty days. Once in the hands of the law, he told everything he knew about the Honoured Society, supplying the authorities with a great many names and evidence to incriminate them. Within forty-eight hours of Castagna's capture, fifty members of the criminal brotherhood were detained. More arrests followed. Apparently the existence of the Calabrian mafia was not quite so 'problematic' after all.

In jail, the Monster of Presinaci even went on to convert the memoir he had sent to the *Carabinieri* into an autobiography. Indeed, he was the first member of the Calabrian mafia ever to tell his own story. *You Must Kill*, as Castagna's autobiography is called, solved the mystery of why its author embarked on his desperate rampage. But it is also a very important historical document: it is post-war Italy's primer on the organisational culture of the criminal brotherhood that is now known as the 'ndrangheta.

Serafino Castagna wrote that he was born in 1921, and grew up in a down-trodden peasant family. He was taken out of school to herd goats, constantly taunted for his disability, and maltreated by his violent father. He first heard about the Honoured Society when he was fifteen. Already, at that age, he would spend long days hoeing the family's field. Working in the adjacent plot was Castagna's cousin, Latino Purita, who was ten years older, and who had just been released from a jail sentence for assault. One day, when the time came for a rest, Latino started to talk to Castagna about 'the honesty that a man must always have', and said that 'to be honest, a man had to be part of the mafia'. Captivated by what his cousin had said, Castagna underwent a five-year apprenticeship, stealing chickens and burning haystacks on Latino's orders. He asserted his manhood by stabbing another youth who had poked fun at his walk. Then, on Easter Monday 1941, he underwent the long oathing ritual that began as follows:

'Are you comfortable, my dear comrades?' the boss asked.

'Very comfortable,' came the reply from the chorus of *picciotti* and ranking *mafiosi* around him.

'Are you comfortable?'

'For what?'

'On the social rules.'

'Very comfortable.'

'In the name of the organised and faithful society, I baptise this place as our ancestors Osso, Mastrosso and Carcagnosso baptised it, who baptised it with iron and chains.'

Respecting the 'social rules' in Presinaci was a low-key business. There were meetings to attend, of course, and procedures to learn. But Presinaci *mafiosi* also spent a great deal of time hanging out in the tavern and spinning yarns. Castagna particularly loved to hear tales of Osso, Mastrosso and Carcagnosso, the Spanish knights who were the legendary founders of all three Honoured Societies.

The Presinaci gang had a court, known as the 'Tribunal of Humility'. Among the minor penalties that could be handed down by the tribunal were shallow stab wounds, or the degrading punishment known as *tartaro*—'hell'. The leadership inflicted 'hell' on any affiliate who displayed cowardice, or arrogance towards his fellows. They summoned him to the centre of a circle of affiliates and told him to remove his jacket and shirt. A senior member then took a brush and daubed his head and torso with a paste made from excrement and urine.

Sex and marriage generated many of the tensions that the Tribunal of Humility tried to manage. One of Castagna's brothers was banned from the tavern for ten days and given a fine of one thousand lire. His offence was to

The Monster of Presinaci. Following his murderous rampage in 1955, Serafino Castagna told the authorities about the Honoured Society of Calabria.

have violated an agreement with another *mafioso* to take it in turns sleeping with a girl they both coveted.

In Presinaci, the Honoured Society always made its presence felt in public spaces, key moments of community life; it monopolised folk dancing, for example. Castagna recalled: 'During religious festivals we in the society always tried to take charge of the dancing, so as to keep the non-members away from the fun.' The *mastro di giornata* ('master of the day', the boss's spokesman) would call each of the gang's members to dance in order of rank. On one occasion that Serafino Castagna recalled, a non-member who tried too hard to join in was clubbed brutally to the ground.

In January 1942, the war brought an early interruption to Castagna's criminal career. Despite his health problems, which included recurrent malaria, he was conscripted into an artillery regiment. After the collapse of the Italian army in September 1943, he managed to escape through both German and Allied lines until, ragged and hungry, he reached home to resume his journey towards the bloodbath of 17 April 1955.

With the Second World War over, life in Presinaci returned to its grindingly poor normality. The Honoured Society began to intensify activities as its leaders came back from wherever they had been scattered by the conflict. The number of arson attacks and robberies increased. Contacts with branches in other places became more regular. The Tribunal of Humility held more frequent sessions. Crimes became more ambitious and violence more frequent: Castagna confronted and stabbed a man against whom he bore a petty grudge. A readiness to kill increasingly became an almost routine test that the gang's leaders set for the members. The climate grew more thuggish still when Latino Purita, Castagna's 'honest' cousin, became boss after his predecessor emigrated.

Castagna first got into serious trouble when he was ordered to exact a fine of one thousand lire from a new affiliate who had been gossiping about the society's affairs to a non-*mafioso*. Castagna's instructions were to execute the offender if the money was not forthcoming. The affiliate in question was Domenicantonio Castagna, the distant cousin whom Castagna tried to kill first of all on the day, five years later, that he committed his outrages. Castagna and Domenicantonio got into a scuffle over money, a municipal guard intervened, and Castagna ended up shooting Domenicantonio in the chest. As luck would have it, Domenicantonio survived. But Castagna was caught and imprisoned for wounding him.

Castagna tells us that the Society failed to help him in prison as he had been promised. Not only that, but when he was released in the final days of 1953, the Society immediately reprimanded him for failing to kill Domenicantonio. He was told that the only way to restore his reputation was by killing the municipal guard who had intervened in the scuffle. Castagna appealed against the decision, and obtained a little breathing space: the bosses decreed that he still had to kill the guard, but that he could wait until his period of police surveillance came to an end in the spring of 1955.

Castagna was trapped. If he committed the murder of a public official, he knew that he would probably spend the rest of his life in prison. But he could also envisage the catastrophic loss of face that would ensue if he betrayed his mafia identity and talked to the authorities: 'Nobody would give me any respect, not even people who did not belong to the Society.' As the deadline for vendetta grew near, he began to be tortured by nightmares about cemeteries, ghosts and wars. In the end, he made the irrevocable decision to refuse to obey, and to kill those who had ordered him to kill. He prepared himself for the coming battle by writing down everything he knew about the Honoured Society, and with it a list of the twenty members he wanted to murder. Then he prepared his last meal of fried eggs.

Castagna's plans misfired grotesquely. Only one of his victims, the last, was a member of the Honoured Society. The others were only obliquely connected to his real targets, if they had any connection at all. This was no grand gesture, but a venting of accumulated rage and desperation.

Much of the criminal subculture that the Monster of Presinaci described in his memoir is still in use in today's 'ndrangheta. Rituals and fables help forge powerful fraternal bonds, moulding the identity of young criminals, giving them the sense of entitlement they need to dominate their communities. If Serafino Castagna's five murders teach us one thing, it is that the 'ndrangheta subculture can exert extreme psychological pressures.

But to the police and judiciary of the 1950s, much of Castagna's account seemed like so much mumbo jumbo. Indeed, this was a picture of the Calabrian mafia that flattered one of Italy's most enduring and misleading misconceptions. Even many of those who were prepared to admit that the mafia existed in places like Calabria and Sicily were convinced that it was a symptom of backwardness. At the time, it was not the problem of organised crime that dominated public discussion of southern Italy, but the issue of poverty. In the South average income stood at about half of levels in the North. In 1951, a government inquiry found that 869,000 Italian families had so little money that they *never* ate sugar or meat; 744,000 of those families lived in the South. If anyone thought about the mafias at all, they thought of them mostly as the result of poverty, and of a primitive peasant milieu characterised by superstition and isolated episodes of bestial violence. In the end, the story of the Monster of Presinaci raised few eyebrows.

The networks of patronage, including mafia patronage, that supported many politicians in southern Italy were an inherently unstable power base. Inevitably, every so often, mafia activity would get out of hand, the violence would escalate, and loyal Christian Democrat supporters would begin to protest. At such times, even governments that were constitutionally averse to drawing attention to the mafia problem were forced to respond. It turned out that the Monster of Presinaci affair was by no means an isolated episode. The year 1955 was a very violent one in Calabria.

One or two journalists picked up signs that all was not well. A correspondent from the Naples newspaper *Il Mattino*, the most influential Christian Democrat daily in the South, visited Calabria a few weeks after Castagna was captured. He discovered that the province of Reggio Calabria was undergoing an alarming crime wave—or at least a crime wave that would have been alarming if it had being going on in any other Italian region. Buses and cars were being hijacked in the countryside, extortion payments demanded from farmers and factory owners, and witnesses were intimidated. Then there was the shocking case of Francesco Cricelli, a *mafioso* from San Calogero in the province of Catanzaro, who was beheaded for stealing a razor from his boss. *Il Mattino* demanded government action to reassert the authority of the law.

By the time these reports were published, somewhere within the courtyards, the loggias and the criss-crossing corridors of the Ministry of the Interior in Rome, the government machinery was already slowly turning its attention to the problem of law and order in the southernmost point of the Italian mainland.

Giuseppe Aloi was an entrepreneur from Reggio Calabria who employed some 150 people making bricks. The day before Serafino Castagna's rampage, Aloi wrote a letter to the Minister of the Interior. He was frightened and angry: his son had recently fought off a kidnapping attempt in the very centre of Reggio. Since then, the family had received threats and demands for money, and the police locally had not been able to identify the culprits. The situation was so bad that he was considering closing down his business. Aloi's letter also pointed out the rising crime in the area and said:

It is a notorious fact that the underworld organisation has reappeared in almost every town in the province. There are numerous *mafiosi* who, despite not having any profession or trade that is useful to society, flaunt an easy and luxurious lifestyle based on suspect wealth; they offer their services to farmers or impose extraordinary tributes on them in return for assurances that property and belongings will be respected.

Two days after the brick-maker wrote his letter, plain-clothes police in two unmarked cars tried to trap the extortionists on a winding mountain road on the northern slopes of Aspromonte. One of the unmarked cars was targeted from the wooded slopes by bursts of machine-gun and hunting-rifle fire. Miraculously, four officers suffered only slight wounds. The Calabrian mafia was heavily armed and prepared to confront the forces of order directly.

Following a request for further information, the Prefect of Reggio Calabria (the Minister of the Interior's eyes and ears on the ground) responded with a report that confirmed Aloi's picture. Calabria had 'a vast network of underworld affiliates' that was able to assure its own immunity from the law through *omertà* and 'a well-ordered system of protection that even reached into politics'; 'often, at election time, these individuals [i.e., *mafiosi*] transform themselves into propagandists for one party or another, and try to influence the election results with the weight of their clienteles'. The Calabrian mafia was beginning to present a problem of public order that could not be dismissed as the work of a single, psychologically fragile peasant.

Soon after taking office in July, a new Christian Democrat Minister of the Interior decided that urgent action was required. There would be an anti-mafia crackdown on a scale that Italy had not seen since the days of the Fascist repression of the late 1920s. A dynamic new chief of police, Carmelo Marzano, was lined up to lead what would become known as the Marzano Operation. Local wags, who could not resist a pun, joked that it was as if Martians (*Marziani*) had landed. Calabria was about to greet invaders from planet law and order.

40

Mars attacks!

The Minister who ordered the crackdown in Calabria was Fernando Tambroni, a Christian Democrat from the Marche region. A timid man in public, Tambroni attracted little press attention. His policy utterances were cagey and abstruse, even by Christian Democrat standards. The only obviously distinctive things about him were his alabaster good looks and his elegance. (He was a loyal customer of Del Rosso, the elite Roman tailor.) In private, Tambroni had a belief system with three pillars: the cult of San Gabriele dell'Addolorata, the influence of his personal astrologer, and a bent for compiling secret dossiers on his allies and enemies.

Despite these personal foibles, when Tambroni announced the beginning of the Marzano Operation it seemed like a good, old-fashioned, right-wing, law-and-order policy of a kind that could be witnessed in other Western European countries. The Marzano Operation was presented as a test run of Tambroni's law-and-order platform—a drive to reinforce the citizens' trust in the state (and thereby in the Christian Democrats). Early in the operation, Minister Tambroni gave a newspaper interview in which he denounced a 'government by organised crime' in Calabria, and promised that he would 'get to the bottom of things' and 'show no favours to anyone'.

Chief of Police Carmelo Marzano's early reports to Tambroni from Calabria were the manifesto of an ambitious man primed for vigorous action. It was no exaggeration, Marzano wrote, to say that the population was 'literally in the grip of terror'. The crime rate was alarmingly high. But many, many more offences went unreported because of public fear. Racketeering was systematic: forestry, taverns and restaurants, the state lottery, the bus service—nothing was allowed to work unless what Marzano called 'certain compromises' were reached. Hundreds of convicted criminals were at large in the province, including fifty-nine murderers; these fugitives paraded the state's failure to impose itself on the territory. One of them, the notorious Brooklyn-born Angelo Macrì, had walked up to a *Carabiniere* in the centre of Delianova and shot him in the head; his status within the Honoured Society had grown immeasurably as a result. Another convicted murderer on the run was the equally notorious boss of Bova, Vincenzo Romeo. Romeo lived openly in his territory, married in the presence of the bosses of the Honoured Society, fathered children, managed his business affairs and cared for his ten beloved dogs. On one occasion, when the *Carabinieri* came looking for him, the women of Bova simultaneously waved sheets from their windows to warn him of the danger.

The new police chief found the state of law enforcement even more shocking than the state of public order. He was horrified by his headquarters, the *Questura*: this poky, filthy building seemed half abandoned; it had no shutters on the windows to keep out the summer heat, and not even any railings on the balconies. Whereas a town of comparable size in the north or centre of Italy might have five or six local stations in addition to the *Questura*, in Reggio, a city that now had one of the highest crime rates in the country, there were no other police stations. So the *Questura* was permanently overrun by citizens from across the province clamouring to report a crime, or to apply for a licence or certificate. There were no cells, and no secluded space where a witness or informer could be interviewed. Visits from grandees making special pleas for arrested supporters were a regular occurrence. The *Questura* seemed less a command centre than a bazaar.

Many of the men now under Marzano's command had taken on the same dilapidated and immobile air as the furniture they sat on. They had close contacts in the community—friendships, family ties, business interests—and thus placed living a quiet life before applying themselves to their more abrasive duties. One officer suspected of conniving with criminals was still doing his job years after a transfer order had been issued. The Flying Squad—the plain-clothes unit whose responsibilities were supposed to include chasing after those fifty-nine convicted murderers—numbered only fourteen men, and less than half of them actually turned up to work with any regularity. Law enforcement in the province lacked even the most basic tools of modern policing: dogs, bicycles, or the radios that were essential if officers searching the wilds of Aspromonte were to coordinate their moves.

The Festival of the Madonna of the Mountain at Polsi was an obvious early opportunity for Police Chief Marzano to show that Minister Tambroni's alien invaders were no joke. The authorities were well aware that the festival was used by the Honoured Society to conceal an annual general meeting of some kind, although quite what happened at the meeting and why was not clear. In 1954, as so often in the past, the pilgrimage had seen a settling of mafia accounts: after the pilgrims had gone home, the corpses of two young men with multiple gunshot wounds were found near the sanctuary. This year, with Marzano in charge, there were roadblocks and patrols in the woods. Fourteen men were taken into custody on charges ranging from carrying weapons to attempted murder and kidnapping. Marzano's line manager, the Prefect of Reggio, telegraphed the Ministry to announce that the pilgrimage had passed off without incident.

Over the coming days and weeks, Minister Tambroni was scatter-gunned with telegrams announcing the recapture of one convicted Calabrian *mafioso* after another. Police arrested two of the men who had tried to blackmail Giuseppe Aloi, the brick manufacturer, and recovered numerous weapons in the same operation. They even managed to collar a town hall employee in Gioia Tauro who was stealing blank identity cards for gangsters who needed to become someone else. Vincenzo Romeo—the fugitive with ten dogs—was arrested, as (eventually) was Angelo Macrì, who had fled back to his native America. Marzano even went on a lone expedition up into Aspromonte, by car and on foot, and single-handedly brought back a renegade murderer from Bova.

Five weeks after arriving in Reggio, hyperactive Police Chief Marzano felt entitled to dictate a toadying dispatch to Minister Tambroni:

> The face of the whole province has been transformed. The citizenry approve of the operation. There has been a tide of beneficial renewal, and trust in the state's authority has been reborn. The citizens know that they owe it all *exclusively* to Your Excellency's decisiveness and resolution. Without any trace of rhetorical exaggeration, I can guarantee that if Your Excellency came to visit Reggio, You would be literally carried shoulder-high.

The public seemed to like what was going on; the press certainly did. Correspondents arrived in Calabria in the kind of numbers previously only attracted by one of the region's frequent natural disasters. Remarkably, as a result of the Marzano Operation, Italy began its first-ever national debate about organised crime in Calabria. Naturally enough, journalists filed copy that contained lots of colourful material about the secret criminal sect that went by the name of 'mafia', or 'Honoured Society', or 'Fibbia' ('Buckle'). Indeed a new name emerged from interviews with local people: 'ndrangheta. Pronounced an-*dran*-get-ah, it means 'manliness' or 'courage' in the Greek-based dialect of the southern slopes of Aspromonte. The word has a long history, but its known association with the Honoured Society only begins in the 1930s. ''Ndrangata' was one of many names used by Calabrian *mafiosi* to surface during Fascist police operations. The publicity created by the Marzano Operation in 1955 ensured that 'ndrangheta soon won out as the brotherhood's official moniker, used by members and non-members alike. After some three-quarters of a century of growing in the shadows, Calabria's version of the mafia had at last attracted enough public attention to merit a commonly agreed-upon name of its own.

The Marzano Operation also caused some Calabrians to recover their memories. One notable example was Corrado Alvaro, the region's best-known writer. He was born in San Luca, the 'Bethlehem of organised crime' on the slopes of Aspromonte whose criminals act as guardians of the Honoured Society's customs. Alvaro was no 'ndrangheta sympathiser. But he could scarcely avoid learning about it as he grew up. The stories from his early life that Alvaro would later publish make it clear that he knew a great deal about Calabria's Honoured Society. After the Second World War, when Alvaro moved to Rome, he became an unofficial spokesman for the voiceless poor of his home region; he turned Aspromonte's downtrodden peasants into archetypes of human resilience. Perhaps through a misguided desire to protect Calabria from bad publicity, or perhaps for darker and more mysterious reasons, Alvaro kept a long silence about the region's criminal brotherhood. In 1949, denouncing the feudal squalor still endured by shepherds and peasants, he wrote that, 'There were attempts to set up criminal societies in imitation of the mafia, but they never took root. Still today, Calabria is one of the safest parts of the country, at any time, and in any isolated corner.' The jotted notes in Alvaro's diary show that these remarks were in bad faith:

> Boss of the Festival of the Madonna (Polsi, San Luca). A provincial boss could not be elected in 1948 because **** [name omitted] had just got out of jail, wanted to live in tranquillity, and did not accept the job. From that moment on the Honoured Society has been divided into three zones: the Ionian coast, the Tyrrhenian coast, and the Straits, with no overall *capo*.

The 'ndrangheta's high-level internal politics were evidently an open secret in San Luca, and even beyond. But in public, Alvaro kept his silence. At around the same time, he jotted an aphorism in his diary that would later become famous: 'The blackest despair that can take hold of any society is the fear that living honestly is futile.' Perhaps Alvaro, better than many, knew what that fear felt like.

In 1955, following the Marzano Operation, Alvaro changed his mind. He wrote about the 'ndrangheta in a column in the *Corriere della Sera*, and memories of the 'ndrangheta from his youth surfaced in his other writings. Indeed he probably did more than anyone to help the new name catch on.

In the end, restoring Corrado Alvaro's memory and naming the 'ndrangheta turned out to be the Marzano Operation's only long-term achievements. And the key obstacle to achieving anything more lasting was Minister Tambroni's refusal to seriously tackle the 'ndrangheta's friends in politics.

The papers from Interior Ministry archives now allow us to peer behind the scenes of the Marzano Operation. Those documents show just how much information Tambroni's civil servants gathered about politicians who were hand in glove with gangsters in Calabria. The Martian invasion of 1955 revealed some darkly comic cameos of bad faith and connivance.

One case in point involved a typical southern grandee: Antonio Capua, an MP from the Liberal Party, one of the Christian Democrats' coalition partners. Indeed, what passed for the 'Liberal Party' in Calabria was actually Capua's personal clientele. Capua also sat across the Cabinet table from Fernando Tambroni, as Junior Minister for Agriculture and Forestry. Given that both agriculture and forestry played a big role in the local economy, Capua's job meant that he had a great many tax-funded favours to bestow on his friends. Tambroni discovered that Capua often pressed officials in private to grant driving and gun licences to known 'ndranghetisti, and his local election agents mingled closely with thugs from the Honoured Society.

Capua was already in the headlines in Calabria before the Marzano Operation began. In a mysterious incident that reeked of the 'ndrangheta, a group of men fired shots at his wife's car as she was driving high on Aspromonte. Capua tried to cover the whole story up. When the press got hold of it, they published a garbled but even more worrying version, saying that Capua himself had been the target of a would-be assassination. An attempt on the life of a government minister was more than local news, and the national newspapers duly took an interest.

When Tambroni's Martians landed in the autumn, the new chief of police investigated both the shooting episode and Capua's underworld friends. But worse was to follow for the Junior Minister: many people jumped to the conclusion that Capua had called the Martians in as a result of the assassination attempt. The 'ndrangheta took the same view, and began to wonder why their favourite grandee had brought so much trouble down on their heads. The Junior Minister was in a desperate predicament; he looked like a crook to the police and a traitor to the 'ndrangheta.

On 14 September 1955, Junior Minister Capua made a desperate bid to save his credibility with *both* the 'ndrangheta and the police. He arranged to meet with Police Chief Marzano because he wanted to discuss the case of a suspect that Marzano was interrogating at the time. The suspect, an 'ndran-

ghetista called Pizzi who was also the mayor of Condofuri, was Capua's election agent for the whole Ionian coast of the province of Reggio Calabria. Capua presumably hoped that his prestige as a Junior Minister would intimidate the chief of police. That, after all, is just how countless *mafiosi* had been protected over the previous century. But the new chief of police was confident enough in his own political backing not to be intimidated. Instead, he calmly showed Capua the damning evidence he had already accumulated against Mayor Pizzi, who was sitting in the room with them. The Junior Minister responded with the kind of brass neck of which only a certain kind of Italian politician is capable. First, he feigned surprise and disappointment. Then he calmly told Marzano that his friend Mayor Pizzi was an honest man who had, despite good intentions, been corrupted by his environment. At that, he turned to Mayor Pizzi and gave him a finger-wagging in tones of plaintive sincerity, telling him to change his ways and collaborate with the police 'from now on'.

Alas, the records do not tell us Fernando Tambroni's reactions when he read this story about his Cabinet colleague. We do not know whether he was shocked, or whether he laughed fit to strain the seams on his Del Rosso suit. But we can make a guess at his thinking. Tambroni might have reasoned that exposing Capua would upset the delicate balance of the coalition government. Or perhaps he simply followed one of the old, unwritten rules of Italian institutional life. Every governing faction, every party clique, had to get into bed at some point or another with politicians who were 'friends of the friends' in Sicily, Campania or Calabria. Start a serious investigation into one of them, and there was no telling where it would end. No matter that law enforcement on the ground in southern Italy said that the mafias could never be eradicated if their political protectors remained untouched. Better to let it all lie. The evidence against Junior Minister Capua was buried.

Capua also managed to smooth things over with his friends in the 'ndrangheta. Or so we must assume, for he was re-elected at the next poll.

Another politician whose nefarious dealings came to light during the Marzano Operation came from the Minister of the Interior's own party, the Christian Democrats. A top-secret report to Tambroni indicated that Domenico Catalano was part of a close-knit group of three DC chiefs who had managed to insert themselves into powerful positions in local quangos and Catholic organisations. There were strong suspicions that all three of these Christian Democrats had links to organised crime. Catalano even boasted publicly that he had arranged for a previous chief of police to be transferred away from Calabria when he became too enthusiastic in his pursuit of 'ndranghetisti. Most worryingly of all, Catalano had a seat on the 'Provincial Commission for Police Measures'. This was a crucial body that ruled on cases in which the police asked for a dangerous suspect to be whisked off into internal exile on a penal colony without a proper trial. (As we have seen, internal exile had been in use in Italy since the days when the *Carabinieri* were equipped with muskets and horses rather than machine guns and jeeps. It was not only highly dubious from a legal point of view, it was also totally counter-productive, since the penal colonies were notorious recruiting grounds for the mafias.)

During the Marzano Operation, the police filed requests for batches of 'ndrangheta suspects to be shipped to the remote penal colony of Ustica, off the northern coast of Sicily. But Minister Tambroni's man on the ground, the Prefect of Reggio Calabria, noticed that Domenico Catalano displayed what they called a 'certain indulgence' towards men with particularly blood-curdling criminal records. A number of parish priests also gave evidence before the Provincial Commission for Police Measures in the same strangely indulgent fashion. But rather than make trouble, the Prefect decided to act in a classic Christian Democrat fashion, and had a quiet word with the Archbishop.

Now the Archbishop of Reggio Calabria at the time was certainly no friend of the 'ndrangheta. He had only recently penned a pastoral letter denouncing 'shadowy secret societies that, under the pretext of honour and strength, teach and impose crime, vendetta and abuse of power'. We can only imagine how disturbed he would have been at the news that Domenico Catalano, a politician who was a senior member of local Church-backed organisations, was in league with organised crime. But rather than create a fuss, the Archbishop decided to act in classic Italian Church fashion, and have a quiet word with Catalano himself. The Archbishop gently persuaded Catalano to take his responsibilities on the Provincial Commission for Police Measures more seriously.

The little chain of quiet words seemed to work. For a while, Catalano voted the same way as everyone else on the commission, which began to send 'ndranghetisti into internal exile.

But then the Provincial Commission for Police Measures was asked to rule on the case of a notoriously powerful criminal who has already played (or rather *danced*) an important role in our story: Antonio Macrì, known as don 'Ntoni, who reputedly joined the *Carabiniere* Master Joe in a *tarantella* at the Festival of the Madonna of Polsi during the last years of Fascism. By 1955, don 'Ntoni was not only the 'chief cudgel' in the market town of Siderno, he was also one of the most powerful bosses in the whole of Calabria. In the autumn of 1953, don 'Ntoni was known to have presided over a plenary meeting of the 'ndrangheta during the Polsi Festival. (A fact that constitutes yet more evidence that the 'ndrangheta has always had coordinating structures of some kind.)

Now, sending a rank-and-file *'ndranghetista* to a penal colony was one thing; confining don 'Ntoni was quite another. On 3 September 1955, with the chief cudgel waiting in the corridor outside the room where the Provincial Commission for Police Measures was sitting, Domenico Catalano got to his feet. He solemnly informed the commission's other members that he felt it was his duty to make a declaration that 'concerned the Vatican'. He then told a tale that left everyone else in the room open-mouthed.

Catalano's tale went something like this. Some years ago, the Bishop of Locri discovered that a number of priests had been stealing money from a Church charity. The Bishop forced the priests to give back the money, Catalano explained. At which the priests hired an assassin to do away with the Bishop. Luckily the Bishop heard tell of the plot to kill him, and wisely sought protection from the dominant *'ndranghetista* in the area, don 'Ntoni Macrì. Don 'Ntoni, Domenico Catalano revealed, had used his good offices to save the Bishop's life. Surely a man capable of such a noble gesture deserved merciful treatment from the Provincial Commission for Police Measures?

The other commissioners were not convinced. Don 'Ntoni Macrì was promptly dispatched to a penal colony, forcing a brief pause in his formidable criminal career. A full report was sent to Minister Tambroni in Rome.

Quite whether there really was any truth in Catalano's highly unlikely story about the plan to kill the Bishop of Locri we will never know, short of a documented declaration by the Papacy. But the whole affair is nonetheless exemplary. Italy's problem with organised crime was not just that mafia influence seeped into the state through private channels. It was also that prefects, politicians and archbishops preferred to use the very same private channels. Instead of respecting the law, they preferred to have a quiet word.

Once again, Minister of the Interior Tambroni read this report and did nothing. No matter that the case involved a clear instance of a politician trying to bend the law in an *'ndranghetista's* favour. Domenico Catalano, the spinner of the strange tale of the bishop saved by the mafia boss, kept his seat on the Provincial Commission for Police Measures for years to come.

On 27 October 1955—a mere fifty-four days after landing—Police Chief Marzano got back into his flying saucer and left Calabria for good. It was hopeless to imagine that less than two months of intensive police activity

could make any long-term difference. All too soon, the *'ndranghetisti* would return from their penal colonies and everything would return to normal.

The Italian state could hardly have given a clearer demonstration of its desperately short attention span. Tambroni's policing apparatus did not even seem keen to really understand the 'ndrangheta as an organisation. The entire chain of command, right down from the Ministry of the Interior in Rome to the junior officers on the ground in Calabria, had at their disposal much of the information needed to build up a convincing picture of the Calabrian mafia. On 28 May 1955, only three months before the start of the Marzano Operation, police and *Carabinieri* had raided a house in Rosarno and found a notebook containing the 'ndrangheta's rules. Two and a half weeks later, the Monster of Presinaci was finally captured, and made clear his intention to tell the police everything. The authorities knew a great deal: the 'ndrangheta's cellular, territorially based structure; its extortion rackets and culture of vendetta; the way it set itself as an alternative to the law, and its ability to forge bonds with the feuding cliques and factions of Calabrian politics. Yet there is not a jot of evidence that Police Chief Marzano was even mildly interested in putting these crucial new sources of intelligence to any practical use. Nor, in the small mountain of official correspondence generated by the Marzano Operation, is there any hint that the authorities had a historical memory of the Honoured Society's development, or of the lessons to be learned from previous attempts to combat it. In short, no one associated with the 'Martian invasion' thought that to beat the 'ndrangheta, it might be a good idea to understand it from the inside.

In parliament in Rome, the Communists suspected that fighting the 'ndrangheta was never the Marzano Operation's real aim. They were convinced that Tambroni's promise to 'show no favours' was hollow and cynical from the outset. The most flagrant instances of organised criminal support for politicians involved Christian Democrats. One Socialist MP said in parliament that Vincenzo Romeo, the boss with ten dogs, had gone round with a machine gun shouting, 'Either you vote Christian Democrat, or I'll kill you.' Yet Marzano was being ideologically selective in the *mafiosi* he rounded up, the Communists protested. The DC mayor of the provincial capital Reggio Calabria had not been detained, despite serious evidence of links to organised crime. By contrast the Communist mayor of the mountain village of Canolo, Nicola D'Agostino, had been arrested and sent into internal exile.

There was definitely some substance in the Communist claims that Tambroni's Martian invasion had an ideological bias. However, the D'Agostino case was probably an unfortunate one for the Communists to cite, because it is clear that this particular mayor was a member of the PCI, while never ceasing to be an 'ndrangheta boss. The police claimed that he used the party to exert his personal power over the town. D'Agostino was not the only case of the kind: the Monster of Presinaci's last victim was a Communist *'ndranghetista*, for example. Communists in southern Calabria had fewer antibodies against mafia infiltration than did their comrades in western Sicily, who could count so many martyrs to the fight against organised crime. Here and there in Calabria, the 'ndrangheta had the power to hollow out even the ideology of its enemies.

That said, it seems that Tambroni had no particularly cunning political plan. He simply rushed into the Marzano Operation, and rushed out again when he realised just how profoundly rooted the 'ndrangheta was. Sensibly, Interior Minister Tambroni decided to take the plaudits for Marzano's easy early victories, dispatch a few gangsters to penal colonies for a couple of years, and then revert to managing Calabria in the normal way. Symptomatic of that return to normality was the final outcome of the Monster of Presinaci case. In September 1957, Serafino Castagna was sentenced to life imprisonment, as was inevitable. But of the sixty-five men implicated by his evidence, forty-six were acquitted and the other nineteen received suspended sentences of between two and three years.

The story of the Marzano Operation and the Monster of Presinaci is typical of the state's response when violence flared up from the underworld. Once that violence faded from the headlines, the authorities resorted to their old habits of cohabiting with mafia power.

41

THE PRESIDENT OF POTATO PRICES (AND HIS WIDOW)

BY THE MID-1950S THERE WERE SIGNS THAT THE ITALIAN ECONOMY HAD ENTERED A period of sustained growth that would finally leave the hardships of wartime behind. In 1950, industrial production overtook pre-war levels. Inflation, which had reached 73.5 per cent per year in 1947, came down to single digits. Unemployment was dropping steadily too. The South still lagged well behind the North, but in the cities of all regions Italians were beginning to spend more. Better food was the first item on the national shopping list, notably the staples of what would later become known as the Mediterranean diet: pasta, and particularly fruit and vegetables.

One place that felt the effects of increased consumption was the wholesale fruit and vegetable market in the Vasto quarter of Naples: roughly 30 per cent of Italy's fruit and vegetable exports were funnelled through it. While other parts of Italy could manage a seasonal trade in one or two specialised crops, the hyper-fertile hinterland of Naples grew every conceivable food plant in year-round abundance. The fresh tomatoes, courgettes, potatoes, peaches and lemons emanating from the region every year were worth some 16 billion lire (roughly $300 million in today's values). A further 12 billion lire ($220 million) came from walnuts, hazelnuts, peanuts, raisins, figs and other dried foods.

Yet, for all its wealth, the wholesale market in Naples was a shambolic spectacle. Here was one of the city's economic nerve-centres, located at the railhead, within easy reach of the port. Yet it was little more than a cluster of skeletal hangars, where rusting wire mesh and crumbling concrete still betrayed damage from the war. A variety of ramshackle vehicles skated through the permanent puddles in the hangars' shade: donkey wagons and lorries, handcarts and tiny cars with comically outsized roof-racks—all of them loaded with teetering crate stacks of aubergines, lettuces, apricots and cherries. The market was serviced by a few cramped offices, a post office and a couple of bank branches in the surrounding streets. There were no teleprinters or rows of phones. Deals, however big, were done on the pavements of via Firenze and Corso Novara, face to face, in stagey exclamations of scorn and disbelief. Now and then, when a serious deal was in the offing or a major account had to be settled, a big-shot vegetable trader from a provincial market town would climb out of his sports car, smooth his hair and his suit, and receive the reverential greetings of agents and labour.

In 1955, one of the most famous murder cases of the era exposed just how powerful and dangerous a caste these fruit and vegetable dealers were. The trial of the 'new camorra', it was called. For, in 1955, Italy began hesitantly to use the 'c' word again. What the case demonstrated, to anyone who cared to look closely, was that the mafias were advancing in step with the growth of the Italian economy. Business was becoming one of the main drivers of mafia history.

Pasquale Simonetti was one of those fruit and vegetable dealers. Two metres tall and thirty-one years old, he had the bulk of a heavyweight and a physiognomy to match: his hard little eyes were pushed far apart by a thick nose (natural or broken, it was hard to tell); his square, burly head was mounted on a neck that defied his tailor's best efforts to restrain it in a shirt collar. He was known, unimaginatively, as Pascalone 'e Nola—'Big Pasquale from Nola' (Nola being a market town not far from the city).

On the morning of 16 July 1955, Big Pasquale was shot twice as he peeled an orange he had just bought from a stall. The shooter, a young blond man in a slate-grey suit, fled unmolested. The victim, abandoned to haemorrhage into the gutter by his sidekicks, died in hospital near dawn the following day. Police moved his body straight to the morgue to avoid an unsightly pilgrimage of mourning by the criminal fraternity from the countryside.

As yet, nobody seemed to want to make the connection between Pasquale Simonetti's death and the huge fruit and vegetable economy. The traditional Neapolitan reticence about mob stories was still in force. The profiles of Big Pasquale that followed his murder did not make it beyond the crime pages of the local dailies. In addition to trading in the produce of Campanian farms, Big Pasquale was already familiar to the local press as

Fruit and vegetable racket. The wholesale market in Naples was a major source of income for the camorra in the 1950s.

a smuggler and enforcer. Some of his deeds had been as flagrantly public as his shooting. In 1951, near the main entrance to the railway station, he had bludgeoned a man with a wrench wrapped in a newspaper; the victim told the police he had not seen anything. Then there was the gun battle in the town centre of Giugliano that had earned him his time in Poggioreale prison, where he became the boss of his wing. In short, Big Pasquale seemed like just another thug from the province, and no one knew or cared much what went on out there. If he had been killed on his home turf rather than in the centre of the city, then the story would not have merited more than a few lines.

Nevertheless, Big Pasquale's death was just news enough for one or two journalists to want to bulk it out with human interest. There were rumours that he had gone straight before he died. The suggested explanation for this unlikely character transformation was his new wife: a broad-hipped, small-town beauty queen from Castellammare di Stabia. While Big Pasquale was in prison, she had written to him every day, vowing to keep him off the 'steep and painful path of sin', and gushing her teenage daydreams: 'I feel truly emotional, and even a little bit afraid, when I think my nice Tarzan will be able to carry me far, far away from this ugly place to go and live in an enchanted castle where fairies live.' Baptised Assunta Maresca, Big Pasquale's young widow was known by her family as Pupetta ('Little Doll'). She was expecting a baby when her husband died.

On 4 October 1955, two and a half months after her Tarzan's murder, a visibly pregnant Pupetta asked to be driven from Castellammare to the wholesale market in Naples; she stopped off on the way to put flowers on Big Pasquale's grave. In Corso Novara, only a few metres from the point where he had fallen, she encountered another prime exemplar of the fruit-and-vegetable-trader type: Antonio Esposito, aka 'Big Tony from Pomigliano'. An altercation ensued, it seems, during which Pupetta's driver ran away. Then the shooting started. Pupetta's FIAT 1100 was hit several times, including once through the seat that the driver had just vacated. Pupetta, who had been firing from the rear seat with a Beretta 7.65 that Big Pasquale had given her, was unharmed. She escaped on foot. However, her target, Big Tony from Pomigliano, caught five fatal bullets.

'Widowed, pregnant beauty queen in gangland gun battle': now here was a story to attract national attention to the strange world of Campanian wholesale greengrocery.

Pupetta toying with a string of pearls. Pupetta stroking her long dark hair. Pupetta leaning against a tree. Pupetta in a prison smock. Pupetta in happier days. Pupetta holding her prison-born baby. When both Corso Novara murders were brought to court in a unified trial, it was Pupetta's photo that newspaper readers were hungry to gaze at, and she obliged them by posing like a Hollywood starlet. But who was the cherubic girl in the pictures, and what had turned her into a murderer? Was she a gangland vamp, or just a widowed young mother, crazed by grief?

Camorra bride. Pupetta Maresca marries her 'President of Potato Prices', Big Pasquale from Nola (1954). She would soon be a widow, and a killer.

Pupetta Maresca gave her own response to these questions as soon as she took the witness stand: her opening gambit was 'I killed for love.' She admitted shooting Big Tony from Pomigliano, and maintained that he, along with another wholesale greengrocer called Antonio Tuccillo (known, prosaically, as '*o Bosso*—'the Boss'), had ordered Big Pasquale dead. Big Pasquale had said as much to her on his deathbed, or so Pupetta claimed. Therefore this was a crime of passion, a widow's vengeance visited on her beloved husband's assassin. One correspondent, recalling Puccini's tragic opera about a woman driven to avenge her murdered lover, toyed with the idea that Pupetta was a rustic Tosca.

This was the Pupetta that the public wanted to see—or at least part of it did. It was blindingly obvious that there was a mob backdrop to the story. Newspapers in the north had started a full-scale debate about the 'new camorra'. But in Naples the idea that the camorra might not be dead after all still put people on edge. *Roma*, the newspaper that supported Mayor Achille Lauro, was as keen as ever to paint a sentimental gloss over organised crime. Lauro's Naples would never give in to any prejudiced northerner who tried to use these tragic murders as a pretext to bring up the camorra again. *Roma*, and with it part of Neapolitan public opinion, took Tosca-Pupetta to its heart and pleaded with the judges to send her home to her baby.

But this was not the real Pupetta. To many in court, it seemed that she was deliberately playing up to the Tosca comparison. She spoke not in her habitual dialect, but in a self-consciously correct Italian. As one correspondent noted, 'Pupetta is trying to talk with a plum in her mouth. She says, "It's manifest that" and "That's what fate decreed"—phrases that wouldn't be at all out of place coming from the mouth of a heroine in a pulp novel written to have an impact on tender hearts and ignorant minds.'

The cracks in both her courtroom persona and her line of defence quickly began to show. Her melodramatic posturing did not sit easily with her lawyer's best line of argument: that she had been threatened and attacked in Corso Novara by Big Tony from Pomigliano, and that she shot him in self-defence. Indeed Pupetta managed to put a hole in her own case with the first words she spoke to the court: 'I killed for love. And because they wanted to kill me. I'm sure that if my husband came back to life, and they killed him again, I would go back and do what I did once more.'

The prosecution did not need to point out that a homicide could be a crime of passion, or a desperate act of self-defence. But it could never be both.

Pupetta was asked whether her family had a nickname in Castellammare. She squirmed, and dodged the issue for a while. When she finally answered she could not help the look of pride that crossed her face: 'They call my family *'e lampetielli,*' she admitted—the 'Flashing Blades'. The Marescas were a notoriously violent lot, with criminal records to go with their nickname. Young she may have been, but Pupetta herself had already been accused of wounding. Her victim withdrew the charges, for reasons that are not hard to imagine.

One of Pupetta's main concerns during the trial was to absolve her sixteen-year-old brother Ciro of any involvement in the murder. Ciro, it was alleged, had been next to Pupetta in the back seat of the FIAT 1100, and had fired a pistol at Tony from Pomigliano. The boy's defence was not helped by the fact that he was still on the run from the law at the time of the trial.

But it may not just have been her brother that Pupetta was trying to shield. Ballistics experts never ascertained exactly how many shots were exchanged—twenty-five? forty?—because the holes spattered across the walls in Corso Novara could feasibly have been the result of previous fruit-related firefights. But it is quite possible that Pupetta and her brother Ciro were not the only people attacking Big Tony. If so, then 'Tosca' had actually been leading a full-scale firing party, and had embarked on a military operation rather than a solitary, impulsive act of vengeance.

Through the fissures in Pupetta's façade, post-war Italy was getting its first glimpses of a deeply rooted underworld system in the Neapolitan countryside, a system that no amount of stereotypes could conceal. Pupetta was a young woman profoundly enmeshed in the business of her clan. And that clan's business included her marriage: far from being a union of Tarzan and a fairy princess, this was a bond between a prestigious criminal bloodline like the 'Flashing Blades', and an up-and-coming young hoodlum like Big Pasquale. The world of the Campanian clans was one whose driving force was not the heat of family passions, but a coldly calculating mix of diplomacy and violence. Shortly before either of the fruit-market murders, a set-piece dinner for fifty guests was held. It seems that the dinner was a celebration of a peace deal of some kind between Big Pasquale and Big Tony from Pomigliano, the man Pupetta would eventually murder. No one could say with any certainty what had been said and agreed round the dinner table. What was obvious was that the peace deal quickly broke down. Yet even after Big Pasquale's death, the diplomatic efforts continued: there were frequent contacts between Big Tony from Pomigliano's people and Pupetta's family. Were they trying to buy peace with the young widow's clan? To stop the feud interfering with business?

These and a dozen other questions were destined to remain without a clear answer at the end of the hearings, largely because, once Pupetta had given evidence, the rest of the trial was a parade of liars. The refrain was relentless: 'I didn't see anything', 'I don't remember'. Only one man was actually arrested in court: he had flagrantly tried to sell his testimony to whichever lawyer was prepared to pay most. But many others deserved the same treatment. The presiding judge frequently lost his patience. 'You are all lying here. We'll write everything down, and then we'll send up a prayer to the Lord to find out which one is the real fibber.'

As the Neapolitan newspaper *Il Mattino* commented, whether they lied for the prosecution or lied for the defence, most of the witnesses were people 'from families where it is a rare accident for someone to die of natural causes'. The young blond man in the slate-grey suit who had gunned down Pupetta's husband was called Gaetano Orlando. His father, don Antonio, had been wounded in an assassination attempt six years earlier. In revenge, Gaetano ambushed the culprit, but only succeeded in shooting dead a little girl called Luisa Nughis; he served only three years of a risible six-year sentence. Big Tony from Pomigliano's family were even more fearsome: all three of the dead man's brothers worked in fruit and vegetable exports with him; all three had faced murder charges; and one of them, Francesco, gave evidence in dark glasses because he had been blinded in a shotgun attack in 1946.

Jailbirds and thugs they may have been, but these were people with drivers and domestic servants, accountants and bodyguards. They owned businesses, drove luxury cars and wore well-tailored suits. Big Pasquale's uncle, a man with an uncanny resemblance to Yul Brynner, now spent much of his time gambling in Saint Vincent and Monte Carlo—this despite having served twenty years for murder in the United States. The grey-suited Gaetano Orlando was the son of a former mayor of Marano, and the family firm had recently won a juicy contract to supply fruit and vegetables to a city hospital consortium. The young killer himself personally took charge of selling produce in Sicily, Rome, Milan and Brescia.

By this stage, the most astute observers of the case were less interested in the beguiling figure of Pupetta than in just how these violent men were making money from the vast agricultural production of the Campania region. Something Pupetta said early in proceedings opened a chink in the wall of *omertà*. She referred to Big Pasquale as the 'President of Potato Prices'. He was the man who determined the wholesale price of potatoes across the marketplace. The other man murdered in Corso Novara, Big Tony from Pomigliano, was also described as a President of Prices.

So what exactly did a President of Prices do? Pupetta put a fairy-tale gloss on her husband's role. Her Tarzan fixed potato prices in the interests of the poor farmers, she said. He was an honest man, who was hated by other more exploitative business rivals. This account is no more credible than the rest of Pupetta's evidence. What seems likely is that a President's power, as is always the case with Italian mafia crime, was rooted in a given territory where he could build an organisation able to use violence without fear of punishment. His men would approach the smallholding farmers offering credit, seed, tools and whatever else was needed for the next growing season. The debt would be paid off by the crop, for which a low price was settled before it was even planted. Bosses like Big Pasquale or Big Tony were able to deploy vandalism and beatings systematically to quell any farmer who had enough cash or chutzpah to try and operate outside of the cartel. By controlling the supply of fruit and vegetables in this way, men who combined the roles of loan shark, extortionist and commercial middle-man could set the sums to be paid when the lorryfuls of produce were unloaded under the hangars in the Vasto quarter of Naples.

The many slippery testimonies at the Pupetta Maresca trial mean that we have to use educated guesswork to put more detail into the picture. It seems likely that the various Presidents from perhaps fifteen different towns in the Naples hinterland (Big Pasquale from Nola, Big Tony from Pomigliano, and so on) met regularly in Naples to hammer out prices between them. Because they all controlled the supply of a variety of different foodstuffs, they agreed to give the initiative in deciding the price of single fruits and vegetables to Presidents whose territory gave them a particular strength in that particular crop: hence Big Pasquale's potatoes.

While this might seem a corrupt and inefficient system, it had distinct advantages for any national or international company that came to source produce at the wholesale market in Naples. Firms such as the producers of the canned tomatoes used on pasta and pizza would look to the Presidents of Prices for guarantees: that supply would be maintained; that prices would be predictable; and that the deals done face to face on the pavements of Corso Novara would be honoured. In return for these services, the Presidents of Prices took a personal bribe. Big Pasquale is reputed to have taken a 100 lire kickback on every 100 kilos of potatoes unloaded at the market. According to one testimony, the President of Potato Prices could send as many as fifty lorry-loads of spuds a day to the market—equivalent to some 750,000 kilos. If these figures are right, Big Pasquale could earn as much as $12,000 (in 2012 values) on a good day. And this does not take into account the money he was bleeding from the poor farmers, and the profit he made on the fruit and vegetables he traded in.

Later investigations showed that livestock, seafood and dairy produce were as thoroughly controlled by the camorra as was the trade in fruit and vegetables. Indeed, Naples did not even have a wholesale livestock market—all the deals were done in the notorious country town of Nola from which Big Pasquale took his name. According to one expert observer, 'The underworld in the Nola area willed and imposed the moving of the cattle market from Naples to Nola.'

Among the questions that remained unanswered by the Pupetta affair was one concerning the links between the rural clans and politicians. It is highly likely that the mobsters of the country towns acted as vote-hustlers in the same way as the *guappi* of the city.

Then there was the question of the relationship between these country clans and the urban crime scene. The wholesale greengrocery gangsters certainly made the *correntisti* of the urban slums look like small-time operators by comparison. The past may provide a few clues as to the links between the two. Big Pasquale from Nola, Tony from Pomigliano and their ilk have a history that remains largely unwritten to this day. Nevertheless, in the days of the old Honoured Society of Naples, the strongest Neapolitan *camorristi* were always the ones who had business links to country towns like Nola. The real money was to be made not in shakedowns of shops and stalls in the city, but upstream, where the supplies of animals and foodstuffs originated. Outside Naples, major criminal organisations certainly survived the death of the Honoured Society, and may well have continued their power right through the Fascist era. So the 'new camorra' revealed by the Pupetta case was not new at all.

If there had been less muddle about the Sicilian mafia in the 1950s, then it might also have occurred to observers of the Pupetta Maresca trial that the camorra families of the Neapolitan hinterland bore a resemblance to the mafia cells of Sicily and Calabria. They all had power built on violence, wealth that straddled the legal and illegal economies, and an insatiable hunger for fruit and vegetables. In March 1955, just seven months before Pupetta shot her husband's killer, a *mafioso* called Gaetano Galatolo, known as Tano Alatu, was shot dead at the entrance to Palermo's new wholesale market in the Acquasanta quarter. A factional battle to control the market then ensued. Southern Calabria had no single wholesale market to compare with those in Naples and Palermo; nor was any blood shed in this period over lettuces and pears. But it is known that the local mob controlled the smaller local markets in Reggio Calabria, Palmi, Gioia Tauro, Rosarno, Siderno, Locri and Vibo Valentia. As Italy recovered from the hungry years of war and reconstruction, and made its first hesitant steps towards prosperity, the mafias established a stranglehold on the South's food supply.

After the events of 1955 in Naples, some of the best current affairs commentators who were not aligned with the PCI came close to these profoundly worrying conclusions. One example was the liberal intellectual and politician Francesco Compagna: his magazine *Nord e Sud* published a number of important analyses of organised crime in the following years. But at a time when the only women within the orbit of organised crime who made themselves visible were the black-clad mafia widows of Sicily and Calabria, even such serious observers struggled to see Pupetta Maresca as anything more than an anomaly. The overwhelming view was that any women who might happen to associate with gangsters did so only because they were typical, family-bound southern females; that they played no active part in the mafia system.

Pupetta received an eighteen-year term for the premeditated murder of Big Tony from Pomigliano. And, despite her best efforts, her brother Ciro was eventually sentenced to twelve years. Many Italians remained hypnotised by the 'Tosca' version of her story. In the wake of the publicity surrounding the murder, the Italian film industry developed a minor obsession with her. The first film came out before the trial, in 1958. Two years after her release, in 1967, Pupetta herself starred in *Delitto a Posillipo* (*Murder in Posillipo*), based loosely on her life. In 1982, she was played in a TV movie by Alessandra Mussolini, the Duce's granddaughter. Another TV dramatisation was transmitted in 2013, attracting criticism for romanticising the camorra. Pupetta established a twin-track career that was destined to last for years: movie celebrity and mob queen.

PART IX

THE MAFIAS' ECONOMIC MIRACLE

42

KING CONCRETE

IN THE LATE 1950S AND EARLY 1960S, INDUSTRY EXPANDED FASTER IN ITALY THAN IN any other Western European nation. The European Common Market was a stimulus for exporters; cheap power, cheap labour and cheap capital created the right conditions for growth at home, and the north of Italy had traditions of entrepreneurship and craftsmanship to draw on. An agricultural country, much of which had still run on cartwheels in the 1940s, was now motoring into the age of mass production. Factories in the North began churning out scooters, cars and tyres in exponentially increasing numbers. This was Italy's 'economic miracle', the speediest and most profound social change in the peninsula's entire history.

Lifestyles were transformed. As tractors and fertiliser modernised agriculture, peasants abandoned the countryside in droves. Italy contracted the consumerist bug. Television began in 1954, and with it advertising for stock cubes, tinned meat, coffee pots, toothpaste . . . Italians learned to worry about armpit odour, lank hair and dandruff. Washing machines, fridges and food mixers promised an end to domestic drudgery for millions of women. Motorways were built for the legions of new car owners.

Italy even became fashionable. Brand names like Zanussi, Olivetti and Alfa Romeo conquered the continent. The Vespa and the FIAT 500 became icons. The world started to crave the peninsula's handbags and shoes. Soon Italy's much sniffed-at food would begin to win converts too.

During the economic miracle, Italy rapidly made itself into one of the world's leading capitalist economies. Here was a shining success story for the Europe that had risen from the rubble of the Second World War.

But the miracle also opened up roads to riches for the mafias. And the mafias' favourite industries knew few of the problems that would come to dog the lawful economy when the boom eventually subsided. No cycles of surge and recession. No obstreperous unions. Little in the way of competition. Through the 1960s, 1970s and 1980s the history of the mafias traces an upward curve of relentlessly growing riches. The mafias' economic miracle would long outlast the first spurt of growth in lawful industry.

From the mid-1950s, Italy's three major criminal organisations followed one another into four new businesses—or at least newly lucrative businesses: construction, tobacco smuggling, kidnapping, and narcotics trafficking. The story of the mafias' economic miracle takes the form of an intricate fugue as, following a trend that was usually set in Sicily, each of the mafias moved in turn through the same cycles of greed, and each of these four businesses in turn increased mafia influence.

The two core skills the mafias deployed to exploit the construction industry, contraband tobacco, kidnapping and drugs were both highly traditional: intimidation and networking, which are what mafia crime has been all about since the outset. All the same, the new era of criminal business did not just make bosses more moneyed than they had ever been, it also profoundly altered the landscape of mafia power.

For one thing, wealth begat wealth. The profits from one illegal enterprise were ploughed into the others, and thereby multiplied. From construction, to smuggled cigarettes, to kidnapping, to narcotics: interlocking chain reactions were set in motion over the coming three decades. The mafias became what Italy's 'mafiologists' describe using an English phrase: 'holding companies'. In some senses that is what *mafiosi* ever were: 360-degree criminals who, in the nineteenth century, would take money from extortion and invest it in stolen cattle, for example. But from the late 1950s there was a quantum leap in the diversification and integration of mafia commerce.

Burgeoning criminal wealth wrought a whole series of other changes. The liaison between organised crime and the Italian state grew both more intimate and more violent. The mafias themselves changed too. They experimented with new rules and new command structures. They grew to look more like one another. *Mafiosi* from different regions increasingly moved in the same circles, doing business together, learning lessons and, sometimes, fighting. *Mafiosi* began to operate more internationally. Entirely new mafias were spawned. In the end, these interlocking changes would plunge all of the mafias into violence of a scale and savagery that had never been seen before.

It all began with a commodity that is set hard at the very foundations of the mafias' territorial authority, and continues to this day to build many of their bridges into the lawful economy and the system of government: concrete.

Naples and Palermo have a great deal in common. Both were glorious capital cities in their time. Both are ports. And both are marked by a long-standing struggle to find an economic *raison d'être* in the era of industrial capitalism. In the early 1950s, Palermo and Naples had ancient enclaves of poverty at their heart: the alleys of the run-down quarters were bomb-damaged, crowded, filthy and poor. Typhoid and tuberculosis were regular visitors. Here the cramped, precarious housing lacked proper kitchens and lavatories. In the alleys, barefoot children played amid open drains and rubbish. Many breadwinners, male and female, lived from hand to mouth as pickpockets, three-card tricksters, pedlars, prostitutes, chambermaids, laundresses and gatherers of firewood, rags or scrap. The bricklayers and plasterers who got occasional work, or the underemployed cobblers and tailors, were all too few. Child labour was one of the mainstays of the slum economy.

Change was urgently needed. To add to the pressure, Palermo was now Sicily's capital again, with the new regional parliament and its army of bureaucrats to accommodate. But instead of planned rehousing and strategic urban development, both cities were ransacked. Building speculation was rampant, and local government proved utterly incapable of imposing any order on the savage concrete bonanza. In the process, through the 1960s, the economic axes of both cities were shifted. Once their livelihoods had depended on land (for the wealthy) and improvisation (for the poor). Now they were rebuilt around state employment, meagre benefits, piecework, sweatshop labour, services—and, of course, construction. For the poor, the transformation meant years of waiting, protesting, and begging for a favour from a priest or politician, before finally moving from a city-centre slum to a bleak housing project a long walk from the nearest bus stop. For the middling sort, the reward was a rented apartment in one of many indistinguishably gaudy, jerry-built stacks on what had once been green space.

But when it comes to organised crime's part in the construction bonanza of the 1950s and 1960s, the contrasts between Naples and Palermo were more striking than the similarities.

In Naples, no one seized the mood of the building speculation boom better than film-maker Francesco Rosi, in his 1963 movie *Le mani sulla città*. *Hands*

Over the City (as it was rather clumsily called in English) was both a prize-winning drama and a stirring denunciation of the political malpractice that fed off the construction industry in Naples. Rod Steiger snarls his way through the leading role as Edoardo Nottola, a rapacious councillor-cum-construction entrepreneur. The movie's opening scene shows Steiger barking out his plans as he gestures with both arms in the direction of a parade of brutalist tower blocks:

> That over there is gold today. And where else are you going to get it? Trade? Industry? The 'industrial future of the *Mezzogiorno*'? Do me a favour! Go ahead and invest your money in a factory if you like! Unions, pay claims, strikes, health insurance . . . That stuff'll give you a heart attack.

There could be no more vivid encapsulation of the cold-blooded credo of what Italians call an *affarista*: a profiteer, a wheeler-dealer, a cowboy businessman. *Affaristi* shirk the risks involved in real entrepreneurship, usually by working in the shadow of the political system where they can arrange little monopolies and sweetheart contracts.

Gangsters prefer to deal with *affaristi* rather than with real entrepreneurs. Yet, although *Hands Over the City* is a searing portrait of a Neapolitan *affarista*, it is telling that the word camorra is never used in Rosi's film; nor does anyone who could be considered a *camorrista* play a front-of-stage role in the story. For once, that absence is not the sign of a cover-up or of moral blindness: rather, it accurately reflects the facts on the ground. In Naples, *camorristi* simply lacked the clout to force their way into a major share in the building boom. At this stage in our story, there were no *camorristi* who doubled as construction *affaristi*.

In Palermo, the situation was strikingly different: here the councillors and construction entrepreneurs were invariably flanked by Men of Honour; *affaristi* and *mafiosi* were so close as to be all but indistinguishable.

In the late 1950s and 1960s, the mafia rebuilt Palermo in its own gruesome image in a frenzied wave of building speculation that became known as the 'sack of Palermo'. There were two particularly notorious mafia-backed politicians who were key agents of the sack. The first was Salvo Lima, a tight-lipped, soft-featured young man whose only affectation was to smoke through a miniature cigarette holder. He looked like the middle-class boy he was—the son of a municipal archivist. Except that his father was also a mafia killer in the 1930s. (That little detail of Lima's background had been buried, along with all the other important information from the Fascist campaigns against the mafia.) In 1956, Lima came from nowhere to win a seat on the city council, a post as director of the Office of Public Works, and the title of deputy mayor. Two years later, when Lima became mayor, he was succeeded at the strategic Office of Public Works by the second key *mafioso* politician, Vito Ciancimino. Ciancimino was brash, a barber's son from Corleone whose cigarette habit had given him a rasping voice to match his abrasive personality. In the course of their uneasy alliance, Lima and Ciancimino would wreak havoc in Palermo, and reap vast wealth and immense power in the process.

Men like Lima and Ciancimino were known as 'Young Turks'—representatives of a thrusting new breed of DC machine politician which, across Sicily and the South, was beginning to elbow the old grandees aside. In the 1950s, the range of jobs and favours that were available to patronage politicians began to increase dramatically. The state grew bigger. Government enlarged its already sizeable presence in banking and credit, for example. Meanwhile, local councils set up their own agencies to handle such services as rubbish disposal and public transport. Sicily's new regional government invented its own series of quangos. As the economy grew, and with it the ambitions for state economic intervention, more new bureaucracies were added. In 1950, faced with the scandal of southern Italy's poverty and backwardness, the DC government set up the 'Fund for the South' to sluice large sums into land reclamation, transport infrastructure and the like. Money from the Fund for the South helped win the DC many supporters, and put food on many southern tables. But its efforts to promote what it was hoped would be a dynamic new class of entrepreneurs and professionals were a dismal failure. As things turned out, the only really dynamic class in the South was the DC's own Young Turks. The Fund for the South would turn into a gigantic source of what one commentator called 'state parasitism and organised waste'. Government 'investment' in the South became, in reality, the centrepiece of a geared-up patronage system. Young Turks began to inveigle their way into new and old posts in local government and national ministries. Journalists of the day dubbed the Christian Democrat party 'the white whale' (i.e., Moby Dick) because it was white (i.e., Catholic), vast, slow, and consumed everything in its path.

In Palermo, for all these new sources of patronage, it was the simple business of controlling planning permission that gave Young Turks like Lima and Ciancimino and their mafia friends such a large stake in the building boom.

The sack of Palermo was at its most swift and brutal in the Piana dei Colli, the flat strip of land that extends northwards between the mountains from the edge of Palermo. It has always been a 'zone of high mafia density', in the jargon of Italian mafiologists. Indeed, it has as good a claim as anywhere to being the very cradle of the mafia: its beautiful lemon groves

The sack of Palermo. From the late 1950s, the construction industry propelled organised crime in Sicily and Calabria to new levels of wealth and power.

were where the earliest *mafiosi* developed their protection racket methods; the Piana dei Colli was the theatre for the 'double vendetta' intrigues of the 1870s that had been investigated by Ermanno Sangiorgi. A century on from those beginnings, the mafia smothered its birthplace in a concrete shroud. The scale of the ruin was immense. The gorgeous landscape of the Conca d'Oro, which for Goethe had offered 'an inexhaustible wealth of vistas', was transformed into an undifferentiated swathe of shoddily built apartment blocks without pavements or proper amenities.

In 1971, when the sack of Palermo was complete, a journalist climbed Monte Pellegrino, the vast rocky outcrop that surges between the Piana dei Colli and the sea. The view below him had once been stunning. Now it was shocking.

> From up there you can cast your eyes across the whole city and the Conca d'Oro. Palermo seems much bigger than you would imagine: long rows of houses spreading out from the periphery towards the orange groves. Concrete has now devastated one of the most beautiful natural spectacles in the world. The huge blocks of flats, all alike, seem to have been made by the same hand. And that hand belongs to 'don' Ciccio Vassallo. More than a quarter of the new Palermo is his work.

Francesco Vassallo, known as 'don Ciccio' ('don Frankie'), or 'King Concrete', was by a distance the dominant figure in the Palermo construction industry in the 1960s. Between 1959 and 1963, under the Young Turks Salvo Lima and Vito Ciancimino, Palermo City Council granted 80 per cent of 4,205 building permits to just five men, all of whom turned out to be dummies. One of the five subsequently got a job as a janitor in the apartment block he had nominally been responsible for building. Behind those five names, more often than not, stood don Ciccio Vassallo.

King Concrete was a fat, bald, jowly man with a long nose, dark patches under his eyes, and a preference for tent-like suits and loud ties. He rose from very humble origins in Tommaso Natale, a *borgata* or satellite village that sits at the northern end of the Piana dei Colli. Reputed to be only semi-literate, he was the fourth of ten children born to a cart driver. Police reports mention Vassallo as moving in mafia circles from a young age; his early criminal record included proceedings for theft, violence and fraud—most of them ended in a suspended sentence, amnesty or acquittal for lack of proof. His place in the local mafia's circle of influence was cemented in 1937 by marriage to the daughter of a landowner and *mafioso*, Giuseppe Messina. With the Messina family's muscle behind it, his firm established a monopoly over the distribution of meat and milk in the area around Tommaso Natale. Vassallo and the Messinas were also active in the black market during the war. When peace came, Vassallo started a horse-drawn transportation company to ferry building materials between local sites. His mafia kinfolk would be sleeping partners in this enterprise, as in the many lucrative real-estate ventures that would come later.

Suddenly, in 1952, Vassallo's business took off. From nowhere, he made a successful bid to build a drainage system in Tommaso Natale and neighbouring Sferracavallo. He had no record in construction; it was not even until two years later that he was admitted onto the city council's list of approved contractors. He was only allowed to submit a tender for the contract because of a reference letter from the managing director of the private company that ran Palermo's buses. The company director would later become Vassallo's partner in some lucrative real-estate ventures. At the same time, Vassallo received a generous credit line from the Bank of Sicily. Then his competitors withdrew from the tendering process for the drainage contract in mysterious circumstances. Vassallo was left to thrash out the terms of the deal in one-to-one negotiations with the mayor, who would also later become his partner in some lucrative real-estate ventures.

In the mid-1950s, King Concrete started to work closely with the Young Turks. Construction was becoming more and more important to the economy of a city whose productive base, such as it was, could not compete with the burgeoning factories of the 'industrial triangle' (the northern cities of Milan, Turin and Genoa). By the 1960s, 33 per cent of Palermo workers were directly or indirectly employed in construction, compared to a mere 10 per cent in Milan, the nation's economic capital. However temporary the dangerous and badly paid work in Palermo's many building sites might be, there were few alternatives for ordinary working-class *palermitani*. Which made construction workers a formidable stock of votes that the Concrete King could use to attract political friends. Friends like Giovanni Gioia, the leader of Palermo's Young Turks, who would go on to benefit from a number of lucrative real-estate ventures piloted by Vassallo.

The notion of a 'conflict of interests' was all but meaningless in building-boom Palermo. The city municipality's director of works became King Concrete's chief project planner. From his political contacts, the rapidly rising Vassallo acquired the power to systematically ignore planning restrictions. The Young Turk, Salvo Lima, was repeatedly (and unsuccessfully) indicted for breaking planning law on Vassallo's behalf. During the sack of Palermo, journalists speculated ironically about the existence of a company they called VA.LI.GIO (VAssallo—LIma—GIOia). They were successfully sued. Rather pedantically, the judges ruled that no such legally constituted company existed.

In the mid-1960s, the market for private apartments reached saturation point. By that stage King Concrete had built whole dense neighbourhoods of condominia that were without schools, community centres and parks. Ingeniously, he then turned to renting unsold apartments and other buildings for use as schools. In 1969 alone he received rent of nearly $700,000 (in 1969 values) from local authorities for six middle schools, two senior schools, six technical colleges and the school inspectorate. The DC press hailed him as a heroic benefactor. In the same year he was recorded as being the richest man in Palermo.

It pays to remember that don Ciccio Vassallo was an *affarista* rather than an entrepreneur. His competitive advantage lay not in shrewd planning and investment, but in corruption, in making useful friends, and of course in the unspoken menace that shadowed his every move. Right on cue, unidentified 'vandals' would cut down all the trees on any stretch of land that had been zone-marked as a park. Any honest company that somehow managed to win a contract from under the mafia's nose would find its machinery in flames. Dynamite proved a handy way of accelerating demolition orders.

In 1957, just as the sack of Palermo was about to enter its most devastating phase, a mafia power struggle began in King Concrete's home village of Tommaso Natale. His own family was soon drawn in. In July 1961 his brother-in-law, Salvatore Messina, was shotgunned to death by an assassin who had sat in wait for him for hours in the branches of an olive tree. Another brother-in-law, Pietro, was shot dead a year later. A third brother-in-law, Nino, only saved himself from the same fate by hurling a milk churn at his attacker when he was ambushed; it is thought he then left Sicily. The fact that don Ciccio himself was not attacked (as far as we know) shows that his power now transcended any local base: he was a money-making machine for the entire political and mafia elite.

Mass migration was one of the most important characteristics of Italy's economic miracle. As the industrial cities of the North boomed, they sucked in migrants. About a million people moved from the South to other regions in just five years, between 1958 and 1963.

Mafiosi also became more mobile in the post-war decades: their trade took them to other regions of Italy. In some places, gangsters went on to found permanent colonies. Those bases in central and northern Italy, as well as in parts of the South not traditionally contaminated by criminal organisations, are one of the distinctive features of the recent era of mafia history. Nothing similar is recorded in previous decades.

Some of the American hoodlums who were expelled from the United States after the Second World War were the first to set up business outside the mafia heartlands of Sicily, Calabria and Campania. Frank 'Three Fingers' Coppola dealt in drugs from a base near Rome, for example.

The earliest signs of mafia colonisation from *within* Italy came in the great North–South migration during the economic miracle. In the mid-1950s, Giacomo Zagari founded one of the first cells of *'ndranghetisti* near Varese, close by Italy's border with Switzerland. The murder of a foreman in the early hours of New Year's Day in 1956 revealed the existence of mafia control among the Calabrian flower-pickers of the Ligurian coast near the French border.

Many northerners resented the hundreds of thousands of new arrivals from the South. Southerners, they said, had too many children and grew tomatoes in the bathtub. News of mafia-related crime, or indeed any crime as long as it was committed by an immigrant, merely served to confirm those anti-southern prejudices. Mafia appeared to be a kind of ethnic affliction that made everyone from 'down there' proud, vengeful, violent and dishonest.

The truth is that mass migration from the South was not to blame for the mafias' spread northwards. *Mafiosi* are a tiny minority of professional criminals; they are not typical southerners. There were plenty of places where immigrants arrived and the mafias did not follow. But migration did create many new opportunities for *mafiosi*—notably, as the flower-pickers of Liguria illustrate, in gangmastering, when immigrants were forced to work for low wages, untaxed, and without the protection of the law. As Italy grew during the economic miracle and afterwards, such criminal opportunities expanded and multiplied.

The criminal opportunities most conducive to long-term mafia colonisation of the North came from the construction industry. The most notorious case is the winter sports resort of Bardonecchia, in the northern region of Piedmont; it is situated in the Alps just a few kilometres from the French border. Bardonecchia is where the inhabitants of Turin, Italy's motor city and one of the capitals of the economic miracle, go to ski. Eventually, in 1995, Bardonecchia became the first town council in northern Italy to be dissolved by central government in Rome because of mafia infiltration. Strikingly, the mafia that had colonised Bardonecchia long before then was the 'ndrangheta. Italy's least-known mafia, the one most frequently associated with a disappearing world of peasant penury, was quick to spot the illegal profits to be made from construction, and put itself in the vanguard of the new era of expansion in the North.

The story of Bardonecchia is like a sequence of time-lapse photographs in a nature documentary. Narrowly focused, as if on the growth of a single poisonous weed, it nevertheless exposes the secret workings of a whole ecosystem. Played in rapid sequence, the images from Bardonecchia take us far ahead in our story. They illustrate how, from small beginnings, and in the right circumstances, the mafias can establish what they call 'territorial control' from virtually nothing.

The first hint of the 'ndrangheta's arrival in Bardonecchia came at past midnight, on 2 September 1963. A heavy rain was falling as Mario Corino, a young primary school teacher, turned into via Giolitti in the old part of town. He was approached by two men, both of them half hidden by umbrellas. The attack was swift — so swift that Corino did not see what type of blunt instrument flashed towards him. He instinctively parried the first blow with his umbrella and his forearm; the second grazed his head before smashing into his shoulder. His screams drove the attackers away. Evidently this was only meant to be a warning.

Initial speculation linked the attack with Corino's work as leader of the local branch of the Christian Democrat Party. More specifically, he had denounced what were politely called 'irregularities' in the local construction industry and the town plan. But within days the two men who attacked Corino had confessed, and the press was able to reassure itself that there was no political background to the assault. The culprits were both plasterers, paid by the square metre of wall they finished; they assaulted Corino because they objected to his attempts to enforce rules against piecework on building sites. Case closed. Or so it seemed.

As it turned out, the original suspicions were correct. Moreover, the assault on Mario Corino was only the first symptom of something much more menacing. The problems began, as Mario Corino had suspected, with a building boom in the early 1960s: tourists and second-homers needed places to stay if they were going to enjoy Bardonecchia's mountain air. Building firms needed cheap hands and a way round safety regulations and labour laws: they turned to 'ndrangheta gangmasters, who were more than happy to provide this service by recruiting from among the droves of Calabrian immigrants. The labourers in Bardonecchia, many of whom had criminal records and little chance of finding more regular employment, lived camped out in semi-squalor. By the early 1970s, an estimated 70–80 per cent of labour in the village was recruited through the mafia racket; many of those workers had to kick back part of their salary to the *capo*. Trades unions found it impossible to set up branches.

But long before then, the 'ndrangheta bosses had gone far beyond labour racketeering. First they set up their own companies to carry out subcontracting work: plastering and trucking were favourite niches. 'Ndrangheta-controlled construction firms were not far behind. Shadowy real-estate companies came and went from the record books. Then, at rival building sites, there were unexplained fires, machinery was vandalised and workers were threatened at gunpoint. Before long most of the honest building companies had been driven out of the market, or driven into the hands of the gangsters.

Meanwhile, the government had done its bit to fill the Calabrian mafia's coffers by building a new highway and a tunnel through the mountains. The 'ndrangheta recruited some local politicians and administrators to help them win contracts and get round regulations. Barely a stone was turned without the say-so of the local *capo*. One city council employee would simply hand out the boss's visiting card to anyone who applied for a licence to start up a new business—just to avoid any messy bureaucratic problems, he claimed. Mario Corino, the schoolteacher-cum-politician who had been attacked in 1963, led a heroic resistance to 'ndrangheta influence over local government when he became mayor in 1972. In 1975 the courts dismissed his alarm-calls as a politically motivated fiction: they said he was using the mafia as a pretext to throw mud at his rivals. Corino's opponents would feign disbelief and outrage when any journalist suggested that there might be a mafia problem in the town. Yet, at the same time, energetic policemen would be mysteriously transferred to other parts of the country. In a phone tap, the local boss was recorded as saying, 'We are the root of everything here, you understand me?'

It was remarkable that Bardonecchia had to wait until as late as 1969 for its first mafia murder. Forty-four deaths would follow between 1970 and 1983. On 23 June 1983, the 'ndrangheta proved how high, and how brutally, it was prepared to strike. Not long before midnight, Bruno Caccia was walking his dog when he was approached by two men in a car; they shot him fourteen times, and then got out to fire three coups de grâce. Caccia was an upstanding investigating magistrate who had refused any dialogue with what was now a thoroughgoing 'ndrangheta power system.

It is unlikely that there was a grand strategy behind the mafias' move north. Rocco Lo Presti, the 'ndranghetista who led his organisation's rise to power in Bardonecchia during the building boom of the 1960s, had been there since the mid-1950s. It seems he came as a humble migrant, albeit one with some fearsome relatives. But he was less interested in getting a job than he was in handling counterfeit banknotes. Thereafter, mafiosi came north for many reasons: to hide from the police or their enemies; to set up temporary narcotics trading posts; to quietly launder and invest their ill-gotten gains, or to capitalise on criminal opportunities opened up by pioneers like Rocco Lo Presti. The full-scale colonisation of a town like Bardonecchia created a pattern to be followed elsewhere. In one bugged conversation, one of Rocco Lo Presti's friends was heard giving him a verbal pat on the back: 'Bardonecchia is Calabrian,' he said. The irony in this remark was that many of the entrepreneurs, administrators and politicians who had helped turn Bardonecchia Calabrian were as Piedmontese as Barolo wine and agnolotti.

In the political sphere, organised crime has always been a problem that affected the North and centre as well as the South. From soon after the birth of Italy as a unified state in 1861, coalition governments in Rome had to recruit clusters of supporters among southern MPs; and southern MPs—some of them, at least—used racketeers to hustle votes. Yet after the economic miracle, thanks primarily to infiltration of the construction industry, the mafias became a national problem in two dramatically new ways. On the one hand, as we have seen, the North became a theatre of operations for southern mobsters. On the other hand, the South became a theatre of cooperation between northern big industry and the mafias. For example, companies from the industrialised North were also dealing on friendly terms with the 'ndrangheta back in Calabria, where concrete proved even more lucrative than it was in Piedmont.

In the 1960s there began a major road-building programme. Its emblem was the so-called 'Motorway of the Sun' that ran down Italy from north to south. The last stretch of that motorway, covering the 443 kilometres from Salerno to Reggio Calabria, carried the burden of enormous hopes: a century on from Italian unification, the 'Salerno–Reggio Calabria' (as it is universally known) would finally end the deep South's isolation from the national transport network. Grand exploits of civil engineering were required to traverse the region's forbidding geology: no fewer than 55 tunnels and 144 viaducts, some of which soar over 200 metres above the forests at the valley floor.

Today the Salerno–Reggio Calabria is notorious—a prodigy of chaotic planning, pork-barrelling and broken political promises. It is still not finished nearly half a century after it was begun. Rather than taking the most logical and direct route along the coast, the Salerno–Reggio Calabria cuts tortuously inland to visit the electoral fiefdoms of long-forgotten ministers. At times the motorway's only purpose seems to be to join a chain of permanent construction sites. Long stretches are so narrow and winding that they have a 40-kilometre-per-hour speed limit. Jams are so frequent that the roadside is permanently lined with chemical toilets to allow desperate motorists to relieve themselves. During peak times, ambulances are parked ready to intervene. In 2002, magistrates in Catanzaro sequestered a whole section of recently modernised motorway because it was so shoddily built as to be acutely dangerous. The Bishop of Salerno recently called Europe's worst motorway a Via Crucis. The Salerno–Reggio Calabria shows the Italian state at its most incompetent.

Since the 1960s, the 'ndrangheta has profited handsomely from the mess. Yet very early on in the story of the Salerno–Reggio Calabria it became clear to law enforcement officers on the ground that the 'ndrangheta carried only part of the blame. One senior *Carabiniere* officer stationed in Reggio Calabria was interviewed by a national newspaper in 1970:

When northern entrepreneurs come down to Calabria to get their projects started, the first thing they do is to go to see the man they have been told is the mafia boss. They pay him a visit out of duty, as if they were calling on the Prefect. They solicit his protection, and pay for it by giving the *capomafia's* friends the sub-contract for earth moving, and by taking on *mafiosi* as guards on their building sites.

Non-Calabrian construction entrepreneurs would offer other favours too: testimonies in favour of *mafiosi* in court; failing to report the many thefts of explosives from their building sites; offering guarantees to the bank when *'ndranghetisti* bought construction machinery on credit. The northern entrepreneurs would then fail to complete their work on time, and blame the local mafia for the delays. Those delays would then allow the entrepreneurs to charge the government more money, money of which the mafia would naturally receive its share. Along the Calabrian stretches of the Salerno–Reggio Calabria, the 'ndrangheta was educated into the ways of a particularly cynical brand of capitalism.

Construction is acutely vulnerable to the mafia's most rudimentary methods. Buildings and roads have to be built *somewhere*. And in any given somewhere, by merely smashing up machinery or intimidating labour, *mafiosi* can force construction companies to sit down and negotiate. Nor, once those negotiations have borne fruit, does it require any great entrepreneurial nous for a boss to buy a few dumper trucks and set up an earth-moving company to take on some generously subcontracted business. More insidiously still, *mafiosi* do not find it hard to convince companies of the advantages that a friendship with organised crime can bring. An entrepreneur does not need to be exceptionally greedy or cynical to lapse into collusion with murderers. He just needs a preference for bending the rules, paying his workers in cash, and dodging red tape. And once he starts operating outside the law, who does he turn to when his machines are wrecked or his builders duffed up? His relief when he does a deal and the harassment stops merges easily with the satisfaction that comes when it is a competitor's turn to suffer. The truth is that there is often a *demand* for the mafias' services—a demand that the mafias themselves are past masters at cultivating.

So muscling in on the construction business is straightforward, up to a point. But success in construction can also be the measure of just how profoundly mafia influence has insinuated itself into the entrails of the state and the capitalist system. Getting zealous policemen moved, corrupting judges, adjusting town plans on demand, manipulating the awarding of government contracts, silencing journalists, winning powerful political friends: these are not activities for mere gorillas whose skills stop at pouring sugar into the fuel tank of a dumper truck. North or South, when a mafia masters these more refined arts, it can vastly increase its power to intimidate. Just as importantly, it can vastly increase the range of services it is able to offer to friendly firms: winning contracts at inflated prices, warding off inspections by the tax authorities, making new friends . . .

43

GANGSTERS AND BLONDES

ITALIANS GOT THEIR FIRST TASTE OF IMPORTED AMERICAN BLEND CIGARETTES LIKE Camel, Lucky Strike and Chesterfield during the Fascist era. They named them 'blondes' because they contained a lighter-coloured tobacco than the dark, air-cured varieties that could be grown in Italy.

Blondes were immediately popular. The state had established a monopoly on the growing, importing, processing and sale of tobacco in 1862; and since that date the state had always struggled to keep pace with consumer demand and changing tastes. The arrival of blondes left the government further than ever from satisfying the public's craving. In fact, no sooner were these glamorous new gaspers introduced in the early 1930s than they disappeared from government tobacco outlets because of the sanctions imposed following Italy's invasion of Ethiopia in 1935. Rationing during the Second World War made smokers' lives even more difficult. And when the Allies invaded in 1943, and Fascism fell, Italy's own capacity to produce tobacco was devastated. Thus British and American troops arrived amidst a tobacco famine, and they arrived with cigarettes in their ration packs. Much of this tobacco was funnelled into the burgeoning black market. By the time rationing ended in the spring of 1948, and domestic production recovered, it was too late: Italy's rapidly growing number of smokers (14 million by 1957) were hooked on imported cigarettes. Perhaps just as damagingly, they were also hooked on the illegal supply channels that made those cigarettes available at tax-free prices. This vast criminal market has shaped the history of organised crime in Italy ever since. It has been compared to the Prohibition period in the United States (1919–33), when the federal government banned alcoholic drinks, and in so doing created a bootleg bonanza. Naples, as the capital of the black market, is the place to watch the unfolding of the lucrative love affair between gangsters and blondes.

In 1963, cinema committed a captivating image of the Neapolitan contraband tobacco trade to popular memory in the first episode of Vittorio De Sica's three-part movie *Ieri, oggi, domani* (*Yesterday, Today and Tomorrow*), which won the Oscar for Best Foreign Film. Sophia Loren plays a girl who sells black-market cigarettes from an orange-box stall. For her, arrest is an occupational hazard. But she discovers that, by law, pregnant women cannot be held in prison, so she cajoles her husband into siring one baby after another, until their one-room apartment is bursting. Eventually, the poor man's reproductive apparatus gives out under the strain. (He is played, with typical harried charm, by Marcello Mastroianni.)

As a piece of cinema, the Loren episode of *Yesterday, Today and Tomorrow* is ultimately a sentimental cliché: yet another song to the gaudy anarchy of Neapolitan street life. Yet the story was rooted in truth all the same. The Loren character was based on Concetta Muccardo, who sold bootleg cigarettes in Forcella, the 'kasbah' quarter of Naples. Muccardo's reputed nineteen pregnancies (seven of them carried to term) kept her out of jail until 1957, when the police finally caught her without a baby on the way, or one in her

Sophia Loren, in the role of a Neapolitan cigarette-seller. Tobacco smuggling, a crucial business for organised crime, is portrayed sympathetically in the 1963 movie *Yesterday, Today and Tomorrow*.

arms. She was sent to prison for eight months and, harshly, a further two years were added to her sentence because she was unable to pay a fine. But Muccardo's notoriety quickly earned her freedom. The generous readers of two newspapers, one from Turin and one from Rome, paid off the money she owed. And in January 1958, following an appeal by Socialist and Communist women MPs, she was granted a pardon by the head of state, the President of the Republic. When Concetta returned to her alley, vico Carbonari, pictures of President Giovanni Gronchi had been set up alongside the images of the Madonna in the local street tabernacles.

The experience of shooting *Yesterday, Today and Tomorrow* in the alleys of central Naples showed De Sica just how close the script came to reality. This was a city where the chronic failings of the economy had left many poor families reliant on contraband to put food on the table. De Sica gave a walk-on part to a well-known local woman with nine children: she boasted she had been in prison a record 113 times for contraband offences. In Forcella there were many other cigarette girls who entered local folklore. A certain 'Rosetta' was the most attractive of a number of women who charged extra for 'fun fags'—cigarettes that customers had to rummage for in her ample cleavage. (A Sophia Loren movie based on Rosetta's story would doubtless not have made it past the censors.)

While De Sica was staying in the Ambassador Hotel, Muccardo's husband introduced himself and demanded a percentage of the film's takings. Rather obliquely, De Sica replied by pointing to a magazine photo of Sophia Loren on set being fitted with a false baby belly. 'Don't you see how beautiful she is? As big as your wife was at that stage.' The husband refused to be wowed: 'Yes, Mr De Sica, but this is a belly full of millions: my wife's is full of air.' Writing to explain the episode to his family, De Sica could find nothing else to say than, 'They are poor people.'

Both De Sica's film, and his reaction to what he witnessed in Naples while shooting it, are a faithful reflection of the dilemma that the Italian authorities also found themselves in. The law against tobacco-trafficking was simply unenforceable at street level. A clampdown seemed to be impossible without hurting the people who were both its operatives and its first victims: the poorest inhabitants of the Neapolitan slums. Indeed this was a dilemma that the Italian state lacked the will to tackle in any other way than by sleep-walking into repression and then recoiling towards tolerance. There was an amnesty for illegal cigarette retailers in the year that *Yesterday, Today and Tomorrow* came out, and another one in 1966. Policies the world over that aim to prohibit or control substances like tobacco and alcohol are difficult to implement at the best of times. When those policies are widely disobeyed, they have a way of making the law seem draconian, unrealistic and inconsistent all at the same time. The vital principle that it is in everyone's interests for the state to create and enforce fair rules can only suffer, and the state itself falls into discredit. In Italy, where that principle has always struggled to hold its own, the damage to the state's credibility was very serious indeed. In Naples, contraband cigarettes were openly on sale in the corridors of government buildings.

Yesterday, Today and Tomorrow came out at a crucial historical moment for contraband tobacco, and thus for all of Italy's mafias. For this was the time when cigarette smuggling became an industry, and that industry became the primary occupation of organised crime.

The decisive event in the gearing up of Italy's bootleg tobacco trade happened in North Africa. In October 1959 Mohamed V, king of a newly independent Morocco, confirmed the fears of smugglers across the Mediterranean: he gave six months' notice that the port of Tangier was to lose its special privileges. Until that point Tangier, which is situated opposite Gibraltar at the mouth of the Mediterranean, had had a large 'International Zone' with few passport controls, very low taxes and no currency restrictions. Banks did not even have to present balance sheets. In short, Tangier was a smugglers' paradise, and the very hub of illegal commerce across the Mediterranean. As one resident, American novelist Paul Bowles, observed: 'I think all Europe's black-market profiteers are here . . . since the whole International Zone is one huge black market.' It was from the safe haven of Tangier that the 'mother ships' packed with contraband cigarettes could fan out along the southern European coastline. When they reached Naples, they would wait in international waters for tiny local craft to come and ferry the cargo to shore.

When King Mohamed announced the closure of the International Zone, the short-term result was that cigarette smuggling became more difficult. And when smuggling becomes more difficult, only the best-organised and best-resourced of smugglers can survive. The only wholesalers who could now prosper were those with international links to shipping companies, cigarette producers and officials in places like the Balkans. For different reasons, the local operators, who ferried the cases of cigarettes from ship to shore, also had to up their game: expensive speedboats were now needed to outrun the *Guardia di Finanza* (Tax Police). As competition in the tobacco business increased, so too did violence. Contraband was no longer a trade for amateurs.

Naples appealed to the new breed of professional trafficker of the 1960s for a number of reasons. One of the most important was the ready supply of cheap criminal labour in the alleys where Concetta Muccardo became a legend. Naples was also the gateway to an Italian market that was in the throes of its economic miracle, and consuming more and more cigarettes as a result. In the 1960s, Naples was also a free port, in the sense that the camorra in the city was still comparatively weak, and there was no dominant local criminal organisation able to throttle competition. So networks of big-time traffickers from Genoa, Corsica and Marseille were drawn to the city under the volcano to find outlets for their cigarettes. But the most important new arrivals after the closure of the International Zone of Tangier—men who would radically alter the course of criminal history in Italy—were from Sicily.

44

COSA NOSTRA: Untouchables no more

IN THE LATE 1950S AND EARLY 1960S, ITALY OBSERVED AS THE UNITED STATES ONCE more addressed its mafia problem. First, in November 1957, there was the spectacular episode at a large estate in Apalachin, upstate New York, when the state troopers stumbled upon a summit of some one hundred mafia bosses. One or two of them came from as far away as California, Cuba and Texas. Sixty men were taken into custody, and as a result the FBI finally admitted the mafia—or national crime syndicate, or whatever name might be applied to it—was something more than a romantic myth. As a result, in 1959, Vito Genovese, chief of the New York Family that bore his name, was sentenced to fifteen years for drug trafficking: the first major blow against a senior stateside boss in the decade and a half since the end of the Second World War.

Meanwhile Robert F. Kennedy, the energetic young chief counsel of a new Senate Labor Rackets Committee, was busy uncovering corruption in the Teamsters Union. Following the Apalachin summit, the committee again used television to good effect by interviewing several of the most prominent men who had been at Apalachin, such as Joe Profaci and Thomas Lucchese. Viewers also saw a federal agent explain the mafia's dynastic politics:

> The intermarriages are significant in that often times you wonder whether these people want to marry each other. Yet the marriages take place. Let's say two people of a prominent status within the Mafia if they have children, you will find that their sons and daughters get married. . . . a leader

within the organization would not have his child marry someone who is a nobody within the organization.

Bobby Kennedy's best-selling account of the investigation he led, *The Enemy Within* (1960), contained vivid cameo portraits of a series of Italian-American gangsters. One such was 'labor relations consultant' Carmine Lombardozzi, who had been ordered to wait in the garage during the Apalachin summit while the other *mafiosi* decided whether to kill him or merely fine him for covertly pocketing money from a juke-box racket. (They opted for the fine.)

In 1961, when his brother became President, Bobby Kennedy became Attorney General. The investigation and repression of organised crime was a key part of his programme. Where there had been nineteen organised crime indictments in 1960, the total rose to 687 in 1964.

Alongside these law enforcement and political developments, the mafia became a hot topic in American culture. In 1959, ABC began transmitting a drama series, based on Eliot Ness's *The Untouchables*, about Al Capone's Prohibition-era Chicago. The show became a hit, largely because it was studded with thinly disguised references to recent gangland news.

As always, there was a good deal of controversy and sensationalism in public discussion. The Order Sons of Italy in America, an ethnic lobby group that was desperate to play down the mafia issue, managed to get all Italian-American characters removed from *The Untouchables* in 1961. Deprived of this key element of authenticity, the show declined in popularity and was taken off air in 1963.

At the other extreme, some wrote about the mafia as if it were a centralised, bureaucratic, calculating monster—an IBM of crime. Ever since then, in both Italy and the States, it has made for good journalistic copy to see the mafia as a dark mirror of cutting-edge capitalism, and to see *mafiosi* as executives with guns. This is an oversimplification with undoubted imaginative power, to both the law-abiding and the outlaw. *The Godfather*—novel and movie—would later draw part of its insidious glamour from the same idea: 'Tell Mike it was only business.' Nothing could be better calculated to make middle-aged, middle-American middle-managers feel dangerous and clever than the suggestion that they and *mafiosi* are pretty much alike—give or take a few garrottings. Conversely, nothing could be better calculated to flatter a hoodlum's ego, and impress his young sidekicks, than the suggestion that he is the incarnation of some sleek, lawless ideal-type of the businessman. But if *mafiosi* are entrepreneurs, then they are entrepreneurs who specialise not in competition, but in breaking and distorting the rules of the market.

The season of intense political and media interest in the mafia in the early 1960s also had a curious side effect: it changed the mafia's name. In 1962 Joe Valachi, a soldier in the Genovese Family, mistakenly suspecting that he was about to be killed on the orders of his boss, bludgeoned an innocent man to death in prison. He then began to talk to the FBI about the mafia, its initiation rituals and structure as he saw them from his lowly and relatively marginal position in the organisation. A non-Italian speaker, Valachi had heard other members of the brotherhood refer to *cosa nostra*—'our thing'. Valachi took this vague description to be the mafia's official name: Cosa Nostra, or la Cosa Nostra. So too did the FBI. And then, once Valachi's testimony had been made public in 1963, so too did American *mafiosi* themselves. Only in 1984 would the world learn that this label had been adopted by the Sicilian mafia too.

The advent of the name Cosa Nostra is only the latest example of the way the mafias have learned their own language from the world outside. Something similar happened a century earlier with the word 'mafia' itself. It only became the most commonly used of the many names for Sicily's elite criminal brotherhood as the result of being used in a successful play about prison gangsters in the 1860s.

Why are the mafias so bad at giving themselves a name? The main reason, as one defector from Cosa Nostra would later explain, is that secret criminal brotherhoods are the 'realm of incomplete speech'.

> Fragmenting information is one of the most important rules. Cosa Nostra is not just secretive towards the exterior, in the sense that it hides its existence and the identity of its members from outsiders. It is also secretive on the inside: it discourages anyone from knowing the full facts, and creates obstacles to the circulation of information.

Mafiosi habitually conduct their affairs in nods and silences, in language marked by an expertly crafted vagueness that can be understood only by those who are meant to understand. Communications within the mafia are like whispers in a labyrinth. So when the outside world says something about the mafia's affairs, it resounds through the labyrinth like a clarion call.

Years of muddled debate about the mafia in the United States still lay ahead. A whole genre of academic studies would decry the notion of an organisation called Cosa Nostra: it was a product of anti-Italian prejudice and a misrepresentation of the immigrant culture of close family ties—or so the sociologists and anthropologists argued. Ironically, in 1972, one of the most successful movies of all time, Francis Ford Coppola's generational saga *The Godfather*, would be based on a systematic confusion between the mafia and the Sicilian-American family, thereby lending a Hollywood gloss to the sceptical views of the academics. But, despite the controversy, the oversimplifications and the perverse side effects, America's open discussion about the mafia in these years was a healthy sign. What it indicates is that the period of relative impunity and invisibility that Italian-American mobsters had long enjoyed was now over for good. The mafia in the United States was no longer untouchable. The question now was how long it would take for Italy to follow Uncle Sam's example.

45

MAFIA DIASPORA

IN OCTOBER 1957, ONLY WEEKS BEFORE THE APALACHIN SUMMIT IN UPSTATE NEW York, Men of Honour from the United States held several days of meetings with Sicilian bosses at the Grand Hotel et Des Palmes in the heart of Palermo. The head of the American deputation was Joe 'Bananas' Bonanno—*capo* of the New York Family that bore his name. Narcotics were almost certainly at the top of the agenda. Unlike what had happened at Apalachin, however, the heavy-lidded eyes of the Palermo police merely registered the meeting. Nothing was done about it.

Business was not the only thing discussed while Joe Bananas was in Palermo. According to the later confessions of a young drug trafficker called Tommaso Buscetta (a man destined to play an epoch-making role in Sicilian mafia history over a quarter of a century later), the 1957 Italo-American summit was the occasion for an important organisational innovation within the Sicilian mafia. It seems that, over dinner one evening, Joe Bananas suggested that Sicily should have a Mafia Commission—a kind of governing body—like the one that had overseen inter-Family relations in New York since Lucky Luciano brought it into being in 1931. The Commission has existed in Sicily, on and off, ever since. Not for the first time, Sicilian *mafiosi* had shown that they were better at learning lessons from America than were Italy's police or politicians.

However, the Commission, as Sicilian historians have now ascertained, was not the novelty that Tommaso Buscetta thought it was. Evidence that Cosa Nostra has had governing bodies of one kind or another is there in some of the earliest documentation we have about it. For example, there were forms of coordination between the different *cosche* of western Sicily—joint tribunals to settle disputes, summit meetings, marriage pacts and the like. In America, there seem to have been consultative meetings of senior East Coast Men of Honour before the First World War. Our best guess, using recent history as a guide to the mysterious moments in the past, is that the mafia has always had a lively constitutional life. Sicilian mafia bosses have constantly invented new rules and procedures to buttress their own authority and keep the peace with their neighbours. But equally, they have constantly broken their own rules and procedures, or found ways to use them as a political weapon against their enemies.

In the late 1950s, however, these nuances of mafia analysis had not even begun to dawn on Italy's rulers. The issue of Sicilian organised crime remained stuck in the political permafrost of the Cold War. Communist politicians took every opportunity they could to raise the mafia issue—and make it count against the DC. But without the power to govern, they remained isolated voices. One of the most astute and caustic of those voices belonged to Pio La Torre, the young leader of the PCI in Sicily:

> The truth is that there is no sector of the economy in Palermo and in vast areas of Western Sicily that is not controlled by the mafia. This has happened in the course of a long process—the same process that has seen the DC regime prosper in Palermo and the rest of the island.

La Torre knew what he was talking about: he was born in Altarello di Baida, a village set amid the lemon groves surrounding Palermo—the mafia's nursery, in other words.

In response to charges like these, the DC all too often fell back on a contradictory rag-bag of myths: the mafia was dying out; it was merely a harmless Sicilian tradition; it was invented by the Left as a way of besmirching Sicily and the DC; it didn't exist; *mafiosi* only kill one another anyway; *gangsterismo* was an American problem.

The Left opposition had not forgotten the Kefauver hearings, and lobbied hard for something similar to happen in Italy: a parliamentary inquiry into the Sicilian mafia. The Christian Democrats were split into shifting and bitterly antagonistic factions. In the heat of the factional struggle, many DC chiefs were very reluctant to look too closely at the ethical standards of their Sicilian lieutenants. So the DC dragged its feet for years, and only gave ground when the Left's lobbying was given extra oomph by mafia dynamite.

Late in 1962, a conflict that later became known as the First Mafia War began in and around Palermo. The conflict's signature weapon was a tactical novelty for underworld wars in Italy: the car bomb. Invariably, it was an Alfa

Romeo Giulietta that was stuffed with explosives. The Giulietta was one of the symbols of Italy's economic miracle. In 1962 it became a symbol of how the Sicilian mafia was keeping up with the pace of growth in the lawful economy.

Although a drug deal gone wrong is known to have been the trigger for the First Mafia War's outbreak, the underlying reasons for it baffled outside observers at the time, and are still uncertain today. Even many of the combatants did not know where the battle lines were drawn. In essence, it seems that the newly revived Commission had been unable to control conflicts over drugs, concrete and territory. Indeed some Palermo *mafiosi* regarded the Commission itself with justifiable suspicion: for them it was not an arbiter in disputes, but an instrument manipulated by some powerful bosses. The Sicilian mafia's constitutional wrangles had taken a bloody turn. Indeed, not for the last time, events in Palermo were pointing the way to the future for organised crime in Italy. Perhaps one hundred people were killed in the First Mafia War—more than in any other underworld conflict since the 1940s. Cosa Nostra had become more volatile in its internal politics, and more flagrant in its violence. Soon the other mafias would follow the same trend.

Against the background of the car bombings and other violence in Palermo, a parliamentary inquiry into the Sicilian mafia was grudgingly approved. Yet it still looked as if it would never get going. Then, on 30 June 1963, another Giulietta detonated in Ciaculli: it blew four *Carabinieri*, two military engineers and a policeman to pieces. The bomb's intended targets were probably the local mafia clan, the Grecos, one of Palermo's oldest and most powerful dynasties.

Remarkably, even on the day of the bomb, the DC remained very touchy about the word 'mafia'. The Christian Democrat notables who occupied the country's most senior institutional posts all issued messages of condolence to the victims' families, and of indignation to the general public. Not one of them mentioned the mafia.

Nevertheless, the public outrage that followed the Ciaculli massacre had rapid effects, both within Cosa Nostra and outside. The First Mafia War came to an immediate halt in the face of a massive police crackdown, with close to two thousand arrests. Cosa Nostra faced one of the worst crises in its history. As a *mafioso* who turned state's evidence later explained: 'After 1963 Cosa Nostra in the Palermo area didn't exist anymore. It had been knocked out. The mafia was about to dissolve itself, and seemed to be in a shambles . . . The Families were all wrecked. There were hardly any murders any more. In Palermo, people did not even pay protection money.'

Mafiosi who were able to flee Palermo did so—men like the boss of the Commission, Totò Greco (known as 'Little Bird'), who emigrated to Vene-

Silent grief. Palermo turns out en masse in 1963 for the funeral of four *Carabinieri*, two military engineers and a policeman murdered by a Sicilian mafia bomb.

zuela. Others fled to Switzerland, the States, Canada . . . The mafia vanished from its birthplace, the province of Palermo.

The Ciaculli bomb also swept away the last resistance to the idea of a parliamentary inquiry into the mafia—an Italian Kefauver, at last. But anyone who expected the inquiry to achieve the kind of spectacular results seen on the other side of the Atlantic was in for both a very long wait and a dull disappointment. The political wrangling only seemed to intensify during the inquiry's hearings. Astonishingly, in 1966, Donato Pafundi, the Senator who chaired those hearings—a Christian Democrat by political affiliation and a prosecutor by profession—denied the existence of the mafia as a criminal organisation, and even blamed Muslims for the problem:

The mafia in Sicily is a mental state that pervades everything and everyone, at all levels of society. There are historical, geographical and social reasons behind this mentality. Above all there is a millennium of Muslim domination. It is hard to shake off the inheritance of centuries. The mafia has ended up in Sicilians' blood, in the most intimate folds of Sicilian society.

Considering views like this, it is hardly surprising that the parliamentary inquiry took no fewer than thirteen years to finish its work.

Nor did Italian politicians have any of the flair for the media that Estes Kefauver and Robert Kennedy had shown. The parliamentary inquiry's final report provided as good a definition of the problem as one could get without using insider sources. It certainly had none of the simplistic sensationalism of Kefauver's vision of a vast, centralised international conspiracy, and none of Donato Pafundi's ignorance. But its abstruse wording was indicative of the problems the inquiry had had in bringing public opinion along with it:

> The mafia has continually reproposed itself as the exercise of autonomous extra-legal power and the search for a close link with all forms of power and in particular state power, so as to collaborate with it, make use of it for its own ends, or infiltrate its structure.

Anyone who was still awake after trying to read a couple of paragraphs of prose like this deserved a medal for endurance.

Predictably, the parliamentary Left also disagreed with the report and issued its own version, placing much more emphasis on the mafia's ties to the highest spheres of Sicilian society: 'The mafia is a ruling class phenomenon.' This, in its own way, was also an oversimplification. The point about the Sicilian mafia, like the nineteenth-century Freemasonry on which it was based, is that it includes members of all classes: both cut-throats and counts can become Men of Honour.

Perhaps the most damning criticism to be made of the 1960s parliamentary inquiry into the Sicilian mafia is that its terms of reference did not include the camorra and the 'ndrangheta. Underestimating the organised crime issue outside Sicily would have dire consequences. And those dire consequences were set in motion scarcely two years after the parliamentary inquiry started work, when the first piece of legislation to issue from the post-Ciaculli climate was passed. Law 575 of 1965 was a parcel of anti-mafia measures that included the policy of 'forced resettlement': suspected *mafiosi* could be compelled to leave their homes and take up residence somewhere else in Italy. Forced resettlement was based on the highly questionable theory that the fundamental cause of the mafia was the backward social environment of western Sicily. If *mafiosi* could be transplanted from that environment into healthier surroundings, so the theory went, then their criminal inclinations would shrivel.

Rather than shrivelling, the mafia spread. As one Man of Honour would later explain: 'Forced resettlement was a good thing for us, because it gave us a way to contact other people, to get to know different places, other cities, zones that weren't already contaminated by organised crime.'

It was not just 'uncontaminated' zones of Italy that hosted resettled *mafiosi*. Incredibly, some of them were even sent to the hinterland of Naples. Despite the fearsome traditions of criminal enterprise that had become visible during the Pupetta Maresca affair, Campania was now deemed socially healthy enough to reform the Sicilian gangster elite. In the late 1960s and early 1970s, some of Sicily's most powerful criminals were forcibly resettled around Naples: *mafiosi* of the calibre of Francesco Paolo Bontate, the boss of Santa Maria di Gesù, and later his son Stefano, a future keystone of Cosa Nostra's Palermo Commission. They were joined there by other *mafiosi* who were on the run from the law. One of these was Gerlando Alberti, who later became famous for a *bon mot*: asked about the mafia by a journalist, he replied, 'What's that? A brand of cheese?'

Through the repression following the Ciaculli bomb, and then by the policy of forced resettlement, Italy had involuntarily created a new diaspora of criminal talent. Naples during the contraband tobacco boom would be one of that diaspora's favourite ports. The stage was set for a crucial new convergence of interests between Sicilian and Campanian organised crime.

46

THE MAFIA-ISATION OF THE CAMORRA

MICHELE ZAZA, KNOWN AS 'O PAZZO ('MAD MIKE'), WAS THE SON OF A FISHERMAN from Portici who became the dominant Neapolitan cigarette smuggler of the 1970s. He had a vast villa in Posillipo, with one of the most splendid views over the bay of Naples—*La Glorietta*, he called it. Interviewed there by a local TV station, he once famously quipped that tobacco smuggling was 'the FIAT of southern Italy'. What he meant was that it created as many jobs as did the Turin-based car giant. Naples could no more survive without smuggling than Turin could without the automotive industry. This was a wisecrack pitched at a ready audience, both in the alleys of central Naples, and in the communities far beyond Naples that had once enjoyed Sophia Loren's sassy performance in *Yesterday, Today and Tomorrow*. As had been the case during Prohibition in the United States, gangsters who operated in a clandestine market, trading a commodity that had a great many non-criminal customers, could easily pose as the good guys.

Mad Mike was no Robin Hood, however. On 5 April 1973, he was part of an assassination squad that tried to kill Chief of Police Angelo Mangano, a Sicilian lawman who had distinguished himself in the fight against the mafia in Corleone. (Mangano survived, despite being shot four times, including in the head.) Why would a Neapolitan *camorrista* try to kill an enemy of the Sicilian mafia? Because that *camorrista* had recently become an initiated affiliate of Cosa Nostra.

By the early 1970s, the Sicilian *mafiosi* who had ended up in Campania had become intimate friends with a number of *camorristi*. The police and *Carabinieri* reported a regular series of meetings between Neapolitan and

388

Sicilian hoods in Naples. The Sicilians even acquired a taste for the sentimental pop melodies that their Neapolitan hosts adored.

The links between the mafia and the camorra were soon formalised. In
the Sicilian mafia's traditional fashion, *mafiosi* established kinship alliances
with the *camorristi*, based on marriage and *comparatico* ('co-parenthood').
Big Neapolitan smugglers were also formally initiated into Cosa Nostra. At
least two Cosa Nostra Families in Campania were created and authorised by
Palermo. One had its seat in the city itself, and was grouped around an extended family, the Zaza-Mazzarellas, including 'Mad Mike' Zaza. The other
was based in Marano, a small town on the northern outreaches of Naples.
Marano was home to the man who had shot dead the 'President of Potato
Prices' in 1955. The murderer's relatives, the Nuvoletta brothers, were now
in charge in the town, and were duly initiated into Cosa Nostra.

Thus Cosa Nostra's new Campanian Families inherited the two main
criminal traditions in the region. 'Mad Mike' Zaza represented the urban
camorra revived by the black market during the Second World War. The
Nuvoletta brothers were just the type of *camorristi* who had long been involved in controlling supply routes from the countryside to the city markets. So in one sense, the novelty of Cosa Nostra's branches in Campania
was also a highly significant return to the past. For the first time since the
days of the old Honoured Society of Naples, a single organisational framework embraced both the urban and rural camorras.

The scaling-up of the trade in bootleg cigarettes, and the close links between the Sicilian and Neapolitan underworlds, was 'mafia-ising' the camorra.
Indeed, not for the first time in history, the very meaning of the word 'camorra'
was undergoing a transformation. Once, if it was used at all, it referred to
small local gangs, or networks of smugglers, or even to isolated *guappi*. Now
camorristi were increasingly functionaries of much bigger groups, with a bigger range of criminal activities and greater financial sophistication.

To the Neapolitans, the incoming *mafiosi* brought many things, such as
organisational skills, and particularly prestige. For who has not heard of the
Sicilian mafia? And who, among criminals, is not afraid of it?

To the Sicilians, Neapolitans like 'Mad Mike' offered excellent smuggling
contacts and a vast distribution network. Bringing them inside Cosa Nostra
was a way of keeping a close eye on them. Indeed, they also did the same
thing, and for the same reason, to a major Palermitan cigarette smuggler,
Tommaso Spadaro.

The Sicilian mafia's decision to absorb some *camorristi* also had strategic military motives. The dominant players in Neapolitan contraband
during the late 1960s were multinational traffickers known collectively

as the Marseillais—because one of their previous bases had been in the French port of Marseille. Between 1971 and 1973, Cosa Nostra's men in Campania deployed their firepower to cut out the competition. A handful of Neapolitan cigarette smugglers were executed, and at least six Marseillais. By mafia standards, this was a very small investment in violence that would reap very big returns. Soon Cosa Nostra and its Campanian friends had the contraband tobacco market to themselves.

Business ballooned. One estimate suggests that, in the late 1970s, the annual turnover of the illegal cigarette business in Campania was some 48.6 billion lire (very roughly $215 million in 2012 values), and net profit stood at somewhere between 20 and 24 billion ($88–$106 million). In 1977, the *Carabinieri* found 'Mad Mike' Zaza with an account book, according to which mafia-camorra tobacco smuggling turned over an astonishing 150 billion lire a year (over $620 million). Between 40,000 and 60,000 people in the Campania region are thought to have found employment in the smuggling economy. The FIAT of southern Italy indeed.

Cosa Nostra got more than its share of the bonanza. Naples, according to a *mafioso* heavily involved in contraband, became the 'El Dorado' of Sicilian organised crime. As Tommaso Buscetta, a veteran cigarette smuggler, recalled:

> The volume of business in the illegal cigarette trade became enormous. In the 1950s, 500 cases were considered a big consignment. Now we'd reached as many as 35–40,000 cases unloaded every time a contraband ship travelled between Naples and Palermo.

Managing the flow of wealth that came to Sicily from across the Tyrrhenian Sea also had profound effects on the Sicilian mafia. For by 1969, most of the Men of Honour charged as a result of the First Mafia War had been acquitted, and they were free to pick up where they had left off at the time of the Ciaculli bomb. They wasted little time letting everyone in Palermo know they were back. At a quarter to seven on the evening of 10 December 1969, five men in stolen police uniforms machine-gunned the occupants of a construction company office in viale Lazio. Five were killed, including one of the attackers and their intended target: the mafia boss Michele Cavataio, who many within Cosa Nostra thought was the mastermind behind the car-bombing campaign of the early 1960s. We now know that the men who carried out the viale Lazio massacre were delegates from different mafia

Families—as if to demonstrate that Cavataio's execution had been decreed by Cosa Nostra as a whole.

Thus, after a six-year hiatus following the Ciaculli bomb, the Sicilian mafia resumed its constitutional life. The first formal shape that Cosa Nostra's politics took was a triumvirate of senior bosses who were entrusted with reawakening the organisation's dormant structures in the province of Palermo. The first triumvir, and probably the most prestigious, was Stefano Bontate, known as the 'Prince of Villagrazia', *capo* of the largest Family in Palermo, a job he had inherited from his father. Bontate was mafia aristocracy. The second triumvir was Gaetano 'Tano' Badalamenti, the boss of Cinisi, where Palermo's new airport provided a huge source of revenue; Badalamenti had long-standing links with Cosa Nostra in Detroit. The third was Luciano Liggio from Corleone.

The triumvirate gave way to the full Commission in 1974, with Cinisi mobster Tano Badalamenti sitting at the head of the table. It was now a subtly different kind of body. When the Commission was set up in the late 1950s, there was a rule that no Family *capo* could have a seat. The ostensible objective was to hear complaints from individual Men of Honour about their bosses, and to protect them from unwarranted bullying. The Commission activated in 1974, by contrast, was composed of the most important bosses in the province of Palermo. It is no coincidence that this new shape emerged at the time that smuggling cigarettes through Naples was one of the mafia's major sources of income. For as well as being a body devoted to managing relations between the Families, the Commission became a tobacco-smuggling joint-stock company.

Mafia sources have given us a remarkable insight into the tense politics of contraband tobacco within Cosa Nostra in the 1970s. Each of the interested parties would take it in turns to take possession of a shipload coming into Campania: one for the Neapolitans, one for each of the groups of *mafiosi* operating in Naples, and then one as a tribute to the Commission. Thus every two months or so, the ship carrying the cigarettes for Palermo would make its way towards Sicily. Tano Badalamenti, in his role as head of the Commission or 'provincial representative', would take responsibility for divvying up the cargo: 1,000 cases for Michele 'the Pope' Greco from Ciaculli; 1,000 for the Corleone Family; 2,000 for the Bontate group, and so on. In other words, each boss who was prestigious enough to be included on the Commission, and rich enough to have the capital to buy cigarettes upfront, became a stakeholder in the portion of the cigarette market that the Commission claimed as its right.

In addition to the Commission's 'joint-stock company', many *mafiosi* ran contraband cigarettes independently, as traffickers in their own right. Rings of smugglers were formed by Men of Honour from different Families, as and when business opportunities presented themselves. The picture was further complicated by the need to work closely with non-*mafiosi* who were not as dependable, and not subject to the mafia's rules. Initiating men like 'Mad Mike' Zaza did not entirely solve the problem.

Mad Mike had manifestly not undergone the same rigorous selection process as the Palermo criminal elite, and he occasionally needed reminding of the self-discipline he was expected to show now that he was a Man of Honour. On one occasion, he was spotted playing cards for large sums in the casino of a luxury hotel on the island of Ischia. The Catania boss Pippo Calderone, one of his partners in the cigarette business, angrily reminded him that ostentatious gambling on that scale was not permitted behaviour for a member of Cosa Nostra.

Mad Mike and other smugglers never lost their reputation for slipperiness within Cosa Nostra. According to Tommaso Buscetta, they had a 'fraudster mentality', and tended 'to play it sly'. Of course, sly behaviour was not an exclusively Neapolitan trait. It is likely that Mad Mike's semi-detached status vis-à-vis Cosa Nostra also made him the perfect accomplice and scapegoat for Men of Honour who were just as sly as him, and who wanted to get more than their allotted share of any given cargo.

Thus the mafia-camorra cigarette oligopoly was born already fissured by mutual suspicion. Some years later, it would become clear that the tensions in the contraband tobacco business had also exposed fault lines *within* Cosa Nostra that would open up into the bloodiest conflict in mafia history.

But in 1978 the tobacco-smuggling boom slowed because an international accord now allowed the authorities to pursue smugglers into international waters. Seizures of cigarettes hit a peak in that year. More significantly, by that time, heroin was opening up a new, more profitable, and much more divisive chapter in Italy's underworld history.

There is a postscript to the story of Concetta Muccardo, the Forcella cigarette-seller played by Sophia Loren in *Yesterday, Today and Tomorrow*. On 27 June 1992, aged sixty-seven, she was arrested for retailing heroin from a doorway in the Sanità neighbourhood; behind the door the police found another fifty wraps of heroin and 350,000 lire ($375 in 2011 values). Long before that date, narcotics were being funnelled through the same channels once used to bring contraband cigarettes into Italy.

THE MUSHROOM-PICKERS OF MONTALTO

The 'ndrangheta, as we have seen, had begun to make inroads into the construction industry in the 1960s. Southern Calabria's long coastline also afforded plenty of sheltered places where cases of contraband cigarettes could be off-loaded. Just as was happening in Sicily and Campania, the money flowing in from concrete and tobacco created a new political climate in Calabrian organised crime.

In 1969, the judicial authorities were given a rare glimpse of the Calabrian mafia's internal politics when, for the first time in history, the police mounted a full-scale raid on the 'ndrangheta's annual general meeting on Aspromonte. The episode briefly propelled Italy's least visible mafia into the headlines for the first time since the 'Martian invasion' of 1955. The story of that 1969 raid, and the trial that resulted from it, allows us to catch up on a crucial process of political change under way within the Calabrian underworld. Just as importantly, it illustrates how the Italian law viewed the sworn criminal sects of both Calabria and Sicily at a time when they were becoming both richer and more dangerous.

At nearly 2,000 metres, Montalto is the highest point on Aspromonte. From here, a statue of the redeeming Christ—were he able to revolve on his axis to follow the line of the horizon—would enjoy one of the most beautiful 360-degree panoramas on the planet: the Aeolian Islands off the

393

northern coast of Sicily, the wooded slopes of Calabria's Serre mountains to the north-east, and the quietly smoking peak of Mount Etna across the Straits. Somewhere in the woods below lies the Sanctuary of the Madonna of the Mountain at Polsi, where the 'ndrangheta has always held an annual reunion early in September. In 1969, the increased attentions of the police had forced a change of date and venue. This year, the chief cudgels of the Calabrian underworld convened in a woodland clearing just below Montalto, on a damp Sunday morning, 26 October. But their countermeasures turned out to be in vain.

A team of twenty-four police and *Carabinieri*, acting on clues derived from weeks of surveillance, came across thirty-five cars parked higgledy-piggledy on the edge of the road near Montalto. Moving swiftly and silently, the police overpowered and gagged the five lookouts. Advancing further into the forest, they heard shouting and applause: the underworld conference was still in session.

The team split into two groups to try and encircle the broad clearing where they could glimpse more than a hundred men, sitting in a circle in animated discussion. But someone gave the alarm. Six officers advanced into the clearing shouting, 'Nobody move! Police!' The gangsters ran off in every direction, firing wildly with pistols, shotguns, automatic rifles and machine guns. No one was hit and, amid chaotic scenes, the police managed to arrest twenty-one of the men at the summit. They also had the cars abandoned by the fleeing 'ndranghetisti to work with. Eventually seventy-two of the estimated 130 men in attendance would face trial. Most of them claimed they had been out picking mushrooms. Some of the younger affiliates cracked under interrogation. One of them, a builder from Bagnara, told police of his initiation ceremony. He and a few others also revealed the gist of what had been discussed at Montalto.

The first striking thing about the debate is how *procedural* some of it was. Before the summit got under way, as tradition dictated, each man present had to stand up and formally greet the others in the name of the clan he represented. An important item on the agenda was the annual meeting itself. Should the Honoured Society continue to gather at the Sanctuary of the Madonna of Polsi every year, now that the police were clearly taking a close interest? Someone proposed a change of location. And surely, with a change of location should come a change of name: it should now be termed the 'Aspromonte meeting' and no longer the 'Polsi meeting'. After much discussion, the conservatives won out: Polsi would remain the venue of choice, although the date could be switched to throw the authorities off. Perhaps understandably, when the men arrested at Montalto came to court, the judge described this discussion as 'formalistic' and 'pedantic'.

Yet there were more substantive issues discussed at the summit, like how to respond to the threat posed by the forces of law and order. The circle of bosses complained loudly about the activism recently shown by the chief of police of Reggio Calabria. This called for a united response, for a show of force. A variety of tactical options were tabled, such as blowing up police vehicles with dynamite, or ambushing the chief of police's car.

Planning dynamite outrages against the common enemy may well have lightened the mood among the 'mushroom-pickers' of Montalto. But the main issue at the summit was potentially much more explosive: addressing the potential for disunity within the 'ndrangheta's ranks. Investigators learned that one of the older bosses from Taurianova in the plain of Gioia Tauro, a veteran felon called Giuseppe Zappia who had been entrusted with the task of chairing the meeting, made a passionate appeal for unity: 'There's no Mico Tripodo's 'ndrangheta here! There's no 'Ntoni Macrì's 'ndrangheta here! There's no Peppe Nirta's 'ndrangheta here! We should all be united. Anyone who wants to stay, stays. Anyone who doesn't want to stay, goes.'

Apart from what is probably a veiled threat in the last line (one wonders what the price of leaving the meeting would have been), this plea sounds very bland: the gangland equivalent of motherhood and apple pie. The police and magistrates looking into the Montalto summit sensed that the appeal was in reality highly significant. But before they could find out much

Giuseppe Zappia, pictured after his arrest at the 1969 Calabrian underworld Summit, where he made this famous plea for unity: 'There's no Mico Tripodo's 'ndrangheta here! There's no 'Ntoni Macrì's 'ndrangheta here! There's no Peppe Nirta's 'ndrangheta here! We should all be united.'

more, the few men arrested at Montalto who had confessed retracted their statements: they had been bullied by the police, they said. As had almost always been the case in the first century of organised crime history in Italy, such vital witnesses were not properly cultivated and protected by the magistrates handling the case; no one will ever know how much more they could have told us about the 'ndrangheta. Instead they joined the chorus of gangsters who claimed to have been picking mushrooms.

To his great credit, the judge in the case, one Guido Marino, would have none of these feeble alibis. Nor did he take very seriously the defence's claims that the 'ndrangheta was like the Rotary Club or the Lions. Judge Marino meant business. He made some devastating criticisms of the way the fight against the 'ndrangheta was being conducted. Investigations were 'superficial' and 'desultory', meaning that the mafia remained 'elusive' in court. Rather than 'solid and patient' investigation, the police all too often fell back on police cautions and internal exile. These preventive measures were entirely counterproductive, he said. 'They have acted like a restorative vaccine in the bodies of these criminal societies, which today are more vigorous and efficient than ever.'

It was the same scandalous story that had been carrying on since Italy had become one country in the nineteenth century. In Calabria, as elsewhere in southern Italy, mafia organisations were thriving on the half-cocked tactics designed to contain them.

Astutely, Judge Marino latched on to what might seem the least sinister aspect of the Montalto summit: the 'formalistic' and 'pedantic' procedural discussion. In his view, this betrayed the fact that the 'ndrangheta was an 'institutionalised' association. Moreover, Judge Marino went on to argue, the gangsters' debate about shared traditions showed that the world of Calabrian organised crime was much more than a scattering of isolated gangs. There was only one 'ndrangheta, and it was a criminal organisation with a long history behind it. (At this point, no one knew how long that history was.)

There is a striking contrast here with the 'Martian invasion' of Calabria in 1955, when the authorities seemed to have only a passing interest in the 'ndrangheta's history and structure. Judge Marino's ruling is the first small sign of what the Italian judicial system could learn by treating the mafias of Calabria and Sicily as what they were: criminal sects that had been embedded in society for decades.

Judge Marino was so keen to delve into the 'ndrangheta's secrets that he compiled biographies of the two most powerful bosses named in the plea for unity at Montalto. Those biographies—the first ever detailed portraits of 'ndrangheta chief cudgels—are worth looking at closely.

The 'Ntoni Macrì invoked by Zappia at Montalto was, of course, the very same don 'Ntoni who had danced the *tarantella* with Master Joe, and had then gone on (reputedly!) to save the Bishop of Locri from being murdered by a gang of vengeful priests. Don 'Ntoni was rich. Apart from his strictly illegal businesses, he induced the local landowners to use his own henchmen as guards on their olive groves; he forcibly regulated lemon prices to suit his own needs as a trader in agricultural commodities; he also had interests in agricultural machinery and construction. In 1957 his wealth and political protection rescued him from the internal exile he had been sentenced to during the Marzano Operation.

A year later he was on the run, charged with murder. In 1961 he was found not guilty, and also acquitted of the supplementary charge of being a member of a criminal association. An arrest for attempted murder came in 1965. Then, in 1967, three of his rivals were shot dead and another two wounded in what became known as the 'massacre of piazza Mercato' in Locri: two men armed with a shotgun and a machine gun opened fire on a group of people who were striking a deal in the wholesale fruit and vegetable market. As always, Macrì was found not guilty on the grounds of insufficient evidence.

But don 'Ntoni's most jaw-dropping coup was yet to come. In 1967, he defrauded the Bank of Naples with the help of the Siderno branch manager. Although the manager was sacked as a result, the Bank of Naples refused to help the police with their investigations. Reviewing the evidence in that case, Judge Marino could only conclude that there was a mafia in the Bank of Naples alongside the mafia run by don 'Ntoni Macrì. The judge was shocked by the number of times, through the 900 pages of don 'Ntoni's criminal record, that he had been shown leniency after important people had defined him as a reformed character. By the time of the summit at Montalto in 1969, the Siderno boss had become what Judge Marino called a 'living symbol of organised crime's omnipotence and invincibility'.

Don Domenico 'Mico' Tripodo was the second boss invoked at the Montalto summit whose biography was assembled by Judge Marino. In the judge's words, Mico Tripodo was a 'proud and indomitable villain, entirely devoted to the mafia cause'. He derived his income from extortion, fruit-market racketeering, armed robbery, counterfeit money and cheques, and, of course, tobacco smuggling and construction. One of the more remarkable features of Tripodo's career is that he escaped confinement three times by the same trick of feigning illness and getting himself transferred to clinics, which were less well guarded and much easier to slip away from. Much of the rest of his time was spent in hiding: he changed his name several times, and even contracted a bigamous marriage in Umbria before finally being recaptured in Perugia. The fact that he was behind bars at the time of the Montalto summit did not stop him running his empire and ordering murders on his turf.

Poring over these biographies understandably left Judge Marino angry and disbelieving. The authorities knew an awful lot about the 'ndrangheta: the summit at Polsi had been an open secret for a while, for example. Yet, as Judge Marino observed, they seemed incapable of making any progress towards hampering its operations and resisting the rise of don 'Ntoni, Mico Tripodo and their ilk.

Judge Marino's diligent and penetrating analysis of the mushroom-pickers of Montalto contrasts strikingly with the trials against Cosa Nostra that took place around the same time. A notable example is the 1968 trial that was intended to bring to justice the participants in the First Mafia War, when Palermo's delinquent elite had blown one another up with booby-trapped Alfa Romeo Giuliettas. The prosecutor who prepared the case against the participants in the mafia war, Cesare Terranova, was certain that the mafia had a centralised coordinating council of some kind. According to a report prepared by the *Carabinieri* in 1963, fifteen senior *mafiosi*, of whom six came from the city of Palermo and nine from the towns and villages of the province, had seats around the table. This council, of course, was what we now know is called the Commission. Yet, as so often in mafia history, this picture of the mafia's inner workings was based on confidential information leaked from within the mafia rather than on formal testimony given in open court. For that reason, it was all but useless as prosecution evidence.

Accordingly, the judge in this case remained agnostic on the question of whether the Sicilian mafia existed or not. He discounted the far-fetched theory that the mafia had 'norms' and 'criteria' common to all its members. He also made concessions to the defence's argument that the mafia was 'a psychological attitude or the typical expression of an exaggerated individualism'. But he also thought it was something more, something illegal but hard to define with any clarity. So he concluded, fuzzily, that it was a 'phenomenon of collective criminality'. All but ten of the 114 defendants were acquitted for lack of evidence.

Law enforcement took its cue from this verdict. In 1974, the very year when, as we now know, the Palermo Commission of Cosa Nostra was reconstituted, the chief of police of Palermo argued that the mafia was only a loose set of unstructured local gangs that coalesced for specific criminal enterprises and then quickly dissolved. It was hopeless to try and fight the mafia *as such*, because it was just a part of Sicilian culture. 'It is impossible to repress the general phenomenon of the mafia! Repress what? An idea?

A mentality?' Cosa Nostra, as so often in its history, was proving very, very adept at concealing its real nature.

So Judge Marino's account of the Montalto summit case gave the Italian authorities a picture of a highly structured and ritualised 'ndrangheta. Moreover, the criminal records of don 'Ntoni Macrì and Mico Tripodo bore a striking resemblance to those of many Sicilian mafia bosses of their generation and earlier: the same violence, the same powerful friends, the same curious train of acquittals for lack of evidence, the same ability to insinuate themselves into the richest sectors of the lawful economy. Yet no one seems to have wondered whether a similar picture of a structured and ritualised criminal brotherhood might fit the evidence in Sicily. The raw truth was that nothing that happened in far-off Calabria was ever likely to wake Italy up to the gravity of its organised crime problem.

Alas, when it came down to it, the revelations that followed the Montalto case did not change anything in Calabria either. Even Judge Marino, who had proved so painstaking in his research and so withering in his condemnation of the state's failings, handed out risible sentences to the 'ndrangheta's leaders. Italy's laws against mafia organisations were feeble. Although a crime of 'mafia association' existed, and made membership of a mafia group illegal, it carried very light penalties. Most of the 'mushroom-pickers' were given two and a half years, and most had two of those two and a half years commuted. The bosses invoked in the chair's appeal for unity, including don 'Ntoni Macrì, were all acquitted of belonging to a criminal association: lack of evidence, yet again. Don 'Ntoni and the others had been *mentioned* at the summit, but they were not arrested at the scene, and there was no proof that they had actually been there. Mico Tripodo was acquitted because he was in prison at the time of the meeting. The judge seemed to be speaking to his own conscience when he tried to explain his reasoning:

> This is an argument that might seem like a travesty if one takes into account the reality that is felt and seen by everyone in this part of the world. But that reality has not been recognised by the criminal justice system in the few extremely serious cases that it has dealt with.

The judge, in other words, was a prisoner of history. The authorities' repeated failure to create a legal precedent by describing the 'ndrangheta accurately, and to convict men like don 'Ntoni, meant that they could not be convicted now.

As well as feeble legislation, Italian law enforcement would continue to betray the same weaknesses that Judge Marino had so acutely identified in his account of the 'ndrangheta's Montalto summit. The mafias would continue to be policed in the haphazard and discontinuous way that had allowed the 'ndrangheta to grow so strong. Much blood would have to be shed before Italy was ready, finally, to create investigating methods and laws that were adequate to the threat it faced.

Years after the summit at Montalto was raided, the memories of a small group of 'ndranghetisti who turned state's evidence helped magistrates understand just how quickly the threat of organised crime was growing in the late 1960s.

For example, the criminal profiles of don 'Ntoni and Mico Tripodo were even more alarming than Judge Marino could know. For, as well as being chief cudgels of the 'ndrangheta, both were also fully initiated members of Cosa Nostra. Here is how one 'ndrangheta defector later recalled don 'Ntoni:

> This man was the overall boss. He embodied what people thought was the Honoured Society—and he wasn't unworthy of embodying it, in my view. We could say that he was the boss of all bosses, and I'm not the only one who has magnified his qualities . . . He was the one and only representative, a fully qualified member of Cosa Nostra . . . He was a personal friend of Sicilian mafia bosses like Angelo and Salvatore La Barbera, Pietro Torretta, Luciano Liggio, and the Grecos from Ciaculli.

Don 'Ntoni's relationship with the Sicilian hoodlum elite was close. He smuggled cigarettes with them. He also borrowed killers from them: it is thought that the shooters in the massacre of piazza Mercato were Sicilians.

Mico Tripodo was a member of Cosa Nostra too. But the Sicilians were not his only friends. Later in his career, Mico Tripodo would spend periods of 'forced resettlement' in various regions. He was arrested for the last time in 1975 in Mondragone, on the northern coast of Campania—a town that had been one of the region's most notorious camorra strongholds for a century. When he was caught, Tripodo was in hiding with two leading *camorristi*. This was just one indicator of the way in which cigarette smuggling and other businesses were weaving high-level ties between the camorra and the 'ndrangheta that were almost as densely meshed as those between Cosa Nostra and the other two organisations.

Gradually, southern Italy was developing a criminal system that was much more unified than it had ever been in the past. Members of Italy's three historic mafias have always had contacts with one another, chiefly through the prison system. But from the 1960s, the cases of 'double affiliation', even 'triple affiliation' would become more and more common. What was happening was *not* the development of a single master mafia, an umbrella organisation of the underworld. Rather it was something much more subtle and efficient: the pooling of contacts, resources and expertise. Because of cigarette smuggling, *mafiosi*, *camorristi* and *'ndranghetisti* were rapidly learning how to work together. The new economic frontiers of mafia power could be exploited more thoroughly when Men of Honour from different criminal organisations worked together.

The evidence of later 'ndrangheta defectors also revealed more about the crucial political changes going on in the Calabrian mob. For about a decade before Montalto, the 'ndrangheta in the province of Reggio Calabria was divided into three territories. Those territories corresponded to the three coastal areas at the bony toe of the Italian boot, and thus to what is almost the natural geographical layout of 'ndrangheta power. In Sicily, about half of Cosa Nostra's total numerical strength is concentrated around the island's capital, Palermo. In southern Calabria, power was and is shared roughly equally between the strip of land facing Sicily that includes the provincial capital of Reggio Calabria; the Ionian coast, looking out into the Mediterranean; and the Tyrrhenian coast, or the top of the boot's toe, which included the plain of Gioia Tauro—the largest and most fertile lowland in the region.

In the 1960s a triumvirate of three bosses, one from each of these three territories, had a great influence over 'ndrangheta affairs. We have already encountered two of the three triumvirs in Judge Marino's conclusions about the Montalto summit. The first was the venerable *tarantella*-dancing don 'Ntoni Macrì, from Siderno, the 'living symbol of organised crime's omnipotence and invincibility', the underworld patriarch whose authority extended along the Ionian coast. The second member of the 'ndrangheta triumvirate was Mico Tripodo, the bigamist whose power centred on the city of Reggio Calabria and its environs.

The third member of the triumvirate was neither present nor mentioned at the Montalto summit (a fact which itself betrayed tensions within the organisation). His name was don Girolamo 'Mommo' Piromalli. Piromalli was the dominant boss in the plain of Gioia Tauro, where the work for the Salerno–Reggio Calabria stretch of the 'Motorway of the Sun' was concentrated. Roughly the same age as Mico Tripodo, he too was a major smuggler of tobacco who had been initiated into Cosa Nostra.

Mommo was the oldest of seven siblings, five of them male. His father Gioacchino, who died in 1956, sat at the root of a vast and spreading genealogy. By the 1960s the Piromallis were busily consolidating their dominant role in the plain of Gioia Tauro by marrying themselves into its major 'ndrangheta bloodlines. Across the province of Reggio Calabria, the spider's web of kinship bonds grew both wider and thicker as the 'ndrangheta immersed itself deeper into the new economic reality.

Together, the three bosses of the triumvirate guaranteed what one *'ndranghetista* called a 'certain equilibrium' in the Calabrian underworld— an equilibrium that was becoming increasingly delicate as the Honoured Society grew richer on concrete and tobacco.

Coordination between the different territorially based cells of Italian criminal organisations is not new. Indeed it has been integral to the mafia landscape since the beginning. Even the most traditional of criminal affairs tend to go better when *mafiosi* from different territories cooperate: rustling cattle, hiding fugitives, borrowing killers from one another, and so on. Nevertheless, the new businesses of the mafias' economic miracle made the rewards of coordination even greater. The Calabrian stretch of the Motorway of the Sun is an obvious example, cutting as it did through numerous 'ndrangheta fiefs along the Tyrrhenian coast. As one senior *Carabiniere* observed in 1970: 'There is always someone who rebels against the monopoly held by some *cosche*, and who then goes and puts dynamite in a cement mixer, under a digger, or in a truck.'

Conflict like this is costly for everyone concerned. So greater cooperation between the rival criminal clans can bring big rewards. The cry for unity that went up at Montalto was one symptom of that new need. And unity, whatever form it actually took, also required more concentrated forms of power. The authority wielded by the triumvirs was a symptom of a drive for greater centralisation. Mommo Piromalli is a good example. In the 1970s, his mighty clan took 55 per cent of the earth-moving and transport subcontracts spun off from a new wave of construction on the plain of Gioia Tauro; the rest went to keep less powerful groups on adjacent territories fed.

Cosa Nostra was undergoing similar changes, a similar distillation of power. As we have already seen, in 1969 the Sicilian mafia created a triumvirate of its own to rebuild the organisation following the dramas of the 1960s. In 1974, the triumvirate was superseded by a full Commission, which was a much more powerful body than the one dissolved in 1963. It was now a direct manifestation of the power of the sixteen or so mightiest bosses in the province of Palermo. Hence the Sicilian Honoured Society underwent a top-down restructuring. Entire Families that had proved troublesome during the early 1960s were disbanded, and their cadres absorbed into neighbouring *cosche*. When a representative was arrested or killed, the Commission reserved the right to impose a temporary replacement, a 'regent', as he was termed.

Yet there is a lethal paradox at the heart of the drive for greater criminal unity in the 1960s and 1970s. For when power became concentrated in fewer hands, then it also brought the risk of greater violence when unity broke down. Mafia history was now caught in a terrible double bind. Criminal organisations had more reasons to negotiate and pool their resources. But greater unity meant that when mafia infighting did explode—as it inevitably would—then the blood-letting would be on a much bigger scale. Where once there had been local squabbles, now there would be all-out conflict. The Italian underworld's intensified peace-making activity—its appeals for unity, its summits, its rules, its governing bodies, its Machiavellian politics of the marital bed—actually served to create the conditions for war. And war became all the more likely because Italy itself was descending into the worst civil strife it had seen since the fall of Fascism. As the 1960s gave way to the 1970s, growing political violence in Italian society helped accelerate the approach of a mafia hecatomb.

48

MAFIOSI ON THE BARRICADES

IN THE LATE 1960S, ITALY ENTERED AN AGE OF POLITICAL TURBULENCE. IT ALL BEGAN IN the autumn of 1967 with the birth of an anti-authoritarian, counter-cultural student movement; a series of occupations of university buildings followed. The protests gained pace in 1968 with a wave of working-class action that culminated in the so-called 'hot autumn' of 1969. There were wildcat strikes, mass meetings, pickets and street demonstrations. New groups of Marxist revolutionaries sprang up to guide the struggle, convinced that—from Vietnam, to South America, to Europe—the Revolution was just around the corner. Agitation on all fronts continued into the early 1970s.

The most sinister response to the new climate of militancy came on the afternoon of 12 December 1969: a terrorist bomb placed in a bank in piazza Fontana, a stone's throw from Milan Cathedral, killed sixteen people and wounded eighty-eight more. Crude police attempts to blame anarchists for the massacre unravelled, but not before one anarchist suspect, Giuseppe Pinelli, had inexplicably fallen to his death from a fourth-floor window in police headquarters. (This was the 'accidental death of an anarchist' on which Dario Fo's famous play is based.) Italy's establishment showed a marked reluctance to dig for the truth about who planted the bomb in piazza Fontana. What remained was the widespread and almost certainly justified suspicion that neo-Fascists linked to the secret services were responsible. This was the 'strategy of tension': an attempt to create a climate of fear that would draw Italian society away from democracy and back towards authoritarianism.

A year later, Junio Valerio Borghese, a recalcitrant Fascist with friends in the military and secret services, mounted an attempted coup d'état in Rome.

The putsch was a flop in the end, but Italians did not even get to hear about it for months: there were suspicions of a secret-service cover-up.

The strategy of tension produced further outrages later in the decade. In May 1974, in Brescia's piazza della Loggia, a bomb was detonated during a demonstration against right-wing terrorism: eight people were killed. Eighty-five people were murdered by a massive bomb placed in the second-class waiting room of Bologna station in August 1980. A familiar sequence of smokescreens and artfully laid false trails ensued. Many in Italy were convinced that these were state massacres, and the credibility of Italy's institutions suffered enduring damage as a result.

In the South, the most shocking result of this dangerous destabilisation of Italian society came in July 1970 when the city of Reggio Calabria rose in revolt. Demonstrations led to police charges, which brought barricades and Molotov cocktails, which in turn provoked gunfire. A few days after the revolt broke out, a train derailed just outside Gioia Tauro station, killing six passengers. There were strong suspicions that a bomb had caused the accident, and troops were sent to guard Calabrian railways. Back in Reggio, there were dynamite attacks on the transport infrastructure and occupations of public buildings. No less than eight months of street fighting were only brought to an end when tanks rumbled along the seafront.

Reggio Calabria erupts. In 1970, an urban uprising marked a turning point in 'ndrangheta history. The revolt was eventually quelled by tanks.

The cause of all the violence was the decision that Reggio would *not* be the administrative headquarters of the new regional government of Calabria. People in Reggio were convinced that politicians from the other two major Calabrian cities, Catanzaro and Cosenza, had formed a devious pact to divide out the prizes of regional government between themselves. At a superficial level, what this meant was that the inhabitants of three of Italy's poorest cities were tussling for the thousands of public-sector jobs that would come with the status of Calabrian capital. But the causes of the Reggio revolt went much deeper than that. Beset by chronic unemployment and a housing crisis that had lasted for generations, Reggio's population had staged a mass rejection of their political representatives. National party leaders were dismayed and baffled by the uprising, which undoubtedly enjoyed widespread local support. It was led first by local dissidents within the Christian Democrat party, and then by a Committee of Action under a rabble-rouser from the Movimento Sociale Italiano, the neo-Fascist party.

Recent testimonies from Calabrian *mafiosi* who have turned state's evidence strongly suggest that there was a criminal subplot to the story of the 1970 Reggio revolt. In the summer and autumn of the year before, Junio Valerio Borghese paid a series of provocative visits to Reggio in the run-up to the coup that he would mount in Rome in 1970. On 27 October 1969, he organised a rally that ended in a riot after a small bomb destroyed a Fascist eagle that dated back to Mussolini's first visit to the city. It later emerged that neo-Fascists themselves had planted the charge as a pretext for the disturbances. It seems that Borghese established contacts with 'ndrangheta leaders at around this time. Some sort of deal between the 'ndrangheta and Junio Valerio Borghese's movement may have been discussed at the 'mushroom-picking' summit at Montalto, which happened the day before the October rally. Sicilian *mafiosi* have also reported discussions with Borghese in the lead-up to his failed putsch.

We do not know whether there was an understanding between Borghese and the Calabrian mafia. What we do know for certain is that *'ndranghetisti* helped man the barricades in Reggio; that *'ndranghetisti* supplied guns and dynamite to the revolt's Committee of Action; and that it was *'ndranghetisti* who provided the explosives used by Fascist terrorists to derail the train near Gioia Tauro. The 'ndrangheta, therefore, had added its weight to the strategy of tension.

But what on earth did *'ndranghetisti* have to gain by allying themselves with Fascists, or indeed with the Reggio revolt? The first thing is that they too had reason to protest about the fact that the privilege of being regional capital was awarded to another, less mafia-infested, city. Several other aspects of this profoundly murky affair seem certain. In the first place, the revolt gave the 'ndrangheta a chance to discredit the police, which had recently stepped up its activity against organised crime. That said, support for the revolt involved only one segment of the 'ndrangheta in Reggio Calabria, whereas outside the city bosses like the old criminal patriarch don 'Ntoni Macrì wanted nothing to do with Borghese. Quite sensibly, rather than the highly risky and uncertain project of plotting an insurgency to bring authoritarian politicians to power, most *'ndranghetisti* preferred the humdrum and much more lucrative business of doing deals with corrupt politicians who already *had* power. What is more, where there *were* contacts between gangsters and right-wing insurrectionaries, they tended to be about one of the few things the two parties genuinely had in common: weaponry. Quite how far beyond this basic convergence of interests the contacts went is unclear. There is much else to this story that is still cloaked in mystery. In subsequent years, some *'ndranghetisti* undoubtedly moved in the same circles as Fascist subversives and their friends in the secret services. However, the main lines of 'ndrangheta history moved along a rather more familiar pathway following the events in Reggio in 1970.

The Reggio revolt is a lesson in how unstable a political system based on patronage, faction politics and mafia influence can be. Eruptions of popular anger are always a possibility, because there are never enough favours to go round.

The national government's response to the Reggio revolt was to increase the supply of favours through a massive programme of investment: the 'Colombo package', named after the Prime Minister of the day. The centrepiece of the Colombo package was a gargantuan new steelworks to be situated on the Tyrrhenian coast at Gioia Tauro.

In the end, as the economic crisis of the 1970s unfolded, the Colombo package would be cut down in size. The steel plant would never actually be completed—a crash in steel prices saw to that. Subsequent plans for a coal-fired power station also failed to materialise. Eventually, the site was transformed into a vast container port—the biggest in the Mediterranean—which opened in 1994. The Piromalli family estate sits on a ridge overlooking both the container port and the cemetery situated next to it: the symbolism is lost on no one.

'ndranghetisti like the Piromallis could not have dreamed of a better outcome to the crisis of 1970: a seemingly permanent building site, right in the middle of one of the most mafia-dominated areas in the whole of Calabria. When the Colombo package was announced, the chief cudgels of the plain of Gioia Tauro scrambled to gather up diggers, cement mixers and

dumper trucks faster than toddlers let loose in a toyshop. The frenzied grab at the contracts and subcontracts generated by the Colombo package would be one of the major causes of what has become known as Calabria's First 'Ndrangheta War.

The First 'Ndrangheta War had other causes too. One of them was the growth of the third big sector of the mafias' economic miracle: after construction and cigarette trafficking came kidnapping.

49

THE KIDNAPPING INDUSTRY

UP AND DOWN ITALY, AROUND 650 CITIZENS WERE KIDNAPPED BY CRIMINALS IN THE 1970s and 1980s. Some of the most famous names in the country became victims, like the singer-songwriter Fabrizio De André, and no less than three members of the Bulgari jewellery dynasty. Of the untold billions of lire paid in ransoms, only the tiny proportion of eight billion (very roughly $37 million in 2011 values) were ever recovered, despite precautions like marking or microfilming banknotes. No wonder that the phrase 'the kidnapping industry' became a journalistic cliché.

From the early 1970s, the kidnapping industry brought organised crime even more riches. Yet it also made the tensions in the whole Italian underworld much more volatile. The lines of cause and effect between the newly profitable business of kidnapping and the risks of mob warfare were not the same in Calabria and Sicily. The 'ndrangheta and Cosa Nostra had very different attitudes to the art of taking hostages. As Antonino Calderone, a Sicilian *mafioso*, explained in 1992:

> The [Sicilian] mafia doesn't run prostitution, because it's a dirty business. Can you imagine a Man of Honour living as a pimp, an exploiter of women? Maybe in America *mafiosi* have got involved in this business . . . But in Sicily the mafia just does not do it, full stop.
>
> Now kidnapping is another matter. Cosa Nostra has no internal rule against abductions. Deep down inside, a Man of Honour accepts kidnapping. He does not view it as something dirty like prostitution.

Sicilian *mafiosi* have a century and a half of collective kidnapping experience; they have snatched away men, women and children since their Honoured Society began. So they know that taking hostages can have many meanings and many motives. A big ransom is always appreciated, but sometimes it is only part of the story. A more important consideration may be the desire to make friends.

To make friends through kidnapping means deploying a role-playing game. The first role is the bad guy: the screaming blackmailer who peremptorily threatens to make your children disappear unless you hand over a fortune. The second role is the mediator who promises to reason with the kidnappers, the quietly spoken friend who can negotiate a reduction in the ransom, get your loved ones home safe and, of course, make sure you are protected from any future dangers.

Both of these roles are played by *mafiosi*. Whether through kidnapping or through extortion (which often works by the same role-playing rules), the mafia has a genius for making itself into *both* your greatest dread *and* the best friend you could hope for in the circumstances. As Machiavelli wrote, 'Men who are well treated by one whom they expected to treat them ill, feel the more beholden to their benefactor.' By simple means like these, the Honoured Society of Sicily has infiltrated the island's ruling class since the mid-nineteenth century. The term 'Stockholm syndrome'—used to describe cases in which kidnap victims form a strong bond with their kidnappers—was only invented in 1973. But for more than a century before that date it could quite easily have applied to large sections of the Sicilian elite.

However, kidnapping tends to be a messy crime. A large team of accomplices is often needed. Hostages have to be restrained, hidden and fed, perhaps for long stretches of time. Those victims are by definition wealthy and, like as not, powerful too—the sort of people whose disappearance embarrasses politicians, leading to loud anti-crime rhetoric and the deployment of large numbers of police. Any mafia boss who pulls off a big kidnapping and does not compensate other bosses for the inconvenience is likely to make himself very unpopular. Any ordinary criminal with an atom of sense knows that carrying out an abduction without the mafia's permission is suicide. In the 1970s, a *mafioso* in prison heard tell that another inmate without mafia connections was thinking about kidnapping someone; his response was simply to mutter *chistu 'avi a moriri*: 'this bloke must die'. The would-be kidnapper was shot dead a week after he was released.

For all these reasons, kidnapping has had its seasons in Sicily: short phases when it has been frequent, and longer periods when it has been rare. For example, *mafiosi*—or bandits who were working for them willy-nilly—took many Sicilian dignitaries hostage in the decade and a half following

Italian unification in 1860. In 1876, the kidnapping of an English sulphur merchant helped trigger a major crackdown on organised crime on the island. Many bandits were betrayed by their mafia protectors and shot down. Kidnapping largely fell out of favour thereafter: a sure indicator that the mafia had reached an accommodation with its friends in the island's ruling class.

So kidnappings, whether they are on the increase or in decline, may also tell us that historically significant change is under way in the Sicilian underworld. That is particularly true of the early 1970s. Most of the bosses released from prison following the trials of the late 1960s—the trials relating to the events of the First Mafia War—were very hard up. As Antonino Calderone, a Man of Honour who knew them all, later recalled:

> Mark my words. When I say that there was no money around at that time, that the mafia didn't have any money, I'm not just saying it by way of exaggeration. After the arrests of 1962–63, after all the men who'd been sent into forced resettlement or who'd spent time in prison, and after the Catanzaro trial in 1968, the money was gone. It had all been spent on lawyers, prison and stuff like that . . . So when they started being released, around 1968, Cosa Nostra's bosses were all skint. Maybe Luciano Liggio had the odd house or property, but he wasn't going to sell. I can tell you that 'Shorty' Riina cried when he told me that his mother couldn't come and see him in prison, in 1966 or 1967, because she couldn't afford the train ticket. So in 1971 or thereabouts a series of kidnappings was organised.

The authors of the new wave of kidnappings were from Corleone, a town in the hinterland some fifty-five kilometres by road from Palermo. We have already had intermittent glimpses of the Corleone Family in mafia history. Kidnapping would turn them into its protagonists. Luciano Liggio began as a petty criminal whose skill with a gun endeared him to the town's boss, Dr Michele Navarra. In 1958 Liggio machine-gunned Navarra to death, triggering a violent fissure in the Family that would make Corleone notorious: 'Tombstone', the press dubbed the town. Eventually Liggio emerged triumphant, thanks in good measure to his fierce young lieutenants, Totò 'Shorty' Riina and Bernardo 'the Tractor' Provenzano. The *corleonesi* had a close working relationship with Vito Ciancimino, the Christian Democrat Young Turk who was instrumental in the sack of Palermo in the early 1960s. Liggio's power base was such that, when Cosa Nostra was reconstituted in 1969, he was one of the triumvirs entrusted with rebuilding the organisation's structure. Since Liggio was often away from Sicily, his place at the triumvirate's meetings, and later on the Commission, was often taken by 'Shorty' Riina, a man who would develop into the most powerful and violent Sicilian mafia boss of all time.

The *corleonesi* first attempted to remedy their shortage of cash on 8 June 1971, when a twenty-eight-year-old man, who had just pulled up outside his home after buying a chilled cake, was grabbed by five assailants and bundled into a car; passers-by were threatened with pistols. Suddenly, bourgeois Palermitans began going out less and wondering who would be taken next. The reason for their fears was that the victim was Pino Vassallo, the son of the notorious 'Concrete King' don Ciccio Vassallo—the very man who had built many of the apartment blocks where much of the Palermitan bourgeoisie now lived. Vassallo had strolled unscathed through all the battles of the 1960s. Now, it seemed, his protection had failed him.

A mafia-backed businessman like the 'Concrete King' (or his son, for that matter) was the perfect hostage. Yet at the same time, abducting him was also a potentially catastrophic move. On the one hand, the crimes that lay behind the Vassallo fortune guaranteed that the whole affair would be handled with discretion. Don Ciccio was never likely to try and involve the police. A ransom estimated at between 150 million and 400 million lire ($1.6 million–$4.3 million in 2011 values) was duly paid, and Pino Vassallo was released. But on the other hand, kidnapping someone protected by another boss was flagrantly offensive. To snatch away someone else's meal ticket was tantamount to a declaration of war. If fighting did not break out after the Vassallo abduction, it may have been because his protection was in abeyance—in that the *mafiosi* closest to him had been the La Barbera brothers, who were the losers in the First Mafia War.

When they received the ransom from the Vassallo kidnapping, Liggio and his boys demonstrated impeccable mafia manners in the way they distributed it equally between the neediest Families in the province of Palermo. So the Vassallo operation served two peaceful purposes: it redistributed wealth, and it cemented the new balance of power that had emerged after the turmoil of the 1960s. But soon the issue of kidnapping would become much more divisive.

After organising the Vassallo kidnapping, the *corleonesi* went on to mount unauthorised operations—such as the August 1972 abduction of Luciano Cassina, the son of the entrepreneur whose contracts to maintain the city's drains and roads made him Palermo's biggest taxpayer. Curiously, the man who posed as a 'friend' to help the Cassina family negotiate with the kidnappers was a priest, Agostino Coppola, who was a nephew of Frank 'Three Fingers' Coppola and close to Luciano Liggio's allies in the Partinico Family

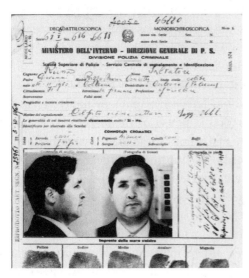

Salvatore 'Shorty' Riina in 1970. The man destined to exercise a dictatorial power over Cosa Nostra would be on the run from the law for the next twenty-three years.

of Cosa Nostra. This time, the *corleonesi* kept the profits from these escapades for themselves.

In mafia terms, there could be little justification for how the *corleonesi* were behaving. Although they were deceitful and evasive when talking to other *mafiosi* about what was going on, it was nonetheless clear that they were mounting a challenge to their rivals' authority that was both calculated and flagrant. In 1972 the other two members of the triumvirate, Tano Badalamenti and Stefano Bontate, were both temporarily behind bars, and therefore less able to react to the provocation. Just as importantly, even if they had wanted to take measures against the *corleonesi*, they would have had trouble finding them. Luciano Liggio had gone on the run again in the summer of 1969. His two lieutenants, Totò 'Shorty' Riina and Bernardo 'the Tractor' Provenzano, had been in hiding since 1969 and 1963 respectively.

The years 1974–5 were politically important for Cosa Nostra. In 1974, after Stefano Bontate's release from prison, the triumvirate that had presided over the organisation in the province of Palermo since 1969 was superseded by a full Commission, largely comprising Bontate allies; Tano Badalamenti sat at the head of the table as provincial representative. Then, in February 1975, a villa set in the central Sicilian countryside near the lofty city of Enna hosted the first meeting of an entirely new body, the Regional Commission, or Region. The Region comprised six bosses representing the six most mafia-infested provinces of Sicily: Palermo, Trapani, Agrigento, Caltanissetta, Enna and Catania. In effect, the mafia Commissions in these six provinces were each sending a delegate to sit on an island-wide coordinating committee for mafia crime. The Region's authority over island-wide mafia affairs was relatively limited, as was symbolised by the fact that the boss chosen to preside over its meetings took the title of 'secretary' rather than *capo*.

The strategic brains behind the Region belonged to Pippo Calderone, whose younger brother Antonino would later turn state's evidence, giving us a priceless insight into this remarkable phase of mafia history. Pippo Calderone, a businessman and Man of Honour from the eastern Sicilian city of Catania, even went to the trouble of drafting a constitution for the new body. The most important article in that constitution, and the first item on the agenda at the Region's first meeting, was an island-wide kidnapping ban—on pain of death. The reasons for the ban seemed wise. Kidnappings might be lucrative in the short term, but made the mafia unpopular with civilians. More importantly, they drew down more police pressure—roadblocks and the like—that made life particularly difficult for *mafiosi* who were in hiding from the law. So it was hard for any of the bosses at the Region's first meeting to disagree with such a statesmanlike measure, and six hands were duly raised to approve it. However, as always in mafia affairs, the kidnapping embargo was a tactical move as well as a practical one: it was aimed at the *corleonesi*, and intended to isolate them within Cosa Nostra. The *corleonesi*, Liggio, Riina and Provenzano, took note.

On 17 July 1975, only a few months after that first meeting of the Region, a little old man was driving an Alfa Romeo 2000 through the crackling heat of a Sicilian summer afternoon. His destination was Salemi, a town clustered round a Norman fortress on a hill in the province of Trapani. But he never reached it: by a petrol pump just outside town, he found the road in front of him blocked by ten men armed with machine guns. As he was being forced out and bundled into another car, the bus from Trapani arrived. Two of the snatch team flagged down the terrified driver and climbed aboard the bus. Silently they then showed their weapons to the passengers. Words were superfluous: nothing had happened, and nobody had seen it happen.

The *corleonesi* had struck again, showing their contempt for the manoeuvres against them in the Region. Moreover, they had struck at a more illustrious victim than ever before. The old man in the Alfa Romeo was Luigi Corleo, a tax farmer. In Sicily, tax collection was privatised and contracted out. Since the 1950s, Corleo's son-in-law, Nino Salvo, had turned the family tax-collecting business into a vast machine for ripping off Sicilian taxpayers. Together with his cousin, Ignazio, Nino Salvo ran a company that now had a near monopoly on revenue gathering, and took a scandalous 10 per cent commission. In effect, one lire in every ten that Sicilians paid in tax went straight into the pockets of the Salvo cousins. Not only that, but the

Salvos managed to engineer a two- or three-month time-lag between harvesting the taxes and handing them over to the state—two or three months in which these huge sums attracted very favourable interest. The pharaonic profits of the Salvos' legalised swindle were invested in art (Van Gogh and Matisse, apparently), hotels, land, and in the political support network needed to ensure that the Sicilian Regional Assembly continued to rubber-stamp the tax-collecting franchise. Both Salvo cousins were also Men of Honour, and both were very close to two members of the triumvirate: Tano Badalamenti and Stefano Bontate, the 'Prince of Villagrazia'. In other words, by kidnapping Luigi Corleo, the *corleonesi* had taken aim at the very heart of economic, political and criminal power in Sicily. Antonino Calderone would later explain that the Corleo kidnapping was 'an extremely serious matter that created a huge shock in Cosa Nostra'. The ransom demand was shocking too: 20 billion lire (not far off $135 million in 2011 values).

The Corleo kidnapping was initially a grave embarrassment for Badalamenti and Bontate, and quickly become an utter humiliation. Despite sowing the countryside around Salemi with corpses, Badalamenti and Bontate failed to either free the hostage, or find any evidence in support of their suspicion that the *corleonesi* were responsible. To cap it all, old man Corleo died while he was still in captivity, probably from a heart attack. Yet Badalamenti and Bontate proved unable even to recover the body.

The *corleonesi* may not have bagged the ransom they had hoped for, but they did gain something that in the long-term would prove far more valuable: a high-profile demonstration that Badalamenti and Bontate had not mastered the basics of territorial control. Plainly, the *corleonesi* could ignore Cosa Nostra's lawmakers with impunity. Across Sicily, other mafia bosses heard the rumours and started to draw conclusions.

The brief sequence of high-profile kidnappings in Sicily coincided with one more important development: a new generation of leader took control in Corleone. Luciano Liggio was gradually side-lined by his deputy, Totò 'Shorty' Riina, who was ably assisted by Bernardo 'the Tractor' Provenzano. Riina it was who directed operations for the Cassina and Corleo kidnappings.

Meanwhile Liggio was still very busy, but in places where Cosa Nostra's rules against kidnapping did not apply. In July 1971 he moved to Milan, where he could orchestrate the hijacking of as many hostages as he liked. Furthermore, in Milan, there were many more rich people available to abduct. Kidnapping in Sicily was more politically significant than it was lucrative or frequent. Between 1960 and 1978, there were only nineteen abductions in Sicily, a very small proportion of the terrifying 329 in Italy as a whole. The word inside Cosa Nostra was that Liggio grew fantastically rich on the off-island trade in captives, and that he was working with the organisation that was rapidly becoming the Italian underworld's kidnapping specialist: the 'ndrangheta.

Cosa Nostra and the camorra were involved in kidnapping to a comparatively limited extent. Cosa Nostra, as we have seen, had severe constitutional reservations about harbouring captives on its own manor. *Camorristi* in the early 1970s performed a number of abductions, but kidnapping did not become a typical camorra crime, probably because they did not have the colonies in the North that would enable them to create a national network for hostage-taking.

To anyone who bothered to read the crime pages of the Calabrian dailies, a pattern of kidnappings had already established itself in the region in the late 1960s. But the victims were all local figures, the ransom demands relatively small, and the periods of captivity short. Things began to change in December 1972 with the abduction of Pietro Torielli, the son of a banker from Vigevano in the northern region of Lombardy. Luciano Liggio and the 'ndrangheta are thought to have been involved. From now on, kidnapping would be a nationwide business for Calabrian organised crime.

Corleonese kidnap king. Sicilian mafia boss Luciano Liggio ran kidnapping operations in northern Italy with his friends in the 'ndrangheta.

There were several reasons why kidnapping became a favourite business for the 'ndrangheta. It had the great advantage of being cheap to organise, for one thing. The ransoms it rendered often served as seed capital for more investment-intensive initiatives, like construction or wholesale narcotics dealing. No mafia had a network of colonies in the North to match the 'ndrangheta's. Nor did any other mafia have Aspromonte. The mountain massif at the very tip of the Italian peninsula had long been a reliable refuge for fugitives. Its crags, its grottoes and its wooded gorges became internationally notorious as hiding places for kidnap victims. Captives would report hearing the same distant church bells from their prisons. A bronze statue of Christ on the cross, situated among the beeches and firs of the Zervò plain above Platì, became a kind of post-box where ransoms would often be deposited. For years the statue had a single large bullet hole in its chest. On Aspromonte the 'ndrangheta's reign of fear and complicity was so complete that the organisation could be confident of keeping hostages almost indefinitely. More than one escaped victim turned to the first passer-by they encountered for help, only to be led back to his kidnappers. The poor 'ndrangheta-controlled mountain villages began to live off the trickle-down profits of kidnapping. Down on the Ionian coast, Bovalino had an entire new quarter known locally as 'Paul Getty'—after the famous hostage whose abduction first propelled the 'ndrangheta to the forefront of the kidnapping industry.

In central Rome, in the early hours of 10 July 1973, John Paul Getty III—the sixteen-year-old, ginger-haired, hippy grandson of American oil billionaire Jean Paul Getty—was bundled into a car, chloroformed and driven away. After an agonising wait, the kidnappers finally communicated their demands in a collage of letters cut out from magazines: ten billion lire, or around $17 million at the time. The eighty-one-year-old Jean Paul Getty, a notoriously reclusive and avaricious man, refused to negotiate: 'I have fourteen grandchildren, and if I pay a penny of ransom, I'll have fourteen kidnapped grandchildren.'

The stalemate dragged on until 20 October when the boy's captors sliced off his right ear, dropped it in a Band Aid packet full of embalming fluid, and mailed it to the offices of the Roman daily newspaper, *Il Messaggero*. The gruesome package included a note promising that the rest of him would 'arrive in tiny pieces' if the ransom were not paid. To increase the Getty family's agony further, the ear was held up by a postal strike and did not arrive for nearly three weeks. The savage mutilation had the desired effect: a month later a ransom amounting to two billion lire ($3,200,000)—a fifth of the sum originally demanded—was deposited with a man wearing a balaclava helmet standing in a pull-off area on the highway.

Kidnap victim. John Paul Getty III
was taken in July 1973. His 'ndrangheta
captors cut off his ear before releasing him.

John Paul Getty was released. But the psychological impact of his ordeal was profound. He was fragile and very young: he had spent his seventeenth birthday in captivity. The trauma seems to have tipped him into drug and alcohol addiction. In 1983 his liver failed, precipitating a stroke that caused blindness and near total paralysis.

It was never proved beyond all doubt that Luciano Liggio masterminded the Getty kidnapping. Nor, for that matter, was anybody ever convicted apart from a handful of small-time crooks—the hired hands rather than the orchestrators. But one thing is certain nonetheless: Getty was held in the mountains of Calabria, and his captors were Luciano Liggio's friends in the 'ndrangheta. And once Luciano Liggio was removed from the scene (he was recaptured in 1974 and never freed again), the 'ndrangheta showed that it was more than capable of running highly lucrative kidnapping schemes on its own.

Kidnapping proved less divisive in the 'ndrangheta than it did in Cosa Nostra. But the new criminal industry did attract media and police attention to Calabria, and therefore controversy within the local underworld. It seems that the *tarantella* dancer and triumvirate member, don 'Ntoni Macrì, made his misgivings about having hostages on his territory known to the other bosses not long after the Getty kidnapping. These misgivings further increased the rivalries between the 'ndrangheta factions that were trying to get their hands on the Colombo package.

Gangsters from the South and Sicily were by no means the only people to profit from the wave of abductions across the country in the 1970s and

1980s. For example, bandits from the island of Sardinia, some of the most active of them operating off-base in Tuscany, had their own tradition of hostage-taking and were particularly active in the 1970s. Many ordinary delinquents latched on to the idea that taking a hostage or two was a short cut to riches. Kidnapping became a criminal craze that was profoundly damaging to Italy's weakened social fabric.

Luigi Ballinari, a drunken, small-time cigarette smuggler of Swiss nationality, recalled the buzz in prison in 1974: 'Our conversations always came back to the crime of the moment, which was now a fashion in Italy: extorting money by kidnapping. It was everyone's dream! We fantasised, we organised, we analysed the mistakes that other kidnappers had made.'

Soon after being released, Ballinari became involved in one of the most atrocious kidnappings of the era. Cristina Mazzotti, nineteen-year-old daughter of an entrepreneur from near Como, on the Swiss border, was taken on 26 June 1975. Her captors stripped, blindfolded and manacled her, blocked her ears, and lowered her into a tiny space below a garage floor. There she was made to consume sleeping pills dissolved in fruit juice for more than two weeks during negotiations with her parents. The plan—one common to many improvised kidnapping groups in the North and centre of Italy—was to sell the hostage on to the real experts: the 'ndrangheta. But in this case, before Cristina could be bartered and sent to a new prison on Aspromonte, her body slowly shut down under the cumulative effect of the drugs; she was loaded into a car boot and buried in a rubbish dump. Her parents, unaware that she was already dead, paid a ransom of 1.05 billion lire ($6.9 million in 2011 values).

Ballinari was later caught trying to launder some of the profits from Cristina's abduction. By the time he buckled under interrogation, and told the whole story, Cristina's body was so decomposed that it proved hard to tell whether she had actually been dead when she was interred.

The horrors of the kidnapping industry were legion. The captives on Aspromonte were particularly badly treated. Shackled and fed on scraps, they were not allowed to wash and their clothes were never changed. In intercepted phone conversations, their 'ndrangheta captors were heard referring in code to the prisoners as 'pigs'. The longest kidnapping was that of teenage student Carlo Celadon from near Vicenza, who was snatched in his own home in 1988. Carlo was kept for a mind-boggling 828 days in a rat-infested grotto scattered with his own excrement. With three chains round his neck, he was subject to constant threats—and to beatings if he dared cry or pray. When he was released, his father commented that he looked like the inmate of a Nazi concentration camp. Carlo's comment on his ordeal was harrowing: 'I asked, I begged my jailers to cut my ear off. I was totally destroyed, I had lost all hope.'

In Italy as a whole, between 1969 and 1988, seventy-one people vanished and were never seen alive again; it is thought that in roughly half those cases, a ransom was paid. In 1981 Giovanni Palombini, an eighty-year-old coffee entrepreneur, was kidnapped by a Roman gang who probably intended to pass him on to the 'ndrangheta. He managed to escape, but was so disorientated that when he knocked on the door of a villa to ask for help, it turned out to be his kidnappers' hideout. He was given a glass of champagne, and then executed. His body was thrown in a freezer so that it could be pulled out for the photographs his family wanted to see to be certain that he was still alive.

Children were not spared: there were twenty-two abductions of children, some no more than babes in arms. Marco Fiora was only seven years old when 'ndranghetisti grabbed him in Turin in March 1987. His ordeal lasted a year and a half, during which time he was kept chained up like a dog in an Aspromonte hideaway. His captors did their best to brainwash him, telling him that his parents did not want to pay the ransom because they did not love him. It seems that the long delay was due to the fact that the 'ndrangheta's spies had greatly overestimated how rich Marco's father was, and refused to believe his claims that he could not afford the ransom. Marco was skeletal when he was released near Ciminà, and his legs were so atrophied that he could barely walk. He knocked on a few doors, but the inhabitants refused to open. So he just sat down by the roadside until a patrol of *Carabinieri* happened upon him. His first words to his mother were, 'You aren't my mummy. Go away. I don't want to see you.'

Some children fared even worse. A little girl of eleven from the shores of Lake Garda, Marzia Savio, was taken in January 1982. Her captor turned out not to be a gangster, but just the local sausage butcher who thought he had found a neat way to make some quick money. He strangled Marzia, probably while he was trying to restrain her, and then cut her into pieces that he scattered from a flyover.

Kidnapping became so common that it acquired its own rituals in the news bulletins and crime pages. The victims' families giving anguished press conferences. Or, conversely, desperately attempting to shun the limelight and avoid provoking whoever was holding their father, their son, their daughter. There was the long, anguished wait for the kidnappers to make known the ransom demands. There were hoax calls from ghoulish pranksters.

Kidnapping is a crime that creates and spreads mistrust. Many families rightly suspected that friends and employees had leaked information to the criminals. Finding reliable lines of communication and intermediaries was often agonising. The family of Carlo Celadon, the young man who was held for a record 828 days, alleged that the lawyer they delegated to transport the ransom had pocketed a proportion of it. (He was convicted of the crime but later benefited from an amnesty before his appeal.) The 'ndrangheta sometimes seemed to know more about how much their hostages earned than did the tax man. For that reason, the media tended to cast suspicion over the finances of even the most honest victims. Hostages' families were often warned against going to the police. And the police were often frustrated by families' silence: some had the indignity of being arrested for withholding information after seeing their loved ones freed.

The poison of mistrust leaked into the public domain. Each high-profile abduction triggered a vitriolic and, for a long time, entirely inconclusive debate between journalists, politicians and law-enforcement officials. There were those who favoured the hard line on kidnapping: refusing to pay ransoms, freezing victims' assets, and the like. Ranged against them were those who thought the 'soft line' (i.e., negotiation) was the only humane and practical option. Some of the more pugnacious entrepreneurs of the North underwent weapons training. The situation became so bad that, in 1978, one magistrate discovered that some wealthy families were taking out special insurance policies so that they would have enough money for a ransom when the masked bandits paid their seemingly inevitable visit. Wealthy citizens—the class of person who, in other Western democracies, would almost automatically be loyal to the powers that be—were angry, alienated and afraid.

There is a photo that makes for an intriguing memento of that terrible era of fear and mistrust. It shows a self-confident young Milanese construction entrepreneur leaning back in a chair. His serious expression shows no hint of the permanent matinée idol smile that would later become his worldwide trademark. He has just removed a pair of aviator sunglasses, and the flared trousers of his suit reveal the trendy ankle boots on his feet. But it is not his dress and accessories that really make the photo symptomatic of the 1970s. Rather it is the holstered pistol that sits on his desk. The entrepreneur's name is Silvio Berlusconi, and around the time the photo was taken, he had the well-grounded dread of kidnapping that was common to many wealthy Italians. However Berlusconi's business factotum, a Sicilian banker called Marcello Dell'Utri, found a more effective way to calm these fears than a pistol in a desk drawer. From 1974 to 1976, Vittorio Mangano, a *mafioso* from Palermo, took a not terribly clearly defined job (groom? major domo? factor?) at Berlusconi's newly acquired villa at Arcore. The Italian courts have recently ascertained that, in reality, Mangano was a guarantee of Cosa Nostra's protection against kidnapping. Moreover, he was also there with the intention of making friends. Or, in the language of a judge's ruling, Mangano was part of a 'complex strategy destined to make an approach

In the 1970s, many wealthy people armed themselves as a defence against mafia kidnappers. Here a young Berlusconi is pictured with a gun on his desk (circled).

to the entrepreneur Berlusconi and link him more closely to the criminal organisation'.

Marcello Dell'Utri has been convicted of a long-standing collaboration with Cosa Nostra that included recommending Vittorio Mangano's services to Berlusconi. He still denies the charges, which he says are the result of a judicial plot against him. The case has gone to the Supreme Court.

Vittorio Mangano was later sentenced to life for two murders, and died of cancer in 2000. He died like a good *mafioso* should, without shedding any light on the case.

Silvio Berlusconi's own public utterances on the affair have been disturbing, to say the least. For example, he gave his view of the *mafioso* in a radio interview in 2008:

[Mangano] was a person who behaved extremely well with us. Later he had some misadventures in his life that placed him in the hands of a criminal organisation. But heroically . . . despite being so ill, he never invented any lies against me. They let him go home the day before he died. He was dying in prison. So Dell'Utri was right to say that Mangano's behaviour was heroic.

Quite whether the kidnapping season was the beginning of a direct long-term relationship between Berlusconi and the Sicilian mafia is not clear. It should be stressed that Berlusconi has never been charged with anything in relation to the Mangano affair.

Every kidnapping was a clamorous demonstration of the governing institutions' inability to protect life and property. Italy was getting visibly weaker at the very same time that the mafias were getting stronger, richer, more interlinked, and closer to descending into war. The state seemed to have lost its claim to a 'monopoly of legitimate violence', as the jargon of sociology would have it. In the 1970s, while the wave of kidnappings spiralled out of control, a new wave of economic and political troubles brought further discredit on the state.

Italy, like the rest of the developed world, had to face a grave economic crisis following a dramatic hike in crude oil prices in 1973. There ensued a decade of stuttering growth, high unemployment, raging inflation, steepling interest rates and massive public debt. Violent social conflict was on the rise. The trades unions that had been so pugnacious since the 'hot autumn' of 1969 now went on the defensive. As a result, some members of Italy's revolutionary groups lost patience with peaceful forms of militancy; they opted instead to form clandestine armed cells. These terrorists, as ruthless as they were deluded, thought of themselves as a revolutionary vanguard who could hasten the advent of a Communist society by maiming or assassinating strategically chosen targets. Italy had entered its so-called 'Years of Lead' (i.e., years of bullets).

The Red Brigades (or BR) would turn out to be the most dangerous of these groups, and many of their earliest actions were kidnappings. The victims—usually factory managers—would typically be subjected to a 'proletarian trial', and then chained to the factory gates with a placard daubed with a revolutionary slogan round their necks. In the spring of 1974, under the new slogan of 'an attack on the heart of the state', the BR hit the headlines by kidnapping a judge from Genoa. The BR's demands were not met, but the judge was released unharmed.

After a wave of arrests brought a lull in their activities in the middle of the decade, the Red Brigades returned with more terroristic resolve than ever. On 16 March 1978, they brought the country to a standstill by kidnapping the former Prime Minister and leader of the Christian Democrat Party, Aldo Moro. Moro's driver and his entire police escort were murdered in the assault. On 9 May Moro was himself shot dead, and his body was abandoned in a car in the centre of Rome. The BR and other groups continued their murder campaign into the following decade. Many young people, in particular, could not find it within themselves to identify with the authorities in their fight against terrorism: 'Neither with the state, nor with the Red Brigades' was one political slogan of the day. This was the state that would soon have to face up to unprecedented mafia violence. Calabria was to be the first place where war broke out.

50

THE MOST HOLY MOTHER AND THE FIRST 'NDRANGHETA WAR

WHEN EVIDENCE OF ORGANISED CRIME'S VAST NEW WEALTH EMERGED IN THE 1960S and 1970s, many observers claimed that, in both Sicily and Calabria, the traditional mafia was being replaced by a new breed. The mafia was now no longer rural, but urban; it was a 'motorway mafia', rather than a donkey-track mafia; these were gangsters in 'shiny shoes' rather than the muddy-booted peasants of yesteryear. The new model *mafioso*, it was claimed, was a young, aggressive businessman. In particular, he had no time for the quaint, formalistic concerns of the Honoured Societies, or for the antediluvian cult of honour. Backward Calabria was where the transformation appeared to be most marked. Here, even many who took the mafia threat seriously thought that initiation rituals; Osso, Mastrosso, Carcagnosso; and the meeting at the Sanctuary of the Madonna of Polsi were bound to be consigned to the folklore museum—if they hadn't been already.

The De Stefano brothers, Giorgio, Paolo and Giovanni, fitted most people's idea of the emergent gangster-manager. The brothers came from Reggio Calabria, the town that was bigamist don Mico Tripodo's realm. As we have already seen, Tripodo spent much of his time away in Campania, cementing close friendships with the *camorristi* of the Neapolitan hinterland. But a boss can only remain away from his territory for so long before the ground shifts behind him. In don Mico's absence the De Stefanos emerged as a power in their own right.

Giorgio, the oldest of the brothers and the most cunning, was referred to by one 'ndrangheta defector as 'the Comet'—the rising star of Calabrian organised crime. The De Stefanos were the most enthusiastic participants in the Reggio revolt, and the keenest to make friends with Fascist subversives. And they were certainly young: none of them was out of his twenties at the time of the Montalto summit. The triumvirs whose authority the De Stefanos would come to challenge were from an older generation: the *tarantella*-dancing don 'Ntoni Macrì could just about have been their grandfather.

One *'ndranghetista* also remembered the De Stefanos as being educated, at least by the standards of the Calabrian underworld, recalling that: 'Paolo and Giorgio De Stefano attended university for a few years. Giorgio was signed up to do medicine, and I think Paolo studied law.' That education was visible. Pictures of Giorgio ('the Comet') and Paolo, the two oldest and most powerful De Stefano brothers, show men with large, sensitive faces and black hair parted neatly at the side. Their up-to-date, clean-cut image could hardly be more starkly different from the grim physiognomies of the triumvirs: Mico Tripodo and the others all had mean little eyes, cropped hair and sagging, expressionless faces; each seemed to have been assembled from the same old kit of atavistic hoodlum features.

As it turned out, these contrasting faces, and the switch from tradition to modernity that they seemed to make visible, proved to be no guide to the winners and losers who would emerge from the unprecedented criminal

The face of the new 'ndrangheta?
Paolo De Stefano in 1982.

wealth and violence of the 1970s. The simplistic 'modernity versus tradition' template that was used to make sense of the events of the 1970s was just a bad fit with reality. For one thing, the rise of ambitious young thugs like the De Stefanos from within the ranks of the organisation is not a novelty. For another, even in Calabria, there is nothing new about *mafiosi* with middle-class credentials. Nor are the mafias traditional in the sense of being very old. On the contrary, they are as modern as the Italian state.

It is much nearer the mark to say that the 'ndrangheta, like Cosa Nostra, is *traditionalist*, in the sense that it has manufactured its own internal traditions that are functional to the demands of extortion and trafficking. When the 'ndrangheta grew richer, through the construction industry, tobacco smuggling and kidnapping, it did not simply abandon its traditions and embrace modernity. From their origins, Italy's mafias have always *mixed* tradition and modernity. Their response to the new era was to *adapt* the mixture. Or indeed, in the case of the 'ndrangheta, to invent brand-new traditions like the one that is the subject of this chapter: the Most Holy Mother. That newly minted tradition is significant for two reasons. First, it provides evidence of just how many friends the mafias, with their new wealth, were making among the Italian elite. Second, the Most Holy Mother became the trigger of the First 'Ndrangheta War. And to understand it, we need to grasp some subtle but important differences between the 'ndrangheta and Cosa Nostra.

The 'ndrangheta and Cosa Nostra are very similar in that they are both Honoured Societies—Freemasonries of crime. Both organisations are careful about choosing whom they admit to the club. No one with family in the police or magistracy is allowed in. No pimps. No women.

Yet there are also some differences in the way the two select their cadres. 'ndranghetisti tend to come from the same blood families. Cosa Nostra, by contrast, has rules to *prevent* too many brothers being recruited into a single Family, in case they distort the balance of power within it. In some cases, two brothers may even enter *different* Families.

Cosa Nostra tends to monitor aspiring gangsters carefully before they cross the threshold of the organisation, often making a criminal wait until his thirties so that he can prove over the years that he is made of the right stuff. The Calabrian mafia admits many more people. A police report from 1997 estimated that in Sicily there were 5,500 *mafiosi*, or one for every 903 inhabitants. By comparison, there were 6,000 *'ndranghetisti* in Calabria, or one for every 345 citizens. In the most 'ndrangheta-infested province,

Reggio Calabria, there was one affiliate for every 160 inhabitants. In other words, proportionally speaking, the 'ndrangheta admits two and a half times as many members. The male children of a boss are initiated willy-nilly. Some even go through a ritual at birth. But that does not mean that the Calabrian mafia has watered-down membership criteria. Rather it suggests that it does much of the business of monitoring and selecting members *once they are inside*. A winnowing process continues through each 'ndranghetista's entire career. Only the most criminally able of them will rise through the ranks. Young hoods may learn to specialise either in business or in violence.

At this point, it helps to recall the stages of a Calabrian mafioso's career. As he acquires more prestige, he progresses through a hierarchy of status levels. An 'ndranghetista starts off as a *giovane d'onore* ('honoured youth'— someone marked out for admission into the organisation, but who is not yet a member). Through day-by-day service to his superiors—issuing threats and vandalising property as part of extortion demands, collecting protection payments, hiding weapons and stolen goods, ferrying food up to the mountain prisons where hostages are kept—he rises to become a *picciotto* ('lad'), and then on up the ladder through a long list of other ranks.

As we have seen, ranks are called *doti* ('gifts'). Being promoted to a higher gift is referred to as receiving a *fiore* (a 'flower'). The giving of each flower is marked by a ritual. But secrets, rather than gifts, are the true measure of status in the 'ndrangheta. Since it began in the nineteenth century, each 'ndrangheta cell has had a double structure made of sealed compartments: the Minor Society and the Major Society. Younger, less experienced and less trustworthy recruits belong to the Minor Society. Minor Society members are insulated from understanding what goes on in the Major Society to which the more experienced crooks belong. Promotion through the ranks, and from the Minor Society to the Major Society, implies access to more secrets.

As profits rose within the 'ndrangheta in the early 1970s, and tensions increased, so too did the tinkering with these peculiarly complicated protocols. Until the early 1970s, the highest gift that any affiliate of the 'ndrangheta could attain was that of *sgarrista*. Literally, *sgarrista* means something like 'a man who gives offence, or who breaks the rules'. (The terminology, like so much else about the 'ndrangheta, dates back to the nineteenth-century prison system.)

Around 1972–3, some chief cudgels began to create a new, higher gift for themselves: *santista* ('saintist' or 'holy-ist'). With the new status came membership of a secret elite known as the Mamma Santissima ('Most Holy Mother') or Santa for short. In theory, the Mamma Santissima had a very exclusive membership: no more than twenty-four chief cudgels were to be admitted.

Becoming a *santista* involved a new ritual, an upmarket variant of the 'ndran-gheta's existing initiation rites. It also entitled the bearer of this new flower to certain privileges, the most important being the right to join the secret and deviant Masonic brotherhoods that were springing up in 1970s Italy.

The most notorious of the new Masonic groups was Propaganda 2 or P2, a conspiracy of corruption and right-wing subversion that reached right to the heart of the Italian establishment. When, in March 1981, a (probably incomplete) P2 membership list of 962 people was found, it included:

> all the heads of the secret services, 195 officers of the various armed corps of the Republic, among whom were twelve generals of the *Cara-binieri*, five of the Tax Police, twenty-two of the army, four of the air force and eight admirals. There were leading magistrates, a few prefects and Police Chiefs, bankers and businessmen, civil servants, journalists and broadcasters.

There were also forty-four members of parliament, including three govern-ment ministers. Among the businessmen on the list was an entrepreneur who could not yet be called a member of the establishment: Silvio Berlu-sconi. It is often not clear what individual members of P2 like Berlusconi thought its aims really were. But the power of the lodge is not in question: in 1977 it took control of Italy's most influential newspaper, *Corriere della Sera*. The very least that can be said about P2 is that it showed how, in the face of the growing influence of the Communist Party (which reached its highest ever percentage of the popular vote in the general election of 1976), key members of the elites of both power and money were closing ranks and establishing covert channels of influence.

P2 was far from the only aberrant Masonic society to emerge at this time. *Mafiosi* wanted in on the act. Cosa Nostra was making similar moves to the 'ndrangheta. According to several defectors from the ranks of the Sicilian mafia, between 1977 and 1979 a number of its most senior men joined Masonic organisations too. The issue of Masonic affiliation was discussed at Cosa Nostra's Regional Commission in 1977.

The mafias' alliance with Freemasonry in the 1970s showed underworld history coming full-circle. For the very origins of Italy's secret criminal broth-erhoods lay in contacts between Masonic conspirators who successfully plot-ted to unite Italy in the first half of the nineteenth century, and the hoodlums those patriotic conspirators recruited as revolutionary muscle. Then, as now, the thing Italy's hoodlums prized most about Freemasonry was contacts. As Leonardo Messina, a Sicilian *mafioso* who defected from Cosa Nostra in 1992, explained:

Many men in Cosa Nostra—the ones who managed to become bosses, that is—belonged to the Freemasonry. In the Masons you can have contacts with entrepreneurs, the institutions, the men who manage power. The Masonry is a meeting place for everyone.

So for the 'ndrangheta, the Mamma Santissima was a new constitutional device for regulating the Calabrian underworld's connections with the upper world of politics, business and policing.

When it was first introduced, the Mamma Santissima was highly controversial: many considered it a 'bastardisation' of the Honoured Society's rules. Indeed the innovation drove a wedge between the members of the triumvirate. Mommo Piromalli supported it, whereas Mico Tripodo was against it. It is said that don 'Ntoni Macrì, the 'ndrangheta's patriarch, the 'living symbol of organised crime's omnipotence and invincibility' who danced a mean *tarantella*, was viscerally opposed.

Why the resistance? Some say that the grounds for don 'Ntoni's opposition to the Mamma Santissima were simply that he was traditional, a man loyal to the old rules. This explanation seems implausible to me, dripping in nostalgia for some good old mafia that has actually never existed. If don 'Ntoni was like every other *mafioso* there has ever been, then he obeyed the traditional rules only for as long as it suited his interests.

No, the real reason why don 'Ntoni Macrì was opposed to the Mamma Santissima was simply that he was excluded from it. In fact, I suspect that the new gift was invented with the precise aim of cutting him out, of isolating him from important secrets. And behind that manoeuvre lay a plan to stop don 'Ntoni meddling in other people's kidnappings, and—even more importantly—to keep his grasping hands away from the Colombo package (the publicly funded construction bonanza that came following the Reggio revolt of 1970). It was through contacts with the local ruling class, and in particular with Masonic brotherhoods, that the bonanza was to be distributed. It is no coincidence that among the main proponents of the Mamma Santissima was don Mommo Piromalli, the triumvir who hailed from Gioia Tauro where the new steelworks was going to be built. In the world of the mafias (and not just the mafias), constitutional innovation is often just a mask for skulduggery.

Between them, the De Stefano brothers' ambitions in Reggio Calabria and the tensions between the triumvirs over the Mamma Santissima and the Colombo package would push the 'ndrangheta into war.

In September 1974, Mommo Piromalli hosted a meeting of the 'ndran-gheta's chiefs in Gioia Tauro. Among those in attendance were not just the other triumvirate members—don 'Ntoni Macrì from the Ionian coast and the bigamist Mico Tripodo from Reggio—but also don Mico's pushy underlings, the De Stefano brothers. Unanimously, the bosses rejected an offer from major construction companies: a 3 per cent cut of profits from construction of the Gioia Tauro steelworks. The 'ndrangheta would not be happy unless its share was fattened out by contracts and subcontracts. Nonetheless tensions within the brotherhood in Reggio spilled over: Mico Tripodo and Giorgio De Stefano exchanged acid words, and only the intervention of don 'Ntoni Macrì—pos-ing, as ever, as the peacemaker—prevented a violent confrontation.

Another attempt to preserve the peace in Reggio Calabria soon followed. This time the occasion was not a business meeting but a wedding reception in the Jolly Hotel in Gioia Tauro. The father of the bride was one of the Mazzaferro clan, close allies of Mommo Piromalli, and the celebrations were attended by chief cudgels from across Calabria. Fearing an ambush, Mico Tripodo did not attend, and paid for his absence by being insulted by the Comet's younger brother Paolo. Again don 'Ntoni tried to calm the waters, and plans were laid for a third meeting on neutral territory—Naples.

But by this time it had become clear to all involved that any outbreak of fighting between the De Stefanos and don Mico Tripodo in Reggio Calabria would draw other 'ndrine in. Behind don Mico stood 'Ntoni Macrì. And behind the De Stefanos stood Mommo Piromalli in Gioia Tauro. So what had initially seemed like a local matter, a familiar confrontation between an older boss and younger men trying to oust him, had grown into a fracture dividing the whole 'ndrangheta into two alliances, both of them prepared for war. The equilibrium that the triumvirate had guaranteed for a decade and a half had been fatally destabilised.

On 24 November 1974, at around eight o'clock in the evening, two killers entered the fashionable Roof Garden bar, a notorious 'ndrangheta hang-out in Reggio Calabria's piazza Indipendenza. Scanning the room, the two quickly identified the table where their targets were sitting. The first assassin pulled out a long-barrelled P38 and shot Giovanni De Stefano in the head from about a metre away. When the gun jammed, his accomplice raised another weapon and blasted two more bullets into Giovanni De Stefa-no's prostrate form before firing at Giovanni's brother Giorgio, 'the Comet'. Although the Comet was badly wounded, he survived the Roof Garden as-sault; Giovanni died at the scene. Retaliation could not wait long. The con-flict was now unstoppable.

Don 'Ntoni Macrì, now that he was too old to dance the *tarantella*, had the habit of playing bowls with his driver every day on the edge of town before heading back home to hold court. On 20 January 1975 he had just finished his game and climbed back into the car when an Alfa Romeo 1750 screeched to a halt in front of him. Four men got out and let rip with pistol and machine-gun fire. Siderno shut down for the old chief cudgel's funeral, and some 5,000 people paid their respects.

The First 'Ndrangheta War, as it is now known, caused more fatalities than Sicily's First Mafia War of the early 1960s. There were 233 murders in three years. Local feuds in Ciminà, Cittanova, Seminara and Taurianova added to the body count. There was savagery on all sides. In one phone tap, Mommo Piromalli was heard telling his wife how he fed one of his victims to the pigs: 'L'anchi sulu restaru' ('Only his thigh bones were left over'), he explained. 'Oh yes!' she replied.

A score of the old bosses fell. The last (and the most important after 'Ntoni Macrì) was the bigamist and triumvir don Mico Tripodo. In the spring of 1976, he was arrested with his camorra friends in Mondragone and sent to Poggioreale prison in Naples. Five months later, on 26 August, two Neapolitan petty crooks cornered him in his cell and stabbed him twenty times on the orders of a camorra *capo*. The De Stefanos had shown that they too had friends in the Neapolitan underworld, and by using them to eliminate their boss and enemy Mico Tripodo, they brought the war to a close.

Or not quite to a close. On 7 November 1977, Giorgio 'the Comet' De Stefano took the risk of leaving his patch in Reggio Calabria to attend an important meeting of the 'ndrangheta's upper echelons up on Aspromonte. Before proceedings got under way, he sat down on a rock to light a cigar. Suddenly, there came a shout: 'Curnutu, tu sparasti a me frati' ('You cuckold, you shot my brother'); it was followed immediately by gunshots. The Comet, the apparent victor of the First 'Ndrangheta War, and the supposed epitome of the modern *mafioso*, had only been allowed a year to enjoy the fruits of his military success.

For a moment, it looked as if the Comet's surviving brother Paolo De Stefano would push the 'ndrangheta into another war. But internal investigations soon discovered that the hit-man was a low-ranking affiliate called Giuseppe Suraci. Paolo De Stefano was told that Suraci just had a personal beef. The other bosses who had seen the Comet die placated Paolo De Stefano's vengeful wrath by presenting him with Giuseppe Suraci's severed head. This grisly gesture re-established the peace that had taken shape after the war of 1974–6.

We now know, however, that the version of the Comet's murder told to Paolo De Stefano by the other 'ndrangheta bosses was an ingeniously crafted lie. The killer Giuseppe Suraci had not acted out of personal vendetta, but because he was ordered to by the De Stefanos' allies in the First 'Ndrangheta

Head of a crime dynasty. Girolamo
'Mommo' Piromalli pictured in 1974,
the year the First 'Ndrangheta War
broke out. Don Mommo would
emerge victorious.

War, the Piromallis. He was then beheaded to prevent him from being interrogated by Paolo De Stefano about why he had *really* killed his brother.

By the time of the Comet's death, Mommo Piromalli was semi-retired,
leaving the clan's day-to-day business to his younger brother Giuseppe. And
Giuseppe had taken objection to the way Giorgio 'the Comet' De Stefano
had extorted a bribe from a building contractor who was already under
Piromalli protection. Thus the Comet had committed a *sgarro*: an insult to
a mobster's authority and honour. That *sgarro* was enough to draw a death
sentence down on its perpetrator. The Piromallis had, deviously and ruth-
lessly, cut their upstart former allies down to size.

So it was Mommo Piromalli's clan who were the real winners of the
First 'Ndrangheta War. The core reason for the Piromallis' success was
their political shrewdness. Mommo Piromalli joined the triumvirate in
keeping the equilibrium for as long as it suited him. He then proposed
the Mamma Santissima when the time came to isolate his enemies. He
used the Comet against his enemies too; and then used a trick to dispose
of him.

Mommo Piromalli was the only member of the triumvirate that ruled
the 'ndrangheta since the 1960s who died of natural causes. Cirrhosis of
the liver carried him away in a prison hospital in 1979. He left behind him
a clan more powerful than any in Calabria. Still to this day, the Piromallis
are a major force. As, for that matter, are their allies in the First 'Ndrangheta
War, the De Stefano family.

By the late 1970s, however, the Mamma Santissima had already been
overtaken. As one 'ndrangheta defector has explained, the number of *santisti* rapidly increased, making it necessary to introduce new, higher gifts
above their rank:

A few years after the Santa was recognised, there was a certain inflation in bestowing the rank of *santista*. Indeed there were no longer just the thirty-three *santisti* envisaged by the rules: more *santisti* were created to keep everyone who aspired to hold that rank happy. So in 1978–80 I heard that a new body was created, called the Vangelo ('Gospel'). I was awarded the rank of *vangelista* ('gospel-ist') between 1978 and 1980 in Fossombrone prison.

In practical terms the Vangelo was restricted to a smaller number of people than the Santa, which had gone from thirty-three people to a much higher number. But then the same thing happened with the creation of the Trequartista ('Three-quarterist') and Quintino ('Fifther').

And so it went on: the business of tweaking and bending the 'ndrangheta's traditional rules so as to suit the needs of the moment. In the mafia world, there is nothing more traditional than that. Tradition helps bind the mafias together. But it can also be used to prepare for civil war. The First 'Ndrangheta War was only a rehearsal for what was to come when narcotics propelled the Italian mafias to the greatest riches they had ever known.

51

A BRIEF HISTORY OF JUNK

> Then Zeus' daughter Helen . . . drugged the wine with the herb nêpenthes,
> which banishes all care, sorrow, and anger. Whoever drinks wine thus
> drugged cannot shed a single tear all the rest of the day, not even though
> his father and mother both of them drop down dead, or he sees a brother
> or a son hewn in pieces before his very eyes.
>
> HOMER, *ODYSSEY IV*, 220-21

OPIUM IS A VERY ANCIENT ORIENTAL DRUG THAT HAS APPALLED AND ENTHRALLED
occidental civilisation since the ancient Greeks. The drug nêpenthes, which
Helen administers in Homer's *Odyssey*, is probably opium.

Heroin, by contrast, is a child of modern, global capitalism; it is a brand
name that was first coined by the German pharmaceutical company Bayer at
the end of the nineteenth century. What Bayer *thought* they were putting on
the market was a new, safe version of the opium derivative morphine—one
that did not carry the same risks of dependency. What they were *actually*
selling was even more addictive than morphine. But it was so reassuringly
packaged and so roundly endorsed by medical opinion that, for the next decade and more, even many children's cough syrups contained it. No wonder
that the United States could count over 200,000 heroin addicts by the time
the First World War came to an end.

In China, the problem of opiate addiction was at least a century older.
By the time heroin was invented, those Chinese hooked on smoking opium

numbered in the millions. Throughout the nineteenth century, British merchants had ferried opium from India to the Celestial Kingdom. At the behest of those merchants, the British government fought two wars to force China to accept the free trade in a drug that was tearing holes in its social fabric. The *Cambridge History of China* calls the British opium trafficking business 'the most long-continued and systematic international crime of modern times'.

In 1912, the United States, China and Britain all signed the first international treaty aimed at controlling narcotics production and distribution; in 1919 its provisions were included in the Treaty of Versailles that sealed the peace at the end of the First World War. A new era of drug control had dawned across the world. From now on, the main suppliers and distributors of heroin and other narcotics would not be pharmaceutical companies, merchants and governments (not openly, at least), but instead criminal syndicates.

The Sicilian mafia was among the earliest players in the world's biggest consumer market for illegal heroin, the United States. With their bases in western Sicily and New York, their transatlantic commercial ties and their wide network of contacts in the United States, *mafiosi* were ideally placed to smuggle. Between the wars, morphine was hidden in hollowed-out oranges, or in crates of other Sicilian exports like anchovies, olive oil and cheese.

But the mafia's heroin business remained artisanal. What is more, the market shrank. By 1924 the number of addicts to all narcotics in the United States was probably no greater than 110,000. The Second World War so badly disrupted supplies of opiates that, at its end, the number of addicts had plummeted to an estimated 20,000.

Trade resumed after the Second World War, as did the mafia's involvement in it. Italy did not have much of a domestic consumer market for drugs at the time. Moreover, until 1951, pharmaceutical companies in the peninsula were able to produce heroin legally for medicinal purposes. Some of that legal heroin found its way to the United States for sale on the black market. Lucky Luciano, like several other *mafiosi* sent back to Italy after the war, was a heroin exporter. Nevertheless, heroin use remained restricted largely to America's black and Puerto Rican ghettoes, and as a result the drug was just one business interest among many for *mafiosi*.

Heroin started to play a more prominent role in Sicilian criminal enterprise after 1956, when the Narcotics Control Act was introduced in the United States. Because the Act established severe new penalties for drug trafficking, the heroin traders of the New York mafia were keen to outsource as much work—and risk—as possible to their Old World cousins. As we have seen, a delegation from New York's Bonanno family came to Palermo in 1957 for a high-level sit-down at the Hotel delle Palme. As a US Attorney would later remark, everyone at the hotel was a 'narcotics track star'. There were other clear signs that Sicily had become a major heroin entrepôt. In 1961, the *Guardia di Finanza* (Tax Police) dismantled an international dope-smuggling ring that was based in Salemi, in the province of Trapani, but included Canadian and American Men of Honour. In February 1962, the First Mafia War was triggered when a mafia drug-dealing consortium comprising bosses from different Palermo Families fell out over a package of heroin destined for the United States. When Cosa Nostra in Palermo disbanded itself following the Ciaculli bomb in 1963, many of the most senior Men of Honour fled to the Americas to immerse themselves full-time in trafficking for the United States market. Thus in the drugs business, as in tobacco smuggling, the Sicilian mafia diaspora of the 1960s dramatically increased the geographical range and profitability of mafia enterprise.

Underlying the Sicilian mafia's increasing commercial activism there also lay a new epidemic of heroin use in America. That epidemic gathered pace from the mid-1960s, as the drug-friendly counter-culture grew, and as American ground forces were deployed in Vietnam. During the war, Laos-based refiners linked to corrupt officers of the South Vietnamese Air Force controlled a fat heroin pipeline to Saigon. In 1971, US Army medical staff calculated that 10–15 per cent of all US troops were using heroin. By the same time, addicts back home in the American market had climbed to half a million—two and a half times the number recorded when heroin was a legal ingredient in many patent medicines. Dope was not a cottage industry anymore.

The world's opium poppy fields are to be found almost exclusively in the highlands that snake across the southern edge of Asia: from the Anatolian Plateau of Turkey in the west, through Iran, Pakistan, Afghanistan and India, to end in the highly productive region known as the 'Golden Triangle', where Burma, Laos and Thailand meet. In the 1960s, most of America's heroin came from Turkey, where the opium poppy could be cultivated legally, but where a large slice of production found its way onto the illegal market. Between Turkish farmers and American junkies there was a long, long chain of middlemen, smugglers and profiteers. Like the police and border guards paid to look the other way. And the camel drivers who fed plastic bags of opium paste to their animals in order to smuggle it over the Turkish border. Or the first-stage refiners, who boiled the raw opium paste with quicklime to precipitate out the morphine. Or the truck drivers who created secret compartments in loads of fruit and vegetables bound for Turkish markets in Germany. Or the technicians who refined the morphine into heroin—a delicate operation that involves heating it with acetic acid to a precise temperature for a precise time. At each of these stages, the price—and the profit margin—rose in geometric progression. Depending on where you were in the chain and, just as importantly, how *many* links of that chain you controlled, heroin could generate shepherd money or oil-magnate money.

At this stage of heroin's history, Sicilian *mafiosi* were not the dominant suppliers to the United States. In the 1960s, the bulk of the heroin consumed in North America came through Corsican hands. The Corsicans were enterprising, with a worldwide network of contacts and a secure base for their refineries in Marseille. Here the Corsican clans won a political shield for their operations by hiring themselves out as strike-breakers and anti-communist thugs, turning the French port city into one of Europe's great criminal capitals. By 1970, Marseille heroin had become famous among American addicts. *Mafiosi* provided access to a distribution network in the United States. Thus the Sicilians were an important but essentially subordinate part of a Corsican business.

The Corsican system was thrown into chaos in the early 1970s. With American public opinion alarmed by the rise in heroin addiction, particularly among combat troops, President Richard Nixon declared a 'war on drugs'. The Turkey–Marseille–New York channel, known as the French Connection, was picked out as the war's strategic objective. The US first offered the Turkish government generous financial persuasion to stop legal opium cultivation, which ceased after the harvest of 1972. Meanwhile, in France, the Corsicans were losing their friends in high places. In November 1971, a French secret-service agent who had been running heroin from Marseille with the Corsicans was indicted in the United States, creating a huge political scandal in France. Moreover, the growing heroin problem in French cities increased the pressure on government to order a clampdown. One by one, the Marseille refineries were shut down and the chemists were arrested.

The Sicilians, who occupied a less strategic segment of America's heroin supply lines than did the Corsicans, looked to have been marginalised by the destruction of the French Connection. American junkies suffered a heroin drought, and the Sicilians occupied a smaller segment of that reduced market. In 1976, the long-awaited final report of Italy's parliamentary inquiry into the mafia used evidence from drug seizures in the States in the early 1970s to argue that 'much of the heroin destined for the United States market is no longer forwarded through Italy as it once was'. The war on drugs, it seemed, was being won.

In reality, all that had happened was that the law of supply and demand was taking its time to work through the global narcotics system. The scarcity of heroin on the American market pushed up the price, which made the risks of setting up new pipelines more worthwhile. Turkish production soon revived after the initial assault. Worse still, as American troops were withdrawn from Vietnam, suppliers of morphine and heroin from the Golden Triangle were avidly seeking new outlets. Between the Asian suppliers and the desperate American addicts there were tempting new opportunities for brokers and refiners. Which is where the Sicilian mafia came in. After the French Connection came the Pizza Connection. Cosa Nostra was about to become addicted.

52

MR CHAMPAGNE: Heroin broker

GASPARE MUTOLO, SON OF A TICKET COLLECTOR ON THE PALERMO TRAM SYSTEM, WAS eased gently into the psychological rigours of life as a professional assassin. Not long after being initiated into Cosa Nostra, he was shown what went on inside a mafia torture chamber. Then he took a hands-on lesson in garrotting technique. He retched as blood started to come out of the victim's nose and ears just before death. Mutolo was then taught how to truss up a body so it could be transported in the boot of a car, and how to bury it with quicklime (so that it would rapidly decompose beyond the reach of forensic science) and fertiliser (so that the site of the burial would be covered in vegetation). He was even shown what a body looks like when it has spent two or three months in one of these specially prepared pits.

The toughening-up process paid dividends when Mutolo carried out the first of many solo murders with calm efficiency, cutting the throat of a dissident Man of Honour during a carefully faked robbery. Giving death soon became routine, as it had done for so many *mafiosi* of previous generations.

> I've never felt fear the evening before a murder. You just have to be convinced about what you are going to do. Sometimes, I've been more thoughtful the night before, and have reflected on how easy it is to kill and be killed . . . On occasions, I've experienced a strange sense of pity, especially when I've had to kill youngsters whose family I maybe knew.

Mutolo was then given a fast-track apprenticeship in all of the major criminal businesses that had been transforming Italy's mafias since the 1950s:

making them richer, broadening their geographical horizons, bringing them into relationships with one another, thickening their ties with politicians. Sent to Naples, he quickly became involved in cigarette smuggling with *camorristi*. Then he was sent into the wealthy northern region of Lombardy to gather information on possible kidnapping targets. Back in Palermo, Mutolo also learned how to make money from public construction projects.

> All you have to do is set up good relationships with a few local administrators. When the Sicilian regional government puts a contract out to tender, there are men linked to Cosa Nostra who manage the negotiations. That way ghost companies win the contracts and pass them on to the mafia group hiding behind them. To give you an idea of the profits: if a contract is worth a billion lire [$2.2 million in 2011], 10 per cent goes to the politician who obstructs the competition and makes sure the contract goes to the right people, and the rest goes to a *mafioso* who will double his money in a year.

Mutolo proved an obedient underling to his boss, Saro Riccobono of the Partanna-Mondello Family. All was progressing well with a good, but unexceptional, mafia career.

Suddenly, in 1975, a new business exploded, a business that would earn the mafia more than tobacco smuggling, kidnapping and construction put together. Mutolo remembers being in a meeting, chatting with other Men of Honour about routine extortion rackets, when Tano Badalamenti burst in. 'Gentlemen, we have the chance to earn ten times as much with drugs.' Badalamenti, head of the Palermo Commission, well connected in the United States, had spotted the gap in the market created by President Nixon's war on drugs, and he was perfectly placed to exploit it.

Initially, Cosa Nostra stepped up its involvement in heroin through the same channels it used to smuggle cigarettes. The merchandise travelled in the same containers as the 'blondes'. Palermo Families pooled their investments in joint-stock ventures in just the same way as they had done for major cigarette cargoes. Payments were made through the same Swiss banks that were used to pass money to some of the major tobacco multinationals. As Mutolo quipped, 'If there are any rascals in the story, it's the Swiss.' Tano Badalamenti himself took charge of the first expedition to meet suppliers in Turkey. The scheme was a roaring success. Within forty days, all of the investors had tripled their money. Cosa Nostra's heroin rush had begun.

Mafiosi plunged headlong into the tide of white powder, adapting their old techniques of networking and corruption, and rapidly acquiring lucra-

Mr Champagne. Gaspare Mutolo became one of Cosa Nostra's leading heroin brokers in the 1980s. With him (left, with striped tie) is Boris Giuliano, a brilliant policeman murdered later in 1979.

tive new skills. Nunzio La Mattina, a Man of Honour from the Porta Nuova Family, underwent retraining of a historically resonant sort. Where he had once used his knowledge of chemistry to test the exact composition of Sicily's lemon juice, now he became a large-scale heroin refiner. Other *mafiosi* learned the same trade by taking lessons from Corsicans who were brought over from Marseille. Among them was Francesco Marino Mannoia, from the Santa Maria di Gesù Family. Each time a bulk delivery of morphine base arrived, Marino Mannoia would spend a week at a time amid the vinegary fumes of one of many laboratories that had sprung up across the island. When he emerged, his skin would be scaly and his lungs scoured. He was known as 'Mozzarella' because he was simple and unflashy, and in restaurants always ordered mozzarella and tomato salad, the simplest and safest item on the menu. His personal habits did not change even when, as Cosa Nostra's most important chemist, he became fabulously rich.

Gaspare Mutolo chose another specialism: he became a broker, contacting the wholesale suppliers in the Near and Far East, bringing batches to Sicily and selling them on to traffickers within Cosa Nostra who had access to America. As a leading heroin broker, Mutolo had a reliable map of the politics and economics of the mafia's trafficking. What that map shows is that Cosa Nostra did not enter the heroin business en bloc. Nor was it transformed into a top-down multinational dope corporation by the late 1970s heroin boom. Rather it acted like what it is, and what it has always been: a Freemasonry of criminals. Each individual member of the club, each little network of friends within it, each of its Families, and each of the high-level coordinating structures like the Palermo Commission, had the capacity to carve out a role. As Mutolo would later explain:

> When it comes to drug trafficking, if deals are small then they can be managed by a Family. Everyone is independent and does what they want. But sometimes someone gets involved in a big consignment that could interfere with other *mafiosi* and their work, with what a whole organisation is doing. Some big deals can take over a whole market. In such cases the Commission may intervene. Members of the Commission can step in to impose organisation on the deal. So the Commission intervenes in all the most important sectors.

A kind of internal market among Men of Honour developed. Some wholesalers would sell consignments of morphine base to refiners they knew in the brotherhood. When it had been transformed into heroin, they would then buy it all back from them. Often the Family bosses did not deal directly in heroin at all, but were content to sit back and 'tax' the dealers they knew: a much less risky way to make money.

In 1976, just as his heroin ventures were really taking off, Mutolo was arrested; incarceration brought a quantum leap in his criminal standing. 'God bless these prisons!', he later proclaimed. Mutolo's cell mate in Sulmona in central Italy was a long-haired Singapore Chinese heroin importer called Ko Bak Kin. Though neither spoke the other's language, Mutolo took a liking to Kin. Over shared meals and through little gestures of generosity, they began to develop the most valuable thing in the treacherous world of international narcotics dealing: trust. When Kin had learned enough Italian to talk business, he said to Mutolo: 'Gaspare, promise me: as soon as you get out, call me. I'll let you have all the drugs you need.' In 1979, just before Kin's sentence ended, Mutolo gave him his gold watch and jewellery to pay for somewhere to stay in Rome, and for a plane ticket to contact his suppliers in Thailand. Kin reciprocated by leaving Mutolo a post-box address in Bangkok.

Soon afterwards, in 1981, Mutolo himself was allowed out on day release. To reintegrate him with the world of honest work, he was allotted a job in a furniture factory in Teramo, in central Italy. But the position of assistant bookkeeper was not best suited to Mutolo's abilities, so he persuaded the owner to make him the factory's Palermo agent. He was also granted periods of leave in Sicily for 'family' reasons. Mutolo had his Ferrari Dino and his Alfa Romeo GTV 2000 brought up to Teramo, so he would roar down to Sicily for his business meetings. He also rented a huge villa by the sea near Teramo, and used a suite in the five-star Michelangelo Hotel as his office. From there he would make calls to Australia, Brazil, Venezuela and Canada.

Mutolo's drug business rocketed. He quickly put together an organisation of common criminals, friends and relatives to handle the hundreds of kilos of heroin imported from Thailand by Ko Bak Kin. When the authorities began to discover some of the Sicilian laboratories, Mutolo and Kin latched on to a scheme that would make refining much safer, and put even more links in the supply chain into their hands. Kin sourced the morphine base in Thailand. A mafia partner of Mutolo's arranged for it to be transported to Europe by ship. On board, there would be a Man of Honour from Mutolo's Family of Cosa Nostra to act as guard. Just as importantly, there would also be a chemist, so that the heroin—as much as 400 kilograms in one go—was ready to put on the market as soon as it arrived.

'1981: my magic moment, the best year of my life,' Mutolo remembered. Armani suits, silk scarves, designer shoes, Cartier watches for his friends . . . Among the lawyers, doctors and professors of Teramo whose company he kept, Mutolo became known as 'Mr Champagne'. Today, having turned state's evidence, he lives a humble life under an assumed identity, and rides a scooter rather than driving a Ferrari. So perhaps it is understandable that he is nostalgic for the luxuries of his past. But he knows deep down that these were fripperies. The phone taps and other evidence that would eventually convict him of heroin trafficking show him carefully using his wealth to dispense favours and make friends. To avoid political tensions within Cosa Nostra, Mutolo made sure that the Palermo Families always got the chance to invest in a new cargo, and that the heroin reaching Sicily was distributed fairly. Mutolo kept his boss happy. He rose in Saro Riccobono's estimation, becoming one of the leading members of the Partanna-Mondello Family. In the end, in Cosa Nostra, money means nothing unless it is converted back into power.

The huge amounts of cheap heroin being channelled through Italy in the 1970s caused an explosion of drug use in the peninsula. In 1970, the presence of a heroin problem had barely registered. By 1980, Italy had more heroin addicts per head of population than did the United States. Anyone who visited a major Italian city in the 1980s can remember the sight of plastic syringes littering the gutters in quiet streets.

Despite the growth in Italian domestic consumption (and therefore in overdose fatalities), the United States market remained the biggest consumer market in absolute terms. Gaspare Mutolo was a big player in the complex pass-the-parcel game of trafficking heroin from the East, through Sicily, and into the United States. But he was a long way from being the biggest. In fact, Mutolo learned very quickly that the *mafiosi* who occupied the most strategic place in the supply chain to America were the ones who straddled the Atlantic.

53

THE TRANSATLANTIC SYNDICATE

ON 22 APRIL 1974, A SMALL GROUP OF MAFIOSI SAT DOWN TO CHAT IN AN ICE-CREAM bar in Saint-Léonard, Montreal's Little Italy. Two of them led the discussion. One was the bar's owner, Paolo Violi, underboss of Cosa Nostra in Quebec. Violi's guest had come directly from Sicily: he was Giuseppe 'Pino' Cuffaro, a Man of Honour who also hailed from the province of Agrigento. The two spoke a common jargon of mafia power politics. A jargon that— through a hubbub of background conversation, a clatter of crockery and the hiss and crackle of a secret microphone—Canadian police were able to record.

Violi began the pleasantries: 'So the journey went well then? Let's kiss one another.'

In reply, Pino Cuffaro could hardly wait to unload his news from Sicily. 'Well, Paolo, before you drink this cappuccino, I've got to announce a nice surprise, an affectionate surprise that is naturally close to our hearts . . . Carmelo has been made representative in our village.'

Then, between sips of coffee, there followed a long bulletin on the latest Cosa Nostra appointments in the far-off province of Agrigento. Who was provincial boss, who were the *capomandamenti* (precinct bosses), who were the *consiglieri*, and who had been initiated. They discussed the state of Cosa Nostra across Sicily, remarking on how the Palermo Commission was still suspended. And they dropped the names of mutual friends, like don 'Ntoni Macrì—the 'ndrangheta boss from Siderno who was also a member of Cosa Nostra (and who, unbeknownst to all, would enjoy his last game of bowls just a few months later).

But Pino Cuffaro had not come all the way to Quebec just to bring his Canadian friends up to speed with the ins and outs of the old country. He had come to resolve a delicate issue of diplomatic protocol. Could a Man of Honour from Sicily arrive in America and assume full citizenship of the Cosa Nostra community there? Underlying this question was the fundamental issue of whether Cosa Nostra was a single transatlantic brotherhood, or whether the American and Sicilian branches were separate entities. The positions were so entrenched, and the argument so strained, that the men had to meet twice.

Paolo Violi, the Canadian gangster, argued for a five-year rule: any Sicilian who arrived in Canada would have to spend five years being monitored before he was granted full status. The Sicilian visitor wanted no barriers to be put up between Sicily and the New World.

Who was right? The short answer is that it does not really matter. In the mafia world, rules are very important, but they are also pliable: *mafiosi*, like the rest of us, tend to interpret rules in ways that suit their own interests. Even a rule as basic as the relationship between the American and Sicilian arms of Cosa Nostra was not permanently fixed.

It is significant that Paolo Violi, the ice-cream-bar owner who was such a stickler for the five-year rule about admission to the American Cosa Nostra, was actually a living example of the rule's flexibility. For he was Calabrian. His bar was called Reggio—after the city in southern Calabria, birthplace of the 'ndrangheta. Like many young Calabrian hoods who emigrated to major centres of organised crime in the Americas, Violi made his career not in the 'ndrangheta, but in the American Cosa Nostra. America was where closer ties between the Calabrian and Sicilian mafias were pioneered, and where those ties persisted. But despite the American mafia's long history of openness to newcomers, even Calabrian newcomers, in the spring of 1974 the Calabrian immigrant Paolo was adamant that Sicilian *mafiosi* would have to spend five years under observation before they were entitled to full membership of Cosa Nostra in the United States.

So the constitutional rights and wrongs of Violi's position are much less important than the question of why he was arguing in that way—of what naked self-interest he was trying to drape in constitutional clothes.

By the time of the ice-cream-bar meeting, the collapse of the French Connection was already beginning to intensify mafia involvement in importing heroin to the United States. Violi was a territorially based boss, not a narcotics trafficker. As such, he felt threatened by this massively lucrative cross-territorial business that he could not entirely control. In the specific case of Quebec, the people who worried Violi were the Cuntreras and Caruanas: two Sicilian mafia bloodlines intertwined over several generations into a single clan-cum-business network. Two members of that clan, Pasquale and Libo-rio Cuntrera, had moved to Canada in 1951—more or less when Paolo Violi arrived. Subsequently, many more members of the Cuntrera-Caruana clan joined the Sicilian mafia diaspora that followed the Ciaculli bomb in 1963. Yet rather than settling permanently in one place, the new exiles converted themselves into roving heroin smugglers, a shifting international network that financed, sourced and shipped heroin in bulk, and then laundered and invested the profits. Over the coming years, their traces would be found in Canada, the USA, Mexico, Brazil, Honduras, the Bahamas, Antigua, the Ca-ribbean tax haven of Aruba, India, Germany, Switzerland—and even in the comfortable London suburb of Woking. Venezuela was the clan's long-term base, an offshore heroin trading post for the US market. Here the Cuntrera-Caruanas owned a vast, fortified cattle ranch near the Colombian border that had its own airport. When Pasquale Cuntrera's son got married, the event was covered on television and the Venezuelan president was a witness.

Giuseppe Cuffaro, the *mafioso* who argued with Paolo Violi at the ice-cream-bar meeting, was a travelling salesman for the Cuntrera-Caruana group. That is why he wanted free entry to the Canadian market for mafia emissaries.

The Cuntrera-Caruana network centred on a set of smart, well-connected and mobile *mafiosi* whose spectacular wealth allowed them to win friends anywhere in the world. The Cuntrera-Caruanas and the other roving heroin traders have been referred to as a mafia in their own right. They formed what we could call a Transatlantic Syndicate whose power floated danger-ously free of the territories controlled by the Sicilian and American branches of Cosa Nostra. Such men could dictate terms to local bosses like Violi in whichever territory they found market or investment opportunities. The loyalty of soldiers to their captain or boss could easily be bought. Thus it was that, on 22 January 1978, Paolo Violi paid the ultimate price for his fin-icky, protectionist interpretation of the mafia's rules when he was shot dead as he played cards in his ice-cream bar.

Canada was not the only place where wire-taps registered the way in which the Transatlantic Syndicate was upsetting the mafia balance of power in the late 1970s. In a justly famous undercover sting, FBI Special Agent Joseph D. Pistone infiltrated New York's Bonanno Family by posing as 'Donnie Brasco'. The memorable 1997 movie of Pistone's story, starring Johnny Depp and Al Pacino, fails to capture the operation's crucial historical context. Pistone/Brasco was a firsthand witness to the rise of the 'zips' or 'greasers'. These were derogatory terms that local *mafiosi* used to refer to Sicilian Men of

Honour who had recently set up shop in America. There were two reasons why New York *mafiosi* were anxious about the new arrivals. First, because the zips had been granted the exclusive right to supply wholesale heroin for New York's Bonanno and Gambino Families. Second, because they formed an autonomous faction whose power within American Cosa Nostra was on the rise. What soldiers in the Bonanno Family called 'zips' were actually members of the Transatlantic Syndicate.

Pistone's body mike recorded two New York wise guys as they reacted to the news that some of the Sicilians were going to be awarded ranks within the American organisation:

> Those guys [the zips] are looking to take over everything. There's no way we can make them captains. We'd lose all our strength.
>
> Them fucking zips ain't going to back up to nobody. You give them the fucking power, if you don't get hurt now, you get hurt three years from now. They'll bury you. You cannot give them the power. They don't give a fuck. They don't care who's boss. They got no respect.

The zips had names and faces. John Gambino was one: he had moved from Palermo to Cherry Hills, New Jersey, in 1964. Salvatore Inzerillo was another: he was the nephew of a Palermo boss. Like the Cuntrera-Caruana clan, these were mobsters with a great many exotic stamps in their passports, and a vast international skein of relatives by blood and marriage to support them. Members of the Transatlantic Syndicate like these were responsible for what became known as the Pizza Connection, a tag coined during the huge US police investigation that eventually cut out a small part of the Transatlantic Syndicate in the mid-1980s.

The members of the Transatlantic Syndicate were frighteningly powerful, and they also worked together. As early as 1971, the Venezuelan secret services looked into the Cuntrera-Caruana cattle ranch, and found that its shareholders included the following: Nick Rizzuto, the Cuntrera-Caruanas' man in Montreal (he would eventually take the reins in Quebec after the murder of Paolo Violi); John Gambino from Cherry Hills; and Salvatore 'Little Bird' Greco, the head of the Palermo Commission at the time of the Ciaculli bomb, who had abandoned Sicily to become a South America–based narcotics importer.

The Transatlantic Syndicate had the keys to the United States heroin market: anyone who wanted to supply bulk dope to the East Coast had little choice but to go through them. Our Sicilian broker, Gaspare 'Mr Champagne' Mutolo, knew that from experience. In 1981, the first of his ships delivered

400 kilograms of ready-refined heroin from Thailand: half of it went to the Cuntrera-Caruanas, and half to John Gambino in Cherry Hills.

Back in Sicily, the Transatlantic Syndicate carried even more clout than it did in Canada or the United States. One member, Salvatore Inzerillo, returned to Palermo in 1973, and his uncle immediately ceded to him his job as representative of the Passo di Rigano Family and then his seat on the Commission. Other bosses who were part of the Transatlantic Syndicate included triumvirate members Tano Badalamenti and Stefano Bontate.

The Transatlantic Syndicate enjoyed the cream of Cosa Nostra's contacts in the world of banking. Some of their narcotics profits were laundered and invested by the notorious fly-by-night financiers and P2 Masonic Lodge members, Michele Sindona and Roberto Calvi. Both Sindona and Calvi would end up dying in circumstances that remain mysterious to this day: Calvi was found hanging under Blackfriars Bridge in London in 1982; Sindona drank a coffee laced with cyanide in prison in 1986.

The Transatlantic Syndicate enjoyed enormous traction in business and politics too. They were close to the Salvo cousins, fabulously wealthy barons of Sicily's privatised tax-collection system. They were also close to Salvo Lima, the Young Turk. Through Lima and the Salvos, but also directly, they had the ear of the most powerful politician in Italy: Giulio Andreotti, seven times Prime Minister by the end of his parliamentary career, and the man whose faction in the Christian Democrat Party included Lima and his Sicilian followers. According to the Italian Supreme Court, in a verdict from 2004, Andreotti displayed 'an authentic, stable and friendly availability' towards Stefano Bontate et al until 1980, when Cosa Nostra's increasing violence alienated him.

Never in the long history of the Sicilian mafia has there been a concentration of might and opulence to compete with the Transatlantic Syndicate. That is why, in 1981, the Transatlantic Syndicate became the target of a war of extermination.

But before war broke out once more in Sicily, the camorra in Campania was revolutionised by the most influential boss of the twentieth century.

54

THE PROFESSOR

RAFFAELE CUTOLO WAS THE CREATOR OF POSSIBLY THE LARGEST CRIMINAL ORGANISAtion in Italian history, the Nuova Camorra Organizzata ('New Organised Camorra'). At its peak in 1980, according to a police estimate, the Nuova Camorra Organizzata (or NCO) counted 7,000 members. Its leader evaded the full force of the law with a regularity that was shocking even by Italian standards. His speciality was obtaining psychiatric reports that absolved him of full responsibility for his deeds. 'While committing criminal acts', one diagnosis declared, 'Cutolo falls under the influence of a typical impulsive-aggressive crisis that completely overcomes and nullifies his will power.' Or, in lay terms: he often gets angry and has people killed—but it isn't his fault. The NCO boss compared himself to Christ and said he could read minds. It is unclear whether he believed this or was merely acting out the psychiatric script.

Whatever Cutolo's precise mental equilibrium was, in 1980 he decided to flaunt his authority architecturally. Overlooking Ottaviano, the town on the north-eastern slopes of Mount Vesuvius where the NCO boss had grown up, was the dilapidated Medici Castle; it had a room for every day of the year. Cutolo bought it through a front company and turned it into both his organisation's HQ and the grandiose symbol of a rise to criminal power as fast and brutally successful as any in the annals of Italian organised crime. And the astonishing thing is that Raffaele Cutolo did it almost entirely from prison.

In 1963, at the age of twenty-one, Cutolo had earned himself a twenty-four-year prison sentence for shooting a man dead in a road-rage incident of illustrative viciousness. Newspaper reports tell us that in Ottaviano's main

Founder of the Nuova Camorra
Organizzata. Raffaele 'the Professor'
Cutolo was the most influential Italian
criminal of the twentieth century.

thoroughfare, Cutolo deliberately drove his car at four young women, braking only at the last minute. When one of the women remonstrated with Cutolo about the stupid stunt, he set about her with his fists. A passing firefighter intervened to save the woman, and Cutolo responded by pulling a Beretta 7.65 pistol from his pocket and firing twice. But what really earned Cutolo the judge's indignation was the way in which he followed the wounded fireman as he staggered into a doorway to take refuge. There, Cutolo emptied the rest of the clip into the luckless man, who died in hospital leaving a widow and three children.

In 1970 Cutolo was freed, pending a ruling on his case by the Supreme Court, and went on the run. He became a junior camorra boss, dealing in extortion and cocaine. Upon his recapture, after a firefight with the *Carabinieri* in March of the following year, he was sent to the infamous penitentiary at Poggioreale. There he would begin to build what became known as the NCO. By 1974 he had already earned the nickname 'the King of Poggioreale' and was involved in a major drug-trafficking ring with senior *mafiosi* from both Sicily and Calabria. By 1977 he had enough power to have himself transferred to the cosier surroundings of the state mental institution in Aversa near Naples. In February 1978 his men blew a wall down with TNT and he scrambled over the rubble to freedom. One plausible theory is that the breakout was staged to avoid the embarrassment that would have been caused had Cutolo merely strolled out of the main gate—as he probably could have done. Be that as it may, the fugitive was not recaptured for fifteen months. In 1981 an appeal verdict said he could not be punished for the escape because of his mental infirmity. As Cutolo himself put it, 'I did not "escape." I wandered away. A little noisily.'

After his recapture, Cutolo never tasted freedom again. Thus, apart from two brief periods on the run, his entire adult life was spent in captivity. But he understood that prison was the perfect base for a criminal empire. Dominate the prison system, and you dominate the underworld. Confinement is an occupational hazard for criminals. And if they cannot go to jail without the fear of being raped in the showers or stabbed in the yard, they become acutely exposed.

In a sense, Cutolo perfected the methods used by prison camorras since the early nineteenth century. At the simplest level, the NCO offered safety in numbers to terrified youths doing their first stretch in an adult jail. Indeed Cutolo specialised in cultivating isolated youngsters who were not affiliated to other gangs. One of his fellow prisoners in Poggioreale described him as a 'talent scout'. Once outside, those young men would kick back part of their earnings to Cutolo so he could support others by sending cash and food to relatives, by corrupting guards and administrators, and by arranging transfers, lawyers and medical visits. So began the circulation of tributes and favours that bound the NCO together. Cutolo's organisation extended its reach from Poggioreale to many other prisons across Italy, and gained the manpower and discipline in the outside world to manage crime on an industrial scale.

The NCO engaged in all kinds of business, ranging from drug dealing and truck theft to defrauding the European Economic Community of agricultural subsidies and infiltrating government building projects. But for the NCO—as for the Sicilian mafia and for the Neapolitan Honoured Society of yesteryear—extortion was the key tool of authority. Cutolo's rackets were run by trusted lieutenants, including his big sister Rosetta. She looked for all the world like the frumpy embroiderer her brother claimed she was. But this was a façade created in part because there were those within the NCO hierarchy who were reluctant to take orders from a woman. Many observers believe that Rosetta was one of the camorra's most powerful female bosses. The money she sent to her brother allowed him to live out his confinement in luxury: in the course of just over a year in 1981–2, he received nearly 56 million lire (equivalent to $133,000 in 2011 values) to take care of his daily expenses; he reputedly spent over half of it on food and clothes.

Cutolo's conspicuous consumption was intended to publicise his power, as was the transparent irony he deployed in interview. During the trial for his escape from Aversa asylum, Cutolo gave an impromptu press conference.

Surviving news footage shows him to be well groomed, with a face both weaselly and self-satisfied. He shifts his weight repeatedly from one foot to the other behind the bars of the defendants' cage, and casts rapid, smirking glances to either side—as if he were a back-row schoolboy seeking complicity from his classmates during a scolding.

'I'm someone who fights injustice. Me, and all my friends.'

'A Robin Hood, so to speak?'

'So to speak.'

'What about the Nuova Camorra Organizzata, the NCO?'

'I dunno. Maybe NCO means *"Non Conosco Nessuno"*—"I don't know anyone."'

'Are you in charge in the prison system?'

Cutolo feigns disbelief with an unpersuasive snigger. 'I'm not in charge, the prison governor is.' [. . .]

'What about the murder of the deputy prison governor? You had previously slapped him and threatened to kill him.'

'Yes I did. Because he was doing some really . . . ' There follows an oily mellowing in Cutolo's tone. 'But he's dead now. It's unkind to talk ill of the dead . . . Anyway, I may be insane, but I'm not stupid-insane. I'm intelligent-insane. So I'm hardly going to slap someone, threaten to kill him, and then go ahead and murder him. I don't fancy collecting life sentences like that.'

Even among professional criminals, there are very few with a public persona as odious as Raffaele Cutolo. Yet his distinctive trait as a boss was the adoration he inspired. The Nuova Camorra Organizzata was founded on a cult of personality and an ideological fervour that no other mafia in Italy has ever matched. At the height of Cutolo's power, a legion of *camorristi* would gladly have died for him. What was the secret of his charisma? For one thing, he had a keen organisational intelligence and used it to construct an elaborate internal culture for the NCO. Its recruits felt they belonged, that they had a shared cause. And for the purpose of building this esprit de corps, Cutolo borrowed rituals and terminology from the Calabrian mafia. Indeed he was almost certainly affiliated into the 'ndrangheta while in prison: two *'ndranghetisti* have spoken to the authorities about how Cutolo was given his 'second baptism' in 1974. Later, Cutolo would put the NCO's new recruits through a very similar ceremony. From the 'ndrangheta, Cutolo also borrowed the terminology that defined ranks within the organisation: *giovane d'onore, picciotto, cuntajuolo, contabile, santista*, etc. Cutolo it was who, on behalf of his Calabrian friends, arranged to have the triumvir

Mico Tripodo stabbed to death in Naples prison in 1976 during the First 'Ndrangheta War.

Camorra history came full circle with Raffaele Cutolo. From Calabrian gangsters, he learned rituals and terminology that the 'ndrangheta had itself inherited from the prison camorra of the early nineteenth century. He then reimported them into the Neapolitan prison system whence they had first come, and where they had died out before the First World War.

Indeed, for a crime boss, Cutolo had a quite extraordinary sense of history. He was dubbed 'the Professor' by his men, partly because he sought out books on camorra history in the prison library, and partly because he wrote verse and short meditations on life, love and *omertà* for his admirers. In 1980 he had his jottings published as *Poems and Thoughts*. The book was seized by the police and possessing it was treated as incriminating. It is not difficult to work out why: Cutolo does little to conceal the terror he wielded. Less obviously, the book also shows the Professor putting his time in the prison library to good use. By way of example, it is worth citing the verses written in praise of the NCO's principal enforcer within the prison system, Pasquale Barra, known as *'o Sturente* ('the Student') or, more appropriately, as *'o 'Nimale* ('the Animal'). Barra was a gaunt, darkly bearded man with a very prominent nose and eyes like a mole's. He had been Cutolo's devoted friend since their teenage years in Ottaviano, and was the first recruit to the NCO. His primary role was stabbing people to death on his old friend's orders. The poem dedicated to him is called simply, 'A Man of the Camorra':

> Pasquale Barra: in our town
> He was called 'the Student'
> When it comes to a *zumpata*, no one is better
> He can even face down an army
> He always pulls off the same move
> His knife-thrusts are totally lethal
> Up under your lungs, so you start to cough
> He makes you spit out a bit of red froth
> He sees you fall to the ground, then leaves you . . .

In his own devious way, Cutolo was here using verse to bestow a certain literary and historical grandeur on his vicious henchman. For 'A Man of the Camorra' is actually cobbled together from lines stolen from a much older poem about the long-dead *camorrista* Gennarino Sbisà. The original author, journalist Ferdinando Russo (1866–1927), often celebrated individual *camorristi*, mixing just enough realistic grit into the verse to make his portraits of noble hoodlums feel authentic and dangerous. Russo it was who penned an elegy for Ciccio Cappuccio ('Little Lord Frankie'), the camorra boss whose lavish funeral was given such sympathetic coverage in the Neapolitan press back in 1892. In Russo's day, the camorra—with its hierarchical management structure and its ceremonial *zumpate*, or knife duels—was very unlike the loose gangs and street-corner bosses that had dominated Neapolitan criminality for most of the twentieth century. And through his poems, Ferdinando Russo became the man most responsible for creating a popular cult around the Honoured Society of Naples.

The echoes of that popular cult still resounded in the 1970s. Cutolo devoured the dewy-eyed fables about the old-time bosses such as Salvatore De Crescenzo and Ciccio Cappuccio—the same *camorristi* once celebrated in the puppet theatres of Naples. As both plagiarising poet and gangster, the Professor was bent on bringing the camorra's historical memory back to life. He explicitly sold the NCO to recruits as a revival of a proud gangster tradition. To be a *cutoliano* was to have roots in the past.

On one intriguing occasion, Cutolo even stage-managed a violent close encounter with camorra history—as personified by Antonio Spavone. Born in 1926 into a family of fishermen in the Mergellina quarter, Spavone and his older brother led a band of black marketeers during the chaos of Allied Military Government in 1943–5 that had launched so many criminal careers. When Spavone's brother was killed during a feud with a rival outfit, Antonio took vengeance in spectacular fashion, by raiding a family celebration in a restaurant and stabbing the opposing gang leader to death in front of a crowd. His gesture earned him both a long prison sentence and the right to inherit his brother's simple but effective nickname: *'o Malommo*—'the Bad Man'.

At some point in 1975, when both *'o Malommo* and Cutolo were in Poggioreale prison, the younger man chose to issue a challenge to a *zumpata*, a knife duel—just like the *camorristi* of the old days. This may well have been a deliberately archaic gesture: the equivalent of slapping *'o Malommo* in the face with a glove. Cutolo's challenge was refused, either because *'o Malommo* was about to be released, or because he did not want to dignify the uppity young hoodlum's impudence with a response. Recalling the episode much later, a prisoner who was in Poggioreale at the time gave a shrewd analysis of how Cutolo managed the prison rumour-machine:

> Nobody witnessed the episode. It was a completely 'virtual' event. Somebody, maybe Cutolo himself, put the rumour into circulation that the duel had not happened because of *'o Malommo*'s cowardice. In cases like this, different versions do the rounds—versions that always suit one side or the other. Cutolo went a long way thanks to a fame that was often built on made-up events. He was skilful at making exploits that never

existed seem credible and legendary. He had an extraordinary talent for promoting his own image.

Even within the straitened confines of a prison, organised crime—however organised it may be—is a domain where information circulates in a confused and fragmentary form. The Professor was a master at making the gaps in any story work for him, in writing his own history.

Cutolo's *Poems and Thoughts* are repulsive, and often trite and clumsy. But they would be much less dangerous if all they did was prompt fake duels in prison corridors or trumpet a killer's feats of savage dexterity. Cutolo's writings did much more. Copies circulated among his acolytes like the scriptures of a new messiah, and provided a seductive emotional script for the Nuova Camorra Organizzata. Analysing that script brings us to the heart of the Professor's charismatic appeal.

Nihilism is the base note of the Cutolo philosophy. We are all beasts, ready to tear one another apart for filthy money. Man is the most treacherous and cruel of all the animals; he ought not to exist. But the psychological trick that the Professor pulls off in *Poems and Thoughts* is to create a criminal value-system that seems redemptive when set against this background of fear and despair.

A good portion of Cutolo's verse voices a prisoner's yearning for his freedom, his mum, and the sights, sounds and smells of home. All of which may seem self-pitying. But it shows that Cutolo was a smart enough leader to identify with the underlying mental vulnerability of his fellow cons. His mawkishness was the first means to a very unsentimental end: moulding a disciplined criminal army.

> The sentence: life imprisonment
> As a youth
> You entered
> The tomb-like cell
> The silent cell
> The suffering cell
> You felt alone, and lost

Cutolo blames social inequality and especially the prison system for the fact that he, like so many others, has turned to crime. But this persecution has had an ennobling effect. As in the following Cutolian maxim: 'Take note: the best men end up as outlaws, fugitives or prisoners. While the people who have done this to them are the hypocrite defenders of the law.'

Cutolo presents the NCO as a fellowship of the downtrodden, bound together against the onslaughts of a hostile world; it is a group of Friends.

For Friendship is the supreme good in the Professor's charismatic world. 'Friendship is sacred, because it is beautiful to share your own moments of bitterness, joy, pain and triumph with a friendly heart.'

And if Friendship came under threat, then death must become the best Friend of all: 'When a battle begins, a boss's first thought must be to make "Death" a Friend . . . Death, my Friend, help me to plant seeds in your land.'

On April Fool's Day 1982, the *Carabinieri* in Ottaviano discovered that Friend Death had planted a seed a few hundred metres away from the Cutolo castle. The body was in the boot of a stolen car. The head, wrapped in cellophane and covered with a towel, was in a plastic basin placed on the front seat. Even in the violence-weary Italy of the early 1980s, a camorra decapitation was guaranteed to attract a deal of media attention. But in this case the victim's name turned the event into front-page news.

Professor Aldo Semerari was the criminal psychiatrist responsible for some of the most clamorous expert opinions on Raffaele Cutolo's mental health. He was also a prime example of the kind of figure who, in the 1970s and 1980s, seemed to be spawned from the murk where organised crime and subversive politics overlapped. An extreme right-wing agitator with links to Italian military intelligence, Semerari had tried to enlist a number of criminal organisations to his Fascist cause. But in the end he only managed to arrange a simple swap: the gangsters received the benefit of his psychiatric expertise and, in return, Semerari's friends were given weapons. But the psychiatrist had been rash enough to try and make the same deal with both Raffaele Cutolo and his camorra enemies. When his headless corpse was found in Ottaviano, it was not clear who had punished him for playing off both sides.

The Semerari case gave Ottaviano a reputation as the town 'where heads fly'. Ten men were murdered there in the first five months of 1982. Journalists flocked to try and diagnose the malaise. But only one of them—a young Milanese writer called Luca Rossi—was patient enough to trace just how deeply the ideas expounded in *Poems and Thoughts* had been imbibed by many of the locals. For the rootless youth that grew up in the 'South Bronxes' of the Neapolitan periphery, Cutolo's poisonous credo was strong magic. The economic downturn of the mid-1970s put thousands of young men onto the market for criminal labour. During Cutolo's reign, Campania was the region with the highest number of juvenile inmates in the country. These *camorristi*-in-the-making were poor, from dysfunctional families, and educated early to the value of violence. By the time these kids were officially recruited, and had the NCO's five-dot insignia tattooed at the base of their right thumb, they professed an indifference to Friend Death that was as pitiful as it was terrifying:

What I've already seen in my twenty-three years is enough for me. I'm already dead. Now I'm just living an extra bit, a bit of life that's been gifted to me. They can kill me if they want.

We're already living corpses. Someone's already got half a foot on my head. And if you put the other half of your foot on my head, then I'll kill you.

You ask me why I behave like this, and why I do certain 'jobs' that even other *camorristi* won't do. The reason is very simple. It doesn't matter to me if I live or die. In fact, in some ways, I'm actually trying to get killed.

An anonymous twenty-year-old girl from Ottaviano interviewed by Luca Rossi set out the most perceptive and chilling dissection of the NCO mentality. This was the voice of a young woman both immersed in camorra culture, and yet able to distance herself from it, as if it were all just a nightmare:

The camorra has some really beautiful things about it. It's an instinctive, animal response. We take what they don't give us, and we take it with force. There are extraordinary, powerful feelings in the camorra. I've seen incredible acts of love and solidarity. They believe in what they are doing like no one believes in political ideologies . . . The strongest among them are the ones who are afraid. You see these kids with a pistol in their hand, and you realise they're fucked. Of all the *camorristi* I know, the most sensitive ones are the most violent. I mean really violent: machine-gun violent, massacre violent.

Raffaele Cutolo gave sensitive, wasted youths an elemental narrative—a reason to die where there seemed no reason to live. His *Poems and Thoughts* was a collective manifesto for living fast and going out in an expensive shirt and a hail of gunfire. The NCO came as close as any mafia has ever done to being a death cult.

And in 1978, Cutolo sent the NCO into a battle that turned into the bloodiest underworld war in Neapolitan history—a war against the Sicilian mafia.

PART X

THE SLAUGHTER

55

Blood orgy

First tobacco. Then construction. Then kidnapping. And finally heroin. The new sources of criminal wealth that developed between the late 1950s and the late 1970s offered huge rewards to *mafiosi, camorristi* and *'ndranghetisti* who could think big and collaborate to achieve their aims. New business networks were assembled: like the joint-stock ventures that pooled investments first in tobacco and then heroin; or the kidnapping gangs that took victims in the north before smuggling them into captivity on Aspromonte; or the heroin-trafficking rings that traversed the globe, linking the Golden Triangle to the United States via Sicily. New economic partnerships were forged, including partnerships that crossed the lines between Cosa Nostra, the camorra and the 'ndrangheta.

Alongside these cycles of commercial inventiveness, there came cycles of political inventiveness too. In Italy, no gangster would last long if he lapsed into believing that he was exclusively a criminal entrepreneur, and forgot that he has no choice but to take part in the permanent scheming and jockeying for position among his criminal peers. Thus, as the mafias grew richer, new arrangements of power were shaped: like the triumvirates in Calabria and Sicily, or Cosa Nostra's Regional Commission, or the Sicilian mafia Families that were set up in Campania. Underworld rules and traditions were overhauled or even invented, such as the ban on kidnapping in Cosa Nostra, or Raffaele Cutolo's revival of the nineteenth-century Honoured Society of Naples, or the 'ndrangheta's Mamma Santissima.

The faster the wheels of the criminal economy turned, and the more frenetic the politicking became, the more the pressures in Italy's underworld increased. The stakes and the risks grew greater and greater until, in the 1980s, there came an explosion of violence without precedent in the annals of mafia history.

How many died? Precision is impossible. Given the number of disappearances, and of mob assassinations that were artfully disguised as crimes of passion or robberies that got out of hand, we will never have an accurate sum. Not unless all the unmarked graves and skeletons in the deep can be located, and some sorcery invented to make the acid baths tell their story. Estimates for the number of fatalities during just the first two years of Sicily's Second Mafia War range between 500 and 1,000 people. More than 900 died in the camorra wars of 1979–83. One journalist has reckoned the total number killed by organised crime across the whole of southern Italy in the 1980s at 10,000. A guess, certainly. But by no means a wild one. More conservatively, the parliamentary inquiry estimated that, between 1981 and 1990, 2,905 murders were committed in Sicily, 2,621 in Campania, 1,807 in Calabria and 757 in Puglia. The vast majority of these were committed by organised crime. If that number is near the truth, it tells us that there were about twice as many victims of organised crime in southern Italy in the 1980s as there were victims of three decades of religious and political strife in Northern Ireland.

Any chronicle of that decade of slaughter must begin in Palermo, where Corleone's Totò 'Shorty' Riina was continuing his ascent. As we have seen, already in the 1970s the kidnappings perpetrated by Riina or his boss Luciano Liggio had begun to split Cosa Nostra into two factions. The make-up of the triumvirate demonstrated the balance of power clearly enough: on the one hand, Riina; and ranged against him Stefano Bontate, the Prince of Villagrazia, and Tano Badalamenti, the first head of the Palermo Commission after it was reconstituted in 1974. On the face of it, the two factions were unfairly matched. Although they were not close allies, Bontate and Badalamenti were nonetheless both part of the greatest concentration of wealth and connections that the Sicilian mafia had ever known. They had the politicians, both local and national. They had the ties with the shadowy world of Freemasonry. They had Palermo's oldest citadels of mafia power in their hands, and—at least in Bontate's case—the prestige that comes with a venerable mafia lineage. Crucially, they were also connected to the Transatlantic Syndicate with its near monopoly on access to the United States heroin market. Riina hailed from Corleone, which historically had been on the edges of the map of mafia power in the province of Palermo. Of the eleven men who had seats on the Commission in 1975, only three, including Riina himself, could be considered opponents of the Bontate and Badalamenti power system.

But Riina had luck and, above all, cunning on his side. Luck, because both Bontate and Badalamenti were arrested in the early 1970s, giving him the time and space to make his initial kidnapping moves. And cunning, because when the narcodollars really began to flood into Sicily, Riina was quick to divine the submerged currents of envy they set in motion.

Everyone in Cosa Nostra was involved in heroin, or at least wanted to be involved in heroin. But not everyone had access to the American market. The Transatlantic Syndicate had created a bottleneck, and was profiting handsomely from it. Many *mafiosi* became rich in the late 1970s drug boom, but only a few became opulent: those like Badalamenti, Bontate and Inzerillo, who were part of the transatlantic heroin elite.

Shorty planned to turn his economic weakness into political strength. He aimed to capitalise on the envy and frustration inspired by the Transatlantic Syndicate so as to win friends and territory in Sicily, and so take control of the Commission. By steadily recruiting the marginal players in the heroin industry, Riina was to transform the *corleonesi* from being just a Family, into being a great alliance of Men of Honour recruited from all the Families.

There was nothing startlingly new about this strategy. In New York, during the Castellammarese War of 1929–31 (the war that ended with Lucky Luciano installing himself at the apex of the New York underworld), Salvatore Maranzano's *castellammaresi* were just such a cross-Family alliance. In the battle for supremacy in Palermo that happened at more or less the same time as the Castellammarese War, Ernesto 'the *generalissimo*' Marasà infiltrated the Families of the province of Palermo in his campaign to become boss of all bosses.

Like his strategy, Riina's tactics were traditional too. The Sicilian mafia is a territorial organisation, and the cult of territory is as old as the mafia itself. As nineteenth-century mafia-fighter Ermanno Sangiorgi put it: 'One of the mafia's canons is respect for another man's territorial jurisdiction. Flouting that jurisdiction constitutes a personal insult.' The point here is that it is not just the mafia's *rules* that are traditional, but also the reasons why those rules are regularly broken—the signals that *mafiosi* send when they break them. Riina showed himself to be a master of maintaining his own territorial authority while sending out signals that undermined other people's. One of those signals was murder.

In January 1974, a retired policeman called Angelo Sorino was shot dead in San Lorenzo, in the Piana dei Colli. (His devotion to the cause was such that he had been helping his former colleagues with their investigations into Riina's allies.) Whoever was responsible for Sorino's death had not informed Cosa Nostra's Commission beforehand, as was supposed to happen with significant hits like this. It was obvious to the police who the culprit was because of the principle of territorial jurisdiction: Filippo Giacalone, boss of the Family whose realm included the murder scene. Giacalone, a friend of Stefano Bontate's, was duly arrested. Needless to say, Giacalone's involvement was even more obvious to his peers in Cosa Nostra. While he was in prison, Bontate demanded an explanation on behalf of the Commission.

As it turned out, Giacalone had not ordered Sorino's death; in fact he was only a patsy in a much bigger plot. Once he was freed, and had time to investigate, he told Bontate that a top *corleonese* killer called Leoluca Bagarella had carried out the murder. But before Bontate could refer these findings back to the Commission, Giacalone vanished. His place on the Commission was taken by the boss of neighbouring Resuttana, a friend of the *corleonesi*.

The Sorino murder was a dual-purpose homicide. It eliminated a threat to one of Riina's friends. More importantly, it loudly proclaimed Bontate and Badalamenti's political weakness.

In 1977, the *corleonesi* carried out another dual-purpose homicide. They killed a zealous colonel of the *Carabinieri* on their own territory, thus eliminating a threat to their own interests. But they also failed to ask permission from the Commission before acting: another political snub to their enemies.

Having used kidnappings and murders to discredit the Bontate-Badalamenti-controlled Commission, the *corleonesi* looked to take it over themselves. By now they already had a prestigious ally: the boss of Ciaculli, Michele 'the Pope' Greco, who proved adept at befogging Bontate with seemingly reasonable explanations for what the *corleonesi* were doing. Behind the smokescreen created by Michele Greco, more and more bosses were coming over to Riina's side.

In 1978 the extent of *corleonese* influence within the Commission became obvious to all when—sensationally—Tano Badalamenti, the boss of all bosses, was expelled from Cosa Nostra. Badalamenti was almost certainly punished because he had failed to give everyone a share of the heroin bonanza. Being expelled—the word *mafiosi* use is *posato* or 'laid down'—is a relatively rare sanction, and often a temporary one. Among men for whom one murder more or less is no cause for handwringing, this was a demonstratively mild penalty. Riina was making a show of playing by Cosa Nostra's traditional rules; he was showing just how *reasonable* he was. Accordingly it was a man of reason, Michele 'the Pope' Greco, who took Badalamenti's place as provincial representative. Greco was little more than a front for *corleonese* power.

Later the same year, the *corleonesi* once more played tricks with the rules of territorial sovereignty. A team of *corleonese* hit men shot dead Giuseppe Di Cristina, a boss who was particularly close to Stefano Bontate. Crucially, the murder took place on territory belonging to another Bontate ally, the zip Salvatore Inzerillo. The killers even abandoned the car used in the assassination in Inzerillo's domain. The message in the murder humiliated a key Bontate ally, and a central figure in the Transatlantic Syndicate. Di Cristina's death also showed that the *corleonesi*'s ambitions were not restricted to the province of Palermo. The son and grandson of mafia bosses, Di Cristina was from the inland town of Riesi in the province of Caltanissetta.

After central Sicily came the turn of the eastern city of Catania. In September 1978, Pippo Calderone—the local boss of Cosa Nostra and the man who had instigated the kidnapping ban at the Regional Commission in 1975—was shot dead by his deputy, another covert member of the growing *corleonese* alliance. At the banquet held by Calderone's men to mark their boss's passing, Shorty Riina had the brass to give a speech. He eulogised the dead *capo* as a peacemaker in the best mafia traditions. Many of the gangsters present were moved to tears.

By 1979 the *corleonesi* had won a clear majority on the Palermo Commission. Just as significantly, they had begun to make inroads into their enemies' own closest circles. One Man of Honour from Stefano Bontate's own Santa Maria di Gesù Family serves as a measure of just how far the *corleonesi* now reached. He was a lawyer, and a major drug trafficker, who resented his boss's overweening manner, and found a sympathetic ear for his complaints among Totò Riina's friends. His name was Giovanni Bontate, and he was the younger brother of the boss.

Cunning exploitation of the mafia's rules and conventions, calculated insults, alliance-building and betrayal: all of the ingredients in the measured *corleonese* advance upon the centres of underworld power in Sicily can be found in the archives of mafia history going back to the nineteenth century. In that sense, the events of the late 1970s and early 1980s were nothing new. All the same, there were at least two novelties. The first was the value of the prize that would accrue to the victors. For once Sicily was won, the Americans would have no alternative but to talk business with Salvatore 'Shorty' Riina. The heroin pipeline would flow through Corleone. The other novelty in Riina's rise to the top was the relentless ferocity with which he executed his plans, the sheer brutality of Sicily's Second Mafia War.

On the evening of 23 April 1981, Stefano Bontate, well dressed as ever, drove his brand-new limited edition Alfa Romeo Giulietta Super through the rain and the habitually frenetic traffic on the Palermo ring road. He had spent the evening quaffing champagne at his own forty-second birthday party, and was now on the way home. When he turned off into a side road, he was stopped dead by blasts from a sawed-off shotgun and a Kalashnikov.

Two and a half weeks later, another Kalashnikov victim was found lying by the gate of a large housing block in via Brunelleschi. The head was so badly pulped by bullets that it took the police five hours to make an identification on the basis of fingerprints and a blood-caked medallion with initials engraved on it: it belonged to Salvatore Inzerillo, boss of Passo di Rigano, whose name had just begun to appear in the papers in association with a major investigation into heroin smuggling.

National public opinion took a while to wake up to the fact that this was something more than another seasonal bout of gangster-on-gangster violence. In newspapers in the North, Salvatore Inzerillo's death attracted coverage comparable to a moderately serious motor accident in Milan or Turin. But as the killings continued in Palermo, people sought explanations for what was happening. Heroin obviously had something to do with it. Not much else made sense.

One by one, all the old journalistic templates for mafia violence were applied, and discarded. Was this a tit-for-tat: perhaps the Bontate and Inzerillo clans were at war with one another? But then it was discovered that the same Kalashnikov was used to kill both bosses.

Another theory—a very old one—was that this was an inter-generational conflict, and that a young mafia of 'forty-somethings' was making an attack on the power of the 'old' mafia. The fact that Bontate was forty-two when he died, and Salvatore Inzerillo thirty-seven, did not square easily with this interpretation.

Some explanations were so wildly off target as to be comical, or exasperating, depending on your point of view. Interviewed by the *New York Times*, the novelist Alberto Moravia argued that 'The Sicilian as such—including the honest Sicilian—is by inclination a Mafioso, in the sense that he shares with the mafia man the yearning for, and obsession with, the "prestige of power."' Nowadays it seems mystifying that anyone should consider a Roman novelist to be an authority worth consulting on the complexities of the mafia. But Moravia's ignorance should serve as a reminder of the appalling state of public knowledge in this key phase of the organisation's century-old history.

The police themselves were more astute than Moravia, but hardly revealing. The chief of the Flying Squad said only that, 'What we have here is a blood orgy: when the war ends, we will manage to understand the new balance of power.' This was the police's traditional approach to the cyclical blood-letting among Palermo's criminal elite: wait for the shooting to stop, and then count the bodies and hope for a tip-off.

The shooting did not stop. The newspapers became a daily catalogue of horrors. Bodies abandoned in slicks of blood in the street, or found crumpled behind shop counters, or left amid burning rubbish on empty lots. Antonino Ciaramitaro was discovered in the boot of a car in two plastic bags—one for his trunk and one for his head. Giovanni Prestigiacomo was shot-gunned to death as he parked his FIAT 1100. His wife heard the detonations and ran outside; she would continue to hold him, screaming 'Don't die. Don't die', long after the life had ebbed from his riddled cadaver.

Desperate for certainties, the newspapers tried to keep a tally. Seventy bodies in the six months between April and October 1981; 148 by the end of the year. But the 'white shotguns' (meaning cases in which a victim simply vanishes and their body is never found) made the counting difficult. Perhaps 112 disappearances in the first nine months of 1982, plus 108 murders. But the numbers were only a veil for confusion.

We now know that what was really going on was not actually a mafia war at all: it was a programme of annihilation. Riina was systematically eliminating his enemies and anyone close to them. The day after Inzerillo's murder, the boss who had stepped into Stefano Bontate's shoes in Santa Maria di Gesù called the dead *capo*'s six most loyal soldiers into a meeting to discuss what was happening. Four of them obeyed and were never seen again: the new boss was Riina's appointment.

The drug broker Gaspare 'Mr Champagne' Mutolo was a witness to what happened next. Emanuele D'Agostino, one of the two men who had wisely decided not to answer the call to visit the new boss of Santa Maria di Gesù, went into hiding. He sought refuge with Rosario Riccobono, Mutolo's *capo*. Riccobono had always tried to maintain a neutral position in the mafia power struggle of the late 1970s. But the initial success of the *corleonese* assault persuaded him it was time to come off the fence: he killed D'Agostino as a token of his new-found loyalty to Shorty Riina. Just in case Riina needed more convincing, Riccobono then set a trap for D'Agostino's son by telling him to bring some clean clothes to his father's hideout. The son followed the father into a shallow grave.

A couple of weeks later, the only survivor from among the six Bontate soldiers, a *mafioso* by the name of Totuccio Contorno, was driving through Brancaccio with a little friend of his eleven-year-old son in the passenger seat. Suddenly, a powerful motorbike pulled out from a side street, and the pillion passenger raked the car with a Kalashnikov as it sped past. Contorno pushed the boy out of the car (miraculously, he had not been hit) and returned fire with a pistol before escaping. Totuccio Contorno would, in time, become one of the most important witnesses who enabled investigators to reconstruct the dynamics of the slaughter.

Hardly had the *corleonesi* finished with the active members of the opposing faction than they moved on to their relatives. Santo Inzerillo, brother of murdered zip Salvatore, was strangled when he tried to make a peace offering to Riina. Another brother, who was only sixteen, had his arm cut off before he was put out of his agony.

News of the slaughter in Sicily caused consternation in New York. John Gambino, the Transatlantic Syndicate boss from Cherry Hills, bravely came back to Palermo to express the American Cosa Nostra's concerns. Shorty Riina's response was an order: the Americans must kill anyone from the Bontate or Inzerillo clans who had managed to escape across the Atlantic. Thus it was that Salvatore Inzerillo's uncle and cousin disappeared; then Pietro Inzerillo, a brother, was taken from a restaurant in Trenton, New Jersey, beheaded by gunfire, and his body dumped in the boot of a Cadillac. One particular detail of Pietro Inzerillo's grisly end caught the public's imagination: dollars were placed in his mouth and on his genitals to show that he had been too greedy. The message here was that his American killers (among whom numbered yet another Inzerillo cousin) were dutifully parroting the *corleonese* justification for the war: the greed of the *mafiosi* who controlled access to the American heroin market.

Having turned the Inzerillo clan against itself, Shorty Riina next purged anyone whose loyalty to him was even remotely in doubt. Just before Christmas in 1982, Saro Riccobono, the Partanna-Mondello representative who had been so keen to cosy up to Riina by betraying and killing Emanuele D'Agostino and his son, was invited to a great barbecue amid the mandarin orange trees of Michele Greco's Ciaculli estate. After a hearty meal and a nap, he was woken by men placing a rope around his neck: 'Saru, your story ends here', they told him. At the same moment, Riccobono's soldiers were being strangled one by one by the other guests at the barbecue. When the stragglers had been hunted down, only three members of Mr Champagne's entire Family remained alive.

The cull extended to other provinces of Sicily. In September 1981, the international heroin traffickers of the Cuntrera-Caruana clan suffered their first victim when Leonardo Caruana was murdered. The *corleonesi* also sponsored particularly vicious fighting in the province of Trapani, where they slowly encircled and conquered the town of Alcamo—the capital of the Bontate-Badalamenti-Inzerillo faction in that province.

Although the Sicilian blood-letting peaked in the years 1981–3, it did not abate entirely, but transformed itself into an endless state of terror. As Riina's power grew, so did his fear. He began to see the young killers who had taken a leading role in the first waves of killings as a potential threat.

The prime case in point was Pino Greco, known as 'Little Shoe'. Little Shoe was the man whose Kalashnikov had put paid to both Stefano Bontate and Salvatore Inzerillo. He was also the Kalashnikov-wielding pillion passenger who led the attempt to eliminate Totuccio Contorno. Little Shoe it was who cut off the sixteen-year-old Inzerillo brother's arm. He is thought to have killed some eighty people. But he was more than just a sadistic butcher. He was also a power in his own right. While he was formally the underboss of Michele 'the Pope' Greco's Ciaculli Family, Pino Greco was in reality the power behind the Pope's throne, making sure that Corleone's will was done. At some point, late in 1985, Little Shoe's own men decided to eliminate him before his ambitions put them in the way of Shorty Riina's wrath.

Such was the dread inspired by the Corleone boss. Shorty had established a kind of military dictatorship. Cosa Nostra would never be the same again. By the time of Little Shoe's death, the new tide of underworld war in Italy had long since engulfed Campania too, and the Sicilian mafia had been drawn into a proxy war against the Professor and his Nuova Camorra Organizzata.

56

THE NEW FAMILY: A group portrait

WHEN RAFFAELE CUTOLO 'NOISILY WANDERED AWAY' FROM THE MENTAL HOSPITAL IN Aversa in February 1978, the growth of his Nuova Camorra Organizzata (NCO) accelerated. The Professor recruited hundreds more young followers, reorganised his command structure, vastly increased the pressure of his extortion rackets, and even made a trip to the United States to seek closer business ties with his contacts in the American Cosa Nostra. All of these initiatives prepared the ground for the audacious demand he then issued to every other camorra organisation: he wanted tribute, in the form of 20,000 lire (equal to some $87 in 2011) for every case of contraband cigarettes that was unloaded in the region. There was no mistaking the scale of the ambition implicit in Cutolo's ultimatum: he was making a bid to become the absolute ruler of the whole Campanian underworld.

Cosa Nostra was the biggest force standing in Cutolo's way. In the early 1970s, the clans affiliated to the Sicilian mafia held the criminal balance of power in Campania, a region traversed by many different gang territories. Canny propagandist that he was, the Professor sold his campaign to his followers as underworld patriotism: the Nuova Camorra Organizzata, heir to the traditions of the Neapolitan Honoured Society of old, was to lead a crusade to free the region of Sicilian influence: 'One day the people of Campania will understand that a crust of bread eaten in freedom is worth more than a steak eaten as a slave. And that day Campania will truly have victory.' Cutolo branded *camorristi* who were loyal to any outside criminal force as traitors: 'In my eyes they were "half *mafiosi*," because they took orders from Sicilian bosses and in that way sold out their own land.' The

Professor's rhetoric was backed by the firepower of his legions of young gunmen. Fighting began to break out across Campania.

The first clans to bond together to resist Cutolo were those from central Naples. The anti-Cutolo front then grew to embrace Cosa Nostra's Campanian Families and other clans in the Neapolitan hinterland too. As it did so, it adopted the name Nuova Famiglia—the New Family—or NF. By early in 1980, the whole of the region was divided between two armed camps, the NF and the NCO. The scale of the armies was absolutely unprecedented in the whole long history of Campanian organised crime. So too was the scale of the bloodshed: an estimated 1,000 dead in the course of five years.

The battle in Campania in the early 1980s was a much messier affair than Shorty Riina's coup d'état in Sicily. Most of the confusion derived from the fact that Nuova Famiglia was a loose alliance rather than a single underworld organisation. It did use improvised initiation rituals. But that fact tells that its leaders were desperate to use any means they could to manufacture loyalty among the recruits they needed to stand up to the greatly superior numbers of the Nuova Camorra Organizzata. The Nuova Famiglia was held together (when it did hold together) only by its opposition to the Professor. Some of the underworld barons within it soft-pedalled on the war-making when it suited their own selfish purposes. Some switched sides halfway through. Cosa Nostra tried to manage the conflict from the outside, while going through a savage conflict of its own back in Palermo.

In 1980, Cosa Nostra first tried to drum up the kind of united resistance to Cutolo's ambitions that would have brought a quick end to the struggle. But the Commission found that even some of the Sicilian mafia's own affiliates in Campania were loath to throw men and money into a war. The leading tobacco smuggler Michele 'Mad Mike' Zaza had been one of the founding members of the anti-Cutolo alliance. But by now he preferred to strike a deal with the Professor based on dividing out territory: the Nuova Camorra Organizzata could have the province to itself, as long as it left the city alone. Lorenzo Nuvoletta, leader of the other Campanian Family of Cosa Nostra, probably had different motives. For narcotics were more important to him than the declining revenue from tobacco smuggling that the Professor wanted to tax.

Frustrated by this lack of warrior zeal, the Palermo Commission sent a killer to dispatch the Professor. But someone must have leaked news of the assassin's arrival, because the assassin himself was shot dead by two men on a motorbike not long after arriving in Naples.

In the summer of 1980 Cosa Nostra tried a different approach. Having failed to nudge Zaza and Nuvoletta into the attack, it urged them to broker an accommodation. But the resultant peace-making seems to have been almost as half-hearted as the war-making, for the cycle of punitive expeditions was not interrupted for long. In the end, Cosa Nostra would sponsor at least three peace conferences attended by large numbers of representatives from both the NCO and NF. Two of those conferences were attended personally by Shorty Riina and his lieutenants, despite the massacre that they were orchestrating in Sicily. But it was all in vain. Once started, the fighting in Campania proved too bitter to stop.

The camorra would go on to murder 364 people in 1982—very nearly one a day. And lest the many innocent victims get lost in the tales of gangland retribution, it is worth citing the case of someone else who died in January 1982: Annamaria Esposito, aged thirty-three, a mother of two who was executed for the sole reason that she witnessed a *camorrista* being murdered in her bar.

A group portrait of the Nuova Famiglia bosses who were fighting against the Nuova Camorra Organizzata for control of this territory tells us a great deal about the past, the present and the future of Campanian organised crime. The story of the camorra stretching forwards into the twenty-first century has its roots in the NF.

The camorra war of the early 1980s brought Pupetta Maresca back to the national headlines again. In 1955, she had first made herself notorious by killing the man who killed her husband, the President of Potato Prices. Pupetta's fame carried weight in the Campanian underworld. In 1970, she started a long-term relationship with a major narcotics trafficker, Umberto Ammaturo. With her new beau, Pupetta was able to turn her fame into a luxurious prominence as a *femmena 'e conseguenza* (a woman with stature), a First Lady of the underworld. The police believed that 'many of the crimes carried out by Umberto Ammaturo were, in reality, dreamed up in her head'.

Pupetta's consort, Umberto Ammaturo, was one of the most aggressive members of the NF. Near Christmas in 1981, he planted a bomb outside Cutolo's Ottaviano palace as a provocation. He would later confess to being the man behind the murder of criminal psychiatrist Aldo Semerari, whose beheaded corpse was also found near Cutolo's palace on April Fool's Day 1982. Raffaele 'the Professor' Cutolo demanded Ammaturo's own head as the price for any peace deal with the NF.

In February 1982, in the middle of this confrontation between Ammaturo and Cutolo, Pupetta Maresca's brother Ciro was arrested and sent to the very maw of the NCO monster: Poggioreale prison. Although he was kept in isolation, his life was in obvious and immediate danger. Pupetta's response showed that she had lost none of her gift for publicity. On 13 February 1982 she called a media conference, no less, in the Naples press association head-quarters. Arriving alone, she made a statement entrance: nearly an hour late, her jewels sparkling as the camera flashbulbs ignited, she was dressed in a black leather skirt and black fur coat, with a leopard-skin choker at her throat and a white blouse that exposed her cleavage. No sooner had she come into the room than she started picking fights with the journalists, responding angrily to queries about her jewellery ('I'd like to see anyone with the courage to mug me') and then demanding order: 'Gentlemen, a bit of silence please! If Cutolo was here instead of me, you wouldn't be making such a racket. Of course, it's because you're afraid. He has shut your mouths with lead.'

The Professor was the target of her unrestrained rage: 'bastard', 'mad-man', 'he wants to become the emperor of the city'. When journalists asked Pupetta if she was speaking on behalf of the Nuova Famiglia, she replied: 'I'm not part of any group. But if some people think like I do—and you tell me that means the Nuova Famiglia—then they are my partners.'

Fighting back tears, she returned to the main purpose of the press con-ference: to issue an ultimatum to Cutolo. 'I want to let that gentleman know that, if he dares touch anyone close to me, I will destroy him and his family down to the seventh generation, women and children included.'

We can only wonder about the emotions that helped drive this extra-ordinary performance. Rage or sorrow? Defiance or fear? Nor do we have an idea whether these emotions were real or staged. Yet it seems certain that they were at least partially the symptom of the psychological strains of a lifetime spent as a camorra queen. Maresca enjoyed status and very probably real power. She also paid a heavy price. She had two children by Ammaturo, twins. She also lost a child: her first son Pasqualino (the baby she had been carrying during the notorious events of 1955) vanished in 1974 during the tobacco-smuggling war between Cosa Nostra and the Marseillais. Pupetta herself strongly suspected that Ammaturo had killed him. Yet she stayed with her man, either because he beat her (above the hairline, so the damage would not show) or because she was too attached to her furs and jewels.

The Professor was even less shy of publicity than Pupetta, and much better than her at getting under his enemies' skin. Dressed in a grey double-breasted suit, he issued his response to her challenge from a Naples court-room: 'Maybe Pupetta said those things to attract attention. Maybe she wants to make another film. You have to say that she's chosen the right moment: Carnival kicks off in a few days' time.'

As the spat between Pupetta Maresca and the Professor demonstrated, the war in Naples was an extraordinarily *public* affair. In Sicily, where Shorty Riina's death squads emerged from nowhere to exterminate his enemies, the citizenry and even the police struggled to make out who was fighting whom. In Campania, by contrast, there were open challenges and proclamations, and nobody was in any doubt where the battle lines were drawn. These contrasting styles of warfare corresponded to a long-standing difference between the public images of the two crime fraternities. The soberly dressed Sicilian *mafioso* has traditionally had a much lower public profile than the *camorrista*. *Mafiosi* are so used to infiltrating the state and the ruling elite that they prefer to blend into the background rather than strike poses of defiance against the authorities. The authorities, after all, were often on their side. *Camorristi*, by contrast, often played to an audience.

There is no clearer illustration of this point than the Giulianos, a clan centred on Pio Vittorio Giuliano and a number of his eleven children, plus some of their male cousins. With its criminal roots in the smuggling boom that took place during the Allied military occupation, the family hailed from Naples's notorious 'kasbah', Forcella.

The Giulianos' reign would persist into the 1980s and 1990s, when the clan eventually began to fall apart amid arrests, deaths and defections to the

'Ice Eyes', early 1980s. Luigi Giuliano led his crime family from their base in the Forcella quarter of Naples—the historical home of the camorra in the city.

state. The brashness of their power—the family occupied an apartment block that loomed like the prow of a huge ship at a fork in the road at the very centre of Forcella—would not have been unfamiliar to nineteenth-century *camorristi* with their gold rings, braided waistcoats and flared trousers. The second Giuliano boy, Luigi (born in 1949), took charge of the family business in his twenties. He was a wannabe actor and poet, a medallion man whose success with the ladies earned him the nickname 'Lovigino'—an untranslatable coupling of the English word 'Love' and the affectionate form of Luigi. Lovigino's menacing good looks and his startlingly blue irises explain his other moniker: 'Ice Eyes'.

It is no coincidence that the Giulianos have left many eloquent photographs of their pomp. By far the most famous image from the Giuliano family album was confiscated during a police raid in February 1986. It shows two of the curly-haired Giuliano boys, Carmine 'the Lion' in a bright red V-neck, and Guglielmo 'the Crooked One' in white jeans. Both are beaming with delight as they recline in the most flamboyant bathtub in the history of plumbing: it takes the form of a giant conch-shell, its top half lifted back to reveal a gold-leaf interior, its surround in black stone, its base in pink marble with a pattern like stone-washed jeans. But the most remarkable thing about the photo is not the questionable taste of the Giulianos' bathroom fixtures and fittings. Lounging between the brothers is a muscular little man wearing a grey and red tracksuit and an even bigger grin than them: Diego Armando Maradona, the greatest talent ever to lace up a pair of soccer boots.

The greatest soccer player of the age, Diego Armando Maradona, poses with members of the Giuliano camorra clan, who were keen to show off their taste in bathroom fittings (mid-1980s).

Argentinian superstar Maradona played for Napoli at his peak, between 1984 and 1992, and won the Serie A national championship twice. He became a demigod in the city, worshipped as no other sportsman anywhere has ever been: still now, his picture adorns half the bars in Naples. The notorious bathtub photo was not the only occasion during his time in the sky-blue shirt of Napoli when his name was associated with organised crime. In March 1989, he put in an appearance at the swish restaurant where Lovigino's cousin was getting married: 'Maradona at the boss's wedding' ran one headline. Four months later, he claimed that the camorra was threatening him and his family, and that he was too afraid to return to Naples for the start of the new season. There were unsubstantiated rumours of match-fixing. This was the summer when the conch-shell bathtub photo was made public. (Mysteriously, it was kept in a drawer in police headquarters for over three years.) It is also worth recalling that it was in Naples that Maradona's well-documented problems with cocaine took a grip.

At the time, 'the Hand of God' denied knowing that the Giulianos were gangsters. His autobiography, published in 2000, is more forthcoming:

I admit it was a seductive world. It was something new for us Argentinians: the Mafia. It was fascinating to watch . . . They offered me visits to fan clubs, gave me watches, that was the link we had. But if I saw it wasn't all above board I didn't accept. Even so it was an incredible time: whenever I went to one of those clubs they gave me gold Rolexes, cars . . . I asked them: 'But what do I have to do?' They said: *Nothing, just have your picture taken.* 'Thank you,' I would say.

The point here is not whether Maradona's links to organised crime were more substantial than he claims. His very visible friendship with the Giulianos was more than enough for their purposes. Many *camorristi*, particularly urban *camorristi*, have always sought good publicity; they have always sought to win the admiration of the section of the Neapolitan population that identifies with well-meaning miscreants. Whether by loud, expensive clothes and flagrant generosity, by shows of piety, by grand public funerals and weddings, or by rubbing shoulders with singers and sportsmen, generations of *camorristi* have won legitimacy in the eyes of the very people they exploit. Maradona's own story, as the pocket genius risen from a shanty suburb of Buenos Aires, was a perfect fit with the camorra's traditional claim that it was rooted in, and justified by, poverty. If the camorra from the slums of Naples had an official ideology, it would be the kind of pseudo-sociology that Lovigino 'Ice Eyes' Giuliano himself articulated:

In Forcella it isn't possible to live without breaking the state's laws. But we Forcella folk aren't to blame. The blame goes to the people who prevent us doing a normal job. Because no one from a normal company is prepared to take on someone from Forcella, we are forced to find a way to get by.

Needless to say, 'getting by' involved extorting money from every money-making activity in Forcella; it involved illegal lotteries and ticket touting for Napoli games; it involved mass-producing fake branded clothes; it involved theft and drug dealing on a huge scale; and it involved appalling acts of violence. When Lovigino 'Ice Eyes' eventually turned state's evidence in 2002, he confessed to the murder of an NCO killer called Giacomo Frattini. Frattini's fresh-faced looks earned him the nickname of *Bambulella*—Doll Face—despite a body covered in jailhouse tattoos. The NF spent a long time planning what they would do to him. One idea was to crucify him in front of the Professor's palace on the slopes of Mount Vesuvius. In the end, in January 1982, an execution party lured him into a trap, tortured him, and then summoned a friendly butcher to lop off his head and hands and cut out his heart. They left the pieces in separate plastic bags in a FIAT 500 Belvedere just off piazza Carlo III. A note from an imaginary left-wing terrorist group was left in a telephone box nearby: it called him the 'prison executioner', the slave of a 'demented, diabetic fanatic'—meaning Raffaele 'the Professor' Cutolo.

Being flash like the Giulianos has never been the only style of criminal authority in Naples. Historically, the area to the city's north is home to a quieter brand of *camorrista* who would also become part of the Nuova Famiglia.

Marano is a small agricultural centre that has long been notorious for camorra influence. In 1955, the son of the town's former mayor, Gaetano Orlando, shot dead Big Pasquale, the 'President of Potato Prices'. During the 1970s and 1980s, Gaetano Orlando's nephews, Lorenzo, Gaetano, Angelo and Ciro Nuvoletta, became the most powerful criminals in Campania. They were initiated into Cosa Nostra during the tobacco-smuggling boom. Their farmhouse, which stood shrouded by trees on a hill just outside town, was the theatre of all the most important meetings during the war between the NCO and the NF.

The Nuvolettas preferred the subdued public image of their brethren in Cosa Nostra. Their wealth was vast, and as was the case with the many criminal fortunes built in the same part of Campania over the previous century, it straddled the divide between lawful business and crime. The clan earned from construction as well as smuggling, property as well as extortion, farming as well as fraud. Sicilian heroin broker Gaspare 'Mr Champagne' Mutolo was initiated into Cosa Nostra on the Nuvolettas' farm. He saw their riches at firsthand: they had warehouses of battery hens because they had a contract to feed all the military barracks in Naples. Thus, even during the new wealth of the 1970s, *camorristi* from the hinterland had not relinquished their traditional grip on the city's food supplies.

This combination of lawful and illegal income explains the Nuvolettas' preference for passing unobserved. For all their riches, their profile was so low that when, in December 1979, the *Carabinieri* captured Corleone *mafioso* Leoluca Bagarella in possession of a photograph of a businessman with salt-and-pepper hair, it took them months to put Lorenzo Nuvoletta's name to the face. No wonder, then, that Lorenzo Nuvoletta was entrusted with being the *capomandamento* ('precinct boss') of the three Campanian Families of Cosa Nostra, the man whose job was to represent Neapolitan interests to the Palermo Commission, through his prime contact, Michele 'the Pope' Greco.

So the Nuova Famiglia reflected all the traditional diversity of organised crime in Naples and Campania. And that diversity also explains why it seemed that the atrocities might carry on without anyone ever achieving a military victory.

57

Catastrophe economy

Giuseppe Tornatore's 1986 film *Il camorrista* is a rambling, rise-and-fall gangster melodrama based on the career of Raffaele 'the Professor' Cutolo. It plays back the embellished highlights of the Nuova Camorra Organizzata story to a soundtrack of plaintive trumpet and clarinet melodies that owe more than a little to *The Godfather*'s genre-defining score. Since *Il camorrista* first came out in 1986, endless reshowings through local TV, bootleg videos, and now YouTube, have irretrievably confused reality and myth in the popular memory of the Professor's reign. The movie's most resonant lines ('Tell the Professor I did not betray him' and 'Malacarne is a cardboard *guappo*') have become slogans—the Neapolitan equivalent of 'I'll make him an offer he can't refuse' and 'Leave the gun, take the *cannoli*.'

Perhaps *Il camorrista*'s most visually arresting scene takes place in prison. The Professor is shown reading a history book in bed, in an immaculately pressed pair of sky-blue pyjamas. A low rumble in the background causes him to look up. The rumble becomes a shaking: first the ornaments on his bedside chest vibrate, then his metal bed frame starts clanking repeatedly against the wall, and his cell window shatters. Wails of panic rise in the background: 'Earthquake!' Staggering to his feet, Cutolo opens his cell door to watch Poggioreale prison plunge into anarchy. Clouds of dust rise from the floor of his wing, and chunks of plaster drop from the ceiling. The guards run hither and thither releasing screaming inmates from the cells. Within seconds, Cutolo has his arms around his two chief enforcers: 'This is a chance sent to us by the Lord above! It's gotta be the apocalypse for the old camorra!'

There then follows a ghastly chiaroscuro carnival of stabbings, clubbings, lynchings and garrottings, as Cutolo's men take advantage of the chaos to dispatch their enemies. From the din and mass panic inside the prison, we then cut to the morning after, to watch a dozen or so pine coffins being loaded into vans in the prison yard.

The earthquake of 23 November 1980 was no cinematic fantasy. With its epicentre in the mountains east of Naples, it killed 2,914 people across Campania. But the film director's job is what it is: Tornatore used a deal of artistic licence when he edited the disaster into his mob movie. The historian's job being what it is, I must indicate a couple of the points at which art and fact diverge. The numbers murdered for example: there were 'only' three fatalities in Poggioreale; plus another three on 14 February 1981 when Cutolo's men went hunting again following a major aftershock. Tornatore makes room for all the extra deaths by stretching the ninety seconds that the real quake lasted into nearly three minutes; he also adds in a few implausible thunderclaps and lightning flashes for effect. In reality, the reign of terror in Poggioreale was more prolonged. NCO killers did not pursue their victims while the quake itself was happening, but rather during the night that followed, after the guards abandoned many wings, leaving the rival criminal factions to battle it out.

Il camorrista embroiders the truth in more insidious ways than these. For example, it turns the squalid road-rage murder that earned Cutolo his first life sentence into an episode where he kills a man for groping his sister. Since the very origins of Italy's mafias, underworld prestige has constantly been confused in the public mind with the defence of women's sexual honour.

Yet even the most nit-picking historian would have to admit that Tornatore's artistic licence was justified in some cases. He was absolutely right to make the earthquake one of the movie's major set pieces, for example. The twenty-third of November 1980, when Cutolo, dressed in his silk dressing gown, directed his teams of killers to eliminate his enemies, was indeed an important date in the Nuova Camorra Organizzata's war. The reason the NF hated Giacomo 'Doll Face' Frattini so much that they beheaded him was because he was one of the Professor's prison killers in November 1980.

The earthquake also marked a seismic shift in the nature of camorra power in Naples. After the earthquake, because of the earthquake, the camorra at last joined the mafia and the 'ndrangheta in plundering the construction business and thereby merging with the political class. One of the many remarkable things about the Professor is that his organisation made that leap into construction while his war against the NF was still going on.

Back in the 1950s, Italy had great hopes that state investment could help the backward South industrialise. By the mid-1970s, the international economic crisis and a long history of politicking, corruption and incompetence in the allocation of the cash had brought these hopes to an end. Italian governments abandoned the long-term ideal of economic development and instead embraced the short-term aims of propping up consumer spending while giving politicians enough money to keep their constituents happy. From now on, the stream of taxpayer's money that went towards the South would no longer be directed in targeted squirts at training and infrastructure. Instead, it would descend as a fine drizzle of benefits and pensions. The same system would prevail even when the Italian economy recovered in the 1980s.

The earthquake of 23 November 1980 cruelly exposed Campania's ills. Prestigious buildings put up with central government money turned out to have been too shoddily built to resist the tremors. An entire wing of one public hospital in the village of Sant'Angelo dei Lombardi flopped to the ground, killing dozens. Clearly, in this, as in many other cases, distributing contracts and jobs had been a higher priority than actually providing an edifice worthy of the name.

The state's response to the challenges of post-earthquake reconstruction was a lesson in bad planning. The professed aim was not just to rebuild, but also to create new economic opportunities for the stricken area. But a proliferation of confused emergency laws created a messy ensemble of spending programmes. Powers and responsibilities were scattered among different special commissars, ministries, regions, provinces and town councils, so that it became impossible to monitor the reconstruction programme properly. Avid politicians rushed to cash in. Two months after the earthquake, in February 1981, 316 town councils were deemed eligible for reconstruction funds; nine months later, the total had risen to 686. The number of damaged buildings reported increased from 70,000 to more than 350,000 over roughly the same period. Either the earthquake had had some very peculiar delayed effects, or a lot of people were telling fibs about the extent of the destruction.

Actually spending the reconstruction money involved a multiplicity of official roles. Technicians to estimate the work required. Commissioners to evaluate those estimates on behalf of the town councils. Planners. Administrators who had to approve the planners' plans. Lawyers to draw up contracts. Construction entrepreneurs. Works supervisors and inspectors. And so on. But because the agencies given money to spend were largely unaccountable, many of these separate roles turned out to have been performed by the same people wearing different hats. Or by groups of friends. Or by

narrow party cliques. The regime of emergency measures that had opened
the door to these vultures turned into a permanent state of affairs.

The results of the shambles were grim. At the end of 1990, ten years after the quake struck, 28,572 people were still living in emergency caravans.
Few of the thousands of jobs that were promised had materialised. Costs
had skyrocketed. Parasites had made fortunes. And vast new political clienteles had been created. The earthquake gave birth to the worst financial
scandal in 1980s Europe. But that scandal was only in its infancy when the
most violent elements in Campania decided that they too could profit from
the disaster.

The episode that exposed the camorra's links to the catastrophe economy
was a terrorist kidnapping.

Ciro Cirillo stood at the very centre of the Christian Democrats' patronage system in Campania. After the 1980 earthquake, he was given responsibility for handling the massive funds channelled through the Campanian
regional government for reconstruction. Soon afterwards, on the evening of
27 April 1981, he was abducted by the Naples column of the Red Brigades.
Five *brigatisti* were waiting for him as he arrived in the underground garage
of his house in Torre del Greco, a town lying on the strip of land between
Mount Vesuvius and the sea. When Cirillo's bodyguard, as usual, stepped
back outside to check that all was well, he was shot dead. Before the driver
could react, he was also killed, and his secretary shot several times in the
legs. Cirillo was pulled from the back seat, pistol-whipped, and led away.

Italy was by then grimly familiar with the routine of terrorist kidnappings. First the call to a newspaper to claim responsibility. Then a short
interlude of worry and speculation: was the claim genuine? Then the proof.
The afternoon after Cirillo was kidnapped, another call was made, this time
to the editorial offices of *Il Mattino*, the biggest circulation daily in Naples.
The instructions were terse: 'At number 275, Riviera di Chiaia, under a rubbish bin, you will find communiqué number one.' When it was retrieved,
communiqué number one contained a Polaroid photo of the captive sitting
in front of the crude, five-pointed star of the Red Brigades, and a slogan,
'The executioner will undergo a trial'. In nearly 150 typed pages of rambling
pseudo-Marxist economico-political analysis of the state of Naples, Cirillo
was described as 'the point man for imperialist reconstruction in the Naples
metropolitan pole'.

The frightened face staring out from the Polaroid did not betray the power
the BR attributed to him: a bald dome of a head, a toothbrush moustache and

features too small for his face. Yet the *brigatisti* had chosen their target well, and despite their delusional ideology, there was a strategic intelligence to their 'Cirillo campaign' (as they termed it). The earthquake had left 50,000 homeless in Naples alone: the terrorists hoped to appeal to this pool of vulnerable and angry people. The BR's regular communiqués denounced the earthquake profiteers and railed against what it called 'deportation of proletarians' from the overcrowded and quake-damaged housing of the city centre. There were other acts of propaganda too: BR posters went up in areas where the caravans of the homeless were concentrated, and two more functionaries involved in the reconstruction were kneecapped. The BR subjected Cirillo to a 'people's trial', tapes of which were released to the media; it showcased DC greed and maladministration. The Christian Democrats in Campania had very good reason to worry. The kidnap victim was a man with many secrets: there was no telling what he might be terrified into saying while in the BR's hands.

On the face of it, Cirillo's chances of surviving his ordeal were not at all good. The DC was officially wedded to a policy of not negotiating with political kidnappers—the same policy that it had adopted when the Party Secretary Aldo Moro had been kidnapped in 1978. Moro ended up dead, as did many other victims. On 9 July 1981 yet another BR communiqué trumpeted that the people's trial had reached 'the only just verdict possible' and that Cirillo's death sentence was 'the most elevated humanitarian act in the circumstances'. He was doomed.

Then, at dawn on 24 July 1981, Cirillo was released, and the BR announced that they had received a ransom of 1 billion 450 thousand lire ($2.5 million in 2011).

The Interior Minister indignantly rejected the notion that Cirillo had been traded for money, saying that he had been freed 'without any negotiation and without any concession on the part of organs of the state faced with blackmail from an armed band'. It would take another twelve years for Italy to learn just how unfounded those denials were. The truth would only emerge after a succession of further denials, of unreliable testimonies, of murdered witnesses and destroyed evidence. During Cirillo's captivity, 'organs of the state' had not just negotiated with the Red Brigades. They had also negotiated with Raffaele 'the Professor' Cutolo's Nuova Camorra Organizzata.

The story goes something like this. A mere sixteen hours after Cirillo's disappearance, a secret agent from Italy's internal intelligence and security agency, SISDE, visited Raffaele Cutolo in prison in Ascoli Piceno. There were further meetings with Cutolo, when the agent was accompanied by two people. The first was a local mayor from Cirillo's faction of the DC who was close to the NCO. The second was the deputy leader of the NCO, Enzo Casillo. Known as 'o Nirone ('Blacky') because of his dark hair, Casillo was the son of a trouser-factory owner; despite these comfortable origins, he had become the NCO's military chief during the war with the Nuova Famiglia.

After these initial meetings, Blacky Casillo and another senior officer in the Nuova Camorra Organizzata roamed the country over the coming weeks under the protective wing of the secret services so that they could take part in negotiation between the state, the BR and the NCO—as well as carrying on their duties in the camorra war.

Yet despite the best efforts of the secret agents of SISDE, the Professor remained standoffish. So a second phase in the negotiations opened on 9 May, when the military intelligence service, SISMI, took over. SISMI had no jurisdiction over domestic security issues, and thus no right to intervene in the Cirillo kidnapping. Nonetheless, things suddenly started to move. Imprisoned BR sympathisers were transferred to Ascoli Piceno to talk to the Professor, and then moved again to jails where BR leaders were being held. Blacky Casillo carried on his work as a roving mediator. Eventually, the ransom was paid and Cirillo was released.

The Cirillo affair illustrated the depths to which the Italian state sank in the course of the 1980s. 'Organs of the state' negotiated with left-wing terrorists through the good offices of the biggest criminal organisation in the country. A dastardly list of characters took part in the talks. The final phase of the negotiations was conducted by a wheeler-dealer called Francesco Pazienza, who had somehow become a consultant for SISMI. (Among other things, he would later be convicted for misleading investigations into the 1980 right-wing terror outrage at Bologna station in which eighty-five people were killed.) Through channels like these, money changed hands— money that the BR then used to pursue its campaign of murder and kidnapping. The DC's reconstruction money magus was saved. But shamefully and tragically, other victims paid the ultimate price instead of him.

Although a parliamentary inquiry could find no direct evidence of a quid pro quo between the secret services and the NCO, very big questions remain unanswered. The Cirillo story is made of many profoundly worrying suspicions and relatively few certainties. A great deal of murk remains. Here are two of the reasons why.

At the time of the Cirillo kidnapping, many senior officers in both SISDE and SISMI were members of the P2 Masonic lodge, which makes their motives very difficult to read. No combination of blackmail, right-wing subversion and corruption can be ruled out.

When Cirillo was released, in a semi-derelict building in the Poggioreale quarter of Naples, he flagged down a passing traffic police patrol. The orders were to take Cirillo straight to police headquarters where he could be cared for and interviewed by the magistrates investigating the kidnapping. But the journey had barely begun when the car was blocked off and surrounded by four more police cars. Citing orders from on high, the officer in charge of the four cars took Cirillo home instead. Once home, Cirillo was examined by a doctor who declared that he was in a state of shock and could not be interviewed by investigating magistrates. These health problems did not, however, prevent senior figures in the DC, including Flaminio Piccoli, the party's national leader, from going to see Cirillo forty-eight hours before the magistrates were eventually allowed access. The timing may have given Cirillo and his DC friends an opportunity to get their story straight about the whole negotiation saga.

What did the Professor have to gain from getting himself involved in the deal to free Cirillo? One thing he definitely pocketed was the chance to boast to the criminal world that he had the ear of the authorities. Irrespective of the real nature of any bargain behind Cirillo's release, the Professor could now present himself as a man with a seat at the top table. But did he receive anything else? And did he give the BR more than money? Several witnesses, including *brigatisti* and *camorristi* turned state's evidence, have cited a whole list of bargaining counters. Such people may of course have been lying. But there is nonetheless evidence to back up what they said.

Some *brigatisti* claimed that Cutolo passed them useful information on potential targets. There are facts that seem to support this allegation. On 15 July 1982, the BR machine-gunned police commander Antonio Ammaturo along with his driver Pasquale Paola. Ammaturo was a common enemy for both the BR and the NCO. He had investigated left-wing terrorism. Moreover, soon after being appointed to the Naples job, he had even had the impudence to raid the Professor's castle in Ottaviano—the first policeman to do so. Ammaturo was also probing into the Cirillo affair at the time of his death. When asked about the murder in court, the Professor was his usual, slippery self:

> I did not give the BR Ammaturo's name so that he could be killed. I'm not ruling out the fact that bumping him off would have been a pleasure for me. But I would have done it myself, directly, because it was a personal vendetta.

The likely scenario—one that illustrates the twisted logic in force in the shadows where violent subversion and violent crime overlapped—is that a left-wing terrorist group killed two good policemen on behalf of the NCO.

According to one *camorrista*, the Professor also converted his intervention as a mediator in the Cirillo affair into a series of favours that further extended his influence within the prison system. Hence, perhaps, the fact that on 27 October 1981, the Appeal Court in Naples ruled that Cutolo was 'semi-insane', and thus deserving of more lenient treatment.

But the biggest item on the Professor's shopping list was a slice of the earthquake reconstruction bonanza. It must be stressed that investigations did not reveal smoking-gun proof of such an exchange. Nevertheless, the courts ruled that entrepreneurs close to the NCO, including the Professor's own son Roberto, *were* awarded contracts worth sixty-seven billion lire ($172 million in 2011 values) to put up prefabricated housing in the Avellino area.

The question of reconstruction contracts leads us into the last, and most controversial, of the mysteries surrounding the Cirillo kidnapping: the question of who authorised the negotiations. Which politicians were involved, and how deeply?

A parliamentary inquiry would conclude that, while there had definitely been negotiations with the BR through Cirillo, there was no absolute proof that favours were exchanged as part of a deal. A number of senior Christian Democrats emerged with their reputations badly damaged by the verdict. For example Flaminio Piccoli, the party's national leader, *must* have known about the negotiations. Francesco Pazienza, the wheeler-dealer linked to right-wing terrorism who conducted the last phase of the bargaining, was a regular visitor to the DC leader's house. But the figure at the epicentre of the controversy, and one of the most powerful politicians in Campania, was Antonio Gava. Gava had just won his first national Cabinet post when Cirillo was kidnapped, and he went on to hold a series of senior Cabinet positions, including Interior Minister and Finance Minister, in the 1980s.

Gava was chief of the local DC faction whose main man on the ground was none other than Ciro Cirillo. Gava went on trial for having links with the camorra in 1993. No less than thirteen years passed before he was finally acquitted in 2006. Gava was suing for damages when he died in 2008. One cannot help but sympathise with the plight of a man on the receiving end of such an appallingly protracted judicial ordeal. Alas, such judicial sagas are all too common in Italy, particularly when it comes to the delicate business of ascertaining the relationship between organised crime and politics. However the final ruling that marked Gava's acquittal, for all its opaque legal phrasing, showed him in a very poor light indeed.

> The court maintains that it has proved with certainty that Gava was aware of the arrangement of functional reciprocity between local politicians in his faction of the DC and the camorra organisation . . . There is also proof that [Gava] did nothing incisive and concrete to fight or

limit that situation, and that instead he ended up enjoying the electoral benefits it brought his political faction.

Gava's behaviour, the judges concluded, was morally and politically reprehensible, but he had done nothing to deserve a criminal conviction.

Camorristi had their hands on the post-earthquake reconstruction before the BR's 'Cirillo campaign' began. On 11 December 1980, a mere two and a half weeks after the quake, the mayor of one damaged town was shot dead because he tried to block companies linked to organised crime from winning rubble-clearing contracts. So the Cirillo kidnapping was ultimately only one symptom of the way the camorra seized hold of the opportunities that came with the disaster of 23 November 1980. In Sicily, the mafia war of the early 1980s was fought for control of the heroin pipeline to the United States. In Campania, the Nuova Camorra Organizzata and the Nuova Famiglia battled for control of the reconstruction riches.

Yet the Cirillo affair would prove to be decisive in another respect: it would bring about the final defeat of Raffaele 'the Professor' Cutolo.

On 18 March 1982—eleven months after the Cirillo kidnapping, and with the mysteries surrounding it still unsolved—the Italian Communist Party daily *L'Unità* published what purported to be an Interior Ministry document that gave full details of the negotiations leading up to Cirillo's release. The letter turned out to be a fake—fake enough to cost the newspaper's editor his job. But many of the details it contained were true—true enough for a formal investigation into the negotiations leading to Cirillo's release to be launched. We now know that the Professor was the likely author of the fake. He created it because he did not feel that he had received his just reward for helping out in the Cirillo kidnapping affair. Leaking the letter to the opposition press was a sly way of sending a warning: if the Professor did not get what he wanted, new revelations, documented revelations, would follow.

The letter backfired horribly. The President of the Republic, outraged by the stories of Cutolo's cushy life behind bars that were then beginning to emerge, arranged for him to be sent to the forbidding prison island of Asinara. From now on, communicating with the rest of the NCO would be impossible. The Nuova Famiglia moved in for the kill. Within days of Cutolo's being transferred to Asinara, Alfonso Rosanova, the construction entrepreneur who managed the business arm of the NCO, was shot dead in the Salerno hospital where he was recovering from a previous attempt on his life; six or seven killers entered the building, disarmed the policemen on duty at his bedside, and shot him many times where he lay. In January 1983 came the mortal blow, when Enzo 'Blacky' Casillo—the Professor's top military commander and the roving negotiator of the Cirillo affair—was blown

Death blow. The car bomb that led to the defeat of the Nuova Camorra Organizzata. Enzo Casillo, the Professor's military chief, was murdered in Rome in January 1983.

to pieces by a car bomb in Rome. The Nuova Famiglia officer who rigged the booby trap would later turn state's evidence and explain to a parliamentary inquiry why Casillo was dispatched in such a spectacular fashion. The message in the murder, he explained, was 'to demonstrate to Cutolo that he was finished, and that he had to stop once and for all with blackmailing the politicians or the people in the state institutions that he had dealt with during the Cirillo kidnapping business'. The same *camorrista* also suspected that the secret services had been the source of the information that allowed him to identify where Blacky Casillo lived.

The Professor had overplayed the hand he had been dealt in the Cirillo affair. The Nuova Famiglia were now determined to punish him, and thereby win over his political friends. The Nuova Camorra Organizzata began to fall apart. Leaderless, Cutolo's zealous young followers were slaughtered by the Nuova Famiglia's well-organised hit squads.

The Professor's legacy was nonetheless enormous. His reign saw the camorra reach a level of wealth and influence that bore comparison with the mafias of Calabria and Sicily. He also had lasting effects outside his own region of Campania. Indeed, the Professor was one of the main reasons why Italy witnessed the birth of two entirely new mafias.

58

THE MAGLIANA BAND AND
THE SACRED UNITED CROWN

THE LATE 1970S AND 1980S WERE NOT JUST A PERIOD OF RECORD VIOLENCE WITHIN Italy's historic mafias. They were also a time when, for the first time in a century, entirely new criminal organisations were created in regions outside the home turf of the Sicilian mafia, the Neapolitan camorra and the Calabrian 'ndrangheta.

Rome was a special case when it came to the spread of mafia power. All three major mafias were present there, kidnapping, dealing in drugs, laundering money, and the rest. Yet none of the three tried to oust the others. Contrary to what one might expect of such ferocious clans, there was no direct military confrontation between *camorristi*, *mafiosi* and *'ndranghetisti* on Roman soil. In Rome, as elsewhere, the three major mafias preferred to profit from peaceful cohabitation rather than endure the costs and dangers of a 'foreign' war. The capital became a kind of free port of criminal influence, its riches open to all for exploitation. In those peculiar circumstances, Rome generated a criminal fraternity of its own in the late 1970s—one entirely independent from the mafia, the camorra and the 'ndrangheta, although deeply indebted to them when it came to methods and contacts.

On 7 November 1977 Duke Massimiliano Grazioli Lante della Rovere, the former owner of Rome's major newspaper, *Il Messaggero*, was kidnapped just outside the city. One night the following March, after months of negotiations, his son heaved a bag containing two billion lire (more than $9 million in 2011 values) over the parapet of a road bridge. From below came a voice: 'Go home and wait. Your father will be freed in a few hours.'

The Duke was never freed. In fact, when the ransom was handed over he was already dead, killed by his kidnappers because he had seen one of them without a mask. His body was propped in a chair, his eyes forced open, and a recent newspaper lodged in his hands so that a photograph proving that he was alive could be sent to his relatives.

The macabre abduction of Duke Grazioli was the first major action carried out by a group named the Banda della Magliana (the Magliana Band), after the newly built suburban neighbourhood of Rome whence some of its members came. The Banda della Magliana's chiefs—variously loan sharks, drug dealers, fences and, particularly, armed robbers—explicitly set themselves the goal of dominating the capital's underworld. Before long, they achieved their aim.

The Banda della Magliana bore many similarities to the mafias of Sicily and Calabria. Its leaders divided out the capital into districts for the purposes of drug distribution, and eliminated any dealers who refused to come under their control. They had a common fund, and used it to support imprisoned members and their families, to corrupt policemen and *Carabinieri*, and to make important friends. Like the traditional mafias, the Banda della Magliana decided its murders centrally, keeping in mind the organisation's strategic aims. They were also a 'holding company' that exploited opportunities for money-making wherever they came, reinvested their profits in new criminal enterprises, and laundered cash through formally lawful ventures, notably property.

From its origins, the Banda della Magliana had an intense pattern of relationships with the traditional mafias. It sourced wholesale heroin from Cosa Nostra—both from the group close to Stefano Bontate and, once Bontate and his friends were exterminated, from Shorty Riina's *corleonesi*. As early as 1975, the police spotted one of the band's future leaders chatting in a Roman restaurant called Il Fungo with *'ndranghetisti* of the highest level, including Giuseppe Piromalli from Gioia Tauro and Paolo De Stefano from Reggio.

The Banda della Magliana also drew inspiration from the Nuova Camorra Organizzata. One of its founders had known the Professor in prison and was a great admirer. Some of the others shared his vision: as one would later confess, 'We decided to try to carry out the same operation in Rome that Raffaele Cutolo was carrying out in Naples.' In 1979, when the Professor was on the run after 'noisily wandering away' from Aversa asylum, he hired a whole floor of a hotel in Fiuggi, a spa town south of Rome, and there held discussions with the Banda della Magliana. The aim of the meeting was to 'find a strategy that was compatible with both groups' aims'. Sh the meeting, the Banda della Magliana deferentially did the Neapolit favour by disposing of a metallic green BMW 733 whose interior was covered in bloodstains—the blood in question had belonged to a construction entrepreneur that Cutolo himself had shot. The NCO and the Banda della Magliana shared a useful friendship with Aldo Semerari, the fascist subversive, ally of the secret services, and professor of forensic psychology who would end up being decapitated near Cutolo's Ottaviano villa. As with the NCO, the Banda della Magliana was offered the chance to take an active part in violent right-wing politics by Semerari; the Romans declined the offer but exchanged weapons for favours instead—just as the NCO had done.

Unlike the NCO or the traditional mafias of Sicily and Calabria, the Banda della Magliana did not use initiation rituals or arcane mythology. Perhaps partly for this reason, despite its wealth and its violence, it failed to set down roots for the long term: in that narrow sense, the Banda della Magliana did not constitute a mafia. By the mid-1980s, it had begun to fall apart, amid the kind of internecine bloodletting and snitching that the traditional mafias have always shown a remarkable ability to survive.

The Sacra Corona Unita ('Sacred United Crown') or SCU is the mafia of Puglia, the region that forms the stacked 'heel' of the Italian boot. Its story begins in 1978 when the conflict between the Nuova Camorra Organizzata and the Nuova Famiglia got under way in neighbouring Campania. The prison authorities tried to defuse the tensions in prisons by moving camorra-affiliated inmates to facilities in other regions, including Puglia. Once installed in Puglian jails in numbers, the Professor's pupils quickly put themselves at the top of the jailbird pecking order, and then began to initiate local crooks into the NCO. In January 1979, Cutolo himself visited Puglia, and held a meeting in a hotel in Lucera at which he 'legalised' more than forty local criminals—meaning he put them through the Nuova Camorra Organizzata initiation ritual. At a second meeting, this time near Lecce, another ninety Puglian criminals were initiated.

In 1981 the Professor, by now back in prison, formally instituted a Puglian branch of the NCO, the Nuova Camorra Pugliese, whose leaders were obliged to kick back 40–50 per cent of their profits to Cutolo. Not content with trying to establish his hegemony over Campania, in other words, the Professor was trying to dominate the entire Puglian underworld too. But in Puglia, as in Campania, the Professor's megalomania was eventually thwarted. As the NCO began its slide to defeat in the wake of the Cirillo kidnapping, some Puglian *camorristi* increasingly hankered after greater autonomy.

The authorities found the first signs that something strange was happening in the Puglian criminal fraternity early in 1984 when a handwritten document was found in a prison cell. Entitled 'The S Code', it listed the articles of faith of a new brotherhood of crime called the Famiglia Salentina Libera (Free Family of Salento—Salento being the farthest part of the 'heel' of Italy). Article 7 of the S Code stipulated that the organisation's aim was 'never to allow any family from other regions to lord it over our territory'. The resistance to the Professor was beginning to take organisational form.

Just a few weeks later, in a prison in Bari, Puglia's biggest city, another statute of another new mafia was found: the Sacra Corona Unita. The statute's author, and SCU's founder and supreme leader, was a murderer called Giuseppe Rogoli. Rogoli was partly driven to found the SCU in 1981 by a desire to resist the Nuova Camorra Organizzata's power in prison. As he would later remark:

> At the time, Cutolo's men felt like they were Lord God Almighty, and wherever they entered the prisons they wanted to commit abuses— things that didn't go down well with us. So a group of us, not just me, decided to constitute this Sacra Corona Unita in opposition to the NCO's excessive power in the prisons.

Looking for a counterweight to the Professor's influence in his region, Rogoli sought backing for his new fraternity from the 'ndrangheta. Rosarno 'ndrangheta boss Umberto Bellocco initiated Rogoli into the Calabrian mafia, and then dictated the rules of the Sacra Corona Unita to him. The Calabrians reserved the right to preside over the rituals that marked the promotion of SCU members to the highest ranks within the Puglian organisation, and also demanded the SCU's collaboration in a series of kidnappings. The SCU, in other words, was a semi-autonomous Puglian branch of the 'ndrangheta.

Rogoli's men embraced the SCU's borrowed mystical rituals with the zeal of converts. One of the new mafia's early leaders, Romano Oronzo, commissioned a painting crammed with the new mafia's symbols. The artist who took the commission would later describe it to a court:

> He wanted me to draw a triangle, the sign of the Holy Trinity, with Jesus's face and a dove, plus the world, and his own eyes, and a hand stopping a bolt of lightning. Before painting it, I asked him to explain why he

wanted those themes, and he told me he felt that he had been sent by God to help the world.

Like the Professor whose power over Puglian territory he sought to resist, Rogoli built his organisation behind bars in the first instance, and then moved on to seek territorial dominance in the outside world. The SCU soon grew to absorb the Famiglia Salentina Libera, and unite criminals from all the provinces of Puglia.

The Sacra Corona Unita did not have a tranquil life, all the same. Members from different parts of Puglia were often reluctant to submit to Rogoli's authority. Rivalries over the growing income from narcotics were also a cause of friction. New mini-mafias were set up in Puglia in opposition to the SCU. In 1986, the internal wrangling had become so bad that Rogoli felt obliged to refound the SCU, renaming his new brainchild, imaginatively, the *Nuova* Sacra Corona Unita. The SCU was given a command body, the Società Riservatissima (or 'Very Confidential Society'), which comprised eight senior bosses—'eight unknown, invisible and well-armed men', in Rogoli's words. They were well armed because they could call on a dedicated death squad, paid for out of the organisation's central fund, to enforce discipline. But even these drastic measures did not stop the internecine conflict and fragmentation.

Thus the Sacra Corona Unita repeated the same basic developments that other mafias had been going through since the 1950s: more profits, greater centralisation and more bloody divisions. Between 1984 and 1992, the number of mafia-related homicides in Puglia tripled, from 45 to 135 per year.

The SCU is still an underworld force today, albeit one that has suffered some heavy blows in recent years. It is too early to tell whether the Sacra Corona Unita will pass the ultimate test of mafia longevity and allow some of its leaders to hand their authority down through the generations.

Puglia, like Rome, was a territory where all three major mafias had a presence. The region's Adriatic coast was a vital point of entry for bootleg cigarettes, as well as other illegal goods. Geographically speaking, it was in the back yard of the 'ndrangheta and the camorra. One of the striking things about the story of the Sacra Corona Unita is that, as in Rome, *camorristi*, *mafiosi* and 'ndranghetisti did not come to blows on Puglian soil. There was even diplomatic cooperation between them. It seems that emissaries from the 'ndrangheta and Cosa Nostra were present as observers when the Professor ceremonially initiated ninety Puglian criminals in Lecce.

Nonetheless, Cosa Nostra, camorra and 'ndrangheta took different approaches to the business of operating on new terrain. As the number and power of mafia outposts in other regions grew during the 1960s and 1970s, through businesses like kidnapping and narcotics, one of the three showed itself to be markedly more successful than the other two at occupying new ground.

Perhaps surprisingly, given that it was the richest and most powerful of the mafias, Cosa Nostra showed only an intermittent interest in formally establishing branches in other regions. In various parts of Italy there were authorised *decine* (ten-man platoons) of Cosa Nostra that were mostly run and staffed by Sicilians. But when they left Sicily for whatever reason, Men of Honour tended *not* to set up their own formalised embassies. Instead, they got along very well by relying on their personal criminal prestige to bind collaborators in the local underworld to them on an ad hoc basis. That is just what Corleone *capo* Luciano Liggio did in the kidnapping phase of his career. Gaspare 'Mr Champagne' Mutolo operated in a similar way when he ran his heroin trafficking from a base near his prison in the Marche region.

Only in Naples were Families of Cosa Nostra established, and non-Sicilians like the Nuvolettas and Zazas put in charge. That unusual move was due to the importance of Naples as the 'El Dorado' of contraband cigarettes. And, as we have seen, Cosa Nostra's influence generated violent resistance from the Professor's NCO. It also spread resentment even among the Sicilian mafia's Neapolitan allies. 'The Sicilians looked down their noses at us,' one camorra boss recalled. 'But what a race there was to suck up to Cosa Nostra. And you call these people *camorristi*! They were ready to offer their arses to the Sicilians just so they could feel a little bit stronger.'

Despite his opposition to the Sicilian influence in his homeland, Raffaele Cutolo adopted a centralised and rather dictatorial strategy when it came to operating outside Campania. Hence the Puglian branch of the Nuova Camorra Organizzata had to pay a heavy tribute to the Professor. His high-handedness backfired when the Sacra Corona Unita was formed to resist him.

The 'ndrangheta took a more subtle and yet also more thorough approach to the problem of expanding outside its home territory. It had powerful emissaries in Campania and Puglia. Yet none of the local criminal groups revolted against the Calabrian presence. Indeed, like the SCU's founder Giuseppe Rogoli, they actively sought it out. A minor mafia, the Rosa dei Venti ('Wind Rose') was set up in Lecce prison in 1990 and also asked for the 'ndrangheta's blessing. Clearly, recognition from Calabria was a great prize for newly formed gangs.

The 'ndrangheta is the mafia that has the richest and most complex repertoire of symbols, traditions, ranks and rituals: it has been collecting them since the nineteenth century. The 'ndrangheta is the last survivor of a broad kin group of Honoured Societies from the Italian mainland that included the original Honoured Society of Naples, and even an organisation called the Mala Vita (literally 'Bad Life', but more accurately, 'the Criminal Underworld'), which was a short-lived nineteenth-century forerunner of the Puglian mafia, the Sacra Corona Unita. Some of the most important new mafias of the 1970s and 1980s, including the NCO and the SCU, drew on the 'ndrangheta's great library of gangland style and structure.

Together with a great many business opportunities in drugs, kidnapping and the like, these cultural offerings were enough to satisfy both the Puglians of the SCU and the 'ndranghetisti they adopted as sponsors. The 'ndrangheta, in short, preferred a hands-off approach. It did not want an empire, just a select band of reliable business partners. Perhaps 'franchising' is the best way to describe the Calabrian approach to the Puglian crime scene.

In the wealthy regions of the North, the 'ndrangheta had long been setting down roots through its involvement in construction and kidnapping. Here the 'ndrangheta spread directly and not by recognising local gangs like the SCU. By the 1980s, 'ndranghetisti had established branches called Locals in many towns and cities across Lombardy and Piedmont. These northern colonies were closely linked to individual Locals back in Calabria by blood ties, organisation and business: through such channels, a regular to-and-fro of drugs, money, assassins, fugitives and kidnap victims was established. Young men born into 'ndrangheta families in the North would come back home to be initiated into the brotherhood. The northern 'ndranghetisti also met among themselves to settle disputes and make sure that Calabrian rules were applied. As one 'ndrangheta defector from the North testified:

In 1982 I took part in a meeting of all the Locals in Piedmont. About 700 people were there . . . The reason for the meeting was because in Turin at that time many Calabrians who were affiliated to the 'ndrangheta were pimping—an activity that the 'ndrangheta considers dishonourable . . . It was decided to order the affiliates to stop pimping. And if they did not obey the order, they would either be expelled from the 'ndrangheta or physically eliminated.

The 'ndrangheta's strategy made it by far the most successful of the three major mafias in other regions. According to one Sicilian *mafioso* who did business in the North: 'In Piedmont, the Calabrians have taken over the region. The little groups of Sicilians don't give any trouble to their organisation.' The

Calabrians were so confident in their power in the North that they accommodated groups of Sicilian *mafiosi* within their structure. The 'ndrangheta, once the poor relation of the mighty Sicilian mafia, had come a long, long way.

While all this was actually going on, the Italian authorities had very little idea of just how far the 'ndrangheta had spread. The Calabrian mafia's softly-softly brand of colonisation proved to be the right formula for expansion into the regions at the heart of the national economy.

However colonisation was not the only measure of mafia reach. The 'ndrangheta may have planted its piratical flag in towns and cities across the North, but Cosa Nostra's narcodollars had earned it a place at the highest tables of Italian finance. Aldo Ravelli was a famously ruthless stockbroker who ran into trouble with the law on several occasions in the course of a career on the Milan stock exchange that traversed the decades. In an interview he ordered to be published only after his death, he gave an insider's take on Italy's financial bourgeoisie, dividing it into three camps. The first was 'semi-clean'. The second was 'unscrupulous'. The third was the Sicilian mafia.

PART XI

MARTYRS AND PENITENTS

59

MAFIA TERROR

IN THE 1980S, THE MAFIAS ACHIEVED GREATER WEALTH, MORE AWESOME MILITARY power, a wider geographical range, and more profound penetration of the state apparatus than at any other moment in their long existence. The story of the people who stood against them at that time is the most tragic and most stirring page in the history of the Italian Republic. Its key dramas took place in the home of what was still the most dangerous of the mafias, Cosa Nostra. The years between 1979 and 1992 were Sicily's longest decade. The island had set the pace of organised crime history since long before the Second World War. Now it was to set the pace of the struggle against the mafias.

The tale told in the following pages was first reconstructed by investigators—the very people who were at the centre of the unfolding events. By journalists too: for many of them, the task of trying to make sense of what was happening around them with such fearful speed in the 1980s became a sacred cause more than a job. Since those terrible days, the story has been told and retold. It is there in the monuments to the fallen, in street names and plaques, and in the ceremonies that mark each passing anniversary of a mafia outrage. It is there in the famous video clips and photographs that have become icons of collective memory. Its grip on the public imagination is no mystery: this, after all, is a narrative that pits good against evil. Nor should we be surprised if, like all great stories, this one is sometimes emptied of its real meaning, hollowed into mere ritual by indifference, turned bland by the cynical lip-service of politicians, or by the cheesy conventions of television dramatisation. All the same, the truths of this story are far too important to be uncontroversial even today; its lingering mysteries still make headline news.

The people who died fighting Cosa Nostra during Sicily's longest decade were martyrs. The word may sound overblown. In those Western countries lucky enough to be able to treat the mafia as if it were little more than a movie genre, such vocabulary now belongs only to the mind-set of religious fanatics. But in the Italian context, it is the only word one can use. The martyrs of the struggle against mafia power died for a cause—one that in luckier European countries might seem banal: the rule of law. They also changed lives by setting an example for others to follow. Inspired by them, many young people found a calling in the police or magistracy—or simply by refusing to rub along with the mafia system that confronted them in their day-to-day lives.

The sacrifices made in the anti-mafia battle changed history too. For what happened in Sicily broke patterns that had remained obstinately in place since Italy first became one country in 1861. The most significant progress was in understanding the mafia. The struggle against Cosa Nostra was also a struggle to find out what it really was. In the 1970s, because more than a century of evidence had been covered up, neglected or forgotten, nobody really knew. Italy did not even know that the Sicilian mafia was called Cosa Nostra by its members. The most widely read academic study of the mafia at the time was written by a German sociologist and translated into Italian in 1973. Filled with penetrating insights into Sicily's social structure, the book was nonetheless dismissive of the suggestion that the mafia might be a secret society: only 'sensation-hungry journalists, confused northern Italian jurists, and foreign authors' made that mistake. There were *mafiosi* in Sicily, of course—mediators, protectors and thugs. But they were part of the island's culture. There was no single organisation that could be labelled 'the mafia'. The results of the most recent trials in the late 1960s seemed to back that view up. By 1992, however, such falsehoods had been decisively overturned: enough proof had been assembled to convince even Italy's Supreme Court to confirm that the Sicilian mafia was indeed a criminal organisation, a secret society. By the end of the longest decade, the Sicilian mafia's most astonishing crime—the claim that it did not even exist—had been exposed at long last.

The years of bloodshed and polemic in Palermo that led to that crucial Supreme Court verdict would have profound repercussions for the camorra and 'ndrangheta, and for Italy's entire criminal power system. In its wake, Italy established institutions whose very founding principle was the need to view the Italian underworld, with its connections to the 'upper world' of politics, the institutions and business, *as a whole*. Finally, after well over a century, the mafias would be viewed as aspects of the same underlying problems.

Such changes are unquestionably profound—profound enough to mark the long 1980s as the bloody passage between two entirely different eras in mafia history. Yet more time must pass before we can tell whether the progress made at such appalling cost is irreversible. That is why the titanic struggle between the mafia and the anti-mafia in those years is a story that must continue to be told. For it will retain its relevance, its urgency, until the day when Italy can say that the mafias have been vanquished for good.

Sicily's longest decade began with five high-profile murders in the space of nine months: 'eminent corpses', as they were called.

In Palermo, on 26 January 1979, Mario Francese was shot in the head outside his house. Francese was the crime correspondent of Sicily's main daily, the *Giornale di Sicilia*. With him when he died was his twenty-year-old son Giulio, who was just a few weeks into his own career as a journalist.

Six weeks later, on 9 March, Michele Reina, the leader of the Christian Democrat Party in the province of Palermo, died in a hail of dumdum bullets at the wheel of his car. His wife, who was beside him, saw the killer grinning as he fired. Reina was the first post-war politician to be murdered by the Sicilian mafia; he left three young children.

The third assassination took place at the other end of the country, in the banking centre of Milan, on 11 July. Giorgio Ambrosoli, a lawyer, had been appointed by a court to dig into the affairs of disgraced Sicilian banker, Michele Sindona. A team of three killers was waiting for Ambrosoli when he got home late in the evening; he too left a wife and three small children.

Ten days later, back in Palermo, Boris Giuliano, the commander of the Flying Squad was shot seven times at the counter of his local bar.

Cesare Terranova was a judge. On 25 September, he and his bodyguard, Lenin Mancuso, were gunned to death in their car. One witness said that the killers wore smiles on their faces.

A journalist, a politician, a financial lawyer, a policeman and a judge. Information, democracy, honest finance, law enforcement and justice. One after another, the mafia's smiling killers had attacked five pillars of Italian society.

None of these murders, taken in isolation, was entirely without precedent for the Sicilian mafia. But coming so close together they made clear an unmistakable and chilling new trend. Sicilian *mafiosi* had never launched such a systematic assault on representatives of the state. The institutions were infiltrated and corrupted, but they were not attacked head on. Now, suddenly, the mafia had taken a terrorist turn.

Comparisons between the mafia and the threat from subversives of Right and Left were on many commentators' lips during the season of terrorism known as the Years of Lead. Cosa Nostra itself had given them a cue. Following both the Reina and Terranova murders, the offices of *Giornale di Sicilia* received anonymous calls claiming to be from terrorist cells. The calls were fake, and intended to mislead investigators. But the parallel between the Sicilian mafia and the Red Brigades was far from spurious. Both killed journalists, politicians, lawyers, police and magistrates. Both arrogantly assumed themselves to be above the law. Both thought the Italian state was so weak, and so discredited, that it could simply be bullied into submission. Violence was used because violence would work—by now, it was part of the language of Italian public life. The Italian people could be relied upon to sit, arms folded, and watch as their country went down.

Yet within some of those murders from 1979 the signs of resistance against the mafia threat were also visible. Cosa Nostra was killing people it feared.

The journalist Mario Francese was a relentless investigator, one of the few journalists who sensed the growing menace of Shorty Riina and his *corleonesi*; he had even dared interview Riina's wife.

Giorgio Ambrosoli had discovered that Michele Sindona had been laundering the profits of the US heroin trade.

Boris Giuliano was a born policeman who had tracked down some of Cosa Nostra's heroin refineries. He also knew how to follow the mafia's money, and the money trail had led him into collaboration with the US Drug Enforcement Administration and to a clear conclusion: 'Palermo's mafia organisations have now become pivotal in heroin trafficking, the clearing house for the United States.'

Judge Terranova had led a large-scale prosecution of the mafia following the Ciaculli bomb outrage back in the 1960s. In 1974, he consigned Luciano Liggio, the boss of Corleone, to a life behind bars. Having spent several years in parliament as an independent MP under the wing of the Communist Party, he had just returned to Palermo, and to the judicial trenches of the anti-mafia struggle, when Cosa Nostra decided to kill him.

The death of Michele Reina, the DC politician, was much more difficult to interpret at the time. Only those closest to the mafia would have been able to decode the meaning in the murder. Everyone else had to be content with the rumours and theories that filled the newspapers. We now have a good idea which of those theories was closest to the truth. Reina was an ambitious man who had had brushes with the law. He had been educated politically in the heart of Palermo's DC machine. He was a 'Young Turk' who belonged to the faction of the party headed by Salvo Lima—one of Cosa

Nostra's most reliable politicians. But now that he was local party chief, Reina's ambition had led him to begin thinking independently. He formed a coalition with the Communist Party: heresy for some. He declared that he wanted to be the leader of a DC that would 'no longer live for the construction industry and off the construction industry'. Dangerous talk: Reina had already received threats. Perhaps Reina does not deserve to be called a martyr, but his assassination was a chilling challenge to the state all the same. In the new era of mafia terror, the penalty for independent thinking in the Sicilian DC was death.

The five murders of 1979 amounted to a declaration of war: Cosa Nostra, for the first time in its history, was directly confronting the state—or at least those few people working within Italy's ramshackle government apparatus who embodied what the state ought to be.

And here lay the crucial *difference* between Cosa Nostra and the Red Brigades, a difference that made the former far, far more dangerous than the latter. The Red Brigades certainly had their spies and their sympathisers. All the same, they were *outside* a state that they wanted to overthrow. Active *brigatisti* operated from clandestine hideouts deep in the most anonymous quarters of Italian cities. Cosa Nostra, by contrast, was an integral part of the state—a state it now wanted to neuter and bend entirely to its own bloodthirsty, rapacious will. Active *mafiosi* operated from the very institutions where people like Mario Francese, Michele Reina, Giorgio Ambrosoli, Boris Giuliano and Cesare Terranova worked. For that reason, standing up to Cosa Nostra required a particular kind of heroism.

The following year, 1980, the assault continued: more eminent corpses fell. And new heroes emerged—heroes who would change the course of Italian history.

On 6 January, Piersanti Mattarella, the Christian Democrat leader of the Sicilian regional government—the most important politician on the island, in other words—was executed just as he got into his car to go to Mass with his wife and son. Mattarella had initiated a campaign to clean up the way government contracts were awarded. His wife saw the killer approach the car, and had time to plead with him not to shoot.

Emanuele Basile was a young captain who commanded the *Carabinieri* in Monreale, a hilltop town overlooking the Conca d'Oro. The night he was killed, 4 May, the streets were crowded, brightly lit and filled with the smell of nougat emanating from street stalls: it was the local festival of the Holy Crucifix. Basile, who was holding his four-year-old daughter Barbara in his arms at the time, was making his way home through the crowds when two assassins appeared behind him. His little daughter's hand was burned by a muzzle flash; miraculously, she was not otherwise hurt. Basile only had time to breathe 'help me' to his wife before he lost consciousness. He died a few hours later on the operating table.

Basile was investigating both the *corleonesi* and the narcotics trade with the United States. The magistrate who was working closely with him on those investigations—a gregarious, chain-smoking Palermitan with slicked-back hair and a trim, sloping moustache—was called Paolo Borsellino. Borsellino was devastated when they called him to break the news about his friend Basile. At forty years old, it was the first time his wife had ever seen him cry. The murder was not just a tragedy, it was also a message—a warning directed at Borsellino himself. But, faced with grief and fear, and the Sicilian mafia's declaration of war, Borsellino responded with resolve. As his wife would later recall, 'The Basile murder made me sure: I had married a man carved out of rock.' Her husband threw himself into his work. In the next few days, he became one of the first Palermo magistrates in the era of eminent corpses to be allocated an armed escort. Paolo Borsellino would go on to become one of the two great champions of the fight against Cosa Nostra.

Three months after the Basile murder, on 6 August 1980, Gaetano Costa, the quietly spoken Chief Prosecutor of Palermo, was shot several times in the face by a single killer who pulled a pistol from inside a rolled-up newspaper. Costa bled to death by a bookstand just across the street from the Teatro Massimo, the giant theatre that is one of Palermo's most famous landmarks. A veteran of the Resistance against the Nazis, he had recently put his name to arrest warrants related to an investigation into Cosa Nostra's biggest heroin traffickers.

As fate would have it, the investigating magistrate working on that very case was a childhood friend of Paolo Borsellino's who was also just getting used to living with the constant company of armed policemen in bulletproof vests. His name was Giovanni Falcone. Falcone's large, friendly face disguised the fact that he was much less outgoing than Borsellino. But he too was a man of granite courage and a voracious appetite for hard work. His meticulous and brilliant research into the finances of heroin trafficking had already unearthed the Sicilian mafia's business dealings with Neapolitan *camorristi* for the first time. Falcone had also encountered the insidious resistance that some of his colleagues put up against anyone who was too diligent. His direct superior had been warned in no uncertain terms by another judge that Falcone was 'ruining the Palermo economy', and that he should be loaded with ordinary casework to prevent him from digging too deep. When Falcone rushed to the scene of Costa's murder, a colleague muttered confidentially to him as he gazed down at the disfigured body: 'Well I never. I was absolutely sure

it was your turn.' Giovanni Falcone was on the way to becoming Cosa Nostra's greatest enemy. With Paolo Borsellino, he would become a symbol of the
struggle against the mafia. The story of the fight against Cosa Nostra in the
1980s and early 1990s is, in large measure, their story.

But to begin the work of challenging Cosa Nostra in earnest, and to do
so within the framework of the law, Falcone and Borsellino would need new
tools. Directly and indirectly, those tools would emerge from the campaign
against terrorism. The Italian state's struggle with the death-bringing ideal-
ists of the Red Brigades during the Years of Lead had crucial consequences
for the history of organised crime.

In 1980 the state acquired its decisive weapon in the fight against the Red
Brigades. Subsequently, the same weapon was deployed with devastating
effect against the mafias.

Law number 15 of 6 February 1980 awarded sentence reductions to
members of subversive organisations who provided evidence against fellow
terrorists. The first member of the Red Brigades to take advantage of the
new law, a carpenter's son called Patrizio Peci, began talking in April of the
same year. Peci was the commander of the Red Brigade column in Turin,
and his testimony almost completely dismantled the Red Brigades in the
north-west.

Peci's story introduced a new and highly controversial figure to the drama
of Italian public life: the *pentito*, or 'penitent', as the newspapers insisted on
calling any terrorist who informed on his associates. In Italy, lawmakers and
magistrates bristle at the very mention of the term 'penitent', and for good
reason. 'Penitence' is one of the most powerful identity narratives in Christian civilisation: it tells of past sins acknowledged and transcended, of a joy-
ful new life born from remorse. But the Christian psychology of penitence
fits badly with the varying motives of *pentiti*. Trading secrets for freedom is
often a self-interested business—even when it does bring valuable truths to
light. Cold-blooded murderers can barter their time behind bars down to
just a few years. Penitents also bring an obvious risk for the legal process: a
pentito who can convincingly fabricate more evidence than he really knows
may be rewarded with greater benefits. 'Penitent', then, is a controversial
term for a controversial thing. (Which perhaps helps explain why none of
the unwieldy alternatives—like 'collaborator with justice', and 'caller into
complicity'—has ever really caught on.)

Yet, for many *pentiti*, the decision to betray former colleagues is an agonising one. (Which is another reason why the term 'penitent' is inadequate,

although inevitable.) Patrizio Peci's decision to collaborate with the state was born of a profound disillusionment with the cause he had killed for. But he contemplated suicide when, after his tip-off, *Carabinieri* got into a firefight with four *brigatisti* in Genoa, killing them all, including two of his closest friends. Peci also paid a terrible price for his repentance when the Red Brigades kidnapped his brother Roberto, subjected him to a 'proletarian trial', and murdered him. Horrifyingly, they even filmed the execution as a deterrent to others. Such inhuman cruelty was powered by the loathing that penitents inspired in those they betrayed. Penitents were more than stool pigeons: they were *infami*—vile, unholy, scum. When *mafiosi* began to turn *pentiti* as terrorists had done, the moral ambiguities, psychological tensions and vindictive violence surrounding judicial repentance were all magnified.

The Red Brigade penitents who braved the loathing of their former comrades encountered a state that was better equipped to make use of their evidence than it had ever been. Italy's police, particularly the *Carabinieri*, learned to operate in specialised, specially trained teams against the terrorists, and they emerged from the fight with a greatly enhanced reputation.

During the Years of Lead, the Italian judicial system also came of age. *In theory*, since the Constitution of the Italian Republic was promulgated in 1948, magistrates and judges had been free from political interference, subject only to their own governing body. *In practice*, genuine judicial independence took much longer to arrive. During the 1960s, the expanding education system and the selection of magistrates through public examinations made a career in the legal system an option for bright young people from many different backgrounds. As a result, the magistracy was becoming less of a caste and more of an open profession.

Some of the magistrates who went to university in the 1960s were the legal professionals who stood in the front line during the Years of Lead. Like the senior police officers, they ran terrible risks: their movements were constantly trailed by terrorist cells spying out any opportunity to strike. The successes that the state eventually won against left-wing terrorism gave the legal system a store of credibility that it could then draw on when taking the fight to Italy's bastions of illicit privilege—corrupt politicians and the mafias.

In Sicily, the conflict within Cosa Nostra that had been rumbling since 1978 exploded in the spring of 1981 when Shorty Riina launched his assault on the mafia's heroin elite. Meanwhile, on the mainland, the Nuova Camorra Organizzata and the Nuova Famiglia were scattering Campania with cadavers. The first penitents from criminal organisations would emerge from the carnage.

60

THE FATAL COMBINATION

ANYWHERE ELSE IN THE WORLD, PIO LA TORRE AND CARLO ALBERTO DALLA CHIESA would have been enemies: the one, a Sicilian Communist militant devoted to radical social change; the other, a rigorous northern military man devoted to defending society from subversives. Cosa Nostra turned them into allies. Then in 1982, Cosa Nostra killed them both.

Few people knew the Sicilian mafia more intimately than Pio La Torre. He was born in 1927 in the village of Altarello di Baida, set among the mafia-controlled lemon groves of Palermo's Conca d'Oro. Life was hard. His father kept a few animals to top up what he could earn as a farmhand. With a stubbornness that would characterise him for the rest of his life, Pio studied by candlelight, laboured to cover his living costs, and worked his way into university. There, in 1945, he joined the Communist Party, soon rising to be a local leader of the Communist agricultural workers' union. He gained his first experience of political action—and had his first clash with the mafia—during the post-war peasant struggle for control of the land. The local boss, always on the lookout for talent, sidled up to him during an election campaign: 'You're an intelligent lad. You'll go far. You just have to come with us . . .' Soon afterwards, the mafia made Pio an offer through his father: he could become a Member of Parliament straight away—all he had to do was change his political colours. 'We just can't stomach this party. Over there in Russia maybe . . . But in Italy, we just don't do that kind of thing.' When La Torre refused, his father woke one morning to find the cowshed door ablaze. The warnings were clear: Pio had to choose between his home and his politics. He packed his bags.

These were acutely dangerous years to be a left-wing militant in western Sicily. Dozens of trades unionists and political activists were murdered by *mafiosi* or by Salvatore Giuliano's bandit gang. In March 1948 Placido Rizzotto, a union leader from the mafia stronghold of Corleone, vanished. La Torre went to take his place. In March 1950, La Torre led several thousand peasants from nearby Bisacquino on a march to occupy part of an under-cultivated estate. Along with 180 others he was arrested and charged with violent conduct based on the false testimony of a *Carabiniere*. He would spend a terrifying eighteen months in Palermo's Ucciardone prison—confined with members of Salvatore Giuliano's gang, among others—before his case even came to trial.

Pio La Torre encapsulated a tradition of Sicilian peasant militancy, and of opposition to the mafia, that went back to the nineteenth century. Again and again, just like La Torre, the peasants had found their hunger for land and a decent living thwarted by a *de facto* alliance between the landowners, the police and the mafia. In the fight for social justice, the rule of law was a mask for repression, and the state was not an ally but an enemy.

But in those earliest years of his career as a militant, Pio La Torre also encountered another face of the Italian state, and a very different tradition of opposition to the mafia—one rooted not in the radical aspirations of the peasantry, but in the patriotic, conservative instincts of the forces of law and order. In 1949, when La Torre first went to serve the proletarian cause in Corleone, he found that a young Captain of the *Carabinieri* had been posted there too: Carlo Alberto Dalla Chiesa.

There is one vignette that captures, better than any description, the value system into which Carlo Alberto Dalla Chiesa was born—and the enormous cultural distance that separated him from Pio La Torre. In 1945, he and his brother Romolo, both of them lieutenants in the *Carabinieri*, both of them in uniform, were waiting anxiously for their father's train to pull into Milan station. The reunion was no ordinary one: General Romano Dalla Chiesa was due to arrive home from a concentration camp. Back in September 1943, Italy had capitulated to the Allies, and the Nazis set up a puppet regime. Like many military men, the General faced a choice between enlisting on the German side or being interned: he opted for the latter, and he had not seen his family since.

At last, the train pulled in, and the two Dalla Chiesa boys saw their father's emaciated figure emerge from the crowd on the platform. Carlo Alberto clicked his heels, stood to attention, and snapped his hand to the peak of his cap. But the emotion of the occasion overcame Romolo, who threw himself into his father's arms.

The following day General Romano Dalla Chiesa sent Romolo a disciplinary notice. *Carabiniere* regulations explicitly state that an officer in uniform may not embrace anyone in public.

Carlo Alberto Dalla Chiesa was a man cut from the same military-issue serge as his father. Like his father, he had faced a stark choice in the terrible September of 1943. At the time, he was billeted in a villa on the Adriatic, charged with supervising the coastguard. When he refused to join the hunt for partisans, the SS came to arrest him. Warned just in time, Dalla Chiesa escaped from a first-floor window and out into the open countryside. He organised a partisan band, and then in the winter of 1943 passed through the battle lines to resume his duties in the liberated South.

Dalla Chiesa had a family connection with Sicily, because his father was a veteran of the Fascist campaigns against the mafia in the 1920s. Two decades later, Carlo Alberto volunteered to join the special force set up to combat banditry on the island. When he reached Corleone, he made a promise to the family of the vanished trade unionist Placido Rizzotto that he would find out who had killed their son. Rizzotto, like Dalla Chiesa, was a former fighter in the Resistance against the Nazis. Thanks to Dalla Chiesa's sleuthing, the wall of *omertà* began to crumble, parts of Rizzotto's body were recovered, and a report—naming an up-and-coming young *mafioso* called Luciano Liggio as the killer—was sent to the prosecuting authorities. Alas, the two key witnesses were intimidated into retracting their statements, and Liggio was released: a dispiriting reprise of countless mafia trials of the past, and a foreshadowing of many more still to come. All the same, Dalla Chiesa's determination would remain impressed in the memory of Corleone's peasants.

After Corleone, Pio La Torre and Carlo Alberto Dalla Chiesa would continue to cross paths. When he was released from prison, La Torre was elected to Palermo city council, where he spent the years of the Sack of Palermo denouncing the corrupt goings-on within the ruling DC. As a trade-union militant, he also campaigned against mafia influence in Palermo docks, where big companies used bosses to recruit casual labour. In 1962 he was elected to the regional leadership of the Communist Party in Sicily, and the following year he won a seat in the Sicilian Regional Assembly. At the end of the 1960s he took up a national role within his party, and in 1972 he became a Member of Parliament, where he took a particularly energetic role in the last years of the parliamentary inquiry into the Sicilian mafia.

Unlikely allies and anti-mafia martyrs: Pio La Torre of the Italian
Communist Party and Carlo Alberto Dalla Chiesa of the *Carabinieri*.

La Torre addresses a local Communist rally   The future General Dalla Chiesa
in Palermo, 1968.   during his time in Corleone, *c.* 1950.

Carlo Alberto Dalla Chiesa testified before the inquiry, by virtue of being commander of the *Carabinieri* legion in Palermo between 1966 and
1973. He provided some of the inquiry's most explosive evidence against
mafia-backed politicians, and compiled reports on, among others, the 'Concrete King', Ciccio Vassallo.

In 1974 Dalla Chiesa was promoted to General, and appointed to a command in north-western Italy, where he created a specialised anti-terrorist
unit to combat the Red Brigades. After the kidnap and murder of former
Prime Minister Aldo Moro in 1978, Dalla Chiesa became the prime figure
in the fight against left-wing terrorism nationally. Dalla Chiesa it was who
convinced Patrizio Peci to become the first *brigatista* to turn penitent. The
General was number two on the Red Brigades' death list in the motor city of
Turin—a list that Peci had helped draw up. (Number one was the FIAT dy-
nast Gianni Agnelli.) He knew that Peci had tried several times to kill him,
and yet dealt with his prisoner in a humane and professional fashion. Dalla
Chiesa personally guaranteed the penitent's safety while he was in prison,
and came to visit him after the Red Brigades tortured his brother to death.
As Peci later recalled: 'His manner was severe but gentle, authoritative but
kind. He never treated you with familiarity, but he didn't make you feel like
a shit either . . . I came to admire him more and more: for his character,
confidence, imagination and ability to command.'

Peci's information led to the dismantling of most of the Red Brigades' structure, and made Dalla Chiesa, with his salt-and-pepper moustache set over stern jowls, a famous face and a national hero. At the close of 1981 he was appointed deputy commander of the *Carabinieri* nationally. Then, in April of the following year, with a nation's plaudits still ringing in his ears, General Carlo Alberto Dalla Chiesa was sent to Sicily to break the mafia in the same way that he had broken the Red Brigades.

In Palermo, there was a bloodbath: Riina's savage mafia coup was in full swing, and the eminent corpses were continuing to fall. One of the most vocal supporters of Dalla Chiesa's appointment as Prefect of Palermo was Pio La Torre, who had also recently returned to his native city, drawn back by the mafia crisis and by the decision to allow the United States to base new cruise missiles at an airbase in the south-east of Sicily.

La Torre was still busy lobbying in support of new anti-mafia legislation that he had proposed the previous year. The planned law was based on the Racketeer Influenced and Corrupt Organizations (RICO) Act that had done such damage to the mafia in the United States since it came into effect there in 1970. The key law enforcement tools that La Torre wanted were two: heavy sentences for anyone proved to be a member of an organisation that used intimidation and *omertà* to gain control of companies and public resources; and the power to confiscate the mafia's illegally acquired wealth. The political irony in La Torre's proposal was clear: once again, it was the Communists who were the keenest to learn lessons from Uncle Sam's experience in fighting organised crime.

A short time before taking up his post as Prefect of Palermo, Carlo Alberto Dalla Chiesa wrote to his sons about what lay ahead. His hopes were high: 'In a couple of years, La Torre and I should be able to get the most important things done.' Faced with unprecedented slaughter in Sicily, the two great but divergent traditions of resistance to mafia power were set to unite their forces after more than a century of suspicion and misunderstanding. Honest Sicilians of all political persuasions would see their champions working together.

Dalla Chiesa's first official duty as Prefect of Palermo was to attend Pio La Torre's funeral. On 30 April 1982, La Torre was trapped in his car in a machine-gun ambush. The driver, Rosario Di Salvo, managed to get off four futile shots against the attackers before dying alongside his great friend. Di Salvo was not a police bodyguard, but a Communist Party volunteer.

Pio La Torre's murder prompted what was now a horrendously familiar public ritual in Palermo. First, on the front pages of the dailies and in TV news bulletins, there would be the macabre images of the victims slumped in ungainly postures in a pool of blood or a bullet-pocked car. Then there came the formulaic condemnations by politicians momentarily distracted from the business of jostling for position and influence. Then finally the funeral, with senior statesmen—representatives of a state that was patently not doing its job—forced to risk the wrath of the mourners and public. (One leading Sicilian politician who tried to speak at La Torre's funeral was heckled with cries of 'Get lost, *mafioso!*')

To anyone with eyes to see, it was clear that Sicilian *mafiosi* were systematically decapitating that part of the state that stood in the way of their lust for power. If a shocking chain of 'eminent corpses' had been seen anywhere else in the Western world, then the most elementary laws of politics would have guaranteed that a national hero like General Carlo Alberto Dalla Chiesa would be given a unanimous and clear mandate to lead the state's response. And when the first reports of his mission appeared, back in March 1982, the elementary laws of politics seemed to be in force: both the government and Communist opposition were agreed that Dalla Chiesa would be granted wide-ranging powers, not limited to Palermo or even to Sicily. 'There should be no political difficulties,' one national paper declared.

Yet, as he mourned Pio La Torre, political difficulties soon became a bigger worry to Dalla Chiesa than the mafia. Through press releases and interviews, the dealmakers of Rome began to send their coded public messages about Dalla Chiesa's appointment. Lukewarm expressions of support were mixed with polite perplexity. Fighting the Sicilian mafia was crucial, but it should not hinder the workings of the market economy, they said. Of course Dalla Chiesa's appointment was a good thing. But Italian democrats needed to be watchful, they said. The General should not be the herald of an authoritarian turn: Sicily didn't need another 'Iron Prefect'. (The reference was, of course, to Prefect Cesare Mori, who had led Fascism's clampdown on organised crime in the 1920s.)

On 2 April, Dalla Chiesa wrote to the Prime Minister to demand an explicit and formal anti-mafia mandate for his new job. 'It is certain that I am destined to be the target of local resistance, both subtle and brutal.' He pointed out that the 'most crooked "political family"' in Sicily was already making sinister noises about him.

There was little mystery about who that political family was: the Andreotti faction of the Christian Democrat Party, headed by the 'Young Turk' Salvo Lima. Dalla Chiesa knew Andreotti well. For the DC magus was Prime

Minister when former premier Aldo Moro was kidnapped and murdered by the Red Brigades. Andreotti it was who conferred special powers on Carlo Alberto Dalla Chiesa to get to grips with the terrorist threat.

Dalla Chiesa was a man who believed profoundly in the values of the state—he had the *Carabinieri* insignia sewn onto his skin, as he often said. Yet he was no ingénue. He was ambitious, and he knew how liquid power was in Italy, how it often coursed through personal channels, and collected in the hands of cliques. He knew the art of modulating relations with his political masters by means of a quiet word, a letter, a leak to a journalist, or a formal newspaper interview. When the list of members of the covert Masonic lodge P2 was discovered in 1981, Dalla Chiesa's name was rumoured to be on it. He explained that he had applied to join, partly out of a desire to monitor the lodge's activities, but that his application was not accepted. The P2 affair cast a shadow over Dalla Chiesa's reputation. Nonetheless, his sense of duty made him an outsider in the Italy of factions and shady schemes. When he reached Palermo, his dealings with Andreotti—the man at the centre of many a shady scheme—showed just how vulnerable that outsider status made him.

On 6 April 1982 Dalla Chiesa was called in to see Giulio Andreotti himself. This meeting was yet another example of just how individualised influence can be in Italy: it resides not in institutions, but in men and their networks of friends. For the spring of 1982 was one of the very rare moments in post-war history when Andreotti did not hold a government post. So he had no official claim to meddle in Dalla Chiesa's Sicilian mission, or request a meeting. Dalla Chiesa answered the summons all the same. As usual, the General did not mince his words: he declared he would show no special favours to Andreotti's supporters on the island. He later told his children, 'I've been to see Andreotti; and when I told him everything I know about his people in Sicily, he blanched.'

Andreotti's typically coded and devious public reply to Dalla Chiesa's statement of intent came in a newspaper column. Sending Dalla Chiesa to Sicily was a welcome initiative, he wrote. But surely the problem was more serious in Naples and Calabria than in Sicily?

This rhetorical question was both disingenuous and alarming. In raw numerical terms, Andreotti was right: at that moment, organised crime was causing more fatalities outside Sicily. But no one could fail to see the vast qualitative difference in the targets of mafia violence in Sicily. Granted, there were a few 'eminent corpses' in Campania and Calabria. In 1980, the 'ndrangheta killed two local Communist politicians. In the same year, the camorra murdered a Catholic mayor and a Communist town councillor who were trying to block the gangsters' access to the earthquake reconstruction goldmine. Lamentable as these crimes were, they did not bear comparison with the long roll of senior policemen, judges and politicians who had been cut down in Sicily. Andreotti knew this. And he knew that everyone else knew this. So he can only have been dropping a hint. The kind of hint that could bring a shiver of fear to even a brave man like Dalla Chiesa.

In the eyes of external observers of post-war Italy, the country's political life could seem confusing to the point of being comic: the same grey suits squabbling and making up, endlessly recombining to form governments that came and went like the rounds of a parlour game. Fear is one of the factors missing from this outside impression. The great string-pullers of Italian politics inspired real fear. For they had the power to take jobs and marginalise, to blackmail, to smear in the media, to initiate Kafkaesque legal proceedings or tax investigations. In Sicily in the 1970s and 1980s, violent death was added to the weaponry of influence.

When Andreotti eventually went on trial accused of working for Cosa Nostra, the Supreme Court ruled that Andreotti's relationship with the bosses rapidly became more tenuous after 1980, when his party colleague Piersanti Mattarella was murdered. Andreotti, the court ruled, knew that Cosa Nostra was intending to kill Mattarella, but did nothing about it. However, he was cleared of any criminal responsibility in the Dalla Chiesa affair. All the same, he must bear a huge moral responsibility for helping to increase the General's exposure to danger, for increasing the impression in the public's mind—and in the mafia's—that the new Prefect of Palermo lacked support.

Dalla Chiesa's job description remained unclear long after he took up residence in the elegant neo-Gothic villa that served as Palermo's prefecture. On 9 August 1982—an unusually cool day by the fierce standards of the Sicilian summer—he voiced his worries to one of Italy's leading journalists. The interview became one of the most famous in the history of Italian journalism. The headline was: 'One man alone against the mafia'.

Dalla Chiesa was as forthright as he had been at every stage of his Palermo journey. Citing events over the past few days, he told how the mafia was flaunting its scorn for the authorities:

> They murder people in broad daylight. They move the bodies around, mutilate them, and leave them for us to find between Police Headquarters and the seat of the regional government. They set light to them in Palermo city centre at three o'clock in the afternoon.

The General laid out his strategic response. First, intensified police patrols to make the state visible to the citizenry. Then the mafia's money must be targeted. The mafia was no longer a problem limited to western Sicily: it invested right across the country, and those investments had to be exposed.

Dalla Chiesa was asked if it had been easier fighting terrorism. 'Yes, in a sense. Back then I had public opinion behind me. Terrorism was a priority for the people in Italy who really count.' There was a bleak truth to Dalla Chiesa's words. There may have been eminent corpses in Sicily—journalists, magistrates, politicians—but they counted for less than victims of equivalent stature in Milan or Rome.

The General also explained the subtle tactics the mafia used to undermine his credibility. The honest police who had fought the mafia since the 1870s, in the teeth of resistance from the island's VIPs, would have read his words with a bitter, knowing smile.

> I get certain invitations. A friend, someone I have worked with, will casually say: 'Why don't we go and have coffee at so-and-so's house?' So-and-so has an illustrious name. If I don't know that so-and-so's house has rivers of heroin flowing through it, and I go for coffee, I end up acting as cover. But if I go for coffee in full knowledge, that's the sign that I am endorsing what is going on by just being there.

Anyone who refused to play along would quickly acquire a reputation for being 'awkward', 'unfriendly' and 'self-important' in Palermo's influential circles. Acquiring such a reputation was often a prelude to being shot dead.

Why had Pio La Torre been killed? 'Because of his whole life. But the final, decisive reason was his proposed anti-mafia law.'

Why was the mafia now murdering so many important representatives of the state? 'I think I've grasped the new rules of the game. Someone in a powerful position can be killed when there is a fatal combination of two things: he becomes too dangerous, and he is isolated.'

From his exchanges with Andreotti, General Dalla Chiesa knew only too well that this 'fatal combination' applied to him. He was a threat, he was isolated, and his life was in very serious peril. Why, then, did he persist, when throughout its history the mafia had defeated everyone sent to fight it?

> I am pretty optimistic—as long as the specific mandate they sent me to Sicily with is confirmed as soon as possible. I trust in my own professionalism . . . And I've come to understand one thing. Something very simple, something that is perhaps decisive. Most of the things the mafia 'protects', most of the privileges that it makes citizens pay a steep price for, are nothing other than elementary rights.

At around ten past nine on the evening of 3 September 1982, Nando Dalla Chiesa, the university lecturer son of General Carlo Alberto, was listening to music on the radio. The telephone rang. 'A normal ring,' he later recalled. It was his cousin, who told him he needed to be strong, very strong. 'What we were afraid of has happened.'

In Palermo's via Carini, General Carlo Alberto Dalla Chiesa, his new wife, and his bodyguard lay disfigured by the Sicilian mafia's Kalashnikov fire. Someone stuck up an improvised poster beside them: 'Here died the hope of all honest Sicilians'.

Back in Dalla Chiesa's apartment in the Prefect's residence, the General's safe was opened and emptied of its contents.

Even in Italy, even in the 1980s, shame could carry political weight. Days after the Dalla Chiesa murder, Italy's two houses of parliament gave an express passage to the anti-mafia legislation that Pio La Torre had been campaigning for: the Rognoni–La Torre law, as it became known.

A hundred and twenty-two years had passed since Italian unification, years when the violence of organised crime had been a constant feature of the country's history. The mafias' methods—infiltrating the state and the economy through intimidation and *omertà*—had been familiar to the police through-

La Torre and his bodyguard were murdered in April 1982. His legacy was the law that underpins the anti-mafia struggle to this day.

'Here died the hope of all honest Sicilians'. Dalla Chiesa, his wife and bodyguard were machine-gunned to death in September 1982.

out. Yet only now had Italy passed legislation tailored to those methods. The delay had been exorbitant. The price in blood had been terrible. Nevertheless, Italy finally had its RICO acts.

The Rognoni–La Torre law had its limits. It explicitly applied 'to the camorra and the other associations, whatever their local names might be, that pursue aims corresponding to those of mafia-type associations'. The 'ndrangheta, typically, was not deemed worthy of name-dropping. More substantially, there were no measures to regulate the use of mafia penitents passed in the aftermath of the via Carini massacre. Dalla Chiesa had fought Red Brigade terror using penitents who had been incentivised by reductions in their sentences. He wanted the same incentives to apply to *mafiosi*. But, for good reasons and bad, Italy's political class remained profoundly wary of what mafia penitents might say. If the ongoing bacchanalia of blood-letting within the world of organised crime ever generated any penitents, and if the police and magistrates wanted to use their testimony to test the Rognoni–La Torre law, then improvisation would be the only recourse.

Right on cue, barely a month after the Rognoni–La Torre law entered the statute book, the first penitent arrived. Not from Palermo, however, but from Naples.

Pasquale 'the Animal' Barra was the first initiate to the Nuova Camorra Organizzata, its second in command, and the lord high executioner of the

Prison assassin. Pasquale 'the Animal' Barra was the Nuova Camorra Organizzata's principal enforcer within the prison system.

Italian prison system. He was a childhood friend of NCO chief Raffaele Cutolo, and the Professor had dedicated a poem to his knife-fighting skills. In August 1981, on the Professor's orders, 'the Animal' murdered yet another inmate, a Milanese gangster. The victim was stabbed sixty times.

The problem was that the gangster in question also happened to be the illegitimate son of Sicilian-American Man of Honour Frank Coppola. The Professor was called to account by Cosa Nostra for the killing. Fearing an out-and-out confrontation with Palermo, he cut his childhood friend loose: he said that the Animal had murdered Frank Coppola's son on his own initiative.

The Animal was now an outcast in the prison underworld, persecuted by the affiliates of every mafia, including his own. He shunned all contact with others, always made his own food and drinks, and took to carrying a clasp-knife hidden in his anus at all times. Eventually, the pressure and his sense of betrayal overcame his blood bond to the Cutolo organisation: the Animal begged the authorities for help. He told investigators the whole story of the Nuova Camorra Organizzata, right from its foundation in Poggioreale prison.

With the NCO disintegrating after the Professor was sent to the prison island of Asinara, more defectors soon joined the Animal. On 17 June 1983, magistrates issued warrants for the arrest of no fewer than 856 individuals across Italy, ranging from prisoners and known criminals, to judicial officials, professionals and priests. They were all charged under the Rognoni–La Torre law. Italy's newest and most important piece of anti-mafia legislation, and the crucial evidence of the penitents, were about to be tried out on the Nuova Camorra Organizzata.

61

Doilies and Drugs

An exercise bike for astronauts. An alarm clock contraption that tipped persistent sleepers out of bed. A drastic cure for the Po valley fog.

A father flown home from Iran to his young family for Christmas. An aged but picky Neapolitan spinster matched with the Spanish flamenco dancer of her dreams.

Talented kids. Fancy dress. Comedy turns. Cheery jazz. Good causes. A set made up to look like a giant patchwork quilt. And a scruffy green parrot that resolutely refused, despite the tricks and blandishments of dozens of studio guests, to squawk its own name: 'Portobello'.

On Friday nights, between 1977 and 1983, 25 million Italian TV viewers had their cockles warmed and their tears jerked by a human-interest magazine show called, like the parrot, *Portobello*. Many thousands of ordinary people took part in the show: their phone calls were answered by a panel of lip-glossed receptionists who sat at one end of the studio floor. The host of *Portobello* skilfully deployed his patrician manners, common touch and toothy smile to hold it all together with aplomb. His name was Enzo Tortora; he had been born into a well-to-do family in the northern city of Genoa in 1928, and *Portobello* made him one of the three or four most popular TV personalities in the country. Between the cosy, warm-hearted Italy that *Portobello* constructed around the clean-living Tortora, and the savage and corrupt world of the Nuova Camorra Organizzata, the distance was astral.

Tortora's show owed its name to London's Portobello Road market for antiques and secondhand goods. The core idea was to stage a televised exchange service for curios. And the idea very quickly caught on. Although RAI, the state broadcaster, sternly told them not to, viewers sent in every conceivable bit of bric-a-brac for barter or auction. The contents of the nation's attics soon filled up the studio's huge storage facilities and spilled into the corridors.

Somewhere, lost among those piles of humble treasure, was a package dispatched from Porto Azzurro prison, on the Tuscan island of Elba; it contained eighteen silk doilies, hand-crocheted by a long-term inmate called Domenico Barbaro. Five years later, Barbaro's doilies triggered one of Italy's most notorious miscarriages of justice. Because of them, *Portobello* went off the air, and Enzo Tortora was accused of being a cocaine dealer to the stars, and a fully initiated member of Raffaele Cutolo's Nuova Camorra Organizzata. The world of *Portobello* and the world of organised crime collided. The resulting explosion inflicted grave damage on the Italian judicial system at the very moment when the power of Italy's mafias was reaching its peak. Just when the Italian state finally had the weapons it needed to combat organised crime, it suffered yet another blow to its legitimacy.

Tortora was arrested before dawn on 17 June 1983, in the luxury Roman hotel that had become a second home. As is so often the case in Italy, fragments of the evidence against him were leaked to the media while he was still being interrogated, creating a widespread assumption that he was guilty. On 21 August—long before any trial—the key testimony against Tortora was published in the current-affairs magazine *L'Espresso*. His principal accuser was another prisoner and *camorrista*, Giovanni Pandico.

Pandico was that rare thing, a con who could read and write; he even had a smattering of legal knowledge, which was enough to make him a Clarence Darrow in the eyes of his fellow jailbirds. His appearance also proclaimed his intellectual gravitas: bland, waxy features hidden behind the boxy black frames of his spectacles. But Pandico was also unstable and very violent. Even as a young man, psychiatrists had defined him as paranoid, and as having an 'aggressive personality strongly influenced by delusions of grandeur'. In 1970, Pandico was released from a short sentence for theft. Someone had to be responsible for his troubles with the law, and that someone had to be important—like the local mayor. As his paranoid reasoning dictated, Pandico rampaged through the Town Hall, Beretta 9mm in hand, killing two people and wounding two others. The mayor only saved himself by tipping over his desk and sheltering behind it.

Pandico began a long stretch behind bars. There his literary and legal expertise were spotted by Raffaele 'the Professor' Cutolo, who initiated him into the NCO and used him as a secretary, a position that gave him access to a great deal of inside information. In a typically self-aggrandising fashion, Pandico would later claim that he had been nothing less than Cutolo's *consigliere*, and thus the acting boss of the NCO after the Professor was transferred to the prison island of Asinara.

Pandico was the second member of the NCO to turn penitent after the Animal. He told magistrates that *Portobello* presenter Enzo Tortora was a cocaine dealer and money launderer for the NCO. Indeed the TV star had been such a successful criminal that he had been initiated into the brotherhood in 1980. But some time after that, according to Pandico's narrative, Tortora's relationship with the NCO had broken down when he failed to pay for a large consignment of cocaine. Pandico claimed to have been entrusted by Cutolo himself with the task of getting the money back. He also said that Tortora received his drugs wholesale through Domenico Barbaro—the same Domenico Barbaro who had sent the doilies to *Portobello* back in December 1977.

Tortora was confronted with these accusations in Rome's historic Regina Coeli prison. He admitted that, yes, he had had indirect contact with Barbaro. Through 1978 and into 1979, Tortora had received a long, indignant and verbose correspondence demanding to know what had become of the doilies. He showed investigators the letters, pointing out their absurd contents: they accused Tortora of stealing the doilies and made far-fetched threats of legal action. One of the letters Tortora received contained the following passage:

> My current status as a detainee who is still bound to the healthy principles of Honour, would oblige me not to inflict damage on you, if I were to see that you forthwith intended, giving tangible proof thereof, to see to the return of the package. As a result, in agreement with my legal advisors, I have decided to suspend the planned penal action as long as you demonstrate your goodwill.

As their pseudo-legalese, rambling logic, paranoia and scarcely suppressed violence betray, the semi-literate Barbaro was not the author of these words. They were the work of Giovanni Pandico, who was an inmate at the same Elba prison as Barbaro at the time of the doilies affair. Pandico had evidently taken charge of pressing the case for the return of the doilies with his usual obsessive persistence.

As a popular TV presenter, Tortora was meticulously protective of his public image, even when the public in question was languishing in jail. So, as he explained to his interrogators, he personally wrote a polite reply to Barbaro/Pandico's complaints, and even arranged for the RAI legal office to compensate the prisoner to the very generous tune of 800,000 lire—some $480 at the time.

Dear Mr Domenico Barbaro,

I am very sorry to tell you that I know nothing about the package you sent and have never seen a trace of it. What concerns me is that you are drawing conclusions from this fact that do not shed a very honourable light either on me, or on the respect that I have always shown to whoever it might be.

Tortora's perfectly reasonable assumption was that these documents would bolster his defence. As it turned out, passages from them would become a central part of the prosecution case. On Pandico's prompting, magistrates decided that these were coded messages: for 'package' read 'consignment of drugs'; for 'doilies' read 'cocaine'. And when 'honour' and 'respect' were mentioned, it was a signal that both parties in the deal adhered to the ethical code of the criminal underworld.

What seemed to give this airy-fairy interpretation the heft of truth was the cascade of NCO defectors, including the Animal, who backed up Pandico's story. The NCO certainly feared the penitents enough to mount violent attacks on them and their relatives in the build-up to the trial. Pandico's own mother died in an explosion only a few days after he had been cross-examined in court. Crucially, there were also two witnesses, an artist and his wife—neither of them prisoners or *camorristi*—who claimed to have seen Tortora actually swapping a small suitcase of cash for a package of white powder in a Milan TV studio.

On 17 September 1985, the huge trial against Cutolo's NCO reached its conclusion: Enzo Tortora was found guilty; he was sentenced to ten years in prison and given a fine of 50 million lire ($80,000 in 2011). For similar offences, Tortora's principal accuser, Giovanni Pandico, received a three-year sentence. The judge's ruling demolished the *Portobello* presenter's character:

Tortora has demonstrated that he is an extremely dangerous individual who for years has managed to conceal his sinister activities and his true face—the face of a cynical merchant of death. His real identity is all the more pernicious because it has been covered by a mask which exudes nothing but courtesy and *savoir-faire*.

The verdict against Tortora seemed to confirm suspicions about the real nature of public life—suspicions that had deep roots in the country's psyche. Many of the millions of ordinary Italians who spent their Friday nights in front of *Portobello* also harboured a half-buried belief that they were witnessing a façade. Behind the televisual world of light entertainment, sport, and above all politics, lay a sordid reality of favouritism, corruption, political shenanigans, and—why not?—organised crime and drug dealing. Indeed, the more suave and convincing the façade, the more cunning and devilish was the truth it concealed. According to this pernicious calculus, Enzo Tortora stood condemned by his own affable public image. The sentimental glow that issued from *Portobello* was reflected back onto its presenter as the incriminating glare of an interrogator's lamp.

The truth of Tortora's off-screen life was anything but lurid. He was exceptionally quiet and bookish by the standards of the media milieu. A non-smoking, non-drinking vegetarian, his favourite author was Stendhal and he liked to spend his spare time reading Livy and Seneca in the original Latin. But before the trial even began, journalists had been hunting for—and finding—evidence of the double life that he *surely* must have led.

To British observers like myself, the Italian legal system's way of doing things can sometimes seem monstrous. That is to say: to anyone raised on an adversarial system that gives judges the power to abandon a trial if the press has said anything likely to prejudice the outcome of the jury's deliberations, the sheer noise that accompanies a prominent case in Italy can be disturbing. Long before the decisive hearings, much of the evidence to be cited by lawyers on both sides is widely available and widely discussed. Witnesses and defendants give lengthy interviews. Multiple media investigations run in parallel to the official legal process. Opinions divide into opposing factions of *colpevolisti* and *innocentisti* (literally 'guilty-ists' and 'innocent-ists'). The actual verdict is frequently not enough to dislodge the most hardened views on the case: it remains only one view among many.

The most important argument in the Italian system's defence is that every stage of a trial, including the preparation of evidence, must be open to public scrutiny. In other words, the axiom 'justice must be seen to be done' applies long before prosecution and defence square up in front of a judge. And this is a strong argument in a country like Italy, where all kinds of undue influences, ranging from a Fascist dictatorship to the mafia, have tilted the scales of justice over the years.

Enzo Tortora certainly had the skills and the influence to fight his corner in the media battle leading up to the trial. Seven months after being arrested, he was granted house arrest for the remainder of his time on remand. He stood for election under the Radical Party banner for the European elections of June 1984. (The Radical Party had a strong civil liberties platform.) Tortora's living room was converted into a TV studio for the campaign, and he was resoundingly elected. In Italy at the time, Members of Parliament, whether in Rome or Strasbourg, had immunity from prosecution. Tortora publicly renounced his immunity.

After being convicted, he took advantage of a period of bureaucratic formalities to visit Asinara maximum security jail as part of a Radical Party initiative highlighting the desperate conditions for inmates. In a bizarre encounter, Tortora even shook hands with Raffaele 'the Professor' Cutolo. 'Very pleased to meet you,' the NCO boss quipped. 'I'm your lieutenant, remember?'

Tortora, who knew that Cutolo had openly called Pandico a liar, accepted the joke in good spirits: 'No, look, you're the boss.'

Between Christmas and New Year 1985, Tortora resigned as a Euro MP. In front of a meeting of thousands of supporters in Milan's vast piazza Duomo, he gave himself up to the police who took him off to begin his jail sentence.

In September 1986, almost exactly a year after Tortora was first found guilty, the Appeal Court overturned his conviction and restored his reputation completely.

The Appeal Court judges' ruling made the first trial seem like *The King of Comedy* rescripted by Franz Kafka. Tortora's main accuser, Giovanni Pandico, was exposed as a vindictive, self-aggrandising fantasist. Flattered by the attention and power that turning penitent brought him, he had taken revenge on the *Portobello* star for 'snubbing' him over the doilies. The other NCO defectors, many of whom were held together in an army barracks for their own protection during the investigation, had simply brought their stories into line with Pandico's. The artist who claimed to have seen Tortora swapping cash for cocaine in a TV studio, it turned out, was a known slanderer desperate to use the publicity surrounding the case to hawk a few more of his execrable paintings.

Portobello returned to the airwaves on 20 February 1987. Tortora, visibly worn down by his ordeal, nonetheless opened the show in his usual gentlemanly style: 'So then, where were we?' It is still one of the most remembered moments in Italian television history, a moment marked with indelible poignancy because Tortora died of cancer a little over a year later.

The whole Tortora story did serious damage to the public's support for the fight against organised crime. The successes of the trial against the Nuova Camorra Organizzata were completely overshadowed. The image of the *pentito* that would remain fixed in the public mind was of Giovanni Pandico in court decrying Tortora's evidence as a mere 'performance', and melodramatically demanding to undergo a lie-detector test.

Just before lunchtime on Monday 16 July 1984, with the Tortora saga still a long way from being resolved in Naples, another penitent from the world of organised crime was going through the formalities of his first interrogation in a police cell in Rome.

> I am Tommaso Buscetta, son of the late Benedetto and the late Felicia Bauccio. Born in Palermo on 13 July 1928. I have not done military service. Married with children. Agricultural entrepreneur. With a criminal record.

Buscetta had once been one of the most charismatic and powerful bosses in Sicily, an international drug lord with contacts on both sides of the Atlantic that earned him the nickname 'the boss of two worlds'. Now, he was a physical wreck. His dark features, which had the noble impassivity of an Aztec prince's, were pale and blurred. Having broken parole and fled Italy in 1980, he had taken refuge on his 65,000-acre farm in Brazil. From there he had watched, impotent, as the *corleonesi* slaughtered his friends and picked off several members of his family.

When the Brazilian police caught up with him, they tortured him: they pulled his toenails out, electrocuted him, and then took him for a ride in an aeroplane over São Paolo and threatened to throw him out. All he said was, 'My name is Tommaso Buscetta.' Just before being extradited to Italy, Buscetta tried to commit suicide by swallowing strychnine. When he landed at Rome airport, he had to be helped from the plane. Soon afterwards, he asked to speak to Giovanni Falcone, who now sat across the desk from him, listening to his every word. When asked if he had anything to declare, Buscetta spoke the following words:

> Before anything else, I want to point out that I am not a stoolie, in the sense that what I say is not dictated by the fact that I intend to win favours from the justice system.

And I am not a 'penitent' either, in the sense that the revelations I will make are not motivated by wretched calculations of what is in it for me.

I was a *mafioso*, and I made mistakes for which I am ready to pay my debt to justice completely.

Rather, in the interests of society, of my children and of young people generally, I intend to reveal everything I know about that cancer that is the mafia, so that the new generations can live in a worthier and more human way.

The most important informer in Italian underworld history. Cosa Nostra's Tommaso Buscetta is brought back to Italy in 1984 after surviving a suicide attempt.

62

WALKING CADAVERS

IN HIS LAST INTERVIEW, GENERAL CARLO ALBERTO DALLA CHIESA HAD SPOKEN ABOUT the 'fatal combination' of being a danger to the mafia, and of being isolated. The same sense of isolation was articulated very clearly by one young magistrate based in Trapani, on the very western tip of Sicily. In 1982 a TV journalist provocatively asked him whether he was mounting a 'private war' against the mafia. The magistrate calmly explained that only certain magistrates would deal with mafia crime, and build up what he called a 'historical memory' about it. For that reason, what those few magistrates were doing in the public interest ended up looking like a private crusade. 'Everything conspires to individualise the struggle against the mafia.' And that, of course, is precisely how *mafiosi* themselves viewed the struggle: as a confrontation between Men of Honour and a few ball-breakers in the police and judiciary. For the *mafiosi*, the lines between private business and the public interest are simply invisible.

The young Trapani magistrate who made this point was a brusque, bespectacled classical music–lover called Gian Giacomo Ciaccio Montalto. One evening, only a few months after the interview, he and his white VW Golf were hosed with bullets. The street where he lay bleeding to death was a narrow one, and tens of people in the overlooking apartments must have heard the gunfire. Yet no one reported the incident until the following morning. Right up to its tragic conclusion, Ciaccio Montalto's battle was an individualised one indeed.

As each 'eminent corpse' fell, seeming to confirm the mafia's barbaric supremacy over Sicily, the tightly knit but isolated group of police and magistrates who were fighting Cosa Nostra somehow found the will to carry on. One of the worst blows came in the summer of 1983 with the death of Falcone and Borsellino's boss, the chief of the investigating magistrates' office, Rocco Chinnici. Chinnici was murdered by a huge car bomb outside his house; two bodyguards and the janitor at the apartment block were also killed in the explosion. This was the most spectacular escalation yet of the Cosa Nostra's terror campaign. Chinnici was one of the first magistrates to understand the importance of winning public support for the anti-mafia cause, of leaving the Palace of Justice to speak in public meetings and schools. His shocking death was intended to intimidate the whole island.

As one hero was cut down, another stepped in to take his place—a volunteer. Antonino Caponnetto was a quiet man, close to retirement, who gave up a prestigious job in Florence to return to his native Sicily. Before he even moved into the barracks that would be his Palermo home, Caponnetto knew what he wanted to do: adopt another lesson from the battle against terrorism in northern Italy. Faced with the daily threat of the Red Brigades, investigating magistrates had decided to work in small groups, or 'pools' (the English word was used), so that the elimination of one magistrate would not cripple a whole investigation. Caponnetto wanted to use the same method against the mafia. The Palermo anti-mafia pool—Giovanni Falcone and Paolo Borsellino, along with Giuseppe Di Lello and Leonardo Guarnotta—would share the knowledge and the risks, uniting the different cases into a single great inquiry. The pool system was the magistrates' response to the 'fatal combination'.

The Palermo pool made steady progress. For example, Gaspare 'Mr Champagne' Mutolo's phone was tapped, and the passages of his heroin trade with the Far East reconstructed. Mutolo's supplier, Ko Bak Kin, was arrested in Thailand and subsequently agreed to come back to Italy to testify. Ballistic analysis had revealed that the same Kalashnikov machine gun was used in a whole series of mafia murders—from that of Stefano Bontate to General Carlo Alberto Dalla Chiesa's. The weapon was a common signature that began to make patterns discernible in the gore. Most importantly, the Flying Squad produced a report on 162 *mafiosi* that included a rough sketch of the battle lines in the war that had led to the extermination of Stefano Bontate, Salvatore Inzerillo and their followers. But as yet, investigators were reliant on secret internal sources from the world of the mafia—men who were far too afraid, and far too mistrustful of the authorities, to give their names, let alone give evidence that could be used in court.

Then, in the summer of 1984, came Tommaso Buscetta, the boss of two worlds. The new penitent's evidence marked a huge leap forward. Buscetta began from scratch by revealing the name that *mafiosi* used for their brotherhood. 'The word mafia is a literary invention,' Buscetta told Falcone. 'This organisation is called "Cosa Nostra," like in the United States.'

Buscetta's interviews with Falcone carried on, almost without interruption, until January 1985. He revealed Cosa Nostra's entire structure, naming everyone he could remember—from the soldiers at the bottom of the organisational pyramid, to the bosses of the Palermo Commission at the top. Drawing on nearly four decades of experience as a Man of Honour (he was initiated into the Porta Nuova Family in 1945), Buscetta taught Falcone about the exotic inner workings of the mafia world, its rituals, rules and mind-set. He identified culprits responsible for a host of murders. Still more importantly, he explained how those murders fitted into the strategic thinking of the bosses who had commissioned them. At last, the entire story of Shorty Riina's rise to power in the Sicilian underworld made sense. The Sicilian mafia was not an unruly ensemble of separate gangs. It was Cosa Nostra: a unified, hierarchical organisation that had undergone a ferocious internal conflict.

Until now, Falcone and his colleagues had been examining the Sicilian mafia from the outside. It was as if they were trying to draw a floor plan of a building by peering in through the keyhole. Buscetta changed everything 'by opening the door for us from the inside', as Caponnetto would later recall. Falcone thought that Buscetta 'was like a language professor who allows you to go to Turkey without having to communicate with your hands'. Following Buscetta's example, more penitents would begin to talk. The most important of them was Totuccio Contorno, the soldier from Stefano Bontate's Family who had narrowly survived a Kalashnikov attack in Brancaccio.

The pool managed to keep Buscetta's collaboration a secret for months. Finally, on 29 September 1984, the secret could be kept no longer. Arrest warrants for 366 *mafiosi* were put into effect at dawn: the operation became known as the St Michael's Day blitz. The police ran out of handcuffs. And when the police's work was done for the day, the pool held a press conference to proclaim to the world that the Sicilian mafia *as such* was to be brought before justice. Borrowing a word used to describe the massive prosecution of the Nuova Camorra Organizzata in Naples, the press began to talk about the forthcoming 'maxi-trial' in Palermo. In the streets where dialect was spoken, the trial became simply *'u maxi*. And the central issue in 'the maxi' would be Buscetta's allegation—the 'Buscetta theorem', it was dismissively labelled—that Cosa Nostra was a single, unified, hierarchical organisation.

The boss of two worlds was perfectly well aware of the historic scale of the trial that was being prepared around his testimony. Indeed a sense of his own historical mission was probably part of the mix of motives that led him to turn to Giovanni Falcone.

When the news first broke that Tommaso Buscetta was helping investigators, many commentators assumed that he was the first Sicilian *mafioso* to break the code of *omertà*. We now know more than enough about mafia history to be certain that Sicilian *mafiosi* have always talked. Both the winners and losers in the Sicilian underworld's constant struggle for supremacy have broken *omertà* over the decades.

The winners talked in order to make a partnership with the police: in exchange for passing on information on their criminal competitors, they would be granted immunity from harassment. At a grassroots level, for the police or *Carabinieri* who demonstratively walked arm-in-arm around the piazza with the local boss, this arrangement guaranteed a quiet life. The Sicilian mafia specialised in a higher level of partnership with authority: when the mafia threatened to make Sicily ungovernable, 'co-managing crime' could become a cynical and covert official policy.

The mafia's losers have broken *omertà* for a reason every bit as sordid: revenge. Abandoned by their powerful friends, out-fought and out-thought by their mafia rivals, they turned to the police as the instrument of vendetta, when no other instrument remained.

Tommaso Buscetta, like generations of *mafiosi* who broke the code of *omertà* before him, was a loser. He was part of the Transatlantic Syndicate that brokered narcotics between Sicily and the United States. As such, he felt the wrath of the *corleonesi* both before and after he decided to speak to Giovanni Falcone: between 1982 and 1984, no fewer than nine members of his family were killed, including two sons and a brother. The boss of two worlds, like many of the mafia's losers before him, had many reasons to seek vengeance through the law. He was also like many mafia witnesses before him in that he told only a part of what he knew: his drug-trafficking friends were barely touched by his revelations.

Buscetta's testimony also followed a script, a narrative about his personal journey that many other defeated *mafiosi* before him had recited. Once upon a time there was a good mafia, he claimed, a Cosa Nostra that adhered to the organisation's true, noble ideals. Now Cosa Nostra had changed. Honour was dead, and greed and brutality held sway. Now the mafia killed women and children—and so he, Tommaso Buscetta, as a true Man of Honour, would have nothing more to do with it. A misleading and self-interested tale, of course.

But if *mafiosi* have always talked, and Tommaso Buscetta was like the many *mafiosi* that had talked before him, why was he so important? Why is he always defined as the 'history-making' penitent? The main reason is that, whether the mafia reabsorbed them, intimidated them or simply killed them, mafia defectors rarely got to repeat their testimonies where it really counted: before a judge. What the prosecutors knew, they could not prove. When the mafia's losers spoke, Italy refused to believe them. And a Sicilian elite that had been profoundly implicated with the killers of the mafia since Italy was unified needed no further invitation to bury what the mafia's defectors said in verbiage: the mafia did not exist, they said; it was all a question of the Sicilian mentality, they said; all those rumours about a secret criminal association were the result of northern prejudices and paranoia; it was all the fault of Arab invaders, centuries ago.

Between talking to the police and testifying to a court, there was a long and difficult journey. For Falcone and the Palermo anti-mafia pool, the challenge was to help the boss of two worlds make it to the end of his journey. Only then could he really be said to have changed the course of history.

Falcone and Borsellino received crucial help in that task from the United States. The investigations into drug trafficking that had first drawn Falcone into the fight against the mafia had taught him just how profoundly linked, by both kinship and business ties, were *mafiosi* on both sides of the Atlantic. Falcone was a pioneer in grasping that anti-mafia investigators had to have the same, international outlook as their foe. Sicilian magistrates and police could make themselves twice as effective by seeking the help of their American counterparts. Buscetta, the boss of two worlds, was almost as important a witness in the United States as he was in Italy. And the United States, unlike Italy, had a proper witness-protection programme to which Buscetta could be entrusted.

Many dark days passed between the day when Tommaso Buscetta first sat down to speak to Giovanni Falcone and his date with the judge. The darkest days of all came in late July and early August 1985.

Beppe Montana was one of the members of the Flying Squad that had been working closely with the pool—his specialism was hunting down the many *mafiosi* who had dodged arrest warrants by going on the run. When interviewed by the press, Montana had summed up the mood of determined fatalism in his unit: 'In Palermo there are about ten of us who are a real danger for the mafia. And their killers know us all. Unfortunately, we are easy targets. If the *mafiosi* decide to kill us they can do it easily.'

On 25 July, two killers surprised Montana as he reached shore after a boating trip with his girlfriend; he died in his swimming trunks, aged just thirty-three. The fatal combination had struck again.

Paolo Borsellino recalled giving Ninni Cassarà, the deputy commander of the Flying Squad, a lift back from the scene of Montana's murder. Cassarà too was working closely with the pool, and Montana was much more than a colleague to him. After a silent journey, ashen-faced, Cassarà could only mutter: 'We'd better resign ourselves to being walking cadavers.' A couple of days later, Cassarà found the composure to give a lucid interview on the political context of Montana's death. By this time, the huge trial against the Nuova Camorra Organizzata was generating a fierce argument over *Portobello* star Enzo Tortora's conviction:

> We keep a very close eye on the worrying events surrounding *both* the build-up to the Palermo maxi-trial, *and* the maxi-trial against the camorra. In Naples we can see exactly what is happening both inside and outside the courtroom. There is a frontal assault on the value of evidence from penitents. We don't know how our Neapolitan colleagues have behaved. What we do know very well is that here we have proceeded by seeking out meticulous, rigorous and even wearying proof to confirm every detail of the penitents' accusations.

What Cassarà did not point out was that, in Naples, it was a criminal organisation in terminal decline that was in the dock. The Palermo maxi-trial set out to prosecute a mafia in its pomp, with most of its leaders still at large. In a more private moment at the end of the interview, Cassarà added a chilling final note. 'Sooner or later all the investigators who really take their job seriously end up getting killed.'

Montana's cruel death pitched the men under Cassarà's command from determined fatalism into desperate rage. Five days later, a young fisherman and amateur soccer player called Salvatore Marino was brought in for questioning. Witnesses placed Marino at the scene of the crime; at his home the police found a bloodied shirt and 34 million lire (about $53,000 today) in cash, part of it wrapped in a piece of newspaper bearing the story of Montana's assassination. (Mafia penitents have since claimed that Marino, although not a mafia affiliate, was indeed the lookout for the murderers.)

None of that excuses what happened to him. While in custody, he was punched, beaten and even bitten. Face up and head leaning back, he was then tied to a desk; a hood was placed over his head, and a hose leading into a bucket of seawater was shoved into his mouth. With a policeman sitting on his stomach, Marino was forced to drink litres and litres. This was a torture known as the *cassetta* ('box'), and it was a relic of Fascist police brutality. Like many victims of the *cassetta* before him, Marino died under torture.

In a panic, the men responsible for his death faked a drowning. Ninni Cassarà found out what had happened, and decided to support the ham-fisted cover-up that his beleaguered men were trying to stage. He went to Falcone's house in the middle of the night to ask for support. The two men had by now been working together for several years, and had become the closest of friends. They paced the room in anguish for hours. Before morning, the investigating authorities were alerted to what had really happened to Salvatore Marino.

On 5 August Salvatore Marino's white coffin, draped in his blue soccer shirt, was taken on a tour of the city to the cry of 'police murderers'. At his funeral, a Carmelite priest gave an angry homily directed at the police. The same Radical Party leader who had offered TV presenter Enzo Tortora a parliamentary seat and a platform for his fight for justice came down to Palermo to decry Marino's killers. There were rumours that the young suspect's death was no accident, and that the Flying Squad had a deliberate policy of 'taking out' mafia captives. Newspaper opinion-makers across the country began to draft well-rehearsed reflections on whether the fight against Cosa Nostra was imperilling citizens' rights. That very evening, before the results of Salvatore Marino's autopsy had even been issued, the Minister of the Interior had the chief of the Palermo Flying Squad and two other senior law-enforcement officers removed from their jobs. The same ministry that had been umming and ahhing for months over whether to replace the Palermo anti-mafia pool's outdated computers had been shaken into absurdly precipitant action by the outrage over Marino's death.

The following afternoon, Ninni Cassarà left work early to find a platoon of mafia killers waiting in two separate firing positions in the apartment block across the road from his house. Three Kalashnikovs and assorted other weapons unleashed 200 rounds. Cassarà's wife, waiting at home with their three young children, saw the whole ambush from a window. Alongside Cassarà died Roberto Antiochia, a twenty-three-year-old Roman boy who had come back early from his holidays after the Montana murder to watch his commander's back.

Between them, the mafia and the politicians had utterly incapacitated the Flying Squad, cutting off the anti-mafia pool's right arm. The rage among the surviving members of the Flying Squad was barely contained. Refusing to let Antiochia lie in state in police headquarters, they kidnapped his coffin, along with the brass posts and cordon that had been positioned around it, and carried them off to the atrium of Flying Squad HQ fifty metres away. The Interior Minister had to be protected from the dead men's colleagues when he came to Palermo for their funeral. There was fighting in the street with men from other forces. Once again, the government was panicked into inappropriate action, sending 800 police and *Carabinieri* to the island to man largely symbolic roadblocks.

The Flying Squad, like the anti-mafia magistrates of the pool, had good reason to feel not only isolated, but misrepresented. In the national and local media, the mafia's friends, or just lazy journalists in search of a polemical angle, could easily shape the frightening isolation in which they worked into a very different story: the men and women in the front line of the anti-mafia struggle were egotists, lone obsessives, loose cannons, self-appointed sheriffs. After Cassarà's death Vittorio Nisticò, a veteran of campaigning anti-mafia journalism in Sicily, berated a number of irresponsible crime correspondents:

> You knew Cassarà. And you understood. The mistake you made was that, when he was alive, you didn't show him for what he was: a modern hero. It would have been a way to protect him. Now, it's too late to tell his story.

While all this was going on, two more modern heroes, Giovanni Falcone and Paolo Borsellino, were hard at work preparing the prosecution case for the maxi-trial—a document that, in the end, would amount to 8,607 lucidly argued pages. (As was normal in the Italian legal system at the time, the investigating magistrates would leave to others the task of standing up before the court and arguing this case to a judge.) Two weeks after the Cassarà atrocity, both Falcone and Borsellino were transferred with their families to an offshore prison so that they could conclude their mammoth labour. Ironically, the island chosen to host them was Asinara, off the north coast of Sardinia, the very same maximum security facility where Raffaele 'the Professor' Cutolo was now being held. For once, the anti-mafia magistrates' isolation was keeping them safe.

63

THE CAPITAL OF THE ANTI-MAFIA

PALERMO'S UCCIARDONE PRISON IS A MONUMENT TO SHATTERED DREAMS OF REFORM. Rising in what was once open countryside near the port, it is a Victorian brick polygon with fat towers at each corner. But its forbidding appearance gives no clue to the enlightened hopes that inspired its construction. It was designed in the 1830s along the lines suggested by the great British philosopher Jeremy Bentham. No longer would men and women, adults and children, the guilty and those awaiting trial, murderers and mere petty thieves, be thrown together in the verminous promiscuity of great dungeons. In the new jail prisoners would be held in separate cells where their God-given consciences would have a chance at last to work on their souls. Rehabilitation would be born from within.

Bad planning, poor resources and a lack of political will soon buried these far-fetched dreams, and transformed the Ucciardone into a filthy, overcrowded mockery of the rule of law. For the police, it became an instrument of blackmail into which suspects would disappear, without due process, for months on end. For the underworld, as one parliamentary inquiry heard in the 1860s, the Ucciardone was 'a kind of government' whence orders were issued in times of political turbulence.

A century later, Palermo prison earned the nickname, the 'Grand Hotel Ucciardone': mafia bosses came and went from their cells in silk dressing gowns, ate lobster and drank champagne, and gave orders for murders and consignments of narcotics. Much of what Tommaso Buscetta told Giovanni Falcone about the personnel of Cosa Nostra was learned in prison. As he explained during their first interviews in the summer of 1984: 'The presence

535

of so many Men of Honour in the Ucciardone at the same time further reinforces the links between them, allowing them to help and encourage one
another.' The Ucciardone was what it had been since the nineteenth century:
the great meeting place for Men of Honour from different Families, a hub of
criminal power.

During the course of 1985, a vast new annexe to the prison was built—a
courthouse with space for up to a thousand lawyers and witnesses, and as
many journalists. Trees were cut down. Buildings requisitioned. Well over
30 billion lire ($48 million in 2011 values) were spent on creating what
looked like a gargantuan bomb shelter. A three-metre-high steel fence was
erected, just in case the reinforced concrete walls were not enough to protect the court's proceedings from a missile attack or an armed assault. Underground passages connected the Ucciardone's cells directly to the cages
arranged in a semicircle around the edges of the courtroom.

Unlike so many other shambolic public works projects of the 1980s,
it was all completed in months. Contractors were rigorously checked to
exclude anyone tied to the mafia. The 'bunker courtroom', as it is known,
was built for one trial: the maxi-trial, in which 475 men were due to stand
accused of being members and leaders of Cosa Nostra, and the Buscetta
theorem would be put to the test.

Like the maxi-trial for which it was built, the bunker courtroom divided
the city of Palermo. For some, despite its forbidding aspect, it was a symbol
of hopes far more down-to-earth than those that had inspired the construction of the Ucciardone 150 years earlier: hopes for justice.

The bunker courtroom certainly showed that the national government,
or at least parts of it, had found the political will to fight Cosa Nostra. In
Rome, ministerial support had swung temporarily behind the anti-mafia
pool: funds were provided not only for the bunker courtroom, but also
for improved security and information technology for the investigating
magistrates.

In Palermo too, there were many who shared the hopes made concrete in
the new wing of the Ucciardone. In 1985 the city elected a new mayor, Leoluca Orlando, whose political mentor was Piersanti Mattarella, the reform-
ing Christian Democrat who was murdered at his own front door in 1980.
Orlando made sure that any planning issues related to the construction of
the bunker courtroom were addressed in record time. He also announced
that the city council would be a civil complainant in the maxi-trial: in effect,
he was announcing his administration's intention to sue the bosses. Where
countless mayors had played the usual game of denying the existence of the
mafia, or pretending that it was just organised crime of a kind that could
be found anywhere, the new first citizen did not mince words. 'Palermo has

always been the mafia's capital city. But I want to express my pride in its ability to be the capital of the anti-mafia too.'

This was not an empty boast. Compared to the other heartlands of criminal power on the southern Italian mainland, Sicily did have a much greater depth and variety of experience when it came to resistance against the mafia. We have already encountered the traditions embodied by Communist leader Pio La Torre and General Carlo Alberto Dalla Chiesa. The investigating magistrates Giovanni Falcone and Paolo Borsellino were themselves, in some senses, the inheritors of those divergent traditions of resistance to the mafia: Falcone was a man of the left, and Borsellino had right-wing sympathies.

The post-war years had seen other, perhaps more sporadic examples of anti-mafia activity. Like the 'Sicilian Gandhi', Danilo Dolci, whose campaign against poverty in the 1950s soon brought him up against one of that poverty's underlying causes. Or the courageous investigative journalists of L'Ora, who were denouncing the mafia in the general silence of the late 1950s. Or the vast public demonstration that accompanied the funerals of the four *Carabinieri*, two military engineers and a policeman killed by the Ciaculli car bomb in 1963. The new dissident left groups that emerged after 1968 also had a strong anti-mafia tendency. In 1977 a small group of militants founded a study centre in Palermo that was destined to be a constant presence in anti-mafia campaigns. Peppino Impastato, the left-wing journalist son of a *mafioso* from Cinisi, near Palermo's airport, for years harangued the local boss Tano Badalamenti—the boss of all bosses in the mid-1970s. Impastato paid with his life for his devotion to the cause: in 1978 he was tied to a railway line and blown up. For a long time, the authorities dismissed his death as a bungled terrorist attack.

The bloody years of mafia conflict after 1979 saw the flowering of new and much more insistent forms of resistance. An estimated 100,000 people packed themselves into Palermo's piazza Politeama for Pio La Torre's funeral in 1982. A mass torch-lit parade followed Rocco Chinnici's death in 1983. Victims' families and their supporters formed support groups and campaigning organisations. Students staged rallies in support of the police. The anniversaries of the worst atrocities, notably the death of General Carlo Alberto Dalla Chiesa, became the occasion for demonstrations and other initiatives. Back in 1972, a Sicilian Communist leader had complained, 'Why are we [i.e., Communists] the only ones who talk about the mafia?' By the time the bunker courtroom was built, his lament was no longer justified.

Mayor Orlando's own story—he was a lawyer close to the Jesuits—spoke of an increasingly vocal strain of Catholic anti-mafia feeling. Priests were beginning to talk about the mafia in their sermons. Groups of Catholic activists embraced the anti-mafia cause. Moreover, extraordinarily, bloodstained

Palermo was witnessing the first hints of a truly epoch-making shift in the attitude of the Church hierarchy.

The Church had rubbed along pretty well with Sicily's Honoured Society for more than a century. As ever, the reasons were political. The Papacy was one of the losers in the process that had made Italy one country with its capital in Rome: the Pope lost all of his earthly territory apart from Vatican City. Thereafter, the Pope banned Catholics from voting or standing for elections in Italy. Alienated from the state, and true to their profoundly conservative instincts, bishops and priests sought out alternative sources of authority in the society around them. And *mafiosi* proved adept at posing as a traditional source of authority. In Sicily, as in Campania and Calabria, local saints' days and processions gave the men of violence the chance to parade their power, while seeming to soften its brutal edges.

By the Second World War's end, Church and state had been reconciled. During the Cold War, Catholicism ceased to be marginal to Italy's political system, and became central. A Catholic party, the Christian Democrats, dominated the political scene and formed a shield against the satanic forces of Communism. The mafia sheltered behind that shield, and found succour in the Cold War fervour of leading clerics. One notorious case was Ernesto Ruffini, the Cardinal Archbishop of Palermo for two decades: he repeatedly denounced any talk of the 'so-called mafia' as a left-wing plot to undermine Sicily.

As the violence grew in 1980s Palermo, Ruffini's successor, Cardinal Archbishop Salvatore Pappalardo, started to send out very different signals. In November 1981, the mafia-backed politicians who were assembled in Palermo Cathedral for the feast of Christ the King squirmed in discomfort as they heard him outline their complicity in murder:

> Street crime, operating in the open, is almost inextricably tied in a complex web with occult manipulators who perform shady business dealings under the cover of cunning protectors. The manual labourers of murder are tied to the men who instigate their crimes. The bullies on every street corner and in every quarter of the city are tied to *mafiosi* whose range and dominion is much more vast.

At General Carlo Alberto Dalla Chiesa's funeral in September 1982, Cardinal Pappalardo's angry denunciation of the government's failure to come to Palermo's aid made headlines even in the Communist daily, *L'Unità*.

At that point, the mafia found its own way to tell the Cardinal what it thought of his anti-mafia turn. At Easter the following year, Pappalardo respected a long-standing custom by going to the Ucciardone to celebrate

Mass with the inmates. But when he reached the prison chapel he found that every single seat was empty. A journalist observed the scene:

> For almost an hour the Cardinal waited in vain for the prisoners to leave their cells. In the end, he came to the bitter realisation that they were absent because they wanted to send him a clear, hostile signal. At that point he got into his little Renault and was driven back to the curia by his assistant.

Yet within the Church, as across Palermo, the sight of the bunker courtroom and the impending spectacle of the maxi-trial provoked unease rather than hope in many. Perhaps because he was unnerved by his experiences in the Ucciardone, or perhaps because someone in the Vatican had a quiet word, Cardinal Pappalardo made a shuffling retreat from his explicit pronouncements against the mafia. Interviewed before the maxi-trial, he blamed the media for sensationalising mafia violence and said: 'The Church is worried that holding such a big trial might attract too much concentrated attention on Sicily. I am anxious about it, and in some ways alarmed. Palermo is no different to other cities.'

The Catholic Church in Italy has always tended to regard the public performance of earthly justice as if it were a distasteful parade of crude state power. As if the courthouse was somehow a sinister rival to the cathedral. Cardinal Pappalardo, like all too many clerics before him, now seemed to have retreated behind the catchall language of evil, suffering and forgiveness: *mafiosi* were just sinners like the rest of us. Despite all the bloodshed, and despite the heroic sacrifices made so far, the Church was not yet ready to take an explicit stand against Cosa Nostra and in favour of the rule of law.

There were still more insidious voices of doubt in Palermo in the run-up to the maxi-trial. Some said that it was going to ruin the city's image. One politician hoped that it would all be over and forgotten soon, so that the bunker courtroom could be turned into something useful, like a conference centre. Sicily's most influential daily, the *Giornale di Sicilia*, was distinctly lukewarm about the whole judicial enterprise, and its editor explicitly sceptical about the key issue of the relationship between the mafia and the institutions of the state:

> Today the mafia is fundamentally unconnected to power. I don't believe it can be said that there are organic links between power and the mafia; just as it can't be said that every corrupt man in public life is necessarily a *mafioso*.

As if to prove this assertion, on the eve of the maxi-trial, the *Giornale di Sicilia* sacked a crime correspondent who had been particularly diligent in his work on mafia issues.

Silently watching the evolving spectacle was a nervous, amorphous, and far from entirely innocent majority of the city's population. Some voices blamed the anti-mafia magistrates for creating unemployment. The argument was groundless, of course: mafia influence had caused scandalous waste and inefficiency for generations. But that did not deaden the ring of truth it had for the architects and civil engineers who profited nicely from the corrupt construction system; for the bankers who did not care where their customers' money came from; for the owners of swanky boutiques and restaurants on via Libertà whose businesses floated high on the trickle-down profits of narcotics; for the idlers who had pulled in favours to get a public-sector job, or for the worker bees of the narcotics and contraband tobacco industries.

Palermo remained hard to decipher in the 1980s. Every pronouncement by a public figure was scrutinised for a coded comment on the work of the anti-mafia pool. Giovanni Falcone gave a resolutely optimistic reading of the public mood in the city of his birth. He talked about the numerous letters of support and admiration that he and his colleagues received. And of how the young people who staged demonstrations in favour of the investigating magistrates were showing great maturity: 'They have shown that, in the struggle against the mafia, party political labels are irrelevant.' The journalists interviewing him probed him further about his increasing fame, and the conflicting views of what he was doing.

> You certainly don't have an easy relationship with this city. There are those who say that you tend to overdo things, that you want to ruin Sicily. Then there are people who, albeit in a whisper, say, 'What we need is a thousand Falcones.' What is your reply?

Falcone gave a typically unassuming response, one designed to play down the familiar and potentially dangerous idea that the anti-mafia cause was a personal crusade. 'I would like to say to this city: men come and go. But afterwards their ideas and the things they strive for morally remain, and will continue to walk on the legs of others.'

The maxi-trial began on 10 February 1986. As it did, Cosa Nostra's guns fell silent while the bosses waited for the curtain to lift on the trial drama.

Meanwhile, as if to remind Italians just how high were the stakes in Palermo's bunker courtroom, the slaughter continued unabated elsewhere—and with it organised crime's insidious hold over the state machinery and the democratic process designed to run it. Palermo may have been living through an optimistic interlude in the run-up to the maxi-trial, but across the country the political system was becoming yet more dysfunctional: a 'rule of non-law'.

64

THE RULE OF NON-LAW

IN CAMPANIA, THE MILITARY AND JUDICIAL DEFEAT OF THE PROFESSOR'S NUOVA
Camorra Organizzata meant that the coalition formed to oppose him, the
Nuova Famiglia, had the region to itself. Once victory was assured, the NF
immediately descended into a bloody internecine struggle to control the
post-earthquake economy. The first signs of that war came in Marano, the
town just to the north of Naples where the Nuvoletta clan—Cosa Nostra's
viceroys in Campania—had their notorious farmhouse.

On 10 June 1984 four cars screeched through the centre of Marano,
firing wildly at one another with machine guns and pistols. A bystander,
Salvatore Squillace, aged twenty-eight, was hit in the head: yet another innocent victim of camorra violence. The *Carabinieri* investigating his death
traced the cars' route back up to a place they knew well, because they had
searched it several times: the farmhouse shrouded by trees that was the operational base of the Nuvoletta crime family. There they found the aftermath
of a huge gun battle. The front of the house was pockmarked by bullets,
and shell cases were strewn all around. Searching further, down an avenue
leading away from the house they found the body of a man, his forehead
flattened by a pistol shot fired at close range: it was one of the younger Nuvoletta brothers, Ciro. Extraordinarily, someone had staged a frontal assault
on the most powerful *camorristi* of all.

The first journalists to report on the incident, well aware of the Nuvolettas' leading role in the resistance to the Nuova Camorra Organizzata,
speculated that the Professor's men were responsible. Was this the sign of
an NCO resurgence? The true significance of the gun battle in Marano only

emerged later. The geography of camorra power was shifting. With the NCO on its way to defeat, the victorious alliance, the Nuova Famiglia, had begun to splinter. The Nuvolettas, the oldest camorra dynasty, the pillar around which Cosa Nostra had built its Campanian protectorate, stood to be eclipsed. And as they were, the Sicilian mafia's influence in Campania came to an end, the camorra came of age, and the face of much of the region was transformed.

The man who staged the spectacular, demonstrative attack on the Nuvoletta farmhouse was Antonio Bardellino. Bardellino was born in San Cipriano d'Aversa, one of three contiguous agricultural towns (the others are Casapesenna and Casal di Principe) to the north of the Nuvolettas' base. Generations of illegal building turned these towns into a two-storey maze of unmapped alleys. The area, known for its fruit trees and its buffalo-milk mozzarella industry, had been notorious for more than a century: Mussolini's repressive drive against the rural camorra in the 1920s was concentrated here.

Although he came from a very traditional camorra territory, Bardellino was something of an upstart compared to the Nuvolettas: he began his career holding up trucks. He was formally a part of the Nuvoletta organisation, and had been put through Cosa Nostra's finger-pricking initiation in the Marano farmhouse. However, the war between the NCO and the NF quickly created tensions between Bardellino and his masters. As we have seen, both Lorenzo Nuvoletta and Michele 'Mad Mike' Zaza were reluctant to commit themselves to the campaign against the Professor. Bardellino, by contrast, opted for a much more aggressive stance. He commanded a committed team of young killers who were one of the Nuova Famiglia's most efficient fighting forces—and more than a match for the numerically superior NCO. One of Bardellino's allies at the time recalled that 'we felt like the Israelis facing up to the Arabs'.

As the war dragged on, further differences between the Nuvolettas and Bardellino surfaced. The Nuvoletta brothers were closely linked to Shorty Riina and the *corleonesi*. Bardellino, on the other hand, was a business partner of some of Shorty's enemies in the Transatlantic Syndicate, and spent increasing amounts of his time with them, away from Campania, on the narcotics route from South America. Thus the same battle lines that were mapped across Sicily during the Second Mafia War in 1981–3 were now being redrawn across Cosa Nostra's Campanian territories.

By 1984, the *corleonesi* knew that Bardellino had been continuing to network with surviving Men of Honour from the losing side in Sicily, thus flouting Shorty Riina's newly established hegemony over Cosa Nostra. Bardellino and his allies, by contrast, were now certain that the Nuvolettas had adopted a duplicitous waiting strategy during the war against the Nuova Camorra Organizzata. On instructions from Corleone, the Nuvolettas had kept their Family out of the conflict, while Bardellino and his killers bore the brunt of the fighting. The Nuvolettas' intention was to wait until the Professor and Bardellino had fought one another to a standstill, leaving them free to mop up.

When Bardellino realised that war with the Nuvolettas was inevitable, he came home from his drug-trafficking base in Mexico especially to lead his men against the Marano farmhouse. Later confessions would make it clear that Bardellino's assault could have been absolutely devastating for the Nuvolettas: the *capo*, Lorenzo Nuvoletta, was due to hold two meetings in his farmhouse at that time, one with his senior commanders and one with the Professor's sister; a last-minute change of plans saved his life.

Thus the Bardellino-Nuvoletta conflict of 1984 was a restaging of the Sicilian war of 1981–3, only on Neapolitan soil. This time, however, the outcome was different.

After the success of the assault on the Nuvoletta farmhouse, Antonio Bardellino returned to his drug trafficking in South America, leaving the campaign against the Nuvolettas in the hands of his main ally, Carmine Alfieri, known simply as 'o 'Ntufato—'Mr Angry'. Alfieri came from another historic stronghold of organised crime in Campania, the cattle-market town of Nola, birthplace of the Italian-American gangster Vito Genovese. 'Mr Angry' was a meat trader and loan shark who had grown up amid the middle-class ferocity that characterises the towns of the Neapolitan hinterland: his father was murdered when he was young. He met Raffaele 'the Professor' Cutolo in jail, and was later invited to join the Nuova Camorra Organizzata. When he refused, the Professor killed his brother. 'Mr Angry' joined forces with the Nuova Famiglia.

'Mr Angry' Alfieri proved to be even more spectacularly ruthless than Bardellino. His first major attack on Nuvoletta allies was one of the worst massacres in Italian gangland history. Late on the morning of 26 August, a battered tourist coach pulled up on the main thoroughfare of Torre Annunziata, just outside a fishermen's club. The streets were crowded with people strolling, or taking coffee, or leaving church. Nobody took any notice of the bus—after all, Torre Annunziata, which lies between Mount Vesuvius, Pompeii and the Sorrento peninsula, was a frequent watering hole for tourist parties. Fourteen killers, carrying a mixture of machine guns, shotguns and pistols, calmly descended the steps of the bus and started shooting at the men playing cards and chatting in the fishermen's club. Eight people were killed. The club, it turned out, was a regular meeting place for the Nuvolettas' local allies, the Gionta clan, whose leader was yet another *camorrista* initiated into Cosa Nostra at the Marano farmhouse.

For Carmine 'Mr Angry' Alfieri, the massacre was a military triumph. Intended to damage the Nuvolettas' prestige as loudly and visibly as possible, it succeeded in its aim. The Nuvoletta clan, who were also reeling from heavy blows inflicted by the police, sued for peace. Cosa Nostra's authority in Campania crumpled. Many Sicilian construction companies operating in Campania immediately abandoned the region, some without even waiting to finish the projects they were working on.

The war against the Nuvolettas left Carmine 'Mr Angry' Alfieri as the most powerful *camorrista* in Campania. But Mr Angry had learned the lessons of Cosa Nostra's colonialism, and of the Professor's megalomania, and he did not try to impose central control. Alfieri's camorra was a confederation, as his lieutenant would later explain. 'Everyone remained autonomous. We weren't like the Sicilian mafia . . . Every group had its boss, with men loyal to him who were the sharpest and most enterprising.'

Alfieri's presiding authority finally guaranteed a measure of equilibrium in Campania's volatile gangland, albeit that the map of organised crime in the region was much more fragmented than it had been at the height of the Professor's power. In 1983, at the conclusion of the war between the Nuova Camorra Organizzata and the Nuova Famiglia, there were a dozen camorra organisations in Campania. Five years later, in 1988, there were thirty-two, many of them the splinters of the NCO and the NF.

One distinguished victim of the upheaval in the camorra was Mr Angry's ally, Antonio Bardellino, who did not live long to enjoy the fruits of victory over the Nuvolettas. In Rio de Janeiro, in 1988, he paid the price for abandoning hands-on management of his territory when one of his underlings battered him to death with a hammer. His successors—the young 'Israelis' who had been in the vanguard of the Nuova Famiglia during the war against the Professor—would no longer have their boss's taste for Cosa Nostra–style rituals. The last trace of Sicilian influence over the Campanian underworld was gone. From now on, the camorra had to stand up for itself.

The fragmentation of some camorra clans in the mid-1980s did not mean that the camorra as a whole was less powerful. Quite the contrary. Cutolo's cultish Nuova Camorra Organizzata, and the fractious Nuova Famiglia that opposed it, certainly had thousands of soldiers and ruled broad expanses of Campanian territory. But because they were only in at the beginning of the post-earthquake construction bonanza, they never achieved as deep a penetration of the economy and political system as did the more territorially circumscribed clans that came in their wake.

The new camorra groups of the mid- and late 1980s were also the beneficiaries of a whole new phase in the blend of economic growth and political failure in late twentieth-century Italy. The Italian economy returned to growth in the early 1980s. Inflation dropped, and there was a stock-market boom between 1982 and 1987. The big success story of the decade was the north-east and centre of the country where small, often family-run businesses produced specialist manufactures for export: luxury fabrics, high-specification machinery, spectacles, ski boots and so on. By 1987, the Treasury Minister could claim that Italy had overtaken the United Kingdom to become the fifth biggest economy in the world. Italy entered the age of remorseless consumerism, driven by a huge growth in advertising on new private TV stations that offered a bountiful diet of soap operas, game shows, Hollywood movies, sport and stripping housewives.

Beneath the glitzy surface, all was not well with the Italian economy. Tax dodging was widespread. The South retained its chronic problems of administrative inefficiency, poor skills and education, and a lack of inward investment. Submerged, unregulated, untaxed businesses were everywhere. Southerners bought their fair share of Levi's jeans and Timberland shoes in the consumerist boom. But what they spent tended to come from public funds rather than productive economic activity. Not coincidentally, Italy's public debt grew inexorably during the 1980s, although the South was by no means the only region responsible for the unrestrained borrowing.

The chief culprits for the debt were the usual suspects: the state and the political system that was supposed to manage it. The old vices of pork-barrel politics, nepotism and clientele-building grew worse in the 1980s—in part because there were fewer restraints. The Communist Party had reached its highest ever percentage of the vote in the 1976 general election. Thereafter, it went into decline, beached by the final retreat of the tide of labour militancy in the early 1980s. The PCI could now only look on from the margins, its leaders bewildered by change.

The decade was dominated by a five-party coalition, centred on the DC and the Socialist Party, which seemed to spend most of its time squabbling over the spoils of office. Endless bargaining, and endless jockeying for position and influence, robbed the executive branch of its ability to make reforms, plan for the future, or put a brake on public spending. The extension of local democracy (Italy's regional governments began in 1970) only spread the same methods deeper down into society. The parties, and party factions, moved in to place their men in every possible position of influence: from government

ministries, national TV stations and nationalised banks to local health authorities. This 'party-ocracy', as it was termed, became entirely self-serving, cutting politics and the state off from the ordinary job of reflecting the people's
will and administering collective services. A new breed of 'business politician'
emerged: a party functionary or state administrator devoted to systematically
taking bribes on public contracts. The business politicians then took home
those bribes or, much more often, reinvested them in the sources of personal
power: a party or party faction, a clique of friends or fellow Masons. Some
money went on conspicuous consumption to advertise political traction and
lack of scruple: a big car, a flash suit or a daughter's lavish wedding. When the
occasional corruption investigation hit the headlines, the governing classes
united in denouncing the magistrates for political bias.

In the South, but not just in the South, this newly degraded political
system was easy prey to the threats and wiles of organised crime. In the
ethics-free world of the party-ocracy, criminal organisations became just one
more lobby group to buy off. For any given political coterie, as for any given
company looking to do business with the public sector, having *camorristi*,
'ndranghetisti or *mafiosi* as friends became a competitive advantage in the
struggle to corner public resources. Even as they became more violent than
ever before, more hooked on the profits of narcotics trafficking, the mafia,
camorra and 'ndrangheta became more deeply entwined with the state—a
state that had occupied more of society and the economy than ever before.

Organised crime had made itself indispensable. Looking back on the
growth of the camorra in the 1980s, a parliamentary inquiry into the
camorra put it this way in 1993:

> In areas dominated by the camorra, society, companies and public bodies
> tend to become dependent on the camorra organisation. The camorra
> becomes the great mediator, the essential junction box linking society
> to the state, linking the market to the state, and linking society to the
> market. Services, financial resources, votes, or the buying and selling
> of goods: all are subject to camorra mediation. The camorra's activities
> create a generalised 'rule of non-law'.

The line between criminal business and lawful business had never been as
blurred. In the construction sector, it was difficult to discern any line at all.
Camorristi were newcomers to the building game, but by the early 1980s every major clan could boast its own cement works. Paying kickbacks became
routine, as did doling out fat subcontracts.

Naples and the towns of Campania were rebuilt in organised crime's
ghastly image. An entire neighbourhood of 60,000 inhabitants, Pianura near

the Nuvoletta capital Marano, was built using mob money and without a single building licence. The whole of greater Naples, in the words of the parliamentary inquiry's report,

> has been transformed into a conurbation that can only be compared to some of the metropolises that have grown up rapidly and chaotically in South America or South-East Asia: it is uninhabitable, and impossible to travel across. This level of disorder helps the camorra prosper and grow vigorous.

Illegal building has corrosive long-term effects. People who live in houses put up without planning permission, or businesses based in illegally built real estate, make up a vast and vulnerable constituency for the most unscrupulous power brokers. They are dependent on favours from on high to have their properties linked up to the electricity grid, to the road network or to water supplies. They need to be protected from any politician or administrator who might take it upon himself to enforce the law and begin demolition procedures. And they seek the help of any politician or administrator above to give them planning approval retrospectively. Such people are the *camorrista*-politician's perfect constituents.

The camorra (and the same could be said for Cosa Nostra and the 'ndrangheta) exploited Italy's political and social weaknesses with cool entrepreneurial rationality. Antonio Bardellino's business manager later explained his clan's strategic thinking:

> In the 1980s we realised that we had to 'industrialise mafia activities' in the way that the Nuvolettas had already done. We needed to do this for several reasons: so as to have capital constantly available; so that we could plan the organisation's future activities; and so that we didn't end up like Cutolo's Nuova Camorra Organizzata, which no longer had the money to pay what was due to its affiliates behind bars. That's the time when [our people] set up CONVIN, an aggregates consortium. In 1982 Antonio Bardellino and I also set up CEDIC, a concrete supply consortium. We entrusted the running of CEDIC to a qualified surveyor, Giovanni Mincione. Before being nominated chairman, Mincione was ritually affiliated to Antonio Bardellino's organisation by having his finger pricked while an image of the patron saint of our village was burned.

Force of arms, and through it the establishment of territorial control, was of course integral to this business plan. After the Torre Annunziata massacre,

Antonio Bardellino's victorious troops ousted the Nuvolettas from the pits that supplied sand and gravel for the building industry.

Carmine 'Mr Angry' Alfieri's territorial control around his home town of Nola was so undisputed that no one would have dreamed of awarding a contract except through his good offices. All the commodities of the modern mob imperium flowed through Alfieri's hands: bribes and votes, narcotics and concrete, contracts and weapons. In just one operation against one of Alfieri's lieutenants in the Sarno and Scafati area to the south-east of Mount Vesuvius, the police arrested a former mayor, a chief of a local health authority and three bank managers.

The Torre Annunziata bus massacre that confirmed 'Mr Angry' Alfieri's pre-eminent position in the camorra in 1984, happening as it did in a tourist hotspot, was the cause for renewed chest-beating by politicians and the media. The Italian state seemed to have lost control of the streets, its right to rule usurped by gangsters who were dragging much of the South and Sicily into a slough of gore. Once the question had been, 'When will it all end?' Now the press was asking, 'When will we even reach the bottom?'

The answer was not yet. Across Calabria, 'ndranghetisti fought one another throughout the 1980s in a seemingly interminable sequence of feuds over local turf. Then in 1985, yet another major conflagration broke out in Reggio Calabria over control of narcotics trafficking and construction. The so-called Second 'Ndrangheta War began with a bang: on 11 October 1985, in Villa San Giovanni, an ugly ferry port north of Reggio, a FIAT Cinquecento stuffed with dynamite exploded, killing three people. The intended target, the local boss Antonio 'Ferocious Dwarf' Imerti, survived. But the criminal balance of power in place since the end of the previous war in 1976 was blown apart.

The First 'Ndrangheta War had left Paolo De Stefano as the dominant boss in the city of Reggio Calabria and its environs. De Stefano's authority in the city had the blessing of the 'ndrangheta's regional institutions. He boasted to one of his lieutenants that, 'He lived to do justice because he was the armed emissary of the Madonna of Polsi, which used him to kill and eliminate all the dishonoured scum and schemers in the 'ndrangheta.'

De Stefano it was who had tried to kill Ferocious Dwarf. Two days later he was cruising on his motorbike round Archi, the ramshackle new quarter of Reggio Calabria that was his fortress, when the assassins caught up with him.

After Paolo De Stefano's death, the underworld in Reggio Calabria again split into two factions, and descended into a seemingly endless slogging match. Bosses from the 'ndrangheta's Canadian colonies tried to intervene to stop the blood-letting, but to no avail. Six years passed, and six hundred lives were lost before a compromise was reached. When judges came to reconstruct the events of the Second 'Ndrangheta War, their narrative of how it all began was tinged with justified fury: 'Great fluctuations in power. Marriages to seal pacts. Secret alliances. These were the warning signs of the conflict—a conflict between opposed criminal personalities who were all just as cunning as they were stupidly determined to carry on with a futile massacre.' By the end, according to the same investigating magistrates, 'the war's protagonists, who had by now been decimated, were irrationally hitting victims chosen at random just so that they could demonstrate—perhaps more to themselves than to their adversaries—that they still existed.'

Mafia war had become its own reason. Sicily, Campania and Calabria stood at risk of becoming narco-regions, swollen empires of graft, nightmarish mockeries of the civilised Europe to which they purported to belong.

65

'U MAXI

THE PALERMO MAXI-TRIAL OPENED ON 10 FEBRUARY 1986 AMID BARELY CONCEALED scepticism in the international press. Foreign correspondents were uniformly puzzled by the sheer scale of the undertaking: 3,000 police occupying the area of the bunker courtroom; an entire spare team of judges and jurors, just in case anything should happen to the first lot; 475 defendants, a quarter of whom were being tried *in absentia*—including, of course, Shorty Riina himself. The *New York Times* summarised the 'Buscetta theorem' in terms that made it sound as if Falcone and Borsellino were tilting at windmills: 'The prosecution will try to prove how individual acts were part of a vast criminal conspiracy born centuries ago and now able to reach from Bangkok to Brooklyn.'

Across the pond, the *Economist* referred to the Palermo Commission, Cosa Nostra's ruling body, as 'semi-mythical'. The *Observer* called the maxi a 'show trial' whose only precedents dated back to the Fascist era. The *Guardian* was more disparaging still, saying that the whole affair had 'overtones of a Barnum and Bailey production'.

There were barely concealed stereotypes at work in these views: the anti-mafia pool's work, like the Fascist campaign against the mafia that it inevitably called to mind, was a typically Italian mixture of the sinister, the melodramatic and the farcical.

It was not only the foreign media who dealt in stereotypes. In Italy, as abroad, Mussolini's anti-mafia drive was frequently evoked as a parallel for Falcone and Borsellino's maxi-trial. But what people meant by 'Fascism' was rarely more than a crude metaphor—the image of a demonic alliance

551

between propaganda and state brutality. In other words, the Fascism of popular memory bore little relationship to the contradictory reality of what had actually happened in the 1920s and 1930s. The truth was that the maxi-trial bore comparison with Fascism only in the minds of its enemies.

Nevertheless, the doubters seemed to have their prejudices confirmed by the inordinately slow opening to proceedings. It took three hours for the judge just to read out the charges; and two days for him to check that all the defendants had lawyers to call on. As they were trained to do, *mafiosi* did their part in trying to discredit the court: some feigned insanity or illness; others brought up endless procedural quibbles, or complained loudly about prison conditions. The presiding judge, Alfonso Giordano, refused to be thrown off course, but also listened to any sensible requests from the defendants and their lawyers. In the coming months, he would show reserves of patience and good sense that would earn him deserved plaudits. The maxi-trial would be many things, but it would not be a farce.

Falcone, Borsellino and Caponnetto responded to the many critics and doubters in a series of interviews. They vehemently denied that their case was founded only on finger-pointing by former crooks. A mountain of evidence had been gathered to back up what Tommaso Buscetta, Totuccio Contorno and the other penitents alleged. Falcone and Borsellino took justifiable pride in claiming that the maxi-trial also included the largest investigation of bank records in Italian history. They also denied that they were trying to deliver herd justice, trampling over the specific circumstances of each individual defendant. As the two magistrates argued, none of the individual crimes made sense outside of the bigger picture of a struggle for power within the whole of Cosa Nostra; these crimes were local battles conducted in the context of a war-fighting strategy. Above all, the magistrates insisted that the maxi was not a gargantuan show. The unitary nature of Cosa Nostra could not be proved without putting a large number of *mafiosi* on trial at the same time.

Falcone and Borsellino were, of course, absolutely correct to say what they said. They were also politically smart to say what they said. Any concession to the idea that they had written the script for a judicial extravaganza would open them up to their enemies' charge that they were merely ambitious showboaters. Nevertheless in Sicily, where the Honoured Society's power had hitherto been as fearsome as it was invisible, the sight of *mafiosi* undergoing cross-examination helped puncture the mafia's aura of invincibility. So it was inevitable that the maxi-trial would be a spectacle.

The spectacle really began on 3 April 1986, when the constant backdrop of argument and chatter from the defendants' cages was finally silenced by Judge Giordano's declaration that Tommaso Buscetta was ready to give evidence. The boss of two worlds was about to live up to his epoch-making promise not to retract his confessions. The accused were rapt as he spoke—first from behind a hedge of policemen, and subsequently from behind a portable bulletproof shield that had been brought in at the insistence of the United States authorities. Over the course of a week, Buscetta confirmed the structure of Cosa Nostra as he had first explained it to Giovanni Falcone, and told the story of the rise of the *corleonesi*. Although this was the prosecution's central contention, it was not news to the watching public: diagrams of the mafia's pyramidal structure had appeared in every newspaper since the pool went public with the news that Buscetta had 'repented'.

Remarkably, one of the defendants asked for the chance to question Buscetta face to face. Pippo Calò was no run-of-the-mill *mafioso*. Initiated into the Porta Nuova Family of Cosa Nostra by none other than Buscetta, Calò had risen to become the Family's representative, and had allied himself with Shorty Riina. In the early 1970s, Calò had transferred to Rome, where he worked closely with the Banda della Magliana, sharing their contacts with right-wing terrorists. The investments he managed on behalf of the Palermo bosses earned him the press nickname of the 'Treasurer of Cosa Nostra'. Calò stood accused of no fewer than sixty-four murders. In a separate case, he had also been charged with planting a bomb on a Naples–Milan train. (The charge was, in the end, confirmed.) On 23 December 1984 the bomb detonated in a mountain tunnel between Florence and Bologna; seventeen people were killed, including Federica Taglialatela (aged twelve), and the entire De

The 'Treasurer of Cosa Nostra'. Pippo Calò's worst crime was the bomb that killed seventeen on a train between Florence and Bologna in 1984. His confrontation with Tommaso Buscetta was one of the highlights of the maxi-trial in 1986.

Simone family, comprising Anna and Giovanni (aged nine and four) and their parents. Calò's aim in planning this slaughter of innocent people was to turn the government's attention away from Cosa Nostra and back towards terrorism. Police investigating the 'Christmas train bomb' (as it was called) found an arsenal in Calò's house that included anti-tank mines.

Now Calò loped across the green floor of the bunker courtroom in a yellow shirt and fawn flared slacks, his grey hair combed back over his ears and collar from a bald pate. His insolent smirk betrayed a supreme confidence that one hundred and fifty years of Sicilian mafia impunity was not about to end. Buscetta was 'ten times a liar', Calò declared; he had cribbed his evidence from *The Godfather*, and he could not be trusted because of his immoral private life. (The history-making penitent had been married three times.)

Buscetta's retaliation was withering. On the subject of family values, Calò had taken part in the Commission meetings that had sentenced Buscetta's own brother and nephew to death: their only 'crime' was being related to the boss of two worlds. Buscetta went on to accuse Calò of strangling another member of the Porta Nuova Family with his own hands.

In response, Calò wavered visibly. Having denied ever meeting the strangling victim, he was forced to admit that he had known him in prison. After this encounter, no other defendant dared challenge Buscetta directly.

More and more evidence of Cosa Nostra's barbarity emerged. Particularly shocking was the testimony of a petty criminal from the slums of Palermo called Vincenzo Sinagra, who gave evidence in an almost impenetrable dialect. Sinagra's relationship with the mafia had begun when he made the terrible mistake of robbing someone with mafia connections—a capital offence in Cosa Nostra's value system. But because he had a cousin who was a Man of Honour, Sinagra was offered the chance to work for the mob during its murder campaign of 1981–3. Arrested after he botched an assassination, Sinagra made an unconvincing attempt to feign insanity. Largely thanks to Paolo Borsellino's extraordinary powers of empathy, this pitiful figure was then persuaded to put his trust in the state, and to confess his every murder. He explained that he had been paid the equivalent of two or three hundred dollars a month to help one of Riina's most ruthless killers torture and strangle his victims, and then dissolve their bodies in acid—a process he described to the court with unassuming clarity and in horrific detail.

Played against the background of evidence like Sinagra's, the words of the bosses seemed grotesquely mannered, separated by an almost ludicrous distance from the realities of their calling. The *capo* whose performance would remain longest in the memory was Michele 'the Pope' Greco, nominally the head of the Commission at the time of the Second Mafia War, but in reality one of Shorty Riina's mere patsies. Greco's Favarella estate in Ciaculli had been the theatre of much of the action in the early 1980s. It had hosted a heroin refinery, and its large cellars were a reliable refuge for killers on the run. Many of the Commission's meetings were held there. Late in 1982, the Pope had hosted the banquet after which Saro Riccobono, the boss of Gaspare 'Mr Champagne' Mutolo's Family, was garrotted in his chair while his men were hunted down amid the fruit trees.

Sitting in a midnight-blue suit before a microphone in the vast space of the bunker courtroom, Greco insisted on prefacing his cross-examination with a lapidary declaration: 'Violence is not part of my dignity. Let me repeat that for you: violence is not part of my dignity.' Greco uttered these words, carefully framed by pregnant pauses, as if he had just enunciated one of the fundamental laws of physics for the first time in history. He gave every indication of thinking that a mere reassurance about his own good character would be sufficient in itself to guarantee an acquittal. He went on to blame the cinema for putting ideas into the penitents' heads. 'It's certain films that are the ruin of human kind. Violent films. Pornographic films. They are the ruin of human kind. Because if [Totuccio] Contorno, instead of watching *The Godfather*, had seen *Moses*, for example, then he would not have uttered such slanders.'

The least spectacular cross-examination in the maxi-trial was among the most revealing and intriguing. On 20 June 1986, Ignazio Salvo entered the bunker courtroom in an elegant light blue suit, carrying a briefcase. For thirty years, before he was brought blinking into the light of publicity and justice by the anti-mafia pool, Ignazio had controlled tax-collecting franchises across much of Sicily with his cousin Nino. The inflated profits of their licensed robbery were reinvested in agribusiness, tourism, property, and in buying the political leverage within the DC that was essential to the whole operation. Nino Salvo, who had died of a tumour just before coming to trial, was a more abrasive man than his cousin. When he was called to the Palace of Justice, his growling voice had uttered an admission (and a veiled threat) that had echoed through the building's marble and glass atrium: 'The Salvos paid all the political parties. Money to all of them: no exceptions.'

Unlike most of the other defendants at the maxi-trial, Ignazio Salvo had not been held in the Ucciardone, but under house arrest. Now, with his reading glasses halfway down his long nose, he addressed the presiding judge with relaxed precision. He began by giving a point-by-point response to Buscetta's allegations, and then embarked on a long and monotonous explanation of the reams of documentary evidence he had in his briefcase. 'You seem bored,' he said at one point to the judge, through a thin smile of contempt. It was as if, by sheer grinding force of tedium, the richest and most powerful man in Sicily hoped to vanish slowly into the background once more.

The Salvos were particularly close to Stefano Bontate, the 'Prince of Villagrazia', and other members of Cosa Nostra's drug-trafficking elite. That friendship had cost the cousins dearly, when in 1975 Nino Salvo's father-in-law was kidnapped by the *corleonesi* and never returned. The Salvos were understandably terrified in 1981, when Shorty Riina began slaughtering Bontate and his allies. For safety's sake, Nino went for a long cruise on his yacht. Meanwhile Ignazio stayed in Palermo frantically trying to contact Tommaso Buscetta to find out what was going on and organise resistance to Shorty Riina's coup. It was to be the beginning of the end of the Salvos' power.

Ignazio Salvo's response to the prosecution's narrative, apart from trying to bore the court to a standstill, was an argument of devilish subtlety:

> For many a long year the state was practically absent from the struggle against the mafia. Connivance and complicity were so widespread that citizens were left defenceless before the power of mafia organisations. The only thing for us to do was to try and survive by avoiding threats, especially to family members, and especially when our activity as businessmen necessarily put us in touch with those organisations. I have never been a *mafioso*. But I am one of the many entrepreneurs who, in order just to survive, has had to strike a deal with these *enemies of society*.

'What could we do?' Ignazio Salvo was saying. We thought we made just enough concessions to the men of violence to be left alone. Alas, we were wrong, and we ended up on the receiving end of a kidnapping. We are not culprits, but victims.

This defence was part admission and part excuse—and all completely disingenuous. Generations of Sicilian landowners and entrepreneurs had produced *exactly* the same argument when their links to *mafiosi* were discovered.

Buscetta and other penitents knew that Ignazio Salvo was a Man of Honour from the Salemi Family of Cosa Nostra—the underboss, indeed. As early as 1971, the then colonel of the *Carabinieri* Carlo Alberto Dalla Chiesa had filed a report stating that Ignazio was a *mafioso* and that his father Luigi had been the town's boss. Falcone and Borsellino's work on bank records showed that the Salvos had been illegally exporting capital—the mafia's profits, likely as not. But the cousins' real sphere of influence lay *outside* the criminal brotherhood. On that score, Buscetta's analysis of the Salvos was a lesson in the subtle relationships between the mafia and Sicily's economic and political system.

The Salvos' role in Cosa Nostra is modest. Yet their political importance is huge, because I know about their direct relationships with extremely well-known Members of Parliament, some of whom are from Palermo, and whose names I will not give.

'Whose names I will not give'—Buscetta was saying that the Salvos were the link between Cosa Nostra and politics. But he would not say *which* politicians. He had warned Falcone at the very beginning of their discussions that he did not think Italy was yet ready for such revelations, which would have been more controversial, harder to prove, and more dangerous. Ignazio Salvo was as close as the maxi-trial was going to get to the explosive subject of the mafia's 'untouchable' friends inside the institutions of government. Yet the message in Ignazio Salvo's presence at the maxi was clear all the same: there were more revelations of political scandal to come.

When the major bosses had finished giving evidence, the maxi still had over a year left to run. Vast quantities of bank data and other evidence needed to be aired. The relatives of mafia victims were given the chance to speak too. It was difficult to tell which of them made the more harrowing sight: those who pleaded tearfully for news of where their loved ones were buried;

Caged defendants look out at proceedings in the history-making maxi-trial against Cosa Nostra, Palermo, 1986–87.

or those who, evidently petrified, recited the familiar refrain of 'I didn't see anything. I don't know anything.'

In April 1987, the prosecution summed up: a process that took more than two weeks. When one of the two prosecuting advocates finally sat down after eight long days of oratory, he found himself unable to get to his feet again and had to wait for the closure of the day's proceedings so he could be carried bodily out of the courtroom by the *Carabinieri*.

One by one, the squadron of nearly two hundred defence lawyers then took the floor to give their final remarks, a process that took months.

Finally, on 11 November 1987, the judges and jury retired to consider their verdict. But just before they did, Michele 'the Pope' Greco made it known that he wanted to address them. His short speech would become the most famous of the whole maxi.

> I wish you peace, Your Honour. I wish you all peace. Because peace, and tranquillity, and serenity of mind and conscience . . . It's for the task that awaits you. Serenity is the fundamental basis for standing in judgement. These are not my words: they are the words of Our Lord, his advice to Moses. May there be the utmost serenity when it comes to passing judgement. It's the fundamental basis. What is more, Your Honour, may this peace accompany you for the rest of your life.

A threat, of course. But one draped in the cloying language that had characterised the Pope's defence throughout: he was a family man, a citrus-fruit farmer, a devout Christian who knew nothing of the mafia and narcotics.

True to his imperturbable self, Judge Giordano replied only, 'That's what we wish for too.'

Five weeks later, some twenty-two months after the opening of proceedings, came the verdict. Life imprisonment for nineteen men, including Shorty Riina, Michele 'the Pope' Greco, and three bosses who, unknown to the rest of the world, had already been dealt a swifter form of justice by Cosa Nostra itself. Pippo Calò was sentenced to twenty-three years. The tax farmer Ignazio Salvo was given six years for being a fully fledged member of Cosa Nostra—an 'enemy of society', to use his own words.

Just as striking as these heavy sentences were the acquittals: fully 114 of them. Even Shorty Riina's *corleonese* mentor Luciano Liggio was acquitted, because the court found that there was not sufficient proof that he had been giving orders from behind bars since the mid-1970s. The 2,665 years of jail handed down to the guilty were 2,002 fewer than the prosecution had asked for in its summing up. Even those who had been sceptical about the maxi-trial now had to admit that it had manifestly *not* delivered summary justice in bulk.

The outcome was a cause for celebration. It was widely viewed as a victory for justice. The penitents had been believed. Buscetta's account of Cosa Nostra and its structure had been confirmed. The Sicilian mafia existed, in other words.

Or at least it did for now. Falcone and Borsellino had always warned that the maxi-trial was just the beginning. An appeal was bound to follow. And the Supreme Court after that. There was still plenty of time for Cosa Nostra to strike back, and then to vanish once more into the mists of history.

66

ONE STEP FORWARD, THREE STEPS BACK

EARLY IN HIS FIRST INTERVIEWS WITH GIOVANNI FALCONE IN 1984, TOMMASO 'THE BOSS of two worlds' Buscetta put the magistrate on notice.

> I warn you, judge. After this interrogation, you will become a celebrity. But they will try and destroy you physically and professionally. They will do the same with me. Do not forget that Cosa Nostra will always have an account to settle with you for as long as you live.

Buscetta's prophecy began to come true in the months and years following the conclusion of the maxi-trial in 1987. What faced Falcone was not just the renewed threat of violence. (As would later become clear, Cosa Nostra's plans to kill him reached an advanced stage at various moments between 1983 and 1986; Shorty Riina had even ordered bazooka tests.) Nor was the danger just the Sicilian mafia's well-practised tactics of spying, intrigue and misinformation. For, in addition, Falcone ran into resistance at the very heart of the judicial system. The outcome was an ordeal both humiliating and terrifying.

Today, Giovanni Falcone is remembered as a national icon. Any nation would have been lucky to have him. But the bland hero-worship to which he is inevitably now subjected, and the hollow tributes paid to him even by the shadiest politicians, still provoke a gritty resentment among those who supported him during his darkest days. They are determined, quite

Giovanni Falcone and Paolo Borsellino photographed in March 1992, on one of the last occasions when the two heroic magistrates were seen in public together. Photographer Tony Gentile's image is now an icon of the anti-mafia movement.

rightly, that both Falcone and Borsellino should remain controversial figures in death as they were in life. For as long as Italy's mafias still exist, and for as long as there is institutional collusion with the mafias, Falcone and Borsellino should retain their divisive charge.

In the late 1980s, Falcone in particular was sucked into a series of nerve-shredding institutional squabbles that would have destroyed a weaker man. The anti-mafia pool and the maxi-trial offended some deeply rooted conservative instincts among judges. The pool system challenged a cherished vision of the magistrate as a solitary figure, answerable only to his conscience and to the law. So some of the resistance to Falcone was well intentioned: the very nature of the magistrate's calling was at stake. But if conservatism had been all Falcone had had to put up with, he would not have been put through such tribulation. Sleazier forces combined to create a quagmire of opposition: professional jealousy; territorial conflicts between factions; a petty obsession with regulations; and the engrained fear of talent within all Italian institutions. All in all, at the very least, Falcone's enemies were guilty of a complete failure to appreciate the dangers that lay ahead for Falcone and his work once the maxi-trial had concluded. They could not grasp just what a threat Cosa Nostra represented, and how insidious were its efforts to marginalise Falcone and dismantle what had been achieved so far, at such an appalling cost in blood. Nor did Falcone's enemies see how vulnerable he was to the 'fatal combination' that General Carlo Alberto Dalla Chiesa spoke of before his assassination in 1982: the magistrate who posed the biggest danger to Cosa Nostra would be pitilessly exposed by any hint that he was on his own.

Many of Falcone and Borsellino's enemies took their cue from Sicily's most celebrated writer. On 10 January 1987, with the maxi-trial still going on, Leonardo Sciascia published a book review in the establishment daily *Corriere della Sera*. The volume in question was a study of Fascism and the Sicilian mafia by a young British historian, Christopher Duggan, who put forward a highly controversial thesis: the mafia did not exist, but Mussolini had puffed up reports of a secret criminal organisation in order to strike at his political enemies on the island. Far more controversial were the parallels that Sciascia drew with the present day: the anti-mafia had once more become an 'instrument of power', he claimed. The novelist cited two examples. One was Mayor Orlando in Palermo, who spent so much time posing as an anti-mafia figurehead that he neglected the most basic duties of running the city, said Sciascia. No one dared oppose him for fear of being branded a *mafioso*. The other example was none other than Paolo Borsellino, who had just been made chief prosecutor in Marsala despite having served much less time in the judiciary than other candidates for the job. As Sciascia concluded, in the snide conclusion to his article, 'If you want to get ahead in the magistracy in Sicily, there's no better way to do it than to take part in mafia trials.'

Borsellino, in other words, was a mere careerist. Sciascia's review predictably detonated an enormous row.

The facts spoke out resoundingly against Sciascia's contrarian griping. It would have been more accurate to say that there was no better way for a magistrate to end up in a box than to take part in mafia trials. Since 1979, four frontline magistrates had been murdered by Cosa Nostra, and a fifth by the 'ndrangheta. Others had been lucky to survive assassination attempts. Yet more would die soon. What drove Borsellino to move to Marsala, in Sicily's most westerly province of Trapani, was certainly not ambition. He knew that Trapani province was a key power base for the *corleonesi*. In 1985, the biggest heroin refinery ever discovered in Italy was unearthed there. Borsellino's promotion was, unusually for Italy, based on merit and not seniority—on his 'specific and very particular professional expertise in the sector of organised crime', as the official explanation of his promotion put it. Yet Sciascia had cited this passage in his review as if it were self-evidently a reason for casting doubt on the legitimacy of Borsellino's transfer.

Sciascia would later come to regret his review, which was a tragically misjudged coda to his career as a voice of intellectual dissent. He deserves to be remembered for the incisive pages he wrote about the mafia back in the 1960s when most other writers refused to tackle the subject. But the regrets came too late. Sciascia had given voice to old Sicilian suspicions about the state; and the title of his review—'*Professionisti dell'antimafia*' or 'Professional anti-mafia crusaders'—had given Falcone and Borsellino's enemies their slogan.

The next blow against Falcone and Borsellino's cause was perhaps the most devastating of all. The Sciascia slogan could be heard being muttered in the Roman corridors of the Consiglio Superiore della Magistratura (High Council of the Magistracy), the body that guarded the judiciary's independence from the government, ruled on appointments and administered discipline within the judicial system. Late in 1987, Antonino Caponnetto, who was Falcone and Borsellino's boss and the man who had overseen the birth of the anti-mafia pool, went into retirement. There was still much work to be done. Two more maxi-trials were in preparation. Since the spring of '87, Falcone had been taking weekly flights to Marseille where an important new penitent, Antonino Calderone, was confessing all. Falcone was the obvious man to replace Caponnetto, and thereby guarantee continuity in the anti-mafia magistrates' work.

That was not how the High Council of the Magistracy saw it. On 19 January 1988, by a small majority, it voted *not* to give Caponnetto's job to Falcone. The post went instead to Antonino Meli, a magistrate twenty years Falcone's senior who had far less experience of mafia cases and no sympathy for the anti-mafia pool's methods. Explaining their decision in opaque legalese, the members of the Council made reference to Falcone's 'distorted protagonism' and the 'personality culture' surrounding him.

Shortly afterwards, the High Council of the Magistracy slapped Falcone down again when he applied to become High Commissioner for the Fight Against the Mafia. The role, created in a political panic after the murder of General Carlo Alberto Dalla Chiesa, was that of a supervisory super-investigator. Falcone knew that the job entailed being a lightning conductor for public criticism of the government's inactivity on mafia issues. Nonetheless, he thought he could achieve something with the powers available. His application was rejected—despite (or perhaps because of) the fact that he was the most qualified candidate by far.

Back in Palermo, the appointment of Antonino Meli proved more destructive than Falcone and his friends had feared. Once in charge, Meli began to override the anti-mafia pool. Mafia cases were entrusted to magistrates with no experience and no formalised links to other magistrates working on the mob. Falcone and his colleagues were loaded with ordinary criminal investigations. All the crucial advantages that the pool had brought—the accumulation and sharing of expertise, the panoramic view of the Sicilian criminal landscape, the mitigation of risk—were being frittered away. In the practical workings of the Palermo prosecutors, Cosa Nostra had already ceased to exist as a single organisation.

In the summer of 1988, Borsellino took his career in his hands by complaining publicly from Marsala about Meli's management of the Palermo investigating magistrates. 'I get the impression that there is a great manoeuvre under way aimed at dismantling the anti-mafia pool for good.' The President of the Republic ordered the High Council of the Magistracy to investigate. Meli demanded Borsellino's head. Falcone confirmed Borsellino's complaints and asked to be transferred. During a drawn-out and exhausting Supreme Council hearing, there were more Sciascia-type noises about Falcone: 'No one is irreplaceable . . . there is no such thing as a demi-god.' In the end, there was a messy compromise: Borsellino received only a slap on the wrist, and Falcone withdrew his transfer request.

On both sides of the Atlantic, Cosa Nostra kept close tabs on the arcane shenanigans within the High Council of the Magistracy. Joe Gambino, one of the Cherry Hill Gambinos, telephoned a friend in Palermo and asked for an update on Falcone:

> — Has he resigned?
> — Things in Palermo are still trouble. He's withdrawn his resignation and gone back to where he was before, to do the same things he was doing before.
> — Shit.

But the mafia had reasons to be optimistic too: Antonino Meli stayed where he was and continued to dismantle the pool. He simply did not believe that Cosa Nostra was a single, unified organisation, and the way he assigned mafia cases reflected his atomised view of it—a view that was already outdated in the 1870s, never mind the 1980s. Cosa Nostra was taking its own precautions, nonetheless. In September 1988, Antonino Saetta, a judge who looked likely to take charge of the maxi-trial appeal, was shot dead along with his son.

In June 1989, the campaign against Falcone took a far more sinister turn. Anonymous letters falsely accused him of using a mafia penitent to kill some of the *corleonesi*. The mysterious source of the letters, dubbed 'the Crow' by the press, was clearly inside the Palermo Palace of Justice because there was just enough circumstantial detail in the accusations to give the slander a vague ring of plausibility. Falcone was again hauled before the High Council of the Magistracy.

Then on 21 June 1989, with the furore about the Crow letters still in the air, a sports bag containing fifty-eight sticks of dynamite was found on the rocks below Falcone's holiday home at Addaura just along the coast from Palermo. Riina and other *mafiosi* were later convicted of planting the bomb, but several aspects of the Addaura attack remain mysterious to this day. Two policemen who were at the scene, and who may have been secret agents involved in saving the magistrate's life, were both murdered within months. Some rumours say that deviant elements within the secret services were to blame. Falcone was not a man given to conspiracy theories. But he was convinced that 'extremely refined minds' were behind the attack, and that the Crow letters had been part of the plan. His logic had an impeccable grounding in patterns of mafia behaviour over a century and a half: first they discredit you, and then they kill you. The magistrate's enemies aired a simpler explanation. They claimed that the attack was a fake and Falcone had orchestrated it himself to further his career.

These were the bleakest and most anxious days of Falcone's life. Over the past eighteen months, he had discovered how many fair-weather friends he had. In May 1986 he married the love of his life—an academically outstanding magistrate called Francesca Morvillo. The couple had already decided not to have children: 'I don't want to bring any orphans into the world,' Falcone said. But after the Addaura attack, he seriously entertained the idea of separating from Francesca so that she would not have to share his inevitable fate. He told his sister, 'I am a walking corpse.'

Falcone's mood improved slightly over the coming months. The prosecutor's office was restructured as part of a far-reaching reform of the judicial system. Falcone was promoted. But he soon found himself at loggerheads with his new boss. As he confided in an off-the-record briefing to a journalist: 'Working here is impossible. One step forward, three steps back: that's how the fight against the mafia goes.'

Falcone continued to be buffeted in the media too. In May 1990, the anti-mafia Mayor Leoluca Orlando used a politics chat show as a platform to accuse Falcone of protecting mafia-backed politicians from prosecution—of keeping sensitive cases 'hidden in his desk drawer'. Here was yet another insidious slur. There was a widespread conviction that the law only ever caught the underworld's lower ranks; that the 'big fish', or the 'real mafia', or the so-called 'third level' were never touched. Such a conviction is impossible to disprove, and plays to a disgust with politics that is dyed into the fabric of Italian public opinion.

Falcone angrily demanded that Orlando prove his allegations, and stated that if he had not charged anyone with having links to the mafia it was for the elementary legal reason that he did not have enough evidence. As Falcone appreciated, Orlando was cynically trying to make himself seem more anti-mafia than the champion of the anti-mafia cause. The episode was also personally hurtful because Falcone had considered Orlando a friend: the mayor had conducted the magistrate's wedding ceremony in 1986. Nevertheless, Orlando would persist in his accusations for months, accusing Falcone of cosying up to the corrupt establishment in Rome.

More serious than all of these personal attacks was the gradual erosion of Falcone and Borsellino's work in the maxi-trial. By early 1989, only 60 of the 342 men who had been convicted at the maxi were still in jail. Many were released because the Italian legal system did not consider anyone guilty until their case had been through all possible stages of the trial process, right up to the Supreme Court. Even those who were still behind bars had managed to find a way to make themselves comfortable. Pippo Calò, the train bomber who confronted Buscetta in the bunker courtroom, had arranged an asthma diagnosis and was now living comfortably in a Palermo hospital.

Worse was to come. In December 1990, the Appeal Court ruled on the maxi-trial verdicts. Seven of nineteen life sentences were overturned, as were Falcone and Borsellino's explanations of a number of high-profile murders, including that of General Carlo Alberto Dalla Chiesa. Doubt was cast on the whole 'Buscetta theorem' and the value of penitents' evidence. The case would soon be passed on to the Supreme Court, which had already demonstrated its deep suspicion of the Palermo magistrates' methods and the theory that the Sicilian mafia was a single organisation. Having been revealed in all its ferocious complexity by the maxi-trial, the mafia was rapidly becoming as legally diaphanous as it had been for the previous century and more.

67

FALCONE GOES TO ROME

DEEP DOWN, BELOW THE SURFACE HEAT OF ITS TERRORIST VIOLENCE, ITS CONSTANT crises and unstable coalition governments, post-war Italy was a country immobilised by the Cold War. In eternal opposition, the Italian Communist Party received funding from Moscow; in eternal government, the Christian Democrats banked money from the CIA. Rot spread in the stagnant political air: in every corner of the state, factions and secret cabals fought over the spoils of power. In a very Italian paradox, ties between the palaces of power and the country 'out there' became both utterly remote and stiflingly intimate. *Remote*, because the obsession with promoting allies and friends, with occupying 'centres of power', made reform close to impossible. The real rights and needs of the Italian people—among them the rule of law— went unserved. Yet also *intimate*, because as the state gradually occupied more and more of society, citizens had to make political allies and friends to get a job, or get anything done. Here was a people that loathed politicians, and yet was more addicted to politics than any other nation in Europe. Here was a state that the mafias were perfectly adapted to infect, and a governing party that had few antibodies to the mafia infection. Here was a society where anyone doing their job properly, anyone taking the initiative, risked being looked on with suspicion, if not outright hostility. The tale of Giovanni Falcone's woes in the late 1980s was a metaphor for the experience of countless other honest citizens.

The fall of the Berlin Wall in November 1989, and the end of forty-two years of Cold War, would profoundly destabilise the system. Its most immediate effect was to provoke the Italian Communist Party into changing its name, and tip it into an identity crisis that rendered it virtually inoperative. The great bugbear of Italian politics was no more. At first, the Christian Democrats and their allies seemed unscathed, victorious. But their system had now lost its chief *raison d'être*: keeping the Reds out. The DC was living on borrowed time.

The man who embodied the most cynical and slippery aspects of Christian Democrat rule, Giulio Andreotti, was Prime Minister between 1989 and the spring of 1992. Even Andreotti and the other grandees of the old system could see that the government now had to take the initiative. The hunger for reform, and the pent-up public disgust at the Italian political class, was seeking outlets. In the Christian Democrat strongholds of the north-east, the Northern League, heaping racist abuse on southerners and spraying vulgar invective against 'robber Rome', began to rake in votes. Fighting crime was a handy way for the politicians who had governed Italy for so long to win fresh legitimacy.

In February 1991, Giovanni Falcone accepted the offer of a senior post in the Ministry of Justice: his brief was to overhaul Italy's entire approach to organised crime. On the government's part, this was a jaw-slackening volte-face. As everyone knew even then, Andreotti had garnered political support from Salvo Lima and the island's 'most crooked "political family"' since the late 1960s. As everyone knows now, Andreotti was on intimate terms with Cosa Nostra until 1980. Yet here he was handing power over key aspects of the justice system to Cosa Nostra's greatest foe. Falcone's appointment was both extraordinarily welcome and cynically expedient.

Many in Palermo, from *mafiosi* to some of Falcone's supporters, were convinced that the anti-mafia's champion had traded in his cause for a fat armchair in a grand Roman office. By sheer attrition, the scandals and disappointments of the years since the maxi-trial had neutralised him. Andreotti had ensnared yet another victim.

On the eve of his departure for Rome, Falcone responded to these accusations in a revealing interview in a restaurant in Catania. He used a humble metaphor for his past achievements and future plans in the fight against the mafia. In Palermo he had built a room, he said. Now the time had come to construct a whole building. And to do that he had to go to Rome.

As the interview progressed, Falcone could not conceal the hurt he felt at being forced to leave Palermo. Most hurtful of all was the insinuation that the Addaura bomb attack had broken his nerve and that, by going to Rome, he was running away. Falcone's response was an uncharacteristic display of anger. 'I am not afraid to die. I am Sicilian,' he said. Grabbing the button of his jacket so hard that he almost ripped it off, he continued: 'Yes, I am Sicilian. And for me, life is worth less than this button.'

Once in Rome, Falcone set to work with his habitual dynamism. The result was an astonishing rebuttal to anyone who thought he had been rendered harmless. He designed a whole series of laws to gear up the fight against all the mafias, nationwide. There were measures to check money laundering and keep the defendants in mafia trials behind bars during the long unfolding of their cases. The government was given the power to dissolve local councils that had become infiltrated by organised crime. A new fund was set up to support the victims of extortion rackets. Politicians and bureaucrats convicted of mafia-related crimes were banned from public office. And, at long last, a law was passed to regulate the incentives that could be offered to penitents in return for reliable information.

Far more important even than any of these laws were Falcone's plans for entirely new structures to investigate and prosecute Cosa Nostra, the camorra, the 'ndrangheta and Italy's other mafia organisations. The Direzione Investigativa Antimafia (Anti-mafia Investigative Directorate), or DIA, was a kind of Italian equivalent of the FBI: it would marshal Italy's various police forces in their war on gangland. For the judiciary, Falcone also took the model of Palermo's anti-mafia pool and proposed replicating it. Specialised teams of magistrates devoting their efforts entirely to the fight against the mafias would be set up in all the prosecutors' offices in the country. These were to be known as the Direzioni Distrettuali Antimafia (District Anti-mafia Directorates), or DDAs. The pool system dismantled in Palermo had now become the template nationwide. The DDAs would be coordinated by a Direzione Nazionale Antimafia (National Anti-mafia Directorate), or DNA, headed by a senior magistrate whom the press soon dubbed the 'Super-prosecutor'. Huge new databases would keep track of the myriad names, faces and connections in Italy's mafia networks.

Falcone had been marginalised in Palermo, and the pioneering efforts of the anti-mafia pool, carried out in the teeth of horrific violence, had gradually been hobbled. Yet with extraordinary lucidity and daring, Falcone had grasped a fleeting moment of political opportunity to apply the lessons of his bitter Palermo experience and utterly transform the fight against the mafias nationwide. It was to be his crowning achievement, his legacy to the country that never embraced him as it should.

For one hundred and thirty years, Italy's response to the mafias had been half-hearted and sporadic at best. No one in power had seen fit to view the three historic gangster organisations—Cosa Nostra, camorra and 'ndrangheta—as a *national* issue, as three faces of the same fundamental set of problems. Most disturbingly of all, Italy had been forgetful. Each new generation of police, magistrates, politicians and citizens had had to rediscover the mafias for itself. Falcone's plans for the DIA, the DNA and the DDAs brought huge improvements, and a new continuity in the anti-mafia drive. From now on, when Italy investigated the crimes of Cosa Nostra, the camorra and the 'ndrangheta, it would do so using Falcone's method. For the first time in its life as a unified state, Italy had been endowed with an institutional memory when it came to mafia crime. Falcone had finally lifted the curse of amnesia, and enabled his country to begin to learn.

While they watched developments in Rome in horror, Sicilian *mafiosi* knew that the Supreme Court verdict on the maxi-trial, due early in 1992, would be crucial to their fortunes. A verdict confirming the Buscetta theorem would set a momentous legal precedent by finally confirming the existence of Cosa Nostra as a single criminal organisation. The bosses of the Palermo Commission also had strong personal reasons to follow the Supreme Court's deliberations closely: most of them risked irreversible life sentences. The wrong outcome of the maxi-trial, from the Sicilian mafia's point of view, would also be a catastrophic judgement on Shorty Riina's dictatorial rule of the Honoured Society. Ten years of unprecedented slaughter had exposed Cosa Nostra to the risk of its worst-ever legal defeat. Countermeasures were in order.

On 9 August 1991, the Calabrian magistrate Nino Scopelliti was on his way home from the beach when he was ambushed on a road overlooking the Straits of Messina. Scopelliti was due to present the prosecution's case in the maxi-trial to the Supreme Court. To this day, his murder remains unsolved, although the most likely scenario is that Cosa Nostra asked the 'ndrangheta to kill him as a favour. It is thought that the peace that finally put an end to the Second 'Ndrangheta War at around this time was brokered by Cosa Nostra as part of the deal. Today, a monument marks the spot where Scopelliti's BMW crashed to a halt: it shows a winged angel on her knees, holding the scales of justice.

Shorty Riina made his men promises. He told them that Cosa Nostra's tame politicians, notably 'Young Turk' Salvo Lima, would pull strings to ensure that the final stage of the maxi-trial would go their way. He claimed that the case would be entrusted to a section of the Supreme Court presided over by Judge Corrado Carnevale, whose tendency to overturn mafia convictions on hair-splitting legal technicalities had earned him newspaper notoriety as the 'Verdict Killer'. Judge Carnevale made no secret of his disdain for the Buscetta theorem.

Despite these promises, by the end of 1991 Cosa Nostra knew that the battle over the maxi-trial was likely to be lost. In October Falcone managed to arrange for the maxi-trial hearing to be rotated away from the Verdict Killer's section of the Supreme Court. Shorty called his men from across Sicily to a meeting near Enna, in the centre of the island, to prepare the organisation's response to the Supreme Court ruling. The time had come to take up their weapons, he said. The plan was to 'wage war on the state first, so as to mould the peace afterwards'. The mafia's dormant death sentences against Giovanni Falcone and Paolo Borsellino were reactivated. As it had always done, Cosa Nostra was going to negotiate with the state with a gun in its hand. But this time, the stakes would be higher than ever.

On 30 January 1992, the Supreme Court issued its ruling and re-established the maxi-trial's original verdict. The Buscetta theorem had become fact. Cosa Nostra existed in the eyes of the Italian law. When the news broke, Giovanni Falcone was in a meeting in the Ministry of Justice with a magistrate who had come all the way from Japan to seek his advice. Falcone smiled and told him what the maxi-trial's final outcome meant: 'My country has not yet grasped what has happened. This is something historic: this result has shattered the myth that the mafia cannot be punished.'

It was equally evident to Falcone's enemies how significant the Supreme Court verdict was. Shorty Riina's brutality had cut Cosa Nostra off from its political protectors. His leadership would be called into question, and his life was inevitably forfeit. The boss of all bosses declared that Cosa Nostra had been betrayed, and was entitled to take vengeance. His leading killer has since told judges that Cosa Nostra set out to 'destroy Giulio Andreotti's political faction led [in Sicily] by Salvo Lima'. Without Lima and Sicily, Andreotti would lose much of his influence within the DC. Thus, less than six weeks after the Supreme Court's ruling on the Buscetta theorem, Salvo Lima received his reward for forty years of service to Cosa Nostra when he was gunned down in the Palermo beach suburb of Mondello by two men on a motorbike.

Falcone understood the ground-shaking implications of Lima's execution. As he said to a magistrate who was with him when the news broke: 'Don't you understand? You must realise that an equilibrium has been broken, and the entire building could collapse. From now, we don't know what will happen, in the sense that anything may happen.'

With the establishment of the DIA, the DNA and the DDAs, the confirmation of the Buscetta theorem, the political orphaning of Cosa Nostra, and finally the murder of Salvo Lima, Falcone's brief months in the Ministry of Justice saw the dawn of an entirely new epoch in the long history of Italy's relationship with the mafias. An epoch we are still living in. An epoch born to the sound of bombs.

PART XII

THE FALL OF THE
FIRST REPUBLIC

68

SACRIFICE

AT 17.56 AND FORTY-EIGHT SECONDS ON 23 MAY 1992, AT THE GEOLOGICAL observatory at Monte Cammarata near Agrigento in southern Sicily, seismograph needles jumped in unison. Sixteen seconds earlier, and sixty-five kilometres away, a stretch of motorway leading back to Palermo from the city's airport had been torn asunder by a colossal explosion.

At the scene of the explosion, three policemen, Angelo Corbo, Gaspare Cervello and Paolo Capuzza, felt a pressure wave and a flash of heat, and were thrown forwards as their car juddered to a halt under a cascade of debris. They were in the third vehicle of a three-car convoy escorting Giovanni Falcone and his wife back home to Palermo for the weekend. Groggy from the impact, they peered in horror at the devastation. Then it dawned on them that there could be a secondary assault, a death squad moving in to finish off the man under their protection. Capuzza tried to grab his M12 submachine gun, but his hands were shaking too much to pick it up. So, like the others, he opted for his service pistol. The three stumbled onto the tarmac. Falcone's white FIAT Croma lay a few metres away, pitched forwards, on the edge of a four-metre-deep crater. Falcone sat in the driver's seat behind a bulletproof door that refused to budge. Gaspare Cervello later recounted the scene: 'The only thing I could do was to call Judge Falcone. "Giovanni, Giovanni." He turned towards me, but he had a blank, abandoned look in his eyes.'

Giovanni Falcone and Francesca Morvillo died in hospital that evening. Three of their bodyguards—Vito Schifani, Rocco Dicillo and Antonio

The Capaci massacre, 23 May 1992. Falcone, his wife and three of their bodyguards were murdered by a bomb placed under the motorway leading back to Palermo from the airport.

Montinaro—were already dead: they were in the lead car of the convoy that took the full force of the detonation.

What makes a hero? Where did Falcone get his courage? After so many set-backs, so much terror? The Italian state was viewed with scorn by many of its citizens; its human and material resources were treated by all too many politicians as mere patronage fodder. Yet it was in the name of that very state that Falcone chose to give his life.

The definitive answer to those questions lies hidden in psychological depths into which no historian will ever be able to reach. All the same, the question is far from being an idle one. Indeed it is extremely historically important. Because Falcone was not alone. His cause was shared by many others—beginning with his wife and his bodyguards. After Falcone, many others would be inspired by his story, just as he had been inspired by the example of those who died before him.

When Falcone's friends and family were asked about what drove him, they spoke of his upbringing, and the patriotism and sense of duty that were instilled in him from a young age. Such factors are undoubtedly important.

But the most insightful account of Falcone's motives came from the man who shared his destiny.

On the evening of 23 June 1992, exactly a month after Giovanni Falcone passed away in his arms, Paolo Borsellino stood up in his local church, Santa Luisa di Marillac, to remember his great friend. As he made his way to the pulpit, the hundreds who had crowded into the candle-lit nave spontaneously got up to applaud him. Hundreds more could be heard clapping outside. Seven minutes later, his voice unsteady, Borsellino began one of the most moving speeches in Italian history:

> While he carried out his work, Giovanni Falcone was perfectly well aware that one day the power of evil, the mafia, would kill him. As she stood by her man, Francesca Morvillo was perfectly well aware that she would share his lot. As they protected Falcone, his bodyguards were perfectly well aware that they too would meet the same fate. Giovanni Falcone could not be oblivious, and was not oblivious, to the extreme danger he faced—for the reason that too many colleagues and friends of his, who had followed the same path that he was now imposing on himself, had already had their lives cut short. Why did he not run away? Why did he accept this terrifying situation? Why was he not troubled? . . .
>
> Because of love. His life was an act of love towards this city of his, towards the land where he was born. Love essentially, and above all else, means giving. Thus loving Palermo and its people meant, and still means, giving something to this land, giving everything that our moral, intellectual and professional powers allow us to give, so as to make both the city, and the nation to which it belongs, better.
>
> Falcone began working in a new way here. By that I don't just mean his investigative techniques. For he was also aware that the efforts made by magistrates and investigators had to be on the same wavelength as the way everyone felt. Falcone believed that the fight against the mafia was the first problem that has to be solved in our beautiful and wretched land. But that fight could not just be a detached, repressive undertaking: it also had to be a cultural, moral and even religious movement. Everyone had to be involved, and everyone had to get used to how beautiful the fresh smell of freedom is when compared to the stench of moral compromise, of indifference—of living alongside the mafia, and therefore of being complicit with it.
>
> Nobody has lost the right, or rather the sacrosanct duty, to carry on that fight. Falcone may be dead in the flesh, but he is alive in spirit, just as our faith teaches us. If our consciences have not already woken, then

they must awake. Hope has been given new life by his sacrifice, by his woman's sacrifice, by his bodyguards' sacrifice . . . They died for all of us, for the unjust. We have a great debt towards them and we must pay that debt joyfully by continuing their work, by doing our duty, by respecting the law—even when the law demands sacrifices of us. We must refuse to glean any benefits that we may be able to glean from the mafia system (including favours, a word in someone's ear, a job). We must collaborate with justice, bearing witness to the values that we believe in—in which we are obliged to believe—even when we are in court. We must immediately sever any business or monetary links—even those that may seem innocuous—to anyone who is the bearer of mafia interests, whether large or small. We must fully accept this burdensome but beautiful spiritual inheritance. That way, we can show ourselves and the world that Falcone lives.

As he spoke these words, Borsellino knew he was next. He knew that Falcone was his shield against Cosa Nostra. His family often heard him say, 'It will be him first, then they will kill me.' When Falcone went to work at the Ministry of Justice in Rome, Borsellino returned from Marsala to Palermo to pick up where his friend left off. Now Borsellino was widely rumoured to be the leading candidate for the job Falcone had designed: 'Super-prosecutor', in charge of the National Anti-mafia Directorate, coordinating organised crime investigations at a national level. Borsellino had prepared the maxi-trial with Falcone. Sicily had chosen him, willing or not, to be Falcone's heir as the symbol of the struggle against Cosa Nostra. He had been informed that the explosive meant for him was already in Palermo.

All of which makes his courage all the more astonishing, and the Italian state's failure to protect him all the more appalling.

On 19 July 1992, a FIAT 126 stuffed with explosives was detonated outside Paolo Borsellino's mother's house in via d'Amelio. The magistrate had just rung the doorbell when he was torn limb from limb.

With Borsellino died his five bodyguards, volunteers all: Agostino Catalano, Vincenzo Li Muli, Walter Eddie Cosina, Claudio Traina, and a twenty-four-year-old female officer from Sardinia called Emanuela Loi. Several times during the previous fifty-six days, Borsellino had gone out alone to buy cigarettes in the hope that he would be shot, thus sparing anyone else from sharing his end.

The via d'Amelio massacre, 19 July 1992. Paolo Borsellino and five police bodyguards were blown apart by a car bomb in Palermo.

At his wife's insistence, Borsellino's funeral was private, held in the very church where he had pronounced his own epitaph on 23 June.

The state funeral of his five bodyguards took place in Palermo Cathedral. It turned into a near riot. The streets around were closed off, and a police cordon tried to deny access—for reasons that nobody could understand. Among the vast crowd of grief-stricken citizens shut outside were members of the dead officers' families. There was screaming, spitting, pushing and shoving. Police fought police, to cries of 'they won't let us sit with our dead'. As one eyewitness commented:

> The state seemed like a punch-drunk boxer throwing his fists in the wrong direction, at the people. The tens and tens of thousands of Palermitans who had shown up in the piazza to protest against the mafia were being treated as if they were a gigantic public order issue.

Eventually, the cordon broke, and the crowd flooded into the cathedral. The coffins of Borsellino's bodyguards were greeted with a chorus of '*GIUS-TIZ-IA, GIUS-TIZ-IA.*' Justice. Justice.

69

THE COLLAPSE OF THE OLD ORDER

THE SUMMER OF 1992 IN PALERMO WAS A TIME OF RAGE, DESPAIR AND DISBELIEF. It was also a time of enormous cultural and political energy as the healthy part of the city sought to broadcast its feelings. There were demonstrations, torch-lit parades, human chains . . . The tree outside Falcone's house in via Notarbartolo became a shrine to the heroes' memory. Balconies across the city were hung with sheets bearing anti-mafia slogans: 'FALCONE LIVES!'; 'GET THE MAFIA OUT OF THE STATE'; 'PALERMO DEMANDS JUSTICE'; 'ANGER & PAIN—WHEN WILL IT END?'

The echoes from Palermo reverberated across a national political land-scape that was in the throes of an earthquake. A many-layered crisis was in the process of utterly discrediting the system that had been in force since 1946. The end of the Cold War was working its delayed effects.

Falcone died on 23 May 1992 in the middle of a power vacuum in Rome. Recent general elections had witnessed a slump in the DC vote. 'Collapse of the DC wall', ran one newspaper headline. Following the elections, the be-ginning of a new five-year parliamentary cycle coincided with the beginning of a new seven-year term for the President of the Republic. A governing co-alition had yet to be formed, and newly elected Members of Parliament and the Senate were still busy haggling over who would be the next President of the Republic. Giulio Andreotti was playing a canny game as ever, waiting for other candidates to be eliminated before putting himself forward. The keys to the Quirinale, the Head of State's palace in Rome, were to be the crowning glory of his long career.

The shame and horror surrounding Falcone's death made Andreotti's candidature unthinkable. In the coming months, the most powerful politician in post-war Italy would be increasingly marginalised. Oscar Luigi Scalfaro, a respected Christian Democrat senior statesman with no 'odour of mafia' around him, was rapidly elected President.

However, Italy was not allowed to regain its equilibrium after 23 May. On the evening of Borsellino's assassination, 28 million people followed the news special on the state broadcaster RAI, and a further 12 million watched the horror unfold on the private channels. 'The mafia declares war on the state', ran one national headline the next day. The war, in actual fact, had been declared more than a decade earlier. It now looked as if the state was about to *lose* that war. Not only that, but the country itself seemed to be falling apart.

On 16 September 1992, after months of pressure on international currency markets, the lira was forced out of the Exchange Rate Mechanism—the forerunner of the planned single European currency. The debts racked up by the party-ocracy had destroyed Italy's financial credibility.

The day after the lira's exit from the ERM, Cosa Nostra killed another key component of what had once been the DC machine in Sicily: Ignazio Salvo, the tax collector brought down by the maxi-trial, was shot dead at the door of his villa. Like Salvo Lima, Ignazio Salvo paid the price for failing to protect Cosa Nostra from Falcone and Borsellino.

Meanwhile, a huge corruption scandal had begun, with investigations into the Socialist Party in Milan. The summer and autumn months witnessed more and more politicians and party functionaries targeted by investigations grouped under the name 'Operation Clean Hands'. The scandal continued to gain momentum until it engulfed the weakened 'party-ocracy'. By the end of 1993, some two hundred Members of Parliament were under investigation. In January 1994, the Christian Democrat Party was formally dissolved. The First Republic, as it is now known, was dead. Cosa Nostra had helped finish it off.

Yet precisely because the old regime was toppling, Italy found the will to respond to public dismay and fight back. By murdering Falcone and Borsellino, Shorty Riina and his entourage brought down the state's retribution not just on themselves, but on the whole Italian underworld. For a brief and extraordinary season, between Borsellino's death in July 1992 and the spring of 1994, Italy's institutions finally called the mafias to account for more than a decade of slaughter. Even crude numbers registered the transformation. Between 1992 and 1994, 5,343 people were arrested under the Rognoni–La Torre anti-mafia law. In 1991 there were 679 mafia-related homicides in Italy; by 1994 the figure had fallen to 202.

Immediately after Borsellino's murder, 7,000 troops were sent to Sicily to relieve the police of more mundane duties. New anti-mafia legislation was rushed through parliament—legislation that arrived more than a century late, but which was welcome nonetheless. A witness-protection programme was set up. Just as importantly, a tough new prison regime was imposed on underworld bosses. At long last, Italy had the means to stop jails like the Ucciardone becoming command centres for organised crime.

The fight against the mafia was also stepped up on the international front. In September 1992, the Cuntrera-Caruana clan, key members of the heroin-dealing Transatlantic Syndicate, suffered a serious blow: three Cuntrera brothers, Pasquale, Paolo and Gaspare, were extradited from Venezuela.

A new Chief Prosecutor from Turin, Gian Carlo Caselli, volunteered to enter the Palermo war zone. Caselli's bravery and absolute professional in-

tegrity were not the only things that made him the perfect man for the job. He had a highly distinguished record investigating the Red Brigades in the late 1970s and early 1980s. He had experience of handling penitents, and of the rigours of life under armed escort. He had also supported Falcone at every stage of his battles with the High Council of the Magistracy. Palermo prosecutors were galvanised as never before.

In January 1993, the very day of Caselli's arrival in Sicily, Shorty Riina was captured as he and his driver circled a roundabout on the Palermo ring road. He had been on the run since 1970. But as with all the many fugitives from justice in Cosa Nostra, 'on the run' was an entirely inappropriate metaphor. In all his twenty-three years of evading capture, Riina had not only

After his capture in 1993, Riina is made to pose before a picture of one of his most illustrious victims, General Carlo Alberto Dalla Chiesa.

masterminded his coup d'état within Cosa Nostra, managed his economic empire and murdered countless heroic representatives of the law, he had also married in church, fathered and schooled four children, and obtained the best medical care money could buy.

Riina's arrest resulted from inside information from his former driver. Since Borsellino's death, magistrates had been offered a flood of such tip-offs. The number of penitents grew exponentially too. Some were encouraged by the new measures to protect them; others were afraid of the new prison regime; and some were just shocked to their human core by what happened to Falcone and Borsellino. Gaspare 'Mr Champagne' Mutolo, the Ferrari-driving heroin broker, turned state's evidence in May 1992 after months of gentle encouragement by Giovanni Falcone. He was the last man to be interrogated by Borsellino. The via d'Amelio bomb removed the residues of Mutolo's reticence, and from then on he held nothing back. Having been in prison with bosses close to Riina until the spring of 1992, he was able to supply the first insider account of Cosa Nostra's strategy following the Supreme Court's ruling on the maxi-trial. He also provided evidence that led to the arrest, on Christmas Eve 1992, of Bruno Contrada, former chief of police of Palermo and Deputy Head of Italy's internal intelligence service. Contrada would ultimately be convicted of collusion with Cosa Nostra.

Most sensationally of all, Mutolo's evidence was also used against seven-times Prime Minister Giulio Andreotti. When Tommaso Buscetta first met Falcone in 1984, he had warned that Italy was not ready for him to talk about Cosa Nostra's links to politics. The tragic events of 1992 convinced Buscetta that the time was now right: he too implicated Andreotti. Another penitent, the heroin refiner Francesco 'Mozzarella' Marino Mannoia, told prosecutors that he had seen Andreotti come to a meeting in the early days of 1980 with Stefano Bontate, the Prince of Villagrazia. On the agenda of the meeting was Cosa Nostra's plan to kill the President of the Sicilian Region, Piersanti Mattarella. Andreotti objected to the plan, according to Marino Mannoia. But Bontate overruled him, went ahead and killed Mattarella. Judges would later declare that this meeting marked the point at which Andreotti would increasingly distance himself from Cosa Nostra. Yet it remains a chilling episode. Andreotti knew in advance that the mafia was planning to kill his party colleague Mattarella, yet he did nothing to save him.

Cosa Nostra tried to terrorise the penitents into silence. Santino Di Matteo, captured a few weeks after Riina, was one of the first men from within the group that had planned and executed the bomb attack on Giovanni Falcone to confess. As a result, Di Matteo's eleven-year-old son Giuseppe was kidnapped and kept in a cellar for more than two years before being strangled and dissolved in acid.

Nonetheless, more penitents followed—including from Shorty's inner circle. In September 1992 a young drug dealer called Vincenzo Scarantino was arrested and charged with planting the bomb that killed Paolo Borsellino and his bodyguards. He too would confess.

Sicily was breathing revolutionary air. The Catholic Church has always been the institution most resistant to change in Italy. Moreover, when it came to the subject of organised crime, it had long been unworthy of the faith shown by believers like Paolo Borsellino, not to mention the priests who have paid with their lives for resisting the mafia over the decades. But even the Pope could not fail to be moved by the mood radiating out from Palermo in 1992–93.

In May 1993, John Paul II came to Sicily for the first time in a decade. In Agrigento soccer stadium, shortly after meeting the family of a young magistrate called Rosario Livatino who was murdered in 1990, the pontiff deviated from his prepared speech to deliver a jeremiad against the mafia and its 'culture of death'. 'Convert! Because one day the judgement of God will come!' The Vatican had abandoned its traditional misgivings about the anti-mafia cause. Cosa Nostra, finally, was anathema.

The camorra suffered almost as much as Cosa Nostra from the bombs in Sicily and the collapse of what was beginning to be called the First Republic.

Camorra boss Pasquale Galasso was a prime example of what it can mean to be bourgeois in southern Italy's organised crime hotspots. He was the son of a 'man of respect' from a small town between Naples and Salerno. His father owned land, traded agricultural produce, ran a dealership selling tractors and diggers, and farmed votes for the local Christian Democrat potentates. Pasquale had a Ferrari when he was barely out of his teens, and enrolled at university to study medicine. In 1975, at age twenty, he shot two men dead. With the help of his father's lawyers, Galasso would eventually be acquitted on the grounds of self-defence. But in the meantime he was sent to Poggioreale prison. There he was taken under the wing of Raffaele 'the Professor' Cutolo.

When the war with the Nuova Famiglia broke out at the end of the 1970s, Galasso received a visit at home from the Professor, who asked him to join the Nuova Camorra Organizzata. Galasso refused, and Cutolo had one of his brothers killed in revenge. Instead of the NCO, Galasso teamed up with the Nuova Famiglia, and in particular with someone else he had met in prison: Carmine 'Mr Angry' Alfieri. The former medical student would be Mr Angry's right arm through the rest of the war; together, the two of them would rise to the top of the Campanian underworld. When the Galasso family villa was finally raided in October 1991, the *Carabinieri* found a hoard of stolen art treasures, including the gilded throne that had once belonged to the last Bourbon King of Naples.

In May 1992 Galasso was captured while chairing a meeting between construction entrepreneurs and members of his clan. Suspecting that he was about to be betrayed by his political friends, he 'repented' later that year and confessed to forty murders. His testimony allowed the police to reconstruct the whole history of the Nuova Famiglia, from its first emergence to its break-up in the wake of the victory over the Nuova Camorra Organizzata.

Galasso's tip-off also led to the arrest of Mr Angry himself, after nine years on the run. Investigators estimated that his wealth amounted to 1,500 billion lire—the biggest patrimony in Italian criminal history, equal to roughly $1,600 million in 2011. The newspapers made much play of the fact that there were heavily annotated copies of Dante and Goethe on Mr Angry's bookshelves, and that he liked to listen to Bach while he was accepting bribes and ordering murders. This most serenely powerful of *camorristi* was sent to the formidable island prison of Pianosa, off the coast of Tuscany. There, after watching the Pope's denunciation of the Sicilian mafia on television, he too resolved to tell all. As a result, the dominant camorra organisation in Campania fell to pieces.

Together Carmine Alfieri and his lieutenant Pasquale Galasso would also do their bit to destroy the DC system of which they had formed an integral part: they named a slew of politicians with whom they claimed to have done business. Many of those politicians belonged to the political machine of Antonio Gava, a former Finance and Interior Minister for the DC.

Like Cosa Nostra, the camorra reacted with ferocity to the threat from the penitents. On the day Mr Angry made his first court appearance, 8 April 1994, killers went looking for his twenty-five-year-old son Antonio. They were told he was staying at a friend's parents' house. They burst into the living room, pointing guns and demanding to know where the Alfieri boy was. In frustration, one of the killers sprayed a darkened bedroom with machine-gun fire. When they were at last convinced that the family did not know their target's whereabouts, they left, but not before kneecapping one of Mr Angry's distant relatives who was there. Only later was it discovered that there had been an innocent victim of the raid. Maria Grazia Cuomo was asleep in the bedroom that had been sprayed with machine-gun fire. She was fifty-five, unmarried, and rarely went out of the house because she was so ashamed of the purple birthmark that covered much of her face.

Mr Angry's son would eventually be killed in September 2002. His brother was shot dead in December 2004.

The increased pressure from the authorities was also felt by the 'ndrangheta. Here too, there was a new batch of penitents whose testimonies launched important new trials, whose memories cast a light backwards into the history of the 'ndrangheta, and whose life stories illustrated the deathly psychological grip of the Calabrian mafia. Here are two examples.

Giacomo Lauro was the son of a sculptor, who carved statues and reliefs for graves in Brancaleone. He was initiated into the 'ndrangheta at eighteen years old in 1960, back in the days when the Honoured Society held its meetings at night, by candlelight, and when *tarantella*-dancing triumvir don 'Ntoni Macrì was the dominant figure on the Ionian coast. After fighting in the First 'Ndrangheta War from 1974 to 1977, Lauro was imprisoned and then sent to internal exile in—of all places—northern Campania. There Lauro hooked up with Nuova Famiglia chiefs Antonio Bardellino and Carmine 'Mr Angry' Alfieri and became one of the link-men between the 'ndrangheta and the camorra. He was a close adviser of Antonio 'Ferocious Dwarf' Imerti during the Second 'Ndrangheta War of 1985–91. He was arrested in Holland, where he had gone to receive payment for a cocaine shipment. In his pocket was found a plane ticket for Colombia. When Falcone and Borsellino were killed, he contacted the Italian embassy and told them he wanted to talk. Lauro's evidence would be crucial in reconstructing the whole history of the Calabrian mafia since the 'mushroom-picking' summit on Montalto in 1969. Lauro's evidence also shed light on the 'ndrangheta's most prominent political murder—that of corrupt Christian Democrat politician Ludovico Ligato in 1989.

Giovanni Riggio came from the southern outskirts of Reggio Calabria. His father was a humble builder. In 1981, when he was eleven years old, his six-year-old brother was killed in a hit-and-run motor accident. Riggio saw the driver. Everyone else in the quarter knew who it was too. But nobody spoke. Riggio's grief-stricken father turned to the authorities but received no help. One day he asked the local *Carabiniere* officer if he could help. The man just shrugged his uniformed shoulders and said, in so many words, that only the local boss could sort things out. Riggio's father cried in desperation. Henceforth, his surviving son would have a burning resentment against the police, and a powerful fascination for the cocksure criminals who hung around in the local bar.

As a teenager, Riggio began to hang around in the bar too. After several petty crimes, the poisonous language of 'respect' and 'honour' entered his bloodstream. In September 1987, he was initiated with the rite of Osso, Mastrosso and Carcagnosso. The following spring, when Riggio bumped into the man who had run over his little brother, he shot him dead on the spur of the moment. 'Everyone saw me, and I immediately thought: now they're going to arrest me. But they didn't. No one said anything. No one talked. On the contrary: the day after, people were smiling at me, letting me know that I had done the right thing.'

By this time, Riggio's Local had been drawn into a territorial conflict. By the end of it, he had committed four murders himself and helped out in another ten. He was twenty-one years old.

Riggio turned state's evidence in September 1993, after falling in love with a girl from Rovigo who would subsequently become his wife. His evidence put his former boss and most of the Local behind bars. Asked what he thinks about the police now, he said, 'Today I feel as if I am completely one of them, because when it comes down to it we're all running the same risks and fighting for the same cause.'

These penitents, as well as the increased police pressure, undoubtedly had their effects. For it was at this time that the 'ndrangheta finally decided that kidnapping attracted too many police into the wooded folds of the Aspromonte massif. The determination of one woman played a part in their decision too. Angela Casella's son Cesare was kidnapped by the 'ndrangheta in January 1988. Several times during his 743-day-long captivity, she made the journey down to Calabria from the family's home in Pavia, near Milan. She earned the press nickname 'Mother Courage' by appealing for help from the people on Aspromonte; she even chained herself to railings in several village squares. By the time her son was eventually released in January 1990, his case had become as well known as the Getty kidnapping. In the early 1990s, Calabrian gangsters duly abandoned the traffic in captives in which they had been the leading force among Italian criminal organisations—the business that had helped launch them into narcotics and construction.

An important phase in the 'ndrangheta's history was over. But of all the three mafias, the Calabrians were the least damaged by the crackdown in the early 1990s. One measure is the number of penitents. In 1995, 381 members of Cosa Nostra were recorded as state's witnesses. There were markedly fewer penitents from the camorra in the same year: 192. But then former bosses like Carmine 'Mr Angry' Alfieri inflicted disproportionate damage. The total of 133 'ndrangheta defectors was the lowest of all the three historic criminal organisations.

Relatively unscathed, the 'ndrangheta could now harvest the rewards of the long history of invisibility that distinguished it from the camorra and Cosa Nostra. Its decision to refuse Shorty Riina's invitation to join Cosa Nostra in his war on the state also paid dividends. After 1992, only the 'ndrangheta among criminal organisations would remain mysterious, its internal structure still only partially understood, its existence as a single criminal organisation—rather than a loose ensemble of local clans—as yet unconfirmed.

70

NEGOTIATING BY BOMB: Birth of the Second Republic

THE SHOCK FROM THE MURDERS OF FALCONE AND BORSELLINO WAS MOST INTENSELY felt among the magistracy: by their colleagues, obviously, but also by young magistrates who could only admire the two heroes from a distance, and try to live up to the spirit of self-sacrifice that they embodied. One such young magistrate summed up the feelings of a generation of his peers: 'After the second bomb we were genuinely all ready to be killed. But we certainly had not resigned ourselves to mafia rule.' The bombs of 1992 blasted out a deep trench between the representatives of the rule of law on the one side, and the criminal power system on the other. The era of dialogue, and compromise, and collusion between the state and the mafia that produced magistrates like Giuseppe Guido Lo Schiavo, the inspiration for the film *In the Name of the Law*, was over for good.

Or at least it should have been. In the years since 1992, magistrates in Sicily and elsewhere have been haunted by questions that refuse to go away. Shorty Riina had set out clear aims for his organisation when the Supreme Court's ruling on the maxi-trial went against him: 'Wage war on the state first, so as to mould the peace afterwards.' Cosa Nostra was trying to negotiate by bomb. But with whom was it negotiating? Did anyone try to appease Falcone and Borsellino's murderers? Was a deal ever struck? Today, twenty years on, investigating magistrates believe they can now glimpse the answers to those questions.

Cosa Nostra's war on the state did not stop with the murders of Giovanni Falcone and Paolo Borsellino in 1992. Nor did the arrest of Shorty Riina in January 1993 bring a halt to the bombing. Indeed later that year, Riina loyalists within Cosa Nostra—bosses who became known as the organisation's 'pro-massacre wing'—launched a series of terrorist attacks aimed at high-profile targets on the Italian mainland.

On 14 May 1993 a car bomb detonated in via Fauro, Rome. The intended victim was Maurizio Costanzo, a leading chat-show host who had been very vocal in his disgust at Cosa Nostra's crimes. Luckily, although many people were wounded, Costanzo's car avoided the explosion and nobody was killed: a massacre had been narrowly averted.

Thirteen days later there was no such luck when a FIAT minivan stuffed with explosives blew up without warning in the shadow of the Uffizi Gallery in Florence. Five people died, including a nine-year-old girl. The van's engine was found embedded in a wall on the other side of the river Arno, and three paintings in the Uffizi were damaged beyond all hope of restoration.

There were five more fatalities in Milan's via Palestro on 27 July. At just after 11 p.m., three firefighters, a police officer and a man who happened to be sleeping on a bench nearby were all caught in the blast from another car bomb.

Barely an hour later, Rome became the next city to be targeted by Cosa Nostra's car bombs. The Catholic Church was made to pay a price for the Pope's denunciation of Cosa Nostra earlier in the year. One device damaged the façade of the Pope's official seat in the city, the Basilica of San Giovanni in Laterano—the huge piazza before it hosts many political rallies. A second explosion destroyed the portico of the Church of San Giorgio in Velabro. There were no victims in either incident.

Rome was also scheduled to be the venue for the worst slaughter of the whole campaign. On 31 October 1993, a Lancia Thema filled with dynamite was parked outside the Olympic Stadium where a soccer match between Lazio and Udinese was taking place. Activated by a remote control, the bomb was directed at supporters leaving the ground, and at the *Carabinieri* supervising the crowds. The device, which could have killed dozens, failed to detonate.

The annals of Italian organised crime contain no precedent for the outrages of 1992–93. Throughout those two terrible years, the pro-massacre wing's intentions remained consistent: 'Wage war on the state first, so as to mould the peace afterwards.' Riina's demands were high: he wanted both to blunt the state's most effective weapons against organised crime (the penitents, the Rognoni–La Torre law), and also to reverse the judicial results that those weapons had obtained (Falcone and Borsellino's maxi-trial).

As the massacres followed one another, Cosa Nostra's need to negotiate grew ever more urgent, and the list of demands longer. In response to Falcone's death, the government imposed a new prison regime, universally known as 41-*bis* ('Clause 41a'), which aimed to prevent leading *mafiosi* communicating with the outside world, and therefore running their empires. (This was yet another of Falcone's ideas.) In the middle of the night of 19–20 July, just hours after Paolo Borsellino's murder, Clause 41a came into effect when military aircraft took 55 bosses from the Ucciardone to join 101 other top criminals in the bleak penal colony on the island of Pianosa off the Tuscan coast. The abolition of the new prison regime was quickly added to Cosa Nostra's war aims.

The whole narrative of the season of mafia massacres in 1992–93 remains worryingly open-ended in a number of crucial respects. For example, some suspect that negligence was not the only factor in play when Paolo Borsellino was left so shamefully underprotected after Falcone's murder.

In the immediate aftermath of Borsellino's own death, his red diary, containing some of his most secret notes, disappeared from the scene of the massacre. (Borsellino's younger brother Salvatore has adopted the red diary as a symbol of his quest for the truth.)

When Shorty Riina was captured in 1993, his villa was left unguarded long enough thereafter for *mafiosi* to enter it, remove property and compromising documents, and even redecorate. Quite how this was allowed to happen has never been satisfactorily ascertained. The episode has led many to suspect that someone within Cosa Nostra betrayed Shorty to the authorities in exchange for favours.

Crucial insights into Cosa Nostra's negotiations with the state came in 2008 when Gaspare Spatuzza began to talk. Spatuzza, known by the nickname of 'Baldy', was a Man of Honour from the Brancaccio Family of Cosa Nostra who was already serving life sentences for his role in Cosa Nostra's bombing campaign on the Italian mainland. Baldy explained that Vincenzo Scarantino, the young drug dealer who had already spent a decade and a half in prison for planting the car bomb that killed Borsellino, could not be guilty—for the simple reason that he, Spatuzza, was responsible. So convincing was the corroboration that Baldy provided to back up his revelation, that Scarantino has since been released and his innocence confirmed. (He had long maintained that he was not guilty, claiming that he was tortured until he confessed.)

Another new mystery about the massacres of 1992–93 was thereby exposed. Was Scarantino framed by overenthusiastic policemen who were desperate to get any kind of result in the climate of emergency following the deaths of Falcone and Borsellino? Or was the shocking injustice he suffered part of a bigger and much more devious plan?

Baldy Spatuzza's evidence has brought new energy to the search for the truth about the negotiations between Cosa Nostra and the state in the early 1990s. Still more worrying fragments of evidence have emerged. Some *Carabinieri* have confirmed that they tried to make contact with Cosa Nostra in the summer of 1992 to try and stop the massacres, but they deny that there were any negotiations.

In the summer and autumn of 1993, while Baldy was placing car bombs in Florence, Milan and Rome, no fewer than 480 *mafiosi* were released from the Clause 41a prison regime by the Minister of Justice Giovanni Conso. Conso has recently offered the explanation that this act of clemency was a purely personal initiative, aimed at sending out an accommodating signal.

Most troubling of all, it has now been confirmed that Paolo Borsellino found out that overtures were being made to Cosa Nostra in the days following Falcone's death—overtures that he vigorously opposed. Shorty Riina's top killer has claimed that Cosa Nostra brought forward its plan to kill Borsellino precisely in order to stop him interfering with the deal-making: 'The ongoing negotiations were the main reason why the plan to eliminate Borsellino was accelerated.'

One of the two most important murders in the entire history of Italian organised crime therefore remains substantially unsolved. Testimonies from Spatuzza and others raise the chilling possibility that Paolo Borsellino was deliberately sacrificed. Some witnesses speak of secret-service involvement both in the negotiations between the mafia and the state, and in the murder of Paolo Borsellino.

As I write, several mafia bosses, including Shorty Riina, stand accused for their part in trying to blackmail the state in 1992–93. Three senior *Carabinieri* and two politicians face related charges. A former Minister of the Interior has been accused of giving false evidence about the negotiations. Their trial has only just begun, and the presumption of innocence can be no mere formality in such an intricate and controversial case.

The charges filed by the investigating magistrates paint a picture of a negotiation that developed over several stages, and involved links between Cosa Nostra and a number of functionaries and politicians, by no means all of them among the accused in the new trial. What the magistrates believe is that, in order to achieve its aims in 1992–3, Cosa Nostra needed to find new political partners—just when Italy's Cold War political parties were breaking up, and the country was negotiating the tumultuous passage between the First Republic and the Second Republic (as we now call them). Among the protagonists of the negotiations on the state's side were politicians of three kinds, according to the as yet untested charges. First, there were those from the First Republic, previously close to Cosa Nostra, who felt threatened by Riina's rage. Second, there were statesmen trying to pilot Italy through its economic and political crisis who were not friendly with the Sicilian mafia, but who may have made or approved misguided attempts to appease the pro-massacre wing. And finally there were the new men trying to assert themselves politically in the chaos of the First Republic's collapse. Men like Marcello Dell'Utri, the Sicilian right-hand man of a media entrepreneur who went on to become the dominant and most controversial figure of the Second Republic, Silvio Berlusconi.

Berlusconi did well out of the close political friendships he made during the First Republic: the Socialist Party leader and sometime Prime Minister, Bettino Craxi, was the best man at his second wedding. The collapse of the old political order was a serious threat to his business interests. It is thought that as early as June 1992 (between the murders of Falcone and Borsellino, that is), Berlusconi's people were taking soundings about founding a new political party. The magistrates contend that, as Berlusconi's political plans took shape, Dell'Utri offered himself to Cosa Nostra as a negotiating partner, promising to grant some of its wishes in return for support. The Second Republic began in March 1994, when Berlusconi led his new party, Forza Italia, to election victory. That was the point in time, according to the magistrates, when 'the new pact of co-habitation between the state and the mafia was finally sealed'.

Marcello Dell'Utri is an old acquaintance to readers of these pages. It was he who hired the *mafioso* Vittorio Mangano in 1974 to protect Berlusconi and his family from kidnappers. Since 1996, Dell'Utri has been the subject of a seemingly endless mafia trial. He currently has an outstanding conviction for helping Cosa Nostra, and a sentence of nine years in prison to serve. But Dell'Utri is still a free man because the verdict remains provisional until the Supreme Court rules. So far, the judges have explicitly rejected the argument that Dell'Utri's relationship with Cosa Nostra was still operative in the early 1990s when the mafia-state negotiations are thought to have taken place. But that too may change. It should also be stressed that an investigation based on the theory that Berlusconi and Dell'Utri had a role in commissioning Cosa Nostra's bombing campaign was shelved because of a lack of evidence in 2002. Berlusconi has never been charged with any crime in relation to Cosa Nostra's bombs. Nor does he appear in the latest trial, except as the victim of an alleged extortion by his friend Marcello Dell'Utri, who is one of the two politicians who face charges that they helped Cosa Nostra with its negotiating strategy.

No period in Italian mafia history is without its lingering uncertainties. Historians live with the constant risk that their work will be unmade when some new document surfaces from the archives, or a new penitent unlocks his or her memory. The transitional years of 1992–4 are more than usually dogged by doubt. Only time—the glacier-slow time of the Italian judicial system—will reveal what truth, if any, there is in all the accusations about Cosa Nostra's plan to negotiate by bomb.

Even if the worst suspicions about the mafia-state negotiations turned out to be true, it would be very rash indeed to conclude either that Silvio Berlusconi's main aim in government was to do Cosa Nostra's bidding, or indeed that a pact with Cosa Nostra explained his political success. There is much, much more to the whole Berlusconi phenomenon than his alleged links to Cosa Nostra.

That said, Berlusconi's priority while in power was to protect his business interests from what he deemed to be a judicial conspiracy. In the process of defending himself, he damaged the anti-mafia cause. In Berlusconi's view, popularity and electoral success exempted him from the rule of law. Many of the measures he introduced, or tried to introduce, displayed a categorical failure to perceive the boundary between his own personal concerns on the one hand, and those of the state and the Italian people on the other. He repeatedly tried to make himself immune from prosecution. He introduced amnesties for people seeking to reimport money that had been exported illegally to foreign or offshore bank accounts (usually to avoid the attentions of the law or the tax authorities). He decriminalised false accounting, and made it harder for magistrates to obtain evidence from financial institutions in other countries. He introduced a law specifically targeted at Gian Carlo Caselli, the Chief Prosecutor who had gone to Palermo after the deaths of Falcone and Borsellino and achieved such extraordinary results. The law tweaked the age qualifications for the job of National Chief Anti-mafia Prosecutor, and was aimed at stopping Caselli getting the job for which he was the outstanding candidate. *Mafiosi*, *camorristi* and *'ndranghetisti* were not the intended beneficiaries of these and other changes, but they will have greeted them with a broad smile nonetheless.

Berlusconi's rhetoric on the issue of organised crime was frequently irresponsible. To one British journalist, he said that he thought that anti-mafia magistrates were 'mad'. 'To do that job you need to be mentally disturbed, you need psychic disturbances,' he asserted. Berlusconi's party attracted electoral support from the mafias. In open court in 1994, 'ndrangheta boss Giuseppe Piromalli said, 'We'll all vote for Berlusconi.' In a sense, that fact is not scandalous: the mafias are attracted by power, whoever holds it. But Berlusconi did little to disown or discourage such supporters.

Whether he was in opposition or in government (which he was in 1994–95, 2001–6, and 2008–11) Silvio Berlusconi was impossible to ignore, inspiring both adulation and loathing. Viewed from abroad, his dominance gave the Italian political scene during the years 1994–2011 an appearance of clarity that was deceptive. If one looks beyond those appearances, one finds a dispiritingly familiar picture of political confusion and paralysis of a kind that has always prevented Italy introducing the reforms it needs, and made the state weak in the face of the threat from organised crime.

The end of the Cold War inaugurated a new series of opportunities and threats for Italy, as for its neighbours and the other developed countries. There was the expansion and deepening of the European Union, with the creation of the Euro and its subsequent crisis. Globalisation introduced Italy for the first time to mass inward migration and the tide of cheap Chinese manufactures. The rise of the information society forced economies worldwide to recalibrate. The end of the Cold War ideologies left many political systems looking for new ways to engage with distracted electors. Old problems—like the balance between social solidarity and economic individualism—were posed in novel forms.

Italy, in particular, had a long and urgent to-do list that it had inherited from the First Republic: its poor education system; the lamentable state of its public finances; one of the worst records for youth unemployment and tax avoidance on the continent; the chronic imbalance between North and South; a serious lack of investment in research and development; a pensions time-bomb; and last but not least, the control that criminal organisations exercised over a good quarter of the national territory. The fall of the First Republic gave Italian politics of all colours a chance to make a fresh start in the task of offering collective solutions to challenges new and old, global and local. On most measures, after two decades of the Second Republic, few observers would view the results as being other than lamentable—left, right and centre.

In the First Republic, parliament and the Senate had been dominated from the centre ground by the vast, formless and irremovable 'white whale' of the DC. The extremes of left (Communist Party) and right (the neo-Fascists) were perpetually excluded from power. Now the white whale was gone. Italy's Catholics, who had once been united in the DC, were scattered across much of the political spectrum. The Communists (mostly) converted to some form of social democracy, and the neo-Fascists (mostly) restyled themselves as a conventional European party of the centre-right. No one was excluded *a priori* from the game of forming governing coalitions. Even the Northern League—a raucous movement that wanted independence for a fictional country called 'Padania', and that was given to racist outbursts unacceptable in any other European polity—was now a sought-after ally.

What many people hoped for at the birth of the Second Republic was that a new clarity would reign. To give Italy effective government, a consensus formed around so-called 'bi-polarism': the idea that two opposing forces of centre-right and centre-left should compete for the voters' loyalties, and form a government or an opposition according to who came out on top. Italian politicians, in other words, would have to get used to winning *and* losing elections. Governments would rule with the knowledge that they would be thrown out by the electorate if they did not perform. Nobody would be able to occupy power in the way that the DC had done for the best part of half a century. No longer would the left have a monopoly on trying to make political capital out of accusations of corruption or complicity with organised crime.

The theory was good. The practice, however, was confusion: partly because of the badly drafted electoral laws designed to promote bipolarism, but mostly because of the familiar Italian spectacle of factional infighting. Minor parties, able to blackmail larger ones by threatening to withdraw their support, continued to proliferate. Catholics and ex-Communists continued to search, in vain, for a political identity. The interests of North and South, lay values and Catholicism, region and nation continued to divide each electoral alliance from within—to say nothing of the more conventional sources of political disagreement over economic and social policy, or indeed of the instability brought by overweening personal ambition. Shamelessly expedient deals were struck between politicians who had previously traded vicious insults. In 1998, Northern League leader Umberto Bossi said there could be 'no agreement with the *mafioso*'. He meant Berlusconi, whom he would subsequently go on to support staunchly throughout their time as coalition allies.

Each election saw a confusing array of new acronyms and symbols, shallow political 'brands' for hastily formed parties and coalitions. Each coalition of parties of centre-right or centre-left that presented itself at the polls started to fall apart almost as soon as it was elected, cripplingly divided as it was. Politicians predictably abandoned governing coalitions as soon as the going got tough. Governments continued to hand out appointments to their political friends. Most obviously, the state television networks, lacking any tradition of independence, continued to be distributed on party lines, and continued to produce boring and biased news coverage that seemed designed to put young people off democracy for life.

The end of the old ideologies killed off some of Italy's few antibodies to the old political maladies of patronage, clientelism and corruption. The country's elected representatives seemed more and more to fit to their caricature: they were a self-interested 'caste', cut off from the population behind the tinted windows of their blue, state-funded, luxury limousines. Meanwhile, the nation's problems went unsolved.

Under the Second Republic, the battle against the mafias has been carried on largely in spite of the political system, rather than because of it. The strange thing is that some quite extraordinary successes have been recorded all the same. And the most extraordinary of these have been in Sicily. If a deal *was* struck between Cosa Nostra and the state between 1992 and 1994, then almost all of the bosses who negotiated that deal are now buried in maximum-security prisons. Since the arrest of Shorty Riina, Cosa Nostra has sunk steadily into the worst crisis in its entire history.

PART XIII

THE SECOND REPUBLIC AND THE MAFIAS

71

COSA NOSTRA: The head of the Medusa

SINCE THE CAPTURE OF TOTÒ 'SHORTY' RIINA IN 1993, SICILY'S ANTI-MAFIA MAGISTRATES, police *Carabinieri*, and *Guardia di Finanza* (Tax Police) have scored a series of victories over Cosa Nostra that have absolutely no historical precedent. By comparison, the Fascist campaigns against the Sicilian mafia in the 1920s and 1930s were clumsy, superficial and fitful. Cosa Nostra continues to pay a very heavy price for its war on the state between 1979 and 1993.

Every *mafioso* accepts a certain amount of prison time as an occupational hazard. Yet he will do everything he can to avoid being convicted: from intimidating witnesses to pulling strings so that judges make 'anomalous' rulings. If he is unlucky enough to be on the receiving end of a guilty verdict, a *mafioso* still has the option of becoming a fugitive. But as we have seen, few Sicilian mafia fugitives from justice actually run away. Most just go to ground in their own fiefdom, take on an assumed identity and carry on running their criminal affairs just as before. There were hundreds of such renegades in Sicily at the start of the 1990s; among them were the bosses responsible for Cosa Nostra's worst crimes. Their charisma seemed magnified by their invisibility: an aura grew up around them—both among *mafiosi* and in the general population. They were a living proclamation of the Italian state's failure to enforce the law, to turn the sentences issued by the courts into years actually served behind bars.

Even before the maxi-trial, Cosa Nostra knew exactly how grave a challenge to its authority any serious attempt to round up fugitives would be. That is why the bosses killed Flying Squad officer Beppe Montana in 1985. His murder—he was shot dead in his swimming trunks when he was using his own free time to follow up leads on mafia fugitives—encapsulates both the dedication and the vulnerability of the forces ranged against Cosa Nostra in the bloody 1980s.

Gian Carlo Caselli was the Piedmontese Chief Prosecutor who stepped into the Palermo hot seat after the murder of Paolo Borsellino in 1993. Caselli would continue in his role until 1999. He immediately made the capture of Cosa Nostra's fugitives from justice a priority. He kept a list of them in his desk drawer, and when one was taken, he would cross the name off in green ink. By the end of Caselli's Palermo stint, over three hundred names had been cancelled out. Penitents gave information that led to the capture of bosses in hiding, some of whom turned penitent in their turn, supplying more valuable leads.

The chain of defections was not the only weapon in the authorities' armoury. In the 1990s, the pursuit of Cosa Nostra's fugitives became increasingly technologically advanced: bugging and tracking devices came into play, and the police and *Carabinieri* acquired ever more expertise in their use. Before Giovanni Falcone died, he turned his experience in the Palermo pool of magistrates into a template for Italy's new national organisations for investigating and prosecuting organised crime. After Falcone's death, Palermo continued to be the model for the rest of the country: it became an elite school for teams of *mafioso* hunters.

Among the many leading fugitives to be rounded up was Leoluca Bagarella, 'Shorty' Riina's brother-in-law. Bagarella was the first boss to step into the huge leadership vacuum created by the arrest of the dictatorial Riina. Bagarella's power was primarily military: he inherited command of Cosa Nostra's specialised death squads. He also inherited Riina's war on the Italian state, a war which Bagarella continued by orchestrating Cosa Nostra's terrorist attacks on the Italian mainland in 1993.

Tracking down a fugitive *mafioso* like Bagarella meant learning everything there was to find out about his territory and his network of contacts, piecing together fragments of information on his personal life and psychology. Once the fugitives were captured, their life stories gave sociologists and psychologists rich insights into the world-within-a-world that is Cosa Nostra. The Sicilian mafia's interior culture seemed utterly distant from our own experience, rendered alien by a constant fear of betrayal and a casual familiarity with violent death. Yet at the same time, mafia life was eerily ordinary, filled with day-to-day stories of love and loss. As so often, Giovanni Falcone's insights into the mafia mentality were proving correct. *Mafiosi* were not monsters, Falcone once pointed out:

Getting to know *mafiosi* has profoundly influenced my way of relating to other people, and also my convictions. I have learned to recognise the humanity even in those who are apparently the worst of beings. I have learned to have a respect for other people's opinions that is real and not just a question of form.

Bagarella's story was a case in point. He married his wife, Vincenzina Marchese, in 1991. Her menfolk were members of the Corso dei Mille Family of Cosa Nostra. So this was a classic union of mafia dynasties, celebrated sumptuously with hundreds of guests. Bagarella had the *Godfather* theme tune recorded over the wedding videos. Yet at the same time, the marriage was unquestionably a love match, and the two were devoted companions. Penitents have since related that, if Vincenzina called to tell Bagarella that his dinner was nearly ready, he would even break off from strangling someone to join her at table.

However the Bagarellas had a secret anguish. Vincenzina struggled to bear the child that she yearned for. She became convinced that this was a divine punishment for what Cosa Nostra had done to Giuseppe Di Matteo—the penitent's young son who was held captive for more than two years and who would eventually be strangled and dissolved in acid. She constantly asked her husband what had happened to the boy, and received repeated reassurances (which were truthful at the time) that he was still alive. But Vincenzina could not be convinced. So, on the night of 12 May 1995, she hanged herself in the couple's hideout. Because he was on the run from the law, Bagarella could not give her a decent burial. He even had to move her from one shallow grave to another. Her body has never been found. During a month of mourning, Bagarella refused to take part in any murders out of respect for his beloved. When he was captured on 24 June 1995, six weeks after his wife's death, he was just planning a return to action. He had her wedding ring on a chain round his neck.

More fugitive members of Cosa Nostra's Palermo Commission fell into the dragnet. On 20 May 1996 came the turn of the man who killed Falcone. Giovanni Brusca was known in mafia circles as 'the Man who Cuts Christians' Throats' or, more simply, as 'U Verru—'the Pig'. He came up with the idea of lying on his stomach on a skateboard to push the barrels of explosive meant for Falcone into a drainage tunnel under the motorway. On 23 May 1992, it was Brusca who pressed the detonator. 'The Pig' had committed so many murders that he had lost count: somewhere between a hundred and two hundred was his disturbingly vague estimate. When he eventually turned state's evidence, magistrates had to bring him a list of all the suspicious deaths and disappearances in western Sicily in the previous twenty years so that he could tick off the ones that were his handiwork.

As the police closed in on Brusca, he was forced to move from one safe house to another. In February 1996, investigators unearthed the bunker that the boss had had built by a construction entrepreneur friend. From the outside, it looked like a peasant's dilapidated homestead. But inside, in the marble floor of the expensively appointed kitchen, there was a concealed entrance worthy of a James Bond villain. When Brusca pressed a remote control, a section of floor would descend like a lift sixteen feet underground into a two-room apartment. One of the two rooms had a metal door with a spyhole, just like a prison cell. This was where Giuseppe Di Matteo, the penitent's son, was held captive, and where Brusca eventually had him strangled and dropped into an acid bath. Branching off from the apartment was a further secret tunnel that led to a large metal tank where investigators discovered the biggest arms cache in Italian history. A human chain of *Carabinieri* spent hours passing out more than four hundred pistols, dozens and dozens of pump-action shotguns and machine guns, explosives of all kinds (including Semtex), several bazookas, boxes and boxes of grenades, and ten RPG-18s—the shoulder-launched antitank missiles that were known as 'Allah's hammer' because the Taliban used them against Russian helicopters in Afghanistan. There were even some collector's pieces, such as a Tommy gun with a circular magazine, just like the ones in the Al Capone–era gangster films. Brusca's arsenal was only one of many taken out of commission in these years.

Brusca's last hideout was far from his territory, in the province of Agrigento in southern Sicily. He was eventually betrayed by his nostalgia for home. He made regular calls to order sausages and meat from the butcher in the town of his birth, San Giuseppe Jato—calls that the *Carabinieri* tapped. Brusca was watching a television programme about Giovanni Falcone when the flash grenades went off and the police burst in on him.

The capture of bosses like Bagarella and Brusca marked the end of the most dangerous phase in the Sicilian mafia's history. Like the entire leadership of Cosa Nostra, these men had approved Shorty Riina's policy of waging war on the state. They had also been part of a smaller group of bosses (the 'pro-massacre wing' of Cosa Nostra) that favoured carrying on with that war once Riina was captured in 1993. But as the roundup continued, the pro-massacre wing lost control of the organisation, and Cosa Nostra entered an even deeper leadership crisis. A new strategy of 'submersion' was implemented in response to that crisis.

The boss responsible for the submersion strategy was Bernardo Provenzano. Provenzano was scarcely a peacemaker by vocation. For most of his criminal career, he formed a solid partnership with Shorty Riina in any question relating to Cosa Nostra's internal politics. Both were *corleonesi*, and both pupils of Luciano Liggio. Provenzano's relentless pursuit of his enemies had long ago earned him the nickname 'the Tractor'. He bore just as much responsibility for the horrors of the 1980s, and for the murders of Falcone and Borsellino, as did any other member of the Palermo Commission. Yet Provenzano also had another nickname that spoke of different skills: 'the Accountant'. To his partnership with Riina he brought greater business acumen, and a more refined aptitude for weaving ties with politicians.

Mafia penitents tell us that when the pro-massacre wing of Cosa Nostra sought to step up their terrorist campaign in 1993 (they even planned to blow up the Leaning Tower of Pisa), Provenzano began to go quiet. Internal divisions that had been kept in check by Riina began to surface once more. The centralisation process that Cosa Nostra had undergone when the *corleonesi* mounted their coup was thrown into reverse. Precinct bosses acquired more autonomy—and more power to create trouble. Try as he might to appear as if he was above the fray, the Tractor was viewed with suspicion by the pro-massacre wing. In 1995, he fought a proxy war with Riina's brother-in-law, Leoluca Bagarella, for control of the town of Villabate at the edge of Palermo. Rightly or wrongly, many within Cosa Nostra were also convinced that Provenzano had betrayed Shorty Riina to the authorities in 1993.

Provenzano was the most experienced fugitive from justice in Sicilian mafia history, having been on the run since 1963. For much of that time, he had even been rumoured to be dead. Once he was in charge, he abandoned Riina's direct challenge to the Italian state, and tried to repair the damage Cosa Nostra was suffering as a result of the reaction to the massacres of 1992 and 1993. His submersion strategy—'walking with padded shoes', as he termed it—aimed to keep Cosa Nostra out of the headlines. Accordingly, the number of murders fell dramatically. The Tractor brought an end to the atrocities committed against penitents and their families. Instead, Cosa Nostra gave renewed support to imprisoned *mafiosi* and their families in the hope that the penitents would retract their evidence. The flood of penitents from Cosa Nostra, which had peaked at 424 in 1996, was reduced to a trickle. One effect of this was that the Tractor's support network proved much harder to disrupt than had been the case with bosses like Bagarella and Brusca.

Provenzano placed a renewed emphasis on cultivating the Sicilian mafia's traditional, covert friendships with corrupt elements in the state and business. Extortion rackets were absolutely central to the submersion strategy. Extortion is the Sicilian mafia's least visible and yet most important crime. Each entrepreneur or criminal who gives in to the local boss's demand for a percentage of takings is not only providing the mafia with its staple income;

he or she is also recognising the mafia's sovereignty, its right to intervene. Extortion is how a boss gathers information about his territory, and how he gets his foot in the door of lawful businesses. What the tax system is for a democratic state, extortion rackets are for the mafias—southern Italy's shadow state.

The submersion strategy certainly managed to buy time. But Provenzano faced perhaps insuperable challenges. For one thing, an old problem for the Sicilian mafia was rearing its head once more: the tendency of politicians to break their promises. The laughably bad Italian that Provenzano used in his typed messages to his network is impossible to render properly in English. But I hope the following extract from a 1997 message gives some idea of the Tractor's concerns when it came to making friends in politics:

> Now you tell me that you've got a good level political contact, whod allow you to manage lots of big works, and before going ahead you wanna know what I fink? If I don't no him I can't tell you nothing. You'd need to no the names? And no how they are set up? Coz today you can't trust no one. Could they be swindlers? Could they be cops? Could they be infiltrators? Could they be time wasters? Could they be massive schemers? If you don't no the road you gotta travel, you can't set off—so I can't tell you nothing.

In this case, as in many others, Provenzano failed to make a clear decision. Truth be told, his power to make policy had severe limits. For one thing, his authority still depended to a great extent on Riina's prestige. The Tractor never sat at the head of the Commission, which had not been convened since Shorty was captured. As Sicilian investigating magistrates have put it:

> Provenzano never underwent a formal investiture by the other precinct bosses. So he exercised his supremacy in substance, but not officially, and he did so only by virtue of the fact that he was considered to be 'the same thing' as Riina.

In other words, the Tractor was a first among equals, and not a *capo di tutti i capi*. He had the authority to *advise*, but not to *order*. In the end, mere advice would not be enough to save Cosa Nostra's leadership—either from the persistent divisions within the organisation, or from the mafia hunters.

The first of Provenzano's inner circle to be caught was his number two, Pietro Aglieri, the boss of Santa Maria di Gesù. Aglieri's story revealed yet more about the strange world of Cosa Nostra, and in particular about the religious beliefs that historically have helped *mafiosi* cloak the real nature of their power. In his youth, Aglieri had studied theology in a seminary. Investigators tracked him down by following a Carmelite priest, Father Mario Frittitta. (He was the same Carmelite who had spoken the homily at the funeral of the soccer player and fisherman suspected of being the mafia's lookout when Flying Squad officer Beppe Montana was killed in 1985.) Father Frittitta, it turned out, was Aglieri's confessor. In the boss's farmhouse hideout, as well as the usual gangland paraphernalia like weapons and a radio for listening to police communications, was a chapel complete with an altar, crucifix, incense-burner, pews, and cushions for kneeling on during prayer.

Was Aglieri's faith genuine? Ultimately, only the Almighty himself can give us the answer to that question. Clearly, what Aglieri believed in was a twisted version of Christianity that he somehow thought was compatible with his vocation as a professional criminal. He may have found in it some kind of justification for the evil he did.

What *is* certain about Aglieri's religion is that it was strategically useful to him at that moment in Cosa Nostra's history. Aglieri, like his mentor Provenzano, was seeking ways to repair the damage to Cosa Nostra's legitimacy caused by the deaths of Falcone and Borsellino, and by the Pope's long overdue condemnation of mafia culture. Making religious noises—of humility and piety—could feasibly help the bosses mend the bonds with the organisation's members and friends that were broken by episodes like the horrific murder of the young penitent's son, Giuseppe Di Matteo. The typed notes through which Provenzano communicated with other bosses, and with his business friends, are full of religious phrases: 'Thanks be to God', 'God willing, I am at your complete disposal'. Whether it expressed any form of devotion, Provenzano's language revealed a political style that contrasted markedly with his old friend Riina's.

In the spring of 2000, the 'devout' boss Pietro Aglieri—now in prison— was one of a group from Provenzano's wing of Cosa Nostra who proposed to dissociate themselves from the organisation. The idea was that they would confess their crimes and repudiate the mafia, but without turning state's evidence and ratting on former comrades-in-arms. In short, Aglieri and his allies would repent in the eyes of God; but they would not turn penitent in the eyes of the state.

The Sicilian mafia being what it is, there was a catch: dissociation would only happen if prison conditions were relaxed and some of Italy's new antimafia legislation repealed. Not long afterwards, it became clear that members of the 'ndrangheta and camorra also supported such a bargain. Life behind bars had created a common front among some of southern Italy's most feared mob bosses.

Investigating magistrates immediately realised that accepting 'dissociation' would be a very bad deal indeed for the state. Moreover, they suspected it was part of a plan to engineer a negotiated settlement to the war between the state and Cosa Nostra—a settlement that would leave Cosa Nostra intact, and pave the way for a return to the traditional partnership between the authorities and the Sicilian mafia's shadow state. The dissociation offer fitted perfectly with the Tractor's submersion strategy, in other words. Worryingly, the proposal received a warm welcome in a newspaper article published in Silvio Berlusconi's newspaper *Il Giornale*. More worrying still, in 2001, the magistrate who did most to oppose the dissociation deal was suddenly removed from his job by Berlusconi's Minister of Justice.

In the end, Aglieri's dissociation proposal never came to anything, thanks to incisive coverage by investigative journalists and political lobbying by anti-mafia magistrates. Nevertheless, it resurfaced now and again over the coming years, as a reminder of Cosa Nostra's ability to strike up an insidious dialogue with elements of the Italian state.

The pursuit of the mafia fugitives continued, meanwhile. In April 2002, the police captured Antonino Giuffrè, known as *Manuzza* ('Little Hand') because his right hand was mangled in a hunting accident. Unlike the devout Pietro Aglieri, Little Hand quickly turned penitent, giving investigators important new insights into the way Bernardo 'the Tractor' Provenzano was restructuring Cosa Nostra and rebuilding its links to business. When he was captured, Little Hand was found with a shopping bag full of letters to Provenzano from *mafiosi* and entrepreneurs in his network.

But it would take another four long years of sleuthing for the Tractor's logistical system to be dismantled and for Provenzano himself to be unearthed. In April 2006, disbelieving journalists from all over the world swooped on Sicily to film the shack near Corleone where Cosa Nostra's great strategist, a man who had been a fugitive from justice for no less than forty-three years, was finally captured. Could a man as powerful as Provenzano really have lived in such humble surroundings, living off ricotta cheese and chicory like some peasant of days gone by? The truth was that he was no peasant: he was a professional criminal. And his home town of Corleone was a last redoubt, a place he had been forced to retreat to when every other operational base had been denied him by the authorities.

Bernardo 'the Tractor' Provenzano. Riina's sidekick tried to repair the damage caused to Cosa Nostra by Riina's war on the state. Provenzano was captured in 2006 after a record forty-three years on the run.

The mafia hunters did not let up even after the capture of Riina's heir. Just over two months later, they arrested another forty-five *mafiosi* in the course of an operation that provided a new understanding of political fissures that had brought Cosa Nostra to the brink of civil war, even while the state closed in on its leaders. The fissures had their roots in the most savage conflict in Cosa Nostra's history: Shorty's war of extermination against the leading mafia drug barons in 1981–3. At the time of that war, *mafiosi* from some of the losing Families, notably the members of the Inzerillo clan (who were closely related by blood to the Gambino Family in the American Cosa Nostra), had fled into exile in the United States. Now there was a move afoot to allow the exiles back to fill out the organisation's thinning ranks and rebuild the transatlantic narcotics pipeline.

The proposal to bring the exiles home had been in the air since Shorty Riina's capture, and it was bound to be inflammatory. No less than twenty-one members of the vast Inzerillo clan had been killed by the *corleonesi*. Others had been forced to buy their own lives by betraying their closest relatives to Riina. An entire *borgata*, Ciaculli, had been ethnically cleansed by the victors in the war. Only a deal brokered by powerful American bosses had stopped the *corleonesi* pursuing their surviving enemies after they escaped to the United States. With the *corleonesi* now weakened, the exiles' return was bound to bring a settling of old scores. 'Tractor' Provenzano lacked the authority to impose a solution. So the issue festered, and Cosa

Nostra divided into two armed camps: one in favour of the exiles' return, and one against. Once the Tractor was hunted down, the last obstacle to civil war was removed.

The most fervent proponent of the exiles' return was Salvatore Lo Piccolo, who was initiated into the same Partanna-Mondello *cosca* of Cosa Nostra as Gaspare 'Mr Champagne' Mutolo, and who had close links with the Gambino Family in the United States.

Lo Piccolo's plan was opposed by Antonino Rotolo, who was one of the older generation of bosses to whom the Tractor had entrusted leadership roles as part of the submersion strategy. Rotolo viewed the return of the exiles with undisguised dread: as a loyal supporter of Shorty Riina, he had personally taken part in the butchery of the exiles, and knew that his life would be forfeit if they were given permission to return. In 2006 Rotolo was serving a life sentence. Or at least he was in theory: for he had faked a heart condition and thereby won the right to serve out his time in the rather more comfortable surroundings of his own house in Villagrazia. Whenever he wanted to meet his men, he would call them to a humble garage that lay just over his garden wall. The garage, however, was bugged by the police, who listened in as Rotolo set out his plans to kill Lo Piccolo. He was arrested before the plan could be put into effect.

Lo Piccolo was left as the most powerful boss in the province. But not for long: in November 2007, he too was arrested. Investigators found a wealth of evidence in the leather bag he had with him at the time. There was a directory of businesses paying protection money: the monthly sums extorted ranged from $650 for a shop, to $13,000 for a construction firm. There were notes discussing murders and political friendships. There was an up-to-date map of the Families of the Palermo area. There was a sacred image inscribed with the oath that affiliates take when they are admitted to the organisation: 'I swear to be faithful to Cosa Nostra. If I should ever betray it, may my flesh burn as this image now burns.'

Last but not least, Lo Piccolo had with him a badly typed piece of paper headed 'Rights and Duties', which was a kind of 'ten commandments' of Cosa Nostra. Rule One, for example, stipulated that, 'You are not allowed to introduce yourself [as a *mafioso*] either on your own or to another friend unless there is a third party [i.e., a Man of Honour known to both] there to do it.' Several other rules proscribe 'immoral' behaviour: no *mafioso* is allowed to look at the wives of 'our friends', or to disrespect his own wife; and no one is allowed to be initiated into Cosa Nostra if they have 'sentimental betrayals' in their immediate family. As ever, the Sicilian mafia was concerned to make sure that affairs of the heart do not interfere with affairs of the gun. Although we are now pretty certain that similar rules have been in force for as long as the Sicilian mafia has existed, to my knowledge no written version of them had ever been captured before. It seemed yet another symptom of the unprecedented trouble that Cosa Nostra was in.

That trouble became even more profound in February 2008, when a joint operation by the FBI and the Italian police led to the arrest of ninety *mafiosi* on either side of the Atlantic. Many of them were from the clans exiled in the 1980s, whom Salvatore Lo Piccolo had hoped to bring back to Sicily. The operation, codenamed 'Old Bridge', prevented the American Cosa Nostra from crossing the ocean to come to the rescue of its Sicilian sister association as it had done so many times in the past. Even in its name, the operation showed that the lessons of history had been learned: close transatlantic collaboration in the fight against organised crime brings big rewards for justice.

The assault on Cosa Nostra was now remorseless. In the spring of 2008, *Carabinieri* tailing mafia boss Giuseppe Scaduto saw him go to a mob meeting in a garage in the city centre. With the surveillance skills they had by now honed to perfection, officers placed listening devices and even cameras in the garage. They then proceeded to watch live as, between 6 May and 27 June, Cosa Nostra's bosses schemed. It emerged that, with Provenzano in prison, the time had come for the bosses still at large to re-organise themselves—to impose the kind of coordinating structure that Cosa Nostra always has when it is working best: 'a Commission to deal with the serious things, with situations, and that way we all stay friends', as one *capo* explained.

> If we all do our own thing, like the Neapolitans do . . . if we do things like they do we'll never get anywhere . . . Instead, everyone takes his precinct and then we sort things out nicely. And in the end we all sit down and try and create a kind of Commission like in the old days.

A *kind of* Commission: the hesitancy of this formulation is striking. The men embarking on this new constitutional initiative were without doubt the most powerful *mafiosi* in Palermo. Yet even now, even fifteen years on from Riina's arrest, they did not feel they had the political authority to reconstitute the *official* Commission. Shorty he may have been, but Riina still cast a long, long shadow over the internal affairs of Cosa Nostra.

The *kind of* Commission never met. On 16 December 2008, after nearly nine months of painstaking investigation, some 1,200 *Carabinieri* made coordinated dawn raids on dozens of addresses in Palermo and across western Sicily. They called it Operation Perseus, after the hero of Greek mythology who beheaded the snake-haired monster Medusa, because the aim was nothing less than to decapitate Cosa Nostra. Among the ninety-nine men arrested were the bosses of nineteen Families, including from mafia territories whose names recur throughout the organisation's long history, such as Santa Maria di Gesù, Monreale, Corleone, Uditore and San Lorenzo. No less than eleven precinct bosses were detained too—the men who presided over three or four Families and took a seat on the Commission to represent their interests. And of course the *capo di tutti i capi* elect was also taken: sixty-four-year-old Benedetto Capizzi. The choice of Capizzi showed that, after 'walking with padded shoes' under Provenzano, Cosa Nostra was ready to don its hobnailed boots again. Capizzi was a former member of Giovanni 'the Pig' Brusca's death squad. Among many other crimes, Capizzi helped plan the kidnap of Giuseppe Di Matteo, the penitent's boy who ended up in an acid bath. Capizzi was a man of action, who could be relied on to deal militarily with anyone who dissented from the new order. One minor drawback was that he was still serving several life sentences. However, he was yet another case of a boss granted house arrest for health reasons, thus giving him the liberty he needed to meet his criminal friends.

Operation Perseus was a stunning blow, which received far less media attention abroad than it deserved—certainly far less than the arrest of Ber-

Rebirth of the Commission. Benedetto Capizzi was at the centre of Cosa Nostra's efforts to reconstruct its governing body, the Palermo Commission. Would-be boss of all bosses Capizzi was arrested in 2008.

nardo 'the Tractor' Provenzano two and a half years earlier. It has left Cosa
Nostra a fragmented organisation. The *mafiosi* who remain at large do not
have the experience or charisma to embark on any major restructuring
along the lines of what Benedetto Capizzi was attempting. Their main priority is now survival: finding enough criminal income to support the heavy
burden of prisoners and their relatives, and to keep the fabric of the Families together.

The damage inflicted on Cosa Nostra over the last decade has helped create
the space for grassroots movements against its protection racket regime. Their
goal is to attack mafia power at its base, and their potential is truly revolutionary. Like much that is good in contemporary Sicily, the anti-racket movement
has its roots in the tragedies of the 1980s and early 1990s.

Libero Grassi was an entrepreneur who ran a factory in Palermo making
pyjamas. When he moved to a new site in the shadow of Monte Pellegrino
in 1990, demands for money started to arrive—a contribution 'for the lads
shut up in the Ucciardone'. Grassi went to the police, and three of the men
who had visited his factory to ask for money were arrested. The demands
then became more menacing. Grassi responded with a public letter to the
press that began 'Dear extortionist':

> I wanted to tell our unknown extortionist that he can save himself the
> threatening phone calls and the money to buy fuses, bombs and bullets,
> because we are not prepared to contribute and we have put ourselves un-
> der the protection of the police. I built this factory with my own hands
> and I have no intention of shutting up shop.

Grassi's cause found painfully little support. The entrepreneurs in the
neighbourhood let it be known that he should wash his dirty linen in private like everyone else. He received only one letter from another businessman expressing solidarity. However, in April 1991, Grassi's campaign took
him onto national TV screens, where the millions of viewers of a popular
politics talk show heard his lucid explanation of how the extortion racket
system worked, and the *omertà* that beset him on all sides. He was becoming a threatening symbol of anti-mafia resistance, and an advertisement
for the weakness of the boss on whose territory his factory was sited. On
29 August 1991, Libero Grassi was shot five times in the face as he left his
house to go to work.

After this appalling murder, many resolved that no one who stood up against the extortionists should ever be left isolated again. The national shopkeepers' association, Confesercenti, founded an anti-racket support group in Palermo called 'SOS Business' in the same year. In 1997, a ruling by the Supreme Court made it clear that paying protection money is a crime. Everyone is obliged turn to the authorities for help against the extortionists, and no one can offer the excuse that they are forced to pay. In 2004, the inheritance of Libero Grassi and other pioneers of the anti-racket movement was picked up by a group of young Palermitans who founded an organisation they called Addiopizzo ('Goodbye Extortion'). Their idea was fresh and beautifully simple: entrepreneurs, shopkeepers, restaurateurs and hoteliers would sign a public pledge not to pay protection money; and consumers would sign a public pledge to patronise businesses that did not pay. The aim was to grow a mutually reinforcing alliance between clean enterprises and honest consumers.

Others followed Addiopizzo's lead. In September 2007, the Sicilian branch of Confindustria (the employers' organisation) announced that it would expel any members found to have been paying protection money or failing to collaborate with the authorities. The days when Sicilian business leaders would grumble that the fight against the mafia was ruining the island's economy were finally gone.

Organising to defy extortion is far from being an empty gesture: it actually works. One mafia penitent from the Family of Santa Maria di Gesù has recently explained why *mafiosi* did not try to extort money from businesses that proclaimed their opposition:

> If a shopkeeper is a member of Addiopizzo or an anti-racket association, we just don't go there, we don't ask for anything. It's more because of the trouble it causes than the money. If they report it to the police, you then get investigations, listening devices, and so it's better just to avoid them.

The rebellion against extortion is potentially life-threatening for Cosa Nostra. In late November 2007, *mafiosi* showed how concerned they were about Confindustria's new stance by performing a clamorous act of intimidation: the employers' organisation's offices in the central Sicilian city of Caltanissetta were vandalised, and a number of CDs containing the names and addresses of its members were stolen.

Despite the threats, a virtuous circle has begun to turn in Palermo. As more businesses go to the police when they receive extortion demands, more *mafiosi* are arrested, and the authorities and anti-racket organisations can demonstrate their growing ability to stand shoulder-to-shoulder with people that resist—with the result that more businesses gain the confidence to turn to the police when they receive extortion demands.

Moreover, as so often in our story, Palermo's example has been followed elsewhere. The anti-racket associations that began in Sicily have spread. For example, in January 2010 Confindustria adopted a *national* policy of expelling members who do business with gangsters.

The hunt for fugitives from justice has also achieved crucial results in both Campania and Calabria. Some of the most powerful camorra and 'ndrangheta bosses have taken to building underground bunkers in the hope of avoiding the ever more determined and expert mafia hunters. Some of these bunkers are just secret compartments in a house: hidey-holes into which a fugitive can dash when the doorbell rings unexpectedly. Others are extraordinarily ingenious and elaborate—miniature apartments, complete with plumbing, air pumps and security cameras. Most are hidden among ordinary houses and farm buildings or on industrial estates, and involve secret passages and moveable walls. The 'ndrangheta are bunker specialists. The Bellocco clan from Rosarno took to burying entire shipping containers, perfectly furnished inside, and disguised by vegetation above. The ground underneath the town of Platì, in Calabria, is criss-crossed by hundreds and hundreds of metres of tunnels connecting bosses' houses to a complex of bunkers and escape routes. Here the 'ndrangheta even opened the street up in the process of building its secret bunker network; nobody in town said a word.

Whatever form they take, today's mafia bunkers are not just refuges: they are command centres. Invariably they are built on a boss's own territory, where he can count on a close network of family and friends to provide for his daily needs and, crucially, to shuttle in and out with orders and requests. Territorial control remains crucial for bosses of all three major criminal organisations. As one mafia hunter from the *Carabinieri* explains:

> The first rule for a boss is to never abandon his ground. Going off to evade justice somewhere else is a sign of weakness. If the throne is left vacant, a boss's competitors go into overdrive, manoeuvring and plotting to take his place.

La presenza è potenza, as *mafiosi* say: presence is power.

The bunkers where some bosses now try to maintain their territorial presence are not unprecedented in the history of the mafias: in Sicily, under Fascism, police chasing down *mafiosi* discovered a range of ingenious secret compartments and sunken shelters. But the bunkers are nonetheless an important sign of the pressure the mafias are now under. Until the 1980s, the dreaded Piromallis of Gioia Tauro could still be spotted presiding over the town square, making their authority visible. Those days are gone. The state has become more serious than ever about fighting organised crime, and so the underworld has gone underground.

Sicily remains the place where the anti-mafia fight is most advanced. And the drop in the number of homicides is only the most obvious indicator of that fact. There were nineteen mafia-related murders in 2009 on the island, eight in 2010 and only three in 2011. These are historical lows. The staggering body count of the 1980s now seems an aeon away.

72

CAMORRA: A geography of the underworld

IN SEPTEMBER 2011, JOURNALISTS FROM THE NEWS MAGAZINE *L'ESPRESSO* SECRETLY filmed an exhibition of underworld power in the Barra suburb of Naples. For anyone with a sense of camorra history, the film provides depressing evidence of continuity over time.

The backdrop was the Festival of the Lilies, one of several similar religious festivals in the region. The 'lilies' in question are actually eighty-foot-high obelisks made from wood and decorated with papier-mâché sculptures. They are built and then shouldered by proud teams of volunteers, known as 'crews', who are sponsored by a local grandee known as a 'Godfather'. The crews compete to attract crowds to their lily with an MC, music and dancing. The film published on the *L'Espresso* website showed activities around one particular lily built by the crew that called itself *Insuperabile*. First the local camorra boss's father arrived in an open-top white vintage sports car to the sound of a saxophone playing *The Godfather* theme. As the crowd cheered, the MC hailed the boss Angelo Cuccaro (recently released from prison), then sang him a song called 'You're great', and finally called for a round of applause 'For all our dead'. Meanwhile the boss himself, dressed in the *Insuperabile* crew's blue T-shirt and white baseball cap, was kissed by enthusiastic supporters.

Investigations by the *Carabinieri* subsequently discovered that the Festival of the Lilies had been a platform for the Barra clan for a long time: they extorted money from businesses under the pretext of spending it on their obelisk; the *Insuperabile* crew's 'Godfathers' were chosen from among entre-preneurs close to the bosses; the festival was used to publicly celebrate new camorra pacts. When the neighbouring town of Cercola came under the Barra clan's control, shopkeepers there were forced to display the *Insupera-bile* crew's blue and red colours in their windows.

In September 2012 the *Insuperabile* crew had their obelisk confiscated and destroyed because, according to the judge who authorised the confiscation,

> The messages it sends, the hidden meaning of that wood and papier mâché, is worth more than a whole arsenal to the clan. Deploying it on the day of the festival means much more than a victory in battle, than the physical annihilation of a rival: it is a sign of authority.

Using community religious celebrations as a chance to parade criminal might is traditional in the Naples underworld. In the nineteenth century, *camorristi* used to take control of the springtime pilgrimage to the sanctuary of Montevergine. Each boss, with his woman next to him decked out in silk, gold and pearls, would drive his pony and trap into the mountains at the head of his followers. The pilgrims' progress would be punctuated by drink-ing bouts, races, more or less stylised knife fights, and camorra summits with the clans of the hinterland.

Similar things characterised mafia life in Calabria and Sicily. In towns and villages controlled by the 'ndrangheta and Cosa Nostra, criminal terri-torial control was advertised by taking over the day set aside to celebrate the local patron saint. Barra is far from being the only place where the tradition continues to this day. In Sant'Onofrio in 2010, the 'ndrangheta reacted an-grily when the local priest tried to enforce the Bishop's order to ban mobsters from taking a leading role in an Easter parade of statues of the Madonna: the head of the confraternity that presided over the festival received a warning when two shots were fired at his front door. The festival was suspended for a week, and when it eventually took place, the *Carabinieri* were out in force.

So has nothing changed in Campania? Is the camorra still the force it once was? Certainly, a 'murder map' of underworld deaths over the last few decades would have its dots concentrated in the same broad area that has been blighted by the camorra since the nineteenth century: the city of Naples and a semicircle of roughly forty-kilometre radius extending out into the towns and villages of the hinterland. An enduring pattern is unmistakable. Yet once we zoom in on the detail of our map of camorra power, it becomes clear that the continuities are less prevalent than they first appeared. Less prevalent, certainly, than in Sicily and Calabria, where the micro-territories demarcated by mafia *cosche* have remained all but

CCTV footage shows a camorra killer calmly finishing off his victim, Naples, 2009.

identical. Places like Rosarno and Platì ('ndrangheta), or Villabate and Uditore (Cosa Nostra) have been notorious for well over a century. In Campania, by contrast, the geography of the underworld has seen some important transformations recently.

The camorra fragmented following the war in the early 1980s between Raffaele 'the Professor' Cutolo and the allied clans of the Nuova Famiglia. There were an estimated thirty-two camorra organisations in 1988; that number had increased to 108 by 1992. The years of the Second Republic have seen no reversal of the fragmentation. The most recent estimates suggest that there are still around a hundred sizeable criminal organisations in Campania, where gangland has assumed a lasting but instable pattern. Camorra clans come and go, merge and break apart, go to war and make alliances. Thus most of these camorras have a very short lifespan compared to the extraordinarily persistent criminal Freemasonries, Cosa Nostra and the 'ndrangheta. In Campania, the lines on the map of camorra power move constantly as the police make arrests, turf wars break out and clans fissure and merge. Increased violence is the inevitable consequence of this fundamental instability: the camorra continues to kill more people than either the

Sicilian mafia or the 'ndrangheta. There have been several major peaks in the murder rate in recent years: there were over a hundred camorra killings each year from 1994 to 1998; and then again in 2004, and again in 2007.

Naples is a port city. That simple fact has shaped the camorra's history ever since the 1850s and 1860s, when Salvatore De Crescenzo's camorra smuggled imported clothes past customs and extorted money from the boatmen ferrying passengers from ship to shore. The port of Naples was where vast quantities of Allied materiel vanished onto the black market during the Second World War. In the 1950s, the travelling cloth-salesmen known as *magliari*, who were often little more than swindlers, would set sail to bring the sharp practices of the Neapolitan rag trade to the housewives of northern Europe. Thereafter, Naples was a point of entry for contraband cigarettes and narcotics. These days, the port is a mechanised container terminal on the model of Rotterdam or Port Elizabeth, NJ. It has assumed new importance as a gateway to Italy for the Far Eastern manufactures that are shipped into the Mediterranean through the Suez Canal. Some of those manufactures—shoes, clothes and handbags, electrical tools, mobile phones, cameras and games consoles—are forged versions of market-leading brands. The Neapolitan tradition of manufacturing counterfeits has gone global. Sometimes, the label 'Made in Italy' or 'Made in Germany' hides a different reality: 'Faked in China'. And in place of the *magliari*, there are international brokers, permanently stationed abroad to find markets for bootleg products. Quite how large this sector is, and quite what proportions of it are run by *camorristi* as opposed to garden-variety shady entrepreneurs, is still subject to investigation.

Naples is a remarkable place for many reasons. One of them is the fact that, where historic poor neighbourhoods in many other European cities have long ago been demolished or yuppified, the centre of Naples still has many of the same concentrations of poverty that characterised it back in the eighteenth century. Forcella, the 'kasbah' quarter we have visited occasionally through this story, is a case in point. The camorra rose from its fetid and overcrowded alleys in the early nineteenth century. Although much is now different in Forcella, not least the sanitation, eking out a living here is still precarious, often illegal, and occasionally dangerous. No visitor can enter without the distinct sensation of being watched. In this and other neighbourhoods, the camorra's territorial purview is still made manifest by the kids who extort money for parking places, and the cocksure teenagers perched atop their scooters who act as lookouts for drug dealers.

Despite the wholesale economic transformation of the last century and a half, in places like Forcella the camorra continues to recruit among a population made vulnerable by hardship and a widespread disregard for the law, just as it did in the nineteenth century. In 2006, it was estimated that 22 per cent of people with any kind of job in Campania worked in the so-called 'black economy'—paid in cash, untaxed and unprotected by labour and safety laws. It seems likely that a sizeable majority of jobs in small- and medium-sized companies are off the books.

Recent economic change seems to have made the situation worse. In Campania, as in much of the South, the new economic mantra of flexible employment has often meant just a bigger black economy. Since 2008, Europe's dire economic difficulties have increased the power of the camorra (and, for that matter, of Cosa Nostra and the 'ndrangheta) to penetrate businesses, and lock the region into a vicious circle of economic failure. In the summer of 2009, Mario Draghi, then the president of the Bank of Italy, argued as follows:

> Companies are seeing their cash flow dry up, and their assets fall in market value. Both of these developments make them easier for organised crime to attack . . . In economies where there is a strong criminal presence businesses pay higher borrowing costs, and the pollution of local politics makes for a ruinous destruction of social capital: young people emigrate more, and nearly a third of those young people are graduates moving north in search of better opportunities.

In hard times, it is not just fly-by-night businesses that are easy prey for loan sharks and extortionists, for gangsters seeking an outlet for stolen goods or a way to launder drug profits. By the nature of the narcotics business, gangsters are cash rich—and just at the moment southern Italy's entrepreneurs are struggling even more than everyone else to get their hands on credit. When times are hard, cash is *capo*.

The camorra's undiminished power to feed off the weaknesses of the Neapolitan economy has helped remould the landscape of criminal influence. Once upon a time, when Naples was an industrial city, factory workers had a tradition of labour organisation and socialist ideals that gave them an inbuilt resistance to the camorra infection. Nowadays, with the factories largely gone, the camorra has spread to quarters like Bagnoli, where the steelworks shut down in the 1990s.

Today, moreover, the urban camorra economy no longer revolves around the old slums of the city centre. The major concentrations of poverty and illegality have moved away from the Naples that tourists know. Even the camorra in Forcella has felt the force of the new. The Giuliano clan (centred on 'Ice Eyes' and his brothers) has been broken by murder, repentance and arrest. More importantly, the most powerful and dangerous clans now emerge from the sprawling periphery of the city, from neighbourhoods that grew anarchically in the 1970s and after the earthquake of 1980. The artisan studios of the city-centre maze cannot compete with the sweatshop factories of the suburbs when it comes to churning out bootleg DVDs and counterfeit branded fashions. With the modernisation of Naples's road network and public transport, addicts now find it cheaper to source their hit from the great narcotics supermarkets operating in the brutalist apartment blocks of Secondigliano or Ponticelli, than to visit the small-time dealers of the Spanish Quarters.

The first fragment of cityscape that springs into the public mind when the word 'camorra' is mentioned is no longer the alleys of Forcella. Rather it is a catastrophically failed housing project in the suburb of Scampia. Known as 'Le Vele' ('The Sails'), it consists of a row of massive, triangular apartment blocks built in the sixties and seventies, and designed to reproduce the tight-knit community life of the city-centre alleyways in multiple storeys. The outcome, with its ugly, dark and insecure interior spaces, feels more like a high-security prison without guards. The blocks were very badly built: lifts did not work, concrete crumbled, roofs leaked, and neighbours could hear everything that went on three doors down. These problems had

The worst housing project in Europe. The camorra turned the triangular tower blocks of Le Vele ('The Sails') into a narcotics shopping mall in the 2000s.

already tipped Le Vele towards slum status when desperate refugees from the 1980 earthquake illegally occupied vacant apartments—some of them before they were even finished. Before long, residents felt besieged by a minority of drug-dealing *camorristi*. The police presence consisted of sporadic and largely symbolic tours. Residents say that some cops took bribes to leave the drug dealers unmolested. A long-running campaign to have Le Vele emptied and demolished met with a sluggish political response. At the time of writing, of the seven original apartment blocks, four are condemned but still standing—and still partially occupied.

In the 1990s and 2000s, drug distribution in Le Vele was under the control of the Di Lauro clan. Its founding boss was Paolo Di Lauro, known as 'Ciruzzo the Millionaire'. His base was in Secondigliano, a neighbourhood next to Scampia on the northern outskirts of Naples that was originally a row of large, elegant nineteenth-century houses ranged along the road out of town, but which hosted huge new developments in the 1970s and 1980s. The Millionaire led a centralised organisation moulded around the demands of the drug business. His closest lieutenants included two of his sons and his brother-in-law. Under them were the so-called 'delegates', who handled the purchase and cutting of the wholesale narcotics. Everything below this top level of the clan was run on a kind of franchising system that kept the risky and messy day-to-day business of dealing at a safe distance. Twenty 'zone chiefs' were granted authorisation to manage sales in various areas of the Millionaire's territory, and handle the salaried pushers, lookouts and enforcers who occupied the lowest tier of the organisation. A pusher would earn $2,600 per month, killers a mere $3,300 per hit. Around 200 people counted as formally recognised members of the clan, but many, many more were employed. At the peak of the Millionaire's power, unverifiable estimates put the organisation's narcotics income at $1.3 billion per year.

In 2002 the Millionaire was forced to go into hiding from the law, and day-to-day control passed to his sons, who struggled to control the ambitions of the organisation's 'delegates'. The result, during the winter of 2004–5, was the most violent of recent camorra wars, known as the 'Scampia Blood Feud'.

The Di Lauro clan was one of the more hierarchically structured camorra organisations of the most recent generation. In the 1970s, *camorristi* learned the advantages of organising themselves as a criminal Freemasonry from members of Cosa Nostra and the 'ndrangheta who were keen to find business partners in Campania. Following the break-up of the Nuova Camorra Organizzata and the Nuova Famiglia in the 1980s, practices such as initiation rituals fell out of favour across Campania. Since then, camorra clans have invented their own structures according to need. Yet, despite the fading of the influence of Sicilian and Calabrian organised crime in Campania, the two fundamental principles of camorra organisation are the same as those that apply to the more formalised Families of Cosa Nostra or the *'ndrine* and Locals of the 'ndrangheta. On the one hand, a camorra clan needs a tight command structure, particularly at the core, and particularly for fighting wars and defending territory. On the other hand, a clan must also be loose enough to allow its bosses to network widely, taking advantage of any criminal opportunity that presents itself at home or abroad. Within the limits set by these two principles, a variety of structures is possible. The term 'camorra' has come to embrace anything from the kind of street drug-dealing gangs that can be found in run-down areas of many Western cities, to major syndicates with iron bonds to the political system and the legal economy.

As was the case with the Di Lauro clan, blood ties often help bind the core members of any camorra organisation together. Camorra bosses are often brought up in a family tradition of violence and 'criminal *savoir-faire*' (to use the words of one Italian expert). Intermarriage between camorra bloodlines on adjacent territories helps consolidate authority and pass this *savoir-faire* down through the generations. One example is the Mazzarella clan, based around three nephews of Michele 'Mad Mike' Zaza, the cigarette smuggler and member of Cosa Nostra who helped turn contraband tobacco into the 'FIAT of the South' in the 1960s and 1970s. In 1996, one of the Mazzarella brothers, Vincenzo, saw his family's prestige augmented when his teenage son married the daughter of Lovigino 'Ice Eyes' Giuliano, the boss of Forcella.

The importance that kinship ties have within the camorra clans helps explain why women closely related to a clan's core group can sometimes take on frontline roles. The cases of Pupetta Maresca and the Professor's big sister Rosetta Cutolo tell us that, even before the 1990s, some camorra women were more prominent than was the case with women in the orbit of the Sicilian mafia or the 'ndrangheta. But in the last two decades women in the camorra have become enormously more visible. There are two reasons for this. The first is that the authorities have shaken off old prejudices that made them blind to women's criminal talents. The second is that, because of increased police pressure, the clans have delegated greater power to women when their menfolk go on the run or get arrested. These trends have also made their effects felt in Sicily and Calabria, where the male-centred Masonic structure of the criminal brotherhoods tends to place more limits on women's power. In 1998, Giusy Vitale took over day-to-day management of the Partinico Family of Cosa Nostra when her brother, the boss, was locked up. She has since turned penitent.

But it is no coincidence that it was a female *camorrista*, Teresa De Luca Bossa, who became the first woman in Italy to be subjected to the tough new prison regime set up in the wake of the Falcone and Borsellino murders in 1992. De Luca Bossa was both the mother and the lover of clan leaders, and showed notable military, managerial and diplomatic skill in keeping the organisation together when her menfolk were arrested.

Nor have Sicily or Calabria seen anything to compare with the vicious battle fought out between the women of the Graziano and Cava clans in 2002. On 26 May of that year, a Graziano firing party including three women chased down and rammed a car containing five women from the Cavas. In the ensuing bloodbath, four Cava women were shot dead and a fifth left paralysed. On both the victims' and the perpetrators' side, several generations of women were involved. The Graziano boss's wife, Chiara Manzi, aged sixty-two, coordinated the attack by mobile phone; the shooters included her daughter-in-law (aged forty) and two of her nieces (nineteen and twenty, respectively). In tapes of their phone conversations in the run-up to the assault, these women can be heard spitting insults at their intended victims: 'gypsies', 'sows'.

Uniquely among the mafias, the camorra has also allowed affiliates from minority sexualities to reach leading positions. Anna Terracciano is one of twelve sisters and brothers from the Spanish Quarters of Naples—eleven of them active in organised crime. Known as 'o Masculone (something like 'Big Bloke'), Anna is a male-identified lesbian who went around armed and took part in military actions on behalf of her clan. She was imprisoned in 2006. Three years later, the police arrested Ugo Gabriele, whom the authorities claim is the first transsexual camorrista on record. Known as 'Ketty', Gabriele is the younger sibling of one of the clan that broke off from the Millionaire's organisation during the Scampia Blood Feud of 2004–5. According to the police, when her brother was promoted, Ketty graduated from pushing cocaine to her clients (she was a prostitute) to a more managerial role in the drug ring. As well as the camorra's reliance on family ties, Ketty's promotion may also owe something to Neapolitan popular culture's traditional tolerance towards male transsexuals—the so-called femminielli.

No tour of the geography of contemporary Campanian organised crime would be complete without a visit to the vast fertile plain to the north of the city, which is sometimes called the Terra di Lavoro (the Land of Work). In a poem from 1956, writer and film director Pier Paolo Pasolini evoked its eerie beauties as seen from a train:

> Now the Terra di Lavoro is near:
> A few herds of buffalo, a few houses

> Heaped between rows of tomato plants,
> Twists of ivy, and lowly palings.
> Every so often, close to the terrain,
> Black as a drainpipe,
> A stream escapes the clutches
> Of the elms loaded with vines.

This distinctive landscape has been the backdrop to some of the most important developments in the history of Campanian organised crime over the past century and a half. In the nineteenth century, when much of the area was a marshy wilderness known as the Mazzoni, production of mozzarella cheese from buffalo milk was notorious for being controlled by violent entrepreneurs. In the drained agricultural land to the south and south-east of the marshes, gangs ran protection rackets on the farms, exploited the labourers, taxed the wholesale fruit, vegetable and meat markets, and controlled the routes by which produce made its way into the city.

If Pasolini were alive and able to journey through Terra di Lavoro today, he would see a landscape radically transformed by the arrival of factories in the 1960s, and by industrial decline and the post-earthquake building boom in the 1980s. But perhaps more than these visible changes, Pasolini would be struck by a new smell. In many parts of the land north of Naples, the stench of rubbish fills the air—rubbish that has become the contemporary camorra's most important new source of wealth.

73

CAMORRA: An Italian Chernobyl

WHEN THE SECOND REPUBLIC WAS BORN, NAPLES AND THE CAMPANIA REGION WERE in the midst of a garbage crisis. No scheme to recycle the waste from homes and shops had yet got off the ground. Dumps were full to overflowing. Worrying signs of health problems among the population near the dumps were beginning to emerge.

Early in 1994, the government declared an emergency and appointed a 'Commissariat' to manage the day-to-day collection and disposal while the regional government prepared a long-term solution. But no long-term solution emerged: it was the usual story of political stasis and confusion. At that point, in 1996, the Commissariat was given the task of planning Campania's way out of the emergency, and the power to override normal planning restrictions and local government controls in order to put the plan into place.

The resulting scheme seemed sleek. Municipal trash was to be sorted and disposed of in stages. First, recyclables would be creamed off at the point of collection. Then there was to be a further, centralised sifting to extract both biodegradable matter and any dangerous substances. The next stage involved mashing and compacting what was left into so-called 'ecobales' that could be used as fuel. And finally those ecobales would be burned to generate clean electricity. Seven plants to produce ecobales would need to be built, and two new incinerator-generators. Once they were up and running, it was claimed, Campania would have a perfect cycle of environmentally friendly refuse collection and reuse. No one heeded the waste-management experts who said that the scheme was unrealistic and based on principles that had already failed elsewhere.

The solution to Campania's rubbish emergency rapidly turned into an environmental disaster. The rubbish-collection cycle was dysfunctional at every stage.

Eighteen consortia were set up in the 1990s to manage collection and recycling in different parts of the region. But for a variety of reasons they did not do their job: trash entered the waste-management system in an undifferentiated state.

At that point in the cycle the most serious problems started. An alliance of four companies, known as FIBE, won the contract to build the ecobale plants and the incinerator-generators. The main reasons FIBE won were the low cost and high speed of their proposals: this was an emergency, after all. FIBE was offered a contract with the Campania regional government that contained inadequate penalty clauses.

FIBE companies promised they would have the incinerator-generators up and running by the end of 2000. But by that date, they had not even obtained planning permission. Only one of the incinerator-generators had been completed by the end of 2007. Plans for the second incinerator-generator were finally cancelled in 2012.

FIBE companies were also given pretty much a free rein in choosing where to build their plants. The first incinerator-generator was built in Acerra, in northern Campania, just a few hundred metres away from a large children's hospital. The second was originally to be sited only twenty kilometres away from the first. This was a part of the country famous for being the centre of buffalo-milk mozzarella production. But even before the first incinerator-generator was built, the area already hosted more than its fair share of legal and illegal dumps, and dioxin poisoning had been discovered in farm animals and crops. The incinerator-generator that was actually built was quickly shown to be working badly, spreading gases over a ten-kilometre radius.

The seven ecobale plants were even worse: a parliamentary report found that the ecobales they produced were just large plastic-wrapped cubes of unsifted rubbish that were too damp and too filled with poisons to incinerate, even if the incinerators had been working. Nothing could be done except stockpile them. Across Campania, grey and white ziggurats of ecobales began to climb skywards. The regional rubbish Commissar told parliament in 2004 that *every month* 40,000 square metres of land was being used up to store ecobales.

Periodically, throughout the early years of the twenty-first century, Campania's broken-down garbage-disposal system seized up entirely. At the worst point in 2007–8, hundreds of thousands of tonnes of waste from homes and shops accumulated in the streets. The authorities responded by forcibly reopening rubbish dumps that had already been deemed to be full. Local people, justifiably worried about the impact on their quality of life, staged angry protests. News cameras from around the world relayed the pictures of both the trash-mountains and the protests, causing untold damage to the reputation of Naples, Campania and Italy. Only in the last couple of years have the authorities begun to get a grip on the situation, it seems, although many piles of ecobales remain to scar the landscape.

The *monnezza* scandal (named after the Neapolitan for garbage) is still subject to legal proceedings: a number of politicians, entrepreneurs and administrators have been charged with fraud or negligence. Irrespective of the precise criminal blame, the story is one of shambolic politics, irresponsible business (including northern business), bad planning, mismanagement, and inadequate monitoring. The problems started at the top: the Commissariat supposed to keep tabs on the whole system stands accused of cronyism and inflated expenses as well as a manifest failure to make sure that the rubbish cycle actually worked.

The *monnezza* affair bears many similarities to the chaos of reconstruction following the 1980 earthquake. For one thing, both of them created opportunities for organised crime. The camorra was late to enter the construction industry when compared to Cosa Nostra and the 'ndrangheta. While Sicilian gangsters were heavily involved in the building boom of the 1950s and 1960s, and the Calabrians followed suit in the 1960s and 1970s, only following the 1980 earthquake did *camorristi* start earning serious money from concrete. But when it came to rubbish, the camorra clans became pioneers and protagonists. 'Eco-mafia' is a term coined by Italian environmentalists to refer to the damage the underworld inflicts on Italy's natural and other resources—from illegal building to the traffic in architectural treasures. The waste sector is the most lucrative eco-mafia activity, and one of the biggest growth areas in criminal enterprise in the last two decades.

As with construction, the camorra infiltrated the rubbish system in a variety of ways, starting with the eighteen consortia set up to manage recycling in different parts of the region. Many of the people employed in these consortia were drawn from militant lobby groups of unemployed people. Some of those lobby groups, which date back to the 1970s, have been linked to the camorra: their leaders have been shown to have extracted bribes from members in return for the promise of a job; quite a few of the members have criminal records. In 2004, the regional rubbish Commissar told a parliamentary inquiry that: 'It's a miracle even if 200 of the 2,316 people [employed by the recycling consortia] actually do any work.' It is estimated that, by the end of 2007, more than forty of the lorries bought to transport recycled rubbish had been stolen.

Cash from trash. Shocking mismanagement of the rubbish system created lucrative opportunities for the camorra, Naples, 2008.

The camorra also moved in on the subcontracts and sub-subcontracts handed out for moving the ecobales around. Since the days of the post-earthquake construction boom, the camorra has had a near-monopoly on earth-moving. There is evidence of camorra profiteering on the deals that were rushed through to buy land where ecobales could be stored.

In some places, notably around Chiaiano, young *camorristi* took control of the protests against reopening old garbage dumps. Inevitably, the demonstrations turned violent. There were probably two reasons why the camorra became involved. First, because their bosses had an economic interest in perpetuating the emergency. And second, because they wanted to pose as community leaders, champions of NIMBYism. Much of the trouble was concentrated at a dump not far from Marano, the base of the Nuvoletta clan. A banner was hoisted above the entrance to the town: 'The state is absent, but we are here'. Nobody needed to be told who this 'we' was.

Mondragone, the buffalo-milk mozzarella capital on the northern coast of Campania, was the base for a waste-management company called Eco4 that was at the centre of a thoroughgoing infiltration of the rubbish cycle by the clans: an illicit circuit of votes, jobs, inflated invoices, rigged contracts and bribes tied together politicians, administrators, entrepreneurs and *camorristi*. In the summer of 2007, one of the Eco4 directors implicated in the case, Michele Orsi, started to give evidence to magistrates. The following May he went out with his young daughter to buy a bottle of Coca-Cola and was shot eighteen times. Other witnesses in the Eco4 case implicated a senior politician close to Silvio Berlusconi. In 2009, Nicola Cosentino was both Junior Minister for Finance and the coordinator of Berlusconi's party in the Campania region when magistrates asked parliament for authorisation to proceed against him for working with the camorra. Berlusconi's governing majority turned down the request. The following year parliament refused to give investigators permission to use phone-tap evidence against Cosentino, although he did resign from his government job later that year when he was involved in another scandal. In January 2012 parliament again sheltered him from arrest under camorra-related charges. Cosentino claimed that he was the victim of 'media, political and judicial aggression'.

However, by far the most worrying aspect of eco-mafia crime in Campania is not directly related to the rubbish emergency and the ecobales affair. In the early 1990s, evidence began to emerge that *camorristi* were illegally dumping millions of tonnes of toxic waste from hospitals and a variety of industries such as steel, paint, fertiliser, leather and plastics. The poisons found to be involved included asbestos, arsenic, lead and cadmium. The picture was confirmed by the investigation known as Operation Cassiopea between 1999 and 2003. Although the camorra's trucks transported and dumped the waste in Campania, they were only the end point of a national system. Agents for camorra-backed waste-management firms toured the north and centre of the country, offering to make companies' dangerous by-products vanish for as little as a tenth of the cost of legal disposal. Obliging politicians and bureaucrats along the toxic-waste route made sure that the paperwork was in order. The *camorristi* tipped the waste anywhere and everywhere in the territory they controlled, ranging from ordinary municipal dumps to roadside ditches. Some of the toxic waste was blended with other substances to make 'compost'. In many cases the waste was placed on top of a layer of car tyres and burned to destroy the evidence, thus poisoning the air as well as the soil and the water table. The camorra also dumped toxic waste into the quarries situated in the hillier parts of the Terra di Lavoro, from which they extracted the sand and gravel for their concrete plants. Many of these quarries were also illegal. In 2005, a judge described the disappearance of whole mountains in what he called a 'meteorite effect'. Hence the harm from one eco-mafia crime was multiplied by that from another.

The profits of this trade were enormous. One toxic-waste dealer who turned state's evidence handed over a property portfolio that included forty-five apartments and a hotel, to a total value of $65 million.

Many of those charged in the trial that resulted from the Cassiopea investigation confessed. Despite that, in September 2011, a judge decided not to carry on with the case because inordinate delays in procedure meant that the crimes would inevitably have fallen under Italy's statute of limitations: according to Italian law, it all happened too long ago for guilty verdicts to be reached. The toxic waste strewn across the Terra di Lavoro recognises no such time restrictions. Generations of citizens living on this sullied land will pay the price for what the magistrate in charge of the Cassiopea investigation called an 'Italian Chernobyl'.

74

GOMORRAH

THE PEAK OF THE NAPLES RUBBISH CRISIS IN 2007-8 COINCIDED WITH THE STARTLING success of a book that has made the camorra better known around the world than it has been since before the First World War. *Gomorrah* (the title is a pun) was published in 2006 by a little-known twenty-six-year-old writer and journalist called Roberto Saviano.

Before *Gomorrah*, the fragmented camorra had once more become the subject of bewildered indifference outside Campania. Reporters who tried to keep the public informed about outbreaks of savagery like the Scampia Blood Feud found that the faces, names and underworld connections proliferated far beyond the tolerance of even the most dogged lay reader.

Gomorrah is, at first glance, an unlikely book to have reawoken public concern about the apparent chaos in Campania. It is a hybrid: a series of unsettling essays that are part autobiography, part undercover reportage, part political polemic, part history. Compelling as they are, none of these ingredients holds *Gomorrah* together. The secret of its remorseless grip on Italian readers resides in the way Saviano puts his own sensibility at the centre of the story. His is a kaleidoscopic and immediate personal testimony rooted in a visceral rage and revulsion. He is not content to observe the holes punched in bulletproof glass by an AK-47; he is morbidly drawn to rub his finger against the edges until it bleeds. He feels the salty swill of nausea rise in his throat as yet another teenage hoodlum is scooped into a body bag from a pool of gore in the street during the Scampia Blood Feud. Anger clutches at his chest like asthma when the umpteenth building worker dies on an illegal construction site. The ground seethes beneath him as he explores a landscape contaminated for decades by illegally dumped carcinogens.

Saviano had every right to make his own feelings so important to his account of the camorra (or 'the System', as he taught Italians to call it). For he hails from Casal di Principe, in the heart of the most notorious part of the Terra di Lavoro. After the eclipse of Carmine 'Mr Angry' Alfieri in 1992, the local clan, the *casalesi*, became the dominant force in the camorra. The core group of *casalesi* were a highly proficient team of killers deployed against the Nuova Camorra Organizzata in the 1980s—the 'Israelis' to the Professor's 'Arabs'. The group evolved into a federation of four criminal families. In 1988, the *casalesi* did away with their own boss, Antonio Bardellino. After a bloody civil war, they were able to take over his concrete and cocaine interests. They also branched into agricultural fraud and buffalo-milk mozzarella. The *casalesi* established a local monopoly on the distribution of some major food brands. Moreover, the Eco4 waste-management business was one of their front companies. The *casalesi* were also the clan responsible for creating the 'Italian Chernobyl' on their own territory with their traffic in toxic refuse. According to a penitent from the *casalesi*, when one of the clan's affiliates expressed doubts to his boss, he received a dismissive reply: 'Who gives a toss if we pollute the water table? We drink mineral water anyway.'

By September 2006, *Gomorrah* had already won prizes as well as tens of thousands of readers, particularly among the young. At that point Saviano returned to his home town to take part in a demonstration in favour of the rule of law. Speaking in the piazza from a raised table in front of an azure backcloth, he was moved to call out to the bosses by name: 'Iovine, Schiavone, Zagaria—you aren't worth a thing!' He then addressed the crowd: 'Their power rests on your fear! They must leave this land!' No one should underestimate the bravery of these words: as Saviano knew, relatives of *casalesi* bosses were watching him from the piazza.

Within days, the authorities received intimations of what was to be the first of several credible threats against Saviano's life. Ever since then, he has lived under armed escort. Gratifyingly, his predicament boosted sales: the latest estimates are that *Gomorrah* has sold well over two million copies in Italy, and has been translated into fifty-two languages. In 2008, a film dramatisation of *Gomorrah*—which in my view is even better than the book—won the Grand Prize at the Cannes Film Festival and went on to bring Saviano's vision to a bigger audience still. *Gomorrah*'s author is now a major celebrity: millions tune in to watch his televised lectures, and his articles reliably boost the circulation of the newspapers that host them.

Gomorrah, and its author, have attracted criticism and even denunciation. Some of the sceptical voices ('He only did it for the money!') patently come from the camorra's supporters, or from people who resent his success, or from the usual chorus that would prefer a decorous silence about organised crime. Less easy to dismiss out of hand are those who point out that *Gomorrah*'s style is overblown and occasionally pretentious, that it contains exaggerations, and that it merges fact with imagination and unfiltered hearsay. Saviano himself defines his work as a 'no-fiction novel', but most of his readers have read it as the unexpurgated truth. *Gomorrah* undoubtedly draws on investigative documents, like the Cassiopea case on the toxic-waste trade, or the major prosecution mounted against the leaders of the *casalesi* (known as the Spartacus trial). But now and again there are also stories that do not come from reliable sources—like the book's arresting opening scene, which depicts the frozen cadavers of illegal Chinese immigrants spilling out from a container hoisted above the port of Naples. Other critics worry that Saviano's personalised approach has helped turn him into an oracle or a guru. (Saviano is not the unique figure that the media outside Italy sometimes present him

Camorra *capo* Michele Zagaria was captured in an underground bunker in his home town of Casapesenna, 2011. His organisation, the *casalesi*, became the most powerful in the Campania underworld in the 1990s.

as being: in the first nine months of 2012 alone, 262 Italian journalists were threatened in the course of their work, many of them by gangsters.)

Nevertheless, there is much that helps tip the balance clearly in favour of Saviano and against his detractors. In the wake of his success, many other anti-mafia voices won the kind of large audience that they would not otherwise have found. One instance is the magistrate Raffaele Cantone, who is from Giugliano in *casalesi* territory. His books distil the insights he gained between 1999 and 2007 when he conducted camorra investigations, and traced the *casalesi's* business interests in the North. After *Gomorrah*, the *casalesi* gained a notoriety that they deserved, and that certainly damaged a criminal cartel that had previously done its best to remain invisible. In the years after the publication of *Gomorrah*, the authorities scored a number of successes against the *casalesi*, radically reducing their power. In December 2011, the last remaining historic boss of the *casalesi*, Michele Zagaria, was captured after a decade and a half as one of Italy's most wanted. Fittingly, in his bunker, he had a copy of *Gomorrah*.

In short, Saviano's book once more made the camorra into what it should always have been: a national scandal. Quite what future historians of Italy will make of the whole Saviano phenomenon is anyone's guess. My sense is that his unusual form of celebrity is only the most prominent sign that, up and down Italy, a generation of citizens too young to even remember the ideological certainties of Cold War politics are finding new ways to express their civic engagement, their intolerance of corruption and organised crime. Saviano's young readers are Campania's best hope for the future.

75

'NDRANGHETA: Snowstorm

HEROIN WAS THE MAFIAS' ILLEGAL COMMODITY OF CHOICE IN THE 1970S AND 1980S, but by the 1990s cocaine had overtaken it.

Since the late nineteenth century, cocaine has followed a similar trajectory to heroin: from medicine, to vice, to valuable criminal business. When it was first successfully extracted from coca leaves in the 1860s, it became a tonic: Pope Leo XIII was a heavy user of a cocaine-based drink called Vin Mariani, and even allowed his image to appear in adverts. In the early twentieth century, the drug was banned in its biggest consumer market, the United States. From then on, it became a source of profit for the underworld. But not until the late twentieth century did a self-reinforcing cycle of increasing supply, falling prices, and more widespread consumption make cocaine more popular than any other drug except cannabis. Soon cocaine prices fell enough for it to cease being a niche drug for the rich. In 2012 it was revealed that the inhabitants of Brescia, a city of just under 200,000 in Lombardy, are sniffing their way through $835,000 worth of white powder every single day. And Brescia is only a microcosm.

Cocaine is a less debilitating narcotic than heroin (at least in the short term); it can be consumed without the unsightly business of injection; it is more socially acceptable, and it even has the false reputation of being non-addictive. Try as they might, the authorities cannot create the same sense of emergency around cocaine as there was with heroin. Cosa Nostra, the camorra and the 'ndrangheta have found an inexhaustible new source of money.

Mafiosi from all the major Italian criminal organisations indulge in trafficking cocaine, and since at least the 1980s they have often formed business partnerships with one another to do so. Giacomo Lauro, a penitent from the 'ndrangheta who was heavily involved in international trafficking throughout the 1980s, has described his dealings with Sicilian *mafiosi* and with *camorristi* of the calibre of Antonio Bardellino. Already at that stage, Italian drug barons made sure that deals went through smoothly by exchanging hostages with the South American producers. A prominent family linked to the Calì cartel were permanently resident in Holland: they acted both as hostages and as business agents for the Colombians.

But in the 1990s, just as the era of mass cocaine consumption really began, the 'ndrangheta became the leading operator in the cocaine sector. Indeed, it is primarily to cocaine that the 'ndrangheta owes its reputation as Italy's richest mafia today. Three police investigations into drug running tell a snapshot story of how the 'ndrangheta overtook Cosa Nostra as Italy's major trafficking power.

On the night of 6–7 January 1988, a Panamanian-registered merchant ship called *Big John* was intercepted off the western coast of Sicily. Hidden in its cargo of fertiliser were 596 kilograms of pure Colombian cocaine—just as an informer within the drug ring responsible had told Giovanni Falcone there would be. Cosa Nostra, it turned out, had paid in the region of twelve million dollars for the drugs, depositing the money with the Medellín cartel's emissary in Milan. The *Big John* investigation showed that Cosa Nostra, now firmly in the fist of Shorty Riina, was trying to turn Sicily into what Spain had been hitherto: the major port of entry for South American drugs bound for the European market. The confiscation of the *Big John's* cargo was not just a big financial loss for the Sicilians: it was a huge embarrassment too. When the news broke, American Cosa Nostra learned that its Sicilian sister organisation had cut it out of the cocaine trade, and was now dealing direct with the Colombian producers. From now on, mafia cocaine brokers in the New World would be looking for more trustworthy business partners.

The second illustrative case involves the discovery, in March 1994, of 5,500 kilograms of 82 per cent pure cocaine in a container lorry near the northern Italian city of Turin. The man who exported the load from South America had a name that should sound familiar: Alfonso Caruana, of the Cuntrera-Caruana clan, the Sicilian *mafiosi* who had moved to the Americas and become key members of the Transatlantic Syndicate during the 1970s heroin boom. Significantly, however, Caruana's cocaine was not destined for his Sicilian brethren. Cosa Nostra was in turmoil following the murders of Falcone and Borsellino, Shorty's attack on the Italian state, and an unprecedented flood in penitents. Instead the shipment had been paid for and imported by an investment club comprising the biggest crime families in Calabria. With Cosa Nostra looking increasingly untrustworthy to its international narcotics partners, and with most of the larger camorra clans in the process of breaking up, the 'ndrangheta was left in prime position to take advantage of the most important commercial opportunity international organised crime had seen for years.

In 2002 investigators from the Italian tax police, the *Guardia di Finanza*, broke into the coded communications used by an international cocaine-trafficking ring comprising both Sicilian and Calabrian gangsters. The bugged conversations told a tale of two brokers. The first was a Sicilian by the name of Salvatore Miceli: a Man of Honour from the Salemi Family—and Cosa Nostra's agent. The second was a Calabrian by the name of Roberto 'Bebè' Pannunzi; he had been brought up among the long-established Italian criminal networks of Canada, and he was the 'ndrangheta's agent. The names of both men had already cropped up again and again in connection with international cocaine deals. The two were old friends as well as business partners: the Calabrian had acted as godfather to the Sicilian's son. But it emerged from the phone taps that, in the early 2000s, the Sicilian managed to lose three separate cargoes of cocaine on circuitous routes between South America, Greece, Spain, Holland, Namibia and Sicily. Understandably, everyone else involved in the trade was furious. The Sicilian had forfeited his credibility, and risked forfeiting his life. Investigators intercepted a telephone call he made to his son: 'We've lost face here . . . we've lost everything . . . any minute they're going to have a go at me . . . everyone has abandoned me.'

Soon afterwards, the Sicilian was kidnapped and held prisoner on a plantation deep in the South American forest. The Colombians wanted their money back. His life was only saved following reassurances issued by the Calabrian, Roberto 'Bebè' Pannunzi. But henceforth the 'ndrangheta decided to cut Cosa Nostra out of its affairs altogether. In 2002, the Calabrian broker moved to Medellín, to join a number of *'ndranghetisti* who were already based there. The twin messages in the story were clear to all. First, that cocaine was being sourced directly in Colombia for the European market. And second, that Cosa Nostra was now, at best, the junior partner in relations with the South American cocaine barons.

Back home in Calabria, the 'ndrangheta received a major boost to its trafficking operations in the early 1990s when work was finally completed on the gargantuan container-transhipment port at Gioia Tauro. The port was the only concrete legacy of the 'Colombo package'—the parcel of industrial investment that was promised in the wake of the urban revolt in Reggio

Cocaine containers. The colossal transhipment port at Gioia Tauro in Calabria is a major entry point for the 'ndrangheta's narcotics.

Calabria in 1970. Despite intensive security measures, cocaine has been passing through the port of Gioia Tauro ever since it opened: as a result of a stepping up of surveillance, more than 2,000 kilograms were confiscated in 2011. Quite what percentage of the total volume of cocaine imports this figure represents is anyone's guess.

Yet the port of Gioia Tauro is only one of many options for 'ndranghetisti seeking a route into Europe for their cocaine. The 'ndrangheta has men stationed in a number of major European ports, notably in Spain, Belgium and Holland. Circa 2003, when the European authorities tried to crack down on imports from South America, the Calabrians also began to use various African countries as cocaine staging posts. Large consignments would be brought into Senegal, Togo, the Ivory Coast or Ghana by ship, and then divided into smaller packages for importation into Italy by boat, plane or drug mule.

The 'ndrangheta also has more local distribution networks. We have already seen how, since the 1950s, the 'ndrangheta has been the most successful of any of the southern Italian mafias at setting up colonies in northern Italy. Today, there are thought to be as many as fifty 'ndrangheta Locals in northern Italy. Given that, by Calabrian mafia law, it takes at least forty-nine Men of Honour to form a Local, that figure suggests there are at least 2,450 members in the North. From gangmastering, construction and kidnapping, those northern Locals have graduated to wholesale cocaine dealing, while intensifying their penetration of local government and the economy.

Nor is this a problem confined to Italy. Since the 1960s, thousands of Calabrians have also migrated to other countries in Europe in search of work. Concealed among the honest majority there were 'ndranghetisti who have set up a network of cells that no other mafia can match. The starkest illustration of the 'ndrangheta's European influence is not directly related to cocaine: it is the story of Gaetano Saffioti, a businessman specialising in concrete who, having paid extortion money to the Calabrian mafia for years, rebelled in 2002 and handed video evidence over to investigators that put dozens of 'ndranghetisti behind bars. Since that time, Saffioti has lived with an armed escort and has not won a single contract in Calabria. When he tried to trade outside of his home region he was thwarted. Seven of his lorries were burned in Carrara, Tuscany. Even more insidiously, he faced a silent boycott everywhere he went in Italy: potential clients would be 'advised' that it was not a good idea to be seen with the Calabrian whistle-blower. Saffioti went further afield in search of business. In 2002–3 his machinery was also burned in France and Spain, and in other European countries the same whispering campaign against him was in force. He now does most of his trade with the Arab world where, he says, there is greater commercial freedom for someone like him.

The 'ndrangheta's reach is not limited to the old continent. Calabrian *mafiosi* have had an uninterrupted presence in Canada since before the First World War. In 1911, Joe Musolino—the cousin of Giuseppe Musolino, the 'King of Aspromonte'—was arrested for leading a gang of extortionists in Ontario. Australia is another example: the 'ndrangheta has been down under since before the Second World War. Back in the early 1930s, Calabrian gangsters who infiltrated the booming sugar-cane plantations of North Queensland were able to order up a killer from Sydney, some 2,500 kilometres away. This was the equivalent of sending someone from Reggio Calabria to London to commit a murder. Needless to say, longstanding international contacts such as these also afford today's 'ndranghetisti unrivalled opportunities for laundering and investing their cocaine profits.

Given the 'ndrangheta's global network of cells, it is hardly surprising that journalists in Italy often refer to it as a 'cocaine multinational' or an 'international holding company'. But this is an oversimplification. Just as was the case with Cosa Nostra in the golden era of heroin trafficking in the 1970s and 1980s, the 'ndrangheta's cocaine business is not a single economic venture. There is no one centre from which the drug trade is run, and no overall cocaine kingpin. Indeed, if there were, the world's police forces would find it a great deal easier to clamp down. Narcotics traders need to keep their business as secret as possible; they constantly change their routes and routines as the authorities close in, or as rivals emerge. Recent investigations indicate that the 'ndrangheta's trafficking operations are even more flexible and wide-ranging than were Cosa Nostra's in the days of the Pizza Connection. Calabrian *mafiosi* have created an intricate and constantly changing pattern of cells and networks, of more-or-less-temporary consortia and partnerships. In the early 1980s, Shorty Riina's men fought the bloodiest mafia civil war in history for control of the heroin route to the United States. To date, there has been no comparable conflict in Calabria. One of the reasons for that is that the cocaine business is just too diversified for any Calabrian boss, however powerful, to even dream of monopolising it.

Yet the 'ndrangheta in Calabria, in the rest of Italy, throughout the world, is by no means confused or centreless. Of that, we have recently become much more certain, because of one of the most important investigations in 'ndrangheta history. In 2010, the *Carabinieri* succeeded in secretly filming the Crime . . .

76

'NDRANGHETA: The Crime

Italy has never been short of information on the Sicilian mafia. The noise of public debate—sometimes loud, and often unproductive—has been a constant accompaniment to every phase of organised crime history on the island. There has only ever been one period when absolute silence was the rule: the last decade of Fascism, when Mussolini muted all coverage of mafia stories in the press. The post-war period has seen the quantity of information increase exponentially. Already, between 1963 and 1976, the first parliamentary inquiry into the Sicilian mafia generated a final report comprising three fat books, plus a further thirty-four volumes of supporting evidence. These days, I would be surprised if the various local and national anti-mafia bodies set up by Giovanni Falcone did not generate more material than that every single year. Today, in mafia affairs, as in every other facet of society, we are in an era of information abundance. It took six years, between 1986 and 1992, for Italy's historic refusal to contemplate the existence of the Sicilian mafia to be destroyed in the courts by Giovanni Falcone and Paolo Borsellino's maxi-trial. These days, the police and *Carabinieri* nonchalantly demonstrate its existence every day, in every home in Italy, by posting compelling footage of their operations on YouTube. Everyone can see and hear what the *Carabinieri* of Operation Perseus saw and heard when Palermo's bosses got together to re-establish the *kind of* Commission in 2008.

Nor is there any shortage of news, comment and documentation about the camorra. Once post-war Naples overcame its reluctance to use the 'c' word, the deeds of *camorristi* were widely reported—at least locally, at least for those who cared. For a while in the 2000s, thanks to Roberto Saviano's *Gomorrah*, Neapolitan gangland stories were national headline news.

By no means everything about the camorra that makes it into the public domain deserves to be taken seriously. As has always been the case, camorra dramas are often acted out in public, and the culture of the camorra intermingles with some trends in Neapolitan culture. Some of the local newspapers in Campania have been criticised for acting as bulletin boards for the clans. Then there are the 'neo-melodic' singers, whose work is sometimes a scarcely disguised apologia for the camorra. In 2010 neo-melodic musician Tony Marciano recorded 'We Mustn't Surrender', in which he impersonates a fugitive from justice railing against penitents who have 'lost their *omertà*' and 'brought down an empire'. In July 2012 Marciano was arrested on suspicion of drug trafficking. The arrest warrant describes him as being very close to the Gionta clan, 'so much so that he was constantly invited to private celebrations planned by that organisation's supporters and members'. Marciano's only comment when the *Carabinieri* took him away was, 'I wouldn't get this many TV cameras if I was putting on a concert.'

For much of its history, the 'ndrangheta has been the odd mafia out: it has failed to capture consistent public attention. Some basic facts help explain why. Calabria is comparatively small: Sicily has a population of 5.05 million, Campania 5.8 million, whereas there are only 2.2 million in the toe of the boot. Calabria is also politically marginal, and its media fragmented: the region's main newspaper, the *Gazzetta del Sud*, is not even based in Calabria, but is instead published across the Straits in Messina, Sicily. For a long time, viewed from Turin or Trieste, the cyclical violence between 'ndrangheta clans in Calabria was all too easily dismissed as something atavistic, incurable and irrelevant. The spate of kidnappings in the 1970s and 1980s only created concern about organised crime in Calabria because many of the victims were northern. Kidnappings apart, what space there was for mafia stories in national news bulletins was taken up by goings-on in Palermo or Naples. Meanwhile, the 'ndrangheta thrived on neglect.

One of the most significant developments of the last few years is that the nation's habitual indifference towards the 'ndrangheta threat has begun to dissipate. The 'ndrangheta's own actions have played a key part in that trend. In October 2005, the Deputy Speaker of the Calabrian Regional Assembly, Francesco Fortugno, was murdered in Locri: the highest-profile politician to be killed by any mafia in the twenty-first century.

Events in the German steel town of Duisburg in 2007 attracted even more attention. In the early hours of 15 August, six men of Calabrian origin, the youngest of them a boy of sixteen, were executed as they sat in a car and a van outside an Italian restaurant. Their deaths were the final act of a sixteen-year-long feud between two branches of the 'ndrangheta, both based in San Luca, up on Aspromonte. The momentum of the feud had spun out of Italy to take in the clans' satellites in Germany.

Grim as it sounds to say it, the Duisburg massacre happened at a good time and in a good place. With Tractor Provenzano's arrest the year before, Cosa Nostra had fallen down the news agenda, leaving space for the 'ndrangheta story to fill. For most Italians, the idea that the 'ndrangheta had spread far beyond the wooded slopes of Aspromonte came as a surprise; to hear that it had strong bases in Germany was a shock.

Important indicators of Italy's newfound concern about the 'ndrangheta soon followed. In 2008, a Calabrian centre-left politician became the author of the parliamentary inquiry's first full-scale report on the 'ndrangheta—roughly one hundred and thirty years after it emerged from the prison system. The Calabrian mob's visibility around the world has grown too: in June of the same year, President Bush included it in the Foreign Narcotics Kingpin Designation Act, a kind of blacklist of traffickers.

2010 was an important year both for acts of high-level intimidation by the 'ndrangheta, and for a response from the Italian state. In January, a bomb detonated outside the Prosecutors' Office in Reggio Calabria—no one was hurt. Eighteen days later a car full of weapons and explosives was found on the morning of a visit to Reggio Calabria by the President of the Republic. Other warning messages followed, including a bazooka left near the offices of the Chief Prosecutor. Later in 2010, the text of the Rognoni–La Torre law, the equivalent of the USA's RICO legislation, was finally modified to include the 'ndrangheta explicitly.

At long last, the 'ndrangheta is news. In 1979, only one book was published in Italian with the word 'ndrangheta in the title. In 1980, there were none at all. In both 2010 and 2011, the total was comfortably over twenty. I have even heard people complain that there are *too many* books published on Calabrian organised crime these days. How short some memories are. The pioneering historians, and the brave Calabrian magistrates and journalists who have been trying to document the 'ndrangheta emergency for decades, and who are now finally getting the national readership they deserve, are not among those grumbling.

The investigating magistrates of Reggio Calabria's District Anti-mafia Directorate (the 'pool', in other words) have recently been producing results to match the public's awakened curiosity. Just as in Sicily, the extraordinary surveillance work carried out by the *Carabinieri* can be seen by all on You-Tube. The most historically resonant film shows a group of men, mostly middle-aged, and all dressed as if they were just ambling down the road for a game of cards and a glass of wine at their local *circolo*. They are shown stopping in front of a small white statue of the Madonna and Child perched on top of a two-metre stone column. For anyone who has been to Polsi, the site is unmistakable: this is the medieval Sanctuary of the Madonna of the Mountain on Aspromonte. According to prosecutors—and so far the courts have wholly endorsed their case—what happens next is a sacred moment in the life cycle of the 'ndrangheta. Each year, early in September, chief cudgels from across Calabria mingle with pilgrims at the Sanctuary to ratify the appointment of the Calabrian mafia's senior officers. Once they have all assembled before the Madonna statue, the men on the grainy film slowly form into a circle, and listen intently as the oldest among them sets out his credentials:

> What we have here just wouldn't exist if it wasn't for me . . . I was awarded the Santa four years before anyone. Then they gave me the Vangelo . . . There's a rule: the *offices* can't be given out whenever we want, but only twice a year, and we have to do it together. We need to be all together! The Crime doesn't belong to anyone: it belongs to everyone!

The Santa and Vangelo are the 'ndrangheta's senior 'gifts'—permanent badges of status, each marked by a special initiation ritual. (The institution of the Santa, or Mamma Santissima ['Most Holy Mother'] triggered the First 'Ndrangheta War in 1974.) These 'gifts' give their bearer access to the higher positions, or *offices*, in the 'ndrangheta's ruling body, the Crime, which is also known as the Province. The man filmed addressing the ring of *'ndranghetisti* at Polsi in September 2009 was seventy-nine-year-old Domenico Oppedisano, who had just been elected *capocrimine* (boss of the Crime), the most senior post

Boss of the Crime? Domenico Oppedisano, arrested in 2010, is alleged to have been elected to the highest office in the 'ndrangheta.

in the 'ndrangheta. (Oppedisano has been convicted and sentenced to ten years. An appeal is under way.)

So what does the Crime do, exactly? And how powerful is the *capocrimine*? According to the prosecuting magistrates, and the judges who have ruled on the case so far, comparisons with the Commission of Cosa Nostra, and with a dictatorial super-boss like Shorty Riina, are a long way wide of the mark. Domenico Oppedisano is no Shorty. For one thing, his new job, like all the other positions in the Crime, was only due to last for a fixed term, and not for life. Oppedisano was chosen as a wise old head, an expert on tradition and procedure, a settler of disputes. The Crime has the power to suspend a Local from the organisation, to recognise a newly established Local, or to decide between two rival candidates for the job of chief cudgel in a Local. As a recent 'ndrangheta penitent explains, the Crime has no power to intervene in day-to-day criminal business:

> In Calabria they get together, but not to say, 'What are we going to do?' or 'Shall we bring in that cargo from Colombia?' They get together exclusively to choose the offices . . . But not to set out what we should do, or who we should kill. Those are decisions that are taken by the towns and villages, the Locals.

The 'ndrangheta has an internal political life that is even more procedurally and politically complicated than Cosa Nostra's. The *Carabinieri* were able to record long and involved discussions over which Locals should get positions on the Crime. However, everyone involved acknowledged that it was right and proper that the top jobs should circulate between the three precincts into which criminal territory in the province of Reggio Calabria is divided: the plain of Gioia Tauro, the Ionian coast and the city of Reggio Calabria. Domenico Oppedisano, it turns out, was a compromise candidate— chosen because he carried little personal power and would offend no one.

One of the most remarkable features of Operation Crime, and the cluster of other investigations centring on it, is that it shows how the 'ndrangheta's political life embraces affiliates up and down Italy. With one or two exceptions, each of the Locals in northern Italy is the clone of a mother-Local in Calabria. One penitent provided a lively image for the relationship: 'a woman gives birth, but the umbilical cord is never cut'. That 'umbilical cord' consists of the close kinship ties between members of the same clans. But the link is also constitutional. Locals outside Calabria have to refer back to the Crime to settle disputes, win approval for the award of senior 'flowers', or have new Locals authorised. (Unauthorised Locals are known as Bastards.)

Locals in Lombardy, Italy's most populous and economically dynamic region, have their own representative assembly, known as 'Lombardia'. In 2008, Carmelo Novella, the chief of the Lombardia, tried to break away from the Crime, awarding senior flowers without approval, and setting up new Locals himself. On 14 July 2008, he paid the price for his unilateral declaration of independence when he was shot dead in his favourite bar. The Crime then set up a temporary body, known as a Control Chamber, to pilot Lombardy through the crisis. The man put in charge of the Control Chamber, Pino Neri, was a Freemason and convicted drug dealer who was born in Calabria but studied for a law degree at Pavia University near Milan. His final-year dissertation was on, of all things, the 'ndrangheta. On 31 October 2009, the town of Paderno Dugnano near Milan was the venue for a meeting at which Neri put forward a solution to the constitutional issues with the Lombardia. In a cultural centre named in honour of Giovanni Falcone and Paolo Borsellino, the Lombardy bosses all raised their hands to approve the plan. The *Carabinieri* made a film of the whole event that is now, inevitably, on YouTube. At the time of writing, Pino Neri has been convicted and sentenced to eighteen years for his leading role in the 'ndrangheta in Lombardy. It is as yet unclear whether he will appeal.

There is much that still needs to be clarified about the 'ndrangheta's internal political life. Investigators believe, for example, that Locals stationed around the world habitually report back to the Crime. The most startling instance is the most distant: in Australia there are reputed to be nine Locals. One of them is based in Stirling, a town of 200,000 people near Perth. In 2009, according to the Italian authorities, the boss of the Stirling Local, a property developer and former mayor called Tony Vallelonga, was bugged when he came back to Calabria to consult a member of the Crime. Vallelonga has declared himself angry and baffled by the allegations of his involvement, which were public in 2011. To date, he has not been extradited.

Recent investigations have not only laid bare some previously puzzling aspects of the organisation's internal political system; they have also revealed new evidence about Calabrian mafia women. The 'ndrangheta's smallest cells, or *'ndrine*, are small groups of male affiliates—often relatives. Clustered around them is a network of male and female relatives by blood and marriage. Some of the 'ndrangheta's womenfolk can have great influence within the kinship groups; they can, as it were, 'borrow' power from their male relatives. Such power goes beyond the usual women's work of inciting their men to vengeance and raising children in the cult of violence, and may even involve more than hiding weapons and ferrying messages to prisoners. A few 'ndrangheta women have even been entrusted with the gang's common fund. There is also evidence that one or two particularly enterprising women have earned a special status in the 'ndrangheta, and with it the title of 'sister of *omertà*'.

Despite the clout that some 'ndrangheta women have, they are entirely *absent* from the command structures identified by Operation Crime: there are no women officers in the Locals, and women are not allowed to be ritually affiliated. Put another way, women may be born or marry into Calabrian gangster bloodlines, but they cannot be part of the 'ndrangheta as an organisation.

Like the other two mafias, the 'ndrangheta weaves together family bonds and organisational ties in a particular way. The 'ndrangheta is as heavily rooted in families as is the camorra; yet like Cosa Nostra, it is also a sworn brotherhood of male criminals, a highly structured Freemasonry of delinquency. This specific blend of characteristics seems to make women in the 'ndrangheta's orbit acutely vulnerable: it would appear that they are liable to suffer even more abuse than their peers in Campania or Sicily. Using evidence from women close to the 'ndrangheta who have confided in the law, magistrates in Reggio Calabria have recently begun to look again at some twenty murder investigations concerning women who had either vanished, or whose deaths had previously been dismissed as either inexplicable or as suicide. A submerged history of 'ndrangheta honour killings may be about to surface. One of the victims was Maria Teresa Gallucci. In 1994, in the northern port city of Genoa, gunmen burst into her flat and shot her dead, along with her mother and niece who just happened to be with her at the time. Maria Teresa was the widow of an *'ndranghetista*. Her crime, in the mob's eyes, was to have offended her husband's memory by starting a relationship with another man.

A similarly disturbing case concerns Domenica Legato, who was found dying in the street outside her family home in 2007. She fell from the balcony, her family said. One female 'ndrangheta penitent thinks that this was a disguised murder. Knife wounds found on her hands may suggest that she was resisting an attack just before her death. Domenica too was an 'ndrangheta widow who had found a new love. It should be stressed, however, that the case was treated as suicide at the time, and no new investigation has been ordered as I write.

Perhaps the most chilling case of all is that of Maria Concetta Cacciola, a mother of three whose husband was an *'ndranghetista* serving a long jail sentence. Maria Concetta turned to the *Carabinieri* in Rosarno in May 2011 after being beaten up by her father, who had discovered that she had started a platonic relationship with another man over the Internet. Maria Concetta was eventually discovered in appalling agony, having drunk hydrochloric acid. Suicide again, the family claimed. Concetta's father, brother and mother are currently on trial for the abuse that resulted in her death, although *not* for her murder. There has been a great deal of public comment about whether that charge reflects what really happened to Concetta.

Tragedies like these inevitably raise historical questions. For how long, before the awakening of judicial interest in the roles of mafia women in the 1990s, have such horrors been part of the everyday life of the 'ndrangheta? In the early phase of the Calabrian mafia's history, as we have seen, pimping was a key business. Thus when the 'ndrangheta began, a great many of the women closest to the gangs were prostitutes. Beating, disfigurement and murder were the Calabrian gangster's favourite tools for managing his working girls. Between the two world wars, the 'ndrangheta learned that it was in its long-term interests to eschew pimping and use women in different ways: notably as pawns on the chessboard of dynastic marriage. If the cases of Maria Teresa Gallucci, Domenica Legato, and Maria Concetta Cacciola are anything to go by, then this long-term transformation of women's roles in the 'ndrangheta has not liberated them from the threat of being injured, maimed or killed in the cause of masculine honour.

The biggest historical questions of all are raised by Operation Crime. How long have we, and indeed the world, been living in ignorance while the 'ndrangheta existed in this form? Readers of this book will know that I believe that the Crime is not an innovation, and that 'ndrangheta has *always* been one brotherhood of crime, with a rich internal political life focused on coordinating institutions (whenever circumstances allowed those institutions to function). Since the 1880s, all 'ndrangheta cells across Calabria have always had roughly the same structure, and have used recognisably similar rituals. By far the most likely explanation for this fact is that the 'ndrangheta has always had a Crime, or something like it.

The footage of the Crime taken by the *Carabinieri* in 2009 is enough to give a historian goose bumps. There has never been such a direct record of the 'ndrangheta's annual gathering. Over the last century and more, fragmentary evidence about the Polsi summit has recurred, and rumours have proliferated. But until Operation Crime no one had managed to puzzle out the exact constitutional function of whatever body it was that met regularly on the upper reaches of Aspromonte. To this day, there is no legal precedent in Italy that states unequivocally that the 'ndrangheta actually exists, as a single brotherhood, with a single structure and a single coordinating body, rather than as a loose collection of gangs who sometimes form temporary alliances. The underlying aim of Operation Crime is to establish just such a precedent. In other words, the 'ndrangheta still awaits the kind of definitive legal description of its workings that Falcone and Borsellino's maxi-trial produced for Cosa Nostra. As was the case with the Sicilian mafia in the 1980s, Italy has only just begun properly to recognise a criminal conspiracy that has almost certainly existed for more than a century.

The 'ndrangheta is without doubt contemporary Italy's most powerful mafia. The beneficiary of years of disregard by the state and public opinion, it has a remorseless grip on its home territory, an unparalleled capacity to colonise other regions and other countries, and vast reserves of narco-wealth that allow it to penetrate the lawful economy and financial institutions. Yet it remains a largely unexplored frontier for investigators. Calabria has yet to develop the rich anti-mafia culture that now flourishes in Sicily. The number of entrepreneurs who have rebelled against protection rackets is tiny. In all kinds of ways, Calabria is a generation behind Sicily when it comes to the fight against organised crime.

77

WELCOME TO THE GREY ZONE

THERE IS ONE MEMBER OF COSA NOSTRA'S PRO-MASSACRE WING WHO STILL REMAINS at large—one boss whose power dates back to the rise of the *corleonesi*. His name is Matteo Messina Denaro. Now fifty years old, he has been on the run for twenty years. According to the Ministry of the Interior, he is wanted for 'mafia association, murder, massacre, devastation, possession of explosives, robbery, and more besides'. Messina Denaro is mafia aristocracy, the son of a great boss. But in some other ways he is less conventional. He has a long-term Austrian girlfriend, and some of his captured communications reveal that he professes no religious faith. His base is in Sicily's westernmost province, Trapani. That fact prevents him taking charge of Cosa Nostra in its capital, Palermo. But he has always had a network of supporters there, particularly in the Brancaccio precinct. And during Operation Perseus it became clear that Messina Denaro was an important influence in the debates within Cosa Nostra over the setting up of the *kind of* Commission in Palermo. Quite whether Messina Denaro is the last of the old bosses of Cosa Nostra, or the first of a new breed, is hard to tell.

Over the last few years, Sicilians have grown used to the scenes when a major mafia fugitive is arrested. Police and *Carabinieri* in ski masks and bulletproof vests punch the air and sound their horns as they bring their captive back to base. Crowds gather outside police HQ to cheer and sing 'We are the real Sicily'. Then there comes the first sight of the captive himself, blinking impassively in the photographers' flashes, as everyone mentally compares his face to the police facial composite.

It is to be hoped that those scenes will soon be repeated in celebration of Matteo Messina Denaro's capture. For when the Castelvetrano boss is finally caught, it will indeed mark yet another historic victory over an old evil.

Historic, but certainly not definitive. Sicilians will have every right to rejoice at the end of Messina Denaro's career. Yet despite all the good news since the tragedies of 1992, few on the island will have any illusions that the Sicilian mafia is gone for good. The reasons why that is so—like the whole history of organised crime in Sicily—are partly to do with the Sicilian mafia's strength, and partly to do with Italy's weakness.

Every six months, the Anti-mafia Investigative Directorate (the FBI-equivalent set up by Giovanni Falcone) issues a report on the state of the fight against organised crime that is thick with data. Among the least conspicuous but most significant figures it records is the number of acts of 'vandalism followed by arson'—a tell-tale sign that racketeers are at work, a proclamation of Cosa Nostra's ability to make good its threats without resorting to murder. In 2011, there were 2,246 cases of vandalism followed by arson in Sicily: the highest in any Italian region, and an increase on the preceding years.

Of course, this figure is far from reflecting the full extent of Cosa Nostra's protection regime. For one thing, extortion operations lie hidden among the figures for many other kinds of crime: a burglary in a warehouse, for example, is often just an invitation to the owner to find the right person to pay. But it does give an idea of just how difficult Sicily finds it to loosen the racketeers' grip.

The anti-racket movement, Addiopizzo, as its coordinators are only too well aware, remains largely restricted to the better-off quarters of Palermo. Its impact in the suburbs and outlying settlements where the Sicilian mafia originated and is still strongest has been much more limited. The number of businesses that have signed Addiopizzo's pledge has been growing steadily since 2004. But at the time of writing, it stands at 723. There is still a long, long way to go.

Why has the current weakness of Cosa Nostra not triggered a full-scale revolt against extortion? Fear is part of the explanation. Sicilians are only too well aware that any lapse in concentration by the authorities will allow Cosa Nostra to regroup, as it did after two separate waves of Fascist repression, for example, or again in the late 1960s. When one of the last remaining bosses from the pro-massacre wing was arrested in 1998, Guido Lo Forte, a magistrate involved in the hunt, issued a note of caution that is still valid today:

> The experience of the last twenty years has helped us understand that there is never a time for triumphalism. Cosa Nostra is an organisation

whose structure was created to dominate territory irrespective of the role of individuals, and it has an enormous power to regenerate and transform itself.

If a mafia boss is captured, his replacement is almost always ready to step up. If thirty bosses are captured, as in Operation Perseus, new leaders emerge from the rank-and-file. Cosa Nostra's soldiers are all generals of crime, as Giovanni Falcone once said. Even when a whole generation of bosses and soldiers ends up behind bars for a while, their sons and nephews—boys brought up by the values of violence and honour—are eager to rise to the challenge. And when old bosses are released from their sentences, they too can step back into leadership roles. No criminal organisation venerates experience more than Cosa Nostra. Among the men identified in Operation Perseus who were due to sit on the re-formed *kind of* Commission was the legendary Gerlando Alberti, aged eighty-one. Alberti has been a constant presence in the crime pages since the 1960s. He was the boss who uttered the cocksure witticism: 'The mafia? What's that? A brand of cheese?'

One of Cosa Nostra's often invisible sources of strength is its control over ordinary criminals. The mafia governs and taxes crime. *Mafiosi* live by extorting money from burglars and drug peddlers as well as from shopkeepers and construction companies. Control of the underworld begins in prison, and extends out into the streets: the local boss takes a cut of everything, on pain of death. There is a convention in Sicily that anyone who robs a heavy goods vehicle has to wait for twenty-four hours while *mafiosi* run checks on the booty; if it belongs to a firm with the right connections, then it has to be returned. Ordinary crime is no more likely to die out in Sicily than it is in any other part of the world, and Cosa Nostra's authority over street criminals will take a long time to eradicate.

Fear has never been the only resource that Sicily's Honoured Society can call on. Nor has the mafia ever been just a club for cut-throats. In 1876, a pioneering sociologist called *mafiosi* 'middle-class felons'—meaning people who are upwardly mobile, judicious in their use of violence. These middle-class felons were experts at corrupt networking who had their hands on some of the most advanced sectors of the Sicilian economy, and who were able to draw on both passive and active support in the society around them. Cosa Nostra owes its ability to regenerate itself in large part to the fact that its members and allies have always included men who can blend in with the economic, professional and political elite, men who can mould a kind of consensus for their authority. The latest journalistic buzzword for such people is the 'grey zone': it is an area of society where complicity with the bosses is hard to detect, and where the partnership between the bosses and the businessmen, or between the gun and the laptop, is by no means always tilted in favour of the former. The grey zone is both invisible and pervasive: it cannot be seen on YouTube.

Michele Aiello, a construction entrepreneur who became the leading supplier of hospital facilities in Sicily, came straight out of the grey zone. He was a front for Bernardo 'the Tractor' Provenzano. When he was convicted in 2011, his colossal $1 billion fortune was confiscated. (Alarmingly, just a few months into his fifteen-year sentence, he was granted house arrest on the grounds that he was allergic to beans.)

Another middle-class criminal is Aiello's friend Giuseppe Guttadauro, a leading surgeon and boss of the Brancaccio precinct of Cosa Nostra. There is a very long line of mafia doctors—men who have not seen any incompatibility between the Hippocratic oath and the vows that Men of Honour make when they are initiated into Cosa Nostra. Infiltrating Italy's semi-privatised health system has been one of Sicilian organised crime's major sources of income over the last two decades.

The most recent man from the grey zone was unmasked in 2010. When Salvatore Lo Piccolo was taken in 2007, his soldiers chose one Giuseppe Liga to succeed him as boss of the San Lorenzo precinct of Cosa Nostra. Liga's nickname in mafia circles is 'the Architect'—for the prosaic reason that he is an architect. He has recently begun a twenty-year sentence.

Politics has been part of the Sicilian mafia's grey zone since 1860. It would be naïve to think that the Andreotti faction of the Christian Democrat Party—the 'Young Turks' like Lima and Ciancimino—were the only ones in cahoots with Cosa Nostra. The overwhelming likelihood is that many of the gangsters' political allies from the 'bad old days' of the 1980s got away scot-free. The mafia's politicians have also been inserting their friends and hangers-on into the state machinery for decades.

In recent years, there have been some successful prosecutions of Sicilian politicians with mob ties. The most prominent case is that of Salvatore Cuffaro, another doctor, and the leader of Sicily's regional government between 2001 and 2008. Cuffaro is now serving a seven-year term for 'aggravated aiding and abetting of Cosa Nostra', and he faces other charges too. Among the crimes that earned him his conviction is that of choosing electoral candidates on the say-so of the surgeon-cum-*capo* Giuseppe Guttadauro. Cuffaro was also deemed guilty of leaking information about criminal investigations into Guttadauro's affairs that he derived from a ring of corrupt *Carabinieri* working in the Palermo prosecutors' office. Despite successful investigations like this, colluding with the mafia remains a difficult crime to prove. Quite how many more Cuffaros there are out there is anyone's guess.

Cosa Nostra is also difficult to destroy because of its ability to win supporters in the lawful economy. Over generations, mafia money and influence have dyed much of the island's economic fabric varying shades of grey. No one knows how many companies in business now were set up with mob cash. Or have *mafiosi* as sleeping partners. Or earn from sweetheart contracts and cartel arrangements negotiated under Cosa Nostra's tutelage. Or whose employees owe their jobs to a boss's friendly word.

All of this political and commercial traction gives *mafiosi* enormous power to buy support. It pays to remember the words that the 'devout' boss, Pietro Aglieri, said to the magistrate who masterminded his capture:

> When you come to our schools to talk about justice and the rule of law, our kids listen to you and follow you. But when those same kids grow up, and start looking for a job, a home, a bit of help with health or finance, who do they go looking for? You or us?

At its edges, the grey zone becomes lighter, spreading out into the sections of the economy, politics and society that are not directly under mob control. There are thousands of enterprises that operate on the borders of the law, paying under the table, cheating on taxes, falsifying accounts, and dodging regulations. Recourse to offshore banking and tax havens is routine among some sections of the bourgeoisie. A large proportion of Sicily's enduringly sluggish economy depends on the state sector, where favouritism, pork-barrel politics and corruption are deeply entrenched vices. Bosses love to offer their own brand of law to such an arthritic and lawless wealth-accumulation system. The 'off the books economy', like the politics of patronage, is inherently susceptible to mafia influence.

Even when it is not in league with Cosa Nostra, a great deal of Sicily's business, like much of its political system and state apparatus, is constitutionally averse to transparency. Whatever shade of grey they are, nobody wants the law looking too closely at what they are up to. Ivan Lo Bello is the head of Sicily's Confindustria (the employers' organisation) who introduced the policy of expelling members who paid protection money. He now lives under escort and has sent his children to be educated abroad. Reflecting on his experience late in 2011, he said the following:

> I'm less worried by the response from the criminal organisations than by the response from politicians. In Sicily, we've been met by silent hostility. We have the feeling that we aren't loved by town councillors, aldermen,

party leaders and state functionaries who have an interest in maintaining the status quo.

There is a broad section of Sicilian society—from the lowliest shopkeeper to the smartest banker—for whom the fight against organised crime is, at best, extremely inconvenient.

Like Cosa Nostra, the camorra and the 'ndrangheta have a long history that testifies to their ability to adapt to new circumstances and recover from adversity. Like Cosa Nostra, but in subtly distinctive ways, they draw on organisational traditions and family know-how to find their way to the future. Moreover, everything I have said about the grey zone in Sicily applies in Campania and Calabria too. The toxic-waste and rubbish scandals demonstrate how bad business and bad politics open the door to the camorra. The 'ndrangheta would not be the 'ndrangheta without its own 'middle-class felons' and its own grey zone. Indeed, in Calabria, where the anti-racket movement is weak, and shady Masonic organisations are notoriously ramified, the grey zone extends even further into society than it does in Sicily. When Confindustria, the employers' organisation, began applying measures against businesses with mafia contacts, other organisations followed its example. One example was the Palermo branch of ANCE, the association of building companies. When the Reggio Calabria branch of the same organisation staged a conference on the rule of law in June 2010, delegates spent their energies *protesting against* a whole range of legislation aimed at prohibiting relationships between *mafiosi* and businessmen.

Historically speaking, the 'ndrangheta, of all the mafias, has also perhaps been the most completely indifferent to ideology. It has always understood that the grey zone has no political colour. The 'ndrangheta's longstanding bases in the North also demonstrate that the grey zone recognises no boundaries between regions. Corrupt politicians and businessmen do deals with *'ndranghetisti* up and down the country.

Even in some areas of the national economy not directly touched by the tentacles of organised crime, sharp practice and corruption are rife—and are found far beyond the South and Sicily. In 2011, the chief of Italy's national anti-mafia prosecutors' office, Pietro Grasso, was talking about the whole of Italy when he said the following:

> The mafia method, which involves promoting illicit privileges and cancelling out competition, has been cloned in some border areas of

politics and the economy where predatory cliques of wheeler-dealers have sprung up.

The Italian state is also doing a great deal to alienate those citizens who do still manage to live according to the rules. Italy's criminal justice system is in a lamentable state. The average length of a case is four years and nine months. There are many examples in the story I have told here of mafia-related trials that have dragged on for years, with verdicts being reversed at each successive tier of the system right up to the Supreme Court. These delays are monstrous for the accused, and bring continual discredit down upon the law. The delays can also be made to work in favour of the crooked. Citizens could be forgiven for thinking that the courts offer near-impunity to any white-collar criminal who can afford the lawyers needed to spin out proceedings until the statute of limitations takes effect.

The mafias latch onto the state at its weakest points. Prisons have always been one of the most shambolic parts of the Italian state and for that reason they have always been theatres of mafia activity. Indeed the camorra and the 'ndrangheta were both born behind bars. Since the nineteenth century, detainees in unsafe and overfull conditions have turned to the mafia orga-nisations in the hope of protection, and *mafiosi* have imposed their own ar-bitrary and brutal rule on their fellow inmates. Italy's penitentiaries are now more overcrowded than those of any European country other than Serbia. The suicide rate is nearly twenty times higher than it is in Italian society as a whole. No wonder that today, as in the nineteenth century, serving a first stretch is a rite of passage for aspiring gangsters, and most camorra recruits are formally enlisted in jail.

The state can even help push honest citizens into the grey zone. For example, it is utterly failing to impose fairness and transparency on the national economy. A vital case in point is the civil courts, dealing with disputes between citizens and companies, which are in an even worse state than the criminal courts. In 2011, the World Bank ranked Italy 158th out of 183 countries for the efficiency of its justice system in enforcing contracts, just below Pakistan, Madagascar and Kosovo, and three places above Afghanistan. At the end of June 2011, there was a backlog of 5.5 million cases in the civil courts. The *average* length of a case is seven years and three months. In Germany, when a supplier takes a customer to court for an unpaid delivery, it takes him or her an awfully long time to obtain a ruling from a judge—an average of 394 days. In Italy, the figure is 1,210 days. Which is an *age* in the life of a business: one could go bust six times over. No wonder some entrepreneurs are tempted to find less peaceful ways of recuperating credit. *Mafiosi* welcome such entrepreneurs with open arms and a crocodile smile.

Too much of Italy is dysfunctional. The state apparatus is mired in ineptitude, patronage and corruption. A large slice of the economy is cash-in-hand, and therefore invisible to the law; whole areas of the visible economy are hobbled by inefficiency and sleaze. Italian society seems incurably addicted to the same vices. Nor is there much prospect that Italians will elect a government honest, determined and authoritative enough to implement the reforms their country needs. For as long as Italy remains in this condition, then enduring victory over Cosa Nostra, the camorra and the 'ndrangheta will remain out of reach.

The Cold War gave the mafias a political shield. Behind it, they plundered, prospered, and pushed Italy to the brink of the abyss. But the mafias were around before the Cold War, and they have survived its end. The headline-grabbing violence of the long 1980s may have abated, but organised crime is still a national emergency and a national shame.

However, Italy has more reasons for optimism today than at any point in the past. The anti-mafia magistrates and police forces of Italy are underpaid, underresourced, and understaffed. They operate in very hostile circumstances. Magistrates in mafia-run areas still have constant armed escorts, and live a monastic life for fear that they could be unwittingly photographed in the wrong company. Yet because of the dedication, courage and professionalism that so many of them display, Italy's gangster fraternities are finding life harder than it has ever been. *Mafiosi* have their meetings bugged. They are tracked down when they flee from justice. Even in the wilds of Aspromonte, the 'ndrangheta is no longer having things entirely its own way. A mountain operations unit of the *Carabinieri*, the *Cacciatori* ('hunters') was founded in the early 1990s and equipped with helicopters to combat kidnapping. Since the 'ndrangheta got out of the kidnapping industry, the *Cacciatori* have had notable success in denying Calabrian mobsters full use of their traditional mountain redoubts.

Although the Italian justice system remains extraordinarily lenient and hyper-protective of the rights of the accused, the long history of mafia impunity seems to be over. Gangsters can now expect to be fairly convicted when they go to court. Despite the agonisingly slow workings of the justice system, *mafiosi*, *camorristi* and *'ndranghetisti* are now serving thousands of years of prison. Just as importantly, billions of Euros of their stolen wealth have been confiscated. Inroads are even being made into the grey zone.

Looking back from today over the history of Italy's relationship with the mafias since the Second World War, and indeed since the very origins of the mafias in the nineteenth century, the single biggest and most positive change is that the police and magistracy are, at long, long last, doing their job.

Now it is over to the Italian people to do theirs.

ACKNOWLEDGEMENTS

LACK OF TIME IS A MAJOR REASON WHY NOBODY HAS EVER BEFORE TRIED TO WRITE A chronicle of organised crime in Italy from its origins to the present day. *Blood Brotherhoods* is the result of a long period of research and writing that it would have been impossible for me to begin, let alone complete, without the support of two institutions. My heartfelt gratitude goes to both the Italian Department, University College London, where my colleagues have created an encouraging and lively environment for teaching and research, and to the Leverhulme Trust, which awarded me a Research Fellowship between 2009 and 2011—a crucial period in the development of the book.

Thanks must also go to my editors and agents who have waited as my submission deadline receded into the distance. My fondest hope for this book is that it constitutes some kind of reward for the saintly patience of Peter Sillem, Rupert Lancaster, Giuseppe Laterza, Haye Koningsfeld, Catherine Clarke and George Lucas. I would also like to thank Kate Miles and Juliet Brightmore at Hodder & Stoughton for their cheerful support. Copy editor Helen Coyle had a much greater influence on the development of the typescript than her official responsibilities imply.

Cosa Nostra, the camorra and the 'ndrangheta show Italy at its worst. Yet the greatest privilege that comes with studying mafia history is that of meeting some of the extraordinary people who dedicate themselves to fighting the mafias, and thereby show Italy at its uplifting best. I would like to thank them for their invaluable help and input of all kinds. The list starts with Nicola Gratteri of the *Direzione distrettuale antimafia* in Reggio Calabria, who impressed me with his courage, energy and rigour—and sent me away laden with fascinating documents. My particular gratitude goes to Michele Prestipino of the *Direzione distrettuale antimafia* in Reggio Calabria: conversations with him have been among the most fascinating moments of my quest to understand and explain the 'ndrangheta. Capitano Giuseppe Lumia of the *Carabinieri* was endlessly resourceful, and colonnello Jacopo Mannucci-Benincasa, head of the Arma's *Ufficio Criminalità Organizzata*, extremely insightful. In the final stages of writing the book, I was lucky enough to talk at length to Alessandra Cerreti (*Direzione distrettuale antimafia*, Reggio Calabria), Catello Maresca (*Direzione distrettuale antimafia*, Naples), colonnello Claudio Petrozziello and capitano Sergio Gizzi (*Guardia di Finanza*), vice questore Alessandro Tocco and commissario Michele Spina (*Polizia di Stato*), colonnello Pasquale Angelosanto (*Carabinieri*), colonnello Patrizio La Spada, tenente Angelo Zizzi, and the men of the *Squadrone Cacciatori* in Vibo Valentia. My encounters with servants of the rule of law like these were both hugely encouraging as well as extremely useful in confirming or qualifying what I thought about the state of the mafias today. I should stress that they cannot be blamed for any misinterpretation I may have made of their words and that what I have written in these pages reflects my own views.

The many debts I owe to other academics and historians are set out in the notes that follow. But I have also had a number of extremely fruitful personal exchanges with a number of Italy's leading experts in the field. It is rare to find a historian who is as open-handed with his time and knowledge as Enzo Ciconte. Enzo sent me some documentation I had had trouble finding and scrutinised an important chunk of the manuscript, making valuable suggestions. I discussed some of the ideas in *Blood Brotherhoods* at length with both Marcella Marmo and Gabriella Gribaudi. The book is much better as a result of their consideration and their profound understanding of the camorra. In Palermo, Salvatore Lupo and Nino Blando have always been willing to be mined for interesting ideas.

In *Blood Brotherhoods* I have tried to reach out beyond academia to explain to as broad a readership as possible what we can (and cannot) know about the history of the mafias. From my fellow academics, I can only crave indulgence for sacrificing many conventions of academic writing in this cause. As always, I have called on a team of friends to read drafts of the book in the hope of making it more readable. The following deserve special recognition for their selfless commitment to that arduous endeavour: Nino Blando, David Brown, Stephen Cadywold, Caz Carrick, John Foot, Robert Gordon, Prue James, Laura Mason, Vittorio Mete, Doug Taylor, Federico Varese.

Very many archivists and librarians have assisted me during the course of my work, but some of them were especially kind: Maria Pia Mazzitelli and the staff at the Archivio di Stato di Reggio Calabria, Salvatore Maffei at the marvellous Emeroteca Vincenzo Tucci in Naples, Maresciallo Capo Salerno and Col. Giancarlo Barbonetti at the Carabinieri Archive, Linda Pantano at the Istituto Gramsci in Palermo, and the staff in Humanities 2 at the British Library.

A number of people in Campania helped me during a field trip to many of the places mentioned in this book: Alfonso De Vito, Marcello Anselmo, Egidio Giordano, and Vittorio Passeggio. My friend Fabio Cuzzola was also my go-to guy in Reggio. His generosity extended far beyond the intellectual and even involved his developing an appreciation of Rory Delap's throw-ins and Ricardo Fuller's footwork. The great Nino Sapone was invaluable to me in many different ways. He knows his way around the Archivio di Stato di Reggio Calabria like few others, and he has a documented feeling for Aspromonte, its people and history; I will never forget our visits to Amendolea, S. Stefano, Montalto, and the Sanctuary at Polsi. Joseph Condello was an extremely helpful and friendly guide when we toured the Plain of Gioia Tauro together. I would also like to express my thanks to Chiara Caprì, one of the founders of Addiopizzo in Palermo, and to the inspirational Gaetano Saffioti in Palmi for his patience in being interviewed twice.

A long list of people have helped me with advice, or by locating sources; some of them also chipped in with good ideas: I would have been lost without Salvo Bottari, Mark Chu, Vittorio Coco, Nicola Crinniti, Fabio Cuzzola, Azzurra Fibbia, Joe Figliulo, David Forgacs, Patrick McGauley, Francesco Messina, Manuela Patti, Marcello Saija, Nino Sapone, Diego Scarabelli, Fabio Truzzolillo, Chris Wagstaff, Thomas Watkin. Since the very earliest stages of my research into the 'ndrangheta, I have been having exceptionally useful exchanges with Antonio Nicaso. Antonio also read a section of the manuscript, patiently and insightfully. Nick Dines deserves a special mention for his astute and creative research on my behalf. Fabio Truzzolillo not only hunted down some important material for me but contributed positively to the content of the book: I hope by now that he has found the right home for his passion for research. For certain localised but important aspects of my research I relied on the help of David Critchley, Tim Newark, and Eleanor Chiari. Christian De Vito was particularly insightful on the history of the prison system. Roger Parker found out what Silvio Spaventa went to see at the opera. Peter Y. Herchenroether generously sent me the results of his research into early Calabrian *mafiosi* in the United States. Alex Sansom, UCL's resident expert on early modern Spain, helped me find out more about Cervantes and the Garduña. Jonathan Dunnage was the source of some very useful prompts on the history of policing. My friend and colleague Florian Mussgnug generously surfed the German press on my behalf. A number of people in Australia offered tips on studying Calabrian organised crime in their country. David Brown was remarkably generous in letting me see his collection of material on the same subject: I regret only that I was not able to analyse that area properly in *Blood Brotherhoods*.

I owe a special debt to Lesley Lewis for allowing me to consult her late husband Norman's diaries—the notes he drew on while writing his profoundly compassionate and yet disillusioned observations in *Naples '44*.

Laura and Giulio Lepschy were for me, as for so many Italianists in the UK, an endless source of linguistic wisdom. Maria Novella Mercuri helped me work out some of the trickier, ungrammatical passages in some manuscripts.

I have had the great boon of being able to consult a number of journalists who are immersed in the subject of organised crime on a day-to-day basis. In Sicily, Lirio Abbate, Attilio Bolzoni, Salvo Palazzolo, and Dino Paternostro offered advice, material or both. In Calabria, Pietro Comito passed on a rare copy of Serafino Castagna's autobiography. Peppe Baldessarro knows as much about the 'ndrangheta as any journalist: it was enriching to chat with him in the course of several visits to Calabria. Several of these names are among the all too many courageous and professional Italian journalists who have had to face death threats from the clans.

Yet again my biggest thank you goes to my wife, Sarah Penny. I am constantly astonished by her ability to juggle work, family and my seemingly endless demands for time. She has my gratitude and my love, always. The book is dedicated to her, to our two children Elliot and Charlotte, and to their baby sister, Iris.

ILLUSTRATION CREDITS

I would like to thank the following for their help in sourcing photographs: Chiara Augliera of the Cineteca di Bologna; Maggiore Antonio Coppola of the Carabinieri's Nucleo investigativo–reparto operativo, Palermo; Fabio Cuzzola; Nick Dines; Cecilia Ferretti of the Archivio Unità; Capitano Giuseppe Lumia and the ROS in Gioia Tauro; Vito Lucio Lo Monaco of the Centro Pio La Torre, Palermo; Gabriele Morabito; Nino Sapone; Fabio Truzzolillo.

NOTES ON SOURCES

FOR SOCIOLOGISTS IT HAS BECOME COMMONPLACE TO TREAT ITALY'S MAJOR CRIMINAL organisations as different aspects of the same set of problems. Historians have been slow to catch up. All the major historians of organised crime in Italy have made often very insightful comparative asides. Yet sustained comparison is very rare indeed. *Blood Brotherhoods* is intended to explore what we can learn by letting the histories of the three mafias run in parallel to one another. It is a task that has presented many challenges, notably at the level of narrative organisation. But the goal is fundamentally a simple one, all the same: a chronicle.

Blood Brotherhoods is also intended for readers beyond Italy, as well as within its borders, for whom the word 'mafia' conjures up visions of Al Pacino before it does the faces of Luciano Liggio, Raffaele Cutolo or the De Stefano brothers. What I hope to do is dissipate some of the confusion generated both by films like *The Godfather*, and by the catchall word 'mafia'. In an effort to make *Blood Brotherhoods* as accessible as possible, I have not used footnotes or endnotes. Those of us who are university lecturers and therefore lucky enough to read for a living all too easily forget the huge efforts that many people have to make to find the time to read—and to read non-fiction in particular. Perhaps the least we can do to meet such readers halfway is to produce a narrative unencumbered by references, nods to obscure academic debates, and the name-dropping of academic allies and opponents.

That said, footnotes fulfill many duties and afford many pleasures. The following pages can be but a poor substitute for them. My hope is that they will at least serve as a stimulus to further reading, a recognition of my many intellectual debts, an indication of what sources I have used to formulate and substantiate my arguments, and a clue to interesting issues that I did not have time to explore or treat fully. Some of the sources cited are not referred to or quoted from explicitly in the text, but I have included them here all the same, generally for one of two reasons: first, because they make points that I did not have the space to explore and illustrate in the text; second, because they add evidential weight. *Blood Brotherhoods*, as a comparative history, can have no pretentions to being an encyclopedic account of the camorra, the Sicilian mafia and the 'ndrangheta. My approach has been to choose stories that I consider to be exemplary. By including the full range of my archival sources on the picciotteria, for example, I hope to show that my choice of exemplary stories has a broad foundation in firsthand research, whether by me or by other people.

My particular gratitude and admiration must go to those who, before me, have written narrative syntheses of the history of Italy's individual criminal organisations. These are the books that have been my constant companions while writing *Blood Brotherhoods*. Salvatore Lupo's *Storia della mafia* (Rome, 1993) is one of the books that anyone interested in the mafias must read and re-read. (If you don't know Italian, be warned that an already dense text is badly served by a very poor English translation: *History of the Mafia*, New York, 2011.) Lupo's more recent *Quando la mafia trovò l'America. Storia di un intreccio intercontinentale, 1888–2008* (Turin, 2008) provides a unique and perceptive 'transatlantic' history of the mafia in both Sicily and the United States. In several chapters here I have tried to follow Lupo's cues about the many-faceted relationship between the two branches of Cosa Nostra and have also profited from his insights into the long-lasting dialogue of the deaf between Italy and the United States when it came to mafia matters. The 'Transatlantic Syndicate' is my coinage for what Lupo, drawing on firsthand sources, calls the 'third mafia'. Given that there were already three mafias in my story, I thought it best to choose another moniker in order to avoid confusion.

Anyone who wants to find out about the history of organised crime in Calabria must start with Enzo Ciconte's pioneering book *'Ndrangheta dall'Unità a oggi* (Rome-Bari, 1992). As well as drawing the main outlines of 'ndrangheta history, Ciconte also brought together for the first time a vast quantity of evidence from the Archivio di Stato di Catanzaro. My approach has been to return to the same documentation but to add a great deal of previously unstudied or understudied material from the Archivio di Stato di Reggio Calabria and the press that I think allows us to reach firmer and clearer conclusions on the early 'ndrangheta than Ciconte felt able to. Ciconte also wrote the first comparative history of the three mafias: *Storia criminale. La resistibile ascesa di mafia, 'ndrangheta e camorra dall'Ottocento ai giorni nostri* (Soveria Mannelli, 2008). His approach is very distinctive—it is thematic rather than chronological—but it has given me a great many leads in preparing *Blood Brotherhoods*.

In its rigour and clarity, Francesco Barbagallo's *Storia della camorra* (Rome-Bari, 2010) stands head and shoulders above all previous attempts to survey the history of organised crime since the nineteenth century in Campania. His earlier books, *Napoli fine Novecento. Politici, camorristi, imprenditori* (Turin, 1997) and *Il potere della camorra (1973–1998)* (Turin, 1999) remain fundamental for the dramatic growth of the camorra in the late twentieth century. I have drawn on them repeatedly. Mention must also be made of Isaia Sales's influential collection of historical essays, *La camorra le camorre* (2nd edn, Rome, 1993), from which I have learned a great deal. P. Monzini, *Gruppi criminali a Napoli e a Marsiglia. La delinquenza organizzata nella storia di due città (1820–1990)* (Rome, 1999), provided a stimulating precedent for a comparative approach, and insights into various moments of camorra history.

The early phases of the mafias' history, from their origins until the fall of Fascism, are the least well known outside specialist circles. I have learned a great deal from scholars working specifically on this period. In the 1980s Marcella Marmo was among the pioneers of the new history of organised crime in Italy, and she is still *the* authority on the camorra from its origins to the Cuocolo trial. Her many essays should be the first items on any reading list about the camorra. Accordingly, I have drawn on them heavily and cited them in the appropriate chapters below. For now it is worth highlighting three essays that offer a broad survey of the Neapolitan Honoured Society: M. Marmo, 'Tra le carceri e il mercato. Spazi e modelli storici del fenomeno camorrista', in P. Macry and P. Villani (eds), *La Campania*, part of *Storia d'Italia. Le regioni dall'Unità a oggi* (Turin, 1990); M. Marmo, 'La camorra dell'Ottocento: il fenomeno e i suoi confini', in A. Musi (ed.), *Dimenticare Croce? Studi e orientamenti di storia del Mezzogiorno* (Naples, 1991); M. Marmo, 'La città camorrista e i suoi confini: dall'Unità al processo Cuocolo', in G. Gribaudi (ed.), *Traffici criminali. Camorra, mafie e reti internazionali dell'illegalità* (Turin, 2009). This third essay makes some important observations about women in the camorra.

Marmo's essay on honour is also essential on one of the key themes that run through organised crime history: M. Marmo, 'L'onore dei violenti, l'onore delle vittime. Un'estorsione camorrista del 1862 a Napoli', in G. Fiume (ed.), *Onore e storia nelle società mediterranee*, (Palermo, 1989).

The 'ndrangheta is the least known and least studied of the three major criminal organisations. And although there has been a recent wave of new publications on the 'ndrangheta today, historical research remains very rare indeed. For a long time, Gaetano Cingari was the only professional historian who took an interest in the Calabrian mafia. I have drawn on the important pages in his *Storia della Calabria dall'Unità a oggi* (Rome-Bari, 1983), *Reggio Calabria* (Rome-Bari, 1988), and of course on his essay on the 'brigand' Musolino: 'Tra brigantaggio e "picciotteria": Giuseppe Musolino', in G. Cingari, *Brigantaggio, proprietari e contadini nel Sud* (Reggio Calabria, 1976). Two other important contributions to the early history of the 'ndrangheta deserve mention. The first is by a magistrate, Saverio Mannino: 'Criminalità nuova in una società in trasformazione. Il Novecento e i tempi attuali', in A. Placanica (ed.), *La Calabria moderna e contemporanea* (Rome, 1997). Mannino's richly documented essay is particularly insightful on the Fascist era. The second contribution, just as richly documented, but with a focus on the pre-Fascist period, is by journalist and campaigner, Antonio Nicaso: *Alle origini della 'ndrangheta. La picciotteria* (Soveria Mannelli, 1990).

Several scholars contributed to the foundation of a new school of history-writing on the Sicilian mafia in the 1980s—they are the people I cited in the bibliography to my *Cosa Nostra. Blood Brotherhoods* tries to apply the many lessons I absorbed from those historians to new material, and to the other criminal organisations. So if space prevents me from citing them and their works all over again here, my debt to them is nonetheless profound. There are some more recent works that do stand out, however. It is an indicator of the quality of Salvatore Lupo's research that newly discovered material—like the documentation from Ermanno Sangiorgi's career that I found in the Archivio Centrale dello Stato—all too often confirms Lupo's fundamental insights. His book-length interview with Gaetano Savatteri, *Potere criminale. Intervista sulla storia della mafia* (Rome-Bari, 2010), is, among many other things, a persuasive argument for the importance of studying the mafia with the tools of the historian. Lupo it was who unearthed the 1938 report by the Royal General Inspectorate for Public Security for Sicily that I have used here. Two researchers working with Lupo, Manoela Patti and Vittorio Coco have analysed the report thoroughly and gone on to make huge advances in the understanding of the mafia under Fascism. Important essays by them, and by other scholars, are collected in a special issue of the journal *Meridiana. Rivista di storia e scienze sociali*, 'Mafia e fascismo' (63, 2008). The Inspectorate's is published in V. Coco and M. Patti, *Relazioni mafiose. La mafia ai tempi del fascismo* (Rome, 2010). Chief of Police Ermanno Sangiorgi's extraordinarily insightful report into the mafia at the turn of the twentieth century—another discovery of Lupo's—is also now available in print: S. Lupo, *Il tenebroso sodalizio. La mafia d'inizio novecento nel rapporto Sangiorgi* (Rome, 2010). (The book also includes my short biography of Sangiorgi, which covers elements I did not find space for here.)

There is now a good body of scholarly work on the role that women and family relations play in mafia life, although it is almost all about the contemporary period. I hope that my study, whether the conclusions it draws are correct or not, at least shows that the comparative historical study of women and the mafia can yield insights about what Alessandra Dino has called the 'submerged centrality' of women in the underworld. The following four studies are recommended as essential starting points:

> A. Dino and T. Principato, *Mafia donna. Le vestali del sacro e dell'onore*, Palermo, 1997.
> A. Dino, *Mutazioni. Etnografia del mondo di Cosa Nostra*, Palermo, 2002. Remarkable, amongst many other reasons, because it shows how much strategic thinking goes into the management of families within the Sicilian mafia.
> O. Ingrascì, *Donne d'onore. Storie di mafia al femminile*, Milan, 2007.
> R. Siebert, *Le donne. La mafia*, Milan, 1994.

All translations from the sources listed in the following pages are my own unless stated.

I have used the following abbreviations:

> ACS = Archivio Centrale dello Stato.
> ASC = Archivio di Stato di Catanzaro.
> ASRC = Archivio di Stato di Reggio Calabria.
> ASN = Archivio di Stato di Napoli.
> ASPA = Archivio di Stato di Palermo.
> Documentazione antimafia = Senato della Repubblica, Documentazione allegata alla relazione conclusive della Commissione parlamentare d'inchiesta sul fenomeno della mafia in Sicilia.
> Istruttoria Maxi = Falcone and Borsellino's history making the prosecution case for the maxi-trial against Cosa Nostra, Ordinanza-sentenza contro Abbate Giovanni + 706.
> Istruttoria Stajano = part of the above was published as C. Stajano (ed.), *Mafia: l'atto d'accusa dei giudici di Palermo* (Rome, 1986).
> Maxiprocesso = 40,000 pages of other material from the maxi-trial can now be viewed online thanks to the Fondazione Falcone, www .fondazionefalcone.org.
> Processo Olimpia = Procura della Repubblica di Reggio Calabria, Direzione Distrettuale Antimafia, Procedimento penale n.46/93 r.g.n.r. D.D.A. a carico di CONDELLO PASQUALE ed altri. 'Processo Olimpia' (this vast trial is the fundamental document for reconstructing the history of the 'ndrangheta from the late sixties onwards).

Sources consulted

Preface to the US Edition

S. Lupo, *Quando la mafia trovò l'America. Storia di un intreccio intercontinentale, 1888–2008*, Turin, 2008. Explains how the name 'Cosa Nostra' took hold among *mafiosi* both in Sicily and the United States following Joe Valachi's testimony to the McClellan committee in 1963.

L. Malafarina, *Il codice della 'ndrangheta*, Reggio Calabria, 1978. There is no canonical form of the legend of the three Spanish knights: it seems never to be reproduced in the same form twice in 'ndrangheta mythology. References to it in 'ndrangheta rituals are reproduced in many sources including Malafarina.

P. Natella, *La parola 'mafia'*, Florence, 2002. Suggests the derivation of *Carcagnosso* from *calcagna*.

To my knowledge the name 'ndrangheta or 'ndranghita does not make a consistent public appearance before press coverage of the so-called 'Marzano operation' in the autumn of 1955. One can see it surfacing, in tentative inverted commas, in 'Il Ministro Tambroni e il sottosegretario Capua in disaccordo nel valutare la situazione esistente nelle province calabresi', *L'Unità*, 10/9/1955; or 'Latitanti che si costituiscono e altri che vengono arrestati', *Il Mattino*, 14/9/1955. The man who seems likely to have been responsible for giving the name a broad currency was Corrado Alvaro, with his article 'La fibbia', *Corriere della Sera*, 17/9/1955.

Introduction: Blood brothers

Relazione annuale della Commissione parlamentare d'inchiesta sul fenomeno della criminalità organizzata mafiosa o similare. 'ndrangheta. Relatore On. Francesco Forgione, 2008. On the Duisburg massacre and the 'ndrangheta's international reach. Can be downloaded from: http://www.camera.it/_dati/leg15/lavori/documenti parlamentari/indiceetesti/023/005/intero.pdf.

Procura della Repubblica Presso il Tribunale di Reggio Calabria, Direzione Distrettuale Antimafia, Decreto di Fermo di indiziato di delitto—artt. 384 e segg. c.p.p. Agostino Anna Maria + 155. I have drawn on this document, which is better known as '*Operazione Crimine*', for an up-to-date insight into the 'ndrangheta's structure based on the most recent investigations.

F. Barbagallo, *Storia della camorra*, Rome-Bari, 2010. Another very good source on the contemporary situation.

G. Gribaudi, 'Guappi, camorristi, killer. Interpretazioni letterarie, immagini sociali, e storie giudiziarie', in *Donne, uomini, famiglie*, Naples, 1999. Also the source for my remarks on the *guappi* after the demise of the Neapolitan Honoured Society.

G. Gribaudi, 'Clan camorristi a Napoli: radicamento locale e traffici internazionali', in G. Gribaudi (ed.), *Traffici criminali. Camorra, mafie e reti internazionali dell'illegalità*, Turin, 2009. An excellent short summary of the camorra today based on judicial sources. Here I owe the observation about the Honda 'Dominator', along with many other points, to Gribaudi's essay.

P. Martino, *Per la storia della 'ndranghita*, Rome, 1988. Suggests the most plausible derivation of *'ndrina*.

L. Paoli, *Fratelli di mafia. Cosa Nostra e 'Ndrangheta*, Bologna, 2000. A fine comparative study of the Sicilian and Calabrian organisations.

R. Saviano, *Gomorra. Viaggio nell'impero economico e nel sogno di dominio della camorra*, Milan, 2006. Saviano's powerful, impassioned and enormously successful book is a shocking denunciation of camorra power today. Compared to Gribaudi and Barbagallo, however, it has the disadvantage for historians of not citing its sources. Readers who do not know Italian will be hampered by the book's dreadful English translation.

A. Zagari, *Ammazzare stanca. Autobiografia di uno 'ndranghetista pentito*, Cosenza 1992.

'Books of The Times; Journey to a Strange Land That Seems Like Home', *New York Times*, 18/7/2003. On the 'unpronounceable name' of the 'ndrangheta.

The United States Consul General's 2008 report on Calabria, as made public by Wikileaks, can be found at: http://racconta.repubblica.it/wikileaks-cablegate/dettaglio.php?id=08NAPLES96.

PART I: *VIVA LA PATRIA!*

ASN, Ministero della Polizia, Gabinetto, f. 1702, incart. 38. Ministero e Real segreteria di Stato della polizia generale, Affari di conferenze con S.M. il Re Nostro Padrone D.G. Undated report, but c. 20/10/1853. On the links between liberals and *camorristi*.

ASN, Ministero della Polizia, Gabinetto, f. 1648, incart. 295. Corrispondenza tra il Prefetto di polizia Farina e il Ministro Romano. On the setting up of a new police force in the summer of 1860.

ASN, Dicastero di polizia e delle luogotenenze, f. 202, inc. 4. Letter from Prefettura di Polizia signed by Filippo De Blasio to Luogotenente del Re Luigi Carlo Farini dated 22/11/1860. On the 'perniciosissima peste della Camorra' and on Romano's policy of co-opting *camorristi* into the police.

ASN, Dicastero dell'Interno e Polizia della Luogotenenza, f. 202, incart. 112. Componimento dello stato dei camorristi in questa città . . . Trasmesso il 21/6/1861 dal questore Tajani al Dicastero di Polizia. A list of '*gamorristi*', by city quarter, drawn up under Spaventa.

ASN, Questura di Napoli. Archivio Generale 1a serie. Archivio dei pregiudicati. Fascicoli personali (1860–1887). B. 1581, numerazione autonoma 53. Salvatore De Crescenzo. Contains De Crescenzo's lengthy criminal record.

Foreign press sources (UK unless stated): *The Times*; *London Daily News*; *Morning Chronicle*.

Other sources drawn on throughout this section:

G. Machetti, 'Cultura liberale e prassi repressiva verso la camorra a Napoli degli anni 1860–70', in M. Marmo (ed.), *Mafia e camorra: storici a confronto*, *Quaderni del Dipartimento di Scienze Sociali dell'Istituto Universitario Orientale*, 2, 1988.

G. Machetti, 'Camorra e criminalità popolare a Napoli (1860–1880)', *Società e Storia*, 51, 1991.

G. Machetti, 'L'impossibile ordine. Camorra e ordine pubblico a Napoli nella congiuntura unitaria', *ParoleChiave*, 7–8, 1995.

M. Marmo, 'Camorra anno zero', *Contemporanea. Rivista di storia dell'800 e del '900*, 1999/3. Reproduces and comments on the two reports on the camorra compiled under Spaventa from ASN, Alta polizia, f. 202, f. lo 4, *Luogotenenza generale del Re* (Carignano), *Gabinetto del Segretario Generale di Stato* (Nigra) *a Dicastero di Polizia*, 5/4/1861.

M. Marmo, 'I disordini della capitale', *Bollettino del Diciannovesimo Secolo*, 6, 2000.

M. Marmo, 'Quale ordine pubblico? Notizie e opinioni da Napoli tra il luglio '60 e la legge Pica', in Macry, P. (ed.), *Quando crolla lo Stato. Studi sull'Italia preunitaria*, Naples, 2003. Among Marmo's essays (already cited above), this one is crucial for its narrative of the events of 1860–63, which I have substantially followed here.

M. Marmo and O. Casarino, '"Le invincibili loro relazioni": identificazione e controllo della Camorra napoletana nelle fonti giudiziarie di età postunitaria', *Studi Storici*, 2, 1988.

M. Monnier, *La camorra. Notizie storiche raccolte e documentate*, Lecce, 1994 (1862). This edition has a useful introduction by Gabriella Gribaudi.

A. Scirocco, *Governo e paese nel Mezzogiorno nella crisi dell'unificazione (1860–61)*, Milan, 1963.

1. How to extract gold from fleas

L. Agnello, 'Castromediano, Sigismondo', in *Dizionario biografico degli Italiani*, vol. 22, Rome, 1979.

P. Bourget, *Sensations d'Italie. (Toscane—Ombrie—Grande-Grèce)*, Paris, 1891.

R. Canosa and I. Colonnello, *Storia del carcere in Italia dalla fine del '500 all'Unità*, Rome, 1984. This remarkable study traces some of the traditions of prison extortionists back to the early modern era.

S. Castromediano, *Carceri e galere politiche*, 2 vols, Lecce, 1895.

W.E. Gladstone, 'First Letter to the Earl of Aberdeen, on the state prosecutions of the Neapolitan government' (1851), in *Gleanings of Past Years, 1843–78*, vol. IV, London, 1879.

E. Martinengo Cesaresco, 'Sigismondo Castromediano', in *Italian Characters in the Epoch of Unification*, London, 1901 (2nd edn).

F. Montuori, *Lessico e camorra. Storia della parola, proposte etimologiche e termini del gergo ottocentesco*, Napoli, 2008. This is the best source on the etymology of 'camorra' and the history of Neapolitan underworld slang more generally. Montuori argues that camorra meant 'extortion' or 'extortion payment' for many decades before we hear of the existence of a secret society called the camorra.

G. Neppi Modona, 'Carcere e società civile' in *Storia d'Italia*, v. 5, *I documenti*, t. 2, Turin, 1973. Still the best starting-point for the history of the prison system in Italy.

R. Shannon, *Gladstone*, vol. 1, *1809–1865*, London 1982.

S. Zazzera, *Procida. Storia, tradizioni e immagini*, Naples, 1984.

There are many sources on the prison camorra in the nineteenth century, and on the continuing influence of organised crime behind bars into the twentieth century:

M. Beltrani Scalia, *Sul governo e sulla riforma delle carceri in Italia*, Turin, 1867.

A. Gramsci, *Lettere dal carcere*, Turin, 1947. Especially the letter of 11/4/1927.

I. Invernizzi, *Il carcere come scuola di rivoluzione*, Turin, 1973.

J.W. Mario, 'Il sistema penitenziario e il domicilio coatto in Italia', I, *Nuova Antologia*, 1/7/1896.

L. Settembrini, *Ricordanze della mia vita*, vol. II, Bari, 1934.

L. Settembrini, *Lettere dall'ergastolo*, Milan, 1962.

V. Susca, *Le isole Tremiti. Ricordi*, Bari, 1876.

2. Co-managing crime

G. Alessi, 'Polizia e spirito pubblico tra il 1848 ed il 1860. Un'ipotesi di ricerca', *Bollettino del Diciannovesimo Secolo*, 6, 2000.

C.T. Dalbono, 'Il camorrista e la camorra', in F. De Bourcard (ed.), *Usi e costumi di Napoli e contorni descritti e dipinti*, vol. II, Naples, 1858. Interesting on how widespread knowledge of the camorra was before 1860. Blames the Spanish for the camorra's origins. The essay also reproduces the camorra's 'National anthem' (see chapter 5).

A. De Blasio, *Nel paese della camorra. L'Imbrecciata*, Naples, 1973 (1901).

S. De Renzi, *Topografia e Statistica medica della città di Napoli . . . ossia Guida medica per la città di Napoli e pel Regno*, 4th edn, Naples, 1845.

C.A. Mayer, *Vita popolare a Napoli nell'età romantica*, Bari, 1948.

J. Murray, *Southern Italy*, London, 1853. Describes via Toledo as the busiest street in the world, and gives sound advice to wary travellers.

C. Petraccone, *Napoli dal Cinquecento all'Ottocento. Problemi di storia demografica e sociale*, Naples, 1974.

A. Scialoja, *I bilanci del Regno di Napoli e degli Stati Sardi con note e confronti*, Turin, 1857.

C. Spadaccini, *Pensieri sulla polizia detta pubblica sicurezza*, Naples, 1820. An early discussion of the *feroci* and their role in policing Naples.

3. The redemption of the camorra / 4. Uncle Peppe's stuff: The camorra cashes in

K. Baedeker, *Italie. Manuel du voyageur*, III, *Italie du Sud et la Sicile*, Coblenz, 1872. Gives an authoritative assessment of Marc Monnier's hotel.

S. Baridon, *Marc Monnier e l'Italia*, Turin, 1942.

'I camorristi', in *Giornale Universale*, 15/9/1860.

C. Cavour, *La liberazione del Mezzogiorno e la formazione del Regno d'Italia, Carteggi di Camillo Cavour con Villamarina, Scialoja, Cordova, Farini, ecc.* 5 vols, Bologna, 1949–54. Vol. 3. Contains Scialoja's letter to Cavour on the *camorristi* being received by ministers under Garibaldi's dictatorship. Vol. 4 contains much material on Spaventa. 'Memorie di Giuseppe Ricciardi' in vol. 5 explains the role of Monnier's hotel for the *Comitato d'Ordine*.

R. De Cesare, *La fine di un regno*, I, *Regno di Ferdinando II*, 3rd edn, Città di Castello, 1908.

R. De Cesare, *La fine di un regno*, II, *Regno di Francesco II*, 3rd edn, Città di Castello, 1909.

P. De Riccardis, 'Una guardia nazionale inquinata: primo esame delle fonti archivistiche per Napoli e provincia, 1861–1870', in M. Marmo (ed.), *Mafia e camorra: storici a confronto*, Quaderni del Dipartimento di Scienze Sociali dell'Istituto Universitario Orientale, 2, 1988.

G. De' Sivo, *Storia delle Due Sicilie dal 1847 al 1861*, vol. 2, Naples, 1964. De Cesare and De' Sivo, two chroniclers from opposite political points of view, are among the richest contemporary sources on the fall of the Bourbons in Naples. Naturally enough they have very different takes on Liborio Romano.

G. Ghezzi, *Saggio storico sull'attività politica di Liborio Romano*, Florence, 1936.

G. Lazzaro, *Liborio Romano*, Turin, 1863.

M. Monnier, *Garibaldi. Histoire de la conquête des Deux Siciles*, Paris, 1861.

M. Monnier, *Garibaldi. Rivoluzione delle Due Sicilie*, Naples, 1861.

L. Romano, *Il mio rendiconto politico*, Locorotondo, 1960.

L. Romano, *Memorie politiche*, Milan, 1992.

XX (i.e., anon), 'Corrispondenza di Napoli', Al Direttore della Rivista Contemporanea, *Napoli* 20/8/1860, in *Rivista Contemporanea*, September 1860. On *la Sangiovannara*.

5. Spanishry: The first battle against the camorra

L. Arsenal and H. Sanchiz Álvarez de Toledo, *Una historia de las sociedades secretas españolas*, Barcelona, 2006. On the myth of the Garduña.

F. Barbagallo, *Il Mattino degli Scarfoglio*, 1892–1928, Milan, 1979. On San Donato's political career.

P. Bevilacqua, 'La camorra e la Spagna', *Meridiana*, 9, 1992. Praiseworthy for its scepticism about the story of the camorra's Spanish origins.

Il Carteggio Cavour-Nigra dal 1858 al 1861, vol. IV, *La liberazione del Mezzogiorno*, Bologna, 1929.

P. Costantini, *Silvio Spaventa e la repressione del brigantaggio*, Pescara, 1960.

E. Croce, *Silvio Spaventa*, Milan, 1969.

J. Davis, *Naples and Napoleon. Southern Italy and the European Revolutions (1780–1860)*, Oxford, 2006. For a good summary of the role of the *Carbonari* (Charcoal Burners) in early nineteenth-century politics in southern Italy.

M. de Cervantes, 'Rinconete and Cortadillo' (1613), in *Exemplary Stories*, Oxford, 2008.

V. de Féréal (pseud. of Madame Suberwick), *Mystères de l'inquisition et autres sociétés secrètes d'Espagne, par V. de F., avec notes historiques et une introduction de M. de Cuendias*, Paris, 1845.The origin of the supposedly medieval sect of the Garduña.

D. Fozzi, 'Una "specialità italiana": le colonie coatte nel Regno d'Italia', in M. Da Passano (ed.), *Le colonie penali nell'Europa dell'Ottocento*, Rome, 2004. A good study of *domicilio coatto*.

G. Machetti, 'Le leggi eccezionali post-unitarie e la repressione della camorra: un problema di ordine pubblico?', in F. Barbagallo (ed.), *Camorra e criminalità organizzata in Campania*, Naples, 1988.

C. Magni, *Vita parlamentare del Duca di San Donato patriota e difensore di Napoli*, Padova, 1968.

L. Musella, *Individui, amici, clienti. Relazioni personali e circuiti politici in Italia meridionale tra Otto e Novecento*, Bologna, 1994. On Spaventa.

E. Peters, 'The Inquisition in Literature and Art' in *idem*, *Inquisition*, Berkeley, 1989. On Mme Suberwick's novel's place in anti-Catholic polemic.

S. Ricci, 'La difesa della rivoluzione unitaria, 1860–64', in S. Ricci and C. Scarano (eds), *Silvio Spaventa. Politico e statista dell'Italia unita nei documenti della biblioteca civica "A. Mai"*, special issue of *Bergomum*, 2–3, 1990.

P. Romano, *Silvio Spaventa. Biografia Politica*, Bari, 1942.

S. Spaventa, *Dal 1848 al 1861. Lettere, scritti, documenti*, Naples, 1898.

PART II: GETTING TO KNOW THE MAFIA

Sources cited throughout this section:

S. Carbone and R. Grispo (eds), *L'inchiesta sulle condizioni sociali ed economiche della Sicilia, 1875–1876*, 2 vols, Bologna, 1968–69. The papers of the 1875–76 inquiry into Sicily. Contains the material on the Uditore *cosca* and Antonino Giammona; Carlo Morena's testimony on the state of justice in Sicily; Rudinì's testimony about the 'benign mafia'; and much information on prominent early *mafiosi* mentioned here.

S. Lupo, *Storia della mafia*, Rome, 1996 edn.

6. Rebels in corduroy

P. Alatri, *Lotte politiche in Sicilia sotto il governo della Destra (1866–74)*, Turin, 1954.

O. Cancila, *Palermo*, Bari, 2000. Also includes much interesting information on the figure of Rudinì.

P. Catalanotto, 'Dal carcere della Vicaria all'Ucciardone. Una riforma europea nella Palermo borbonica', *Nuovi Quaderni del Meridione*, 79, 1982. I have referred to the Palermo prison as the Ucciardone here to avoid confusion with the Vicaria in Naples.

G. Ciotti, *I casi di Palermo. Cenni storici sugli avvenimenti di settembre 1866*, Palermo, 1866.

M. Da Passano (ed.), *I moti di Palermo del 1866. Verbali della Commissione parlamentare di inchiesta*, Rome, 1981. Includes both Rudinì's testimony and Chief of Police Albanese's notorious statements about 'getting the mafia interested' in helping maintain order.

W. Dickinson, 'Diario della rivoluzione siciliana dalla notte del 9 al 10 gennaio 1848 sino al 2 giugno 1849', in vol. 1 of *Memorie della rivoluzione siciliana dell'anno MDCCCXLVIII pubblicate nel cinquantesimo anniversario del XII gennaio di esso anno*, 2 vols, Palermo, 1898. On Turi Miceli in the revolution of 1848.

G. Fiume, *Le bande armate in Sicilia (1819–1849). Violenza e organizzazione del potere*, Palermo, 1984.

Gazzetta Ufficiale del Regno d'Italia, 18/10/1866, 'Relazione del marchese Rudinì, Sindaco di Palermo, sugli ultimi avvenimenti di quella città'.

Gazzetta Ufficiale del Regno d'Italia, Supplemento al n. 302, 3/11/1866, 'Relazione del Sindaco di Palermo, marchese Di Rudinì, sui fatti avvenuti in quella città nel settembre scorso.'

Gazzetta Ufficiale del Regno d'Italia, 20/11/1866, 'Relazione al Ministro del l'Interno del questore della città e circondario di Palermo sui fatti del settembre 1866'.

N. Giordano, 'Turi Miceli. Il brigante-eroe monrealese nei moti del 1848, 1860 e 1866', *Il Risorgimento in Sicilia*, 1, 1, 1965.

S. Lupo, *Il giardino degli aranci: il mondo degli agrumi nella storia del Mezzogiorno*, Venice, 1990. On organised crime and the citrus fruit business.

A. Maurici, *La genesi storica della rivolta del 1866 in Palermo*, Palermo, 1916.

G. Moncalvo, *Alessandra Di Rudinì. Dall'amore per D'Annunzio al Carmelo*, Milan, 1994.

G. Pagano, *Sette giorni d'insurrezione a Palermo. Cause—fatti—rimedî*, Palermo, 1867.

'The Week's Republic in Palermo, 1866', *Quarterly Review*, vol. 122, no. 243, January 1867.

L. Riall, *Sicily and the Unification of Italy. Liberal Policy and Local Power, 1859–1866*, Oxford, 1998. Also includes the quotation about *camorristi* in Turi Miceli's entourage.

U. Santino, *La cosa e il nome. Materiali per lo studio dei fenomeni premafiosi*, Catanzaro, 2000. One of the many places that cites the 1838 report from Trapani on the 'Unions or brotherhoods, sects of a kind'.

7. The benign mafia / 8. A sect with a life of its own: The mafia's rituals discovered

ACS, Ministero dell'Interno, Direzione Generale Affari Generale e del Personale, Fascicoli del personale del Ministero, Ia e IIa Serie, B. 542. Albanese, Giuseppe. Personal papers on the shady figure of Chief of Police Albanese showing how Rudinì was responsible for appointing him.

ACS, Ministero di Grazia e Giustizia, Direzione generale degli affari penali. Miscellanea B. 44, Fasc. 558, 1877 Sicilia. Associazioni di malfattori. Including the files on the various associations discovered across Sicily, and Carlo Morena's letter denying any link between them.

ACS, Ministero di Grazia e Giustizia, Ufficio superiore personale e affari generali, Ufficio secondo, Magistrati, fascicoli personali, primo versamento 1860–1905, Morena, Carlo.

ASPA, Gabinetto Prefettura serie I (1860–1905), b. 35, fasc. 10, 1876, Denuncia Galati—Malfattori all'Uditore. Il Questore Rastelli al Procuratore del Re, Palermo 29/2 (1876). The first document reproducing the mafia's initiation ritual.

A. Crisantino, *Della segreta e operosa associazione. Una setta all'origine della mafia*, Palermo, 2000. Contains a great deal that is useful about policing and the mafia between the Right and the Left.

P. Pezzino, 'Stato violenza società. Nascita e sviluppo del paradigma mafioso', in idem, *Una certa reciprocità di favori. Mafia e modernizzazione violenta nella Sicilia postunitaria*, Milan, 1990.

D. Tajani, *Mafia e potere. Requisitoria (1871)*, P. Pezzino (ed.), Pisa, 1993. On the Albanese affair.

9. Double vendetta

ACS, Ministero dell'Interno, Direzione Generale Affari Generale e del Personale, Fascicoli del personale del Ministero (1861–1952) IIa Serie, B. 256. Sangiorgi Ermanno, Questore. Sangiorgi's career file, containing the documentation on the 'fratricide' case and much else besides. Most of what I have written about Sangiorgi is from this source.

ACS, Ministero di Grazia e Giustizia, Dir. Gen. Aff. Penali, Miscellanea, b. 46, fasc. 589. The correspondence concerning Carlo Morena's defence of Pietro De Michele, including Sangiorgi's evidence against the latter.

A. Cutrera, *I ricottari. La mala vita di Palermo*, Palermo, 1979 (1896). On the differences between *ricottari* and *mafiosi*.

J. A. Davis, *Conflict and Control*, London, 1988. Good for contextual information on policing in Liberal Italy.

J. Dunnage, *The Italian Police and the Rise of Fascism*, London, 1997. Contains a good brief summary of policing history in Italy before Fascism.

I. Fazio, 'The family, honour and gender in Sicily: models and new research', *Modern Italy*, 9 (2), 2004. An exceptionally useful survey of the vast literature on the Sicilian family.

C. Guerrieri, 'L'azione repressiva di Giovanni Nicotera contro mafia e camorra', in A. Bagnato, G. Masi and V. Villella (eds), *Giovanni Nicotera nella storia italiana dell'Ottocento*, Soveria Mannelli, 1999. For the background to the whole Sangiorgi-Morena-De Michele story told here.

P. Pezzino, '"La Fratellanza" di Favara', in *idem*, *Una certa reciprocità di favori. Mafia e modernizzazione violenta nella Sicilia postunitaria*, Milan, 1990.

'Processo Amoroso e compagni', in *Giornale di Sicilia*. Series of articles covering the trial begins on 29/8/1883 and ends on 20/10/1883. The trial is a classic instance of the way only the mafia's losers were successfully prosecuted. The trial is, among other things, an unexplored source on the role of women in the mafia.

G. Vaccaro, *Notizie su Burgio*, Palermo, 1921. One of the few published sources of information on the history of this Sicilian agrotown. Suspiciously, it portrays De Michele as a victim of the 1848 rebellion.

PART III: THE NEW CRIMINAL NORMALITY

10. Born delinquents: Science and the mob

G. Alongi, *La maffia nei suoi fattori e nelle sue manifestazioni: studio sulle classi pericolose della Sicilia*, Rome, 1886.

G. Alongi, *La camorra. Studio di sociologia criminale*, Turin, 1890.

G. Alongi, 'Polizia e criminalità in Italia', *Nuova Antologia*, 1/1/1897. Summarises police accommodation with organised crime after the crucial years of 1876–77.

A. Cutrera, *La mafia e i mafiosi. Origini e manifestazioni*, Palermo, 1900. The best of the policemen writing in the era of positivism.

C. D'Addosio, *Il duello dei camorristi*, Naples, 1893.

A. De Blasio, *Usi e costumi dei camorristi*, 2nd edn, Naples, 1897.

A. De Blasio, *Il tatuaggio ereditario e psichico dei camorristi napoletani*, Naples, 1898.

A. De Blasio, *Nel paese della camorra. (L'Imbrecciata)*, Naples, 1901.

A. De Blasio, *Il tatuaggio*, Naples, 1905.

C. Fiore, 'Il controllo della criminalità organizzata nello Stato liberale: strumenti legislativi e atteggiamenti della cultura giuridica', *Studi Storici*, 2, 1988.

C. Lombroso, *L'uomo delinquente in rapporto all'antropologia, alla giurisprudenza ed alle discipline carcerarie*, 4th edn, 2 vols, Turin, 1889.

F. Manduca, *Studii sociologici*, Naples, 1888. An interesting and contradictory text by a leading former magistrate with experience in both Sicily and Naples. In positivist style he blames ethnic factors for the mafia and camorra, but runs against the consensus of the time by believing that the mafia, like the camorra, is an organisation with a hierarchy.

A. Niceforo, *L'Italia barbara contemporanea*, Milan, 1898.

11. An audience of hoods

La fondazione della camorra is covered in *Il Mattino, Roma* and *Corriere di Napoli*, October–November, 1899. The photograph of a scene from *La fondazione della camorra* can be viewed at: http://archiviteatro.napolibeniculturali.it/atn/foto/dettagli _foto?oid=127417&descrizione=stella&query_start=10.

The letter from the Ispettorato Vicaria to the Questura (Police HQ) in Naples on the *Fondazione della camorra*, dated 4/11/1899 was available on the same site, but now seems to have been taken down.

V. Bianco, *La mala vita ovvero I camorristi nella Vicaria,* manuscript play held in Biblioteca Lucchesi Palli, Biblioteca Nazionale, Naples.

V. Bianco, *La mala vita'* o *'E carcere 'a Vicaria,* manuscript play held in Biblioteca Lucchesi Palli, Biblioteca Nazionale, Naples.

V. Bianco, *La mala vita o 'O zelluso d' 'o Mercato* (1923), manuscript play held in Biblioteca Lucchesi Palli, Biblioteca Nazionale, Naples.

G. Castellano, *'E guappe 'a Vicaria*, manuscript play held in Biblioteca Lucchesi Palli, Biblioteca Nazionale, Naples.

F.P. Castiglione, *Il segreto cinquecentesco dei Beati Paoli*, Palermo, 1999.

E. De Mura (ed.), *Enciclopedia della canzone napoletana*, Naples, 1969, vol. III. See the entries on the San Ferdinando and on Edoardo Minichini.

S. Di Giacomo and G. Cognetti, *Mala vita*, Naples, 1889. A camorra play by one of the best-known Neapolitan authors of the era.

S. Di Giacomo in (various authors), *Napoli d'oggi*, Naples, 1900. On the camorra in the theatre, the San Ferdinando, Stella, etc.

S. Di Giacomo, 'Il "San Ferdinando"', in *idem, Napoli. Figure e paesi*, Naples, 1909.

V. Linares, 'I Beati Paoli', in *idem, Racconti popolari*, Palermo, 1886.

F. Mancini, 'I teatri minori' in F. Mancini and S. Ragni (eds), *Donizetti e i teatri napoletani nell'Ottocento*, Naples, 1997. On the San Ferdinando.

G. Montemagno, *Luigi Natoli e i Beati Paoli*, Palermo, 2002.

F. Renda, *I Beati Paoli. Storia, letteratura e leggenda*, Palermo, 1988.

G. Tessitore, *Il nome e la cosa. Quando la mafia non si chiamava mafia*, Milan, 1997. On modern-day *mafiosi*—men of the criminal caliber of Totuccio Contorno, Gaetano Badalamenti, Totò Riina and Gaspare Mutolo—who believe, or profess to believe, that their organisation is the modern form of the *Beati Paoli*.

G. Trevisani (ed.), *Teatro napoletano. Dalle origini a Edoardo Scarpetta*, 2 vols, Bologna, 1957.

V. Viviani, *Storia del teatro napoletano*, Naples, 1969.

12. The slack society

ACS, Archivio di Francesco Crispi, Crispi Roma, fasc. (79) 320, Relazioni e promemoria relativi alla organizzazione della PS e dei CC specie in Sicilia, 1888.

ACS, Archivio di Francesco Crispi, Crispi Roma, fasc. (222) 321, Relazione d'inchiesta sul personale e sull'organizzazione delle guardie a cavallo di Pubblica Sicurezza nelle provincie di Palermo, Trapani, Girgenti e Caltanissetta, 1887. Contains Sangiorgi's report dated 25/10/1888. There is also material on Sangiorgi's mission to Sicily at this time in his career file (see above). Davis, *Conflict and Control*, also covers the mission.

Il Mattino. For coverage of Ciccio Cappuccio's funeral, 7–8/12/1892; and 9–10/12/1892 for Ferdinando Russo's poem about the *camorrista*.

La Gazzetta Piemontese is a very useful press source on the disturbances of August 1893. The profile of Sangiorgi when he was appointed police chief in Milan is in the issue of 14/2/1889.

A.G. Bianchi (ed.), *Il romanzo di un delinquente nato. Autobiografia di Antonino M.*, Milan, 1893.

G. Fortunato, *Corrispondenze napoletane*, Cosenza, 1990. A collection of classic writings on the Southern Question originally published 1878–80. See particularly, 'La camorra'.

M. Marmo, *Il proletariato industriale a Napoli in età liberale*, Naples, 1978. On the camorra-backed cab drivers' strike. Davis, *Conflict and Control* is also useful on this.

S. Pucci, 'Schizzo monografico della camorra carceraria', in *Allegazioni e discorsi in materia penale*, Florence, 1881. Article by a magistrate involved in prosecuting the prison camorra.

F.M. Snowden, *Naples in the time of cholera, 1884–1911*, Cambridge, 1995.

P. Turiello, *Governo e governati in Italia*, P. Bevilacqua (ed.), Turin, 1980 (1882).

P. Villari, 'La camorra', in *idem.*, *Le lettere meridionali ed altri scritti sulla questione sociale in Italia*, Florence, 1878.

PART IV: THE 'NDRANGHETA EMERGES

Court rulings on the emergence of the 'ndrangheta:

ASRC:

Tribunale Reggio Calabria, Sentenze, 16/7/1890, n. 301, Arnone Alessandro + 36. Based in Reggio. One of several cases where prostitutes testify against the *picciotti*.

Ditto, 12/3/1896, Triveri Giacomo + 4. A group tried for petty thefts in Gherio. The criminal association element of the prosecution is not proven.

Ditto, 16/11/1896, n. 1028, Attinà Domenico + 18. A group based in Condofuri, Casalnuovo and Roccaforte. One witness blames the railways for the spread of the picciotteria. Several local notables testify against the *picciotti*, despite having relatives in the gang, whose members have 'trying it on with women' among their aims.

Ditto, 7/9/1897, Arena Michele + 57. A large group based in Reggio.

Ditto, 7/10/1899, n. 22. A case based in Melito, which sees *picciotto* Beniamino Capri sentenced to six months for rape and membership of a criminal association.

ASC:

Corte di Appello delle Calabrie, Guzzi Giovanni + 2, 4/9/1877. A case in Nicastro involving ex-cons.

Sezione accusa, Zema Demetrio + 5, 23/10/1878. A case in Gallina (just outside Reggio Calabria) where a man imprisoned for assault in 1872 was released in 1876 and formed a criminal association. The gang, who practised extortion, are accused of shooting a man in the head for offending Zema's 'concubine'.

Sezione accusa, Serraino Giuseppe + 7, 23/12/1879. Here the 'criminal association' charge is dismissed.

Sezione accusa, Battista Antonino + 16, 17/12/1879. A group of thieves, one of whom had a record as a prison *camorrista*, but who do not create a formal criminal association; based in the Palmi area.

Sezione accusa, Voce Vincenzo + 2, 30/06/1882. A classic tale of factional rivalry between wealthy families rather than an organised crime episode. Three brothers in Bruzzano are accused of hiring a killer to eliminate one of the opposing clan; one of the brothers is a judge.

Sezione accusa, Barbaro Felice + 6, 23/4/1883. Municipal corruption in the Locride. As yet no criminal association element, it would seem. This case and the previous one show the Calabria that would prove vulnerable to the emergence of the picciotteria.

Corte di Appello delle Calabrie, Crocè Paolo + 3, 22/3/1884. Four *picciotti* from Reggio Calabria appeal against their convictions.

Sezione accusa, Anania Giuseppe + 27, 21/4/1884. The first signs of the picciotteria in Nicastro, dating back to 1883. All of the accused are ex-cons, and they have links with Ciccio Cappuccio, the 'Little Lord Frankie' of the Neapolitan camorra. Pimping is their primary source of income.

Sezione accusa, Romeo Bruno + 27, 7/12/1899. *Picciotti* from S. Cristina.

Sezione accusa, Auteri Felice + 316, 7/12/1899. The picciotteria centred in Iatrinoli, Radicena and Cittanova in the Plain of Gioia Tauro. A vast prosecution based on the evidence of a killer from the gang who was not offered help by his comrades once he had been arrested. The leader is a 39-year-old shepherd. He and his men stole cattle and forced landowners to take *picciotti* on as guards.

Corte di Appello delle Calabrie, Auteri Felice + 229, 25/2/1901. A later stage in the same trial—the document is particularly insightful on the *picciotti*'s attitude to women. Ciconte reads this trial as an example of dynastic marriages in the picciotteria. But while there are two marriages mentioned, it seems to me that we are still clearly in a milieu dominated by face-slashings and petty conflicts of 'honour' over prostitutes, of a kind familiar from the world of the Neapolitan camorra. The bosses, nonetheless, are said to have 'risen from squalor' and 'accumulated a fortune'.

Sources consulted throughout this section:

P. Bevilacqua, 'Uomini, terre, economie' in P. Bevilacqua and A. Placanica, *Storia d'Italia. Le regioni dall'Unità a oggi, La Calabria*, Turin, 1985. Another fundamental study, which is particularly good on the vulnerability of the peasantry.

Again it would be interesting to match this account of the family's role in the peasant economy with what we know about the nature of the picciotteria. For the moment, it is the *contrast* between the peasant family and the gangs that is most striking.

V. Cappelli, 'Politica e politici', in P. Bevilacqua and A. Placanica, *Storia d'Italia. Le regioni dall'Unità a oggi, La Calabria*, Turin, 1985. Particularly important for the effects of the electoral reforms of the 1880s.

E. Ciconte, *'Ndrangheta dall'Unità a oggi*, Rome-Bari, 1992. Ciconte in particular identifies evidence of what he believes is a mafia presence in Calabria before the 1880s. My interpretation of that evidence, broadly speaking, is that it represents localised instances where the prison camorra established a temporary bridgehead in the outside world—a bridgehead that would turn into a full-scale colonisation in the 1880s and 1890s. The quotation about 'the wails of the wounded and dying' being audible before the Angelus is cited from Ciconte, p. 211.

G. Cingari, 'Tra brigantaggio e "picciotteria": Giuseppe Musolino', in *idem, Brigantaggio, proprietari e contadini nel Sud*, Reggio Calabria, 1976.

G. Cingari, *Storia della Calabria dall'Unità a oggi*, Rome-Bari, 1983.

G. Cingari, *Reggio Calabria*, Rome-Bari, 1988.

Cronaca di Calabria. This weekly has occasionally good coverage of the picciotteria emergency. For the quotation from the initiation ritual ('Are you comfortable? Very comfortable!'), see 'La mala vita a Palmi', 30/09/1896. The Trimboli testimony on the myth of the Spanish knights is in 'La mala vita a Palmi', 11/03/1897. On the 'innately wicked' well-to-do *africoti*, see 12/03/1896.

F. Piselli and G. Arrighi, 'Parentela, clientela e comunità', in P. Bevilacqua and A. Placanica, *Storia d'Italia. Le regioni dall'Unità a oggi. La Calabria*, Turin, 1985. Important on society and the economy in the Plain of Gioia Tauro, but does not square that socio-economic profile with the available evidence on the nature of the early picciotteria.

13. Harsh mountain

K. Baedeker, *Italy. Handbook for Travellers.* Third Part: *Southern Italy and Sicily*, London, 1869.

P. Borzomati, *La Calabria dal 1882 al 1892 nei rapporti dei prefetti*, Reggio Calabria, 2001. Contains the first reports on a substantial mafia presence in Reggio.

L. Costanzo, *Storia delle ferrovie in Calabria,* Cosenza, 2005.

L. Franchetti, *Condizioni economiche ed amministrative delle province napoletane*, Florence, 1875. Franchetti does use the m-word on one occasion, on p. 155. 'I hear tell that quite a few big landowners who live in the big cities are, as it were, excluded from their estates by a kind of maffia of middle-class people who rent those estates. But this phenomenon is not as generalised as some people seem to believe'. Franchetti does not give enough information for us to be able to interpret this observation. We know of course that he would go on to write a famous study of the 'middle-class villains' of Sicily (his term), so we can be sure that the Tuscan intellectual had no qualms about denouncing the mafia when he saw it. The best we can do, perhaps, is to add this isolated note to the list of fragmentary sightings of Calabrian *mafiosi* before the 1880s.

F. Manduca, *Studii sociologici*, Naples, 1888. Manduca, a magistrate, tells us that as chief prosecuting magistrate (*procuratore del Re*) in Reggio Calabria he was friends with some politicians who had been imprisoned under the Bourbons who, they alleged, put *mafiosi* and *camorristi* in their cells to provoke them and cause trouble; they had to defend themselves with knives. We can add this reference to the list of early mentions of organised crime in Calabria.

G. Verga, 'Fantasticheria', in *idem*, *Vita dei campi*, Milan, 1880.

U. Zanotti-Bianco, 'Tra la perduta gente—Africo', in *idem*, *Tra la perduta gente*, Milan, 1959.

The following maps allow one to trace the progress of railway construction through the areas of 'high mafia density' (to use an Italian phrase) in Calabria:

Corpo di Stato Maggiore, *Carta delle strade ferrate del Regno d'Italia in esercizio nell'Aprile del 1869*.

Comando del Corpo di Stato Maggiore (Direzione Trasporti), *Carta delle ferrovie e delle linee di navigazione del Regno d'Italia*, Istituto Topografico Militare, gennaio 1877.

Ditta Artaria, *Carta speciale delle ferrovie e della navigazione in Europa*, Milan, 1878.

Comando del Corpo di Stato Maggiore (Direzione Trasporti), *Carta delle ferrovie e della linee di navigazione del Regno d'Italia*, Istituto Geografico Militare, 1883.

Carta delle ferrovie, telegrafi, tramways a vapore e corsi d'acqua navigabili del Regno, Milan, 1886.

Cesare Ramoni, *Ferrovie italiane nel 1890. Carta completa delle reti ferroviarie*, Milan, 1890.

Istituto Geografico Militare, *Carta delle ferrovie e delle linee di navigazione del Regno d'Italia*, Edizione giugno 1891.

Carta della ferrovie e delle linee di navigazione del Regno d'Italia, Istituto Geografico Militare, gennaio 1894.

The figure of 1,854 people successfully prosecuted for membership of the picciotteria between 1885 and 1902 comes from a speech by the prosecutor Sansone in the Musolino trial, as reported in *Giornale d'Italia*, 1/5/1902.

14. The tree of knowledge

I have used the following documents to try and reconstruct the emergence of the 'ndrangheta in the Plain of Gioia Tauro chronologically:

ASC, Sezione Accusa. Corte d'appello di Catanzaro, Lisciotto Francesco + 23, v. 133, 18/1/1889.

ASC, Sezione Accusa. Corte d'appello di Catanzaro, Sciarrone Giovanbattista + 95, v. 137, 21/2/1890.

ASC, Corte d'appello delle Calabrie. Tripodi Carmine, v. 323, 27/8/1890.

ASC, Corte d'appello delle Calabrie. Calia Michelangelo + 65, v. 324, 14/10/1890.

ASC, Corte d'appello delle Calabrie. Marino Francesco + 147, v. 336, 9/9/1892. The trial that mentions the two oathed women members of the picciotteria.

ASC, Corte d'appello delle Calabrie. Saccà Rocco + 45, v. 364, 31/5/1897. This is the trial based on the testimony of Pasquale Trimboli, who gives us our first evidence of the myth of the three Spanish knights.

La Ragione. This local paper was threatened by the picciotti and covered its emergence in Palmi in 1888 closely. The paper was also concerned about the relationship between the police and the gangs: 'the police should not trust anyone they pay for information, because such people perhaps belong to the gangs themselves: instead of uncovering the criminal cabals, these informers help cover them up' (1/4/1888).

Zivì. A radical paper that on 16/6/1895 complains about the overly friendly relations between the police and picciotti in Palmi.

F. Arcà, Calabria vera. Appunti statistici ed economici sulla provincial di Reggio, Reggio Calabria, 1907.

G.A. Carbone, 'Cenni sull'agricoltura ed industrie agrarie del circondario di Palmi', L'Agricoltura e le Industrie Agrarie, 15/4/1893. The first of a series of articles running until 15/10/1893 that are essential on the economic background to the emergence of the picciotteria.

N. Marcone, Un viaggio in Calabria. Impressioni e ricordi, Roma, 1885.

15. Darkest Africo

The following court documents from the ASRC constitute the most concentrated documentation from any early 'ndrangheta trial. They include the voluminous court papers, including witness statements, and the judges' rulings from the four trials of the Africo picciotteria: three groups of defendants prosecuted separately as part of the same criminal association and a smaller group accused of murdering the main witness in the case, Pietro Maviglia.

ASRC, Tribunale penale di Reggio, b. 750, inv. 68, vol. 1, 2. Associazione a delinquere 1887–1894.

ASRC, Tribunale penale di Reggio, b. 154, inv. 68, fasc. 4. Assise RC. Procedimento contro Callea Domenico +10 per l'omicidio di Maviglia Pietro 1894.

ASRC, Tribunale penale di Reggio, b. 543, inv. 68, no. 3069. Procedimento contro Ioffrida Domenico di Roghudi + 39 associazione a delinquere 1896.

ASRC, Tribunale Reggio Calabria, Sentenza 25/3/1896, Velonà Filippo + 29.

ASRC, Tribunale Reggio Calabria, Sentenza 27/4/1896, n. 210, Ioffrida Domenico + 39.

ASRC, Tribunale Reggio Calabria, Sentenza 26/5/1896, n. 444, Favasuli Bartolo + 29.

C. Alvaro, Polsi nell'arte, nella leggenda, nella storia, Reggio Calabria, 2005 (1912).

G. Chirico, Una vicenda giudiziaria di associazione per delinquere di tipo mafioso nella provincia di Reggio Calabria (1890–1900), Tesi di Laurea, Facoltà di Scienze

Politiche, Università degli Studi di Messina, 1989–90. A precocious analysis of part of the above material.

P. Martino, 'Per la storia della 'Ndrànghita', *Biblioteca di Ricerche Linguistiche e Filologiche*, vol. 25, no. 1, 1988. Very useful on the jargon of the picciotteria and its derivation.

G. Postiglione, *Relazione statistica dei lavori compiuti nel circondario del tribunale civile e penale di Palmi nell'anno 1890*, Palmi, 1891.

J. Steinberg, *The Number. One man's search for identity in the Cape underworld and prison gangs*, Johannesburg, 2004.

F. Varese, *The Russian Mafia. Private Protection in a New Market Economy*, Oxford, 2001. An excellent account of the Russian mafia.

16. The King of Aspromonte

Archival sources:

ASRC, Gabinetto di Prefettura, n. 1089, Associazione a delinquere in S. Stefano, b. 27, inv. 34. Mangione's reports on the picciotteria in Musolino's hometown. Includes remarkable material on Musolino's sisters.

ASRC, Gabinetto di Prefettura, Serie prima, affari riservati. Bandito Musolino. The vast collection of documents on the Musolino case.

See for example:

Ditto, b. 2, fasc. 11. Delegati di PS impegnati nella cattura di Musolino, sottofasc. Mangione. On the policeman who investigated the picciotteria in Santo Stefano.

Ditto, b. 2, fasc. 23. Stampa. Notizie sul brigante Musolino. Press clippings on Musolino that show how worried the authorities were about the growth of his mythical status as an innocent avenger.

Ditto, b. 2, fasc. 13. Favoreggiatori. A collection of false leads from all over Italy and the USA.

Press:

I have followed the Musolino trial in *Giornale d'Italia* and *Avanti!* (April–June, 1902).

G. Cingari, 'Tra brigantaggio e "picciotteria": Giuseppe Musolino', in *idem*, *Brigantaggio, proprietari e contadini nel Sud*, Reggio Calabria, 1976. Fundamental for all aspects of the Musolino case. The brigand's open letter to *La Tribuna*, dated 28/3/1900, is quoted from Cingari.

N. Douglas, *Old Calabria*, London, 1983 (1915).

E. Morselli and S. De Sanctis, *Biografia di un bandito. Giuseppe Musolino di fronte alla psichiatria ed alla sociologia*, Milan, 1903.

M. Pascoli, *Lungo la vita di Giovanni Pascoli*, Milan, 1961.

A. Rossi, 'Alla ricerca di Musolino', *L'Adriatico*, 11/2/1901. The first of a brilliant series of twenty articles (most published under the title 'Nel regno di Musolino') running until 6/4/1901.

PART V: MEDIA DONS

17. Bankers and Men of Honour / 18. Floriopolis / 19. Four trials and a funeral

ACS, DGPS, aa.gg.rr. Atti speciali (1898–1940), b. 1, fasc. 1, 'The Sangiorgi Report'. It is worth noting that there were some links between Palizzolo and the *mafiosi* detailed in Sangiorgi's report. The MP provided character references for some of the Men of Honour whose gun licences the chief of police confiscated. Palizzolo's favourite Villabate *cosca* sold stolen cattle through the same Palermo butcher who hosted summits attended by Antonino Giammona, Francesco Siino, *et al.*

There is information on Sangiorgi's activities as chief of police of Palermo in the Sangiorgi career files, including the transfer notification telegram I quote.

The best accounts of the Notarbartolo affair are in:

S. Lupo, *Storia della mafia*, Rome, 1996. The quote from the police on Palizzolo as 'the mafia's patron' is quoted on p. 115. Lupo also describes Ignazio Florio's free ride during the trial as 'miraculous'.

G. Barone, 'Egemonie urbane e potere locale (1882–1913)', in M. Aymard and G. Giarrizzo (eds), *Storia d'Italia. Le regioni dall'Unità a oggi. La Sicilia*, Turin, 1987. Florio on the mafia as 'an invention created to calumny Sicily' is quoted on p. 317. The quotation about the fear among honest journalists is from p. 314. Cosenza quoted on the 'priests of Themis' is on p. 325.

There are also useful points in:

F. Renda, *Socialisti e cattolici in Sicilia (1900–1904)*, Caltanissetta, 1972.

F. Renda, *Storia della mafia*, Palermo, 1997. The quotation on 'the high mafia planned the murder long in advance' is on p. 147.

N. Colajanni, *La Sicilia dai borboni ai sabaudi (1860–1900)*, Milan, 1951.

L. Notarbartolo, *Memorie della vita di mio padre*, Pistoia, 1949. On the *Tribuna Giudiziaria* being close to Cosenza, see p. 365.

R. Poma, *Onorevole alzatevi!*, Florence, 1976. Quotes the lines on the Florence verdict hailed as a sign of national unity.

S. Sonnino, *Diario 1866–1912*, vol. 1, Bari, 1972. On the possibility of an early election due to the first Notarbartolo trial.

I followed the various trials in a number of newspapers:

Avanti! On Palizzolo's convulsive laughter at the verdict 1/8/1902.

Corriere della Sera. On Palizzolo 'accessible to the voters', 1–2/10/1901 (quoted in Lupo, *Storia della mafia*, p. 111).

Daily Express. On the Florence verdict, 25/7/1904.

Giornale di Sicilia. 'La questione Avellone', 2–3/4/1892 (quoted in O. Cancila, *Palermo*, Bari, 2000, pp. 234–5). For the new prefect's proclamation of a campaign against extortion, see 14–15/9/1898. On how well respected the Giammona family were, 13–14/5/1901. On the Giammonas' generosity: 20–21/5/1901. On the mafia as a 'hypertrophy of individualism', 24–25/5/1901. Interestingly the full quote comes word-for-word from Cosenza's 1900 speech opening the judicial year (see Renda, *Socialisti e cattolici*, p. 408). Cosenza also quotes Giuseppe Falcone, a lawyer of Palizzolo's and the man responsible for trying to smear Sangiorgi at the end of the story. On Sangiorgi's death, 4–5/11/1908.

Il Mattino. On Sangiorgi's death, 4–5/11/1908.

Morning Post. On the hypocrisy at the pro-Notarbartolo demonstration, see 22/12/1899.

L'Ora. On the mafia as 'rustic chivalry' 5–6/6/1901. For the letter slandering Sangiorgi, 19–20/11/1903. On Sangiorgi's death, 4/11/1908.

Resto del Carlino. Sangiorgi on 'the mafia is powerful', 30–31/10/1901.

The St Louis Republic. 'The bandit-king's levee' (anon), 14/1/1900. For the scene at Palizzolo's bedroom receptions.

The Times. On Leopoldo Notarbartolo's 'sobriety, scrupulous attention to fact', 18/10/1901.

Tribuna Giudiziaria. See 29/11/1903 and the article 'Commedia poliziesca' for Sangiorgi's 'slanderous' testimony.

22. The criminal Atlantic

C. Alvaro, 'La fibbia', *Corriere della Sera*, 17/9/1955. For the anecdote about the 'association' in San Luca.

G. Cingari, *Storia della Calabria dall'Unità a oggi*, Rome-Bari, 1983.

G. Cingari, *Reggio Calabria*, Rome-Bari, 1988. On the picciotteria in the aftermath of the earthquake of 1908.

D. Critchley, *The Origin of Organised Crime in America. The New York City Mafia, 1891–1931*, London, 2009. Marshalls a vast amount of excellent documentation but is marred by its lack of knowledge of the best Italian studies on the mafia, which leads, for example, to his taking the Sicilians like Joe Bonanno at their word on 'honour' and such like. All the same, Critchley's book is important in that it is the first to assemble an overview involving both Campanian and Calabrian gangs as well as Sicilians. I have drawn on Critchley for Erricone's time in New York, among other things.

P.Y. Herchenroether, *Helltown. The Story of the Hillsville Black Hand*, unpublished typescript, kindly provided by the author. On picciotteria-style gangs among miners in Pennsylvania.

S. Lupo, *Quando la mafia trovò l'America. Storia di un intreccio intercontinentale, 1888–2008*, Turin, 2008. Among many other things, Lupo quotes Antonio Musolino's statement to the police.

New York Times. 'By order of the mafia', 22/10/1888. Salvatore Lupo identifies this first mafia murder in the USA. Walter Littlefield, 'Criminal band that murdered Petrosino in police coils', 11/9/1910.

The ASRC contains some interesting files on the re-importation of the Black Hand into Calabria and on links between Calabrian gangs and the mining communities of the USA:

Tribunale penale Reggio Calabria, 1906, b. 981, fasc. 11156, Leone Antonino +63, Associazione a delinquere mano nera.

Ditto, b. 993, fasc. 11732. Ignoti: minacce.

Ditto, b. 1028, fasc. 12896. Romeo Francesco e altri (11/1907).

20. The 'high' camorra / 21. The camorra in straw-yellow gloves / 23. Gennaro Abbatemaggio: Genialoid / 24. The strange death of the Honoured Society

F. Barbagallo, *Il Mattino degli Scarfoglio, 1892–1928*, Milan, 1979.

F. Barbagallo, *Stato, parlamento e lotte politico-sociali nel Mezzogiorno (1900–1914)*, Naples, 1980. On Peppuccio Romano, among other things.

F. Barbagallo, *Storia della camorra*, Rome-Bari, 2010.

R. Canosa, *Storia della criminalità in Italia, 1845–1945*, Turin, 1991. The request from the *Carabinieri* for more money to pay witnesses is quoted on p. 291.

E. Ciccotti, *Come divenni e come cessai di essere deputato di Vicaria*, Naples, 1909. On the election and the camorra in tricolour cockades once more.

E. De Cosa, *Camorra e malavita a Napoli agli inizi del Novecento*, Cerchio, 1989 (1908).

G. Garofalo, *La seconda guerra napoletana*, Naples, 1984.

G. Machetti, 'La lobby di piazza Municipio: gli impiegati comunali nella Napoli di fine Ottocento', *Meridiana*, 38–39, 2000.

M. Marmo, '"Processi indiziari non se ne dovrebbero mai fare." Le manipolazioni del processo Cuocolo (1906–1930)', in M. Marmo and L. Musella (eds), *La costruzione della verità giudiziaria*, Naples, 2003.

M. Marmo, 'Il reato associativo tra costruzione normativa e prassi giudiziaria', in G. Civile and G. Machetti (eds), *La città e il tribunale. Diritto, pratica giudiziaria e società napoletana tra Ottocento e Novecento*, Naples, 2004.

M. Marmo, 'L'opinione pubblica nel processo penale: Giano bifronte, ovvero la verità giudiziaria contesa', *Meridiana*, 63, 2008.

F. Russo and E. Serao, *La camorra. Origini, usi, costumi e riti dell' 'annorata soggietà'*, Naples, 1907. The source of the quote on absinthe and debt.

R. Salomone, *Il processo Cuocolo*, Arpino, 1930. Contains Abbatemaggio's recantation and information on his life; also Erricone's speech at the verdict, p. 102.

F. Snowden, *The fascist revolution in Tuscany, 1919–1922*, Cambridge, 1989. On Abbatemaggio's life under Fascism.

F.M. Snowden, *Naples in the time of cholera, 1884–1911*, Cambridge, 1995.

A. Train, *Courts, Criminals and the Camorra*, London, 1912. The 'bear garden' quote is from p. 184. The 'best dressed' *camorristi* from p. 211. The 'excitability' of Italians, p. 202.

The press on the Cuocolo trial:

The Advertiser (Australia). Abbatemaggio as 'a rascal of almost inconceivably deep dye' 13/7/1912.

Bulawayo Chronicle. For the damning verdict on the Cuocolo trial, 8/9/1912.

Il Mattino. Unless otherwise stated, I have quoted from *Il Mattino*'s copious coverage. For example: Abbatemaggio's initial testimony begins on 25–26/3/1911; Abbatemaggio questioned on his theatregoing, 3–4/5/1911; Abbatemaggio's 'mnemonic and intuitive capacities', testimony of Prof Polidori 14–15/3/1911; Erricone on 'the gramophone', 29–30/3/1911; Erricone on the 'sons of Vesuvius', 1–2/4/1911; on the pederast / spitting episode, 3–4/5/1911; Fabroni's testimony, with its accusations against Abbatemaggio, begins on 13–14/7/1911; Simonetti testimony, 9–10/6/1911; Catalano testimony, 22–23/6/1911; Ametta testimony and Erricone's outburst, 23–24/6/1911; on the *camorrista*'s printed defence and 'rustic chivalry', 20–21/3/1911.

New York Times. 'The greatest criminal trial of the age', 11/9/1910; 'Camorrist told all to win his bride', 6/3/1911; 'the black vitals of the criminal hydra', 11/9/1910; 'one of the most remarkable feats of detection', 15/1/1912.

Otautau Standard and Wallace County Chronicle (New Zealand). One of many papers across the world to use the Sherlock Holmes parallel.

La Stampa. Curiously, Gennaro Abbatemaggio kept himself in the headlines by claiming to know important inside details of the Matteotti murder; he gave evidence at the trial. See 'Le rivelazioni di Abbatemaggio sulla premeditazione dell'assassinio Matteotti', *La Stampa*, 7/9/1924. After the war, Abbatemaggio tried and failed to get a film of the Cuocolo trial made, and was also prosecuted in 1954 for falsely claiming to have crucial information on the notorious Montesi murder case. See 'Gennaro Abbatemaggio arrestato per le sue false dichiarazioni', *La Stampa*, 24/8/1954.

Washington Times, 12/9/1910.

PART VI: MUSSOLINI'S SCALPEL

25. Sicily: The last struggle with the mafia / 31. Sicily: The slimy octopus

ASPA, Questura, Affari generali, 1935, b. 2196. Questura di Palermo. Archivio Generale b. 2196 Anno 1935. R. Ispettorato generale di PS per la Sicilia—Nucleo centrale Carabinieri reali, Processo verbale di denunzia di 175 individui responsabili di associazione per delinquere (16 luglio 1938).

Manchester Guardian. Ascension Day speech, 27/5/1927.

New York Times. 27/5/1927; 'signs of increasing megalomania', 29/5/1927.

M. Allegra, 'Come io, medico, diventai un mafioso', *Giornale di Sicilia*, 22–23/1/1962.

M. Allegra, 'La mafia mi ordinò di entrare in politica', *Giornale di Sicilia*, 23–24/1/1962.

M. Allegra, 'Tutti gli uomini della "cosca"', *Giornale di Sicilia*, 24–25/1/1962. Intriguingly, Allegra mentions Ernesto Marasà, says he has more to say about him, and then does not return to the subject.

M. Andretta, 'I corleonesi e la storia della mafia. Successo, radicamento e continuità', *Meridiana*, 54, 2005.

A. Blando, 'L'avvocato del diavolo', *Meridiana*, 63, 2008.

A. Calderone, *Gli uomini del disonore*, (ed. P. Arlacchi), Milan, 1992.

V. Coco, 'Dal passato al futuro: uno sguardo dagli anni trenta', *Meridiana*, 63, 2008.

V. Coco and M. Patti, 'Appendice', *Meridiana*, 63, 2008. A breakdown of trials following the Mori operation.

V. Coco, 'La mafia dell'agro palermitano nei processi del periodo fascista', in G. Gribaudi (ed.), *Traffici criminali. Camorra, mafie e reti internazionali dell'illegalità*, Turin, 2009.

F. Di Bartolo, 'Imbrigliare il conflitto sociale. Mafiosi, contadini, latifondisti', *Meridiana*, 63, 2008.

M. Di Figlia, 'Mafia e nuova politica fascista', *Meridiana*, 63, 2008.

C. Duggan, *Fascism and the Mafia*, New Haven, 1989. Duggan's study remains important for the context to the Mori Operation. But the book is best known for the thesis that the mafia-as-organisation was invented by Fascism as a pretext to exert political control over Sicily. That thesis was controversial at the time of publication, and it is now contradicted by a crushing weight of evidence.

S. Lupo, *Storia della mafia*, Rome, 1996. Mori 'on heat' for the nobility, quoted p. 182.

C. Mori, *The Last Struggle with the Mafia*, London, 1933.

C. Mori, *Con la mafia ai ferri corti*, Naples, 1993 (1932).

B. Mussolini, 'Discorso dell'Ascensione', 26/5/1927, in *idem*, *Opera Omnia*, ed. E. Susmel and D. Susmel, 44 vols, Florence, 1951–80, vol. 22.

M. Patti, 'Sotto processo. Le cosche palermitane', *Meridiana*, 63, 2008.

V. Scalia, 'Identità sociali e conflitti politici nell'area dell'interno', *Meridiana*, 63, 2008.

A. Spanò, *Faccia a faccia con la mafia*, Milan, 1978. For Mori's lifestyle in Palermo, p. 38.

I have estimated the extent of Marasà's wealth using www.measuringworth.com (the unskilled wage index) 1938–2009.

26. Campania: Buffalo soldiers / 30. Campania: The Fascist Vito Genovese

Comando Generale dell'Arma dei Carabinieri. Ufficio Storico, various reports from the career of Vincenzo Anceschi, including *Bollettino Ufficiale dei Carabinieri Reali* 1919 (p. 214), 1927 (p. 109), 1929 (pp. 330, 461, 585, 871), 1930 (p. 882).

E. Anceschi, *I Carabinieri reali contro la camorra*, Rome, 2003. Includes the article from *Il Mezzogiorno*, 2–3/6/1927 on which I base my description of the Mazzoni.

L. Avella, *Cronaca nolana. Dalla Monarchia alla Repubblica*, vol. 7, *1926–1943*, Naples, 2002. For the quote on Vito Genovese's donation.

F. Barbagallo, *Storia della camorra*, Rome-Bari, 2010. On 'Little Joey', pp. 86–88.

O. Bordiga, *Inchiesta parlamentare sulle condizioni dei contadini nelle provincie meridionali e nella Sicilia*, vol. IV, *Campania*, tomo I, *Relazione*, Rome 1909. On the 'tribes' of the Mazzoni.

P. Frascani, 'Mercato e commercio a Napoli dopo l'Unità', in P. Macry, and P. Villani, (eds.), *Storia d'Italia. Le regioni dall'Unità a oggi. La Campania*, Turin, 1990.

G. Gribaudi, 'Guappi, camorristi, killer. Interpretazioni letterarie, immagini sociali, e storie giudiziarie', in *Donne, uomini, famiglie*, Naples, 1999. On the *guappo*.

M. Marmo, 'Tra le carceri e il mercato. Spazi e modelli storici del fenomeno camorrista', in P. Macry and P. Villani (eds), *La Campania*, part of *Storia d'Italia. Le regioni dall'Unità a oggi*, Turin, 1990. The best starting point for the history of the camorra outside Naples itself.

P. Monzini, *Gruppi criminali a Napoli e a Marsiglia. La delinquenza organizzata nella storia di due città (1820–1990)*, Rome, 1999. On the obscure fate of the camorra after the Honoured Society, pp. 53ff.

H.S. Nelli, *The Business of Crime. Italians and Syndicate Crime in the United States*, New York, 1976. On Genovese and Fascism.

C. Petraccone, *Le "due Italie." La questione meridionale tra realtà e rappresentazione*, Rome-Bari, 2005. On Fascism's ban on 'Mezzogiorno', p. 190.

Il Mattino. The articles triggered by the Nola murders run through August and September, 1911. See esp., 9–10/8/1911 'Il brigantaggio nell'Agro nolano'; and on the 'crass ignorance' and 'bloodthirsty instincts' in the Mazzoni, 'Brigantaggio nei Mazzoni di Capua', 18–19/9/1911. I have followed Anceschi's operation in *Il Mattino* (November 1926 to May 1927).

Roma. Also contains extensive coverage of Anceschi's operation (November 1926 to June 1927). On the funeral interrupted by Anceschi's men, 1/1/1927, 'I maggiori maladrini avversani tratti in arresto mentre accompagnano in camposanto la salma del loro "capintesta"'.

27. Calabria: The flying boss of Antonimina / 28. Calabria: What does not kill me makes me stronger / 29. Calabria: A clever, forceful and wary woman / 32. Master Joe dances a *tarantella*

Overview of archival sources on the 'ndrangheta under Fascism:

ASRC:

Tribunale di Reggio Calabria, Sentenze, 6/6/1923 n. 15, Battaglia Giuseppe + 46, vol. 206.

Ditto, 1/12/1924, Callea Giovanni + 8, vol. 210.

Ditto, 18/2/1924, Calù Clemente + 25, vol. 208.

Ditto, 23/9/1924, Palamara Francesco + 6, vol. 210. A Casalnuovo-based group that decide to punish anyone who voted Fascist in the local elections. They are acquitted on the grounds of insufficient evidence.

Ditto, 15/4/1926, n. 192, Minniti Antonio, vol. 215.

Ditto, 2/8/1926 n. 395, Mafrici Stefano + 13, vol. 216.

Ditto, 7/5/1927 n. 153, De Gaetano Andrea + 28, vol. 218. Three of the accused get themselves photographed with pistols pointing at a sheet of paper and raising hands as if to take an oath. They are all acquitted.

Ditto, 29/3/1927, Schimizzi Giacomo + 64, vol. 217. In Melito the gang initiation oath emerges from insider evidence: 'before us there is a tomb covered in flowers, and he who breaches secrecy will receive five dagger blows to the chest'. The judge explains why such insider evidence often emerges: 'judicial psychology teaches us, members of criminal associations always betray one another'.

Ditto, 13/7/1928 n. 395, Bruzzaniti Giovanni + 51, vol. 224. A case in Africo where there was an upsurge in picciotteria violence after the First World War. The judge lamely blames 'social causes' and reduces the sentences on the grounds that the culprits are reformed characters.

Ditto, 19/6/1928, Putortì Vittorio +5, vol. 223.

Ditto, 14/8/1930, Passalacqua Giuseppe + 19, vol. 234. A nasty case involving the rape of a mentally handicapped prostitute.

Ditto, 26/5/1930 n. 341, Curatola Francesco, vol. 232.

Ditto, 12/6/1931 n. 524, Altomonte Carmelo + 8, vol. 238.

Ditto, 16/7/1931 n. 752, De Gaetano Domenico + 20, vol. 239. Describes a battle for territory in San Roberto (near Villa San Giovanni) between Fascists and *picciotti*. The latter have a close web of kinship and marriage ties between them.

Ditto, 6 *aprile* 1933 n. 174, Spanò Demetrio + 106, vol. senza numero *Anno* 1933—dal 15 *gennaio al* 30 *aprile*. Trial of a whole network of picciotteria groups in Reggio Calabria. The leaders pimp and extort money from junior members. A detailed picture of the organisation emerges. There is, as always, a *Società minore* and a *Società maggiore*, but the latter is further divided between the *Società in testa* a.k.a. *Gran criminale* grouped around the boss, and the *Società indrina* of which there are several based in different quarters of the city.

ASC:

Corte di Appello di Catanzaro, Sentenze, 7/6/1922, De Paola Gregorio + 11, vol. 486.

Ditto, 8/8/1923, Noto Domenico + 46, vol. 489. The flying boss.

Ditto, 14/11/1923, Alfinito Donato + 36, vol. 489. Prosecution of a group in Petronà. Two women accused of being in the *cosca* are acquitted for insufficient evidence. The boss was unseated because his wife betrayed him, ostensibly.

Ditto, 16/4/1923, Costa Salvatore + 6, vol. 488.

Ditto, 19/7/1924, Bruzzi Camillo + 18, vol. 491. From Radicena and Gioia Tauro. The gang's practice of forced initiation produces a witness for the prosecution.

Ditto, 11/3/1925, Cotela Giuseppe + 14, vol. 492. Some members admit the existence of the association, based in Serrata. Forcible enlisting of members still practised, at least according to some witnesses.

Ditto, 19/12/1925, Barbara Antonio + 35, vol. 494.

Ditto, 26/1/1925, Panucci Gesuele + 17, vol. 492.

Ditto, 22/5/1926, Fabrizio Giuseppe + 26, v. 495. Like many rulings, this one shows an organisation divided between *picciotti* and *camorristi*. Once again the evidence is from turncoats inside the group.

Ditto, 6/2/1926, Pandurri Pietro + 14, vol. 495.

Ditto, 10/2/1926, Facchineri Giuseppe + 18, vol. 495.

Ditto, 12/4/1926, Notarianni Vincenzo + 34, vol. 495. Dagger duels.

Ditto, 13/2/1926, Mascaro Camillo + 3, vol. 495.

Ditto, 17/3/1926, De Caro Vincenzo, vol. 495. A group in the ethnically Albanian village of Santa Sofia d'Epiro. The group kept women's clothes for disguise purposes.

Ditto, 26/4/1926, Albanese Domenico + 26, vol. 495. The ruling describes the disorder following demobilisation in Rosarno.

Ditto, 28/6/1926, Gullà Francesco, v. 496. Gullà, from Celico in the province of Cosenza, has ties with the Black Hand in the USA.

Ditto, 10/10/1927, Biancamaro Arturo + 6, vol. 500.

Ditto, 4/12/1928, Bumbaca Vincenzo + 45, vol. 505. One of several cases where the prosecution case fails to stand up.

Ditto, 8/6/1928, De Santis Giuseppe + 21, vol. 503.

Ditto, 9/7/1928, Lucà Luigi + 38, vol. 504. In Gioiosa Jonica the picciotteria calls itself the 'Montalbano family'.

Ditto, 12/11/1928, Speranza Stefano + 26, vol. 505.

Ditto, 17/12/1928, Cristiano Giuseppe + 13, vol. 505. The *Carabinieri* fail to produce enough evidence against this group from Staiti.

Ditto, 18/8/1928, Saccomanno Antonio + 11, vol. 504. The defendants are acquitted because, in the judge's view, the prosecution has not proved that this society was a *criminal* association, despite several confessions.

Ditto, 2/5/1929, Palermo Rinaldo + 48, vol. 507. Interesting case from Gerace in which the picciotteria extort bribes on marriages. Two wealthy members were acquitted on the flimsy grounds that 'it was implausible that they would have shady dealings with what was essentially a bunch of beggars'.

Ditto, 17/5/1929, Napoli Pasquale + 7, vol. 507. A spike in thefts follows the return of a *picciotto* from the United States.

Ditto, 25/11/1929, Gareri Domenico + 13, vol. 509.

Ditto, 26/9/1929, Romeo Stefano + 75, vol. 508. Important trial of the picciotteria in San Luca. Giuseppe Delfino uses the evidence of an informer (subsequently murdered) to dismantle the local cattle-rustling operation.

Ditto, 1/4/1930, Gullace Domenico + 20, vol. 512.

Ditto, 6/12/1930, Spanò Vincenzo + 33, vol. 517.

Ditto, 11/7/1930, Vallone Giuseppe + 6, vol. 514.

Ditto, 13/6/1930, Carioti Francesco, vol. 513.

Ditto, 15/11/1930, Corio Santo + 144, vol. 516. Several women are involved in this clan from Palmi, Gioia Tauro and Rosarno.

Ditto, 20/10/1930, Sorace Salvatore + 9, vol. 515.

Ditto, 25/11/1930, Annacorato Vincenzo + 93, vol. 516. A 'Montalbano family' in Nicotera, Polistena and Gioia Tauro. One boy is initiated at age eleven. The judge is unsurprised that most of the evidence comes from turncoats inside the picciotteria: 'It is natural that underworld trials grow from the revelations of gangsters who betray the secrets of the sect that they were affiliated to'.

Ditto, 29/11/1930, Mollica Vincenzo + 41, vol. 516.

Ditto, 29/8/1931, Ponzano Gaetano+ 10, vol. 521.

Ditto, 1/3/1932, Lupino Giovanni + 16, vol. 525.

Ditto, 25/11/1932, Argentano Menotti + 12, vol. 529.

Ditto, 12/5/1933, Piccione Francesco + 10, vol. 531.

Ditto, 21/9/1934, Pollifrone Rocco + 22, vol. 536. The picciotteria in the Locride smuggles its stolen animals to market in the Plain of Gioia Tauro.

ASC:

Corte di Assise di Catanzaro, Sentenze, 2/11/1931, Pugliese Francesco + 4, vol. 62.

Ditto, 21/5/1932, Rosello Francesco + 2, vol. 63. A *Carabiniere* is murdered for trying to prevent an underworld marriage alliance. He may have got too close to one of the factions involved.

ASC:

Corte di Assise di Locri, Sentenze, 2/2/1933, Andrianò Vincenzo + 8, b. 1.

Ditto, 19/7/1937, Commisso Francescantonio + 56, b. 3. The boss rules that a man spreading rumours about his wife must die, and orders a sixteen-year-old boy to perform the deed.

Ditto, 8/2/1938, Oppedisano Francesco + 5, b. 3.

Ditto, 6/9/1939, Macrì Francesco + 141, b. 4. The case involving Maria Marvelli.

Ditto, 9/2/1939, Canario Vincenzo + 26, b. 4.

ASC:

Corte di Assise di Palmi, Sentenze, 11/6/1937, Vicari Francesco, b. 3.

Ditto, 18/3/1937, Romeo Procopio + 2, b. 3. A butcher in a *frazione* of Oppido Mamertina is hit by shotgun pellets in the thighs, genitals, scrotum, penis and left hand while excreting in an olive grove. There follows a chain of attacks that the judge puts down to family rivalries.

Ditto, 6/12/1938, Vinci Alfonso + 10, b. 3. Acquittals despite an outbreak of razor slashes to the face in Cittanova.

Ditto, 8/4/1938, Corso Rocco + 1, b. 3.

Ditto, 7/3/1940, Barone Michele + 37, b. 4. The gang, under the leadership of Michele Barone convicted of smothering an old lady in her bed and throwing a prostitute off a bridge, seems not to have been part of the picciotteria, despite operating in the classic 'ndrangheta territories of Polistena and Taurianova.

ASC:

Gabinetto di prefettura, Affari gen. e disposizioni riguardanti la P.S.—b. 14. On the picciotteria that has 'almost been crushed', see letter from chief of police to the Prefect, 21/11/1931.

Gabinetto di prefettura, Ordine Pubblico—b. 609.

Ufficio Storico Stato Maggiore Aeronautica (USSMA), Fondo aviatori Grande Guerra, b. 132, fasc. 14. Noto Domenico. The flying boss's war record.

Comando Generale dell'Arma dei Carabinieri. Ufficio Storico, various documents on the career of Giuseppe Delfino including: *Bollettino Ufficiale dei Carabinieri Reali* 1911 (p. 289), 1919 (p. 285), 1927 (p. 104); Comune di San Luca, 'Deliberazione del consiglio comunale', 4/12/1915 and another dated 14/7/1921; Partito Nazionale Fascista, Sezione de Platì, 'Deliberazione', 20/12/1926; letter from the Procuratore del Re, Gerace Marina, 3/6/1929.

Cronaca di Calabria. Has low-key coverage of the picciotteria during the early Fascist years, 1922–28. On the actions of Giuseppe Delfino, see 'Vasta associazione a delinquere', 8/12/1927.

Gazzetta di Messina e delle Calabrie, 1924–27. On Giuseppe Delfino's tireless work, see, 'Da Platì. Un maresciallo dei carabinieri che si fa onore', 3/4/1927.

G. Buccini, 'I due Delfino, carabinieri, e i boss Nirta: un'epopea a Platì', *Corriere della Sera*, 16/10/1993. Delfino family lore.

L. Malafarina, 'La leggenda di Massaro Peppe', *Gazzetta del Sud*, 9/9/1986. An interview with Delfino's son.

P. Bevilacqua, *Le campagne del Mezzogiorno tra Fascismo e dopoguerra. Il caso della Calabria*, Turin, 1980.

V. Cappelli, *Il fascismo in periferia. La Calabria durante il Ventennio*, Lungro di Cosenza, 1998.

F. Cordova, *Il fascismo nel Mezzogiorno: le Calabrie*, Soveria Mannelli, 2003.

L. Izzo, *Agricoltura e classi rurali in Calabria dall'Unità al Fascismo*, Geneva, 1974.

E. Miséfari, *L'avvento del fascismo in Calabria*, Cosenza, 1980. On 'acute factionitis', p. 116.

A. Placanica, *Storia della Calabria*, Rome, 1999 (1993).

J. Steinberg, 'Fascism in the Italian South: the case of Calabria', in D. Forgacs (ed.), *Rethinking Italian Fascism. Capitalism, Populism and Culture*, London, 1986.

33. Liberation

ASRC, Tribunale di Locri, Sentenza 20/3/1937, Macrì Antonio + 12, vol. 286. Don 'Ntoni has one of his early brushes with the law.

La mafia a Montalto. Sentenza 2 ottobre 1970 del Tribunale di Locri, Reggio Calabria, 1971. Includes a detailed criminal profile of don 'Ntoni Macrì.

National Archive, London

Italy. Zone Handbook Sicily. WO 220/277.

Italy. Zone Handbook no. 3. Calabria. WO 220/278.

Italy. Zone Handbook no. 6. Campania. WO 252/804.

WO 204/9719, Sicily and southern Italy: reports on social, economic and political aspects of provincial living conditions. 1943 Oct–1944 Jan. Includes Lord Rennell's report from Calabria.

WO 204/11462, Psychological Warfare Branch. PWB and OSS activities reports. 1944 Dec–1945 May. Includes accounts of food riots in traditional picciotteria areas but no mention of gang activity.

WO 204/12625, Italy. Political situation. Naples and Campania. For figures on prostitution in Naples see the report reviewing the situation since Liberation, dated 19/4/1945. On the food supply from the hinterland see report dated 2/5/1945.

WO 204/12627, Italy. Political situation. Naples and Campania. On the 'fantastic gangland situation' in the hinterland north of the city see report of 21/2/1946 .

WO 204/6313, Psychological Warfare Branch. Naples: weekly reports on economic and political conditions. 1944 Apr.–Aug. Report dated 3/5/1944 on the police cut on goods coming out of the port, and on the main black market sales points in the city. Report of 23/6/1944 on the problems of those on fixed incomes. Report of 30/6/1944 on class distinctions disappearing.

WO 204/6314, Psychological Warfare Branch. Naples: weekly reports on economic and political conditions. 1944 Aug.–Oct. Report of 16/8/1944 on two kinds of spaghetti. Report of 28/9/1944 on the inactivity of the Military Police. Report of 5/10/1944 on the old crone tipping a bank clerk for counting her money. Report of 26/10/1944 (interview with woman) for the role of street-corner bosses.

WO 204/6315, Psychological Warfare Branch. Naples: weekly reports on economic and political conditions. 1944 Nov.–1945 Jan. Report of 23/11/1944 on a Casoria gang that stages train robberies between Rome and Naples.

WO 204/6277, Psychological Warfare Branch. Italy: reports on conditions in liberated areas. 1944 Jan.–Mar. Report of 28/3/1944 on the Caputos sentenced to seven years.

C. Alvaro, 'Il canto di Cosima', in idem, L'amata alla finestra, Milan, 1994.

F. Barbagallo, Storia della camorra, Rome-Bari, 2010. On the Giuliano boys in Forcella, p. 103.

E. Ciconte, 'Ndrangheta dall'Unità a oggi, Rome-Bari, 1992. On mafia mayors and what little we know about this under-researched period of 'ndrangheta history, pp. 239–44.

E. Ciconte, Storia criminale. La resistibile ascesa di mafia, 'ndrangheta e camorra dall'Ottocento ai giorni nostri, Soveria Mannelli, 2008. On Delfino pp. 283–4.

D. Ellwood, Italy 1943–1945, Leicester, 1985. Also quotes Lord Rennell on mayors from an 'American gangster environment', p. 59.

N. Gentile, *Vita di capomafia*, Rome, 1993.

A. Gramsci, *Lettere dal carcere*, Turin, 1947. For an example of the prison gangs as viewed by a political prisoner under Fascism. When Antonio Gramsci, the founding member and leader of the Italian Communist Party, was jailed by Mussolini, he witnessed a camorra initiation in a Naples prison. He also saw a 'fencing academy' and a friendly duelling tournament conducted according to the rules of what he termed the 'four realms of the southern Italian underworld (the Sicilian realm, the Calabrian realm, the Puglian realm, and the Neapolitan realm)'. The weapons, in this case, were harmless: spoons rubbed against the wall so that whitewash marked hits on the duellers' clothing. But even so, the rivalry between Sicilians and Calabrians was so intense that they did not even fight with spoons in case the battle escalated. See particularly the letter dated 11/4/1927.

J. Huston, *An Open Book*, London, 1988 (1980).

N. Lewis, *Naples '44*, London, 2002 (1978). I have used Lewis's classic work of reportage here, but sparingly. After reading the manuscript notes upon which the text is based, I felt that the references to the '*zona di camorra*' in *Naples '44* were not sufficiently reliable to be used as historical evidence, and that they may well have been a product of literary licence based on Lewis's later visits to Naples and his encounters with films such as *La sfida*.

C. Malaparte, *La pelle*, Rome-Milan, 1950. 'Two dollars the boys, three dollars the girls!' p. 19.

T. Newark, *The Mafia at War: Allied collusion with the mob*, London, 2007. Quotes the OSS report ('theirs for the asking', dated 13/8/1943), pp. 209–10. On 45 per cent of Allied military cargo stolen, Newark quotes the report from Allied Civil Affairs to the War Cabinet in London 19/4/1944 (National Archive, MAF 83/1338), p. 217.

V. Paliotti, *Forcella. La Casbah di Napoli*, Naples, 2005.

E. Reid, *Mafia*, revised edn, New York, 1964. Reproduces Dickey's testimony, pp. 163–89.

C. Stajano, *Africo*, 1979. On Delfino's dancing.

'Lord Rennell', obituary in *The Geographical Journal*, vol. 144, No. 2 (July 1978).

PART VII: FUGGEDABOUTIT

34. Sicily: Banditry, land and politics

V. Coco and M. Patti, *Relazioni mafiose. La mafia ai tempi del fascismo*, Rome, 2010.

S. Di Matteo, *Anni roventi. La Sicilia dal 1943 al 1947*, Palermo, 1967.

D. Ellwood, *Italy 1943–1945*, Leicester, 1985.

N. Gentile, *Vita di capomafia*, Rome, 1993.

F.M. Guercio, *Sicily. The Garden of the Mediterranean. The Country and its People*, London, 1938. See pp. 64, 88 for the proclamations of the Sicilian canker's demise.

R. Mangiameli, 'La regione in guerra', in M. Aymard and G. Giarrizzo (eds), *La Sicilia, Storia d'Italia. Le regioni dall'Unità a oggi*, Turin, 1987.

P. Pezzino, *Mafia: Industria della violenza*, Florence, 1995. The October 1946 report on the 'occult organisation' is by *Carabinieri* General Amedeo Branca to the Comando Generale dell'Arma, and is reproduced on pp. 190–91.

U. Santino, *Storia del movimento antimafia. Dalla lotta di classe all'impegno civile*, Rome, 2009 (updated edn). On the Santangelo brothers and other aspects of the mafia's political atrocities in this period.

A. Spanò, *Faccia a faccia con la mafia*, Milan, 1978. 'The mafia has never been as powerful and organised as it is today', p. 130.

The Scotten report on the mafia is in the National Archives, FO 371/37327.

Meridiana, 63, 2008. Monographic issue on *Mafia e fascismo*.

New York Times, 'Mafia chiefs caught by Allies in Sicily', 10/9/1943; 'Mafia in Sicily', 11/9/1943.

35. Sicily: *In the Name of the Law*

O. Barrese, *I complici. Gli anni dell'antimafia*, Milan, 1978. The quotation from Scelba is on p. 7.

A. Blando, 'L'avvocato del diavolo', *Meridiana*, 63, 2008.

Dizionario biografico dei meridionali, vol. 2, Naples, 1974, 'Lo Schiavo Giuseppe Guido'.

D. Forgacs, *Rome, Open City*, London, 2000. André Bazin's famous 1946 quotation about the 'skin of History peels off as film' is discussed on p. 23.

E. Giacovelli, *Pietro Germi*, Rome, 1991.

G.G. Lo Schiavo, 'La redenzione sociale nelle opere del Regime', *Politica Sociale*, X, August, 1937.

G.G. Lo Schiavo, *Piccola pretura*, Rome, 1948. The quote comparing the mafia boss to Buddha is on p. 114. The novel would go on to form part of a trilogy of novels with equally questionable visions of the mafia. The trilogy was published together as *Terra amara* (Rome, 1956). The other two episodes in it are *Condotta di paese* (1952) and *Gli inesorabili* (1950). This latter novel was turned into an alarmingly bad film of the same name (dir. Camillo Mastrocinque, 1950), which was issued in the United States as *The Fighting Men* and can be viewed at http://archive.org/details/fighting_men. Charles Vanel reprises his role as a mafia boss—this time as a caped righter of wrongs: 'we protect all honest people'.

G.G. Lo Schiavo, 'Nel regno della mafia', *Processi*, 5, 1955. Contains Lo Schiavo's fond recollections of Calogero Vizzini.

G.G. Lo Schiavo, *100 anni di mafia*, Rome, 1962. Contains many of Lo Schiavo's writings, including his original 1933 response to Puglia, 'La mafia siciliana', with the addition of some very strange new footnotes in which he tries to wriggle out of his earlier opinions.

G.G. Lo Schiavo, 'Il cinema alla luce del costume e della libertà', Trieste, 1963 (extract from *L'osservatore economico e sociale*, V, 1). Also contains biographical information.

G.G. Lo Schiavo, 'La mafia della lupara e quella dei colletti bianchi', *Nuovi Quaderni del Meridione*, 4, 1963.

L. Sciascia, 'La Sicilia nel cinema' in *La corda pazza*, Turin, 1970.

M. Sesti (ed.), *Signore e signori: Pietro Germi*, Siena, 2004.

V. Spinazzola, *Cinema e pubblico. Lo spettacolo filmico in Italia 1945–1965*, Rome, 1985.

In nome della legge (dir. Pietro Germi), 1949, is available on DVD from Cristaldi Film and on YouTube.

36. Calabria: The last romantic bandit

C. Cingari, 'Tra brigantaggio e "picciotteria": Giuseppe Musolino', in *Brigantaggio, proprietari e contadini nel Sud*, Reggio Calabria, 1976.

G.G. Lo Schiavo, *100 anni di mafia*, Rome, 1962. Reproduces 'Requisitoria del Sostituto Procuratore Generale del Re dr. Vittorio Barbera' (Messina, 27/2/1932) in the case against Anile Giuseppantonio + 89: on the Criminale.

A. Sapone, *Sant'Alessio in Aspromonte. Uomini e storie dell'antico Casale di Alessi*, Reggio Calabria, 2001.

F. Truzzolillo, '"Criminale" e "Gran Criminale." La struttura unitaria e verticistica della 'ndrangheta delle origini', *Meridiana*, 77, 2013.

Crescenzo Guarino was the journalist who wrote about the aged Musolino most often, such as in the following articles: 'A colloquio con Musolino', *La Stampa*, 16/1/1950; 'La manìa di grandezza del brigante Musolino', *Stampa Sera*, 18–19/1/1950; 'Una poesia inedita di Pascoli per il brigante dell'Aspromonte', *Il Mattino*, 3/7/1955; 'Arde sempre in Musolino la fiamma della vendetta', *Il Mattino*, 5/7/1955; 'È morto il brigante Musolino', *La Stampa*, 24/1/1956; 'L'ultimo "brigante romantico" viveva tra i fantasmi del passato', *Stampa Sera*, 24/1/1956.

The key archival material on Musolino is in the Archivio di Stato di Reggio Calabria: Gabinetto di Prefettura, n. 1089, Associazione a delinquere in S. Stefano, b. 27, inv. 34; and Gabinetto di Prefettura, Serie prima, affari riservati. Bandito Musolino.

37. Naples: Puppets and puppeteers

P.A. Allum, *Politics and Society in Post-war Naples*, Cambridge, 1973.

'Camorra', in *Enciclopedia Italiana*, VIII, BUC–CARD, Milan, 1930.

M. Figurato and F. Marolda, *Storia di contrabbando. Napoli 1945–1981*, Naples, 1981.

G. Gribaudi, *Donne, uomini, famiglie. Napoli nel Novecento*, Naples, 1999.

G. Gribaudi, 'Les rites et les langages de l'échange politique. Deux exemples napolitains', in D. Cefaï (ed.), *Cultures politiques*, Paris, 2001. Very insightful on Navarra.

M. Marmo, '"Processi indiziari non se ne dovrebbero mai fare." Le manipolazioni del processo Cuocolo (1906–1930)', in M. Marmo and L. Musella (eds), *La costruzione della verità giudiziaria*, Naples, 2003. On the trial that destroyed the Honoured Society of Naples.

G. Marotta, *San Gennaro non dice mai no*, Milan, 1948, especially 'I "pupanti"' on puppets, 'Re Giuseppe' on Giuseppe Navarra.

G. Marotta, 'L'angelo degli autocarri', *La Stampa*, 13/10/1953, on the *correntisti*.

L. Musella, *Napoli dall'Unità a oggi*, Rome, 2010. A short history of Naples that is rich in ideas for several periods including this one.

'Feroce delitto in Sezione Vicaria. Ucciso un giovane con due coltellate da un camorrista in via A. Poerio', *Il Mattino* 13/7/52. On the murder by *'O Grifone*. His story is followed up over the following days in the same newspaper.

'La caccia ai "correntisti." Drammatico inseguimento per i vicoli del Mercato', *Il Mattino*, 1/8/52. For the quotation on the 'fluid' *corrente*.

Gennaro Abbatemaggio was an intermittent presence in the northern press throughout the 1950s. See for example: 'Lauro sorpreso a Napoli a strappare manifesti', *La Stampa*, 25/5/1952, on Abbatemaggio working for Achille Lauro; 'Il piccolo e feroce uomo dai baffi neri all'insù', *Stampa Sera*, 4/7/1952; 'Gennaro Abbatemaggio fa la prima comunione', *La Stampa*, 4/7/1952; 'Gennaro Abbatemaggio arrestato per le sue false dichiarazioni', *La Stampa*, 24/8/1954; 'Don Gennaro Abbatemaggio derubato da un borsaiolo', *La Stampa*, 24/7/1958; 'Abbatemaggio chiede di esibirsi al Musichiere', *La Stampa*, 9/1/1959; 'Gennaro Abbatemaggio promette sensazionali rivelazioni sulla camorra', *La Stampa*, 22/4/1959.

'Incontro c' 'o rre', Paolo Monelli, *Nuova Stampa Sera*, 30/9/1947, one of many portraits of Navarra in the press; this one includes the quotation about his Bourbon nose.

Navarra was interviewed on 6/3/1952 on the TV programme *La Settimana Incom*, and the interview can be seen via the Istituto Luce archive website: 'Intervista con il Re di Poggio Reale'.

'Il Tesoro di S. Gennaro trasportato a Napoli dal "Re di Poggioreale"', *Roma d'Oggi*, 7/3/1947. 'Il fortunoso viaggio del tesoro di S. Gennaro', *Roma d'Oggi*, 8/3/1947. These are the only press articles I can find on the Navarra San Gennaro story that date from when the event is supposed to have happened.

38. *Gangsterismo*

H. Erickson, *Encyclopedia of Television Law Shows: Factual and fictional series about judges, lawyers and the courtroom, 1948–2008*, Jefferson, N.C., 2009.

S. Gundle, 'L'americanizzazione del quotidiano. Televisione e consumismo nell'Italia degli anni Cinquanta', *Quaderni Storici*, vol. XXI (1986), p. 62. I could not avoid citing the most cited article in contemporary Italian studies!

E. Kefauver, *Crime in America*, New York, 1968 (original edn 1951). Quotations taken from pp. 14–21. (Published as *Il gangsterismo in America*, Turin, 1953.)

W.H. Moore, *The Kefauver Committee and the Politics of Crime, 1950–1952*, Columbia, 1974. The seagull death rattle quote is on p. 190 from a newspaper source.

G. Prezzolini, 'Una catena di delitti nei più ricchi docks del mondo', *Stampa Sera*, 11–12/2/1953.

G. Prezzolini, 'La "mafia" nel rapporto del senator Kefauver', in *America con gli stivali*, Florence, 1954.

G. Prezzolini, *Tutta l'America*, Florence, 1958, for Italy's borrowings from America.

'Sfilano gli "eroi" della democrazia americana', *L'Unità*, 7/4/1951.

PART VIII: 1955

39. The Monster of Presinaci

S. Castagna, *Tu devi uccidere*, Milan, 1967 (and Vibo Valentia, 2008). The contents of this memoir were widely reported in the press in 1955.

E. Ciconte, *'Ndrangheta dall'Unità a oggi*, Rome, 1992. On the 'Martians' see p. 245.

C. Guarino, 'Sulla intera Calabria l'ombra dell'Aspromonte', *Il Mattino*, 13/7/1955. On the state of law and order in Calabria.

S. Lanaro, *Storia dell'Italia repubblicana: dalla fine della guerra agli anni Novanta*, Venice, 1992. The statistics on poverty are from p. 165.

The physical description of Castagna is from *L'Unità*, 21/4/1955, and the 'problematic' existence of the Calabrian mafia is from *L'Unità*, 26/4/1955. The same paper provides detailed coverage of Castagna's rampage.

Aloi letter dated 16/4/1955 in ACS, Min. Int., Gabinetto, 1953–56, b. 4, fasc. 1066–1.

Prefect's report dated 14/5/1955 in *ibid.*, b. 4, fasc. 1066–1.

40. Mars attacks!

The archival sources I have consulted on the Marzano Operation are the following:

ACS, Min. Int., Gabinetto, 1953–56, b. 4, fasc. 1066–1.

Ibid. (hereafter 'ACS Marzano'), b. 4, fasc. 1066–2.

Ibid., b. 293, fascc. 5160–23.

Ibid., b. 352, fascc. 6995–23.

Ibid., b. 363, fascc. 6995–66.

Report by Marzano to Min. Int. dated 6/9/55 in ACS Marzano, b. 4, fasc. 1066–2 for 'literally in the grip of terror' and further details of Marzano's work.

ACS Marzano: telegram 3/9/54 in b. 4, fasc. 1066–1, aftermath of Polsi pilgrimage the year before; telegram, 2/9/55 in b. 4, fasc. 1066–1, pilgrimage without incident; telegram 26/10/55 b. 4, fasc. 1066–1, arrest of Aloi blackmailers; telegram 25/9/55 in b. 4, fasc. 1066–1, identity card forger; prefect's telegram 19/9/55, b. 4, fasc. 1066–2, Marzano solo operation; letter 30/9/55 from Marzano to Tambroni. b. 4, fasc. 1066–2, Marzano's 'toadying' dispatch.

Capua story: report by prefect dated 4/1/56 in ACS Marzano, b. 363, fascc. 6995–66.

Capua's friendships with gangsters: prefect's report 20/9/55 in b. 4, fasc. 1066–2.

Catalano: see prefect's report to Min. Int. 28/10/55 in b. 4, fasc. 1066–2.

On raiding a house and finding notebook containing the 'ndrangheta's rules, see telegraph dated 29/5/1955, ACS Marzano, b. 4, fasc. 1066–1.

Some indications on the longer term ineffectiveness of the Marzano Operation can be gleaned from ACS, Min. Int. Gab. 1957–60, b. 4, fasc. 11001/66, 'Relazioni prefetto Reggio Calabria 1957–60'.

G. Bocca, 'Delianova Paese del West', *L'Europeo*, 11/09/1955.

G. Cervigni, 'Antologia della fibbia', *Nord e Sud*, 18, 1956, quotes Tambroni on 'showing no favours', p. 66, and the pastoral letter from the Archbishop of Reggio Calabria, p. 65.

E. Ciconte, *'Ndrangheta dall'Unità a oggi*, Rome, 1992, on the Marzano Operation is essential reading for the whole episode. See particularly: sheets to warn of danger, p. 251; 'either you vote DC or I kill you', p. 273.

L. Radi, *Tambroni trent'anni dopo. Il luglio 1960 e la nascita del centrosinistra*, Bologna, 1990.

Il Mattino provides interesting coverage of the whole Marzano Operation, such as 'Nella zona dell'Aspromonte non esistono più "intoccabili"', 7/9/1955, on Romeo.

Sources on Corrado Alvaro:

C. Alvaro, 'La gran cuccagna degli usurai sul cumulo di antiche miserie', *La Stampa*, 30/11/1949: denies existence of Calabrian mafia.

C. Alvaro, 'I briganti', *Corriere della Sera*, 18/5/1955.

C. Alvaro, 'La Fibbia', *Corriere della Sera*, 17/9/1955.

C. Alvaro, *Ultimo Diaro (1948–56)*, Bompiani, Milan, 1959, for his memories of the 'ndrangheta including, intriguingly, the failure to elect the 'capo della provincia' in 1948. The same episode is treated in the fictional (?) short story 'Angelino' from *Parole di notte*, in C. Alvaro, *Opere, Romanzi brevi e racconti, Settantacinque racconti* (1955), Milan, 1994.

A. Balduino, *Corrado Alvaro*, Milan, 1965.

G. Carteri, *Corrado Alvaro e la Madonna di Polsi*, Soveria Mannelli, 1995.

G. Cingari, *La 'politica' di Corrado Alvaro*, Rome, 1978, especially S. Staiti, 'Un incontro con Alvaro', which reports Alvaro as saying during the Marzano Operation that the Calabrian mafia, unlike the Sicilian, was 'un'autentica forma di cavalleria', p. 108.

A.M. Morace and A. Zappia (eds), *Corrado Alvaro*, Reggio Calabria, 2002.

L. Vento, *La personalità e l'opera di Corrado Alvaro*, Chiaravalle Centrale, 1979.

Sources on Nicola D'Agostino, the left-wing mayor of Canolo associated with organised crime (D'Agostino's son took part in the Montalto summit and was shot dead in 1976):

ACS, Min. Int., Direzione Generale Pubblica Sicurezza, Divisione Polizia Giudiziaria, Confino di Polizia e Confino Speciale per mafiosi (sez. II) 1945–56, D'Agostino Nicola, b. 4.

E. Ciconte, *'Ndrangheta dall'Unità a oggi*, Rome, 1992, pp. 265ff.

U. D'Errico, *Criminalità organizzata e politica in Calabria fra XIX e XX secolo*, Università degli Studi di Roma 'La Sapienza', Facoltà di Lettere e Filosofia – Corso di Laurea in Lettere, Cattedra di Storia Contemporanea (degree thesis), 2009.

A. Fiumanò and R. Villari, 'Politica e malavita ("L'operazione Marzano")', *Cronache meridionali*, II, 10, 1955.

N. Gratteri and A. Nicaso, *Fratelli di sangue*, Milan, 2010, on the D'Agostino clan.

E.J. Hobsbawm, *Primitive Rebels. Studies in Archaic Forms of Social Movement in the 19th and 20th Centuries*, London, 1965 (original edn 1959).

R. Longone, 'Il ministro Tambroni e il sottosegretario Capua in disaccordo nel valutare la situazione esistente nelle province calabresi', *L'Unità*, 10/9/1955.

G. Manfredi, 'Mafia e società nella fascia ionica della provincia di Reggio Calabria: il "caso" di Nicola D'Agostino', in S. Di Bella (ed.), *Mafia e potere: società civile, organizzazione mafiosa ed esercizio dei poteri nel Mezzogiorno contemporaneo*, 3 vols, Soveria Mannelli, 1983–84.

On another left-wing mayor associated with the Calabrian mafia, see the famous case of Pasquale Cavallaro from Caulonia in the following sources:

ACS, Min. Int., Dir. Gen. Pubblica Sicurezza, Divisione polizia giudiziaria, Confino per comuni e mafiosi, b. 47. Contains Fascist reports on Cavallaro's 'subversive' activities that led to his period of internal exile.

I. Ammendolia and N. Frammartino, *La repubblica rossa di Caulonia*, Reggio Calabria, 1975.

A. Cavallaro, *La rivoluzione di Caulonia*, Milan, 1987.

A. Cavallaro, *Operazione 'armi ai partigiani'. I segreti del Pci e la Repubblica di Caulonia*, Soveria Mannelli, 2009.

E. Ciconte, *All'assalto delle terre del latifondo. Comunisti e movimento contadino in Calabria (1943–1949)*, Milan, 1981.

P. Cinanni, *Lotte per la terra e comunisti in Calabria (1943–1953): 'Terre pubbliche' e Mezzogiorno,* Milan, 1977.

P. Crupi, *La repubblica rossa di Caulonia. Una rivoluzione tradita?*, Reggio Calabria, 1977.

G. De Stefano, 'La "repubblica di Caulonia"', *Il Ponte*, 1950.

O.R. Di Landro, *Caulonia. Dal fascismo alla repubblica*, Reggio Calabria, 1983.

A. Fiumanò and R. Villari, 'Politica e malavita ("L'operazione Marzano")', *Cronache meridionali*, II, 10, 1955.

S. Gambino, *In fitte schiere*, Chiaravalle, 1981.

G. Mercuri, *Cavallaro e la repubblica di Caulonia*, Catanzaro, 1982.

S. Misiani, *La Repubblica di Caulonia*, Soveria Mannelli, 1994.

A. Paparazzo, 'Lotte contadine e comportamenti culturali delle classi subalterne. Il caso della rivolta di Caulonia' in M. Alcaro and A. Paparazzo (eds), *Lotte contadine in Calabria (1943–1950)*, Lerici, 1976.

V. Teti, 'La "banda" di Cavallaro', *Quaderni del Mezzogiorno e le Isole*, November, 1977.

Other documentation from the Fascist era on Cavallaro is in ACS, Min. Int., Dir. gen. amministrazione civile, Podestà e consulte municipali, Reggio Calabria, Caulonia, b. 241.

41. The President of Potato Prices (and his widow)

Il Mattino is the main contemporary source for my narrative from the time of both the murder and the trial. Like Marmo, I found Etta Comito's articles very perceptive.

Federico Frascani wrote two articles that are important for understanding the role of the President of Prices: 'Due testimoni importanti', 14/4/1959; and 'Svelato il retroscena del mercato ortofrutticolo', 15/4/1959. For the trial more generally, see: E. Marcucci, 'Le lettere di Pupetta al fidanzato "Pascalone"', 14/4/1959, 'My nice Tarzan'; 'Drammatico confronto tra Pupetta e l'autista "Sansone"', 10/4/1959, 'You are all lying here'; E. Comito, 'Due mani nervose ed un fazzoletto', 9/4/1959; 'Pascalone confidò anche allo zio i nomi dei presunti mandanti', 22/4/1959, on 'Yul Brynner'; for the other figures of the trial and Gaetano Orlando, see various articles on 1/4/1959.

I supplemented *Il Mattino* with articles from other dailies from the period, such as 'Pupetta maresca piange e svela i segreti di spietate rivalità', *La Stampa*, 5/4/1959, 'I killed for love'.

S. Gambino, *La mafia in Calabria*, Reggio Calabria, 1975. On the wholesale markets in Calabrian towns.

C. Guarino, 'Dai mafiosi ai camorristi', *Nord e Sud*, 13, 1955, provides figures for the trade in fruit and vegetables through the market.

S. Lanaro, *Storia dell'Italia repubblicana: dalla fine della guerra agli anni Novanta*, Venice, 1992, on the recovering economy.

M. Marmo, 'La rima amore/onore di Pupetta Maresca. Una primadonna nella camorra degli anni cinquanta', *Meridiana*, 67, 2010. By far the most insightful source on Pupetta.

P. Ricci, 'La gran mamma. 150 anni di malavita napoletana', *Vie Nuove*, 1959, nos. 16–23.

I. Sales, 'La sfida: il mercato ortofrutticolo', in *Le strade della violenza. Malviventi e bande di camorra a Napoli*, Naples, 2006.

R. Trionfera, 'Sparava con due pistole per vendicare il marito', *L'Europeo*, 16/10/1955.

G. Tutino, 'Camorra 1957', *Nord e Sud*, 37, 1957. Including on the cattle market in Nola.

The Pupetta affair also seems to have coincided with an increased interest in the so-called *magliari*: 'Più di cento corone da ieri in via Baldacchini', *Il Mattino*, 21/7/1955; 'Un carro a dieci cavalli per il "magliaro" Pasquale Balsello', *Il Mattino*, 22/7/55; 'Rivalità, rancori e vendette alla base del nuovo delitto dei "magliari"', *Il Mattino*, 8/7/1955; I. Montanelli, 'Le sorprendenti risorse dei famigerati "magliari"', *Corriere della Sera*, 8/10/1959.

PART IX: THE MAFIAS' ECONOMIC MIRACLE

42. King Concrete

J. Chubb, *Patronage, Power and Poverty in Southern Italy*, Cambridge, 1982. On Naples and Palermo, the Young Turks and Ciccio Vassallo. 'State parasitism and organized waste', quoted by Chubb, p. 32 from A. Statera, 'Chi semina miliardi raccoglie onorevoli', *L'Espresso*, 23/6/1974.

V. Coco and M. Patti, *Relazioni mafiose. La mafia ai tempi del fascismo*, Rome, 2010. On Salvo Lima's father, p. 35.

L. D'Antone, *Senza pedaggio. Storia dell'autostrada Salerno–Reggio Calabria*, Rome, 2008.

P. Ginsborg, *A History of Contemporary Italy. Society and Politics, 1943–1988*, London, 1990. On the miracle.

Mafia e potere politico. Relazione di minoranza e proposte unitarie della commissione parlamentare d'inchiesta sulla mafia, Rome, 1976. On Ciccio Vassallo pp. 62ff.

F. Rosso, 'Gli spietati clan di Sicilia', *La Stampa*, 14/3/1976. On Vassallo's life and the Riccobono family.

U. Santino and G. La Fiura, *L'impresa mafiosa*, Milan, 1990. On Ciccio Vassallo, pp. 128ff.

J. Walston, *The Mafia and Clientelism: Roads to Rome in post-war Calabria*, London/ New York, 1988.

'Relazione sulle risultanze acquisite nel corso dell'ispezione straordinaria svolto presso il comune di Palermo dal dottor Tommaso Bevivino', in Documentazione antimafia, vol. IV, tomo VI.

'Don Ciccio Vassallo impassibile attende "un colpo di telefono"', *Stampa Sera*, 10/6/1971 for the view from Monte Pellegrino.

'Cade colpito da due rivoltellate mentre torna dal brindisi di capodanno', *Stampa Sera*, 2/1/1956. On Calabrian flower-pickers.

'Avrebbe movente politico l'aggressione al segretario della dc di Bardonecchia', *Stampa Sera*, 3/9/1963. This and other articles in September 1963 from *La Stampa* describe the Corino attack.

'Ora c'è la mafia delle autostrade', *La Stampa*, 3/3/1970. 'When northern entrepreneurs come down to Calabria'.

Bardonecchia has become something of a classic case of mafia expansion, thanks to two excellent accounts that I have drawn on here:

R. Sciarrone, *Mafie nuove, mafie vecchie. Radicamento ed espansione*, Rome, 1998. 'We are the root of everything here', quoted p. 267.

F. Varese, *Mafias on the Move: How Organized Crime Conquers New Territories*, Princeton, NJ, 2011.

43. Gangsters and blondes

G. Dagel Caponi, *Paul Bowles. Romantic Savage*, Carbondale, Ill., 1994. 'I think all Europe's black-market profiteers are here', p. 146.

V. De Sica, *Lettere dal set*, Milan, 1987.

G. Diana, 'La storia del tabacco in Italia', *Il Tabacco*, from issue 7(2), 1999. Five articles downloadable from the website of the Istituto Nazionale di Economia Agraria, http://www1.inea.it/ist/lista.htm.

M. Figurato and F. Marolda, *Storia di contrabbando. Napoli 1945–1981*, Naples, 1981.

M. Gershovich, *French Military Rule in Morocco. Colonialism and its Consequences*, London, 2000.

N. Guarino, 'Sigarette di contrabbando: il traffico illecito di tabacchi a Napoli dal dopoguerra agli anni novanta', in G. Gribaudi (ed.), *Traffici criminali. Camorra, mafie e reti internazionali dell'illegalità*, Turin, 2009.

S. Gundle, *Bellissima: feminine beauty and the idea of Italy*, New Haven, Conn./London, 2007.

V. Paliotti, *Forcella, la kasbah di Napoli*, Naples, 1970.

C.R. Pennell, *Morocco since 1830. A History*, London, 2000.

L. Vaidon, *Tangier. A Different Way*, Metuchen, NJ, 1977.

'Graziata la donna che ogni anno diventava madre per evitare il carcere', *La Stampa*, 23/01/1958.

44. Cosa Nostra: Untouchables no more

P. Arlacchi, *Addio Cosa Nostra. La vita di Tommaso Buscetta*, Milan, 1994. 'Realm of incomplete speech', pp. 84–5.

L. Bernstein, *The Greatest Menace. Organized Crime in Cold War America*, Boston, 2002. 'The intermarriages are significant', Federal Bureau of Narcotics agent Martin Pera, quoted p. 138; figures for organised crime indictments, p. 171.

R.F. Kennedy, *The Enemy Within*, New York, 1960.

S. Lupo, *Quando la mafia trovò l'America. Storia di un intreccio intercontinentale, 1888–2008*, Turin, 2008.

45. Mafia diaspora

A. Calderone with P. Arlacchi, *Gli uomini del disonore*, Milan, 1992. 'After 1963 Cosa Nostra in the Palermo area didn't exist anymore', p. 72.

L. Gay, 'L'atteggiarsi delle associazioni mafiose sulla base delle esperienze processuali acquisite: la camorra', *Quaderni del Consiglio Superiore della Magistratura*, 99, 1996.

P. La Torre, *Comunisti e movimento contadino in Sicilia*, Rome, 1980.

S. Lodato, *Venti anni di mafia*, Milan, 1999. 'What's that? A brand of cheese?', p. 48.

S. Lupo, *Storia della mafia*, Rome, 1993.

P. Pezzino, *Mafia: Industria della violenza*, Florence, 1995.

F. Renda, *Storia della mafia*, Palermo, 1997.

W. Semeraro, 'Lo scandalo di Agrigento impallidisce dinanzi ai fatti che abbiamo in archivio', *Giornale di Sicilia*, 6/8/1966. 'The mafia in Sicily is a mental state'.

N. Tranfaglia, *Mafia, politica, affari*, Rome–Bari, 1992. Extracts from the final reports of the Parliamentary Commission of Inquiry quoted p. 55, p. 154.

'Dichiarazione del compagno La Torre', *L'Unità*, 1/7/1963. 'The truth is that there is no sector of the economy . . . '.

46. The mafia-isation of the camorra

P. Arlacchi, *Addio Cosa Nostra. La vita di Tommaso Buscetta*, Milan, 1994. 'Now we'd reached as many as 35–40,000 cases', p. 183; 'fraudster mentality' 'to play it sly', p. 185.

F. Barbagallo, *Il potere della camorra (1973–1998)*, Turin, 1999. On Zaza's turnover, p. 7.

A. Calderone with P. Arlacchi, *Gli uomini del disonore*, Milan, 1992.

P. Monzini, *Gruppi criminali a Napoli e a Marsiglia. La delinquenza organizzata nella storia di due città (1820–1990)*, Rome, 1999. Arlacchi quote, p. 127, provides the statistics for the turnover of tobacco smuggling.

Istruttoria Stajano.

I. Sales, *La camorra le camorre*, Rome, 2nd edn, 1993.

'Ritorna in prigione la contrabbandiera', *Corriere della Sera*, 28/6/1992. On the arrest of Concetta Muccardo on heroin-dealing charges.

47. The mushroom-pickers of Montalto

P. Arlacchi, *La mafia imprenditrice. Dalla Calabria al centro dell'inferno*, Milan, 2007 (original edn 1982). On 55% of the earth-moving and transport sub-contracts going to Piromalli, p. 104.

S. Boemi, 'L'atteggiarsi delle associazioni mafiose sulla base delle esperienze processuali acquisite: la 'ndrangheta', *Quaderni del Consiglio Superiore della Magistratura*, 99, 1996.

E. Ciconte, *'Ndrangheta dall'Unità a oggi*, Rome, 1992.

D. Gambetta, *The Sicilian Mafia*, London, 1993.

S. Gambino, *La mafia in Calabria*, Reggio Calabria, 1975.

La mafia a Montalto. Sentenza 2 ottobre del Tribunale di Locri, Reggio Calabria, 1971. 'There's no Mico Tripodo's 'ndrangheta here!' p. 27; 'superficial' and 'desultory', p. 128; 'restorative vaccine in the bodies of these criminal societies', p. 207; 'living symbol of organized crime's omnipotence and invincibility', p. 258; 'This is an argument that might seem like a travesty', p. 258.

S. Lupo, *Storia della mafia*, Rome, 1993. 'Repress what? An idea? A mentality?', p. 181.

F. Pierini, 'I mafiosi si difendono sull'Aspromonte. Non abbiamo sparato', *L'Europeo*, 13/11/1969.

Processo Olimpia. 'This man was the overall boss', from 'Parte II°: Anni Settanta: 'Da Montalto al convegno di contrada Acqua del Gallo', p. 288, words of 'ndrangheta defector Giacomo Lauro.

F. Silvestri, 'Dinasty della Piana', *Narcomafie*, February, 1999.

'Sentenza, emessa il 22 dicembre 1968 dalla Corte di Assise di Catanzaro, nei confronti di Angelo La Barbera ed altri, imputati di vari omicidi, sequestri di persone, violenza privata ed altri reati', in Documentazione antimafia, vol. 4, tomo 17.

'Ora c'è la mafia delle autostrade', *La Stampa*, 3/3/1970. 'There is always someone who rebels against the monopoly held by some *cosche*'.

48. *Mafiosi* on the barricades

E. Ciconte, *Processo alla 'Ndrangheta*, Rome–Bari, 1996.

F. Cuzzola, *Reggio 1970. Storie e memorie della rivolta*, Donzelli, Rome, 2007.

P. Ginsborg, *A History of Contemporary Italy. Society and Politics, 1943–1988*, London, 1990.

Processo Olimpia.

49. The kidnapping industry

L. Ballinari and C. Castellacci, *Carceriere fuorilegge: la storia del sequestro di Cristina Mazzotti (Fatti e misfatti)*, Milan, 1978. 'Our conversations always came back to the crime of the moment', p. 39.

A. Calderone with P. Arlacchi, *Gli uomini del disonore*, Milan, 1992. 'The mafia doesn't run prostitution', p. 5; 'the mafia didn't have any money', pp. 85–6; Corleo kidnapping 'an extremely serious matter that created a huge shock in Cosa Nostra', p. 130.

O. Cancila, *Palermo*, Bari, 2000.

E. Deaglio, *Raccolto rosso: la mafia, l'Italia e poi venne giù tutto*, Milan, 1995.

B. Fontana and P. Serarcageli, *L'Italia dei sequestri*, Rome, 1991. On 650 citizens kidnapped by criminals, p. 214.

D. Gambetta, *The Sicilian Mafia*, London, 1993. ' . . . this bloke must die', p. 178.

S. Gambino, *La mafia in Calabria*, Reggio Calabria, 1975.

N. Machiavelli, *The Prince*, translated by N.H. Thomson, New York, 1914.

G. Moroni, *Cronista in Calabria. Storie di 'Ndrangheta, sequestri di persona, delitti eccellenti nel racconto di un giornalista-testimone*, Cosenza, 1993. 'I asked, I begged my jailers to cut my ear off. I was totally destroyed, I had lost all hope', p. 120; between 1969 and 1988, seventy-one people vanished and were never seen alive again, Pier Luigi Vigna cited p. 220.

J. Pearson, *Painfully Rich. J. Paul Getty and His Heirs*, London, 1995. 'I have fourteen grandchildren', p. 176.

Istruttoria Stajano.

O. Rossani, *L'industria dei sequestri*, Milan, 1978.

Berlusconi's views on Mangano ('[Mangano] was a person who behaved extremely well with us') were given during the radio programme *28 minuti*, *RadioDue*, 9/4/2008. Consulted via YouTube: http://www.youtube.com/watch?hl=it&gl=IT&v =PD4ixdKJzOE.

'Rapito il figlio di Vassallo', *L'Unità*, 9/6/1971.

Tribunale di Palermo II Sezione Penale, Sentenza nei confronti di Dell'Utri Marcello e Cinà Gaetano, 11 dicembre 2004. ' . . . complex strategy destined to make an approach to the entrepreneur Berlusconi', p. 171.

50. The Most Holy Mother and the First 'Ndrangheta War

P. Arlacchi, *La mafia imprenditrice. Dalla Calabria al centro dell'inferno*, Milan, 2007 (original edn 1982). 'Paolo and Giorgio De Stefano attended university for a few years', quoted on p. 129; 3% cut of profits from construction of the Gioia Tauro steelworks, p. 115.

L. Barone, 'L'ascesa della 'ndrangheta negli ultimi due decenni', *Meridiana*, 7–8, 1989–90.

S. Boemi, 'L'atteggiarsi delle associazioni mafiose sulla base delle esperienze processuali acquisite: la 'ndrangheta', *Quaderni del Consiglio Superiore della Magistratura*, 99, 1996. The quotation from Leonardo Messina, p. 13.

E. Ciconte, *Processo alla 'ndrangheta*, Rome–Bari, 1996. On 233 murders in three years, p. 108.

S. Gambino, 'Calabria: i nuovi "malavitosi"', *Il Ponte*, 11–12, 1976.

P. Ginsborg, *Italy and its Discontents*, Penguin, London, 2001. 'All the heads of the secret services, 195 officers of the various armed corps of the Republic', pp. 144–45.

Processo Olimpia. 'Bastardisation' of the Honoured Society's rules: the expression is from 'ndrangheta defector Gaetano Costa, p. 319.

R. Sciarrone, *Mafie nuove, mafie vecchie. Radicamento ed espansione*, Rome, 1998. For the comparative statistics on membership of Cosa Nostra and 'ndrangheta, pp. 53–54.

F. Silvestri, 'Dinasty nella Piana', *Narcomafie*, February, 1999. ' . . . only his thigh bones were left over', p. 19.

'Caccia ai due killer del night di Reggio C.', *L'Unità*, 26/11/1974. For the Roof Garden attack.

51. A brief history of junk

Homer, *The Odyssey. Rendered into English Prose by Samuel Butler*, London, 1900. Book IV, verses 220–21.

C. Lamour and M.R. Lamberti, *The Second Opium War*, London, 1972. On over 200,000 heroin addicts in USA by end of First World War, p. 7.

A.W. McCoy, *Drug Traffic. Narcotics and Organized Crime in Australia*, Sydney, 1980. In 1971, 10–15% of all US troops were using heroin, p. 23.

A.W. McCoy, *The Politics of Heroin: CIA complicity in the global drug trade*, New York, 1991.

P. Pezzino, *Mafia: Industria della violenza*, Florence, 1995. Reproduces important passages on narcotics from the Commissione Parlamentare d'Inchiesta.

C. Sterling, *The Mafia*, London, 1990. 'Narcotics track star', quoted p. 71.

D. Twitchett and J.K. Fairbank (eds), *The Cambridge History of China*, vol. 10, *Late Ch'ing, 1800–1911*, Part 1, edited by J.K. Fairbank. F. Wakeman Jr, 'The Canton trade and the Opium War'; J.K. Fairbank, 'The creation of the treaty system'. 'The most long-continued and systematic international crime of modern times', p. 213.

W.W. Willoughby, *Opium as an International Problem. The Geneva Conferences*, Baltimore, 1925. 'By 1924 no more than 110,000 addicts in the United States', p. 6.

52. Mr Champagne: Heroin broker

P. Arlacchi, *La mafia imprenditrice. Dalla Calabria al centro dell'inferno*, Milan, 2007 (original edn 1982). By 1980, Italy had more heroin addicts per head of population than did the United States, p. 187.

O. Barrese (ed.), *Mafia, politica, pentiti: la relazione del presidente Luciano Violante e le deposizioni di Antonio Calderone, Tommaso Buscetta, Leonardo Messina, Gaspare Mutolo: atti della Commissione parlamentare d'inchiesta sulla mafia*, Soveria Mannelli, 1993. 'When it comes to drug trafficking, if deals are small then they can be managed by a Family', p. 420; 'God bless these prisons!', p. 497.

E. Deaglio, *Raccolto rosso: la mafia, l'Italia e poi venne giù tutto*, Milan, 1995.

L. Galluzzo, F. La Licata, S. Lodato (eds), *Rapporto sulla mafia degli anni '80*, Palermo, 1986. Suite in the five-star Michelangelo Hotel as his office, p. 322.

Istruttoria maxiprocesso, vol. 9. Ferrari Dino and Alfa Romeo GTV 2000, p. 1763.

L. Paoli, *Mafia Brotherhoods: organized crime, Italian style*, Oxford, 2003.

V. Scafetta, *U Baruni di Partanna Mondello. Storia di Mutolo Gaspare mafioso,pentito*, Rome, 2003. 'I've never felt fear the evening before a murder', p. 55; 'All you have to do is set up good relationships with a few local administrators', p. 61; 'Gentlemen, we have the chance to earn ten times as much with drugs', p. 63; 'If there are any rascals in the story, it's the Swiss', p. 62; 'Gaspare, promise me: as soon as you get out, call me', p. 65.

A. Stille, *Excellent Cadavers*, London, 1995. A fine journalistic reconstruction of the dramatic events in Sicily in the 1980s that I have drawn on for this chapter and several following.

53. The Transatlantic Syndicate

T. Blickman, 'The Rothschilds of the Mafia on Aruba', *Transnational Organized Crime*, Vol. 3, No. 2, 1997.

Corte Suprema di Cassazione, Seconda parte penale, Sentenza Andreotti, 15/10/2004. 'An authentic, stable and friendly availability', p. 83.

Istruttoria maxiprocesso, vol. 5, p. 847. Reproduces the conversation in the ice-cream bar in Saint-Léonard, Montreal's Little Italy.

A. Jamieson, 'Cooperation Between Organized Crime Groups Around The World', *Jahrbuch für internationale Sicherheitspolitik*, December, 1999. For the international traces of the Transatlantic Syndicate, and the marriage of Pasquale Cuntrera's son, p. 68.

S. Lupo, *Quando la mafia trovò l'America. Storia di un intreccio intercontinentale, 1888–2008*, Turin, 2008. For an astute analysis of this episode, and (what Lupo calls) the 'third mafia'.

J.D. Pistone, *Donnie Brasco*, New York, 1989.

54. The Professor

F. Barbagallo, *Il potere della camorra (1973–1998)*, Turin, 1999. 7,000 NCO affiliates, p. 13.

E. Ciconte, *Processo alla 'ndrangheta*, Rome–Bari, 1996. Cutolo's initiation into the 'ndrangheta, pp. 108–10.

R. Cutolo, *Poesie e pensieri*, Naples, 1980.

S. De Gregorio, *Camorra*, Naples, 1981. Quotes the extracts from the psychiatric analyses of Cutolo, p. 34.

M. Jacquemet, *Credibility in Court. Communicative Practices in Camorra Trials*, Cambridge, 1996. Juvenile inmates in Campania, p. 29; Cutolo's living expenses in prison, p. 43.

M. Jouakim, *'O Malommo*, Naples, 1979.

A. Lamberti, '"Imposture" letterarie e "simulacra" poetici. Il ruolo di Ferdinando Russo nella costruzione dell'immaginario di massa sulla "camorra"', in P. Bianchi and P. Sabbatino (eds), *Le rappresentazioni della camorra*, Naples, 2009.

L. Rossi, *Camorra. Un mese a Ottaviano il paese in cui la vita di un uomo non vale nulla*, Milan, 1983. Contains the harrowing interviews with young *camorristi* I have quoted here, and has a very useful introduction on the 'South Bronxes' of Campania by Pino Arlacchi.

M. Savio (with F. Venditti), *La mala vita. Lettera di un boss della camorra al figlio*, Milan, 2006. This camorrista close to Cutolo is the source for Cutolo's challenge to 'o Malommo and his aptitudes as a 'talent scout', pp. 35–37.

La Stampa: on Cutolo's first murder, 'Sfiora una ragazza con l'auto, provoca un litigio e uccide il paciere', 26/2/1963 and 'Ergastolo all'automobilista che uccise a rivoltellate un passante dopo un incidente', 29/12/1965; on Cutolo as drug-dealer, 'Dirigevano dal manicomio il traffico di stupefacenti', 13/10/1974.

PART X: THE SLAUGHTER

55. Blood orgy

P. Allum and F. Allum, 'The resistible rise of the new Neapolitan Camorra', in S. Gundle and S. Parker (eds), *The New Italian Republic*, London, 1996. More than 900 died in the camorra wars of 1979–83, p. 238.

L. Brancaccio, 'Guerre di camorra: i clan napoletani tra faide e scissioni', in G. Gribaudi (ed.), *Traffici criminali. Camorra, mafie e reti internazionali dell'illegalità*, Turin, 2009.

For deeper analysis of numbers:

Commissione parlamentare antimafia, Camorra e politica: relazione approvata dalla Commissione il 21 dicembre 1993, Rome, 1994. For the estimate of murders between 1981 and 1990, p. 3.

E. Deaglio, *Raccolto rosso: la mafia, l'Italia e poi venne giù tutto*, Milan, 1995. Estimate of total deaths in mafia wars and comparison with N. Ireland, p. 9.

P. Hofmann, 'Italy gets tough with the mafia', *New York Times*, 13/11/1983. For the opinions of Alberto Moravia.

F. Messina, 'Cosa Nostra trapanese: gli anni del dominio corleonese', unpublished PhD chapter, 2011.

Sutton Index of Deaths. Online resource for calculating number of victims in the Northern Ireland Troubles: http://cain.ulst.ac.uk/sutton/.

'Palermo capitale mondiale dell'eroina', *La Stampa*, 10/10/1981. 'Blood orgy'.

'Altro omicidio ieri a Palermo', *La Stampa*, 31/12/1982. 'Don't die!'
The figures for the number of dead are from various dates in *La Stampa*.

56. The New Family: A group portrait

Corte di Assise di Santa Maria Capua Vetere, Sentenza contro Abbate Antonio, + 129, 'Sentenza Spartacus', 15/9/2005.

S. De Gregorio, *I nemici di Cutolo*, Naples, 1983. ' . . . many of the crimes carried out by Umberto Ammaturo were, in reality, dreamed up in her head', p. 38; 'If Cutolo was here instead of me, you wouldn't be making such a racket', p. 33.

L. Gay, 'L'atteggiarsi delle associazioni mafiose sulla base delle esperienze processuali acquisite: la camorra', *Quaderni del Consiglio Superiore della Magistratura*, 99, 1996.

C. Longrigg, *Mafia women*, London, 1997.

D.A. Maradona, *El Diego*, London, 2004 (original edn 2000). 'I admit it was a seductive world', pp. 98–9.

M. Marmo, 'La rima amore/onore di Pupetta Maresca. Una primadonna nella camorra degli anni cinquanta', *Meridiana*, 67, 2010.

I. Sales, *Le strade della violenza: malviventi e bande di camorra a Napoli*, Naples, 2006. 'One day the people of Campania will understand that a crust of bread eaten in freedom' and 'In my eyes they were "half *mafiosi*"', p. 154; 'In Forcella it isn't possible to live without breaking the state's laws', p. 173.

'Ucciso e mutilato un uomo di Cutolo', *La Stampa*, 22/1/1982. 'Demented, diabetic fanatic'.

'Pupetta Maresca sfida il "boss" Cutolo', *La Stampa*, 14/2/1982.

'Il boss replica alla Maresca', *L'Unita*, 20/2/1982. 'Maybe Pupetta said those things to attract attention.'

'Morti ammazzati 515 e 130 desaparacidos di lupara', *Stampa Sera*, 7/1/1983. On 364 killed; Annamaria Esposito murder.

'Maradona alle nozze del boss', *L'Unità*, 14/3/1989.

'"Bambulella," il camorrista decapitato. Dopo 27 anni trovati i suoi assassini', *Corriere del Mezzogiorno*, 13/2/2009.

57. Catastrophe economy

F. Barbagallo, *Napoli fine Novecento: politici, camorristi, imprenditori*, Turin, 1997.

F. Barbagallo, *Il potere della camorra (1973–1998)*, Turin, 1999.

J. Chubb, 'Three earthquakes: political response, reconstruction and the institutions: Belice (1968), Friuli (1976), Campania (1980)', in J. Dickie, J. Foot, and F.M. Snowden (eds), *Disastro! Disasters in Italy Since 1860: culture, politics, society*, Palgrave, 2002.

Commissione parlamentare antimafia, Camorra e politica: relazione approvata dalla Commissione il 21 dicembre 1993, Rome, 1994. On Cirillo and patronage, p. 135; 'to demonstrate to Cutolo that he was finished', p. 165.

I. Sales, *La camorra le camorre*, (2nd edn), Rome, 1993. 'I'm not ruling out the fact that bumping him off would have been a pleasure for me', p. 80.

R. Saviano, *Gomorra: viaggio nell'impero economico e nel sogno di dominio della camorra*, Milano, 2006. On the lasting resonance of *Il camorrista*, p. 275.

M. Travaglio, 'Un altro martire', blog from www.voglioscendere.ilcannocchiale.it, 10/8/2008. For the extracts from judge's ruling on Gava.

La Storia Siamo Noi: Il caso Cirillo. TV documentary containing many interviews with protagonists at www.lastoriasiamonoi.rai.it/puntate/il-caso-cirillo /798/default.aspx. 'At number 275, Riviera di Chiaia, under a rubbish bin, you will find communiqué number one.'

'Il Pci si chiede "Chi ha pagato?"', *La Stampa*, 25/7/1981. 'Without any negotiation and without any concession on the part of organs of the state faced with blackmail from an armed band'.

58. The Magliana Band and the Sacred United Crown

E. Ciconte, *Storia criminale. La resistibile ascesa di mafia, 'ndrangheta e camorra dall'Ottocento ai giorni nostri*, Soveria Mannelli, 2008. For very interesting observations on the increasing ties between the mafias, and on the Mala Vita.

'Commissione parlamentare d'inchiesta sul fenomeno della mafia e sulle altre associazioni criminali similari', *Mafia, politica, pentiti: la relazione del presidente Luciano Violante e le deposizioni di Antonio Calderone, Tommaso Buscetta, Leonardo Messina, Gaspare Mutolo*, Soveria Mannelli, 1993. 'In Piedmont, the Calabrians have taken over the region', testimony of Leonardo Messina, pp. 321–2.

G. Di Fiore, *Io, Pasquale Galasso, da studente in medicina a capocamorra*, Naples, 1994. 'But what a race there was to suck up to Cosa Nostra', p. 141.

P. Ginsborg, *Silvio Berlusconi: television, power and patrimony*, London, 2005. The first was 'semi-clean', quoted from F. Tamburini, *Misteri d'Italia*, Milan, 1996.

M. Massari, *La Sacra Corona Unita: potere e segreto*, Rome, 1998. 'Never to allow any family from other regions to lord it over our territory', p. 15; 'At the time, Cutolo's men felt like they were Lord God Almighty', p. 17; 'He wanted me to draw a triangle, the sign of the Holy Trinity', pp. 18–19; 'eight unknown, invisible and well-armed men', p. 32.

'Rapporto del Questore di Bari al Procuratore del Re rivelante l'esistenza in Bari della Mala Vita', 22/8/1890. Reproduced in C. D'Addosio, *Il duello dei camorristi*, Napoli, 1893, pp. 141ff. The Mala Vita was also widely covered in the press, even in the UK. Its emergence bears many similarities to that of the 'ndrangheta at the same time. The Mala Vita, however, does not seem to have put down roots.

R. Sciarrone, *Mafie nuove, mafie vecchie. Radicamento ed espansione*, Rome, 1998. 'In 1982 I took part in a meeting of all the Locals in Piedmont. About 700 people were there', p. 235.

Tribunale Penale di Roma, Ufficio Istruzione, Ordinanza-Sentenza contro Abbatino Maurizio + 237 (Banda della Magliana). 'We decided to try and carry out the same operation in Rome that Raffaele Cutolo was carrying out in Naples', p. 65.

'Così fu ucciso il duca Grazioli', *Corriere della Sera*, 5/10/1993. 'Go home and wait. Your father will be freed in a few hours.'

PART XI: MARTYRS AND PENITENTS

59. Mafia terror

A. Dino (ed.), *Pentiti. I collaboratori di giustizia, le istituzioni, l'opinione pubblica*, Rome, 2006.

Gruppo Abele (ed.), *Dalla mafia allo Stato. I pentiti: analisi e storie*, Turin, 2005.

H. Hess, *Mafia and Mafiosi. Origin, Power and Myth*, London, 1998. 'Sensation-hungry journalists, confused northern Italian jurists, and foreign authors', p. 3.

F. La Licata, *Storia di Giovanni Falcone*, Milan, 2002. A fine biography that I have used repeatedly in the following chapters. 'Ruining the Palermo economy', p. 61; 'Well I never. I was absolutely sure it was your turn', p. 54.

U. Lucentini, *Paolo Borsellino*, Cinisello Balsamo, 2003. Another fine biography that I have used repeatedly in the following chapters. 'I had married a man carved out of rock', p. 59.

S. Palazzolo, *I pezzi mancanti. Viaggio nei misteri della mafia*, Rome–Bari, 2010. 'Palermo's mafia organizations have now become pivotal in heroin trafficking, the clearing house for the United States', p. 39.

'Giornalista assassinato a Palermo', *L'Unità*, 27/1/1979.

'Noi politici siamo indifendibili', *L'Ora*, 10/3/1979. 'No longer live for the construction industry and off the construction industry'.

'S'intese col PCI e gli sparì l'auto', *Giornale di Sicilia*, 11/3/1979.

60. The fatal combination

G. Anremi, *La strategia vincente del Generale Dalla Chiesa contro le Brigate Rosse . . . e la mafia*, Rome, 2004.

P. Arlacchi et al., *Morte di un generale. L'assassinio di Carlo Alberto Dalla Chiesa, la mafia, la droga, il potere politico*, Milan, 1982.

G. Bascietto and C. Camarca, *Pio La Torre. Una storia italiana*, Rome, 2008. 'In a couple of years, La Torre and I should be able to get the most important things done', pp. 26–7.

G. Bocca, 'Quell'uomo solo contro la mafia', *Repubblica*, 10/8/1982.

G. Burgio, *Pio La Torre. Palermo, la Sicilia, il PCI, la mafia*, Palermo, 2010. 'You're an intelligent lad. You'll go far', p. 47; 'We just can't stomach this party. Over there in Russia maybe . . . ', p. 47.

C.A. Dalla Chiesa, *Michele Navarra e la mafia del corleonese*, ed. F. Petruzzella, Palermo, 1990.

C.A. Dalla Chiesa, *In nome del popolo italiano*, ed. N. Dalla Chiesa, Milan, 1997.

N. Dalla Chiesa, *Delitto imperfetto. Il generale, la mafia, la società italiana*, Milan, 1984. 'Get lost, *mafioso*!', p. 45; 'I've been to see Andreotti; and when I told him everything

I know about his people in Sicily, he blanched', p. 34; 'What we were afraid of has happened', p. 122.

N. Dalla Chiesa, *Album di famiglia*, Turin, 2009.

C. De Simone, *Pio La Torre. Un comunista romantico*, Rome, 2002.

G. Frasca Polara, 'Una vita contro la mafia', *L'Unità*, 1/5/1982.

P. La Torre, *Comunisti e movimento contadino in Sicilia*, Rome, 1980.

P. La Torre, *Le ragioni di una vita*, Palermo, 1982.

M. Nese and E. Serio, *Il Generale Dalla Chiesa*, Rome, 1982. The anecdote about Dalla Chiesa's father's return to Italy, p. 9.

S. Palazzolo, *I pezzi mancanti. Viaggio nei misteri della mafia*, Rome–Bari, 2010.

D. Paternostro, *A pugni nudi: Placido Rizzotto e le lotte contadine a Corleone nel secondo dopoguerra*, Palermo, 2000.

P. Peci, *Io, l'infame*, Milan, 1983. 'His manner was severe but gentle, authoritative but kind', p. 189.

Pio La Torre. 30 aprile 1982. Ricordi di una vita pubblica e privata, Palermo, 2007.

D. Rizzo, *Pio La Torre. Una vita per la politica attraverso i documenti*, Soveria Mannelli, 2003.

Repubblica, 29/3/1982. 'There should be no political difficulties'.

61. Doilies and drugs

G. Ascheri, *Tortora. Storia di un'accusa*, Milan, 1984. 'Aggressive personality strongly influenced by delusions of grandeur', p. 46; 'My current status as a detainee who is still bound to the healthy principles of Honour', p. 39.

F. Coppola, 'Ecco perché Tortora è innocente', *Repubblica*, 18/12/1986.

M.V. Foschini and S. Montone, 'Il processo Tortora', in L. Violante (ed.), *Storia d'Italia. Annali 12. La criminalità*, Turin, 1997.

L. Galluzzo, F. La Licata, S. Lodato (eds), *Rapporto sulla mafia degli anni '80*, Palermo, 1986. On Buscetta's treatment in Brazil, see the interview with Falcone, p. 35.

M. Jacquemet, *Credibility in Court. Communicative practices in the Camorra trials*, Cambridge, 1996.

R. Lumley, 'The Tortora Case: The Scandal of the Television Presenter as Media Event', *The Italianist*, 6, 1986.

R. Lumley, 'The Tortora Case: Restoring the Image and Putting the System of Justice on Trial', *The Italianist*, 7, 1987.

Maxiprocesso: Tribunale Penale di Palermo, Ufficio Istruzione Processi Penali, Processo verbale di interrogatorio dell'imputato Tommaso Buscetta, 16/7/1984.

'C'era una volta Portobello', episode of TV series *La storia siamo noi*: available at www.lastoriasiamonoi.rai.it.

'Tra Tortora e il boss Cutolo stretta di mano all'Asinara', *Repubblica*, 3/12/1985. 'No, look, you're the boss'.

62. Walking cadavers

D. Dolci, *Banditi a Partinico*, Bari, 1955. On the *cassetta*, p. 282.

G. Falcone and M. Padovani, *Cose di Cosa Nostra*, Milan, 1991. 'Was like a language professor who allows you to go to Turkey without having to communicate with your hands'.

L. Forte, '20 anni fa', *Repubblica*, 28/7/2005. 'In Palermo there are about ten of us who are a real danger for the mafia'.

S. Lodato, *Trent'anni di mafia*, Milan, 2008. 'Everything conspires to individualise the struggle against the mafia', p. 120; 'Sooner or later all the investigators who really take their job seriously end up getting killed', pp. 166–7; 'We keep a very close eye on the worrying events surrounding both the build-up to the Palermo maxi-trial, and the maxi-trial against the camorra', pp. 166–7.

U. Lucentini, *Paolo Borsellino*, Cinisello Balsamo, 2003. 'We'd better resign ourselves to being walking cadavers', p 122.

S. Lupo, 'Alle origini del pentitismo', in A. Dino (ed.), *Pentiti. I collaboratori di giustizia, le istituzioni, l'opinione pubblica*, Rome, 2006.

V. Vasile, 'La normalità a Palermo', *L'Unità*, 8/8/1985. 'You knew Cassarà. And you understood.'

Antonino Caponnetto interview with Gianni Minà from 1992 available in various versions on YouTube. (Buscetta changed everything 'by opening the door for us from the inside'.)

'Gian Giacomo Ciaccio Montalto', episode of TV series *Blu notte*. Episode first transmitted in 2008. The street where he lay bleeding to death was a narrow one.

Interview with Procuratore della Repubblica Bernardo Petralia.

63. The capital of the anti-mafia

N. Alongi, *Palermo. Gli anni dell'utopia*, Soveria Mannelli, 1997. 'Why are we [i.e., Communists] the only ones who talk about the mafia?', p. 95; 'Street crime, operating in the open, is almost inextricably tied in a complex web with occult manipulators', p. 16; 'For almost an hour the Cardinal waited in vain for the prisoners to leave their cells', p. 29.

P. Catalanotto, 'Dal carcere della Vicaria all'Ucciardone. Una riforma europea nella Palermo borbonica', *Nuovi Quaderni del Meridione*, 79, 1982.

L. Galluzzo, F. La Licata, S. Lodato (eds), *Rapporto sulla mafia degli anni '80*, Palermo, 1986. 'They have shown that, in the struggle against the mafia, party political labels are irrelevant', and the rest of the interview with Falcone, pp. 39–40.

A. Jamieson, *The Antimafia: Italy's Fight against Organized Crime*, London, 2000.

S. Lodato, *Trent'anni di mafia*, Milan, 2008. 'Palermo has always been the mafia's capital city. But I want to express my pride in its ability to be the capital of the anti-mafia too', p. 212; 'the Church is worried that holding such a big trial might attract too much concentrated attention on Sicily', p. 179; 'Today the mafia is fundamentally unconnected to power', p. 182.

Maxiprocesso: Tribunale Penale di Palermo, Ufficio Istruzione Processi Penali, Processo verbale di interrogatorio dell'imputato Tommaso Buscetta, 16/7/1984–. 'The presence of so many Men of Honour in the Ucciardone at the same time further reinforces the links between them', p. 376.

U. Santino, *Storia del movimento antimafia*, Rome, 2009 (updated edn).

J.C. Schneider and P.T. Schneider, *Reversible Destiny: mafia, antimafia, and the struggle for Palermo*, Berkeley, CA, 2003.

F.M. Stabile, *I consoli di Dio*, Caltanissetta, 1999.

64. The rule of non-law

F. Barbagallo, *Napoli fine Novecento: politici, camorristi, imprenditori*, Turin, 1997.

F. Barbagallo, *Il potere della camorra (1973–1998)*, Turin, 1999.

F. Barbagallo, *Storia della camorra*, Rome-Bari, 2010. 'In the 1980s we realised that we had to "industrialise mafia activities"', p. 154.

Commissione parlamentare antimafia, Camorra e politica: relazione approvata dalla Commissione il 21 dicembre 1993, Rome, 1994. Estimate of number of camorra clans, p. 10; 'The camorra's activities create a generalised "rule of non-law"', p. 55; construction of Pianura without a single building licence, p. 61; 'a conurbation that can only be compared to some of the metropolises that have grown up rapidly and chaotically in South America or South-East Asia', p. 62; arrest of a former mayor, a chief of a local health authority and three bank managers, p. 47.

Corte di Assise di Santa Maria Capua Vetere, Sentenza contro Abbate Antonio, + 129, 'Sentenza Spartacus', 15/9/2005.

S. De Gregorio, *I nemici di Cutolo*, Naples, 1983.

D. Della Porta, *Lo scambio occulto: casi di corruzione politica in Italia*, Bologna, 1992.

G. Di Fiore, *Io, Pasquale Galasso, da studente in medicina a capocamorra*, Naples, 1994. 'Everyone remained autonomous. We weren't like the Sicilian mafia', p. 148.

L. Gay, 'L'atteggiarsi delle associazioni mafiose sulla base delle esperienze processuali acquisite: la camorra', *Quaderni del Consiglio Superiore della Magistratura*, 99, 1996. 'We felt like the Israelis facing up to the Arabs', said by Pasquale Galasso; Sicilian construction companies operating in Campania immediately abandoned the region.

Processo Olimpia. 'He lived to do justice because he was the armed emissary of the Madonna of Polsi', p. 517; 'Great fluctuations in power. Marriages to seal pacts. Secret alliances', p. 558; 'the war's protagonists, who had by now been decimated, were irrationally hitting victims chosen at random', p. 653.

I. Sales, *La camorra le camorre*, Rome, 1993. Figures on numbers of camorra clans, p. 7.

'Assalto alla villa del boss camorrista: tre morti e 2 feriti', *L'Unità*, 11/6/1984.

65. 'U maxi

G. Ayala, *Chi ha paura muore ogni giorno. I miei anni con Falcone e Borsellino*, Milan, 2008.

Istruttoria Stajano. 'For many a long year the state was practically absent from the struggle against the mafia', p. 328.

F. La Licata, 'La "finta giustizia" di Cosa Nostra', *La Stampa*, 4/10/1994.

G. Lo Forte, 'L'atteggiarsi delle associazioni mafiose sulla base delle esperienze processuali acquisite: la mafia siciliana', *Quaderni del Consiglio Superiore della Magistratura*, 99, 1996.

Maxiprocesso: Tribunale Penale di Palermo, Ufficio Istruzione Processi Penali, Processo verbale di interrogatorio dell'imputato Tommaso Buscetta, 16/7/1984–. 'The Salvos' role in Cosa Nostra is modest. Yet their political importance is huge', p. 465.

F. Viviano, *Michele Greco il memoriale*, Roma, 2008.

'Anti-mafia trial to open in Sicily', *New York Times*, 9/2/1986. 'The prosecution will try to prove how individual acts were part of a vast criminal conspiracy born centuries ago'.

'Cast assembles for Mafia show trial', *Observer* 9/2/1986.

'Trial a challenge to might of mafia', *Guardian*, 10/2/1986. 'Overtones of a Barnum and Bailey production'.

'The Mafia is not dead', *Economist*, 15/2/1986. The Commission as 'semi-mythical', p. 55.

'Anche Salvo non sa nulla', *La Stampa*, 21/6/1986. 'The Salvos paid all the political parties. Money to all of them: no exceptions'; 'You seem bored'.

'Sgomento a Palermo', *La Stampa*, 10/10/1986. 'And they call themselves Men of Honour!' 'We join the Domino family in their grief.'

'Maxiprocesso alla mafia', RAI documentary available on YouTube. Includes Michele Greco's infamous 'peace' wishes.

66. One step forward, three steps back

C. Duggan, *Fascism and the Mafia*, New Haven, London, 1989.

G. Falcone and M. Padovani, *Cose di Cosa Nostra*, Milan, 1991. 'I warn you, judge. After this interrogation, you will become a celebrity', p. 44.

L. Galluzzo, F. Nicastro, V. Vasile, *Obiettivo Falcone. Magistrati e mafia nel Palazzo dei veleni*, Naples, 1989. ' . . . distorted protagonism' and 'personality culture', p. 205; 'No one is irreplaceable . . . there is no such thing as a demi-god', p. 267; 'Has he resigned? Things in Palermo are still trouble', p. 280.

F. La Licata, *Storia di Giovanni Falcone*, Milan, 2002. 'I am a walking corpse', p. 113; 'One step forward, three steps back: that's how the fight against the mafia goes', p. 120.

L. Sciascia, *A Futura memoria (se la memoria ha un futuro)*, Milan, 1989.

67. Falcone goes to Rome

Corte d'Assise di Caltanissetta, Sentenza nel procedimento penale contro Aglieri Pietro +40 (the trial for the murder of Falcone, his wife and bodyguards). 'Wage war on the state first, so as to mould the peace afterwards', p. 1242; 'destroy Giulio Andreotti's political faction led by Salvo Lima', p. 825.

P. Ginsborg, *Italy and its Discontents. Family, Civil Society and the State 1980–2001*, London, 2001.

A. Jamieson, *The Antimafia: Italy's Fight against Organized Crime*, London, 2000.

F. La Licata, *Storia di Giovanni Falcone*, Milan, 2002. 'Yes, I am Sicilian. And for me, life is worth less than this button', p. 14; 'My country has not yet grasped what has happened. This is something historic: this result has shattered the myth that the mafia cannot be punished', p. 163; 'Don't you understand? You must realise that an equilibrium has been broken, and the entire building could collapse', p. 166.

PART XII: THE FALL OF THE FIRST REPUBLIC

68. Sacrifice

Corte d'Assise di Caltanissetta, Sentenza nel procedimento penale contro Aglieri Pietro +40 (for the details of the Capaci bomb). 'Giovanni, Giovanni', p. 146.

S. Lodato, *Venti anni di mafia*, Milan, 1999. 'The state seemed like a punch-drunk boxer', p. 305.

U. Lucentini, *Paolo Borsellino*, Cinisello Balsamo, 2003. 'While he carried out his work, Giovanni Falcone was perfectly well aware that one day the power of evil, the mafia, would kill him', pp. 260–62; 'It will be him first, then they will kill me', p. 243.

69. The collapse of the old order

R. Alajmo, *Un lenzuolo contro la mafia*, Palermo, 1993.

F. Barbagallo, *Storia della camorra*, Rome-Bari, 2010.

B. De Stefano, *I boss della camorra*, Rome, 2007.

G. Di Fiore, *Io, Pasquale Galasso, da studente in medicina a capocamorra*, Naples, 1994.

N. Gratteri and A. Nicaso, *La malapianta*, Milan, 2010. On invitation from Riina for 'ndrangheta to join massacre campaign, p. 63.

Gruppo Abele, *Dalla mafia allo Stato*, Turin, 2005. 'Everyone saw me, and I immediately thought: now they're going to arrest me', p. 461; 'Today I feel as if I am completely one of them, because when it comes down to it we're all running the same risks and fighting for the same cause', p. 469.

D. Parrini, 'Collaboratori e testimoni di giustizia. Aspetti giuridici e sociologici', in *L'altro diritto. Centro di documentazione su carcere, devianza e marginalità*, available at: www.altrodiritto.unifi.it/ricerche/law-ways/parrini/cap1.htm#60.

Some of the sheets of protest hung up in Palermo in the summer of 1992 can be viewed here: http://www.rainews24.rai.it/it/foto-gallery.php?galleryid=165442&photoid=392267.

'La mafia dichiara guerra allo Stato. Dopo Falcone, uccisi Borsellino e cinque agenti', *La Stampa*, 20/7/1992.

70. Negotiating by bomb: Birth of the Second Republic

S. Ardita, *Ricatto allo Stato*, Milan, 2011. 'After the second bomb we were genuinely all ready to be killed', p. 7.

S. Colarizi and M. Gervasoni, *La tela di Penelope. Storia della Seconda Repubblica*, Rome, 2012. 'No agreement with the *mafioso*', p. 103.

Corte d'appello di Palermo, 29/6/2010. Sentenza d'appello nei confronti di Dell'Utri Marcello.

N. Farrell and B. Johnson, 'Forza Berlusconi', *The Spectator*, 6/9/2003. 'To do that job you need to be mentally disturbed, you need psychic disturbances,' p. 16.

P. Ginsborg, *Silvio Berlusconi: television, power and patrimony*, London, 2005.

Procura della Repubblica presso il Tribunale di Palermo, Memoria a sostegno della richiesta di rinvio a giudizio, 5/11/2012. 'The new pact of co-habitation between the state and the mafia was finally sealed', p. 20.

N. Tranfaglia, *La mafia come metodo*, Milan, 2012. 'The ongoing negotiations were the main reason why the plan to eliminate Borsellino was accelerated', p. 129.

Tribunale di Palermo. II Sezione penale presieduta da Leonardo Guarnotta. Sentenza nei confronti di Dell'Utri Marcello e Cinà Gaetano, 11/12/2004.

I have also drawn on the newspaper coverage of the negotiations between the state and Cosa Nostra; the articles are too numerous to be cited here.

M. Fuccillo, 'Vogliono colpirmi a tutti i costi . . . ', *Repubblica*, 20/3/1994. 'We'll all vote for Berlusconi'.

PART XIII: THE SECOND REPUBLIC AND THE MAFIAS

71. Cosa Nostra: The head of the Medusa

E. Bellavia and M. De Lucia, *Il cappio*, Milan, 2009. 'Now you tell me that you've got a good level political contact', p. 244.

C. Caprì with P. Maisano Grassi, *Libero. L'imprenditore che non si pieg ò al pizzo*, Rome, 2011. 'For the lads shut up in the Ucciardone', p. 77.

A. Dino, *La mafia devota: Chiesa, religione, Cosa Nostra*, Rome, 2008.

A. Dino, *Gli ultimi padrini: indagine sul governo di Cosa Nostra*, Rome, 2012.

Direzione Investigativa Antimafia, Relazione secondo semestre 2011.

G. Falcone and M. Padovani, *Cose di Cosa Nostra*, Milan, 1991. 'Getting to know *mafiosi* has profoundly influenced my way of relating to other people', p. 70.

A. Galli, *Cacciatori di mafiosi*, Milan, 2012. 'The first rule for a boss is to never abandon his ground', p. 12.

P. Grassi, 'La svolta: ora Confindustria può cacciare le mele marce', *Corriere del Mezzogiorno*, 29/1/2010.

Procura della Repubblica presso il Tribunale di Palermo, Direzione Distrettuale Antimafia, N. 18038/08 R. mod. 21 D.D.A. Fermo di indiziati di delitto, art.

384 segg. c.p.p. Adelfio Giovanni + 98 ('Operazione Perseo'). 'If we all do our own thing, like the Neapolitans do', p. 1139; 'Provenzano never underwent a formal investiture by the other precinct bosses. So he exercised his supremacy in substance, but not officially', p. 26; 'a Commission to deal with the serious things, with situations, and that way we all stay friends', p. 1139.

Procura della Repubblica presso il Tribunale di Palermo, Direzione Distrettuale Antimafia, Fermo di indiziati di delitto, Casamento Filippo + 29, 2/2008 (Operazione 'Old Bridge').

A. Sabella, *Cacciatore di mafiosi: le indagini, i pedinamenti, gli arresti di un magistrato in prima linea*, Milan, 2008.

U. Santino, *Storia del movimento antimafia. Dalla lotta di classe all'impegno civile*, Rome, 2009 (updated edn).

United States District Court, Eastern District of New York, Indictment against Joseph Agate and others, 6/2/2008 (Operation 'Old Bridge').

My thanks to Chiara Caprì for passing on the quotation about Addiopizzo from the Cosa Nostra penitent.

72. Camorra: A geography of the underworld

F. Barbagallo, *Storia della camorra*, Rome-Bari, 2010. This source is used for the following chapters too.

R. Cantone, *Solo per giustizia*, Milan, 2008.

R. Cantone, *I gattopardi: uomini d'onore e colletti bianchi: la metamorfosi delle mafie nell'Italia di oggi*, Milan, 2010.

G. Gribaudi (ed.), *Traffici criminali. Camorra, mafie e reti internazionali dell'illegalità*, Turin, 2009. Especially the following essays: G. Gribaudi, 'Introduzione', 'criminal *savoir-faire*', p. 13; L. Brancaccio, 'Guerre di camorra: i clan napoletani tra faide e scissioni' for statistics on the murder rate, and the market in fake goods; G. Gribaudi, 'Clan camorristici a Napoli: radicamento locale e traffici internazionali'; A.M. Zaccaria, 'Donne di camorra'; R. Sommella, 'Le trasformazioni dello spazio napoletano: poteri illegali e territorio', 22% in Campania in the 'black economy', p. 367; L. Mascellaro, 'Territorialità e camorra: una proposta di lettura geografica dell'attività criminale'; L. D'Alessandro, 'Città e criminalità: il commercio come chiave interpretativa', on *magliari* and today's international commerce; F. Beatrice, 'La camorra imprenditrice'; A. Lamberti, 'Camorra come "metodo" e "sistema"'; M. Anselmo, 'L'impero del calcestruzzo in Terra di Lavoro: le trame dell'economia criminale del clan dei casalesi', cites the Pasolini poem.

G. Marino, 'L' ordine di morte arrivò dal telefonino', *Repubblica*, 29/5/2002. Mentions 'gypsies', 'sows'.

M. Marmo, *Il coltello e il mercato: la camorra prima e dopo l'unità d'Italia*, Naples, 2011.

P.P. Pasolini, *Le Ceneri di Gramsci. Poemetti*, Milan, 1957.

C. Tucci, 'Draghi: la crisi ha reso le aziende più aggredibili dalla criminalità. Le mafie avanzano in Lombardia', *Il Sole 24 Ore*, 11/3/2011. 'Companies are seeing their cash-flow dry up, and their assets fall in market value', also quoted in Barbagallo, *Storia della camorra*, p. 270.

The video of Festival of Lilies can be viewed at: http://espresso.repubblica.it /multimedia/home/30547536.

'Ketty, una trans capeggiava gli Scissionisti', *Corriere del Mezzogiorno*, 12/2/2009.

'Festa gigli: distrutto l'Insuperabile. Ma i fan sfilano comunque con i loro colori', *Corriere del Mezzogiorno*, 29/9/2012. 'The messages it sends, the hidden meaning of that wood and *papier mâché*'.

73. Camorra: An Italian Chernobyl

F. Barbagallo, *Storia della camorra*, Rome-Bari, 2010.

R. Capacchione, *L'oro della camorra*, Milan, 2008. For the property portfolio that included forty-five apartments and a hotel, to a total value of $65 million, p. 167.

G. Corona and D. Fortini, *Rifiuti. Una questione non risolta*, Rome, 2010.

G. Gribaudi, 'Il ciclo vizioso dei rifiuti campani', *Il Mulino*, 1, 2008.

Meridiana, 64, 2009, *Napoli emergenza rifiuti*. Especially the following essays: G. Corona e M. Franzini, 'Capire l'emergenza rifiuti a Napoli. Un'introduzione'; D. Fortini (G. Corona, ed.), 'Ormai sono venti anni che il Paese è in emergenza rifiuti'; A. Di Gennaro, 'Crisi dei rifiuti e governo del territorio in Campania'; M. Andretta, 'Da *Campania Felix* a discarica. Le trasformazioni in Terra di Lavoro dal dopoguerra ad oggi'; D. Ceglie, 'Il disastro ambientale in Campania: il ruolo delle istituzioni, gli interessi delle organizzazioni criminali, le risposte giudiziarie', 'meteorite effect', p. 129; E. Giaccio, 'Chiaiano 2.0', 'The state is absent, but we are here', p. 152.

P. Rabitti, *Eco balle*, Rome, 2008.

The regional rubbish commissar's testimony to parliamentary inquiry: http:// www.camera.it/_dati/leg14/lavori/stenbic/39/2004/0727/s020.htm. 'It's a miracle even if 200 of the 2,316 people actually do any work'.

'Camera nega arresto a Cosentino. Il deputato: "Ringrazio Parlamento, non Lega"', *Repubblica*, 1/12/2012.

Biùtiful cauntri (2007), documentary film. 'Italian Chernobyl', stated by magistrate Donato Ceglie.

74. *Gomorrah*

A. Dal Lago, *Eroi di carta. Il caso Gomorra e altre epopee*, Rome, 2010.

D. Del Porto, 'Minacce camorriste a Roberto Saviano. Finisce sotto scorta l'autore di Gomorra', *Repubblica*, 13/10/2006. 'Iovine, Schiavone, Zagaria—you aren't worth a thing!'

J. Dickie, 'Gang rule', *The Guardian*, 12/1/2008. Some of the phrases in this chapter are borrowed from my own review of Saviano's book.

V. Faenza, 'Casalesi e l'affare rifiuti: "Inquinamento? Che ce ne frega, noi beviamo la minerale"', *Corriere del Mezzogiorno*, 4/2/2011.

M. Marmo, 'Camorra come Gomorra. La città maledetta di Roberto Saviano', *Meridiana*, 57, 2006.

U. Santino, *Don Vito a Gomorra. Mafia e antimafia, tra papelli, pizzini e bestseller*, Rome, 2011.

R. Saviano, *Gomorra: viaggio nell'impero economico e nel sogno di dominio della camorra*, Milano, 2006.

See http://www.ossigenoinformazione.it/ for up-to-date information on threats to journalists.

75. 'Ndrangheta: Snowstorm

T. Bendinelli, 'Cocaina, Brescia "sniffa" 625 mila euro al giorno', *Corriere della Sera*, 11/12/2012.

A. Bolzoni, 'Palermo chiama Medellin', *Repubblica*, 23/2/1990. On *Big John*.

D. Brown, unpublished research paper on Calabrian *mafiosi* in Queensland in the 1930s.

E. Ciconte and V. Macrì, *Australian 'Ndrangheta: i codici d'affiliazione e la missione di Nicola Calipari*, Soveria Mannelli, 2009.

F. Forgione, *Mafia Export. Politici, manager e spioni nella Repubblica della 'Ndrangheta*, Milan, 2012. 'We've lost face here . . . we've lost everything', p. 64.

N. Gratteri and A. Nicaso, *Fratelli di sangue*, Milan, 2009. On Joe Musolino, p. 237.

A. Nicaso, *'Ndrangheta. Le radici dell'odio*, Rome, 2007.

G. Pignatone and M. Prestipino, *Il contagio. Come la 'ndrangheta ha infettato l'Italia*, Rome-Bari, 2012. On 2,000 kg cocaine confiscated in 2011, p. 91.

Processo Olimpia. For Giacomo Lauro testimony, esp. Chapter 7.

A. Sabella, *Cacciatore di mafiosi: le indagini, i pedinamenti, gli arresti di un magistrato in prima linea*, Milan, 2008.

R. Sciarrone, *Mafie nuove, mafie vecchie. Radicamento ed espansione*, Rome, 1998. On 5,500 kg of 82% pure cocaine in a container lorry near Turin, p. 245.

Istituto di ricerche farmacologiche 'Mario Negri', Milan. A report on research on cocaine in the river Po is available at: http://www.marionegri.it/mn/it/pressRoom /comStampa/archivioComunicat05/cocainaPo.html.

76. 'Ndrangheta: The Crime

L. Abbate, 'Calabria: la strage delle donne', *Espresso*, 24/7/2012.

F. Forgione, *'Ndrangheta. Boss, luoghi e affari della mafia più potente al mondo. La relazione della Commissione Parlamentare Antimafia*, Milan, 2008.

Meridiana, 67, 2010, *Donne di mafia*. A series of essays with the most up-to-date research on women and all the mafias. For the 'ndrangheta see especially: O. Ingrascì, 'Donne, . . . 'Ndrangheta, 'Ndrine. Gli spazi femminili nelle fonti giudiziarie'.

G. Pignatone and M. Prestipino, *Il contagio. Come la 'ndrangheta ha infettato l'Italia*, Rome-Bari, 2012.

Procura della Repubblica presso il Tribunale di Reggio Calabria, Direzione Distrettuale Antimafia, Decreto di Fermo di indiziato di delitto, Agostino Anna Maria + 155 (Operazione Crimine).

Tribunale di Reggio Calabria, Sezione Gip - Gup, Sentenza resa nell'Operazione Crimine contro Agnelli Giovanni + 126, 8/3/2012. 'In Calabria they get together, but not to say, "What are we going to do?"', p. 101; 'a woman gives birth, but the umbilical cord is never cut', p. 101; on Tony Vallelonga, pp. 819–20.

'Arrestato Tony Marciano, il "re dei neomelodici" cantava per il clan', *Corriere del Mezzogiorno*, 4/7/2012.

The video of the Polsi meeting in 2009 can be watched at: http://www.youtube.com/watch?v=A79oXiOt5WI.

The video of the 2009 meeting in Paderno Dugnano can be watched at: http://www.youtube.com/watch?v=aR7WQhq7TTI.

77. Welcome to the grey zone

E. Bellavia and M. De Lucia, *Il cappio*, Milan, 2009. On truck thefts, p. 103.

G. Bianconi, 'Così si mimetizzano le mafie. Silenzi, complicità, omissioni: perché il contagio si allarga', *Corriere della Sera*, 12/11/2011. 'I'm less worried by the response from the criminal organizations than by the response from politicians'; 'the mafia method, which involves promoting illicit privileges and cancelling out competition'.

P. Davigo and L. Sisti, *Processo all'italiana*, Rome-Bari, 2012.

N. Delgrande and M.F. Aebi, 'Too much or not enough? Overcrowding in European prisons. An analysis based on SPACE statistics', Université de Lausanne, Institut de criminologie e de droit pénal, downloadable from http://ebookbrowse.com/overcrowding-cdap-rome-delgrande-121020–3-pdf-d432188927.

G. Di Girolamo, *Matteo Messina Denaro. L'invisibile*, Rome, 2010.

A. Dino, *Gli ultimi padrini: indagine sul governo di Cosa Nostra*, Rome, 2012.

L. Franchetti, *Condizioni politiche e amministrative della Sicilia*, vol. 1 of L. Franchetti and S. Sonnino, *Inchiesta in Sicilia*, 2 vols, Florence, 1974.

C. Macrì, '"Rapporti sospetti con le cosche." Sciolto il Comune di Reggio Calabria', *Corriere della Sera*, 9/10/2012.

G. Pignatone and M. Prestipino, *Il contagio. Come la 'ndrangheta ha infettato l'Italia*, Rome-Bari, 2012. On Calabrian delegates of ANCE, p. 87.

A. Sabella, *Cacciatore di mafiosi: le indagini, i pedinamenti, gli arresti di un magistrato in prima linea*, Milan, 2008. 'When you come to our schools to talk about justice and the rule of law', p. 246.

A. Ziniti, 'Processo Talpe alla Dda, 7 anni a Cuffaro, riconosciuto il favoreggiamento alla mafia', *Repubblica*, 23/1/2010.

'Cosa Nostra, in manette l'erede di Riina', *Repubblica*, 14/4/1998. 'The experience of the last twenty years has helped us understand that there is never a time for triumphalism'.

Ministero dell'Interno, Approfondimento. Direzione Centrale della Poliza Criminale—Programma Speciale di Ricerca—MESSINA DENARO MATTEO: www.interno.gov.it/mininterno/export/sites/default/it/sezioni/sala_stampa/notizie/polizia/latitante matteo_messina_denaro.html. 'Mafia association, murder, massacre, devastation . . .'

Direzione Investigativa Antimafia, Relazione secondo semestre 2011. On 2,246 cases of vandalism followed by arson in Sicily, p. 24.

World Bank, *Doing Business 2012*. Report downloadable from http://www.doing business.org/ For statistics on Italian legal system.

www.addiopizzo.org/. For updates on subscriptions.

Index

Poppy Berry

JOHN DICKIE is professor of Italian Studies at University College, London, and an internationally recognised expert on many aspects of Italian history. In 2005 he was awarded the title Commendatore dell'Ordine della Stella della Solidarietà Italiana. He is the author of several books, including *Delizia!*, which won the special commendation in the André Simon Food and Drink Book Awards and in France was voted food book of the year in *RTL/Lire* magazine's prestigious poll. *Cosa Nostra*, his history of the Sicilian mafia, has been translated into twenty-one languages, has sold over 750,000 copies, and won the Crime Writers' Association Award for Non-Fiction.

www.johndickie.net

PublicAffairs is a publishing house founded in 1997. It is a tribute to the standards, values, and flair of three persons who have served as mentors to countless reporters, writers, editors, and book people of all kinds, including me.

I. F. STONE, proprietor of *I. F. Stone's Weekly*, combined a commitment to the First Amendment with entrepreneurial zeal and reporting skill and became one of the great independent journalists in American history. At the age of eighty, Izzy published *The Trial of Socrates*, which was a national bestseller. He wrote the book after he taught himself ancient Greek.

BENJAMIN C. BRADLEE was for nearly thirty years the charismatic editorial leader of *The Washington Post*. It was Ben who gave the *Post* the range and courage to pursue such historic issues as Watergate. He supported his reporters with a tenacity that made them fearless and it is no accident that so many became authors of influential, best-selling books.

ROBERT L. BERNSTEIN, the chief executive of Random House for more than a quarter century, guided one of the nation's premier publishing houses. Bob was personally responsible for many books of political dissent and argument that challenged tyranny around the globe. He is also the founder and longtime chair of Human Rights Watch, one of the most respected human rights organizations in the world.

. . .

For fifty years, the banner of Public Affairs Press was carried by its owner Morris B. Schnapper, who published Gandhi, Nasser, Toynbee, Truman, and about 1,500 other authors. In 1983, Schnapper was described by *The Washington Post* as "a redoubtable gadfly." His legacy will endure in the books to come.

Peter Osnos, *Founder and Editor-at-Large*